FOLKLORE STUDIES
IN THE
TWENTIETH CENTURY

Proceedings of the Centenary Conference
of the Folklore Society

The clock tower and quadrangle at Royal Holloway College where the Centenary Conference was held.

FOLKLORE STUDIES
IN THE
TWENTIETH CENTURY

Proceedings of the
Centenary Conference of the
Folklore Society

Edited by Venetia J. Newall

D. S. BREWER · ROWMAN AND LITTLEFIELD

Published by D. S. Brewer, an imprint of
Boydell & Brewer Ltd., P.O. Box 9, Woodbridge, Suffolk IP12 3DF
and Rowman & Littlefield, 81 Adams Drive, Totowa, N.J. 07512, U.S.A.

ISBN 0 85991 064 4

Printed in Great Britain by
St Edmundsbury Press, Bury St Edmunds, Suffolk

CONTENTS

List of Illustrations		*vii*
List of Participants		*ix*
Note on Tale-Types and Motifs		*xiii*

Venetia J. Newall	*Introduction*	*xv*

INTRODUCTORY PAPERS

J. R. Porter	*The Place of the Folklore Society in Folklore Studies:Presidential Address at the Opening of the Conference*	1
Richard M. Dorson	*The Founders of British Folklore*	7

PLENARY SESSION PAPERS

Dan Ben Amos	*The Concept of Motif in Folklore*	17
Alan Dundes	*Wet and Dry, the Evil Eye; An Essay in Semitic and Indo-European Worldview*	37
Iona and Peter Opie	*Certain Laws of Folklore*	64
Roger Pinon	*From Illumination to Folksong: the Armed Snail, a Motif of Topsy-Turvy Land*	76
Lutz Röhrich	*Folklore and Advertising*	114

GENERAL CONFERENCE PAPERS

Roger Abrahams	*Play*	119
Issacher Ben-Ami	*Miraculous Legends of Wartime*	123
Sandra Billington	*Early Dance Phenomena and Possible Fish Imitation*	128
Philip Brady	*Volk or Proletariat? Folklore and Agitprop*	135
Katharine Briggs	*Some Unpleasant Characters among British Fairies*	143
Alan Bruford	*Some Aspects of the Otherworld*	147
David Buchan	*Social Function and Traditional Scottish Rhymes*	153
Michael Chesnutt	*The Colbeck Legend in English Tradition of the Twelfth and Thirteenth Centuries*	158
Manuel Dannemann	*Fox Hunting; A Form of Traditional Behaviour Providing Social Cohesiveness*	167
H. R. Ellis Davidson	*Folklore and Folly*	170
Indra Deva	*The Future of Folklore*	177
Tekla Dömötör	*The Cunning Folk in English and Hungarian Witch Trials*	183
L. P. Elwell-Sutton	*The Persian 'Passion Play'*	188
Douglas Gifford	*The Theme of Twins in Relation to that of the Trickster in Latin American Mythology and Folklore*	192
Olga Goldberg-Mulkiewicz	*The Folk Artist in Yemenite Jewish Society in Yemen and Israel*	199
Rayna Green	*Culturally-Based Science; The Potential for Traditional People, Science and Folklore*	204

L. V. Grinsell	*A Century of the Study of Folklore of Archeological Sites, and Prospects for the Future*	213
Robin Gwyndaf	*The Welsh Folk-Narrative Tradition*	218
Herbert Halpert	*Supernatural Sanctions and the Legend*	226
Maria Luisa Herrera	*Some Typical Spanish Traditions*	234
Bengt Holbek	*Oppositions and Contrasts in Folklore*	236
Rosaleen Howard	*Turkey Buzzard Tales of the Ecuadorean Quichua*	240
Hiroko Ikeda	*The Thomas Rymer Ballad and the Urashima Legend*	247
John Irwin	*The Axis Mundi and the Phallus; Some Unrecognised East-West Parallels*	250
Michael Owen Jones	*Perspectives in the Study of Eating Behaviour*	260
Mária Kosová	*The Social as a Folklore Category*	266
Mária Kresz	*Festive Functions of Hungarian Pottery*	269
Mary Ellen Lewis	*Some Continuities between Oral and Written Literature*	272
Demetrios Loukatos	*A Commentary on the Presidential Address of W. H. D. Rouse in 1905*	278
Brid Mahon	*Beliefs and Customs associated with Dress in Ireland*	284
J. J. Maitlis	*The Didactic Story in Old Yiddish Folk Literature*	289
Lynwood Montell	*The Hanging of Calvin Logsdon*	291
Vidosava Nedomački	*The Embroidery and Costume Collections of the Jewish Historical Museum, Belgrade*	303
Venetia Newall	*The Black Outsider; Racist Images in Britain*	308
W. F. H. Nicolaisen	*Time in Folk-Narrative*	314
John Niles	*Storytelling by the Very Young*	320
J. O. Ojoade	*The White Man in African Proverbial Sayings*	332
Trefor Owen	*The Ritual Entry to the House in Wales*	339
Martin Puhvel	*Circumambulation and Medieval English Literature*	344
Anna Birgitta Rooth	*Pattern Recognition, Data Reduction, Catchwords and Semantic Problems*	348
Claire Russell	*A Study in the Folk Symbolism of Kinship; The Tooth Image*	365
W. M. S. Russell	*Plutarch as a Folklorist*	371
Stewart Sanderson	*Why Was It a de Soto?*	379
A. E. Schroeder	*Traditional Song Current in the Midwest*	384
Haim Schwarzbaum	*The Value of Ibn Zabara's 12th-century Sepher Sha'ashu'im ('Book of Delight') for the Comparative Study of Folklore*	391
Linda-May Smith	*Aspects of Contemporary Ulster Fairy Tradition*	398
Nai-tung Ting	*The Collection and Study of Folktales in Twentieth-Century China*	405
Kenneth Varty	*The Lion, The Unicorn and The Fox*	412
Vilmos Voigt	*Folklore and 'Folklorism' Today*	419
Barry Ward	*Guineas and Other Englishmen; Folklore and Race in a Tri-Racial Community*	425
Karl P. Wentersdorf	*Witchcraft and Politics in Macbeth*	431
Beatrice White	*Fact, Fancy and the Beast Books*	438
John Widdowson	*Folklore and Regional Identity*	443
Maria Znamierowska-Prüfferowa	*Some Problems Concerning the Folklore of Polish Fishermen*	454
Index		459

LIST OF ILLUSTRATIONS

Frontispiece The clock tower and quadrangle at Royal Holloway College

Plate I   The Rev. Professor J. R. Porter and Dr Venetia J. Newall welcoming the participants   xxxiii

Plate II   The Hooden Horse of Kent which entertained guests at the opening reception   xxxiii

Plate III   The Convener and Hon. Secretary, Dr Venetia J. Newall   xxxiv

Plate IV   The Conference in session   xxxiv

Plate V   Professor Dan Ben-Amos and Professor Anna-Birgitta Rooth   xxxv

Plate VI   Professor Alan Dundes delivering his plenary session paper   xxxv

Plate VII   The Minehead Sailors' Hobby Horse which entertained participants on the last day   xxxvi

Plate VIII   A performance by the Kennet Morris Men of Reading on the final evening   xxxvi

Plate 1   Archer aiming at a snail from a thirteenth-century MS.   89

Plate 2   Snail attacked by soldiers, from a Viennese manuscript   89

Plate 3   Snail confronting a soldier who is urged on by a woman. From the fourteenth-century Amiens *Missale Romanum*   90

Plate 4   Reynard carrying a snail in a wheelbarrow. From the *Bréviaire du Saint-Sepulchré de Cambrai*   90

Plate 5   Knight fighting a snail, carved on a fourteenth-century draughtsman (British Museum)   91

Plate 6   Illustration of *Le débat des gens d'armes*, from the *Grand Compost du XVe siècle*   91

Plate 7   One version of *Le débat des gens d'armes*   92

Plate 8   Second version of *Le débat des gens d'armes*, after the MS. calendar illuminated by Antoine Vérard   93

Plate 9   Slovenian beehive front   94

Plate 10   Slovenian beehive front   94

Plate 11   Drawing of the Langholm 'cross'   251

Plate 12   Medieval 'Market Cross' and phallic stone at Clackmannan, near Stirling   251

Plate 13   Phallic stone (*bauta*), Denmark   252

Plate 14   Twelfth-century Romanesque granite phallus with cross ornamentation, in Tφmmerby Church, north Jutland   252

Plate 15   Drawing of a typical medieval Śiva-liṅga   253

Plate 16   Artist's reconstruction of the Aśokan Pillar at Sarnath, north India   254

Plate 17   The 'Gosforth Cross' or Rood, from Gosforth in Northumberland   254

Plate 18   Misericord in Knowle Parish Church, Warwickshire, showing the Lion, the Unicorn and the Fox   413

Plate 19   Woodcut by Wynkyn de Worde showing the Lion, the Unicorn and the Fox   414

Plate 20   The duel of the Wolf and the Fox, from the Wynkyn de Worde series   417

Plate 21   Wynkyn de Worde illustration of the Lion sparing the Fox's life   417

Plate 22   The fox as trickster   440

Plate 23   A carving from New College, Oxford, showing hedgehogs gathering fallen fruit on their spines   440

A series of 8 maps, illustrating Professor Anna-Birgitta Rooth's paper, appears on pages 356-63.

LIST OF PARTICIPANTS

This list includes those who were present at the Centenary Conference, as well as those who were prevented from attending, but who sent papers which were read at the appropriate sessions. All those who presented papers, whether in person or otherwise, are in bold print in the list, those who were not present being additionally marked with an asterisk. A few papers were not available for publication, as can be seen by comparison of the present list with the list of contents, and in one case (Professor Dorson) a different paper was substituted for that read at the Conference. Professor Dorson's unique knowledge of the history of folklore studies in England made his *Times Literary Supplement* article on this subject specially relevant to the proceedings, and permission was therefore obtained for it to be reprinted here.

Professor Roger ABRAHAMS*, University of Texas, Austin
Professor Bo ALMQUIST, University College, Dublin
Mrs Florence BAER, The Folklore Society, London
Mr J. BALLANTYNE, The Folklore Society, London
Dr F. R. BASFORD, The Folklore Society, London
Mrs Kathleen BASFORD, The Folklore Society, London
Dr Issacher BEN-AMI, Hebrew University, Jerusalem
Professor Dan BEN-AMOS, University of Pennsylvania, Philadelphia
Miss Sandra BILLINGTON, University of Cambridge
Dr Carmen BLACKER, University of Cambridge
Miss Janice BLAYNEY, University of Wellington, New Zealand
Dr Philip BRADY, University of London
Dr Derek BREWER, University of Cambridge
Dr Katharine BRIGGS, The Folklore Society, London
Dr Alan BRUFORD, University of Edinburgh
Dr David BUCHAN, University of Stirling
Professor Frank de CARO, University of Louisiana, Baton Rouge
Dr Michael CHESNUTT, University of Copenhagen
Miss Joyce COLEMAN, The Folklore Society, London
Professor Manuel DANNEMANN, University of Chile, Santiago
Dr Hilda R. Ellis DAVIDSON, University of Cambridge
Mr Richard DAVIDSON, Cambridge
Professor Indra DEVA*, Ravishankar University, Raipur
Professor Tekla DÖMÖTÖR, University of Budapest
Mr G. DORAN, The Folklore Society, London
Distinguished Professor Richard M. DORSON*, Indiana University, Bloomington
Professor Alan DUNDES, University of California, Berkeley
Professor Laurence ELWELL-SUTTON, University of Edinburgh

Miss FINNEY, Stockton, California
Mr Derek FROOME, The Folklore Society, London
Professor Douglas GIFFORD, University of St Andrews
Dr Jacob GOLDBERG, Hebrew University, Jerusalem
Dr Olga GOLDBERG-MULKIEWICZ, Hebrew University, Jerusalem, & Israel
    Museum
Dr Rayna GREEN, American Association for the Advancement of Science,
    Washington, D.C.
Mr Leslie GRINSELL, O.B.E., Bristol City Museum (retired)
Mrs Elesi GWYNDAF, Cardiff
Mr Robin GWYNDAF, Welsh Folk Museum, Cardiff
Professor Emeritus Herbert HALPERT, Memorial University, St John's,
    Newfoundland
Mrs L. HARPER, Washington, D.C.
Mr T. HASHIUCHI, University of Leeds
Mrs Maria Luisa HERRERA, Museo del Pueblo, Madrid
Miss HERRERA, Madrid
Dr Bengt HOLBEK, University of Copenhagen
Dr D. HOLLIDAY, University of S.W. Missouri, Springfield
Miss Rosaleen HOWARD, University of St Andrews
Professor Hiroko IKEDA, University of Hawaii, Honolulu
Mrs Kimie IMURA, Cambridge
Mr John IRWIN, Victoria & Albert Museum, London (retired)
Miss M. ISHII, University of Cambridge
Mrs Charlotte JOHNSON, The Folklore Society, London
Professor Michael JONES, University of California, Los Angeles
T. Vaughan JONES, Welsh Folk Museum, Cardiff
Professor Rosan JORDAN, University of Louisiana, Baton Rouge
Dr A. KLEIN-FRANKE, Israel Museum, Jerusalem
Dr Mária KOSOVÁ, University of Bratislava
Dr Mária KRESZ, Neprajzi Museum, Budapest
Professor Mary Ellen LEWIS, Indiana University, Bloomington
Rivanna LICHMAN, Leeds
Simon LICHMAN, University of Leeds
Dr Michael LOEWE, University of Cambridge
Dr S. H. LONSDALE, London
Professor Emeritus Demetrios LOUKATOS, University of Jannina
Mr LOUKATOS, Athens
Miss Brid MAHON, University College, Dublin
Dr Joseph MAITLIS, London
Mrs MAITLIS, London
Dr Jan Krzysztof MAKULSKI, Ethnographic Museum, Warsaw
Toshiko Lady MARKS, The Folklore Society, London
Professor Lynwood MONTELL, Western Kentucky University, Bowling Green
Miss S. NAKANO, Tokyo
Dr Vidosava NEDOMAČKI, Jewish Historical Museum, Belgrade
Dr Venetia NEWALL, University of London
Lady C. NICHOLSON, The Folklore Society, London
Professor Wilhelm NICOLAISEN, University of New York, Binghamton
Professor John NILES, University of California, Berkeley
Professor Dov NOY, Hebrew University, Jerusalem

Dr J. Olowo OJOADE, University of Jos, Nigeria
Miss Jos O'KELLY, The Folklore Society, London
Iona OPIE, The Folklore Society, London
Peter OPIE, The Folklore Society, London
Trefor OWEN, Welsh Folk Museum, Cardiff
Dr Alicia PERCIVAL, The Folklore Society, London
Neil PHILIP, The Folklore Society, London
Mrs Andrea PINON, Liège
M Roger PINON, Commission Royale Belge de Folklore, Liège
Mrs R. POPE, The Folklore Society, London
The Rev. Professor J. Roy PORTER, University of Exeter
Professor Martin PUHVEL, McGill University, Montreal
Mrs Joan ROCKWELL, University of Reading
Professor Lutz RÖHRICH, University of Freiburg
Mrs RÖHRICH, Freiburg
Professor Anna Birgitta ROOTH, Institute of Ethnology, Uppsala
Mrs Ruth ROSS, The Folklore Society, London
Mrs K. RUBY, The Folklore Society, London
Mrs Claire RUSSELL, Reading
Dr William M. S. RUSSELL, University of Reading
D. Roy SAER, Welsh Folk Museum, Cardiff
Stewart F. SANDERSON, University of Leeds
Professor A. E. SCHROEDER, University of Missouri, Columbia
Theodor SCHUCHAT, Washington, D.C.
Dr Haim SCHWARZBAUM, Institute for Jewish and Arab Folklore Research,
    Kiron, Israel
R. J. SIMS, The Folklore Society, London
J. B. SMITH, The Folklore Society, London
Miss Linda-May SMITH, Ulster Folk Museum, Holywood
Miss Margaret STEINER, Indiana University, Bloomington
Dr Annelise TALBOT, The Folklore Society, London
Mr Harry THOMAS, The Folklore Society, London
Dr Hilary THOMPSON, Acadia University, Wolfville
Dr Raymond THOMPSON, Acadia University, Wolfville
Professor Nai-tung TING*, University of Illinois
Mrs TOCK, Liège
Mrs Jean TSUSHIMA, The Folklore Society, London
Dr Jean URE, University of Edinburgh
Professor Kenneth VARTY, University of Glasgow
Roy VICKERY, The Folklore Society, London
Dr Vilmos VOIGT*, University of Budapest
Dr Barry WARD, University of West Virginia, Morgantown
Mrs Janice WARD, Morgantown
William WARD, The Folklore Society, London
Dr Elizabeth WARNER, University of Hull
Dr Karl P. WENTERSDORF, Xavier University, Cincinnati
Mrs WENTERSDORF, Cincinnati
Professor Emeritus Beatrice WHITE, University of London
Dr John WIDDOWSON, University of Sheffield
John YEOWELL, The Folklore Society, London
Professor Maria ZNAMIEROWSKA-PRÜFFEROWA, Ethnographic Museum,
    Toruń (retired)

NOTE

Mentions of Tale-Types or Motifs in the text or notes refer, where no other indication is given, to the following:

Antti Aarne and Stith Thompson, *The Types of the Folktale* (Helsinki, 1964); Stith Thompson, *Motif-Index of Folk-Literature* (Bloomington, 1966; 6 vols).

Introduction

VENETIA NEWALL   University of London

THERE is no universally accepted definition of folklore. *The Standard Dictionary of Folklore, Mythology and Legend*, published in 1949, contains 21.[1] They have been proliferating ever since, and indeed there are almost as many definitions as there are folklorists. I would agree with Jan Brunvand, author of *The Study of American Folklore* (1968), who defines folklore as the traditions of a people which reveal a common life of the mind below the level of formal culture.[2]

This corresponds closely to views expressed by Professor Ronald Fletcher, former head of the Department of Sociology at York University. Writing in Bullock and Stallybrass's *Dictionary of Modern Thought*, he specifically relates folk culture to subculture, which he describes as a 'body of attitudes, values, beliefs, and behavioural habits, shared by members of a particular group or stratum within a society, which has significant determining effects upon them as individuals, and is distinguishable from the commonly accepted culture (or majority culture) held to be characteristic of the society as a whole. The slum-dwellers of a large city, for example, may have a subculture of their own, distinct from that held by the governing culture of the whole city. Similarly ethnic, regional, linguistic and other groups may each have their distinctive subculture.'[3] Folklorists might regard this as too constricting a definition, if we are to relate it to our own subject. For example, not only the slum-dwellers, but the bourgeoisie, the aristocracy and any other class one cares to mention may have their own subcultures, and the term 'governing culture' obscures the fact that majority culture is effectively little more than a conglomeration of subcultures, in which certain common denominators generally act as important signposts.

Alan Dundes, one of the leading scholars in the field, takes up this point when writing of the folk: 'The term "folk" can refer to any group of people whatsoever who share at least one common factor. It does not matter what the linking factor is — it could be a common occupation, language or religion — but what is important is that a group formed for whatever reason will have some traditions which it calls its own.'[4]

Tradition, as used here by Professor Dundes, is associated with the importance of establishing a link with the past, or, at its very lowest, provides an accepted link with previous behaviour. This is a pattern which arises in all group activities, for example, in a group meeting occasionally for any purpose, where certain individuals adopt the practice of sitting in a particular chair, and this is recognised by others present. From this point of view tradition can loosely apply even to individual isolated behaviour, but folklore concerns itself with social activities, so that this would fall more accurately within the field of a psychologist.

What, then, is the actual field with which the folklorist now concerns himself? In fact this varies from country to country. The *Great Soviet Encyclopaedia*, to take one example, gives a clear, but rather limiting, definition of *folklore*: 'the artistic activity of the working people: the poetry, music, theatre, dance, architecture, and fine and applied art existing among the popular masses. The collective artistic activity of the common people reflects their work, social organization and everyday life, knowledge of life and nature, and religious practices and beliefs. . . . Having absorbed the age-old experience of the popular masses, folk arts are distinguished by a profound artistic grasp of reality, verisimilitude of imagery, and powerful generalizations.'[5] Certainly, the first two sentences quoted define the cultural activity of a particular subculture, though many would not accept the limitation of our field to the study of one particular social class or group of classes. But it is the final sentence here which raises complex issues. Cultural expressions of a profound grasp of reality, verisimilitude of imagery and powerful generalizations are, it seems to me, precisely not the aspects of life with which we are concerned. These are aspects of life to be studied by social anthropologists, whose discipline certainly uses much of our data, as well as that of sociologists, but the conceptual framework is different.

Folk culture is seen in this way by a western sociologist: 'The social heritage — the institutions, customs, conventions, values, skills, arts, modes of living — of a group of people feeling themselves members of a closely bound community, and sharing a deep-rooted attachment and allegiance to it.' This is close to the Soviet definition, stripped of its overt ideological slant and devoid of particular reference to the popular masses.[6] Indeed, in certain countries the borderline between folklore studies and those of sociology seem even less clearly defined than that between our discipline and social anthropology in, for example, Britain and the United States.

The common history of folklore and social anthropology in this country will be mentioned later, but one should note here that at times the data studied by the two disciplines, and even the use made of it, was remarkably similar. This was most obviously true when both disciplines concentrated on the so-called 'primitive'. Both have now moved away from this rather specific concern, and both now look at society more generally. Despite the similarity of certain data employed by the two disciplines, social anthropologists tend to adopt a viewpoint differing from ours. For them, cultures are categorized as 'particular historical realizations of the common human potential', to quote Maurice Freedman, with the corollary that there is a major stress on societies as real, viable entities.

A justified and often-repeated criticism of folklore in the past was that it did exactly the opposite. It picked up what were seen as the left-overs of outmoded civilizations and social functions, and handled them as museum pieces, scarcely relevant to modern, developed society. Few, if any, folk-

lorists would now view customary lore in this manner. Indeed, for society, for the community, tradition justifies its existence and provides it with a form of foundation charter. It supplies a sense of importance and adds meaning and significance to life to feel that one is doing what one's predecessors did before. This applies particularly to groups like modern mummers and participants in seasonal festivals. Its role is essential in an age like ours, which has seen great social and political changes: the end of Empire and world supremacy, entry into the Common Market, upheavals in the class structure, increasing lack of interest in the established church and organised religion, and so on.

It is often difficult for an individual to stand alone and face life and the link with the past gives strength. Some landed families possessed heirlooms on which their luck depended. Handed down from one generation to another, they represented continuity and tradition. A green glass goblet, the Luck of Eden Hall, preserved the fortunes of the family of Eden Hall in Cumberland. The story goes that it was snatched from the fairies, and if it was ever broken, the family mansion would be destroyed. The Luck of Muncaster, a glass bowl enamelled in gold and white, is the talisman of another Cumberland family, the Penningtons of Muncaster Castle. Henry VI is supposed to have given it to Sir John Pennington, who sheltered him after the defeat at the Battle of Towton (1461), blessing the bowl and saying the family would flourish as long as it remained intact.

The desire for roots is a basic human need. It expresses the wish for order in a changing world, which is also an important function of religion. In the words of a well-known hymn:

> Change and decay
> In all around I see;
> Oh Thou who changest not,
> Abide with me.

But it is not enough simply to have respect for the discipline's subject matter, or to observe its every-day, on-the-ground effect. Social functions, the norms of society, that which is accepted as 'real', have to be further analysed, so that ultimately the whole of society can be seen as virtually an amalgam of past 'lore'. A term coined by the structuralists, the *vraisemblable*, con-

xvi

veniently describes the 'reality' with which the folklorist must concern himself. It correctly suggests the mechanics of the customary attitude to reality – in so far as this is capable of analysis – the method by which the customary itself becomes synonymous with the real. An ideological adjunct of structuralism is generally an emphasis on the need for revolutionary social change, a controversy into which our discipline need not necessarily enter. On the other hand, a respect for the functioning of traditional society, which folklorists may share with many social anthropologists, need not lead to an uncritical reverence for the activities which we choose to study. Here structuralist theory has real insights to offer. Roland Barthes, for example, discussed in *S/Z* the way in which the seemingly real is simply a compound of general opinions and commonplaces, of previous representations: culture is transformed into a *vraisemblable* which is henceforth regarded as 'nature'.[7]

The same point was taken up by Stephen Heath in *The Nouveau Roman*. The '*vraisemblable* is not recognised as such, but rather as precisely, "Reality", its function is the naturalization of that reality articulated by a society as *the* "Reality" and its success is the degree to which it remains unknown as a form, to which it is received as a mirror of "Reality". . . .'[8] Heath is referring to an all-pervading *vraisemblable*, a conglomeration of constructed 'absolutes' which dominates every society and every subculture within that society. Nazi Germany is the most notable example of a set of easily identifiable *vraisemblables* rapidly becoming tagged on to the existing norms within a given society, and representing a subculture – for National Socialism was, vis à vis accepted social principles, a subculture – ideally suited to study by folklorists.

More generally, the extent to which what we class as folklore contributes to 'the lived relation of men to their world' is again made clear by Heath: ' "Reality" . . . needs to be understood not as an absolute and immutable given but as a production within which representation will depend on (and dialectically contribute to) what the French Marxist theoretician Louis Althusser has described as "practical ideology", a complex formation of montages of notions, representations, images, and of modes of actions, gestures,

attitudes, the whole ensemble functioning as practical norms which govern the concrete stance of men in relation to the objects and problems of their social and individual existence.'[9]

Darwin, as will be mentioned later, inspired early theories in folklore, whereas, as Heath points out, the notion of the *vraisemblable* acknowledges a debt to that other great innovator in nineteenth-century social theory, Karl Marx. Obviously, it has moved far from the original Marxian scriptures, incorporating much modern psychological and sociological theory on its way. Yet the idea is less esoteric than it seems, and its distant forerunners may be seen, for example, in the views of Thomas Hardy, a thoughtful and sensitive observer of the role of customary lore:

> The practice of divination by Bible and key, the regarding of valentines as things of serious import, the shearing-supper, the long smock-frocks, and the harvest-home, have . . . nearly disappeared in the wake of the old houses . . . The change at the root of this has been the recent supplanting of the class of stationery cottagers, who carried on the local traditions and humours, by a population of more or less migratory labourers, which has led to a break of continuity in local history, more fatal than any other thing to the preservation of legend, folk-lore, close inter-social relations, and eccentric individualities. For these the indispensable conditions of existence are attachment to the soil of one particular spot by generation after generation.[10]

In my first year as Secretary of the Folklore Society, I presented a short paper on Thomas Hardy at the Anglo-American Folklore Conference.[11] As a folklorist, Hardy was a careful collector, and used the material meticulously in his works. He himself tells us so in a reply to a correspondent: 'To your question, – if the legendary matter and folklore of my books is traditionary and not invented, – I can answer yes, I think, in every case, this being a point on which I was careful not to falsify local beliefs and customs.'[12] In any discipline, the assembly of data, its presentation in useful form, and attempts at its classification are essential. Indeed, as Professor Ben Amos points out in his contribution to the present volume, it was long held that the essential pre-requisite for transforming any knowledge into a scientific discipline was a classification system. This assumption prompted Stith Thompson to compile his Motif-Index, and while few would now regard this as the sole necessary attribute of a discipline, it is certainly one of its functions. More relevantly, it must have, as some people would put it, a specific methodology, or, to use a simpler and more apt expression, a distinctive viewpoint.

This, of course, folklore has always had. A correspondence between Thomas Hardy and Edward Clodd, a fellow Darwinian and later President of the Folklore Society, illustrates the ideology of the day. Hardy quoted Clodd's letter in his diary for 18th December, 1890: 'Mr. E. Clodd this morning gives an excellently neat answer to my question why the superstitions of a remote Asiatic and a Dorset labourer are the same: "The attitude of man," he says, "at corresponding levels of culture, before like phenomena, is pretty much the same, your Dorset peasants representing the persistence of the barbaric idea which confuses persons and things, and founds wide generalisations on the slenderest analogies." '[13] Shorn of its pejorative content, the remark may seem little more than a truism which, in a straightforward manner, is true. Clodd's view of the Dorset 'peasantry' provides, incidentally, an illuminating contrast to that of the *Great Soviet Encyclopaedia* towards the popular masses — profound grasp of reality, verisimilitudes of imagery, and powerful generalizations are precisely, almost word for word, what he found lacking in Hardy's subjects.

A further correspondence took place six years later, which throws still more light on the current ideology. At the Folklore Society's meeting on 17th November, 1896, Clodd, who by then was President, read aloud two letters, The first ran as follows:

Max Gate, Dorchester,
October 30th 1896.

My Dear Clodd,
     Here is a bit of folklore that I have just been reminded of.
     If you plant a tree or trees, and you are very anxious that they should thrive, you must not go and look at them, or look out of the window at them, 'on an empty

stomach'. There is a blasting influence in your eye then, which will make them pine away. And the story is that a man, puzzled by this withering of his newly-planted choice trees, went to a white witch to enquire who was the evil-worker. The white witch, after ascertaining the facts, told him it was *himself*.

     You will be able to classify this, no doubt, and say exactly where it belongs in the evolutionary chain of folklore . .
                    Yours sincerely,
                    Thomas Hardy.[14]

Clodd thought the explanation lay in the fact that a hungry man looked at the trees, which became sympathetically starved and died.[15] He sent this suggestion to a notable member of the Folklore Society, who replied as follows:

Trinity College, Cambridge.
November 1st, 1896

Dear Mr. Clodd,
     The superstition you mention was unknown to me, but your explanation of it seems highly probable.
     As explained by you, the superstition is a very interesting example of the supposed sympathetic connection between a man and a tree. As you say, it bears very closely on my explanation of the connection between the priest of Diana at Aricia and the sacred tree, he having to be always in the prime of health and vigour in order that the tree might be so too. I am pleased to find my theory (which I confess often seems to me far-fetched, so remote is it from our nineteenth century educated ways of thought) confirmed by evidence so near home. It is one more indication of the persistence of the most primitive modes of thought beneath the surface of our civilisation. Thank you for bringing it to my notice. . .
                    Yours very truly,
                    James G. Frazer.[16]

This brief correspondence is, incidentally, of some interest, because the sympathetic connection between a man and a tree is a belief which Hardy used to great effect in one of his finest novels, *The Woodlanders*;[17] a theme which he utilised in such a way as to illustrate an inseparable connection between folk belief and the material culture of the people from which it springs.

Nowadays it is generally unfashionable to adopt a classification system grouping people as, for instance, to use an example taken from the correspondence just quoted, believers in a sympathetic relationship between trees and men. Basically this was Frazer's method, and his books, though still highly regarded as such, are today looked upon as little more than funds of valuable source material. The tendency has, in my view, gone too far. Just as Marx oversimplified the laws relating man to his economic environment, so Frazer adopted an excessively rule-of-thumb attitude *à propos* our cultural reaction to events confronting us. But, leaving aside a detailed criticism of his classification system, useful insights into human psychology and, to use Heath's phrase, 'the lived relation of men to their world', can still be gained from reference to his work.

The group-classification system used today is generally a paraphrase of that evolved by sociologists: e.g. sex — the folklore of women, the folklore of homosexuals; age — the folklore of children, of teenagers; nationality — Scottish folklore, Polish folklore; race — Jewish folklore, black folklore; region — Cambridgeshire folklore, Tyrolean folklore; geographical features — coastal folklore, mountain folklore; the family unit; mental attitude — the folklore of the oppressed; class — public schools' folklore, factory folklore; location — urban folklore, and so on. In other words, a definition of 'the folk' should not be narrow and limited by factors such as social class, occupation, level of earnings, age, or environment. With one or more such frames of reference, 'the folk' can mean everybody, or, to put it the other way round, we can none of us be excluded from a concept of 'the folk'. However, the peasant connotations of the term have lingered on and are still cherished by some scholars in Europe and South America.[18] For the traditional definition of the folk was of backward, illiterate people, living in a rural community, old-fashioned, and at the lowest level of so-called civilised society. This was contrasted with the urban literate class. A distinction was also made between folk — the object of study for the European discipline of folklife or regional ethnology — and primitive, which became the province of social anthropology.[19]

The main categories of folklore are myths, legends, folktales, riddles, proverbs, folk speech, folk song, games, rhymes, jokes, dance and drama, folk costume and folk art, custom and belief, traditional medicine, festivals, the supernatural, traditional food and methods of presentation, and material culture — in other words, customs and customary behaviour.

The word folklore, subsequently adopted by many other European languages, was coined in England by William Thoms in 1846, to replace an earlier and more cumbersome term, 'popular antiquities'. Of course the field is much older than that. Descriptions of the customs of foreign peoples are of ancient origin, and there was an almost universal interest in antiquities. Herodotus in the fifth century B.C., for example, described the habits of the Persians and Scythians, and Tacitus in the first century A.D. left us an account of the customs of the Teutonic tribes.[20]

However, the beginnings of serious studies by professional scholars are comparatively recent. In Germany the work of the Brothers Grimm was of major importance. The publication of the first volume of their *Kinder- und Hausmärchen* in 1812 was a landmark and its influence was felt throughout Europe. The stories were taken down from the lips of the narrators and though by modern standards they had been too much touched up, yet this represented a new technique.[21] The volume was enthusiastically received and this encouraged the Brothers to urge on other collectors of myths, legends, and magic tales. Jacob corresponded with Sir Walter Scott and together the Brothers translated the first field collection from Britain the same year that it was published. This was T. Crofton Croker's *Fairy Legends & Traditions of the South of Ireland*, which appeared in 1825. They inspired interest in the collection and publication of folklore in contemporary Russia, Denmark, Hungary, Greece, Albania, Romania and Sicily[22] and maintained personal contact with leading foreign folklorists; Peter Asbjörnsen (1812-85) and Jorgen Moe (1813-82) in Norway, Emmanuel Cosquin (1841-1921), author of *Contes Populaires de Lorraine* (1886) in France, and Elias Lönnrot in Finland.

Polygenesis and diffusion, rival theories of the origins of tales, were hotly debated in their day.

The Grimms favoured diffusion. This posited the invention in one place of one item which then spread elsewhere. Polygenesis recognised the independent invention of similar materials in different places.[23]

Diffusionists and followers of the historical-geographical method were both concerned with patterns of distribution of similar folktales.[24] The historical-geographical school was known as the Finnish Method, in recognition of the distinguished Finnish scholars who developed it — Kaarle Krohn and his student Antti Aarne. Its aim was to collect all the known variants of an international tale in order to plot its likely place of origin and subsequent spread; a hypothetical original form was then constructed. The result was the life history of an international folktale.[25]

Today the great debate between polygenesis and diffusion is a dead issue. We are less interested in the hypothetical search for origins and recognise that such hard and fast lines cannot be drawn. Some scholars still use the historical-geographical method, which has been very influential, but it undoubtedly encouraged a lack of interest in analysis of meaning.[26]

Another outlook which dominated nineteenth-century thinking was the doctrine of survivals. During the eighteenth and nineteenth centuries degeneration was a standard theological argument flung at those optimists who maintained that human nature inevitably progresses. In the nineteenth century the theory of degeneration was adopted by Archbishop Richard Whately (1747-1863), Professor of Political Economy at Oxford, Archbishop of Dublin, and influential author of various works on logic and theology. It was partly to oppose Whately, and to vindicate the theory of developmentalism, that Sir Edward Burnett Tylor (1832-1917) formulated the theory of survivals in his *Primitive Culture* (1871).[27] Patterned on the biological evolution proposed by Charles Darwin in *The Origin of Species* (1859), it put forward a parallel notion of cultural evolution: that all societies pass through similar stages, from lower to higher forms, progressing from savagery to civilisation.[28] This encouraged the study of analogies, the notion underlying polygenesis.

The appearance of Darwin's theories in the middle of the nineteenth century was one of various factors which stimulated interest in

tradition; nineteen years later the Folklore Society was founded here in London.[29] The British anthropological school of Folklore, led by Andrew Lang (1844-1912), adopted the idea of cultural evolution, regarding the materials of folklore as a means by which culture is expressed.[30] Folklore was held to be a survival from the past and folklorists used it to reconstruct the prehistory of mankind. They focused on cultural data that appeared to be functionless, crude, and superstitious. Illiterate peasant societies were thought to retain these fossilized survivals of pagan detritus, souvenirs from an earlier, more primitive stage of existence. This approach, which saw folklore as, in effect, archaeology of the mind, reflects the view that the movement of time is linear.[31]

So did a theory diametrically opposed to survivals. *Gesunkenes Kulturgut*, proposed by Hans Naumann, a German scholar, in 1922, maintained that folklore consists of debased material, fragments which sank down from former courtly sources and learned tradition, from the educated to the peasants. This theory never gained much academic support, but it helped to explain two important categories of folklore — astrology and magic.[32]

Another German, the orientalist Theodor Benfey (1809-1881), saw the ancient literature of India as the source of the traditional oral narratives of Europe. In his 1859 edition of the *Panchatantra*, a fifth-century Indian literary tale and fable collection, he maintained that the original stories had travelled from India along the trade routes to Europe. Joseph Bédier (1864-1938) crushed this India-diffusionist theory in his *Les Fabliaux* (1893) by showing that medieval fabliaux did not reveal a debt to India; out of a corpus of 400 tales, he traced only 13 in oriental collections.[33]

However Sanskrit had been recognised as the key language of the Indo-European family and the theories of Max Müller (1823-1900) drew on the developing study of comparative linguistics, which was to have so significant and continuing an influence on folklore studies. Müller looked at the names of the gods in different cycles of mythology and compared them with the Sanskrit names of the heavenly bodies. He decided that these names represented solar phenomena. His linguistic reconstructions — no doubt an attempt to explain the grossness and irrationality of much traditional narrative — reduced myths to allegories of nature, and in fairy tales a frog in a pond, for example, was said to represent the sun sinking in the water. His followers carried Müller's solar mythology to great lengths, but the scholars of the British anthropological school, and others, laughed his theories to scorn — Gaidoz even used these methods to prove that Müller and his house in Oxford were nothing but solar myths — and they have had no further influence. [34]

There were many Victorian folklore scholars who gathered large quantities of undigested and unclassified material, without any obvious underlying purpose — what one might call the butterfly-collecting approach. Today, since the early decades of this century, structure has become a key term in modern thought, thanks partly to the influence of *Gestalt* psychology. [35] Reacting against the older, atomistic approach, *Gestalt* theory views an organism as a whole. According to Frederick Perls (1893-1970), founder of the *Gestalt* school of psychotherapy, the *Gestalt* outlook is the original, natural and undistorted approach to life. [36] Most people, he maintained, have lost their wholeness and need to heal the dualism of their thinking in terms of mind and body. The German word is difficult to translate, but it implies a configuration, a structural relationship, and a meaningful, organised whole. [37]

We may say that the twentieth century has been noted for a configurational bias, [38] and for significant progress in the study of language. [39] The French scholar, Claude Lévi-Strauss (1908-) was stimulated by structural linguistics and applied their approach to studies of kinship and mythology. His essay, 'The Structural Study of Myth', in which he attempts to apply the principles of structural linguistics to folklore, was published in the *Journal of American Folklore* in 1955. The Russian scholar, Eleazer Meletinsky, refers to it as having the character of a scientific manifesto. [40]

The discipline of structural linguistics was founded by the Swiss scholar, Ferdinand de Saussure (1857-1913), whose posthumous *Cours de Linguistique Générale* (1916) was the fruit of lectures delivered to his students from 1906-11. [41] Before Saussure, interest in language centred on historical philology. His originality lay in his insistence that language must be regarded as a coherent, orderly system or structure — a social

phenomenon. [42] Its elements do not exist in isolation, but in relation to each other; [43] it is a systematic arrangement of parts. [44]

Saussure saw two interdependent aspects of language: *langue*, the underlying system of relations, or the structure, and *parole*, the individual speech acts that realise the system. [45] He also distinguishes between two types of linguistic approach, the synchronic and the diachronic. These terms, which roughly correspond to the difference between structural and historical research, [46] are widely used by modern folklorists.

Saussure and Roman Jakobson (born 1896) are the leading exponents of modern linguistics. [47] Jakobson assumes a binary structure in the materials of language. [48] The sounds of all known languages can be described by using a dozen pairs of sounds, and these are grouped according to the presence or absence of distinctive features. [49] Lévi-Strauss met Jakobson when they were academic colleagues in New York at the end of the War and the binary form of Jakobson's phonemic analysis is very prominent in his work. [50]

It is not perhaps too exaggerated to say that Lévi-Strauss has been one of the most influential anthropological theorists of recent times. He has used structural linguistics as a model for his study of anthropological material. [51] His intention is to show that binary oppositions are laws which represent a basic structure of the human mind, and that all thinking is structured accordingly. [52] His so-called 'primitives' are said to organise and perceive their world in terms of binary oppositions: soft/hard, wet/dry, raw/cooked, and so on. Our mental processes are the same.

There is undoubtedly some truth in these observations in that the existence of a concept must be assumed to posit, or to derive from, an alternative, but are they sufficient? The problem is still debated. The notion that language can serve as a conceptual model for other aspects of culture has been criticised. [53] Can one apply linguistic procedures to the analysis of social data? Is it correct to assume that the binary oppositions of the human mind are the most effective mode of analysis? Critics like Makarius believe that Lévi-Strauss wanted to illustrate a philosophical position and used anthropology as convenient for his purpose. [54] Leach has said: 'Lévi-Strauss is obsessed with his search for universals and contemptuous of ethnographic evidence'.[55] Using the phraseology of Saussure, it seems that he would like to view social facts as *parole*, and describe them in terms of an underlying system, *langue*.[56]

Lévi-Strauss believes that anthropology has suffered from too much empiricism. He is interested in the organisation of human ideas, the basic mental processes, rather than in social facts and their meaning, and considers the way phenomena are related, rather than the data itself.[57] The literal meaning of myth, the content, is of no interest to him. His aim is to unravel the unconscious meaning and show how it operates in the mind at that deeper level. Our unconscious, in his view, conceals the mechanism that creates cultural dichotomies and resolves them.[58]

In his analysis of myth Lévi-Strauss disregards the sequence of the narrative, focusing instead on elements and characters that can be paired in binary oppositions.[59] His paradigmatic structural analysis aims to reveal the pattern supposedly underlying the text. The myth is broken up. Elements are taken out of order and regrouped into fundamental oppositions of life and death, male and female, light and dark, and so on. I would agree with Dundes when he says that this type of analysis is highly speculative.[60] Nor is it new. It was used by the Church Fathers when they reconciled the Old and New Testaments by assuming the first to have prefigured the second. Thus Adam was the type of Christ, and so on.[61] The method invents tortuous ways of linking different items and relies heavily on subjective, arbitrary judgements.[62] Makarius has gone so far as to say that Lévi-Strauss is wrong in his basic assumption. He argues that, when taken separately, phonemes have no meaning; when combined to form words, they have. On the other hand, social phenomena do possess meaning and richness of sociological content, unlike linguistic signs.[63]

The work of Lévi-Strauss has been very influential in folklore studies. In particular, Elli Köngäs-Maranda, a recent candidate for the Presidency of the American Folklore Society, and her husband Pierre, who edited a *Festschrift* for Lévi-Strauss, developed a structural methodology; they felt it should not be reserved for myths, but also applied to other folklore genres.[64]

The emphasis on structure in linguistics arose partly as a result of the problems of understanding languages which were not a part of the traditional groups within which earlier methods had developed. We may mention in this connection the publication of Franz Boas' *Handbook of American Indian Languages* in 1911. Once Americans began to look at the languages of the Indians in their continent, new ideas were introduced which helped to develop their own structural studies. It was necessary to get rid of presuppositions derived from historical and comparative studies of Indo-European languages.[65] Now each language had to be considered on its own terms.[66]

It was not until the 1950s that structural analyses of folklore were published in America.[67] More recently folklore research at the University of Pennsylvania, a leading centre for the study of the discipline, was greatly assisted by the decision of Dell Hymes, the distinguished linguistic anthropologist, to move from the Department of Anthropology into folklore.[68]

Members of the Prague linguistic circle are said to have been the first to note structure and form in folklore.[69] Founded by Prince Nikolai Trubetzkoi (1890-1938), who became Professor of Slavic Languages in Vienna, and Roman Jakobson (1896-) who was a younger friend of his, this influential group was still active in the middle third of the twentieth century.[70] Thus structuralism appeared in Czechoslovakia soon after the Second World War and its outlook was related to Russian formalism. In the Soviet Union itself structuralism as an intellectual approach has been supported by Eleazer Meletinsky and his colleagues.[71]

Much structural analysis is formalist in approach, that is, it separates and elevates form over content.[72] It was in the early 1920s that this trend made a brief appearance in Russian literature and folklore studies. It was not to last long. By the end of the same decade it had been attacked by the Soviet authorities as 'narrow and impractical academism'.[73] The classic work of this short-lived school was Vladimir Propp's *Morphology of the Folk Tale*. Published in 1928, it remained almost unknown until structural analysis became more fashionable. When an English translation appeared in America, thirty years later in 1958,[74] it was greeted with enthusiasm and used as a model of structural analysis in folklore. Whereas Lévi-Strauss concentrated on bundles of relationships, the underlying conceptual framework, Propp focuses on the narrative line, the syntax, as it were, of the magic tale; his structural model is linear. He follows, in chronological order, the elements in the text and determines the structure of a magic tale according to the functions of its *dramatis personae*. According to his analysis of exclusively Russian material, there are 7 actors – hero, villain, etc. – and 31 functions, e.g. hero returns, hero uses magical agencies, and so on. The arrangement of these in a sequence constitutes the form of the magic tale.[75] Alan Dundes, who wrote the Introduction to the new edition, used Propp's method of analysis in his own study, *The Morphology of North American Indian Folktales*, published in 1964 by the Folklore Fellows of Helsinki.

We have seen that as the discipline of folklore developed, and the materials gathered, it was clear that a classification system would be needed. But listing of narratives according to Tale Types – the plots – and motifs, elements within the plots, again resulted in a tendency to make research more formalised. Tales were lifted out of their context and environment and listed, much as botanists classify plants. The focus was text-orientated, onto the objects, which were grouped according to genre and studied for their context and structure. Scholars worked with texts as if they were abstract forms with an independent life of their own, and the material was stressed to the exclusion of the human element from which it derived.[76]

In the early 1930s the eminent Swedish folk-lorist, Carl von Sydow (1878-1952), realised the importance of a sociological approach and urged that traditional narratives should be studied within their environment, but it is only more recently that this approach has become more popular and textual analysis placed on a socio-cultural basis.[77] Here again, a delayed debt to anthropology must be acknowledged, to the functionalist approach of Bronislaw Malinowski (1884-1942), the Polish-born British anthropologist who said that the mere text of a folktale is lifeless and can only be properly observed during the telling to an audience.[78]

The new movement, which Richard Dorson has labelled 'contextual', leans towards the social sciences, especially of course anthropology, and is closely concerned with the environment of the material. The performance of a narrative is thought important and it is argued that an item of folklore is not a mere text but an event in time, when it is performed or communicated.[79] The text alone is not enough; the whole of the occasion must also be recorded.

I should now like to turn to various movements and ideas which either directly or indirectly, resulted in what one might term abuse of folklore. During the latter part of the eighteenth century, the peasant became a focus of interest. Linked with the noble savage of Montaigne (1533-92), and Rousseau (1712-78), there was a romantic tendency to see him as the shining source of all morality, symbol of a nobler, purer age, in contrast with degenerate urban society. This was how the Romantics saw the peasant and his poetry. As Linda Dégh points out,[80] this trite notion had been popular since ancient times. Now it was to be taken up by Johann Gottfried Herder (1744-1803), the Brothers Grimm, and Bishop Percy (1729-1811), author of *Reliques of Ancient English Poetry* (1765), a collection of ballads, sonnets, historical songs and metrical romances, which did much to promote revival of interest in older English poetry. Percy's *Reliques* filled Herder with enthusiasm. He came to look on folksongs as embodiments of the national spirit, urged other Germans to collect them, and edited a volume himself. His work in turn stimulated the Brothers Grimm.[81]

At this period in England romanticism had created a corresponding fashion for imitation ruins, usually in Gothic style. Joseph Pocklington owned an island on Derwentwater, where he built a bogus stone circle, a make-believe church, and an imitation fort. William Gilpin in his *Observations Relative to Picturesque Beauty made on a Tour to Cumberland & Westmorland* (1786) wrote: 'It is not every man who can execute a ruin'.[82] In 1800, on another island in Derwentwater, Sir Wilfrid Lawson built a 'Hermitage', with a thatched roof, portico of rough tree-trunks, and 'Gothick' windows. It was not uncommon at this time for landscape dilettanti actually to hire imitation hermits to live in grottoes on their estates.[83] This was all symptomatic of a romantic back-to-nature outlook, very much divorced from reality.

In Germany, as Professor Lutz Röhrich remarked to me recently, folklore was a byproduct of the nationalism and romanticism which flourished in the nineteenth century. With the political ideal of the national unity of the Germans before their eyes, the Brothers Grimm strove to create a nationalistic science of German studies, seeing ancient Teutonic myth as the source of German folktales, a theory no longer given any credence.[84] It was, of course, only natural that German intellectuals at the beginning of the nineteenth century were obsessed with their cultural heritage. Political disunity apart, they had been invaded and overcome by the French. A Bonaparte ruled as King of Westphalia and Jacob Grimm himself was his librarian.

Not only in Germany but throughout Europe, and elsewhere, the growth of interest in folklore and folklore studies has been linked with the rise of nationalism. It has stimulated individual folklorists, as we have seen, and has helped to gain any practical support that may have been forthcoming from State or private sources.[85] The earlier notion of the virtuous peasant crystallised into 'the folk' which, so it was romantically thought, preserved the old traditions and values and, in doing so, reflected the spirit of the nation.[86]

Nationalists in general have struggled to restore what they saw as the cultural heritage of their people — of which folklore formed and important part — to show that they were ready for political independence.[87] In Ireland, to give the best example from the British Isles, various literary personalities, concerned by what they saw as the English threat to Irish culture, developed an interest in Irish folklore. Lady Gregory (1859-1932) and the poet William Butler Yeats (1865-1939) organised field trips and published their findings. Their friend, Douglas Hyde (1860-1949), the dramatist and poet, saw the collection of folktales and renewal of the language as one and the same issue. Hyde, Professor of Irish Language and Literature at the National University in Dublin, was founder and President of the Gaelic League. He became first President of the Irish Free State.[88]

In Ireland the language issue was closely involved with the cause of folklore, and Irish patriots reacted against the use of English. Today many of our Irish colleagues have changed their names to their Gaelic forms. Similarly in Finland there was hostility to the spread of Swedish, and in Norway the people did not wish to speak Danish.[89] There, too, the interest in folklore coincided with the rise of nationalism and romanticism. In 1814 Norway became independent from Denmark and during the rest of the century endeavoured to build up a sense of national identity. It is possible, I suppose, that the lack of a language issue is one reason why folklore studies have not flourished as they should in England, France and Italy.[90]

In Israel where more than 50 languages have been spoken, and immigrants must learn Hebrew as a new tongue, folklore has been used for political utilitarian purposes to help build up the new state and arouse feelings of national unity in a very mixed population.[91] In the same way, soon after Nasser had established himself in Egypt and started campaigning for Pan-Arabism, a Folklore Centre was opened in Cairo.[92]

Linda Dégh has referred to the struggle for national independence of East European peoples living under Turkish rule. The first Serbian collection of folklore, edited by Stepan Karadzić, was published in 1815, the year of liberation, This small volume was very influential.[93] Greece also displays a close link between nationalism and folklore studies. It became a nation state in 1821 and scholar-patriots were concerned to demonstrate continuity between ancient and modern Greeks.[94]

In the United States the picture is, of course, rather different. During the late nineteenth and early twentieth centuries, Americans were anxious to reject anything that revealed the foreign origins of their families — national dress, language, foodstuffs, and any other evidence from their homeland was firmly suppressed, in keeping with the 'melting-pot' outlook. The Clarkes have also suggested that these were things which may have carried the stigma of slum origins.[95] Today this no longer applies and it is becoming an increasing part of American patriotism to affirm proudly one's ethnic origins.

The subject of nationalism inevitably leads to folklorism, a rather cumbersome term used by German folklorists, and widely known throughout Europe, though not, as yet, in the British Isles. At the 1967 Conference of the International Folk Music Council in Ostend, Dr Felix Hoerburger spoke of the distinction to be drawn between folk practices as wholly belonging to the innermost life of the people, or as something adopted or imposed for some understood or ulterior reason. This he categorised as the first and second existences of the custom.

Hans Moser has defined folklorism as 'the presentation of folk culture at second-hand';[96] often, though not necessarily, it is linked with tourism, entertainment, and business, or political interests. Folklorism may be used for commercial, patriotic, romantic, propagandistic, and genuinely artistic purposes. It is a growing world-wide phenomenon and is not unique to our time. Examples of folklorism, and they are legion, would include: the conscious wearing of national dress, for instance at political demonstrations; the use of folk melodies by composers like Chopin, Vaughan Williams and Bartok; the use of ethnic ornamentation in architecture, folklore and myth in, for example, the work of Thomas Hardy, as well as Shakespeare, Pushkin, T. S. Eliot and innumerable others; the 'ethnic' souvenir industry; intellectuals who decorate their homes with examples of folk art; television displays of 'picturesque' folklore, and so on.

Lutz Röhrich, whose interesting illustrated paper on *Folklore and Advertising* was presented at the Centenary Conference, and a summary of which appears elsewhere in this volume, made some comments on similar issues at Visegrad in 1979: 'Reading materials of the masses have now become the legitimate subject of folk-narrative research. Folklorists, in addition to working with more traditional genres, are now analyzing contemporary popular reading materials. The question has arisen as to whether, and how, orally transmitted tales can be compared with popular reading materials. It has indeed been determined that there is a whole series of thematic, typological and functional relationships between traditional folk tales and comics. One has, above all, noted a structural relationship between traditional folk tales and comics.'[97]

The most striking use of folklorism is for political purposes of various kinds. In August 1968, when Russian tanks entered Prague, a producer and a group of technicians escaped from the television centre and sent out clandestine broadcasts from a half-finished apartment building in the suburbs. They were able to do this because a tree placed on the roof is part of the traditional 'topping out' ceremony and hence passed unnoticed, and behind this they were able to conceal the transmission antennae.[98]

This is a very literal example of the conscious use of the materials of folklore. On a more esoteric level, Frances Yates in her masterly study *Astraea* (1975), illustrates the political use of Astraean imagery in the cult of Elizabeth I. Astraea ruled during the Golden Age, and left the earth when men became evil. She symbolised the rule of justice and peace in an ideal realm. At that time the monarchy functioned as a unifying symbol in a land troubled by dissension between Protestants and Catholics, which threatened chaos.[99]

The Soviet authorities are well aware of the importance of folklore for propaganda purposes. Precisely because it has so much significance for the people, folklore is used, like other forms of scholarship, as a means of achieving socialism and communism.[100] It is their policy to regard folk traditions as part of the national heritage and, like other governments of Eastern Europe, they support academic research into folklore.[101] Since the 1920s Soviet folklorists have concentrated on the social importance of folklore, rather than on problems of origin and diffusion. Traditional satires on the clergy, for example, have been collected and used as a part of anti-religious propaganda.[102]

Soviet scholars have emphasized the changes in *byliny*, the traditional heroic epics, and *Märchen* under Soviet rule. Sokolov, the Russian folklorist, who published the results of his work during Stalin's lifetime, relates storytelling in the Soviet Union to the Five Year Plans. Here one can clearly see how traditional tales were deliberately altered. He comments on the moral self-consciousness of the storytellers, the curtailment of the old fantastic and miraculous tales, the new stress on realistic, satirical narratives of everyday life, and emphasises the role of such stories in revolutionary ideology. Modern details are introduced into old tales of wonder and magic. Korguyev, the White Sea storyteller who 'corrects many of the old concepts' is typical. Contemporary vocabulary like 'comrade' and 'manager' is introduced, and the hero, who uncharacteristically refuses to marry the Tsar's daughter, travels not by eagle but by aeroplane. The Tsar himself has become a stupid, cruel or comic figure. Sometimes he is executed.[103] In their treatment of traditional tales storytellers reflect 'our contemporary Soviet period. They strive to compose new tales ... expressing ... their own new world view, their attitude towards the October Revolution and the whole Soviet regime'.[104] In one such story, presumably no longer fashionable, three collective farmers wander through the Soviet Union in search of The Most Precious Thing. They discover, after many adventures, that it is the Word of Comrade Stalin.[105]

The most sinister example of folklore used for political purposes in recent world history is undoubtedly that of Nazi Germany — the general relationship of its ideology to folklore has already been mentioned. It was not difficult to set in motion. When Hitler came to power in 1933 there were a number of different groups concerned with esoteric traditions — more in Germany than elsewhere in Europe. The first neo-pagan Germanic religious sects appeared in the early twentieth century. They were the products of nationalism, romanticism, and the *völkischen* movement, which identified with everything Germanic and looked to old pagan religious beliefs as a source of strength. It was in decline by 1933 but its legacy remained and all the related Nazi apparatus of ancient symbolic legends, runes and swastikas became highly significant.[106]

Himmler was interested in the Edda sagas, astrology, and runes. He chose the *sig* rune as symbol of the SS.[107] Contemporary accounts describe Nazi Midsummer Festivals, Nazi Harvest Festivals on the Bückeberg, last sheaves, Christmas trees and Maypoles decorated with swastikas. An ugly photograph in *Der Stürmer*, the scurrilous anti-semitic newspaper published by Julius Streicher, shows the children of Schönfeld in Baden in 1935, attaching a copy of the newspaper to a noticeboard on the village Maypole. The noticeboard is headed 'The Jews are our misfortune'.[108] Children attending school for the first time were given the traditional cornucopoeia filled with sweets, and decorated with swastikas. When the Nazi period finally came to an end, Martin Bormann's wife compared the downfall of the Third Reich to the *Götterdämmerung*.[109]

The Nazis used folklore to support their notion of a master race. During the period of slavery in the southern United States, and after, the whites, who considered themselves superior to the blacks, kept them under control by exploiting their fear of the supernatural. To prevent unauthorised movement, especially at night, for what were regarded as subversive meetings, the overseers and slave-masters disguised themselves as spirits and created rumours of haunted places; the black scholar, Gladys Fry, quotes a maid who actually saw her master dress up as a ghost and go out thus.[110]

The men rode dark horses and wore black shirts and trousers; only their white hats and shoes were visible, creating an eerie effect. They rattled chains or cow-bones, and tied tin-cans to the horses' tails to make ghostly noises.[111] They used white sheets and headless disguises, and sometimes walked on stilts so that, like apparitions, they seemed to glide above the ground. The Ku Klux Klan, which was founded in 1865, wore grotesque disguises and spread the notion that they were the ghosts of the Confederate dead. Indeed they often met in graveyards, since the large, old-fashioned box-tombs were useful for hiding all their bulky paraphernalia.[112] Gladys Fry has made a full study of the subject.

Slavery, colonialism and notions of racial superiority were closely linked to the now discarded theory of unilinear evolution. In 1969, Ruth Finnegan wrote scathingly — and perhaps rather unjustly, since folklore studies even in this country were already undergoing a revival — that:

When (the) concept of unilinear evolution came to be rejected the whole foundation of the 'science of folk-lore' collapsed with it. The study of primitive society developed other interests and theoretical preoccupations and was, under the name of 'social anthropology' adopted into several British Universities. Among academic anthropologists and fieldworkers the term 'folklore' came to be reserved as a synonym for the old evolutionist and uncritical position held by earlier writers in the subject, and by now totally rejected. Those 'folklorists' who cling, and still cling, to the old theoretical framework and write, for example, about 'the folklore of the British Isles' in terms of odd local customs, by-ways, 'survivals', old superstitions, or 'ancient fertility cults', are regarded with scorn by modern professional anthropologists — often rightly so — as dilettante, uncritical, and addicted to a totally out-dated theoretical framework. It is not surprising in view of this that 'folklore' has become almost a term of abuse among social anthropologists today.[113]

This was, of course, written eleven years ago. She goes on to say that in the heat of the reaction against folklore, anthropologists also dropped the study of oral literature.[114] A revival of interest in that field during the last decade or so has been largely due to the scholarly, sensible and imaginative work of Ruth Finnegan herself.

Today it is recognised that the art of storytelling is just as important as the tales themselves, which need to be studied within their cultural context. Ruth Finnegan's African research shows clearly how each narration constitutes a performance in itself. The storyteller makes use of mimicry — perhaps the noise of a swimming tortoise — gestures to portray the various characters, and uses subtle alterations in the timbre of his voice. An African audience will respond to the storyteller, clapping their hands, and exclaiming and laughing at suitable points in the course of the narrative. Sometimes a member of the audience is specially singled out to do this. Audience participation and interested listeners provide encouragement and help the narrator to give a better performance.

Eminent scholars like the Chadwicks[115] thought in terms of an 'heroic age'; others have written studies of 'ballad society'. The notion of an oral 'storytelling society' is just as oversimplified and misleading. Much anthropological thinking during the last hundred years has posited a somewhat romantically conceived homogeneous, non-industrial, rural community with its own pure and uncontaminated oral culture.

Ruth Finnegan sensibly points out that isolation and self-sufficiency are both relative. It is all too easy to overlook the influence of traders, missionaries, administrators, educators, foreign observers and others. Many cultures described as primitive in the Middle East and Africa have flourished on the borders of a literate tradition; centuries of contact with the world's major religions — Christianity, Hinduism, Islam — are conveniently overlooked. In Europe ethnic communities have become cosmopolitan and oral tradition and literacy continually overlap and borrow from each other.

Jerome Mintz's book *Legends of the Hasidim* (1968) attempts to describe and analyse this particular culture through the rich oral tradition that has flourished in hasidic communities for more than two hundred years, first in Central and Eastern Europe, and now in America, Israel and London.[116] It has to be said, however, that hasidic society is somewhat unusual in this respect. For hasids regard the printed word, or at least the printing of their own stories, with great suspicion. They are afraid an editor may tamper with the didactic legends, whose function is to teach their faith and religious way of life. The Baal Shem Tov (1700-60), their founder, taught orally, using tales and parables, and was sceptical of attempts to write down his teachings. His followers have tried to prevent stories of their rabbis from being published. They might, so it was felt, be tainted by the fictional associations of the printed word. Indeed some of the rabbis forbid their followers to read printed legends, for they may contain untruths.[117] But even in this closed and rigid community the modern world has made itself felt.

In their book *Urban Folklore from the Paperwork Empire* (1975), Alan Dundes and Carl Pagter firmly knock the traditional notion that folklore is always oral. Literacy, as we have seen, was often a factor in defining 'the folk', who were thought of in the nineteenth century as the illiterate element within a literate society.[118] Many folklorists still tend to regard folklore as orally transmitted, though I have already mentioned Lutz Röhrich's work on comics.[119] There are other forms to which the same applies, for instance folk art and graffiti. The materials in Dundes and Pagter's book were transmitted by modern methods like photocopying and typing, and through manuscripts. It is time, they say, that the long-standing oral definition of folklore is scrapped,[120] and they are certainly right.

The confusion between folklore and anthropology also needs to be overcome, and one of the aims of this *Introduction* has been to clarify our position as folklorists. Even twelve years ago, in a review of Richard Dorson's monumental work, *The British Folklorists*,[121] Dennis Potter discussed folklore and 'the huge fish which was eventually to swallow it almost entire: anthropology'.[122] Potter was wrong: no gullet large enough has yet been found to swallow us — hence the success of the Conference documented by this volume. To an extent we share a common basis with the anthropologists. Sir Edward Tylor (1832-1917), sometimes referred to as the father of anthropology, was among the founder members of the Folklore Society; so were Andrew Lang (1844-1912) and Sir James Frazer (1854-1941), author of *The Golden Bough* (1890-1936). In England, and perhaps in certain other countries, the anthropologists have found their feet better than we have, and there will be those who may look for evidence of this in these conference proceedings. But, in general, a definable trend is clear in the field of folklore research and analysis, a trend which will continue and will confirm our independent position in the academic world.

Notes

1. Maria Leach, *Dictionary of Folklore, Mythology and Legend* (New York, 1949), 398-407.

2. Jan Brunvand, *The Study of American Folklore* (New York, 1968), 1.

3. Alan Bullock and Oliver Stallybrass, eds., *The Fontana Dictionary of Modern Thought* (London, 1977), 238, 609.

4. Jan Brunvand, *A Guide for Collectors of Folklore in Utah* (Salt Lake City, 1971), 4; Alan Dundes, *The Study of Folklore* (Englewood Cliffs, 1965), 2.

5. A. M. Prokhorov, ed., *Great Soviet Encyclopaedia*, tr. Maxine Bronstein a.o. (New York and London, 1978), XVII, 57.

6. Ronald Fletcher in Bullock and Stallybrass, 238.

7. Roland Barthes, *S/Z* (Paris, 1970), 129; quoted in Victoria Barnsley, *Realism: A French Perspective* (unpublished M.A. dissertation, York University, 1979), 27-8. I am also grateful to Victoria Barnsley for drawing my attention to Heath's exposition of this theory.

8. Stephen Heath, *The Nouveau Roman* (London, 1972), 20.

9. *Ibid.*

10. Thomas Hardy, *Far From the Madding Crowd*. The quotation is from the 'Preface' to the (London) edition of 1895, expanded in 1902.

11. The First Anglo-American Folklore Conference, which I was privileged to help organise, was held at Ditchley Park, Oxfordshire, in Autumn 1967.

12. J. S. Udal, *Dorsetshire Folk-Lore* (Hertford, 1922), 176.

13. Florence Emily Hardy, *The Early Life of Thomas Hardy* (London, 1928), 301-2.

14. *Folk-Lore*, VIII (1) (1897), 11.

15. *Ibid.*

16. *Ibid.*, 11-12; see also J. G. Frazer, *The Golden Bough* (London, 1911), I, 136 and n.6. The first edition of Volume I appeared in 1890.

17. First published in 1887.

18. Brunvand (1968), 2; Barre Toelken, *The Dynamics of Folklore* (Boston, 1979), 4.

19. *Ibid.*; Benjamin Botkin, 'The Folkness of the Folk', *Folklore in Action*, ed. Horace Beck (Philadelphia, 1962), 46; Alan Dundes and Carl Pagter, *Urban Folklore from the Paperwork Empire* (Austin, 1975), xiv-xv, 221; William P. Murphy, 'Oral Literature', *Annual Review of Anthropology* (Palo Alto, 1978), VII, 115.

20. Kenneth and Mary Clarke, *Introducing Folklore* (New York, 1963), 8; Rosalie H. Wax, *Doing Fieldwork* (Chicago, 1971), 21-2.

21. Botkin, 45; Clarke, 9; Richard Dorson, 'Foreword', *Folktales of Germany*, ed. Kurt Ranke (London, 1966), v, xvii-xviii.

22. Linda Dégh, 'Folk Narrative', *Folklore and Folklife: An Introduction*, ed. Richard Dorson (Chicago, 1972), 54-5; Felix Oinas, 'Folklore Activities in Russia', *Journal of American Folklore*, LXXIV (1961), 362.

23. Brunvand (1968), 83.

24. William Bascom, 'Four Functions of Folklore', *Journal of American Folklore*, LXVII (1954), 339.

25. Brunvand (1968), 121-2; Daniel Crowley, *I Could Talk Old-Story Good: Creativity in Bahamian Folklore* (Berkeley, 1966), 1.

26. Murphy, 115-7.

27. John Rogerson, *Anthropology of the Old Testament* (Oxford, 1978), 23.

28. Brunvand (1968), 84; Clarke, 31.

29. Toelken, 4.

30. Brunvand (1968), 84; Clarke, 28; Linda Dégh, 'Folklore and Related Disciplines in Eastern Europe', *Journal of the Folklore Institute*, II (1965), 106-7.

31. Brunvand (1968), 21; Murphy, 118; Rogerson, 23; Toelken, 5; Richard Dorson, *American Folklore* (Chicago, 1959), 1.

32. Brunvand (1968), 21, 192; Toelken, 5; Åke Hultkrantz, *General Ethnological Concepts: International Dictionary of Regional Ethnology and Folklore*, Vol.I (Copenhagen, 1960), 158-9. See also Hans Naumann, *Grundzüge der deutschen Volkskunde* (Leipzig. 1922).

33. Clarke, 28, 41; Dorson (1966), xvii; *idem*, 'Foreword', *Folktales of France*, ed. Geneviève Massignon (London, 1968), viii, x-xi.

34. Bascom, 339; Brunvand (1968), 84; Dorson (1966), xvi; Murphy, 119. See Henri Gaidoz, 'Comme quoi M. Max Müller n'a jamais existé', *Mélusine*, II (1884).

35. Mary Douglas, *Purity and Danger* (London, 1966), 7; Claude Lévi-Strauss, *Structural Anthropology* (London, 1968), 324-5; Raymond Williams, *Keywords: A Vocabulary of Culture and Society* (Glasgow, 1976), 253.

36. F. S. Perls, R. F. Hefferline and Paul Goodman, *Gestalt Therapy* (London, 1973), 14.

37. *Ibid.*, 16; Michael Lane, ed., *Introduction to Structuralism* (New York, 1970), 22.

38. Francis L. Utley, 'Introduction', Max Lüthi, *Once Upon a Time* (New York, 1970), 4.

39. Rosalind Coward and John Ellis, *Language and Materialism* (London, 1977), 1.

40. Eleazar Meletinsky, 'Structural-Typological Study of Folktales', *Soviet Structural Folk-loristics*, ed. P. Maranda (The Hague, 1974), 25.

41. Lane, 27; Lévi-Strauss, 20; Frank Kermode, 'Foreword', Pierre Guiraud, *Semiology* (London, 1975), vii.

42. Barnsley, 9, 12; Lane, 27.

43. Lane, 28.

44. Coward and Ellis, 14.

45. Barnsley, 9, 12.

46. *Ibid.*, 12; Dégh, 119; 'Saussure', *Encyclopaedia Britannica*, ed. Warren E. Preece (Chicago, 1972), XIX, 1096.

47. Coward and Ellis, 96.

48. John Lotz, 'Roman Jakobson', *Encyclopaedia Britannica*, XII, 849.

49. Rogerson, 106.

50. Lane, 12; David Kronenfeld, 'Structuralism', *Annual Review of Anthropology* (Palo Alto, 1979), VIII, 514, 516; Edmund Leach, *Lévi-Strauss* (London, 1970), 27-8.

51. Coward and Ellis, 15; Kronenfeld, 505; Rogerson, 106.

52. Lane, 32; Rogerson, 19-20, 106; Raoul Makarius, 'Structuralism − Science or Ideology?' *Socialist Register 1974* (London, 1974), 195-6, 201.

53. Lévi-Strauss, xii; Rogerson, 106, 110; Umberto Eco, 'Looking for a Logic of Culture', *The Tell-Tale Sign*, ed. Thomas Sebeok (Lisse, 1975), 14; Peter Munz, *When the Golden Bough Breaks* (London, 1973), 5.

54. Makarius, 211.

55. Edmund Leach, 97-8.

56. Rogerson, 106.

57. Lévi-Strauss, x, xi; Makarius, 203; Don Brenneis, '(Review) Edmund Leach, *Culture and Communication: The Logic by which Symbols are Connected*', *Journal of American Folklore*, XCII (1979), 493.

58. Makarius, 203; Murphy, 120.

59. Rogerson, 109.

60. Alan Dundes, 'Introduction to the Second [English Language] Edition', V. Propp, *Morphology of the Folktale* (Austin, 1968), xi.

61. Munz, 6.

62. Makarius, 197.

63. *Ibid.*, 203-4.

64. Meletinsky, 25.

65. Williams, 254; William M. Austin, 'Linguistics', *Encyclopaedia Britannica*, XIV, 69.

66. Williams, 255.

67. Meletinsky, 25.

68. Richard Dorson, 'Is Folklore a Discipline?' *Folklore*, LXXXIV (1973), 196.

69. Mihály Hoppál and Vilmos Voigt, 'Models in the Research of Forms of Social Mind', *Acta Ethnographica*, XVIII (1969), 365.

70. Austin, 69.

71. Hoppál and Voigt, 385; Pierre Maranda, 'Structuralism in Cultural Anthropology', *Annual Review of Anthropology* (Palo Alto, 1972), I, 334. In North American English 'cultural anthropology' is practically equivalent to our term 'social anthropology'.

72. Williams, 258.

73. Oinas, 364.

74. See Note 60, above, which refers to the second edition ten years later.

75. Dundes (1968), xi; Meletinsky, 19, 29; Oinas, 364; Richard Dorson, *Folklore and Folklife: An Introduction* (Chicago, 1972), 34-6.

76. Botkin, 46; Murphy, 131.

77. Linda Dégh, *Folktales and Society* (Bloomington, 1969), 46, 48; Carl von Sydow, *Selected Papers on Folklore* (Copenhagen, 1948), 207-19.

78. Bronislaw Malinowski, *Myth in Primitive Psychology* (London, 1926), 29-30, 34-5, 54.

79. Dorson (1972), 45.

80. Dégh (1965), 103-4.

81. *Ibid.*; Dorson (1966), vi; E. J. Lindgren, 'The Collection and Analysis of Folk-Lore', *The Study of Society*, ed. Frederic Bartlett (London, 1939), 338.

82. Edmund Hodge, *Enjoying the Lakes* (Edinburgh, 1957), 48.

83. *Ibid.*, 108.

84. Bascom, 339; Brunvand (1968), 84; Dégh (1965), 104; Dorson (1966), xvii.

85. Dorson (1959), 2-3; Lindgren, 329.

86. Murphy, 115.

87. Dégh (1965), 104-5.

88. Richard Dorson, 'Foreword', *Folktales of Ireland*, ed. Seán O'Sullivan (London, 1966), xiii, xxiii, xxvi.

89. *Idem*, 'Foreword', *Folktales of Greece*, ed. Georgios Megas (London, 1970), xiv.

90. *Idem*, 'Foreword', *Folktales of Norway*, ed. Reidar Christiansen (London, 1964), v.

91. Clarke, 115.

92. Dorson (1959), 3.

93. Dégh (1965), 104-5.

94. Dorson (1970), xi.

95. Clarke, 99.

96. Hans Moser, 'Vom Folklorismus in unserer Zeit', *Zeitschrift für Volkskunde*, LVIII (1962), 177-209.

97. Lutz Röhrich, 'Comics, Advertising, Mass-Lore', *Current Trends in Folk Narrative Theory*, ed. Lutz Röhrich (Freiburg, 1979), 34.

98. *Sunday Times*, 1st September 1968.

99. Frances A. Yates, *Astraea: The Imperial Theme in the Sixteenth Century* (London, 1975), xii.

100. Clarke, 2; Oinas, 366; Richard Dorson, 'Foreword', *Folktales of Hungary*, ed. Linda Dégh (London, 1965), vi.

101. Dégh (1965), 111.

102. Oinas, 365.

103. *Ibid.*; Venetia Newall, 'Tell us a Story', *Not Work Alone*, ed. Jeremy Cherfas and Roger Lewin (London, 1980), 212-3; Y. M. Sokolov, *Russian Folklore* (New York, 1950), 661-8.

104. *Ibid.*, 663-4.

105. *Ibid.*, 664.

106. Ellic Howe, 'Neo-Pagan German Cults', *Man, Myth and Magic*, ed. Richard Cavendish (London, 1971), V, 1964, 1966; George L. Mosse, *The Crisis of German Ideology* (London, 1966), 149-311.

107. Ellic Howe, 'National Socialism', *Man, Myth and Magic*, V, 1944, 1948.

108. *Der Stürmer*, No.35 (1935).

109. Franz Kolbrand, 'Gedenken und Anregungen zum Erntefest des deutsches Volkes', *Heimatleben*, No.8 (1939); George L. Mosse, *Nazi Culture* (London, 1966), 122-6; Robert J. O'Neill, *The German Army and the Nazi Party* (London, 1966), illus. following 56; H. R. Trevor Roper, ed., *The Bormann Letters* (London, 1954), 177, 198.

110. Gladys-Marie Fry, *Night Riders in Black Folk History* (Knoxville, 1975), 3, 71.

111. *Ibid.*, 87, 143.

112. *Ibid.*, 70-1, 143.

113. Ruth Finnegan, 'Attitudes to the Study of Oral Literature in British Social Anthropology', *Man*, IV (New Series) (1969), 62.

114. *Ibid.*

115. H. M. and N. K. Chadwick, *The Growth of Literature*, 3 vols (Cambridge, 1932-40).

116. Jerome R. Mintz, *Legends of the Hassidim* (Chicago, 1968), 1-4.

117. *Ibid.*

118. Dundes and Pagter, xv, 221.

119. The work of Professor Rolf Brednich at the University of Freiburg should also be mentioned in this connection.

120. Dundes and Pagter, xvi.

121. Richard Dorson, *The British Folklorists* (London, 1968).

122. *The Times*, 18th January 1969.

Plate I. The Rev. Professor J. R. Porter, President of the Folklore Society, and Dr Venetia J. Newall, Hon. Secretary, welcoming the participants at the opening reception.

Plate II. The Hooden Horse of Kent (Barnett Field) which entertained the guests at the opening reception.

Plate III. The Convener and Hon. Secretary, Dr Venetia J. Newall, beside the statue of Queen Victoria at Royal Holloway College.

Plate IV. The Conference in session: seated in the front row (right to left) Dr H. R. Ellis Davidson, Vice-President of the Folklore Society, with her husband, Richard Davidson; Dr Katharine Briggs, Vice-President; Brid Mahon (University College Dublin); Professor Dan Ben-Amos (University of Philadelphia); Dr John Niles (University of California at Berkeley); Dr Bengt Holbek (University of Copenhagen).

Plate V. Professor Dan Ben-Amos (University of Philadelphia) in conversation with Professor Anna-Birgitta Rooth (University of Uppsala) during an interval between sessions.

Plate VI. Professor Alan Dundes (University of California at Berkeley) delivering his plenary session paper. In the foreground (left to right) Dr Venetia J. Newall, Hon. Secretary of the Folklore Society; Dr J. Olowo Ojoade (University of Jos, Nigeria); the Rev. Professor J. R. Porter, President of the Folklore Society.

Plate VII. The Minehead Sailors' Hobby Horse which entertained participants in the quadrangle on the last day of the Conference.

Plate VIII. A performance by the Kennet Morris Men of Reading which took place after the Banquet on the final evening.

INTRODUCTORY PAPERS

The Place of the Folklore Society in Folklore Studies *

J. R. PORTER   University of Exeter

ON behalf of the Folklore Society, I want to welcome all of you most warmly to this conference. You have come from all over the world and we in the Folklore Society of this country greatly appreciate your joining us on this occasion. The organising of international conferences of this kind has always been a particular concern of the Folklore Society and the first of these, held in 1891, was an indication of how firmly the Society had established itself during the first twelve years of its life and was an important milestone in its history. We like to feel that your presence here is a sign of your appreciation of what the Folklore Society has been able to achieve in the study of our subject during the last hundred years and that you are honouring the memory, not only of the illustrious scholars who have been associated with it, but also of the thousands of others, not so well-known, whose devotion and enthusiasm have contributed so much to its existence and to its activities. We are glad to see you here, we hope you will enjoy yourselves and we know you will learn a great deal.

So, of course, I want to say a special word of thanks to those of you who are reading papers. They cover an immensely wide range and one's only regret is that one will not be able to listen to all of them. The title of our conference is 'Folklore Studies in the 20th Century' and, speaking for myself, I am particularly interested to note the number of contributions concerned not only with the study of folklore *in* the 20th century but with the study of folklore *of* the 20th century — that is, with folklore not just as a survival, which was how the pioneers of the subject tended to regard it, but with folklore as something which human beings are creating all the time, just because they are human beings. We have come a

long way from the time in 1878 when the Folklore Society could see its purpose almost exclusively as 'the *preservation* and publication of Legendary Ballads, Local Proverbial Sayings, Superstitions and Old Customs,' although it is fair to say that in fact it has never entirely confined itself to that. I note also that when the original rules of the Society spoke of the preservation of Old Customs, the words were added in brackets 'British or Foreign'. Those adjectives seem today to have a rather insular, not to say imperialistic ring about them, but that very fact shows how the study of folklore has now developed into a clearly recognisable discipline, to which scholars of all nations can contribute to their mutual benefit and understanding. There is something which can properly be called folklore which is not simply the amalgam of the traditions and customs of a particular society, country or race. And I think the words I have quoted show that the founding fathers of the Society at least glimpsed the possibility of the future development which has occurred. Certainly their work was one of the chief factors in making folklore a distinctive scholarly discipline, by giving it in their time a theoretical frame-work and a sound methodology. They would surely have rejoiced to see a conference like this, and those of us who have been concerned with planning and organising it have been immensely encouraged and excited by the ready response to our request for papers from so large, so widely representative and so distinguished a body of scholars.

What I have just been saying leads me on to a few brief remarks about the Folklore Society and about the present position of folklore studies in this country in general. I hope you will not feel I am being unduly domestic in this. I can only plead in defence my own very limited knowledge

---

* Presidential Address, delivered at the opening of the conference.

and it would be folly to parade my ignorance before people who have a far greater acquaintance with, and direct experience of, the world situation of folklore studies than I have. The cobbler had better stick to his last and anyway one aspect of this conference is as a little celebration of the centenary of the Folklore Society. Now I do not propose to survey the history of that Society as it has unrolled so far and this for two reasons. First I do not feel that I could do so adequately at this point, and it has already been excellently done by others who are far more capable than I. Perhaps I may be allowed to mention two such contributions. There is the introductory essay to the Society's Centenary Volume, *Animals in Folklore*, by Dr Katherine Briggs, the product of one who has had an unrivalled knowledge of the Society's life over many years, and then the article by Professor Richard Dorson in the current *Times Literary Supplement*, with its delightfully evocative opening, describing the scholarly chaos of the Society's library just after the war. I did not myself know it then, but I feel it was the sort of library I should rather have enjoyed, because somehow it is only there that you come across the vital books you had never stumbled upon before, as indeed Professor Dorson himself did. However, all that has long ago been put right, and if any of you who have not already done so are able to visit our unique library housed in University College London, I am sure you will find it very well organised and a pleasant place in which to read.

But my second reason for not dealing much with the history of the Folklore Society is that we have surely to consider its future as well as its past. After all, a centenary is an artificial event, a hundred years is only a section of the ever rolling stream of time. Nor is there anything particularly valuable or meritorious in just having lasted: the answer of the French aristocrat, when asked what he had done in the Revolution, *j'ai survécu*, I survived, no doubt had great significance for him, but probably not for anybody else. It is always a good thing for an organisation to ask itself where it thinks it is going and whether it is still fulfilling any useful function. I am led to these reflections by the tone of some comments which I have seen in connection with the Society's centenary, comments which we should certainly not resent, because the truth, if it is the truth, is always

important and there are few things more valuable than informed criticism. The comments I have in mind suggest that the great days of the Society are over and that it can no longer be the formative influence in the progress of Folklore studies that it was at the turn of the century, when its leaders were able to enunciate what might almost be called a set of laws by which folklore could be seen to operate. In particular, the study of folklore must now be seen as a definite academic discipline, its future lying with professional full-time scholars and finding its home in universities and research institutes, requiring, and being able to call upon, vastly greater resources than are ever likely to be at the disposal of such a body as the Folklore Society. In this situation, what is the role of the Folklore Society, and similar societies in other countries? More radically, has it any longer got one at all?

Now, it is almost certainly true that the Folklore Society cannot expect to play the same creative and dominant part in the study of folklore in the future as it once did in the past. But I do not think that any other group or organisation, still less any individual, can expect to do so either. And this is precisely the price of success, the success of the Folklore Society in establishing folklore as a subject for serious academic study in this country, and in attracting serious scholars to devote their attentions to it. When this happens, the subject becomes too diverse and too complex, and particular areas within it become too specialised, for any single theory or overall view of it to continue to be viable. Nor is this peculiar to folklore. The same could be said of the approach to virtually every academic discipline in the 20th century in contrast to the climate of opinion in, let us say, the 19th.

Within this situation, it seems to me that there remains, and is likely to remain, an important and significant place for the activities of a body such as the Folklore Society, and this in a variety of ways. In the first place, the Society can provide a bridge between the work of professional folklorists and that wider public which takes an interest in what they study. That interest is certainly there but it is often ill-informed and popular attention becomes concentrated on the trivial, sentimental and sensational aspects of what is taken to be folklore. The busy professional scholar has little time, and often less opportunity, to combat such misconceptions.

A society with a broader base than the purely academic, and with wide support, can do much more in this direction, by keeping its members in touch, through its meetings and publications, with what is going on in the area of folklore studies and so enabling a better understanding of their real nature to spread throughout the wider community. I can think of no agency other than something like the Folklore Society which would be equally effective in carrying out this task of education and, if you like, propaganda: to paraphrase Voltaire's famous words, if the Society did not exist it would be necessary to invent it.

Secondly, the primarily non-academic basis of such a Society corresponds in important respects to the character of the study of folklore itself. If I may be allowed to quote Professor Dorson again, in a lecture to the Folklore Society, he spoke of the emergence of new groupings in the humanities that 'seek to overturn the elitist, highbrow, rarefied and to a large extent stultifying approach of the established disciplines and get closer to the flavour of common life' and he went on to say that 'in this new thrust folklore studies will clearly play a key role.' In other words, the study of folklore is concerned with the traditions and customs of the mass of ordinary people, if one may speak rather vaguely, with what the early practitioners of the subject meant when they talked about 'the folk': and, if this is so, there must surely be a large role, larger than in some other disciplines, for those who are in close daily touch, in work and leisure, with those ordinary people, in a way which is not always easy for those engaged primarily on the academic level.

I quoted earlier the Folklore Society's original statement of its purpose as the preservation and publication of popular traditions and customs and all subjects relating to them and I believe that this remains as important and as primary as it ever was. The lifeblood of our particular studies, without which they cannot exist, is the continual identification, observation and collection of the basic material, and this is growing, and is in danger of disappearing unrecognised, all the time, because, as I mentioned earlier, folklore does not simply consist of past survivals, but is always being created, and will go on being created, as long as mankind exists. Now, when it comes to the collecting and preserving of the immense amount of basic material which is available to us, the rule must be 'the more the merrier'. The more people who can be made interested in this task, the more rapidly and the more soundly will folklore studies progress, provided — and it is an all-important proviso — that the observers and collectors go about their job in the right way, with a proper understanding of a truly scientific approach to what they are doing. It has been the aim of the Society from its foundation to try and inculcate this proper approach among its membership and to remove the labels bearing the legends quaint, picturesque and entertaining which hung, and still hang, round the neck of folklore. The professional scholar will continue to rely to a considerable extent on the material produced for him by the amateur — and I use that term in no derogatory sense, but in its original meaning of one who loves his subject, whether he pursues it professionally or not. Certainly, in this country, and particularly in the circumstances of financial stringency which are likely to be with us for a long time, few University departments or institutes concerned with folklore studies are going to be able to mount research programmes requiring long and intensive fieldwork on anything like the scale that is needed. We shall continue to require the active participation of a much larger body of interested people working on their own and, to put it bluntly, doing it for nothing.

Such people have always formed the backbone of the Folklore Society and have given it its distinctive character. I do not believe that their day is over and I think that the Society has as important a function as ever as a forum for the presentation and co-ordination of their work. Similar considerations apply to publication — up to a point, 'the more the merrier'. The more serious and scientific articles, monographs and books on folklore that can be published, the better it will be for the advancement of our subject: indeed, without such publication, the subject can hardly progress at all. But again the proviso is important. It would appear to be not too difficult to find a publisher for rubbish in almost any field, but folklore has perhaps suffered more than most other subjects in this respect. And no doubt this largely accounts for the scorn and suspicion with which it is still regarded by many educated people, especially in academic circles. But scholarly publication is difficult and, once more, in the present financial climate, becomes increasingly so. The Folklore Society has always had the publication of learned works as one of its main objectives and it has a distinguished record in this field. Its resources for publishing have never been large, but it has done a great deal and often in the past it has almost stood alone in producing and fostering truly serious and scholarly writing on folklore subjects. Further, its journal *Folklore*, through its articles and reviews, has always provided a means by which what is written about folklore can be discussed, assessed and, where necessary, exposed: here again, journals devoted to the furtherance of sound scholarship have an essential part to play in the advancement of any discipline. Happily, but again not least because of the Society's own efforts, excellent and thoroughly scientific studies of folklore subjects can more readily find a publisher than was once the case. But there will always be a good deal of such work which will not be a commercial proposition. It is work of this kind which the Folklore Society tries to bring to the light of day and, for the reasons I have indicated, the need for this aspect of the Society's work is unlikely to grow any less. Of course, it may be said that we cannot do very much, but, if I may be trite again, every little helps. Indeed, I would go further and claim, modestly, I hope, that our tally of publications in the last few years, during which learned societies in this country have faced unprecedented difficulties, is not unworthy of the Society's great record in the past, both as regards quantity and quality. Anyway, our recent endeavours are on display at this conference and I hope that those of you who may have not come across them will take the opportunity to inspect them and judge for yourselves.

I referred earlier to one of the functions of the Folklore Society as being the encouragement and co-ordinating of the work on folklore that is done by a wide range of individuals and groups in different walks of life and in different parts of the country. I would like to say a little more about this, because I think it is an area where perhaps the Society should go further ahead and be more active than it perhaps has been in recent years — indeed, the long-suffering members of the Committee of the Folklore Society who are present will recognise that the President's King Charles' head is now about to be reared once more. But actual hobby-horses are a prominent feature of this conference, so perhaps you will allow me to ride my metaphorical one for a few moments. The Society from its foundation has always had its base in London and it is right, not to say inevitable, that this should be so. A library, which is one of the most valuable facilities we can provide for the furtherance of folklore scholarship, has to be located somewhere: important papers by distinguished scholars, which again are one of the chief means by which scholarship in our field is advanced, have to be read, and, no less importantly, discussed, somewhere. But work on the ground, that vital observation and collection of the raw material of folklore, has to be done locally. In the past, in this country there have existed many flourishing local and regional folklore societies, some of which happily still survive. But a number have, for various reasons, ceased to exist over the years and others, I think it fair, if perhaps unkind, to say, are somewhat moribund. For the general health of folklore studies, I am sure that such societies ought to be increased and revived. And I believe that the Folklore Society, with its long experience and the knowledge it has accumulated in its hundred years of existence, can take the lead in this task. It is not a question of the Society trying to tell local groups what they ought to be doing, for folklorists are traditionally, and understandably, jealous of their independence. Rather, I see the existing members of the Society in a particular area as taking steps to constitute the nucleus of a local group and the central organs of the Society itself providing help and guidance about programmes of study which they might undertake and making the results more generally available, through our journal and in other ways, so that they can be fed into the whole continuing process of folklore studies and be made known to the general body of those working in the area. Perhaps we are not at the moment specially well-equipped for this very necessary task, but, frankly, I do not quite see who else is to do it, and we have in fact already made a modest start on it. Several local folklore groups have recently come into being as a result of the Society's encouragement — perhaps I may be permitted just to single out the group recently formed in London which has already begun, under its own auspices, to publish material collected by its members on the very rich folklore which our capital city provides.

Let me conclude this part of my remarks with a few observations about the role of the professional folklorist and the happily increasing recognition and development of folklore studies in Universities and Institutes. From what I have said, you will have gathered that I see no ground for conflict between University or Institute-based folklore study and what I might call Society-based folklore study, nor do I think that the latter must inevitably be displaced by these newer developments. Its function has now to be seen in a new context and certainly more thought needs to be given to precisely what its future role should be. On the contrary, I envisage a fruitful interaction between the two, something which already exists and should surely continue. University disciplines which, we must never forget, are always threatened to some degree, require to be sustained and buttressed by a strong and sympathetic non-academic constituency of common interest. One only needs to mention the role of such bodies as the Classical Association or the Historical Association or the various similar scientific or language societies, in relation to their respective academic subjects, to realise the importance of this. And it is such a role in relation to professional folklore studies that the Folklore Society and similar bodies ought surely to fulfil.

May I make two further points in this connection? First, it has often been observed, and quite rightly, that folklore is still viewed with a good deal of suspicion by academics and is frequently regarded as not being a subject worthy of study at University level. And even when some serious and informed consideration is given to it, it often seems to be viewed primarily as something ripe for a take-over bid by one or other of the more firmly established disciplines. Folklorists are frequently abused for being woefully ignorant about anthropology, or sociology, or psychology, or history, or oral literature or even comparative linguistics, and told that if only they knew more about them, they would realise that folklore was really only a branch of one or other of these fields of study. No doubt there is a good deal of truth in these criticisms on specific matters of detail — I myself have had cause to criticise the very odd remarks folklorists sometimes make about religion. But all too often these criticisms are misplaced, because they

fail to accept the fact that the study of folklore is a subject in its own right, that while the folklorist must always take account of other disciplines, he is not actually pursuing them, that he approaches the phenomenon that we call folklore from a different standpoint from theirs, and seeks to answer different questions from those which they ask. It is just here that I think the Folklore Society can be of great significance. The Society has always numbered among its members distinguished scholars whose main concern and expertise has lain in fields other than folklore and I think it is true to say that they have made an increasingly important contribution to its whole life and work in recent years. Many of them will not be in close or direct contact with a professional centre of academic folklore study and for the reasons already mentioned, may well not be so for a long time ahead. It is largely through their participation in the Society that they can begin to understand what folklore is really all about, that they can come to realise how their own particular knowledge can contribute to it, rather than dominating it and how it, from its own distinctive standpoint, can illuminate many areas of the subjects with which they are professionally engaged. This is one way, surely, in which the study of folklore may hope to gain sympathy and support in academic circles. If I may speak personally again, this has certainly been my own experience as a member of the Folklore Society: but I am confident that here I do not stand alone.

Secondly, it has also often been observed, and again rightly, that England has lagged far behind other countries in the degree of actual academic recognition, measured by the establishment of research and teaching posts, which it has given to folklore studies. When one considers the background of so many of the participants in this conference, the number of Universities and Research Institutes that they represent, one can only regretfully acknowledge England's backwardness in this respect — I say 'England' advisedly, because matters have long been better ordered among our Celtic neighbours. But even in darkest England, there are glimmers of light and recent years have seen the arrival of folklore studies as a distinct discipline in its own right on the University scene. Outstanding examples are the Institute of Dialect and Folk Life Studies at the University of Leeds, of which Mr Stewart Sanderson is the Director, and the Centre for English Cultural Tradition and Language, founded as a result of the tireless labours of Dr John Widdowson, with its archives, its artefacts and its own journal. Beginning in 1969, other Universities have established appointments specifically in folklore and there are now at least six Universities where folklore is accepted as part of first degree courses. Nor as I have tried to show, does this list exhaust the interest in folklore, nor the work being done in that area by academics who do not hold a post specifically with that title. We were late on the scene, we have only made a beginning, but we hope it may mark the beginning of the end of the neglect of our subject in this country's institutions of higher education. What I would emphasise again is that these developments, and I trust future ones, have not come about in complete isolation from the Folklore Society itself. It has been part of the background of most of them and all of the people I have mentioned are, I think, members of the Folklore Society and many of them have taken an active part in its work, by serving on its Committee and in numerous other ways. Everyone must welcome the academic developments I have briefly outlined, but, for the forseeable future, folklore studies will still need both their academic and their non-academic bases if they are to realise their full potential.

I hope you will not feel that I have been unduly parochial in devoting most of what I have tried to say to the situation of folklore in England and to the role in them of the English Folklore Society. But this conference is being held in commemoration of that Society's centenary and I thought I must therefore comment on it, with the object of giving you some idea of how things look to your hosts, before we were engulfed by the wider, and, doubtless more stimulating, topics that will claim our attention for the next three busy days. We certainly do not forget that this conference is above all international; it is to share our common research in the field of folklore study and to express our common devotion to the subject that we have come together at all.

I began with an expression of thanks, and I want to end with another. Of course, a considerable number of people have been concerned with planning and running this conference and I hope we shall have an opportunity of expressing our appreciation to at least some of them on a later occasion. But we would never have got off the ground at all without our Secretary, Venetia Newall: it will come as no surprise to the many here who know her that all the hard work has fallen on her shoulders. Only those who have ever tried to organise an international conference can have any idea how hard that work really is — only those of us who have seen Venetia Newall tackling it can know how much better she does it than one could even dream of doing oneself. As always, and in so many ways, she has given unstintingly of her time and energy to the work of the Society, but we can never forget that her first concern is always with scholarship. Indeed, her whole career as, on the one hand, an independent scholar and writer, and, on the other, as a lecturer and teacher, exemplifies that link between the Folklore Society and the University world of which I spoke earlier, and is in the great tradition of the Society. She has for some years been Honorary Research Fellow in Folklore at University College London and only the other day she was awarded the degree of Doctor of Letters, for her numerous writings on folklore, by St Andrews, her old University and one, which she has reminded me, has had long and close connections with folklore studies. It is a great and well-deserved honour to Venetia Newall herself -- Dr Newall as we shall have to learn to call her — but I am sure she would want to say that it also honours the study of folklore in general, and the Folklore Society in particular. I am delighted to be able to announce it at the very outset of this conference which, without her, simply could not have taken place at all.

Ladies and gentlemen, in the words of T.S. Eliot, in my end is my beginning: my purpose has been to welcome you all most warmly in the name of the Folklore Society, to thank you for your presence on this great occasion in the Society's history, to hope that you will greatly enjoy your time here.

The Founders of British Folklore*

RICHARD M. DORSON   Indiana University

EARLY in the summer of 1948 I made my first visit to London, where my sister lived with her English husband, and in the course of drinking in the sights and sounds of that wondrous city I stopped at the office of The Folklore Society in Bedford Square. At that time the Royal Anthropological Institute handled the affairs of the smaller society. The secretary informed me that the society held no meetings during the summer, but that I might wish to look at the Society's library, housed in University College close by. Disappointed at not finding fellow-folklorists about, I trudged down Gower Street and after some inquiries located the folklore collection, temporarily housed in some rear stacks in the medical library, because a bomb had hit the main library. Books lay cluttered on the shelves and spilled on to the floor, and when I picked some up clouds of dust rose to the ceiling. But many of the books held me spellbound, and I returned each day to sample these English folklorists, whom I had all to myself, as not more than three visitors showed up throughout the summer.

None of the authors were familiar to me, although I was fairly deep into folklore teaching and research. Two years earlier I had attended a summer folklore institute at Indiana University directed by Stith Thompson, the foremost folklore scholar in the United States, who had praised folklore studies and investigations beginning with the brothers Grimm in Germany and culminating with the Finns, but he had never mentioned any folklore work in England. Later, when I attended international folklore congresses, I discovered that the Continental folklorists regarded the state of their subject in England as a joke. And English dons also, I would learn, laughed at the Folklore Society and dismissed its activities as antiquarian curio-hunting.

Yet here under my eyes lay exciting books and journals written by English folklorists of a generation past. Within the year I returned on a fellowship, and a year after that on sabbatical, and twenty years after stirring the dust I completed The British Folklorists, A History, with two companion volumes of selections, Peasant Customs and Savage Myths. The history reconstructed the narrative of an accelerating interest in English antiquities that began with Camden's Britannia in 1586, came of age with the minting of the word 'folklore' in 1846 by William John Thoms as a substitute for 'popular antiquities', and reached a climactic period with the founding of the Folklore Society in 1878. This year the Society celebrates its centenary with an International Folklore Conference at Royal Holloway College from July 17 to 21 which folklorists from twenty-three countries will attend.

The first mention of 'A Folk-Lore Society' appeared in a short communication under that caption to Notes and Queries on February 12, 1876, signed 'St Swithin'. Steps should be taken, urged the writer, 'to form a Society for collecting, arranging and printing all the scattered bits of folklore which we read of in books and hear of in the flesh'. On July 1, in the same journal, 'An Old Folk-Lorist' declared his disappointment that St Swithin's proposal had not elicited greater res-

* First published on 14th July, 1978, in The Times Literary Supplement's issue commemorating The Folklore Society's Centenary. Reprinted here by kind permission of the Editor, The Times Literary Supplement.

ponse from readers. 'As one who suggested upwards of thirty years ago the advisability of collecting the remains of our popular mythology and superstitions before they were quite trampled out by the iron horse,' recalled the Old Folk-Lorist, 'I venture to say that not a day should be lost in organising such a society'.

Particularly did he encourage ladies to take part in the work, opining that they must often come across old world customs and beliefs in the course of their ministrations to poorer neighbours. Support for the Old Folk-Lorist came from Andrew Lang, who wrote 'On Founding a Folk-Lore Society' in *The Academy* for December 1 and 15, 1877. The next year the society was organised, issued the initial volume of the *Folk-Lore Record*, and drew up a set of rules, the first of which stated its purpose: 'The Folk-Lore Society has for its object the preservation and publication of Popular Traditions, Legendary Ballads, Local Proverbial Sayings, Superstitions and Old Customs (British and Foreign), and all subjects relating to them'.

The Old Folk-Lorist was none other than Thoms, long-time clerk in the House of Lords, who for thirty years encouraged correspondents to submit items of curious customs and usages to the columns of *The Athenaeum* and *Notes and Queries*. From these bygones Thoms hoped to reconstruct the mythology of the ancient Britons, just as Jacob Grimm, whose *Deutsche Mythologie* he vastly admired, had pieced together from peasant tales and superstitions the outlines of a once glorious Germanic mythology. But no English pantheon of obscured deities emerged from Thoms's search and folklore had relapsed into the old antiquarianism when an exciting new concept revitalised the subject.

The concept of survivals traced folklore back to the childhood of mankind. Edward B. Tylor, father of modern anthropology, formulated the concept in his *Primitive Culture* in 1871. In his system of cultural evolution, an extension of Darwin's biological evolution, mankind marched up the ladder from savagery to barbarism to civilisation, but the peasantry, lagging behind the educated classes, still clung to vestigial practices and ideas — survivals — once central in the life of prehistoric man. Who would know the mind of early man should collect this folklore of the contemporary peasant. Tyler drew the comparison between peasant and savage

in a passage that, if it reads oddly today, made folklorists of Lang and his fellows:

Look at the modern European peasant using his hatchet and his hoe, see his food boiling or roasting over the log-fire, observe the exact place which beer holds in his calculation of happiness, hear his tale of the ghost in the nearest haunted house, and of the farmer's neice who was bewitched with knots in her inside till she fell into fits and died. If we choose out in this way things which have altered little in a long course of centuries, we may draw a picture where there shall be scarce a hand's breadth of difference between an English ploughman and a negro of Central Africa.

Writing in a volume of essays presented to Tylor on his seventy-fifth birthday, Lang recalled his delight at reading Tylor's chapter on 'Survival in Culture' and finding it so persuasive that anyone could scan it and 'become a folklorist unawares'. On that equation between peasant customs and savage myths Lang built his theory of folklore, first outlined in 1873 in a revolutionary article in the *Fortnightly Review* on 'Mythology and Folktales' that reversed the whole trend of mythological criticism. Not philology but ethnology should be used to analyse the meanings in folktales and customs. By 1884 Lang could bring related articles of his together in a book, *Custom and Myth*, frequently reprinted, whose opening chapter explained 'The Method of Folklore'. That method was to compare the peasant custom or idle tale with an equivalent but functioning practice or myth among contemporary savages, and thereby to comprehend the original character of such customs and myths in antiquity. Lang illustrated this idea with a homely example:

Suppose you tell a folklorist that, in a certain country, when any one sneezes, people say 'Good luck to you', the student cannot say *a priori* what country you refer to, what race you have in your thoughts. It may be Florida, as Florida was when first discovered; it may be Zululand, or West Africa, or ancient Rome, or Homeric Greece, or Palestine. In all these, and many other regions, the sneeze was welcomed as an auspicious omen. The little superstition is as widely distributed as the flint arrow-heads. Just as the object and use of the arrow-heads became intelligible when we found similar weapons in actual use among savages, so the salutation to the sneezer becomes intelligible when we learn that the savage has a good reason for it. He thinks the sneeze expels an evil spirit.

This method of folklore aroused and excited other private scholars who joined forces with Thoms and Lang to organise the Folklore Society. Lang with .four other charter members of the society, George Laurence Gomme, Edward Clodd, Alfred Nutt and Edwin Sidney Hartland, who all subscribed to the anthropological theory of folklore-as-survivals, made up what I have called the Great Team of English folklorists. I so group them because of their close working relationship in the society, their similar lifestyles as busy men of affairs who practised scholarship in the evenings and at weekends, their dedication to folklore among other lively interests, their zest in debate, their prodigious output. The five served successively as Presidents of the society from 1888 until 1901, after ten years of titled figurehead Presidents, and held other posts as well. Gomme was elected the first secretary, and then succeeded Thoms as director upon the latter's death in 1885. Clodd, known in London circles as the literary banker, served as treasurer. Nutt, who inherited the publishing house of his father, published the society's journals and monographs. Hartland served on the council and reviewed nearly two hundred books in the society's journal. Lang presided over the International Folklore Congress of 1891 hosted by the society. Collectively they filled the society's publications with essays, addresses, notes, reviews, collectanea, proposals and exchanges, in addition to their own independent writings.

With all their valiant efforts as folklorists their reputations and honours rested largely on activities outside folklore. Gomme, statistical officer and Clerk of the London County Council, was knighted in 1911 for his civic service and his five books on the history and governance of London. Hartland, a solicitor, served a term as Mayor of Gloucester. Nutt published a full line of books,

specialising in foreign and educational titles, as well as the folkloric. Lang enjoyed fame as a universal man of letters, 'editor-in-chief to the British nation'. After his death a dozen lecturers invited to St Andrews University addressed themselves to Lang's gargantuan output, which fills seventeen pages in the British Museum catalogue. In these appraisals (ten were published in 1949 under the title *Concerning Andrew Lang*), the speakers considered Lang as a classicist, a historian, a biographer, a poet, a writer on sports, anthropology, primitive religion, Joan of Arc, the House of Stuart, the Scottish border – but no lecturer dealt with Andrew Lang and folklore

The range of intellectual interests and breadth of acquaintance characterising the Great Team come to view in the volume *Memories* Edward Clodd pieced together in 1916 from his letters and anecdotal recollections. His biographer, Joseph McCabe, recalled how *Memories* 'set our entire press discussing the singular catholicity and high equality of his friendships'. Clodd dined and corresponded with novelists, poets, artists, philosophers, mathematicians, astronomers, explorers, surgeons, liberal clergymen, and university dons. He devoted the longest sections in *Memories* to George Meredith, who called him 'Sir Reynard', and George Gissing who regularly wrote to Clodd from health resorts in France and Spain. As president of the Omar Khayyam Club, Clodd invited Meredith to a dinner, where the guest remarked how as publisher's reader he had recommended the first novels of Gissing and Hardy, who were flanking Clodd at table.

One theme recurring throughout the *Memories* is Clodd's stance against a rigid theology and his affinity with like-minded rationalists. The banker held special affection for the free-thinkers Grant Allen and Thomas Henry Huxley, and prepared memoirs on both. Allen first learnt of Clodd when as a school teacher in Jamaica he chanced on Clodd's primers on evolution in the home of a mulatto woman. Of Huxley, Clodd wrote, 'It was worth being born to have known him'. Gissing heralded Clodd's *Thomas Henry Huxley* as 'an epoch in the intellectual and social history of England'. Throughout the *Memories* Clodd evinces his joy in clubs, dinners, 'tall tales', smoking dens, and weekend gatherings at his Suffolk sea-coast home in Aldeburgh, where good talk flowed, poems were written, ideas were honed. Yet he did not neglect his business: 'Horrible that you should be at the bank till eleven at night!' Gissing wrote to him in commiseration.

Each member of the Great Team carved out his special area of experience on which he wrote books still highly readable and informative, though little read. Gomme reconstructed tribal institutions in prehistoric Britain through the evidence of folklore survivals, such as rituals connected with water worship and fire worship, in *Primitive Folk-Moots: or Open-Air Assemblies in Britain* (1880), which he dedicated to Thoms, and *Folk-Lore Relics of Early Village Life* (1883). In his crowning work, *Folk-Lore as an Historical Science* (1908), he broadened his thesis to say that the folklorist could distinguish between Aryan and pre-Aryan layers of tradition and could further sub-divide the Aryan into Celtic, Roman and Saxon survivals. Folklore could be used therefore as a kind of historical archaeology. For example: a treasure legend associated with London Bridge reveals the strategic value of London in Roman times; a Scottish prejudice against white cows harks back to a pre-Aryan worship of a sacred animal; an Irish family belief that no Coneely can kill a seal without incurring bad luck reflects an ancient totemic guardian of Coneelys, who were thought to have once been seals.

In an extended statement on 'The Science of Folk-Lore' in 1885, Hartland declared that 'the time may come when the conquests of folklore shall be received among the most remarkable, and in their results the most important achievements of inductive reasoning'. He set about proving his point with *The Science of Fairy Tales* (1890), in which he analysed the uniform laws governing the tales about little beings who carried off mortals to their enchanted abode. (Since village people told these accounts as true happenings, folklorists call them fairy legends, not fairy tales). Thus to eat the food of the fairies prevents the mortal from ever leaving their land. Should he avoid the taboo and return to his home, thinking that a brief time has elapsed, he will discover that a generation or more has passed. Such are the rules that obtain in the fairy world and point to an archaic faith of early man.

Between 1894 and 1896 Hartland published three volumes of a majestic work, *The Legend of Perseus,* that in its day rivalled Frazer's *The Golden Bough* in its celebrity. Patiently and exhaustively he dissected the mythic narrative into its primal elements, such as the Supernatural Birth, the Life Token, and the Witch and her Evil Eye, and followed their trials through chains of folktales, customs, rituals and beliefs extending from 'the shores of the arctic Ocean to the islands of the Southern Seas'. Hartland found that the literary treatments of the farflung legend, by Ovid, and Strabo, Pausanias and Lucian, had discarded its coarser incidents, such as the delousing of the sleeping hero by his maiden lover.

In 1899 he wrote a pamphlet of special interest, *Folklore: What Is It and What is the Good of It*? setting forth for the lay reader the evolutionary theory of folklore. For illustration he cited the common belief in curing warts by brushing them against a piece of meat or potato; as the food decays, the wart dries up. This seemingly idle superstition had its counterpart in magical beliefs and practices traceable back to primitive man. How many lives might have been spared, lamented Hartland, if colonial administrators had understood the modes of thought of the lower cultures! It was not too late to remedy this defect by acquainting colonial governors with the traditional customs, usages and inner life − the folklore − of the savage populations under their rule.

If Thoms never found the mythology of the ancient Britons behind his folklore, Alfred Nutt perceived a clear line of continuity linking the old Celtic mythology of the Tuatha de Danaan to the mediaeval fairy-romances and the living tales of Irish peat-farmers. Nor were these folktales debased forms but a still flowering tradition of the oral poetry once sung by Celtic bards. In 1888 Nutt brought together his published papers on this theme, *Studies on the Legend of the Holy Grail, with Especial Reference to the Hypothesis of its Celtic Origin*, and he contributed to the 1895-97 edition of *The Voyage of Bran*, translated from a mediaeval manuscript by Muno Meyer, 'An Essay upon the Irish vision of the happy otherworld and the Celtic doctrine of rebirth', that occupied over 200 pages in the first volume and all of the second.

Not only did Nutt publish many folklore books but he added comparative notes, forewords and postscripts to titles in his list of Celtic-Gaelic folktales. The scholar-publisher exulted in his folklore province of Ireland, unspoilt by Reformation interference, where the older pagan and the newer Roman Catholic creeds blended harmoniously and the saints took over the roles of the pagan wizards. Over a thousand-year stretch Irish literature and fairy-lore had maintained their connections, and peasants still tell tales about Finn and Cachulainn. Where usually the folklorist has only the ancient record or modern folklore with which to work, in Ireland, Nutt claimed, he possessed both links of the chain.

In an autobiographical fragment Edward Clodd recalled the excitement generated in the 1860s by Darwinianism and the Higher Criticism, when Huxley and Tylor extended evolutionary thought to man's mental and spiritual nature. Clodd's interests in liberal religion and folklore overlapped, and led to his publishing, in 1875, *The Childhood of Religions, Embracing a Simple Account of the Birth and Growth of Myths and Legends*, a work widely reprinted and translated. At that time Clodd still separated primitive from revealed religions, but eventually he reached the position that the one fed into the other. In *Myths and Dreams* (1885) he explored primitive man's animistic view of the world and the tales he wove around talking animals and angry stones and the spectres in his dreams.

When he addressed the Folklore Society as President in 1896 he was prepared to carry the doctrine of survivals to its ultimate conclusion and to assert the heathen basis of the Christian sacraments. Clodd set forth the evidence: the exorcism of the priest recalls the incantations of the shaman; the rite of baptism derives from primitive water worship; the ceremony of the Mass confirms the savage idea that the eater of a great warrior acquires his strengths. Two shocked members of the society wrote to Clodd requesting that he suppress the address, but it had already gone to the printer, and on reading it, William Ewart Gladstone, a charter member, resigned. The Catholic Truth Society issued a furious denunciation of the address, beginning 'The inspiring doctrine of man's essential bestiality has no more enthusiastic and devoted apostle than Mr Edward Clodd'.

Unmoved by these criticisms Clodd continued his exploration of folklore survivals in 1898 with *Tom Tit Tot or Savage Philosophy in Folktale*, which he expanded in 1920 as *Magic in Names*. The book grew from a prime example of a *Märchen* or fairy-tale told in his native Suffolk, locally known as 'Tom Tit Tot' but generally known as 'Rumpelstiltskin' in the Grimms' collection, whose plot hinged on the hero's learning the name of the ogre and thereby thwarting his designs, and rescuing the princess. This idea of the power accruing to one who possessed the name, or the image, or a lock of hair or piece of clothing of another, Clodd illustrated with many instances reported in primitive societies and among the lower classes in modern society. The Virgin Mary conferred mana on her worshippers; the name of Jesus is powerful magic.

In addition to his evolutionist's folklore hat, Andrew Lang increasingly wore the hat of a 'psycho-folklorist', his own term to describe his interest in spiritualism and occult matters. He looked closely at accounts of second-sight, crystal-gazing, premonitions, apparitions, poltergeists, hallucinations, dousing, conjuring tricks, spirit rappings and *déjà vu*, and pondered their meaning for the folklorist. In an essay on 'The Comparative Study of Ghost Stories' in 1885 in *Nineteenth Century* he urged the student of folklore to search out examples recorded in the past that corresponded to current ghost stories and so identify their mythical tendencies. Why were the same ghostly tales told over the centuries, such as the legend of the Ghostly Compact in which the revenant as proof of his return sears a scar into the hand of his living partner? Lang gathered his papers on ghostly subjects into *Cock Lane and Common-Sense* (1894) and *The Book of Dreams and Ghosts* (1897), well aware of scoffings at psychical research, but determined to sift fraudulent from genuine visions. The Scot had witnessed mysteries himself; he had bet a literary lady £100 that her vision of a stranger thrusting a knife into the left side of a friend would not be fulfilled, but he lost the bet when the lady some months later met a surgeon who had just operated on her friend's left side. Not only savages and peasants, but English gentlemen and ladies carried folklore, Lang concluded.

If the members of the Great Team went some distance along their own paths, they took pains to keep each other honest and vigorously cross-examined one another's pet theories. Clodd belaboured Lang for succumbing to spiritualism, which was no more than 'the old animism writ large', with spirits and mediums replacing fairies and witches. The banker felt that crystal-gazing scenes which so intrigued Lang should be ascribed to a disordered liver. Gomme chided Lang for lowering his standards in his multicoloured series of rewritten fairy tales. Lang and Hartland each critically reviewed Gomme's *Folk-Lore as an Historical Science*. In Lang's view Gomme had failed to recognise the migratory nature of local traditions, as in the treasure legend of London Bridge, which was told of many other bridges, and in Hartland's view Gomme had erred in relating the totemism of a nomadic society to the ritualism of an agricultural society. Hartland challenged Lang's counter-evolutionary argument that Australian aborigines believed in 'high gods'. Nutt and Gomme engaged in vigorous debate over the evidence for literary versus institutional survivals in folklore.

But Lang and company could not afford too many side issues for a foe at the gates threatened the foundations of their evolutionary system and forced them to close ranks. This enemy was the diffusionist theory that accounted for the similarity of tales and customs among widely scattered peoples not by comparable stages of cultural evolution but by the slow creep of transmission from one culture to another. The International Folklore Congress of 1891 held in London, in which all the Great Team played prominent roles, served as a showcase for the survivalists and a battleground against the diffusionists. So seriously did the congress members take the issue that *The Times* printed an appeal by one to avoid unseemly heat during the discussions. Few readers could have escaped knowing about folklore in the autumn of 1891, for the British press reported the congress in feature articles, editorials, communications, and drawings.

In the end the evolutionary folklorist lost not only their cause of survival theory to the diffusionist school, but the cause of folklore as well. After the First World War the Folklore Society languished. The size of its journal shrank along with its membership, and no new blood replaced the founders. Professorships and chairs, institutes and archives of folklore never took root in England as they did on the Continent, or even to some extent in Ireland, Scotland and Wales, where struggling languages and cultures gave stimulus to folklore enterprises. Why did the Great Team go into eclipse and folklore in England lapse into the doldrums? One

answer appears to be the conservatism of the universities. As John Holloway pointed out in a very fine essay in the November 26, 1976 *Cambridge Review* on 'Folklore, Fakelore, and Literature', educational policy makers of the 1960s during an expansionist period in England simply did not know the existence of folklore as an academic discipline with possibilities for urban, ethnic, and working-class studies in contemporary society. As a consequence, he concludes, 'the virtually complete absence of folklore studies from our universities is likely to bring loss of intellectual collaboration and so of intellectual vigour'.

Folklore studies have flourished most consistently in countries with strong national aspirations and ideological convictions. Finland is a case in point, where the publication of the *Kalevala* by Elias Lönnrot in 1885 spurred continuous studies in folklore, language, and literature keyed to Finnish nationalism and shifting with the political currents. The Soviet Union and the East European bloc make extensive and avowed use of folklore research as aids to socialist propaganda. In Nigeria and Ghana the universities are just beginning to add professional folklorists to their faculties to direct research and teaching of the proto-national oral cultures. Something of a folklore-folklife-oral-history boom can be perceived now in the United States, responding to the interests in minority cultures and family trees epitomised by the success of Alex Haley's *Roots*. But the professional standing of folklore in American universities remains a haphazard affair, dependent on the initiative and reputations of individual faculty members who explain to their administrations that folklore is no longer past-minded and present-minded but a study involved with the modern world and urban, industrial life.

Although the English universities, save for Leeds, have neglected folklore, some excellent private scholars continue the illustrious tradition of the Folklore Society. In a hortatory paper on 'England, the Great Undiscovered', Peter Opie, former President of the Society, outlined rich possibilities for fieldwork yet today. Some of these possibilities are already realised in the reports of agricultural magic obtained by George Ewart Evans from farmers and farriers, and the discovery by Enid Porter, former council member, of an extraordinary spinner of local tales from the Fenns,

W.H. Barrett. Among the active leaders in the society who have published major works one thinks of Peter and Iona Opie, with their collections of games, rhymes, and lore of school children; of Katharine Briggs, compiler of the splendid four-volume *Dictionary of British Folk-Tales* and author of discerning studies of English fairy and witch lore; and of Venetia Newall, energetic Secretary of the Folklore Society, who has written *An Egg at Easter* and developed a modern series on folklore of the English counties. The centenary conference of the society will have reason to honour the achievements of present members as well as the founders who made folklore — the word and the idea — known around the world.

PLENARY SESSION PAPERS

The Concept of Motif in Folklore

DAN BEN-AMOS   University of Pennsylvania

Introduction

MOTIF has become a distinctive concept in folklore. The ability to use Stith Thompson's *Motif-Index of Folk Literature* is, according to Richard Dorson,[1] a skill which is indispensable to the folklorist, and the defining trait that separates him from all other students of culture. Yet, in spite of the deep impression that the term has made on our discipline, the concept that it represents has remained vague and varied, subject to abuse and rebuke, and has often been regarded as an obstacle rather than a vehicle for research.[2] However, there are now hints that suggest renewed interest in the idea of motif. Some of them come from the same ranks of the structural-formalist folklorists who were the most hostile critics of this concept.[3] Before these novel voices are lost in the waves of trends and counter-trends, and lest their sound turns into a whimper, we should review the emergence and fall of the concept of motif in folklore, examine the reasons why the historic-geographic school adopted the concept in the first place, compare it with the historically available alternatives, and analyse the qualities that made motif a superior concept. Once the diverse usages and meanings of the concept of motif outside folklore are clarified, it will be possible to examine the transformation of the concept within the discipline of folklore itself. As a result of such a theoretical-historical survey we will be in a better position to assess the importance and usefulness of the concept of motif in current folklore studies, and to respond effectively to future developments in this direction.

Minimal narrative units and the Historic-Geographic Method

The historic-geographic method evolved in Finland as a nationalistic and empirical response to nineteenth-century speculative controversies about folktale origins.[4] It purported to depose specific countries such as India, Greece,[5] or the Middle East,[6] or specific stages of evolution — either savagery, barbarism or civilised life[7] — from their privileged position as the sole source of all folktales. In order to achieve these objectives, the historic-geographic school set as its research goal the discovery, or rather recovery, of the original form (*Ur*-form), of each known folktale, as it was created in a distinct time and place, tracing back the migration routes and thematic transformations of its narrative elements.

Essential for the success of this research method was first, the identification and classification of all internationally known tales, and secondly, the delineation, definition, and classification of minimal narrative units. While the first task was to provide a common frame of reference for the historic-geographic study of narratives,[8] the second task, our present concern, was to offer the basic analytical tools with which it would have been possible to pursue the search for the original forms of the folktale.

Implicit in this analytical procedure is the notion that narratives are formed and change in terms of elementary episodes which over time combine into elaborate tales. Stories, like Locke's ideas, are distinguishable as simple and complex and the former necessarily evolve into the latter. The primary search on the *Ur*-form trail should unravel this process through a minute analysis of content variations that exist in the texts along the way. The complete tale is too complex and cannot be subjected to the reconstruction of its past unless it is divided into minimal narrative units beforehand. Karl Spiess stated in 1917, and later, in 1924, Kaarle Krohn quoted him with approval, that:

> The folktale as a whole is too variable in its design to serve as an object for comparison; in addition, the fact that the relationship is often restricted to completely isolated characteristics indicates that those characteristics lead, so to speak, an independent existence, detaching themselves with relative ease from one context and, with equal ease, entering another. They are firmly outlined, have a well-delineated size, and are of a material content that can be characterised with a few words. Therefore, they are manageable enough to be used for comparison studies.[9]

Spiess calls these narrative characteristics 'motif' (*Motiv*) or trait (*Zug*), which are 'the smallest thematic units of the *Märchen*.'[10] In spite of Krohn's general agreement with Spiess' methodological approach, they differ in their fundamental idea concerning the ontology of narrative motifs and complete stories and the relationship between them. Spiess regards motifs as context-free units that have an independent existence and therefore have the capacity to enter into innumerable narrative relations. The complex tales represent variations on such combinations between motifs and groups of motifs, and hence, while there is a limited number of motifs, the number of tales is infinite.[11]

In contrast, Kaarle Krohn assumes that 'every Märchen prototype has its own special motifs,'[12] and therefore, the combination of narrative traits has an historical priority over the minimal units themselves. The tale as a whole, however complex it may be, emerges in a distinct time and place. Any resulting similarity between tales is due to historical changes and the transference of motifs from one story to another. Krohn proposes, at least as 'a working hypothesis . . . the assumption that virtually every motif originally belonged to some one particular prototype from which it has migrated.'[13] In either case, the smallest narrative entity remains the basic analytical unit in the pursuit of historical folktale forms.

Different as they are, these two theories about *Märchen* origins established the importance of the minimal narrative unit as an analytical concept in historical-comparative folktale research. Krohn's *Die folkloristische Arbeitsmethode* — which was both a summative and a programatic research statement of the Finnish school — fixed the isolateable narrative trait as the research vehicle for the recovery and the reconstruction of prototypical folklore forms and the tracing of their historical changes. Furthermore, as a research programme *Folklore Methodology* aimed at an even more ambitious goal, namely, the establishment of scientific principles for historical folklore research.

For that purpose the method had two immediate requirements. First there was a need for a precise, unambiguous definition of the folktale minimal narrative unit, and secondly there was a need for a classification system that would enable the organised registration of all these units as they appear in narratives the world over. Theoretically, such a catalogue should have been a list of basic narrative elements that vary as tales diffuse. In practice Krohn recognised that variations occur not necessarily within the most basic elements, but rather within major narrative divisions such as 'episodes' or 'formulas'. Within them it is possible to isolate even smaller divisions 'that can be called "factors" (*Momente*). . . . Each small part of a major component contains in turn several *primary* or *foundation* traits that are more precisely characterised by *secondary elements* or *details*.'[14] Although Krohn specifically avoids the term 'motif' for that purpose, the distinction between it and the smaller narrative divisions is not completely clear, and on occasion he considers them synonymous.[15]

Regardless of vagueness in terminology, for cross-cultural purposes the primary research need was therefore a list of minimal units to which tales are analysable on any level, and which occur in more than one story. Stith Thompson's *Motif-Index of Folk Literature* was to answer this particular need. Thompson based the plan of his *Motif-Index* on the assumption, accepted since Linnaeus, that a classification system is the primary prerequisite for transforming any knowledge into a scientific discipline. For that purpose he employed the concept of the 'motif' that was already in use in folklore and was also current in literary and art criticism and scholarship.

Looked at historically, the concept of motif was not the only one that could have served the purposes of historical-geographic narrative research. Back in 1866 the Reverend Sabine Baring-Gould (1834-1924),[16] a popular and prolific writer who was 'said to have more books to his credit in the British Museum catalogue than any man alive,'[17] borrowed the concept of 'root' from comparative philology[18] and proposed it as a minimal narrative unit.

> 'Every language,' he argued, 'has its primary roots and these roots united together, expanded, somewhat altered with wear-and-tear, become words. The number of radices is fixed. It is small; the words formed from them are innumerable and continually changing. . . . Much the same may be said of household tales. In all nations belonging to the same stock there exist stories resembling each other in many particulars, and differing from each other in others; yet with an unmistakable radical unity about them, which makes it easy to reduce them to a primeval root. Who can doubt,' he says, concluding his statement with an example, 'that *jardin* and *garden* are indentical in significance, though they differ somewhat in spelling and in pronounciation? Sometimes in the same nation one radical had developed into several distinct ideas; as garden and warden: so with stories, they may not resemble each other in much that is superficial, yet a critical eye can often perceive their radical identity.'[19]

On the basis of these assumptions, Baring-Gould proposed a classification system for story radicals which he lifted, with minimal changes, from J. G. von Hahn, *Griechische und albanesische Märchen* (1864).[20] He divides the 'story radicals' into two groups of 'family stories' and 'various' themes. The social relationships are the main concern in the first group, and the supernatural world in the second.

I. Family Stories

    A. Relating to Husband and Wife
    B. Relating to Parents and Children

    C. Relating to Brothers and Sisters
    D. Relating to Persons Betrothed

II. Various

    A. Men and the Unseen World
    B. Men Matched with Men
    C. Men and Beast
    D. Luck Depending on the Preservation of Palladium (a statue of Pallas Athene whose preservation was believed to ensure the safety of Troy)

This classification system and the concept of story radicals had little impact upon folklore scholarship. William Ralston and Joseph Jacobs revised and modified his classification,[21] but since neither Stith Thompson nor any of the Finnish scholars relate their own efforts to Baring-Gould's work, his contribution to narrative analysis and classification remains mostly unnoticed.[22] In fact, Baring-Gould's system had a closer affinity in concept and theory to the Finnish scholars than they later realised or admitted. First, the very effort to construct a closed classification system implies the idea that there is a finite number of narrative elements, a principle that Baring-Gould made explicit. Secondly, his notion of 'story radicals' as the narrative kernel anticipates Krohn's ideas about the formation of tales and the association of motifs with particular stories. Both consider narratives to develop out of an initial core, the continuous existence of which in all of its versions is responsible for the similarity between them. Thirdly, the distinction between thematic centrality and marginality enables Baring-Gould to avoid the theoretical differences that could be later discerned in the respective ideas of Krohn and Spiess. Baring-Gould reserved narrative stability for the story root, and admitted free thematic variations into the periphery of the story.

In spite of these theoretical affinities, the notion of 'story radicals' was not suitable for the needs of historical comparative research. The focus upon the central thematic unit that many narrative versions share in common diverted attention from the peripheral and volatile story elements that vary from one version to another, yet could offer clues to the tale's history. The appropriate minimal narrative unit should be able to include both constant and variable themes. Change itself should be an optional rather than an obligatory aspect of the unit. The concept of motif, it appears, fulfilled these qualifications.

'Motif' in German Romanticism

Like the idea of folklore itself, the concept of motif emerged in the writings of the German romantics. Respectively, the two notions drew upon the nationalistic and the aesthetic-psychological currents in romantic thoughts. The term motif (*Motiv*) refers to the motivating elements in the plot, to the causes that activate the characters and advance the narrative. For example, Jean Paul (Johann Paul Richter, 1763-1825) considers motifs, along with plot and character, as the principal elements in the epic, the drama, and the novel. He regards motif as a literary-psychological factor, the motivation that contributes to the plot is development.[23] Similarly, Johanne August Eberhard (1739-1809) distinguishes between elements (*Gliedern*) and motifs (*Motiven*) as the two categories into which fantasy orders images. Motifs then represent the dynamic relations, the actions and their causes, between elements.[24]

The term 'motif' occurs in the correspondence between Goethe and Schiller,[25] and the essay 'On Epic and Dramatic Poetry' that grew out of this exchange includes a systematic delineation of the kinds of motifs in terms of their effects on the plot. Accordingly there are five kinds of motifs:

(1) Progressive, which advance the action . . .

(2) Retrogressive, which draw the action away from its goal . . .

(3) Retarding, which delay the progress of the action . . .

(4) Retrospective, which introduce into the poem events which happened before the time of the poem.

(5) Prospective, which anticipate what will happen after the time of the poem.[26]

The principal criterion for Goethe's classification is that the motifs function within a literary context, without any reference to their themes or genres. Although he attempts to differentiate between epic and drama, the motifs themselves, their subject or form, do not serve as a distinctive feature that separates one form from the other. Rather, they can occur in both genres, since the sole distinction between them is the relation of narrative to time. 'An epic poet narrates an event as completely past, while the dramatist presents it as completely present.'[27]

However, functional description is still not a substantive definition. Goethe is not clear as to precisely what he means by the term motif. In his letters and conversations the term motif appears to have dual, though related, meanings of theme and motivation. He refers to the 'death by thirst' motif, to 'astrological motifs', and he describes the situation in the *Odyssey* involving the agitation of a woman's heart by the arrival of a stranger as 'the loveliest motif'.[28] In *Wilhelm Meister's Apprenticeship*, in a discussion of Hamlet, Wilhelm says:

> My project therefore is, not at all to change those first-mentioned grand situations, or at least as much as possible to spare them, both collectively and individually; but with respect to these external, single, dissipated and dissipating *motives* [my italics], to cast them all at once away, and substitute a solitary one instead of them.[29]

And later on, in the discussion between Wilhelm Meister and Serlo, Wilhelm says: 'Hamlet returns; for his wandering through the churchyard perhaps some lucky motive may be thought of.'[30] While in these usages of the term 'motif' the notion of motivation is implicit, in other cases the term refers to a specific theme. On February 25th, 1824 Eckermann noted, echoing the words of Goethe: 'To-day Goethe showed me two very remarkable poems, both highly moral in their tendency, but in their several *motives* so unreservedly natural and true, that they are of the kind which the world styles immoral.'[31] About a year later, on January 18th, 1825, Eckermann quotes Goethe, commenting upon some poems of a poetess they knew, and about whom he wrote an essay: 'I have in a few words, characterised these poems according to their chief subjects, and I think you will be pleased with the valuable *motives*.' After reading such characterisations as 'Modesty of a Servian girl', 'conflict in the mind of a lover', and 'The lover comes from abroad, watches her by day, surprises

20

her at night', Eckermann remarked: 'These mere motives excited in me such lively emotions, that I felt as if I were reading the poems themselves, and had no desire for the details.' Goethe comments in his reply: 'No one dreams that the true power of a poem consists in the situation – in the *motives*. And for this very reason, thousands of poems are written, where the *motive* is nothing at all, and which merely through feeling and sounding verse reflect a sort of existence.'[32] In this instance Goethe employs the term 'motif' not only as meaning a theme, but also as a succinct description of a situation. In that sense he probably reflects an idea of the Italian playwright Carlo Gozzi (1720-1806) who contended that there are thirty-six basic plots to all tragedies. Frederic Soret (1795-1865) noted a comment that Goethe made in a conversation on February 14, 1830: 'Gozzi would maintain that there are only six-and-thirty tragical situations. Schiller took the greatest pains to find more, but he did not find even so many as Gozzi.'[33]

All these variations in use and meaning, in fact, do not contradict but complement each other. In Goethe's letters, conversations, and essays, the term 'motif' refers to a dramatic situation and its reductive description. The succinct summation of a situation must encapsulate its essential characteristic and this could be accomplished only by referring to the motivating force, the active cause that moves the characters in the plot. In that sense, motif, is not the minimal narrative unit, but the reduction of a narrative to a minimum.

From this perspective the ultimate motive for action becomes identical with the abstract idea that is dominant in a narrative situation, or even, by extension, in the entire work. In the context of Goethe's search for thematic and formal unity in art, the concept of motif relates to the fundamental idea that provides unity to an epic, a drama or a novel. This notion has become the accepted meaning of motif, so much so, that a dictionary of aesthetics from that period describes the term as 'the mainspring of the plot, the primary cause of the gradually self-realising operation that the poet ... must make in order to establish unity.'[34]

As developed by the German romantics there is an inherent polarity in the concept of motif, connoting both the minimal and the maximal, the concrete and the abstract aspects of any work. The minimal narrative unit becomes in this case, the indispensable motive for action, without which the entire story is rendered meaningless. By the virtue of its import this motive also encapsulates the essential meaning of the work, and hence conveys the abstract idea which the author wishes to express in his poem or story. Since the motive could theoretically be also hidden or implicit, there is no necessary textual representation for the motive and it could be inferred from the relations between actions and characters, or reconstructed on the basis of interpretation. If art is a world unto itself, then the romantic motif is its grain of sand.

Ruskin's aesthetics and the Motif

John Ruskin extricates the concept of 'motif' from the ambiguity in which the polarity of meanings trapped it, but in the process he reverses the term's connotations. Motif is no longer a minimal unit, either narrative or visual. Rather for him, motif is 'a leading emotional purpose,'[35] of any work of art. He shifts the focus of motif from initial to final causes, and explains art teleologically by its ultimate purpose. Unlike the Romantic notion of motif, the minimal unit does not encapsulate the core idea of a single situation or a whole work, but contributes to its expression. He asserts that 'the minutest portion of a great composition is helpful to the whole.' In defiance of the imagined reader's incredulity he states emphatically: '. . . it is inconceivable. But it is a fact.'[36]

In accordance with such an approach every discernible minimal part, be it a line, a colour, or a form, contributes to the emotive effect the art work would have on its viewers. An artist achieves the leading purpose of his art work by selecting the appropriate 'minutest details' and harmoniously relating them to form a whole. 'Undulating lines, for instance are expressive of action; and would be false in effect if the motive of the picture was one of repose. Horizontal and angular lines are expressive of rest and strength; and would destroy a design whose purpose was to express disquiet and feebleness. It is therefore necessary to ascertain the motive before descending to the detail.'[37]

Ruskin shifts meanings around, and consequently he puts even a greater emphasis on the import of the minimal unit. Like Goethe he considers the motif in terms of its function within the context of the individual art work, though he relates it to the artistic purpose rather than to the plot progression. He is concerned with aesthetic evaluation and therefore would examine the minimal units in terms of their correlation to each other and correspondence with the purpose of the whole. However, in spite of such specific analysis Ruskin implicitly assumes that the minimal units have an absolute and general meaning. They are the morphemes of a universal visual language, extending beyond culture and relative perception, and having a definite effect in any context. Motives vary, but the minimal units are constant, limited in number and distinct in their meaning. They enter into unlimited combinations, but to be aesthetically effective, any composition must rely on the meanings inherent in these forms and lines.

Some sixty years later the art historian Erwin Panofsky (1892-1968) would renew the concept of visual motifs, restoring the term to its earlier meaning of a minimal unit, and formulating an analytical framework that was suggestive, though rarely applied systematically.[38] But before such development becomes possible it was necessary to transfer the term of motif from the vocabulary of literary criticism and aesthetic evaluation to the terminology and concerns of literary research.

Motif: From aesthetic evaluation to Literary research

The two scholars that laid the foundation for the analytical use of the concept of motif in literary, art, and subsequently folklore research were Wilhelm Scherer (1841-1886) and Wilhelm Dilthey (1833-1911). Wilhelm Scherer was 'the most influential German literary historian in the later [nineteenth] century.'[39] He proposed applying Comte's positivism to literary history. Like Henry T. Buckel (1821-1862)[40] in England and Hyppolyte Taine (1823-1893)[41] in France, Scherer sought to establish the relations between society and literature on an empirical basis. According to him, such a study required a precise and rigorous

analysis of 'heritage, experience, and learning' (*Erbertes, Erlebtes, Erlerntes*) — three concepts that parallel Taine's *la race, le milieu et le moment* — as the three determining factors that influence art and literature of a nation at any given period.[42]

Through the examination of traditional culture, historical experience and social and religious ideas, Scherer sought to establish empirically the unique character of a nation as it is manifested in language, poetry, and literary history. As a student — and the first biographer — of Jacob Grimm,[43] Scherer regarded philology as the science that comprises all the cultural manifestations of a nation, and he wished to demonstrate the validity of this view by the study of German literary history in particular.[44] His interest in the uniqueness of a national group logically required the identification of all elements that do not fit the ideal model of the group, as inherently foreign to the national ethos. Consequently there was a need to trace their origin to external sources. In the context of such an endeavour the concept of motif had a crucial role. Scherer maintained that 'the history of the motif was to be pursued carefully, especially with regards to borrowing and parallels,'[45] since in this way it would be possible to sift out the alien from the indigenous cultural elements.

Such research requires a clear idea and a precise definition of the nature of motif. For Scherer, who was interested in cultural mores and their literary manifestation, 'the doctrine of motifs' was primarily a doctrine of cultural ethics.[46] The motif itself was an idea, a topic, a theme and a subject,[47] an abstract notion that had a literary formulation. In narratives and songs motif was 'an elementary unitary part of a poetic theme.'[48] But since, according to Scherer, poetry essentially challenges the possible and the probable through 'the relationship between action and character,'[49] it is implicit in his 'doctrine of motifs' that the unitary part of a theme is such a relationship. The central idea of a literary work that becomes apparent through the relations between actions and characters is, by definition, the main motif (*Hauptmotive*) of a poem, a story or a drama. But in realisation of the fact that a single motif cannot encapsulate the ethical principles of a work in completion, Scherer recognises also the existence of supplementary motifs (*Nebenmotiven*) that support the principle literary action.

Scherer proposes a classification system of motifs that is based on the possible relationship between action and character. Only an outline, this classification system includes the following categories:

Relations between Human Beings
    Unnatural love
    Natural love to a girl; reciprocal and non-reciprocal
    [Natural love] to a wife
    [Natural love] to another man's wife

Marriage
    Selfishness of man
    [Selfishness] of wife
    Devotion of man
    [Devotion] of wife
    A wife who refuses her husband (Aristophanes' Lysistrata)
    Mock-marriage
    Wife accused unjustly

Relationship between parents and children
    King Lear
    Orestes the mother-killer[50]
    The father who sacrifices his child (Abraham ·and Isaac) or executes him (Brutus)[51]
    The mother who kills her children (Gretchen the child-murderess)[52]
    Brother-murder (Cain and Abel)

Illicit Liaisons
    Mother-marriage (Oedipus)
    Incest
    Adulterous affair (Phaedra)
    Brother and sister who unknowingly fall in love with each other (Goethe's 'Brother and Sister')[53]

Friendship
    Friends who pledge their lives for each other (Damon)[54]
    Good intention with bad results (Carlos in 'Clavigo')[55]

Master and Servant
    The slave in the Roman theatre
    The flatterer
    Don Quixote and Sancho Panza

Mutual sacrifice
    Servant for the master
    Wolfdietrich[56] for the people

Relations between individuals, however not between one another, but between a single person and a group, a community, a social circle and their general interests:
    The hero in his relations with the state, or the people (Codrus, Arminius)[57]

Relations between one people and another:
    Iliad

Relations toward property:
    The miser

Relations toward spiritual matters:
    Toward science (the unsatisfied researcher: Faust)
    Toward justice (Michael Kohlhaas)[58]

These latest motifs belong to the part of relations of men toward themselves.

Relations to God
    Religious heroes
    Jesus Christ as a literary subject
    Muhammad[59]

Such a system, in which social relations are the crucial taxonomic principle, can theoretically serve as an analytical framework for the empirical relationship between literature and society. In different stages of human development, or in different nations, there should be a different distribution of literary motifs reflecting social reality. Unlike the Reverend Sabine Baring-Gould, who used a similar criterion in constructing his classification system, but who designed it for the sole purpose of literary comparisons, Scherer's conception of motifs and their classification, inconsistencies disregarded, allows the delineation of smaller units and the examination of their preponderance in a body of literature.

Scherer assumes motifs to be clearly delineated literary units, each expressing a unitary idea, and each corresponding to the cultural-historical heritage, experience, and learning that generate a national literature. In this way his 'doctrine of motifs' is a doctrine of culture, comprising all values as they are represented in literature. According to his view, there is a correspondence between society and literature and hence it is possible, even necessary, to consider literature as a social document that reflects social-cultural changes. The use of the motif in such an analysis makes it possible to separate indigenous ideas from alien elements.

The 'Motif' in Wilhelm Dilthey's Poetics

In its assumptions and goals, the poetics of Wilhelm Dilthey contrasts sharply with Scherer's theory of literature. Though they were contemporaries, even acquaintances during their student days, and though they both attended Jacob Grimm's lectures in Berlin,[60] their reaction to the intellectual scholarly trends of the 19th century could not have been farther apart. While Scherer applied to literary studies research models developed in the natural and social sciences, Dilthey insisted upon the comprehension of 'human life in its own terms,'[61] emphasising the priority of subject matter over methodology. Only in this way it would be possible, according to him, to account for the complexity, often unobservable, of human life. Still seeking generalisations based on empirical grounds, Dilthey asserts that:

> Starting from the most universal concepts of a general methodology the human studies must work towards more definite procedures and principles within their own sphere by trying them out on their own subject-matter, just as the physical sciences have done. We do not show ourselves genuine disciples of the great scientific thinkers simply by transferring their methods to our sphere; we must adjust our knowledge to the nature of our subject-matter and thus treat it as the scientists treated theirs. We conquer nature by submitting to it. The human studies differ from the sciences because the latter deal with facts which present themselves to consciousness as external and separate phenomena, while the former deal with the living connections of reality experienced in the mind. It follows that the sciences arrive at connections with nature through inferences by means of a combination of hypotheses while the human sciences are based on directly given mental connections. We explain nature but we understand mental life. Inner experience grasps the processes by which we accomplish something as well as the combination of individual functions of mental life into a whole. The experience of the whole context comes first; only later do we distinguish its individual parts. This means that the methods of studying mental life, history and society differ greatly from those used to acquire knowledge of nature.[62]

Consistent with his general approach, Dilthey formulates outlines for poetics[63] in which motif functions along with other concepts such as theme (*Stoff*), poetic mood (*poetische Stimmung*), plot (*Fabel*), character (*Charakter*), action (*Handlung*), and means of presentation (*Darstellungs-mittel*). The understanding of literature becomes possible through the analysis of all these elements within a particular work. Such an examination illuminates the working of the creative imagination in its psychological dimensions, and would bring insights into the 'inner' mental life of the artist.[64]

Dilthey develops the general concept of motif in terms of a holistic view of the literary work and does not employ the concept for purposes of cultural comparisons, nor does he engage the motif in the cultural-historical reconstruction of the course of evolution.

Unlike Scherer, Dilthey conceives of the poetic process in psychological rather than social-evolutionary terms. He does not assume a direct correspondence between the realities of social ethics and cultural beliefs and the realities of literary works. Rather, he considers artistic creativity as a selective process that incorporates into literature only a limited number of situations that are qualitatively unique. Once such situations are within a poetic context, their meaning may change in adjustment to their position within the artistic work and to their relations with the other elements that are active in literature such as theme, plot, character, and action.

Like his romantic predecessors Dilthey considers motifs in terms of dramatic situations. This is the force that both motivates and unifies the action. Like them, he assumes the existence of only a limited number of motifs, and makes provision, like Scherer did, for the occurrence of dominant and supplementary motifs in the same work. But with clear departure from earlier conceptions of motif, he assumes these situations to be not only products of the fictive imagination, but rather actions rooted in life experience.

According to Dilthey, a motif is a situation of life (*Lebensverhältnis*) that becomes art. Such a transformation of themes occurs through the effects of various contrasting poetic moods and it is dependent upon the artist's ability to grasp the meanings and emotions that the life situation signifies. The motif, then, is a situation of life that has undergone artistic transformation and is subject to the meanings and logical consequences that are brought to bear upon it by a unifying poetic motivating force.

> Several motifs are operating with a larger poetic work. Among them one must have the dominant motivating force toward the establishment of a unity within the entire work. The number of possible motives is limited, and it is the task of comparative literary history to describe the development of individual motives.[65]

In Dilthey's poetics motif functions in a dual capacity both as a life experience and as its artistic transformation. On the one hand, it is a situation of life that has the potentiality of becoming poetry, on the other hand it is a situation of life that has already undergone artistic transformation and has acquired additional significance. The concept of motif as an experience is conceived as effecting the psychological process of artistic creativity, while as a literary element, motif is understood in its relationship to other concepts of poetics, as well as to other motifs.

By formulating a theory of poetics that contains this dual function of motif, Dilthey sets up a framework for historical poetics that transcends national, social, and linguistic boundaries, yet remains empirical and substantive. He rationalises the comparative study of motifs. The quest into the changing artistic perception of reality provides a psychological basis for historical poetics, and the comparative motif analysis demonstrates the differing artistic transformations of similar situations.

Motif as a folklore concept

Theoretically, Dilthey's concept of motif and his framework for comparative historical studies would have been most appropriate for the purposes of folklore research and the needs of *Ur*-form reconstruction. The cross-cultural and historical study of individual motifs, either as constant narrative cores or as variable elements in them, is, after all, the basis of the historical-geographical method. Dilthey's recognition of the potential universality of motifs provides for flexibility in the comparative pursuit of original forms. No doubt, a synthesis between compatible aspects of Scherer's and Dilthey's theories of poetry could have been a further methodological improvement. The notion that a motif is an idea expressed in the relations between actions and characters offered a greater degree of precision than the concept of motif as a 'situation of life'.

In fact, however, neither theory of poetics had a direct effect on folklore research. Only the concept of motif remained to haunt and stimulate students of folktales. During the end of the nineteenth and the beginning of the twentieth centuries the term 'motif' gained popularity, and with it many meanings already discussed, until it lost its analytical value. 'The motif,' wrote Julius Petersen, 'is, in general the most overused, and therefore unclear concept that is employed in the analysis of poetry. No other word has been brought, for no apparent reason, to such use. It is possible to call it a "sponge word" because it has absorbed and was burdened with all kinds of expressions.'[66]

No wonder then, that with the existence of such a conceptual muddle, Stith Thompson pointedly stated upon the conclusion of his revision of the *Motif-Index of Folk Literature* that this work 'is not based on any philosophical principles at all, but mainly upon practical experience, upon trial and error.'[67] But the avoidance of issues does not make them disappear. The preference for practical solutions over philosophical principles certainly has some useful value, but it is also responsible, partially at least, for the 'sterility' and 'pointlessness' which Stanley Edgar Hyman finds in the method in general.[68]

Unfortunately, although Thompson opted for a short term solution to the immediate needs of folklore scholarship, he nevertheless produced a book destined to longevity because, in spite of its flaws, it is an indispensible encyclopedic reference work. He himself regarded his *Motif-Index of Folk Literature* as a mere tool for future research, not research *per se*. 'The work has the same relation to future folklore research as a dictionary has to the writer of literature, or the map to the explorer who needs to keep his bearing.'[69] But the analogy is erroneous. Motifs are not the folklore equivalents of words in a language. They are not the items that make up folklore, but only constructed entities that Thompson and his students abstracted and named within a particular body of narrative tradition. While words, or better, morphemes, have symbolic meanings in a spoken or written language, motifs are constructed symbols in the language of meta-folklore, that is, the discourse of scholars about folklore. Motifs are signs for elements that exist in tales, but not the narrative elements themselves. The delineation and the naming of these narrative units depends completely upon the classification system that Thompson formulated. When Thompson begins to assume that motifs 'persist in tradition'[70] he is like Cassirer's 'primitive man' who believes in the actual existence of the forces he names.[71]

An example could clarify this point. Motif B291.2.1 *'Horse as Messenger,'* chosen at random, is a conceptual abstraction based upon numerous actions performed by the animal but in itself is not a minimal narrative unit, occurring in any folktale. The motif so named refers to an idea that is expressed in various actions or could be inferred from them, but it does not function in narratives as a word does in a language. Certainly, among the many motifs there are differing degrees of abstraction, ranging from a summary of specific incidents such as F1041.1.13.2. *'Woman dies of shame at seeing naked man (husband)'* to a very general idea, G303.3.3 *'The devil in animal form'*, but in all cases, *contra* Thompson, the motifs are not the minimal units that tales are made of.

Indeed Thompson defines motif as 'the smallest element in a tale', albeit he adds two modifications, '[(a)] having a power to persist in tradition. In order to have this power it must have [(b)] something unusual and striking about it.'[72] Size is a necessary but no longer sufficient criterion in delineating motifs. In order for this unit to have any value in comparative studies and in the historical reconstruction of tales it is necessary to add a qualitative requirement to the existing quantitative measure. Only with recurrence in the tradition of at least a single culture but preferably many cultures could a theme become part of a historical-geographical study. The continuous existence of a narrative element depends further on a psychological factor, namely its effect upon the narrators and the listeners.

Thompson not only defines but explains the existence of motifs. Basically he views motif, not as the minimal narrative unit, but as the minimal unit in tradition that has the capacity to become part of a narrative. This element is not bound by the particular story in which it appears since, according to Thompson's definition, it must occur in several tales before being recognised as motif. Thus the same terms that define the motif also explain its existence.

At this particular point Thompson implicitly departs from Arthur Christensen's definition of motif in which the psychological aspect contributes to the formulation of a notion of a dynamic, evolving motif.[73] According to Christensen, a motif is the simplest part into which it is possible to analyse a narration, whether historical or fictitious. These narrative elements are episodes that captivate the audience by their strangeness or by their tragic or comic effects. Oddity is thus the inherent quality of the motif that makes its persistence in social memory and tradition possible, an explanation that Thompson adopted. Once a narrative element ceases being at odds with the culture of narrators and audience it is no longer a motif, and vice versa, episodes that become strange and unusual to the listeners, acquire the quality and transform into motifs:

> We call *motifs* such meaningful elements that are 'catching', according to an undefineable psychological law, and which are detached with greater or lesser ease from their primitive connection in order to enter into new combinations. If one compares the narrations of primitive people with the tales of the peoples of a superior civilisation, it is possible to see that the primitive narrations that are supposed to be historical accounts, resemble a true story which is composed of elements of simple narrations, in which the motifs properly speaking are absent. At the age of totemism, the talking animals, the magic acts, the transformation of man into animals, the sexual relationships between man and animals were as ordinary and as natural events as in other periods episodes of war and hunting. However, a trait that at that period was a simple element of a narration, could have become a motif in

another degree of civilisation in which the transformation and the magical acts and so forth, are considered extraordinary things.[74]

Such a shifting concept of motif in which episodes can change their narrative status depending upon their cultural context was not suitable for a compendium of a universal scope. Therefore, while Thompson incorporated Christensen's idea of strangeness into his definition of motif, he eliminated the principle of cultural relativity that is implied by this feature.

Once having formulated his definition, Thompson distinguishes among the entire body of motifs three classes of actors, objects and actions. 'First are the actors in a tale — gods, or unusual animals, or marvellous creatures like witches, ogres, or fairies, or even conventionalized human characters like the favourite youngest child or the cruel stepmother. Second come certain items in the background of the action — magic objects, unusual customs, strange beliefs and the like. In the third place there are single incidents — and these comprise the great majority of motifs.'[75] Alan Dundes has already pointed out that 'if motifs can be actors, items, and incidents, then they are hardly units. They are not measures of a single quantity. ... In addition, the classes of motifs are not even mutually exclusive. Can one conceive of an incident which does not include either an actor or an item, if not both?'[76]

In fact, Thompson's distinction of motif classes, appears to be an *a posteriori* observation rather than an initial basis for classification. In his attempt to introduce order into 'the traditional narrative material of the whole earth',[77] Thompson follows two separate models of biological and bibliographical classifications. He deliberately avoids the alphabetical ordering of narrative elements as arbitrary, linguistically narrow, and hence of limited use.[78] The classification system that he proposes should have provided folklore with a scientific foundation, like the Linnaean classification had done for biology. At the same time his notation method, like that of the Library of Congress, should have fascilitated registration and retrieval of motifs.

However, the method of classification that resulted from this intended synthesis is no more 'scientific' than any previous system. Most important, the analogy to the biological order of things is a mere illusion. Through his classification, Linnaeus actually discovered an existing order and existing relations in nature. His classification is based upon features that are inherent in the species of animals and plants. In contrast, bibliographical classification involves an imposition of order upon reality. It is an arbitrary order that depends not upon the qualities of the subject, but on external means, like the availability and the shape of signs, like the alphabet that has no intrinsic relations to the subject matter of oral tradition. Utility, convenience and criticism not withstanding, at the hands of Thompson the motif was transformed from a minimal unit of narration into a minimal unit of classification. He shifted the concerns with units from their function in the formation and transmission of narratives, and from their relations within the tale context, to a focus upon their position in a classification system.

While the attempt to categorise motifs into classes began with Goethe, as soon as the term gained some conceptual significance the initial system involved the formulation of relations between minimal units within a narrative or dramatic form. In the course of the nineteenth century, when the diffusion of literary themes and their bearing upon culture and society occupied central positions in scholarship, motifs became research tools in the service of broader goals. Thompson never lost the focus of these global aims of folklore scholarship,[79] but in the process of preparing the way for their attainment, the means overtook the ends, undermining issues and problems that are still in search of solution.

Motif as a minimal folk-narrative element

The most puzzling, and most elusive of these are still the most fundamental problems, namely the very idea of a minimal narrative unit, its ontology, and its position within a narrative, a poem, a play, or within a tradition at large.[80]

Comparative studies and the historic-geographic search for *Ur*-forms cast the motif in a dual perspective. On the one hand it is the fundamental theme of a story, the primary moving force within a distinct plot; but on the other hand it is the most elemental narrative particle that has the power to move from one story to another. Motif is 'the smallest element of narrative that has the capacity (strength) to exist in transmission. . .'[81] This definition implies the complete de-contextualisation of narrative elements. Motifs become the perennial moving elements in inter- and intra-spheres of tradition. They have an equal capacity to enter in and out of narrative combinations. The categorisation of motifs as major and supplementary that appeared in previous studies, becomes related not to meaning but to the transitory capacity of these narrative elements.

According to Anna Birgitta Rooth, for example, the principal motifs are the least detachable and cannot be omitted from the composition without effecting the essential structure of the story. In contrast, 'the detail motifs are those of minor importance; they cleave to the principal motifs but may be eliminated without causing any notable alteration in the plot.' A combination of a principal and several detail motifs constitutes a motif-complex which is 'the smallest unit of composition within a tale.' In Rooth's distinction only a motif-complex, not a motif alone, 'may be regarded as being independent, even self-sufficient. The motif is only a single element in this structure; hence it can neither be preserved nor related in isolation, . . . it is at all times dependent on one or more motifs with which it can form a motif-complex or unit . . .'[82]

Similarly Boris Tomashevsky distinguishes between two types of motifs, those 'which cannot be omitted are *bound motifs*; those which may be omitted without disturbing the whole causal-chronological course of events are *free motifs*.'[83]

This idea of motifs in musical chairs requires the designation not only of free and bound motifs, but also the consideration of motifs that are in free variation with each other, that is, those that can serve as substitutes in similar narrative contexts. For them, Christensen suggests the term *corresponding motifs*.[84]

The bonds between the moving motifs and their narrative contexts depend upon the logical position of the element within the whole. Essence and meaning are no longer a consideration in formulating the relations between a motif and a narrative situation. The idea of motif as an element wandering in the realms of literature cannot involve any semantic connections between an isolateable narra-tive particle and the entire work.

Consequently, it is necessary to make a terminological and conceptual distinction between actions and meanings. There is no necessary direct relationship between motifs and ideas, actions and meanings. Christensen distinguishes between the concrete and the abstract aspects of the smallest narrative elements, referring to the first as motif, and to the latter as theme. 'By the word theme [he] understands the fundamental idea expressed by a motif or a combination of motifs . . . there are tales that have a theme and others that do not. . . . In other tales the theme is secondary, the interest lies mainly in the amusing character of the motifs or the combination of motifs. The more the tale approaches an historical account (voyage adventure, historic legend, local etiology) the more weak is the theme; the more the tale approaches a fable, the more dominant is the theme.'[85] It becomes apparent that according to this distinction the themes are the morals of stories, the messages communicated by tales, whereas motifs are sheer plots and actions; themes are the meanings of motifs, the abstract notions that concrete actions convey. Ina-Maria Greverus echoes this distinction when she states that the theme is abstracted from the content, and that in this way she avoids the confusion between motif and theme. 'By theme I understand the basic thought that is derived from a tale and that the tale embraces. These basic thoughts are realised in the narrative substance. The substance consists of the smaller subject-units, the motifs. . . .'[86]

The analytical separation between motifs and themes is implicitly an attempt to resolve the double bind of the romantic concept of motif, designating the minimal narrative unit as motif, and its essential, and maximal meaning as theme. A folktale, and for that matter any work of art, can have a dominant theme, but many motifs. In that light it is possible also to understand Veselovskij who, at the end of the nineteenth century, regarded themes as a complex of motifs. In the spirit of his time he viewed motifs as formulae by which early man answered metaphysical questions about nature. Such formulae have the capacity to expand and grow through a conscious artistic selection, combination and schematisation and then become a complete theme. Veselovskij regards the theme as the artistic, rather than the philosophical abstraction of a motif,[87] similar to the Wagnerian notion of the relations between motifs and a grand theme in music.[88]

From this perspective repetition becomes an essential feature in the relationship between motif and idea. But this is no longer a repetition that occurs in narrative transmission and is due to the special capacity of motif to survive the hardship of time. Rather, the conceptualisation of a minimal narrative unit as a motif results from a deliberate meaningful repetition of the same episode, even metaphor, in different contexts of the same general tradition, or a single work. The very occurrence of the motif in variable literary contexts constitutes its significance and function. The motif serves to interrelate different narrative contexts, reflect them upon each other, and unify them into a notional, if not a narrative, whole. This idea echoes the romantic motif in so far that 'the fundamental motif' becomes synonymous with 'the underlying idea',[89] albeit with two basic exceptions. First this motif is not a necessary moving force for actions within a situation; at most it becomes a rhetorical force used by the speaker or the writer. Secondly re-occurrence in at least two distinct historical occasions is one of its essential features. This idea of motif has been articulated in religious studies and, discussing its place in Old Testament studies Shemaryahu Talmon offers the following definition:

> A literary motif is a representative complex theme which recurs within the framework of the Old Testament in variable forms and connections. It is rooted in an actual situation of anthropological or historical nature. In its secondary literary setting, the motif gives expression to ideas and experiences inherent in the original situation, and is employed to reactualize in the audience the reactions of the participants in that original situation. The motif represents the essential meaning of the situation, not the situation itself. It is not a mere reiteration of the sensations involved, but rather a heightened and intensified representation of them.[90]

By the virtue of its multiple connections, such a motif is no longer a minimal, or elementary unit, but rather a 'representative complex theme' that

has historical dimensions. Its significance becomes apparent in the phenomenological study of religion as it is, as Peter Berger defined it 'a specific pattern or gestalt of religious experience that can be traced in a historical development.'[91] The meaning of such a motif is completely dependent upon its primary and subsequent contexts, and it derives its rhetorical effect from its inherent inter-textuality.

The notion of a rhetorical motif contrasts sharply with the idea of the wandering motif that the historic-geographic school espouses. It implies meaning and intention, and deliberate manipulation of symbols versus free floating themes, with neither control nor guidance, that move from one tale to another, from one language to the next over time. The idea that motifs roam through folk-literature with no constraints at all was a necessary assumption for the start of a search for an *Ur*-form. Yet, critical observation correlating forms with theme indicated that, even in this apparently cluttered world, order exists. Motifs appear in particular positions in a narrative, or are associated with distinct genres. In other words there is an intrinsic literary regulatory system that governs the migration of motifs, and their transference from one text to another follows some discoverable principles; their diffusion is not erratic, nor necessarily influenced by social and cultural contacts,[92] but has a folkloric-literary basis. For example Robert Petsch distinguishes between Frame-motive (*Rahmenmotive*), core-motive (*Kernmotive*), and completing motive (*Füllmotive*) that supplement and conclude narrative characteristics. Each of these motifs has its sphere of action within a narrative to which it is confined. Motifs that occupy different positions within narratives are not interchangeable with each other. In other words there is a positional formal definition for each motif, that governs its movements within literary spheres.[93]

Albert Wesselski, who criticised the entire historic-geographic method, suggested the existence of a thematic-formal correspondence in folk-tale, according to which motifs occur in particular genres and no others. The basis of his distinction is the attitude of the people toward the narratives, a criterion that has served to describe genres. Hence he distinguishes between myth motifs (*Mythenmotive*), that are believed to be facts but are not; realistic motifs (*Gemeinschaftsmotive*), that are believed and are facts, and culture motifs (*Kulturmotive*) which are neither believed to be nor are facts. Each of the narrative folk genres, the *Märchen*, the novella, the *Sage*, has its own kinds of motif which are not interchangeable, except under shifting cultural conditions that involve a decline or increase of belief in certain ideas that have thematic representation.[94] Wesselski's distinction is not merely an alternative motif classification; his approach has important implication to the theories of narrative formation and motif migration. Each genre, according to him, has a limited number and kind of appropriate motifs and the transgression of these literary formal boundaries requires first a change in cultural attitudes toward these themes.

Although Wesselski was a literary scholar, he challenges the historic-geographic concept of motif as an anthropologist would, introducing cultural attitudes as a necessary dimension in delineating minimal narrative units. In the analysis of verbal art, questions of culture, meaning and their representation often suffer from conventions in the understanding of symbols in verbal narratives. In contrast, the analysis of visual art, with its tangible forms, and the iconic basis of its symbols, brings the relationship between units of meaning and units of form into a sharper focus; such an analysis could in turn illuminate some of the difficulties that folklorists have encountered in their attempts to delineate a minimal narrative unit.

In his attempt to formulate iconography systematically, Erwin Panofsky employed the same pair of terms, motif and theme, that folklore and literary scholars have used for many years. In doing so he first distinguished between the universal and cultural forms as primary and secondary subject matter respectively. The universal configurations are either factual or expressive forms that are recognised by all, cross-culturally. Shapes of men, animals and plants are factual forms; expressive gestures like a smile, mournful decline of the head, are universal as well. In contrast, the secondary or conventional subject matter, consists of the particular gestures associated with specific figures in each culture, or a period, like the various positions and gestures associated with different saints in medieval paintings. The primary and universal forms are visual *motifs* and the secondary and particular subjects are themes. In the association between a gesture and a specific person 'we connect artistic *motifs* and combinations of artistic *motifs* (compositions) with themes or concepts. Motifs thus recognised as carriers of a secondary or conventional meaning may be called *images*.'[95]

By introducing the distinction between motifs and themes in terms of the universal and cultural, Panofsky reverses the relations between the concrete and the abstract aspects of the elementary artistic unit. If followed in folklore the delineation between bound and free motifs, and the designation of some motifs as corresponding with each other, would be formulated in new terms: the motifs, as classes of actors, objects and actions, would remain constant, and hence more abstract and universal, and the themes would have been variable and culturally specific.

But methodologically such a formulation would have defeated the purposes of discovering the process of narrative formation and migration at which the historical-geographic method aimed, and would have pushed motifs over the brinks of history into the domain of structural and symbolic analysis.

Conclusion

In his work Stith Thompson deliberately ignored these issues and possibilities. For him they represented an interference with the practical need of his classification plan. However, now there is a revived interest in the concept of motif. The question of minimal narrative units becomes viable again in the light of structural studies, text-grammar analysis, and inquiry into the symbolic meaning of narrative. Meletinsky suggests that 'the next step [in folktale research] must be the analysis of motifs in the perspective of structuralism. One has to take into consideration here that the distribution of motifs within the theme is structurally also reducible to the above mentioned formula. But if this formula itself represents a specific mechanism for the synthesis of folktales, then the motif is the most essential element of that analysis.'[96]

It well might be. But a renewed interest in the motif cannot be confined to the concept as it is present in the *Motif-Index of Folk Literature*. It must relate to the entire gamut of ideas and controversies that were part of its development from romanticism to structuralism.

Notes

1. Richard M. Dorson, 'Introduction: Concepts of Folklore and Folklife Studies', *Folklore and Folklife: An Introduction*, ed. Richard M. Dorson (Chicago, 1972), 6.

2. Recent critique of Thompson's *Motif-Index of Folk Literature* (Bloomington, 1955-58) ranges from concern with the adequacy and utility of the classification plan of the book as in John Greenway, *Literature among the Primitives* (Hatboro, Pa., 1964), 291-2, to the adequacy of the motif as an analytical unit as in Alan Dundes, 'From Etic to Emic Units in the Structural Study of Folktales', *Journal of American Folklore*, LXXV (1962), 95-105, to questioning the very worthiness of motif analysis as in Melville Jacobs, 'A Look Ahead in Oral Literature Research', *Journal of American Folklore*, LXXIX (1966), 423. Most of this criticism emerged in the early sixties, after the publication of the revised edition of the *Motif-Index* was completed in 1958. More recently Ronald Grambo criticises the definition of the motif as 'a *mixtum compositum* of many varied elements', in 'The Conceptions of Variant and Motif, A Theoretical Approach', *Fabula*, XVII (1976), 251.

3. For example see Lubomír Doložel, 'From Motifemes to Motifs', *Poetics*, IV (1972), 55-90; E. Meletinsky, S. Nekludov, E. Novik and D. Segal, 'Problems of the Structural Analysis of Fairytales', *Soviet Structural Folkloristics*, ed. Pierre Maranda (The Hague, 1974), I, 91, and Eleazar Meletinski, 'Principes sémantiques d'un nouvel index des motifs et des sujets', *Cahiers de Littérature Orale*, II (1977), 15-24. In this connection see also the suggestion of applying to folklore the concept of motif as developed in religious and biblical studies made by Gerald E. Warshaver, 'A Comparative Study according to the Traditio-Historical Method', *Folklore Forum*, V, ii (1972), 38-54, and Grambo, *op. cit.* Simultaneously, the concept of the motif functions in the analysis of ancient and medieval oral epics. See for example, Michael N. Nagler, *Spontaneity and Tradition: A Study in the Oral Art of Homer* (Berkeley, 1974), 64-130, and Joseph J. Duggan, *The Song of Roland: Formulaic Style and Poetic Craft* (Berkeley, 1973), esp. 160-212. See also David E. Bynum, *The Daemon in the Wood: A Study of Oral Narrative Patterns* (Cambridge, Mass., 1978), 79-81.

4. See Kaarle Krohn, *Folklore Methodology*, tr. Roger L. Welsch (Austin, 1971), 4-5, 174-7; Jouko Hautala, *Finnish Folklore Research 1828-1918* (Helsinki, 1969); William A. Wilson, *Folklore and Nationalism in Modern Finland* (Bloomington, 1976), 53-66.

5. Auguste-Louis-Armand e.g. Loiseleur-Deslongchamps, *Essai sur les fables indiennes et sur leur introduction en Europe* (Paris, 1838); Theodor Benfey, *Pantschatantra: Fünf Bücher indischer Fablen, Märchen, und Erzählungen*, (Leipzig, 1859), 2 vols, Stith Thompson, *The Folktale* (New York, 1946), 15-16, 373-9. In his theory of the Indian origin of folktales Benfey concedes to Greece the position of the cradle of animal tales and fables, given the historical priority of Aesop.

6. Emmanuel Cosquin, *Études folkloriques, recherches sur les migrations des contes populaires et leur point de depart* (Paris, 1922); *idem, Les contes indiens et l'Occident* (Paris, 1929)

7. Andrew Lang, 'Introduction', *Grimm's Household Tales*, tr. and ed. Margaret Hunt (London, 1884), xli-lxx; Edwin Sidney Hartland, *The Science of Fairy Tales: An Inquiry into Fairy Methodology* (London, 1891); John Arnott MacCulloch, *Childhood of Fiction: a Study of Folk Tales and Primitive Thought* (New York, 1905).

8. The 'tale type' served this purpose. On the concept of folktale types see Krohn, 28-33, 126-34; Stith Thompson, *The Folktale*, 415, 426; Heda Jason, 'Structural Analysis and the Concept of the "Tale Type"', *Arv*, XXVIII (1972), 36-54; *ibid.*, 'The Russian Criticism of the "Finnish School" in Folktale and Scholarship', *Norveg*, XIV (1970), 285-94; Kenneth Laine Ketner, 'Identity and Existence in the Study of Human Tradition', *Folklore*, LXXXVII (1976), 192-200.

9. Originally published in Karl Spiess, *Das deutsche Volksmärchen* (Leipzig, 1917), 37; quoted here from Krohn, 29-30.

10. Spiess, 37

11. Compare with Johann Georg von Hahn, *Griechische und albanesische Märchen* (Leipzig, 1864), 43. Hahn recognises the similarity between narratives of different peoples, and hence, while he retains the idea of the potentiality of traits for infinite combination, in actuality, he observes, these combinations are rather limited.

12. Krohn, 31.

13. *ibid.*; see also 105-6.

14. *ibid.*, 31.

15. *ibid.*, 126-7.

16. For biographical studies see William Addison, *The English Country Parson* (London, 1947); William Purcell, *Onward Christian Soldier: a Life of Sabine Baring-Gould, Parson, Squire, Novelist, Antiquary, 1834-1924* (London, 1957); Bickford H. Dickinson, *Sabine Baring-Gould, Squarson, Writer, and Folklorist, 1834-1924* (Newton Abbot, 1970). See also his own memoirs: S. Baring-Gould, *Early Reminiscences 1834-1864* (Detroit, 1967); *idem, Further Reminiscences 1864-1894* (Detroit, 1967).

17. Richard M. Dorson, *The British Folklorists: A History* (Chicago, 1968), 295

18. For discussions of the use of the concept of 'root' in linguistics see Holger Pedersen, *The Discovery of Language: Linguistic Science in the Nineteenth Century*, tr. John W. Spargo (Cambridge, Mass., 1931), 1-30; Otto Jespersen, *Language, its Nature, Development and Origin* (London, 1922), 367-95; R. H. Robins, *General Linguistics: An Introductory Survey* (Bloomington, 1964), 206-13. I would like to thank John Fought for these references.

19. Sabine Baring-Gould, 'Household Stories', Appendix to W. Henderson, *Notes on the Folklore of the Northern Counties of England and the Borders* (London, 1866), 209-300.

20. Dorst, John and Dan Ben-Amos, 'From the History of Folklore Notebook', in preparation. While Baring-Gould does not acknowledge his indebtedness to J. G. von Hahn, the relationship between these two schemes did not escape William Ralston who writes: 'The most elaborate attempt at a classification of folk-tales yet made is that due to J. G. von Hahn, who prefixed to his collection of Greek and Albanian Tales (1864) a scheme for the reduction of such stories to their original elements, and their arrangement in divisions and groups. His plan was afterwards employed and modified by Mr Baring Gould, whose classification of "Story Radicals" is appended to Mr Henderson's "Folklore of the Northern Counties".' W. R. Ralston, 'Notes on Folk-Tales', *The Folk-Lore Record*, I (1878), 76.

21. William R. S. Ralston, 'Notes on Folk-Tales', *The Folk-Lore Record*, I (1878), 77-78; George L. Gomme, *The Handbook of Folklore* (London, 1887), 117-35 and later modified by Joseph Jacobs, 'Some Types of Indo-European Folktales', *The Handbook of Folklore*, ed. Charlotte S. Burne (London, 1913), 344-55.

22. An exception is Richard M. Dorson who notes that 'Baring-Gould ingeniously anticipated the *Type-Index of the Folk-Tale*'. See 'Foreword', *Folktales of England*, eds., Katherine M. Briggs and Ruth L. Tongue (Chicago, 1965), xvii. See also his *The British Folklorists*, 295-7, 390.

23. Jean Paul, *Vorschule der Aesthetik* (Hamburg, 1804), section 68.

24. Johanne August Eberhard, *Handbuch der Gesthetik für gebildete Leser aus allen Ständen in Briefen herausgegeben* (Halle, 1803-5), I, 98.

25. Stewart Chamberlain, ed., *Briefwechsel zwischen Schiller und Goethe* (Jena, 1910), 48, 132, 146, 151, 152, 181, 191, 193, 271.

26. J. E. Spingarn, ed., *Goethe's Literary Essays* (New York, 1964), 101.

27. *ibid.*, 100.

28. *ibid.*, 152, 188-193, 48.

29. Johann Wolfgang von Goethe, *Wilhelm Meister's Apprenticeship*, tr. Thomas Carlyle (New York, 1962), 280.

30. *ibid.*

31. John Oxenford, tr., *Conversations of Goethe with Eckermann and Soret* (London, 1874), 63.

32. *ibid.*, 106-7. At this point the translator adds a note worth quoting in full. He writes: 'This "motive" (German, *motiv*) is a very difficult and unmanageable word, and like many words of the sort does not seem always to preserve the same meaning. According to the definition of lexicographers, the German expression is almost the same as the English one, and a poem is said to be well "motived" (*motiviert*) when it is well organised as a whole, – that is to say, when there is a sufficient motive for the different effects produced. But in the passage above, "motive" seems rather to mean "theme" for a poem, and it will be remembered that "motive" has that sense in music. Wherever *motiv* occurs it will be represented by *motive* in italics, and the reader will do his best to understand it from the context.'

33. *ibid.*, 439. For a study on the influence of Gozzi on the German romantics see Hedwig Hoffmann Rusack, *Gozzi in Germany* (New York, 1930). The idea of the limited number of tragical situations was further developed in Georges Potti, *The Thirty-six Dramatic Situations*, tr. Lucile Ray (Ridgewood, N.J., 1916).

34. Ignaz Jeitteles, *Aesthetisches Lexicon: Ein alphabetisches Handbuch zur Theorie der Philosophie des Schönen und der Schönen Künste. Nebst erklärung der Kunstausdrücke aller aesthetischen Zweige* (Vienna, 1835-37), II, 98.

35. John Ruskin, *Modern Painters* (New York, 1872), V, 175.

36. *ibid.*

37. *ibid.*

38. Erwin Panofsky, *Studies in Iconology: Humanistic Themes in the Art of the Renaissance* (New York, 1939), 18-31.

39. René Wellek, *A History of Modern Criticism: 1750-1950* (New Haven, 1965), IV, 297.

40. See his work *Civilisation in England*, (New York, 1870), 2 vols.

41. *Histoire de la litterature anglaise* (Paris, 1863-4) and *Philosophie de l'art* (Paris, 1865).

42. The deterministic tradition in literary and folklore scholarship was not limited to the nineteenth century, and continued well into current scholarship. One of the latest efforts in that direction is Heda Jason, 'A Multi-dimensional Approach to Oral Literature', *Current Anthropology*, X (1969), 413-26.

43. Wilhelm Scherer, 'Jacob Grimm', *Preussische Jahrbücher*, XIV (1864), 632-680; XV (1865), 1-32; XVI (1865), 1-47, 99-139. Later the biography appeared as a separate monograph, *Jacob Grimm* (Berlin, 1865).

44. His major study on the subject is *Geschichte der deutschen Litteratur* (Berlin, 1883). English translation by F. C. Conybeare, ed. F. Max Müller, *A History of German Literature* (New York, 1886).

45. Otto Wirth, *Wilhelm Scherer, Joseph Nadler, and Wilhelm Dilthey as Literary Historians* (Chicago, 1937), 7. See Wilhelm Scherer, *Geschichte der deutschen Dichtung im elften und zwölften Jahrhundert* (Strassburg and London, 1875), 1-10.

46. Wilhelm Scherer, *Poetik* (Berlin, 1888), 213. This work was published posthumously, edited by his student Richard Moritz Meyer on the basis of Scherer's own material and some notes of Scherer's lectures of 1885.

47. *ibid.*, 212.

48. *ibid*', See also Wellek, IV, 299.

49. Scherer, *Poetik*, 214.

50. See Aeschylus, *The Libation Bearers*, 892-1062; *The Eumenides*, 585-613, and Euripides, *Orestes*.

51. Lucius Junius Brutus who witnessed the execution of his sons after their conviction in the trial of the conspirators who plotted to

restore the deposed king Tarquinius Superbus to the throne. See Virgil, *Aeneid*, VI, 817-23.

52. In Goethe's *Faust* (1808), Vol.I.

53. One act play, *Die Geschwister* (1787); written in 1776.

54. Damon and Phintias (erroneously Pythias), the two friends from Syracuse. When Damon was condemned to death he asked permission to go and see his wife and children before he died. At first the request was denied, but on his way to execution he encountered his friend Pythias who was ready to die in his stead if he did not return in time. Damon went to visit his family and, in spite of obstacles, came back just in time. Both were forgiven. See Cicero, *Tusculan Disputations*, V, 63, xxii. The classical story was dramatised by Richard Edwards, *Damon and Phithias* (1571) and John Banim, *Damon and Pythias* (1825). See *Gesta Romanorum*, Tale 108.

55. Clavigo's friend in Goethe's tragedy *Clavigo* (1774).

56. The hero of a Middle High German epic written before 1250.

57. Codrus, the last king of Athens. When he learned, during the Dorian invasion of the Peloponnesus, that the Delphic Oracle prophesised that the Athenians would be defeated if his life was spared, he deliberately courted death at the enemy camp. When the Dorians learned about his death, they retreated. See for example, Pausanias, *Description of Greece*, II, 19, 6; VII, 25, 2; VIII, 52, 1; Lycurgus, *Contra Leocratem*, 84-7. Arminius (c.18- or 16 B.C. -A.D. 19 or 21), Tacitus, *Annals*, I, 63-8; II, 9-18; known in later ages as Hermann der Cheruske. As a chief of the Cherussi he led a revolt against the Roman forces in A.D. 9 upon his return from service at Rome to his native home in northern Germany. He is celebrated in many German romantic novels and plays.

58. A hero in a novel by Heinrich von Kleist (1777-1811) that was based on an old chronicle and appeared in his *Erzählungen* (1810). Kohlhaas is a hero who is driven to crime through circumstances and his strong sense of justice.

59. Schere, *Poetik*, 214-6.

60. See Wilhelm Dilthey, 'Wilhelm Scherer zum persönlichen Gedachtnis', *Deutsche Rund-* schau, XLIX (1886), 132-46; Peter Salm, *Three Modes of Criticism: The Literary Theories of Scherer, Walzel, and Staiger* (Cleveland, 1968), 6.

61. Wilhelm Dilthey, *Gesammelte Schriften* (Stuttgart, 1914-74), V, 4. See also Horace L. Friess, 'Wilhelm Dilthey', *The Journal of Philosophy*, XXVI (1929), 11.

62. Quoted from H. P. Rickman, ed., *W. Dilthey: Selected Writings* (Cambridge, 1976), 89. Original text that was published in 1894 is now available in Dilthey, *Gesammelte Schriften*, V, 143-4.

63. The essay 'Die Einbildungskraft des Dichters: Bausteine für eine Poetik', (1887) was reprinted in *Gesammelte Schriften*, VI, 103-241. Notes toward a further revision have been published in VI, 307-320.

64. See in particular *Gesammelte Schriften*, VI, 216-28.

65. *ibid.*, 216. See also Rudolf A. Makkreel, *Dilthey: Philosopher of the Human Studies* (Princeton, 1975), 194-6; Kurt Müller-Vollmer, *Towards a Phenomenological Theory of Literature: A Study of Wilhelm Dilthey's Poetik* (The Hague, 1963), 173-4. The idea in this quotation contradicts a previous statement of Dilthey, cited by Wellek, in which he denies the possibility of a genealogical sequence of poetic schools, and hence states that 'the changes which occur with a type or motif, cannot be arranged in fixed series'. See *Gesammelte Schriften*, VI, 124 and Wellek, IV, 324.

66. Julius Petersen, 'Das Motiv in der Dichtung', *Dichtung und Volkstum: Neue Folge des Euphorion, Zeitschrift für Literaturgeschichte*, XXXVIII (1937), 45. Compare this situation with the use of the term 'structure' in the second half of the twentieth century. See Roger Bastide, ed., *Sens et usages du term structure dans les sciences humaines et sociales* (The Hague, 1962); Jean Viet, *Les méthodes structuralistes dans les sciences sociales* (The Hague, 1965); Raymond Boudon, *The Usages of Structuralism*, tr. Michalina Vaughan (London, 1971).

67. Stith Thompson, *Narrative Motif-Analysis as a Folklore Method* (Helsinki, 1955), 7.

68. Stanley Edgar Hyman, 'Some Bankrupt Treasuries', *The Kenyon Review*, X (1948), 485.

69. *ibid.*, 9. Compare with Munro S. Edmonson who wrote that 'Motifs in folklore are like the phonetic dimensions of linguistics or like patterns, themes, configurations, and values in general cultural theory. They are, to a first approximation, structural units.' *Lore: An Introduction to the Science of Folklore and Literature* (New York, 1971), 47. He seems to interpret Thompson in a way that is not consistent with Thompson's own ideas about his work.

70. Thompson, *The Folktale*, 415.

71. See Ernst Cassirer, *Language and Myth*, tr. Susanne K. Langer (New York, 1946), 44-62.

72. *ibid.*

73. Arthur Christensen, *Motif et Theme* (Helsinki, 1925). Thompson refers to this work, but considers it too 'philosophical' for his particular needs; see *Motif-Index of Folk Literature*, I, 10-11.

74. *ibid.*, 5-6. Compare with the notion of 'de-familiarisation' (*ostraneniye*) that the Russian formalist Victor Shklovsky develops in his essay 'Art as Technique', in *Russian Formalist Criticism: Four Essays*, tr. and ed. Lee T. Lemon and Marion J. Reis (Lincoln, Nebrask, 1965), 3-24, and the concept of 'foregrounding' that Czech structuralist Jan Mukarovský proposes in his essay 'Standard Language and Poetic Language', in *A Prague School Reader on Esthetics, Literary Structure, and Style*, tr. and ed. Paul L. Garvin (Washington, D.C., 1964), 17-30.

75. Thompson, *The Folktale*, 415-6.

76. Dundes, 97. See also Grambo, 243-56.

77. Thompson, *Motif-Index*, I, 10.

78. Attempts to arrange ideas, motifs or titles in alphabetical order were made by Friedrich Hebbel in a review of *Deutsche Sagen von Adolph Bude* (1839). In *Sämtliche Werke*, ed. Richard Werner (Berlin, 1904), X, 390-2, and in the work of Scherer's student Otto Brahm, *Das Deutsche Ritterdrama des achtzehnten Jahrhunderts. Studien über Joseph August von Törring, seine Vorgänger und Nachfolger* (Strassburg, 1880), 145-167.

   In America, under the suggestion of Franz Boas, the following lists of American Indian tales were made: A. L. Kroeber, 'Catch-Words in American Mythology', *Journal of American Folklore*, XXI (1908), 222-7, and R. H. Lowie, 'Catch-Words for Mythological Motives', *Journal of American Folklore*, XXI (1908), 24-7. Kroeber discussed the relationship between motives and types (p.226) in a way that is similar to the use Thompson was later to employ.

79. See Stith Thompson, 'The Challenge of Folklore', *PMLA*, LXXIX (1964), 357-65.

80. For a bibliography, a survey and a few selected discussions of the concept of motif in literature in general see the following: Franz Anselm Schmitt, ed., *Stoff-und Motivgeschichte der deutschen Literatur: Eine Bibliographie* (Berlin, 1965), and see especially pp.3-4 for a list of general discussions of the concept of motif in literature (the first edition of this bibliography was edited by Kurt Bauerhorst in 1932, and other editions appeared in 1959 and 1976); Elizabeth Frenzel, *Stoff -und Motivgeschichte* (Berlin, 1966); Z. Czerny, 'Contribution à une théorie comparée du motif dans les art', in *Stil-und Formprobleme in der Literatur. Vorträge des VII Kongress der Internationalen Vereinigung für moderne Sprachen und Literaturen in Heidelberg*, ed. Paul Böckmann (Heidelberg, 1959), 38-50; Sophie-Irene Kalinowska, 'A propos d'une théorie du motif litéraire: les formantes', *Beitraege zur Romanischer Philologie*, I (1961), 78-82; Oskar Katann, 'A Review of August C. Mahr, *Dramatische Situationsbilder und Bildtypen* (Stanford: Stanford University Press, 1928), *Euphorion: Zeitschrift für Literaturgeschichte*, XXXII (1931), 97-101; Wolfgang Kayser, *Das sprachliche Kunstwerk* (Bern, 1951), 61-78; Joseph Körner, 'Erlebnis – Motiv – Stoff', *Vom Geiste neuer Literaturforschung: Festschrift für Oskar Walzel*, ed. Julius Wahle and Victor Klemperer (Wildpark-Potsdam, 1924), 80-90; Willy Krogmann, 'Motiv', *Reallexicon der deutschen Literatur-geschichte*, eds. Werner Kohlschmidt and Wolfgang Mohr (Berlin, 1965), II, 427-432; idem, 'Motivübertragung und ihre Bedeutung für die Literarhistorische Forschung', *Neophilologus*, XVII (1932), 17-32; idem, 'Motivanalyse', *Zeitschrift für angewandte Psychologie*, XLII (1932), 264-272; August C. Mahr, *Dramatische Situationsbilder und-Bildtypen: Eine Studie zur Kunstgeschichte des Dramas* (Stanford, 1928), 9-15. For the use of the term in philosophy see Rudolf Eisler, *Wörterbuch der Philosophischen Be-*

griffe Historisch-Quellenmässig Bearbeitet, ed. Karl Roretz (Berlin, 1929), II, 184-9; William P. Alston, 'Motives and Motivation', *The Encyclopedia of Philosophy* (New York, 1967), V, 399-409.

81. Max Lüthi, *Märchen* (Stuttgart, 1962), 18. See also his discussion in 'Europäische Volkliteratur: Themen, Motive, Zielkräfte', *Weltliteratur und Volksliteratur*, ed. Albert Schaefer (Munich, 1972), 66-79.

82. Anna Birgitta Rooth, *The Cinderella Cycle* (Lund, 1951), 31-3; see also 237-40.

83. Boris Tomashevsky, 'Thematics', *Russian Formalist Criticism: Four Essays*, 67.

84. Christensen, 6.

85. *ibid.*, 8.

86. Ina-Maria Greverus, 'Thema, Typus und Motiv: Zur Determination in Erzälforschung', *IV International Congress for Folk-Narrative Research in Athens* (1.9.–6.9. 1964), ed. Georgios A. Megas, *Laographia*, XXII (1965), 135.

87. A. N. Veselovskij, *Istoričeskaja poètika*, ed. V. M. Zirmunskij (Leningrad, 1940), 493-5. The essay on 'Thematic Poetics', 493-596, in which Veselovskij discusses the relationship between motif and theme, was published posthumously, edited by his students V. F. Sismarev and V. M. Zirmunskij. It is based on his manuscript and on students' notes taken in his lectures on 'Thematics' given in the years of 1898-1903. I would like to thank G. Saul Morson for a summary of Veselovskij's essay and lengthy discussions about the subject. See also V. Propp, *Morphology of the Folktale* (Austin, 1968), 12-13, for a discussion of Veselovskij's ideas about motif and theme.

88. For a brief discussion and further bibliographical references see the entries for 'Leitmotiv',

and 'Motif', in *Harvard Dictionary of Music*, ed. Willi Apel (Cambridge, Mass., 1969), 465-6, 545-6.

89. Anders Nygren, *Agape and Eros*, tr. Philip S. Watson (London, 1953), 37.

90. Shemaryahu Talmon, 'The "Desert Motif" in the Bible and in Qumran Literature', *Biblical Motifs: Origins and Transformations*, ed. Alexander Altmann (Cambridge, Mass., 1966), 39. See Warshaver, note 3, for a proposal to adapt such a concept of motif for folkloric analysis.

91. Peter L. Berger, 'The Sociological Study of Sectarianism', *Social Research*, XXI (1954), 478.

92. See Franz Boas, *Race, Language and Culture* (New York, 1940), 437-45, 451-90 (originally published in 1891 and 1914 respectively).

93. Robert Petsch, 'Motiv, Formel und Stoff', *Zeitschrift für deutsche Philologie*, LIV (1929), 378-94.

94. Albert Wesselski, 'Märchen des Volkes un der Literatur', *Märchen des Mittlealters* (Berlin, 1925), xvii; *idem, Versuch einer Theorie des Märchens* (Hildesheim, 1974), 12, 33-7. See also Emma Emily Kiefer, *Albert Wesselski and Recent Folktale Theories* (Bloomington, 1939), 38-58.

95. Erwin Panofsky, *Studies in Iconology: Humanistic Themes in the Art of the Renaissance* (Oxford, 1939), 6. See also 3-17, for the exposition of the ideas summarised here.

96. Meletinsky *et al*, 51. See also further studies cited in note 3 and other works such as Gerald Prince, *A Grammar of Stories: An Introduction* (The Hague, 1973).

Wet and Dry, the Evil Eye; An Essay in Semitic and Indo-European Worldview*

ALAN DUNDES   University of California (Berkeley)

THE evil eye is a fairly consistent and uniform folk belief complex based upon the idea that an individual, male or female, has the power, voluntarily or involuntarily, to cause harm to another individual or his property merely by looking at or praising that person or property. The harm may consist of illness, or even death or destruction. Typically, it is the victim's good fortune, good health, or good looks, or unguarded comment about them, which seem to invite or provoke an attack by someone with the evil eye. If the object attacked is animate, it may fall ill. Inanimate objects such as buildings or rocks may be caused by the evil eye to crack or burst. Symptoms of evil eye caused illness may include loss of appetite, excessive yawning, hiccoughs, vomiting, and fever. If the object attacked is a cow, its milk may dry up; if a plant or a fruit tree, it may suddenly wither and die.

Preventive measures include wearing apotropaic amulets, making specific hand gestures or spitting, and uttering protective verbal formulas before or after praising or complimenting an individual, especially an infant. Another technique consists of concealing, disguising, or even denying good fortune. One may elect to symbolically disfigure good looks, e.g., by purposely staining the white linen of a new dress or placing a black smudge of soot behind a child's ear,[1] so as not to risk attracting the attention of the evil eye. This may be the rationale behind such behavior as disparate as veiling in Arab cultures, the refusal in Jewish culture to say 'good' when asked how one's health or business is — the safe reply is 'not bad' or 'no

complaints' — , the common tendency among millionaires in Europe and America to insist upon dressing in rags, and the baseball custom in the United States of not mentioning that a pitcher has given up no hits. The mere mention of a possible 'no-hitter' would supposedly jinx a pitcher and would thereby result in a batter's successfully getting a basehit of some kind.

In the event of a successful attack by the evil eye, there are prescribed diagnostic and curative procedures available. One may first need to ascertain whether or not it is a true case of the evil eye and secondly, if it is, who is responsible for causing it. Sometimes, the agent who was perhaps an unwitting one is involved in the ritual removal of the evil eye and its ill effects from the victim, e.g., he may be asked to spit on the victim's face.[2]

Although widespread throughout the Indo-European and Semitic world, the evil eye belief complex is not universal. In the most recent cross-cultural survey Roberts found that only 36 percent of the 186 cultures in his world sample possessed the evil eye belief,[3] and he suggested that the belief 'probably developed in the old world, particularly in India, the Near East, and Europe'.[4] From this and other surveys (e.g., Andree, Seligmann), one may observe that the evil eye appears to be largely absent in aboriginal Australia, Oceania, native North and South America, and sub-Saharan Africa. The few rare reports in Africa, apart from the Maghreb where it flourishes, suggest Islamic influence. In Latin America, the evil eye was surely part of the general Spanish

* I should like to dedicate this essay to the memory of Ernest Jones whose brilliant application of psychoanalytic theory to the materials of folklore has served as a continual inspiration to me over the years. I must also thank Stanley Brandes, Robert Coote, Osama Doumani, George Foster, Steve Gudeman, Barbara Kirshenblatt-Gimblett, Wenday O'Flaherty, Felix Oinas, Saad Sowayan, and Tim White for valuable references and suggestions.

and Portuguese cultural legacy, Yet within the Indo-European and Semitic world, it is difficult to think of a more pervasive and powerful folk belief than the evil eye.

The scholarship devoted to the evil eye goes back to classical antiquity. Many of the ancients referred to it and Plutarch (46-120 A.D.) featured it in one of the dialogues in his *Table Talk*: 'On those who are said to cast an evil eye'.[5] The dialogue begins as follows: 'Once at dinner a discussion arose about people who are said to cast a spell and to have an evil eye. While everybody else pronounced the matter completely silly and scoffed at it, Mestrius Florus, our host, declared that actual facts lend astonishing support to the common belief.' Sometimes the passing references indicated belief in the evil eye, sometimes disbelief. Saint Basil, writing in the fourth century in his perspicacious homily *Concerning Envy*, remarked, '...some think that envious persons bring bad luck merely by a glance, so that healthy persons in the full flower and vigour of their prime are made to pine away under their spell, suddenly losing all their plumpness, which dwindles and wastes away under the gaze of the envious, as if washed away by a destructive flood. For my part, I reject these tales as popular fancies and old wives' gossip.'[6]

One of the issues often discussed was whether the evil eye was a conscious or unconscious power. The famed Arab historian Ibn Khaldûn (1332-1406) tended to consider the power of the evil eye as deriving from an involuntary act and for this reason it was to be distinguished from intentionally malicious sorcery. In section 27 of chapter 6 of the *Muqaddimah*,[7] Ibn Khaldûn commented on the evil eye calling it a natural gift, something which is inate and not acquired, not depending upon the free choice of its possessor. He ends his discussion as follows: 'Therefore it has been said: "A person who kills by means of sorcery or a miraculous act must be killed, but the person who kills with the eyes must not be killed." The only reason for the distinction is that the person who kills with the eyes did not want or intend to do so, nor could he have avoided doing so. The application of the eye was involuntary on his part.' Ibn Khaldûn's distinction, somewhat analogous to the modern differences between first degree and second degree manslaughter, is not held by all writers on the evil eye. Some suggest that certain cases of the evil eye reflect an evil disposition on the part of the person possessing the power, while others who are believed to have the power are 'innocent of any ill design'.[8]

From the fifteenth to the seventeenth centuries, a number of treatises were devoted to the evil eye. Representative are Enrique de Villena's *Tradado del Aojamiento* of 1422, Leonarus Vairus's *De Fascino* of 1589, Martinus Antonius Del Rio's *Disquisitionum magicarum* of 1599-1600, Joannes Lazarus Gutierrez's *Opusculum de Fascino* of 1653, and Joannes Christianus Frommann's *Tractatus de Fascinatione* of 1675. These and subsequent surveys often contain valuable data. For example, Nicola Valletta in his *Cicalata sul fascino volgarmente detto jettatura* of 1787 ended his discussion with a series of thirteen queries about the evil eye and the *jettatura*, the casters of the evil eye, queries which were designed very much like the modern questionnaire. Valletta's queries were: (1) Is the evil eye stronger from a man or from a woman? (2) Is it stronger from someone wearing a wig? (3) Stronger from someone who wears glasses? (4) Stronger from a pregnant woman? (5) Stronger from monks and, if so, from which order? (6) If the evil eye does approach, after the attack, what effects must be suffered? (7) What is the range or limit of the distance at which the *jettatura* can be effective? (8) Can the power come from inanimate objects? (9) Is the evil eye stronger from the side, from the front, or from behind? (10) Are there gestures, voice quality, eyes and facial characteristics by which *jettatura* can be recognised? (11) What prayers ought to be recited to protect us against the *jettatura* of monks? (12) What words in general ought to be said to thwart or escape the *jettatura*? (13) What power then have the horns and other things?[9] Valletta then followed his questions with a request that anyone who had had experience with the evil eye should please get in touch with him and that he would be happy to pay for any information furnished.

The steady flow of treatises continued in the nineteenth century. Italian scholars in particular were intrigued with a phenomenon which flourished unabated in their country. Typical are Giovanni Leonardo Marugj's *Cappricci sulla jettatura* of 1815, and Michele Artidi's *Il fascino, e l'amuleto contro del fascino presso gli antichi* of 1825, and

Andrea de Jorio's *La Mimica degli Antichi* of 1832 which was especially concerned with the traditional gestures used to avert the evil eye.

Modern scholarship on the evil eye may be truly said to have begun with Otto Jahn's pioneering essay, *Über den Aberglauben des bösen Blicks bei den Alten* which appeared in 1855.[10] It, like so many of the early treatises, concentrated upon ancient Greek and Roman examples of the evil eye, but it differed in its honest and erudite consideration of all facets of the evil eye complex including the obviously phallic character of so many of the apotropaic amulets. By the end of the nineteenth century, numerous essays had been written on the evil eye, though most of them were limited to descriptive reports from one particular area. Among the more general surveys of the subject would be Jules Tuchmann's remarkably detailed series of articles on *La Fascination* which appeared in the French folklore journal *Mélusine* from 1884 to 1901.[11] Tuchmann's massive and impressive collection of citations on the evil eye from a huge variety of sources in many languages may well have been the inspiration for folklorist Arnold van Gennep's delightful parody of the doctoral dissertation writer who tried but failed to write the definitive work on the evil eye.[12] A better known nineteenth century survey work is Frederick Thomas Elworthy's *The Evil Eye*, first published in 1895.

The next major effort, which was perhaps the most ambitious of any to date, was the encyclopedic two volume work by occulist S. Seligmann, *Der böse Blick und Verwandtes* which was published in 1910. This or the 1922 revision *Die Zauberkraft des Auges und des Berufen* remains probably the best single source of information on the subject, at least in terms of sheer quantity of ethnographic data. Other landmark studies of the evil eye in the twentieth century include Westermarck's extensive consideration of the evil eye in Morocco[13] and Karl Meisen's two comprehensive essays in the *Rheinisches Jahrbuch für Volkskunde*,[14] first covering the evil eye in the ancient and early Christian eras and second treating the medieval and modern periods. Also worthy of mention are occultist Edward S. Gifford's *The Evil Eye: Studies in the Folklore of Vision* in 1958, classicist Waldmar Deonna's marvellously learned and brilliant *Le Symbolism de l'Oeil*, posthumously

published in 1965, psychiatrist Joost A. M. Meerloo's *Intuition and the Evil Eye: The Natural History of Superstition* in 1971, and a collection of anthropological essays on the evil eye, *The Evil Eye*, edited by Clarence Maloney in 1976. This latter group of fifteen essays consists primarily of ethnographic description and makes little reference to the voluminous literature devoted to the evil eye in classics, folklore, and psychiatry. It does, however, include a lengthy, important paper by John M. Roberts, *Belief in the Evil Eye in World Perspective* which carefully canvasses 186 diverse cultures to see if the evil eye occurs and if so, with what other cultural variables it might be meaningfully statistically correlated.

The works mentioned thus far are essentially overviews of the evil eye belief complex, but it should be noted that there are a number of valuable book-length or monographic treatments of the evil eye in a single culture. Among the best of these are investigations in Scotland, R. C. Maclagan's *Evil Eye in the Western Highlands* in 1902, in Spain, Raphael Salillas' *La Fascinación en España* in 1905, in Finland, Toivo Vuorela's *Der böse Blick im Lichte der Finnischen Überlieferung* in 1967, and in Sardinia, Clara Gallini's *Dono e Malocchio* in 1973. When one adds to these the literally dozens on dozens of notes and articles which discuss the evil eye either *en passant* or in some depth, it is clear that one has an unmanageable number of sources available to consult for relevant information.

Despite the enormous bibliographic bulk of the evil eye scholarship, it would not be unfair to say that there have been few attempts to explain the evil eye belief complex in terms of a holistic integrated theory. By far the majority of the discussions of the evil eye consist solely of anecdotal reportings of various incidents. Anthropologist Hocart summed up the situation aptly when he said 'There is a considerable literature about the evil eye, but it does little more than add instances to instances.'[15] Unfortunately, the situation has not changed and as Spooner puts it, 'Permutations of practice do not appear to lead to a satisfactory formulation of theory.'[16]

Formulations of theories of the evil eye do exist. Recent speculations about the possible origin and significance of the evil eye have included the suggestion that it is related to gaze behaviour perhaps involving aversion among numerous forms of animal life.[17] With regard to gaze behavior, Erikson proposes that it is the unresponsive eye of an adult to an infant which the latter experiences as a rejecting, hostile environment or 'Other' (as opposed to self). Thus according to Erikson, 'the unresponsive eye becomes an evil one.'[18] It has also been claimed that the evil eye is an ancient type of hypnotic phenomenon.[19] But probably the most widely accepted theory of the evil eye contends that it is based upon envy. Sumner in his celebrated *Folkways* first published in 1906 argued that the evil eye depended upon primitive demonism and envy. According to Sumner, 'It is assumed that demons envy human success and prosperity and so inflict loss and harm on the successful.'[20]

There is no question that envy is somehow closely related to the evil eye. This is clear in the earliest Near Eastern texts we have. The word envy itself is etymologically derived from the Latin *invidia* which in turn comes from *in videre,* thus ultimately from 'to see' or 'seeing' as Cicero first observed.[21] To see something is to want it, perhaps. It is enough to see a desired object but equally common is to verbally admire it. An expression of admiration or praise is thus understood to imply at least a tinge of envy. Envy can accordingly be expressed either by eye or by mouth or by both. Schoeck in 1955 posited the evil eye as a universal expression of malevolent envy, but Spooner has criticised the envy theory, noting that 'although it is perfectly valid and necessary at one stage of analysis, the anthropologist should attempt to build models at a higher stage of abstraction.'[22] Spooner might also have realized that no theory could be persuasive unless or until it enables one to explain the particulars of detail in a given custom or segment of human behavior. How does the notion of envy explain, for example, the specific details of fruit trees withering, the common symptom of yawning, or the various apotropaic gestures such as spitting, employed to ward off the evil eye. Spooner does remark that since envy is probably in some form universal, how is it envy leads to the evil eye only in some societies but not in others?[23] One can only conclude that whereas envy is surely a component of the overall evil eye complex, it is not sufficient in and of itself to explain the complex in all of its concrete detail.

Much the same difficulties inhere in suggestions that the evil eye complex provides an outlet for the expression of aggression, or that it acts as an agent of social control. The question which must be addressed is why does the evil eye manifest itself precisely in the forms that it does? How would these notions explain why very young children, even infants, are especially susceptible to the effects of the evil eye? Or why the butterfat content of milk in a churn is magically removed?

Psychoanalytic interpretations of the evil eye have also been partial. Inasmuch as many of the apotropaic amulets and gestures have unmistakable phallic elements,[24] it was perfectly obvious that the male genitals were involved in some way with the evil eye complex. If a phallic gesture like the *fica*[25] was effective in warding off the evil eye, or if a male touched his genitals upon seeing a priest or other individual thought to have the evil eye,[26] then it was not unreasonable to assume that the evil eye threatened impotence.[27] But if the evil eye constituted a danger to masculinity, how was it that the ability to inflict an evil eye could be caused by a person who as a weaned infant had been returned to the breast and why was it that an evil eye was especially damaging to *female* animals such as cows? Roberts in his cross-cultural survey attempted a factor analysis of various features associated with the evil eye and he found the highest correlation with milking and dairy production though he was unable to explain this linkage.[28] Of course, psychoanalysts have also argued that the eye could be a female symbol[29] with 'the pupil representing the vagina, the lids the labia, and the lashes the pubic hair.'[30] Is the eye a phallus, a vagina, or is it both, or neither? And how would this possibly relate to injury to cows and their milk supply?

Géza Róheim in his analysis of the evil eye suggests that the key to the whole evil eye belief is oral jealousy and oral aggression.[31] This would illuminate the apparent connection with nursing children as well as the appropriateness of the use of spitting or oral incantations to avoid the evil eye. But in this case, it would not be so obvious why phallic means should be equally effective. Róheim does not succeed, in my opinion, in reconciling the oral and phallic elements in the evil eye complex.

Freud himself in writing in his 1919 essay on

the 'uncanny' about the evil eye considered its origin to be fear of envy, coupled with the device of projection. 'Whoever possesses something at once valuable and fragile is afraid of the envy of others, in that he projects onto them the envy he would have felt in their place.'[32] Tourney and Plazak follow this psychiatric tact by emphasising the eye as an organ of aggression. They suggest 'with the utilisation of the projective mechanism, fear of the evil eye may represent the manifestation of one's own aggressive impulses attributed as being apart from the ego and acting in turn against it. A need for punishment because of guilt over hostility and aggression can be realised in the suffering of a recipient from the influence of the evil eye.'[33] Through projection, the original would-be aggressor is spared feelings of guilt because 'I hate you' or 'I envy you' has been transformed into 'You hate me' or 'You envy me.' By means of this projective transformation, the active becomes the passive, the aggressor becomes the victim. This might very well help explain why the rich and powerful are so often thought to have the evil eye, e.g., popes and nobility have frequently been said to have had the evil eye. The poor envy the rich and powerful, but this envy is transformed into the rich casting an evil eye at the poor. But this psychiatric notion does not really explicate all the particulars of the evil eye belief complex either.

A plausible theory of the evil eye must be able to account for most if not all of the elements in the complex including the manifestly male and female components. Consider the following modern Greek cure for the evil eye which involves the formula 'If it is a woman who has cast the eye, then destroy her breasts. If it is a man who has cast the eye, then crush his genitals.'[34] In a variant, 'If a man did it, may his eyes fall out. If a woman did it may her eyes fall out and her breasts burst.'[35] Moving from Greece to India, we find the same alternation of male and female attributes. According to Thurston, 'When a new house is being constructed, or a vegetable garden or rice field are in flourishing condition, the following precautions are taken to ward off the evil eye:

a. In buildings:
   1. A pot with black and white marks on it is suspended mouth downwards.
   2. A wooden figure of a monkey, with pendulous testes, is suspended.

   3. The figure of a Malayali woman, with protuberant breasts, is suspended.

b. In fields and gardens:
   1. A straw figure covered with a black cloth daubed with black and white dots is placed on a long pole. If the figure represents a male, it has pendent testes, and, if a woman, well developed breasts. Sometimes male and female figures are placed together in an embracing posture.
   2. Pots, as described above, are placed on bamboo poles.'[36]

Since the evil eye is equally dangerous to female breasts, including cow's udders, as to male genitals, it is necessary for the magical counter-measures to defend against each threat. The question is: what theoretical underlying principle or principles, if any, can explain the total range of phenomena believed to be caused by the evil eye, e.g., the withering of fruit trees, the loss of milk from cows, and impotence among males. The striking similarity of evil eye reports from different cultures strongly suggests that whatever the rationale for it might be, it is likely to be cross-culturally valid.

I suggest that the evil eye belief complex depends upon a number of interrelated folk ideas in Indo-European and Semitic worldview. I should like to enumerate them briefly before discussing them in some detail.

1. Life depends upon liquid. From the concept of the 'water of life' to semen, milk, blood, bile, saliva, etc., the consistent principle is that liquid means life while the loss of liquid means death. 'Wet and Dry' as an oppositional pair means life and death. Liquids are living; drying is dying!

2. There is a finite, limited amount of good, e.g., health, wealth, etc. such that any gain by one individual can only come at the expense of another.[37] If one individual possesses a precious body fluid, e.g., semen, this automatically means that some other individual lacks that same fluid.

3. Life entails an equilibrium model. If one has too little wealth or health, one is poor or ill. Such individuals constitute threats to persons with sufficient or abundant wealth and health. This notion may be in part a projec-

41

tion on the part of well-to-do individuals. They think they should be envied and so they project such wishes to the have-nots. On the other hand, the have-nots are often envious for perfectly good reasons of their own.

4. In symbolic terms, a pair of eyes may be equivalent to breasts or testicles. A single eye may be the phallus — especially the glans — the vulva, and occasionally the anus. The fullness of life as exemplified by such fluids as mother's milk or a male's semen can thus be symbolised by an eye and accordingly threats to one's supply of such precious fluids can appropriately be manifested by the eye or eyes of others.

I am not claiming that any of the above folk ideas or principles are necessarily consciously understood by members of Indo-European and Semitic cultures. They may or may not be. What I am proposing is that they are structural principles of thought among the peoples of these cultures. I hope to show that they explain not only the evil eye but a vast range of traditional behavior ranging from tipping to some specifics of burial customs.

Documentation for the folk idea that life is liquid is amply provided by Richard Broxton Onians in his brilliant study, *The Origins of European Thought about the Body, the Mind, the Soul, the World, Time, and Fate* published in 1951. Onians is able to explain one of the rationales behind cremation. Burning the dead expedites the 'drying' process, the final removal of the liquid of life. He remarks on the Greek conception of life as the gradual diminishing of liquid inside a man.[38] I would add that the metaphor probably made sense in the light of what was empirically observable in the case of fruits among other items. Juicy grapes could become dry raisins; plums could become prunes, etc. With increasing age, the human face becomes wrinkled and these inevitable wrinkles could be logically construed as signs of the same sort of drying process which produced the wrinkles in raisins and prunes. It should also be pointed out that this Greek conception is also a manifestation of the notion of limited good.[39] Man is born with only so much life force and he is therefore ever anxious to replenish it. Milk and

wine are obvious sources of liquid noted Onians and he correctly observes the content of toasts in this connection.[40] One drinks 'healths.' What Onians failed to understand is that healths are supposedly drunk to *others,* e.g., accompanied by such verbal formulas as 'Here's to you,' 'Here's to your health,' or 'Here's long life to you.' What this means in terms of limited good, I submit, is: 'I drink but not at your expense.' I am replenishing my liquid supply, but I wish no diminution in yours. The very fact that a drinker mentions another person's *health* before drinking implies that if he did not do so, that person's health might suffer. In other words, drinking without a formulaic prophylactic preamble might be deleterious to the other person's health. In an unusual volume published in 1716 entitled *A Discourse of Drinking Healths,* we find this thought articulated: 'And what strange Inchantment can there be in saying or meaning, As I drink this Glass of Wine, So let another Man perish.'[41]

Lévi-Strauss in a rare instance of ethnographic fieldwork reports on a custom observed in lower-priced restaurants in the south of France. Each table setting includes a small bottle of wine but etiquette demands that one does not pour the contents of the bottle into one's own glass. Rather the wine is poured into the glass of an individual at a neighbouring table. This individual will normally reciprocate by pouring the contents of his bottle into the initial pourer's glass. Lévi-Strauss explains this custom in terms of a structural principle, namely the principle of reciprocity: 'Wine offered calls for wine returned, cordiality required cordiality.'[42] This is not an implausible explanation, but this custom which reflects a remarkable difference in attitude towards the wine as opposed to the food, as Lévi-Strauss himself notes, may also exemplify the special rules governing the incorporation of liquids among Indo-European and Semitic peoples. The notion of limited good — as applied to the essential liquids of life — requires one to offer beverages to others. If one drinks without regard to one's neighbours, one risks being envied and becoming the object or victim of an evil eye. The reciprocity of courtesy is demonstrated in a Gaelic incantation against the evil eye reported from the island of Skye in the Hebrides. Recited when washing in the morning, an individual might say:

Let God bless my eye,
And my eye will bless all I see;
I will bless my neighbour
And my neighbour will bless me.[43]

Numerous reports attest to the fact that it is the act of eating in public which is especially dangerous with respect to the evil eye. Westermarck, for example, notes 'The danger is greatest when you eat. To take food in the presence of some hungry looker-on is the same as to take poison; the evil — *i-bas,* as the Moors call it, then enters into your body. When you commence eating, everybody must either partake of the meal or go away.'[44] In Egypt, Lane reports that his cook would not purchase the fine sheep displayed in a butcher's shop because since 'every beggar who passes by envies them; one might, therefore as well eat poison as such meat.'[45] A report which appeared in the Russian paper *Ilustriravansk Mir* in 1881, quoted by Gordon, reflects a similar belief: 'The Russian government turned over a convict sentenced to die to the Academy of Science for the purpose of testing the powers of the evil eye. The prisoner was starved for three days during which a loaf of bread was placed in front of him of which he was unable to partake. At the end of the third day, the bread was examined and found to contain a poisonous substance.'[46] Gordon himself observes that while the story proves nothing — the bread could easily have been spoiled by being kept in a damp cell for three days — the very fact that a newspaper could print the report shows the readiness of the public to believe in the power of the evil eye.[47]

One technique used in restaurants to avert the dangers of the evil eye is to offer onlookers some of one's food. In Spanish restaurants, for example, an individual waiting to be seated at a table is frequently invited by patrons already eating if he would like to join them or share their food. This formulaic offer is inevitably refused but the point is that the invitation is made. Foster has described this very well: 'In Spain and Spanish America — to this day in small country inns — a diner greets each conceptual equal who enters the room with *Gusta [Usted comer]*? ('Would you care to share my meal?'), thereby symbolically inviting the stranger (or friend) to partake of the good fortune of the diner. The new arrival ritually replies *Buen provecho* ('Good appetite,' i.e., may your food agree with you), thereby reassuring the diner that he has no reason to fear envy, and that he may eat in peace. The entrant normally would not think of accepting the invitation, and the courtesy appears to have the double function of acknowledging the possible presence of envy and, at the same time, eliminating its cause.'[48]

After commenting upon the probable similar functioning of such ritual pre-dining formulas as the French *bon appetit,* Foster proceeds to discuss the necessity for offering something to a waiter in a restaurant. Since a waiter may also envy a diner, he needs to be given something to ensure his good will, namely a tip. In a fascinating brief survey of analogues to the word tip in a number of European languages, e.g., French *pourboire,* German *Trinkgeld,* Spanish *propina,* Portuguese *gorgeta,* Polish *napiwek,* Swedish *drincs,* Finnish *juomarahaa,* Icelandic *drykkjupeningar,* Russian *Chaevye [den'gi]*, and Croatian *Napojinica,* Foster concludes that the English word tip must come from 'tipple' which means to drink. This is obviously much more likely than the folk etymology often encountered that 'tip' is an acronymic formation from 'to insure promptness' or 'tips' from 'to insure prompt service'. While Foster is surely correct in stating that 'A tip, clearly, is money given to a waiter to buy off his possible envy, to equalise the relationship between server and served,' he fails to comment on the possible significance of the fact that the waiter is invited to *drink,* as opposed to eat.[49] In the light of the present argument, it is precisely liquids which must be offered to avert the evil eye.

The use of a liquid bribe so to speak is also found in other evil eye contexts. For example, in Scotland, 'A well-informed woman, an innkeeper, said that in cases where a person possessed of the Evil Eye admired anything belonging to another, no injury could follow if some little present were given to the suspected person on leaving . . . In the case of churning the small present naturally takes the form of a drink of milk to be given to anyone suspected of the Evil Eye, and so a reciter said that one should always, for safety's sake, give a visitor a drink of milk, and stated further that the beneficial effect was added to if the one who gives it first takes a little of it herself before handing it to the stranger.'[50]

The suggestion that the efficacy of the 'tip' is increased if one takes first a litte of the milk before offering it to the stranger is reminiscent of one of the folk theories of the evil eye which claims a connection exists between breast-feeding practices and the evil eye. One notion is that if the infant is allowed to drink freely from both breasts rather than from just one, he will grow up to have the evil eye. Another notion is that if an infant once weaned is allowed to return to the breast, he will likewise grow up to have the evil eye. Representative ethnographic data includes the following. In India, 'One, and perhaps the most common theory of the Evil Eye is that "when a child is born, an invisible spirit is born with it; and unless the mother keeps one breast tied up for forty days, while she feeds the child with the other in which case the spirit dies of hunger, the child grows up with the endowment of the Evil Eye, and whenever any person so endowed looks at anything constantly, something will happen to it".'[51] In Greece, 'it is known, however, that if a new-made mother suckles her infant from both breasts without an interval between, her glance will be baleful to the first thing on which it rests afterwards. Again, should a mother weakly yield to the tears of her newly weaned son and resume feeding him, he will, in later life, have the evil eye.'[52] This belief could function as a socially sanctioned charter or justification for mothers weary of breast-feeding and anxious to finalise weaning. Similarly, in Greece, one of the things that can cause the evil eye is 'if the baby resumes breast feeding after having been interrupted for a few days or weeks.'[53]

Analogous informant testimonies concerning the presumed casual relationship between reversing the weaning act and the evil eye have been reported in the Slovak-American tradition [54] and in Romania.[55] The folk theory that weaning reversal can cause the evil eye would seem to offer support to psychanalyst Melanie Klein's claim that the primary prototype of envy in general is the infant's envy of the 'feeding breast' as an object which possesses everything – milk, love – the infant desires.[56] In all these cases, the infant is displaying what is construed as greedy behaviour. Either he wants both breasts, when one is deemed sufficient, or he wishes to return to the breast after having been weaned, and is perhaps thus depriving a younger sibling of some of the latter's rightful supply of the limited good of mother's milk. An infant who gets more milk in this way is likely to become an adult who also attempts to get other forms of material good in this same way, that is, at someone else's expense. Thus he will be an adult with the evil eye, a greedy individual, who craving more than he deserves, or needs, may seek to take from the bounty of others. One wonders if the yawning symptom of victims of the evil eye might not be reminiscent of weaning anxiety insofar as the mouth in the act of yawning is constantly opening without obvious material benefit.

Confirmation of the importance of weaning and sibling rivalry in the evil eye belief complex comes from a curious detail in a remarkable legend which itself serves as a charm against the evil eye. The text typically involves the personification of the evil eye, usually as a female demon, perhaps a Lilith, child-stealing figure. A saint or archangel encounters the demoness and forces her to reveal all of her names, through the later recitation of which she may henceforth be controlled, and to return any infants she has already carried off or devoured.[57] In a Slavonic version of the charm cited by Gaster,[58] it is the devil who steals and swallows a sixth infant after having similarly disposed of five previous ones. The mother Meletia dispatches her brother Saint Sisoe to recover her infants. When he confronts the devil and demands the return of the infants, the devil replies, 'Vomit thou first the milk which thou hast sucked from thy mother's breast.' The Saint prays to God and does so. The devil, seeing this, regurgitates the six infants who are safe and sound. In two seventeenth century Greek versions cited by Gaster, the same motif recurs. Two saints Sisynnios and Sisynodoros, demand that the villain Gylo return the children of their sister Melitena. The female demon Gylo replies, 'If you can return in the hollow of your hand the milk which you have sucked from your mother's breast I will return the children of Melitena.' The saints pray and 'they vomited at once into the hollow of their hand something like their mother's milk.' Gylo then brings up the abducted children and reveals her other names.[59]

If the brother's regurgitation of mother's milk equals the restoration of infants, then one might logically assume that swallowing mother's milk is symbolically equivalent to destroying infants. Since the protagonists are brother and sister, we appear to have a case of sibling rivalry revolving around the allocation of mother's milk. Incidentally, the name of the personification of the evil eye, Gylo, may, according to Perdrizet[60] who has studied the legend in some detail, be related to the Arab *ghūl* which may in turn be related to the Babylonian *gallou* which means demon. The root may possibly be related to a variety of Indo-European words associated with greediness in drinking. Consider French *goulu* meaning gluttonous or *gueule* meaning the mouth of an animal, with *gueulee* meaning a large mouthful. In English, it may be related to such words as gullet, glut, gulp, gully, and possibly gurgle, gobble, gorge, and gurgitation. Gulch once meant drunkard or to swallow or devour greedily while gulf once referred to a voracious appetite and may derive from the Greek for bosom. To engulf means to swallow.

Water is, of course, necessary for the sustenance of life, and life itself is empirically observed to begin in some sense with an emergence from a flood of amniotic fluid, perhaps providing a human model or prototype for creation myths involving supposed primeval waters or floods,[61] but it is the metaphorical and symbolic quests for water which are most relevant to our consideration of the evil eye. Onians explains that the idea that life is liquid and the dead are dry accounts for the widespread conception of a 'water of life'.[62] The search for the water of life in fairy tales[63] which is found throughout the Indo-European and Semitic world, as well as the common quest for the fountain of youth,[64] certainly support the notion that liquid is life. Hopkins distinguishes the two motifs 'Fountain of Youth' and 'Water of Life' arguing that the first comes from India while the second stems from Semitic tradition.[65] In any case, the magic liquid can cure wounds and even bring the dead back to life. It can also rejuvenate, making the old young again. If the passage of life consists of the gradual diminution of finite fluids, then the only logical way to reverse the process would be to increase one's fluid supply. Whether fluids were taken internally, e.g., by drinking, or externally, e.g., by bathing, baptism, or being annointed, the life giving or renewing principle is basically the same.

If increases in liquid mean health, then decreases might signify the opposite.[66] I think it is quite possible that the English word 'sick' comes ultimately from the Latin *siccus* which means dry. The total loss of liquid, that is, loss of life, would mean death. And this is why in the Indo-European and Semitic world, the dead are specifically perceived to be thirsty. The following custom is typical:[67] 'Water is not only essential for the living but also for the dead. As in ancient days so also now the Palestinian is accustomed to place for the dead a jar containing water; the only difference is that we often find on the tombs a shallow or deep cup-like cavity. Some believe that the soul of the dead visits the tomb and expects to find water to quench its thirst; therefore they that visit the tombs of the dead fill these cups with water.' Onians in writing of the thirst of the dead notes that in Babylonia the provision of water to the dead fell to the deceased's nearest kinsman.[68] This kinsman was known as a man's 'pourer of water.' One form of Babylonian curse consisted of 'May God deprive him of an heir and a pourer of water.' The widespread distribution of the conception of the thirsty dead has been amply described.[69]

Certainly the presumed thirst of the dead is a major metaphorical feature of ancient Egyptian funerary ritual. According to Budge, one of the oldest of the ceremonies performed for the dead was called the 'Opening of the Mouth.'[70] The deceased was told 'Thy mouth is the mouth of the sucking calf on the day of its birth.'[71] Various offerings of food and libation were presented to the deceased, most of them specifically said to come from the Eye of Horus. 'Accept the Eye of Horus, which welleth up with water, and Horus hath given unto thee.'[72] The Eye of Horus as a breast or other body part containing liquid is understood to refresh the deceased by offering him the necessary additional 'fluid of life' to replace the fluids lost before death or during the process of mummification.[73]

In the light of the centrality of liquid as a metaphor for life, it makes sense for envy to be expressed in liquid terms. The 'have nots' envy the 'haves' and desire their various liquids. Whether it is the dead who envy the living, as in vampires who require the blood of the living and who are commonly referred to as 'bloodthirsty', or the old who envy the young, the barren who envy those with children, it is the blood, the sap or vitality of youth, the maternal milk or masculine semen which is typically at stake. The notion of limited good means that there is not really enough liquid to go around. Thus an admiring look or statement of praise is understood as a wish for precious fluid. If the looker or declarer receives liquid, then it must be at the object of the look or praise's expense. So the victim's fruit tree withers from a loss of sap or his cow's milk dries up. The point is that the most common effect of the evil eye is a drying up process.

There have long been clues revealing the dessicating nature of the evil eye. A thirteenth-century Dominican, Thomas of Cantipré, claimed that a man who is seen first by a wolf cannot speak because the rays from the wolf's eye dry up the *spiritus* of human vision which in turn dries up the human *spiritus* generally.[74] At the beginning of the twentieth century, twenty-three informants in Spain mentioned the concept of *secarse,* drying out, as one of the characteristic symptoms of the evil eye.[75] An interesting clinical parallel is provided in a case of schizophrenia where a nurse believed a private eye — not a detective but an actual eye — was watching her and that it had the power to draw vital body fluids from her.[76]

One of the oldest texts extant which treats the evil eye is a Sumerian one and it too confirms the association with water. It begins, 'The eye *ad-gir,* the eye a man has . . . The eye afflicting man with evil, the *ad-gir.* Unto heaven it approached and the storms sent no rain.' The evil eye even takes away water from the heavens. The Sumerian text suggests the cure involves 'Seven vases of meal-water behind the grinding stones. With oil mix. Upon (his) face apply.'[77] One may compare this with a Neapolitan charm from Amalfi which is nearly four thousand years later: 'Eye of death, Evil Eye, I am following you with water, Oil and Jesus Christ.' The protective power of fluids including water is apparent in many ancient texts referring to the evil eye. For example, in the *Berakoth,* a book of the Babylonian Talmud, we read, 'Just as the fishes in the sea are covered by water and the evil eye has no power over them, so the evil eye has no power over the seed of Joseph.'[78] On a portal plaque from Arslam Tash in Upper Syria, we have a Phoenician incantation text inscribed in an Aramaic script of the early seventh century B.C. which urges the caster of the evil eye to flee.[79] It begins, according to Gaster, 'Charm against the demon who drains his victims.'[80] This suggests the antiquity of the idea that the evil eye constitutes a threat against body fluids.

In modern Saudi Arabia, a person who is accused of having the evil eye may be labelled by the adjective *ash-hab* which means grey and dessicated. An individual with the evil eye is thus one who is dried out, in need of liquid refreshment.

Once it is understood that the evil eye belief complex depends upon the balance of liquid equilibrium, it becomes possible to gain insight into the various techniques employed to avoid or cure the evil eye. For example, on the back of a large number of ancient amulets used to keep the evil eye away appears a Greek inscription meaning 'I drink.' Bonner and other scholars puzzled by this inscription felt that this meaning was inappropriate and suggested alternative translations such as 'I am hungry' or 'I devour.'[81] But if these meanings were intended, one might ask, why should 'I drink' appear so often. Bonner even went so far as to suggest that 'perhaps the "error" occurred on the first specimen manufactured in some important workshop and was slavishly copied.' The point is surely that the folk know, in some sense, what they are doing — even if scholars do not. In the light of the present hypothesis, 'I drink' makes perfect sense as the inscription of an anti-evil eye amulet.

Or consider the following detail of a contemporary Algerian Jewish custom. The individual who removes the effects of the evil eye from someone afflicted evidently runs some risk of having the effects transferred to him: *Pour éviter que le 'mauvais oeil' enlevé au malade ne pénètre en lui, l'opérateur après avoir terminé absorbe un verre d'un liquide quelconque (eau, anisette, vin, etc.) que lui offrent les parents de malade.*[82] Clearly, the incorporation of liquid — whether it is water or wine is immaterial — is thought to guard against the dangerous effects of the evil eye.

Structurally speaking, the various apotropaic methods employed to avoid or cure the evil eye ought to be isomorphic. But how is showing a phallus or the *fica* isomorphic with spitting? I would argue that all these amulets or gestures signify the production of some form of liquid. Whether the liquid is semen or saliva, it provides proof that the victim's supply of life-force is undiminished. Spitting is also an act of insult and it is quite likely that spitting as a counteractant to the evil eye represents a devaluation of the victim. In other words, a beautiful baby whether praised or admired or not represents a potential object for attack by an evil eye. If one spits on the baby, or asks the possessor of the evil eye to spit on the baby, one is mitigating the praise or admiration expressed. It is as if to say this is not a beautiful, admirable object and that it should not be subject to an evil eye attack. On the other hand, spitting involves the projection of liquid for all to see. Crombie was quite right in remarking that saliva seemed to contain the element of life,[83] but he did not realise that saliva can also be symbolically equivalent to semen.[84] The initial consonant cluster of 'sp' occurs in both sputum and sperm, suggesting the emission of liquid, but even more persuasive is the unambiguous metaphorical evidence provided by the idiom 'spitten image' which refers to an infant being physically similar to his father.[85] The symbolic equivalance is also attested to in jokes. Legman reported the following abbreviated text collected in Scranton Pennsylvania, in 1930: 'Two twins are conversing in the womb. "Who's that bald-headed guy that comes in here every night and spits in my eye?" '[86]

The important role of saliva in the evil eye belief complex is confirmed by an interesting practice reported in Greece and Saudi Arabia. In the Oasim district in north central Saudi Arabia, in cases where someone is afflicted by the evil eye and it is not known who caused the misfortune, someone representing the victim, a small male child, stands in a public area, e.g., outside a mosque, with a small bowl half filled with water and the child asks each male passer-by to spit into it. This is done so as not to embarrass anyone in particular by accusing that person of having the evil eye. After everyone or a goodly number of individuals has expectorated into the container or made a pseudo-spitting gesture, the container is taken to the victim who drinks half the contents and anoints his body with the other half. In eastern Greece at the beginning of this century, a village girl fell ill. Her mother fearing that the cause was the evil eye hired a female curer to go to the church to collect forty spits in a glass from individuals going into the church. The curer kept track of the number of spits by counting kernals of corn. When she counted forty kernels, she brought the glass to the victim who drank it. The victim recovered within a few days. However esthetically unpleasing or hygienically unsound such a practice may be adjudged by non-members of the cultures concerned, the cure certainly does exemplify the principle of liquid intake as a counteractant to the evil eye.

The details of the Malabar custom of displaying a figure with pendulous testes or protruberant breasts to ward off the evil eye can also be understood as liquid bearing symbols. The large testes or breasts presumably represent an abundance of semen or milk. The overturned pot may suggest that the abundance is so great that hoarding is not necessary. The symbolic equivalence of breasts and eyes is suggested by a variety of evidence. In ancient European iconography, the same symbols, e.g., circles with short lines radiating from the circumference were used for both eyes and breasts.[87] In contemporary German folk speech, dozens of idioms support the fact that *eine der merkwurdigsten Gleichsetzungen im Vokabular der Sexualsprache ist Auge = Brust.*[88] The interchangeability of eyes and breasts is also obvious from an examination of different versions of the folktale or legend *Present to the Lover*[89] whose summary reads 'Maiden sends to her lecherous lover (brother) her eyes (hands, breasts) which he has admired.'[90] Data is also available from contemporary tattooing. 'Open eyes are tattooed on American sailors' lids or around their nipples because the sailors believe that such tattoos will keep watch for them when they are tired or asleep,'[91] a belief probably identical to the one which accounts for the widespread Indo-European custom of painting eyes on each side of the bow of ships and boats.[92] But the important point here is that the eyes are apparently drawn around the nipples which would exemplify the breast-eye equation.

Similar folkloristic data suggests that testicles and eyes may be symbolically equivalent on occasion. In Irish mythology, we find motif J 229.12, *Prisoners given choice between emasculation and blinding,* an alternative which is reminiscent of Oedipus's self-imposed punishment of blinding for a sexual crime,[93] One may note the same allomotifs in another European narrative setting. The plot summary of Aarne-Thompson tale type 1331, *The Covetous and the Envious,* is as follows: 'Of two envious men one is given the power of fulfilling any wish on the condition that the other shall receive double. He wishes that he may lose an eye.' Legman reports a version from

New York City in 1936: 'A Jew in heaven is told that whatever he asks for, Hitler will get double. He asks that one of his testicles be removed.'[94] This kind of incontrovertible data strongly supports the idea that testicles and eyes are in some sense interchangeable. We can now better understand why in the modern Greek formula cited earlier, it is wished that the evil eye possessor suffer crushed genitals or burst breasts, in other words, that his or her vital fluids be wasted. The wish for breasts to burst might also imply a wish for the death of a female evil eye caster's infant — an event which might tend to cause the mother's unused breasts to swell to the bursting point.

One detail which we have not yet explained is the singularity of the evil eye and I mean singularity in the literal sense. Why is it the evil eye instead of the evil eyes (plural)? This single eye holds true for the idiom in most languages. To my knowledge, none of the previous scholarship devoted to the evil eye has even raised this elementary but intriguing question. Any plausible theory of the evil eye should be able to account for the singularity of the phenomenon.

In order to better understand this facet of the evil eye belief complex, we may profitably examine ancient Egyptian data. According to Moret, all living things were created by eye and voice. Life was an emission of fecund light from the Master of rays. Above all, it was the sun Ra who was the primary creator using his eye, the sun 'Eye of Horus.'[95] The solar virtues of the gods were transmitted to the pharaoh through a magical fluid called *sa*. That which flowed in the veins of the pharaoh, son of Ra, was the 'liquid of Ra,' the gold of the sun's rays. The fluid or *sa* was emitted by a process termed *sotpou*, a term used in contexts meaning the shooting forth of water, flames, arrows, and the ejaculation of semen.[96] Another source of life, incidentally, in addition to the liquid of Ra, was the milk of Isis,[97] which suggests that the symbolic equivalence of semen and milk is of considerable antiquity.[98]

The curious verb *sotpou* with all its nuances reminds us of the term ejeculation for the action of the evil eye. Francis Bacon in 1625 spoke of the act of envy producing an 'ejaculation' of the eye and many of the reports of the evil eye among Greeks and Greek-Americans specifically use the term 'ejaculate' in speaking of preventatives, e.g.,

ejaculating the phrase 'garlic in your eyes.'[99] The eye shoots forth its rays just as the Egyptian sun, the eye of Horus, emitted its life force liquid, *sa*. The sun's rays, according to Ernest Jones are often regarded as 'a symbol of the phallus as well as of semen.'[100] The phallic interpretation of the sun, with its rising perceived as a metaphorical form of erection, has been suggested for more than a century[101] and it certainly puts solar mythology into a new light. What is important in the present context is that the sun is both phallus and eye. Noteworthy also is that the common term in southern Italy for the possessor of an evil eye is *Jettatore,* a word which derives from the same Latin root from which ejaculation comes.

In 1910, Ernest Jones remarked, in the course of discussing the power of the eye in hypnotism, on various beliefs in magical fluids including so-called 'magnetic fluid.' In this connection it is of interest that a report of the evil eye mechanism in Corsica suggests that the force involved may be a kind of fluid, a fluid which is released after an unguarded compliment or expression of admiration.[102] Jones noted the magnetic fluid was principally emitted from the hypnotist's eye and he suggested that such a belief in the influence of the human eye, for good or ill, took its origin in the notion that the eye and its glance were symbolically regarded as the expression of the male organ and its function.[103] Freud too spoke of 'the substitutive relation between the eye and the male member which is seen to exist in dreams and myths and phantasies.'[104] In the case of the phallus, one is tempted to observe, the glance might come from the glans. If one looks at the glans of a penis, it would not be impossible to imagine it as an eye, the urinary meatus serving as a surrogate pupil.

What is startling about this notion is that iconographic representations of the phallus with an eye do occur. A number of scholars have noted the existence of the *Phallus oculatus*,[105] but none have discussed its significance. The idea of a phallus with an eye is no stranger than contemporary risqué puns on 'cockeye.'[106] Even more germane is some striking evidence from Arabic folk speech. According to the fifteenth century Arabic classic *The Perfumed Garden*,[107] epithets for the sexual parts of man include *El aâouar*, the one-eyed, and *Abou aïne,* he with one eye. The Arabic word for eye is similar to the Hebrew word *ayin* which means both eye and well.[108] One of the biblical verses used in phylacteries to ward off the evil eye was *Genesis* 49:22, 'Joseph is a fruitful bough, even a fruitful bough by a well', because of the understood play on words. Joseph and his descendants were fruitful even though adjacent to a well (= eye). The strength of the liquid metaphor even in the twentieth century is perhaps signalled by the fact that '*Maiyeh*, water, in colloquial Arabic is also used as the name of male semen, the life medium.'[109]

The folk notion of the penis as the one-eyed also occurs in Walloon folklore. According to an anonymous report in *Kryptadia* one of the traditional epithets for the phallus is *Li bwègne* which is a dialect form of *le borgne* which means 'one-eyed.'[110] We are told that this remarkable appellation can be understood by the *ressemblance vague que la gland et ses lèvres présentent avec un oeil et ses paupières*. However, the resemblance cannot be all that vague if we find the identical one-eye idiom in other cultures. The traditionality of the Walloon metaphor is confirmed by the reporting of an additional illustration *sain-nî-s-bwègne* which is explained as *saigner son borgne, c'est-à-dire pisser*. If bleeding or more figuratively draining the one-eye refers to urination, then this would certainly support the idea that eye containing liquid might represent a phallus.

We need not go so far afield as Arabic and Walloon folklore for the idea that the third eye, like the third leg, can be a circumlocution for the phallus. The fact that the phallus is the *third* eye or leg would be in accord with the phallicism of the number three in Indo-European tradition with the phallus *cum testiculos* perceived as a threefold cluster.[111] The phallus as one eye has been reported in American folklore. One of the 'unprintable' folk beliefs from the Ozarks collected by Vance Randolf in 1946 has been published by G. Legman. It concerns the custom of the so-called dumb supper by means of which young women learn the identify of their future husbands. In most versions of the custom, the girls prepare a supper in total silence and then await the arrival of the first male visitor, who is supposedly a spouse-to-be. In Randolf's account of a prank played around the turn of the century, a 'local ruffian' overhears the plans of two young girls near Green Forest, Arkansas. Here is part of the story: 'Exactly at

midnight the two girls sat down and bowed their heads. The door opened very slowly, and in came a big man walking backwards, clad only in a short undershirt. Approaching the table he bent forward, took his enormous tool in hand, and thrust it backwards between his legs, so that it stuck right out over the food on the table. One of the girls screamed and fled into the "other house" crying "Maw, maw, he's thar! He's come a long way, an' he's only got one eye!"[112] Whether or not the prank actually occurred is immaterial in the present context. What is important is that a narrative collected in 1946 specifically refers to a phallus as a one-eyed man.

Even more striking is the widespread joke reported in America and in Europe in which fleas conceal themselves in various parts of the female anatomy, agreeing to meet the next day to compare notes. The flea who spent the night in the vagina reported that a baldheaded and in some versions a one-eyed man entered and spat on him.[113] This not only underscores the phallus as single eye but also exemplified the equivalence of spitting and ejaculation.

If a healthy eye, that is a phallus, can spit or ejaculate, then an unhealthy one cannot. Given this logic, it is not impossible to imagine that a larger, more powerful eye has robbed a given eye of its ability to produce liquid, or of the precious liquid itself. The idea that an evil eye absorbs or sucks up liquid as opposed to a good eye which emits liquid is paralleled by an analogous folk belief attached to snakes and serpents. La Barre in his important discussion of the phallic symbolism of serpents observes that snakes are commonly endowed with such body image features as feathers or hair, despite the fact that 'No snake in the world has either hair or feathers.'[114] In similar fashion, snakes are believed to be able to suckle human breasts and to drink milk.[115] The point is that phalluses in the form of snakes and also as evil eyes are thought to have the power of stealing precious liquids.

If the phallus is referred to as the 'one-eyed,' then it is at least within the realm of reasonable speculation that one-eyed objects or individuals in folklore might have phallic connotations. The single eye of the Cyclops as exemplified in the tale of Polyphemus might be examined in these terms.[116] Odysseus makes his escape by thrusting a burning mass into the giant's single eye. It may be of interest that one technique reported in removing the threat of an evil eye is to 'blind the eye,'[117] while another entails a 'symbolic burning of the eye'[118] which would be an extreme form of dessicating it. Analogous perhaps to the rationale of cremation discussed earlier, this technique would remove all liquid from the hostile eye.

With respect to Polyphemus, Comhaire remarks that while Homer consistently speaks of the one eye of the Cyclops, he does mention eyebrows, in the plural.[119] This suggests that the eye may be a non-literal or symbolic one. As early as 1913, Reiter suggested that the eye of Polyphemus represented the father's phallus and that Odysseus's blinding of Cyclops represented a son's castration of his father. Reiter's Freudian discussion began, however, with a consideration of a curious Austrian wooden folk toy which consisted of a little man. When the man's head was pushed down, a potent phallus emerged from under his clothing. Not only does this toy equate the head with the phallus, but the head in this case possesses three eyes. Besides the usual two eyes, a third eye appears above them right in the middle of the forehead. Reiter assumes the third eye represents the phallus.[120]

In folk tradition, the one-eyed giant has the eye centred.[121] Onians presents much evidence attesting to the fact that the head is the male genital organ displaced upward.[122] If the head can represent the male genital organ, and if the phallus is perceived as a single eye, then it would be perfectly appropriate for the eye to be centrally located. One must remember, after all, that single eyes situated in the middle of foreheads do not occur in nature. We are dealing with fantasy. The importance of the middle of the forehead is also signalled by the idea in Lebanese-American custom that a counteractant blue bead against the evil eye 'to be truly effective should suspend from the forehead to lie between the child's eyes.'[123] The location of the third eye in the 'middle' of the forehead is also paralleled by the efficacy of the middle finger, the so-called *digitus infamis* or *digitus impudicus*[124] in warding off or curing the ill effects of the evil eye. Typically, spittle is placed on the middle finger and applied to the infant's forehead.[125] The phallus is often considered to be a third leg placed obviously in the middle between the two actual legs.

The equivalence of eye and phallus may be suggested in ancient Egyptian mythology when Horus battles Set. Set tears out an eye of Horus, but Horus counters by tearing off one of Set's testicles. In this connection, it is interesting that the Eye of Horus presented to the deceased in Egyptian funeral ritual is said to be the one devoured by Set who later vomited it up[126] and even more significantly the deceased is told 'The Eye of Horus has been presented unto thee and it shall not be cut off from him by thee.'[127] In a variant text, 'The Eye of Horus hath been presented unto thee, and it shall not be cut off from thee.'[128]

In Irish mythology, we find Balor, a famous robber, who had an eye in the middle of his forehead.[129] Interestingly enough, Balor's was an evil eye and he used it to steal a wonder cow. The use of an evil eye to steal or subvert cattle is, of course, very much a part of the evil eye complex in the Celtic world and elsewhere. The evil Balor is eventually slain by his grandson Lug who as prophesied 'thrust a red-hot bar into Balor's evil eye and through his skull so that it came out on the other side.'[130] The antiquity of a male third eye is suggested by its possible occurrence in Sumer, e.g., where Enki (Ea) allegedly bore the epithet 'Nunigi-ku, the god with the gleaming eye.' Reportedly this was described as 'the god with the holy eye in his forehead.'[131] In Indic mythology, Siva has a third eye. In the light of the hypothetical phallic association of the eye in the forehead, it is of more than passing interest that Siva's cult consisted largely of the worship of his phallus.[132] The third eye of Siva has been interpreted in an erotic sense.[133]

I should like to suggest a logical, albeit magical paradigm which also supports the idea that there is a phallic component of the evil eye. The paradigm is based upon the principle of homeopathic magic in which a form of a dangerous object is itself used as a prophylactic counteragent. In Turkey and surrounding areas, for example, blue eyes are considered to be dangerous, perhaps evil eyes.[134] Lawson who had blue eyes reported how difficult this made the conduct of fieldwork in Greece.[135] He was often taken aback at having his ordinary greeting salutation 'health to you' answered only by the sign of the cross. Yet the colour blue in the Near East is also regarded as protective against the evil eye.[136] The 'like against like' principle also applies to eyes themselves. Eye amulets are commonly used.[137] Bonner has noted that 'The commonest of all amulets to ward off the evil eye consists of an atropaic design which has been found on numerous monuments and which though subject to slight variations, remains the same through several centuries. It represents the eye, wide open, subjected to various injuries and assailed by a variety of animals, birds and reptiles.'[138] The technical name of this design Bonner discovers, is reported in a passage in the *Testament of Solomon,* an important source for the study of demonology dating perhaps from early in the third century.[139] In this passage, each of the thirty-six decans or segments of the zodiac is required to tell the king his name, his power, and the means of guarding against him. The thirty-fifth says, 'My name is Rhyx Phtheneoth. I cast the glance of evil at every man. My power is annulled by the graven image of the much suffering eye.' Conybeare's translation of the relevant passage is 'The thirty-fifth said: "I am called Phtenoth. I cast the evil eye on every man. Therefore, the eye much-suffering, if it be drawn, frustrates me." '[140]

The paradigm then can be sketched as follows. The colour blue caused the evil eye, but the colour blue is used on amulets to ward off the evil eye. An eye causes the evil eye but an image of an eye is used to ward off the evil eye. Now something, that is, something analogous to an algebraic unknown, causes the evil eye, but an amulet or gesture representing a phallus or vulva wards off the evil eye. If our paradigm is valid and our reasoning is correct, then one of the 'causes' of the evil eye must be the phallus or vulva.

The use of a horseshoe or crescent moon to ward off the evil eye could represent the female genitals. The symbolic equation of eye and female gentials is substantiated by a well-known pretended obscene riddle. A version recounted by Bessie Jones of Georgia to enliven a discussion workshop at a folk festival in Berkeley, California, in 1963, is representative: 'What's round and hair all around it and nothin' but water comes out?' The answer is 'Your eye.'[141] The vulva as maleficent object would also explain Frachtenberg's observation that 'The glance of the eye of a woman during her menstruation period was extremely dreaded by the Zoroastrians.'[142] Clearly a woman who was losing blood, a life fluid, would represent a threat to the life-fluids possessed by others — potential victims of the evil eye: the loss of menstrual blood would require making up the liquid deficit, at someone else's expense.

The association between the eye and the genital areas may also explain the curious belief that too much coital activity[143] or excessive masturbation will lead to blindness. Masturbatory ejaculation would imply a loss of liquid and thus the eye would reflect this by dimming with each successive loss. Gifford reminds us of Francis Bacon's note that the ancient authorities believed 'much use of Venus doth dim the sight.'[144] Bacon was puzzled that eunuchs were also dim sighted but if their organs could not produce semen, then this lack of liquid life force might be responsible for poor vision, at least according to the folk theory. The logic is remarkably consistent. If the loss of liquid causes blindness, then the addition of liquid can cure blindness. Urine, for example, was commonly used to cure the effects of the evil eye as well as for eye diseases generally.[145] Mother's milk is as effective a form of eye-medicine as liquid from a male source. Numerous reports related that 'A few drops of mother's milk directly from the breast is also a favourite remedy for inflamed eyes.'[146] 'If a few drops of his mother's milk are poured into his eyes, the child will have good eyesight' reads a typical Hungarian superstition.[147] Urine and mother's milk are evidently effective male and female curative fluids.

The phallus or the vulva as a liquid-seeking evil eye would explain why the evil eye was singular. But it may not be entirely clear why a phallus or a vulva should be perceived as liquid seeking. To understand this, it is necessary to consider an important folk theory of sexuality, namely, that coitus is dangerous and debilitating insofar as it may result in a loss of liquid. Legman refers to the fantasy that 'sexual intercourse is "weakening" to the man, but not to the woman, because he "loses" a fluid, the semen, which she receives.'[148] He relates this fantasy to the notion of the succubus. Earlier Ernest Jones had suggested the 'the simple idea of the vital fluid being withdrawn through an exhausting love embrace' was related to the vampire belief.[149] Jones also cited the fascinating folk belief that the devil has no semen and that he can impregnate a woman only by having first obtained some semen by acting as a Succubus to a man.[150]

51

The crucial point with respect to the evil eye complex is that it is not far-fetched to claim that the eye as phallus or vulva poses a threat to the victim's vital fluids. The widespread idea that hunters should refrain from sexual intercourse just prior to a hunt, or warriors prior to warfare, or athletes prior to a game, is very likely related to the notion that a man has a finite amount of energy and this energy might be unwisely siphoned off or drained by the female genitals. The empirically observable fact that a man can manage only a limited or finite number of erections, hence sexual acts, within a given period of time in contrast to a woman, who, at least in theory — and fantasy — can indulge in an infinite number of sexual acts might account for the idea that males have 'limited good' with respect to semen.[151]

In like manner, the Arab practice of *Imsák* which is devoted to the special art of delaying the male orgasm[152] is probably selfishly intended to decrease the loss of precious semen rather than altruistically increasing the sexual pleasure of females. The idea that 'women emit a special fluid at orgasm similar to the semen in men', which Legman calls a superstition 'once almost universally believed at the folk level,'[153] would encourage such a practice. If the male succeeded in drawing fluid from the female genital while at the same time retaining his own fluid, he would presumably suffer no diminution in the finite amount of his life force. The fact that most males are unable to prevent ejaculation no doubt accounts for the widespread fear of female demons, who threaten to suck a male victim dry in one way or another.[154]

The hypothetical delineation of a battle of the sexes for precious liquid of life is made quite explicit in Chinese sexual theory. In this theory, the Yang-Yin distinction includes a male-female component. According to one authority, the Chinese believed that 'while man's semen is strictly limited in quantity, woman is an inexhaustible receptacle of Yin essence.'[155] Men are supposed to retain their semen insofar as possible and to use the sexual act as a means of 'absorbing the woman's Yin essence.' According to the folk theory, 'This art of sexual intercourse with a woman consists of retraining oneself so as not to ejaculate, thus making one's semen return and strengthen one's brain.'[156] Since men wanted children, especially sons, they were 'supposed to ejaculate only on

those days when the woman was most likely to conceive ... On all other days the man was to strive to let the woman reach orgasm without himself emitting semen. In this way the man would benefit by every coitus because the Yin essence of the woman, at its apex during the orgasm, strengthens his vital power ...' The goal is absolutely clear. Man was to retain his vital essence, while drawing the essence from his female sexual partner. In Chinese folklore, one finds dangerous beautiful women who delight in draining their male sexual victims dry.[157] While the evil eye was reported 'to be no less common amongst the native population of northern China than it was and still is in Europe,'[158] it seems to be largely absent from China.[159] But even though the evil eye complex is not a major element in the Chinese folk belief system, the Chinese perception of coitus in terms of gaining or losing sexual fluids seems to be paralleled by similar folk theories among Indo-European and Semitic peoples.

In Uttar Pradesh in northern India, it is reported that excessive sexual activity may cause minor illness and specifically that 'Sexual intercourse is thought to make men in particular weak and susceptible to disease because the loss of one drop of semen is considered the equivalent of the loss of 40 drops of blood.'[160] Moreover, 'the longevity of several men is attributed to complete abstinence in their later years.' Clearly the loss of vital fluids through ejaculation is believed to diminish a finite supply of life energy. An Andalusian expression, collected in Andalusia by my colleague Stanley Brandes in 1976, confirms the same traditional reasoning in Spain: *Si quieres llegar a viejo, guarda la leche en el pellojo* 'If you want to reach old age, keep your semen within your skin.'

Essentially the same folk idea is described in Kinsey's *Sexual Behavior in the Human Male.* 'For many centuries, men have wanted to know whether early involvement in sexual activity, or high frequency of early activity, would reduce one's capacities in later life. It has been suggested that the duration of one's sexual life is definitely limited, and that ultimate high capacity and long-lived performance depend upon the conservation of one's sexual powers in earlier years. The individual's ability to function sexually has been conceived as a finite quantity, which is fairly limited and ultimately exhaustible. One can use up those

52

capacities by frequent activity in his youth, or preserve his wealth for the fulfillment of the later obligations and privileges of marriage.'[161] Kinsey goes on to remark that medical practitioners have sometimes claimed that infertility and erectal impotence were the results of the wastage of sperm through excessive sexual activity in youth and that Boy Scout manuals for decades informed countless youths 'that in order "to be prepared" one must conserve one's virility by avoiding any wastage of vital fluids in boyhood', which presumably was an attempt to appeal to self-interest to curb self-abuse, the common euphemism for masturbation. The idea that a woman's genital area is perceived as a dangerous mouth posing a threat to the male genitals is confirmed not only by the *vagina dentata* motif[162] but perhaps also by the Latinate nomenclature of labia for the outer and inner folds of skin and mucous membrane of the vulva. Labia, of course, means lips[163] and lips incorporate liquid among other things.

In the context of the evil eye belief complex, I suggest that showing the phallus or making the *fica* gesture, which symbolically shows a phallus in a vagina, affirms the prospective victim's ability to produce semen. The ability to produce liquid is explicit in a curious detail in Lebanese-American custom. An exorcist who specialised in combating the effects of the evil eye maintained that a child was not cured until he had urinated. She insisted that 'no one should kiss a child while he is being read over and not until he has urinated after the eye has been expelled.' Asked why this was necessary, she replied, 'it's just natural. That's the way it is supposed to be.'[164] From the present perspective, the child's cure from the ill effects of the evil eye is demonstrated by his ability to make water, to produce liquid normally. This would also be consonant with the fact that urine is sometimes reported to be effective agent in curing the effects caused by the evil eye.[165] It is, in sum, entirely consonant with the wet-dry hypothesis.

There is yet another way of blinding the evil eye and this is by defecating upon it. An unusual marble bas-relief reported by Millingen in his paper delivered in 1818 shows a man lifting his clothing to allow his bare buttocks to sit upon a large eye which is also being attacked by a host of animals.[166] This belongs to the same tradition as the painting unearthed at Pompeii adjacent to a latrine in which

a man squats in a defecating position between two upright serpents next to a woman whose feet are pierced by a sword. Above the squatting man is inscribed *'Cacator cave malum.'*[167] Seligmann notes that excrement is sometimes used to counteract the effects of the evil eye, for example in the case of a cow whose milk has gone dry, but he offers no explanation of why excrement should be so used.[168] Róheim suggests that 'the magical value of excrement is based on the infantile anal birth theory' in which very young children equate the act of defecation with the act of giving birth.[169] Thus according to Róheim, 'The defecating child is the mother; the excrement, the child.' Róheim remarks that in Scotland, a calf can be protected against the evil eye if some of its mother's dung is put into its mouth and he interprets this as meaning the witch cannot 'eat' the child with her evil eye because the child is eating the witch (bad mother, excrement).[170] For Róheim, 'To possess the evil eye means to have oral aggression or a desire to eat the child.'[171] If the production of faeces is equivalent to giving birth to a child, then defecation could be construed as an alternative means of proving one's fertility. But like spitting, the act of defecation can also have an insulting aspect. Defecating on the evil eye could also be a means of repudiating and defiling it. If the eye were that of an all-powerful and ever-watchful parent or all-seeing god, then a child, or an adult considering himself a child *vis-à-vis* his parents or a deity, might take pleasure in depositing faeces in or on that eye.[172]

Deonna reminds us of a formula employed in Asia Minor by a mother attempting to keep the evil eye away from her child. The mother addresses the possible possessor of the evil eye as follows: *'Que ton oeil soit derrière de mon enfant'*. Deonna wonders if wishing that the eye be positioned at the child's rear might be related to the curious custom of painting an eye at the bottom of chamber pots sold at fairs.[173] Such chamber pots are reported in England, Scotland and France among other places, where they are commonly used in wedding customs.[174] In Stockport, Cheshire, a premarriage ceremony includes the groom's friends presenting him with a chamber pot. It is decorated with the names of the bride and groom and a large eye is painted on the bottom of it with the words 'I can see you.'[175] Later the man and his friends take the pot to a tavern and everyone drinks from it. In Scotland, a chamber pot filled with salt was given as a wedding present to the groom. Miniature chamber pots were sold at the Aberdeen market in the mid 1930's 'usually inscribed with the words "For me and my girl" or with an eye at the bottom.'[176]

French versions of the custom reported by van Gennep include one called *Saucée* from Revel-Tourdan in the Dauphiné district in which melted chocolate was poured into a chamber pot with an eye design at the bottom in such a way as to leave the eye clear. After the chocolate hardened, other ingredients were added, for example white wine or champagne, grated chocolate, balls of chocolate, creams, etc. The concoction was taken later to the nuptial chamber after the bride and groom were considered to be asleep. The bride had to drink first and then the groom.[177] Monger suggests a possible though admittedly highly speculative connection, to a supposed ancient eye goddess cult in the Middle East (Crawford).[178] However, it is more likely that it is a fertility ritual. Salt, as Ernest Jones convincingly demonstrated, is a symbolic substitute for semen,[179] and thus a chamber pot filled with salt is a container full of semen given to the groom. Newly-weds are especially concerned with performing the sexual act satisfactorily. Tourney and Plazek observe that 'the nuptial pair may fear impotence, frigidity or sterility' and that the use of apotropaic charms is to demonstrate that the threatened genitalia are safe.[180] If the eye at the bottom of the chamber pot represents the parental or peer group's attempt to observe the first connubial act of intercourse then the act of pouring in chocolate, a sweet sublimated substitute for faeces, might be analogous to defecating upon the evil eye.

If the evil eye represents the threat of impotence and/or the lack or loss of the necessary sexual fluids, then it would make sense to drink *from* an evil eye container. The chamber pot, an obvious receptacle for the passing of liquid, is converted through ritual reversal into a drinking goblet allowing for the incorporation of a potent liquid. The ritual may also signal that a part of the body hitherto associated primarily with excretion will be employed in a new and different way.

In the context of defecating upon the evil eye, it might be worth conjecturing that the common phrase 'Here's mud in your eye,' said as a drinking toast, may stem from the same psychological source. The person who drinks is incorporating the liquid of life. The liquid is taken at someone else's expense. This other person, rather than taking in vital fluid, receives the end product of digestive incorporation in his eye. Certainly the above mentioned wish 'May your eye be at the posterior of my child' is not all that different from 'Here's mud in your eye.'

In terms of the possible symbolism of body parts, it is conceivable that the anus could constitute a metaphorical eye. This is suggested by a number of standard joke texts. One traced by Legman back to the late 18th century tells of a man who puts his artificial glass eye in a glass of water before retiring and swallows it by mistake. He visits a proctologist who after examining him exclaims, 'I've been looking up these things for thirty years, but this is the first time anyone ever looked *back* at me!'[181] Another involves a drunk who attempts to convince a bartender that he is sober: 'Drunk? Hell, I'm not drunk. I can see. Look at that cat coming in the door there. It's got only one eye, hasn't it.' The bartender replies that the cat has two eyes and besides it is not coming in but going out.[182] In both Italian and Spanish, there are metaphorical references to the anus as an eye. From Liguria in Italy, we have the following example. A young girl refused to drink her coffee because she noticed coffee grains in it. Her mother asked, *'Ti ae puia che o te o l'euggio de cu?'* which might be rendered 'Are you afraid that it will stop up the eye of your ass?' – i.e., cause constipation. Similarly, *ojo* means *culo* in Andalusia. In this connection one recalls Chaucer's reference at the end of his celebrated Miller's Tale to duped Absolon kissing Alison's 'naked ers' with the words 'And Absolon hath kissed hir nether ye.' The nether eye was thus known in the fourteenth century.

To the extent that the evil eye has an anal cast, it would be perfectly reasonable to confront a threatening anus with anal power. In this light, an unusual Spanish ritual and charm against the evil eye might be cited.[183] According to the account, since in general, the individuals who give the evil eye are known, when they are seen coming, one turns a child's back or an animal's butt towards them. Then one thinks mentally or recites in a low voice the following text:

Tres garbanzitos	Three little chick peas (or garbanza beans)
tiene en el culo:	He has in the arse:
quitale dos,	Away with two
déjale uno.	Leave one.
Virate p'al monte	Turn toward the mountain
virate p'al mar.	Turn towards the sea
virate el culo	Turn your arse
y déjalo andar.	And let it go.

This would seem to be consistent with the *Cacator cave malum* pattern noted earlier.

Most folklorists eschew symbolic analysis and they may therefore be sceptical of the analysis of the evil eye proposed in this essay. But even without the symbolic dimensions, one cannot avoid the obvious psychological aspects of the evil eye. Sometimes the possessor of an evil eye used the power for both psychological and mercenary advantage. In Scotland, fear of the evil eye led people to bribe or buy off the potential evil eye inflictor.[184] One informant reported that Mrs. MacE. 'was believed to have the Evil Eye very strongly, and people would do almost anything rather than offend her, so general was the impression that she could injure any person if she wished to do so.'[185] The same holds true for Italy. According to one account, 'I know also a most disagreeable woman whose daily task of running errands is made profitable by propitiatory tips, lest she blight her patrons, their children, or their cattle.'[186] Similarly, 'One case in Philadelphia came up before a magistrate recently in which a dark-haired little old Italian woman was terrorising the neighbourhood. For many years she had extracted large sums of money from those who came under the influence of the evil eye. She also sold charms made out of bones of the dead, articles of ivory, stones, and herbs, wrapped in rag bags.'[187] These are surely examples of transforming what might be a liability into a kind of asset.

Occasionally, there have been attempts to put the power of the evil eye to good use. One of the most unusual of these attempts took place in Sassari in Sardinia near the end of the last century. According to the report, the evil eye was enlisted to battle a plague of locusts: 'Not long ago, Sassari elected a mayor who openly scoffed at the priests. This gentleman was not, however, a thorough type of the modern Sassarese. For though he condemned religion, he was sufficiently in the thrall of superstition to give his earnest sanction to the employment of a youth gifted with the evil eye. The country happened to be plagued with locusts. There was no remedy except the evil eye. And so the lad was perambulated about the district, and bidden to look his fiercest at the insufferable ravagers of vineyards, gardens, and the rich orchards of the north. Even when the locusts remained unmoved by this infliction, the mayor's faith in the remedy was unchanged. They had requisitioned an "evil eye" of comparative impotency, that was all. It behoved them, therefore to find a person better gifted than the lad they had used.'[188]

Evidently, humans are more likely to be intimidated by the evil eye than locusts are. In 1957, a committee of the U.S. Senate charged with investigating possible connections between organised crime and labour, interviewed an Italian racketeer from New York City. The committee was told that the evil eye had been used to keep unhappy employees on the job. According to Gifford's account the racketeer was hired by one employer simply to come in once or twice every week or so, to glare at the employees. The employer found that it was enough to have this individual come in and look at the workers to keep them at their work.[189]

Most of the time, however, the possessor of the evil eye is shunned and ignored. In Morocco: 'A person who is reputed to have an evil eye ... is not allowed to take part in feasts or gatherings ... he must not pitch his tent near the tents of others.'[190] Similar to accusations of witchcraft, accusations of possessing the evil eye give social sanction to ostracising an individual, often transforming him into a pariah figure. Pitrè is one of the relatively few scholars to express sympathy for the poor soul who may be unfortunate enough to be victimised by an accusation of possessing the evil eye: 'The *jettatore* has no name, no friends, nor the possibility of a social life ...'[191]

The evil eye, like so many forms of human custom and superstition, is condemned automatically by so-called educated members of Western élitist societies. But it should be realised that the evil eye, again like most forms of custom, serves an invaluable function of displacement. When an infant becomes ill or dies, there is potentially a great deal of guilt and shame felt by parents. The evil-eye belief complex provides a nearly fool-proof mechanism which allows the anxious parents to shift the responsibility and blame for the misfortune upon someone else, perhaps even a total stranger who happens to have eyes of a colour different from that of the parents. Similarly, if a cow's milk dries up or a favourite fruit tree withers, it is not the owner of the cow or tree's fault. It was the evil eye which caused these calamities.

Even the diagnostic and protective techniques involved in the evil-eye belief complex may provide important psychological supports. A small child who feels ill is assured of a great deal of parental attention. In Italian and Italian-American tradition, a bowl or shallow dish filled with water and a drop of olive oil may be placed on his head to determine whether or not his discomfort has been caused by the evil eye. Whether the child or parents believe in the efficacy of the procedure or not, most children surely enjoy being the cynosure of all eyes. Thus whatever evil results from the evil eye, there is also a beneficial aspect of the belief complex.

The concern in this essay has been not so much with the evil eye *per se*, but with the attempt to understand the folk ideas or world view principles which underlie it. The delineation of the wet-dry opposition and the idea of limited good is, however, not just an idle intellectual exercise. There are applications to be made which may lead to a better understanding of cultural differences. For example, in the United States, the principle of limited good is not as common as in the old world. Instead, it has been argued that a principle of unlimited good prevails.[192] In theory, as opposed to practice, there is enough 'good' for everyone to have their fair share. One could also argue that the collective guilt felt by citizens of the United States for their relatively high standard of living accounts for their attempts at 'tipping' less fortunate countries by offering them substantial foreign aid. Just as many wealthy individuals turn to philanthropy as a means of salving conscience, for having accumulated more goods than one needs to simply physically survive, so the have-nations feel impelled to help the have-nots by offering grain surpluses and other subsidised aid.

But there are some substantive differences. In American culture, praise is not only permitted but expected. One can praise the beauty of an infant or a friend's new house or dress without giving offense or causing anxiety. But Americans need to remember when they travel in other parts of the Indo-European and Semitic world that praise can be considered threatening. When a new acquaintance literally gives a visiting American the shirt off his back, which the American may have admired, it is not necessarily because of friendship so much as because of fear of the evil eye. By the same token, Americans who as infants are accustomed to hearing and receiving lavish praise for even the slightest deed should not be offended when praise is not forthcoming from colleagues from cultures in which the evil-eye belief complex remains a vital force. One American woman married to an eastern European told me she had never understood why her in-laws so rarely praised her or her children. She took it personally, not realising that their unwillingness to indulge in the public praising so common among Americans might have been due to the cultural imperatives demanded by the evil-eye complex. To praise is to invite disaster in evil-eye cultures.

The contrast between American socialisation conventions and socialisation patterns in evil-eye cultures is quite pronounced. American children are typically asked to perform and show-off, so to speak, in front of family and friends, and sometimes even strangers. Not so in evil-eye cultures. The case of the Syrian and Lebanese Americans is instructive. 'Experience taught that to show off a "smart" child in front of people, especially strangers is to invite the eye to strike him.'[193] The same is reported for northern India: 'Because of the belief in the evil eye, a visitor who followed the American custom of admiring the baby, praising its unusual healthiness, good looks, or well-kept appearance would cause panic rather than pride, and a village mother would no more show off her baby to the admiration of a visitor than an American mother would deliberately expose an infant to a contagious disease.'[194]

For most of the Indo-European and Semitic world, the philosophy articulated by Herodotus and Horace prevails with respect to fame and fortune and the praise thereof. Herodotus in Book VII, chapter 10, of the *Persian Wars* speaks of lightning striking the tallest trees. 'See how god with his lightning always smites the bigger animals, and will not suffer them to wax insolent, while those of a lesser bulk chafe him not. How likewise his bolts fall ever on the highest houses and the tallest trees. So plainly does he love to bring down everything that exalts itself.' Horace in Book II of his *Odes*, remarks in like fashion in Odeton: 'It is the mountain-top that the lightning strikes.' A low profile is essential if one is to avoid the envy of peers or the gods. Certainly one element of the evil-eye complex is the 'fear of success'.[195] This is analogous to the underdog theme in American culture whereby politicians and athletic teams prefer to be the underdog because they ardently believe that front runners and the favoured are likely to be overtaken and defeated. Horace in the very same ode suggested 'Whoever cultivates the golden mean avoids both the poverty of a hovel and the envy of a palace.' This is an ideal — to be neither envied nor envier. One thinks of the advice of Polonius to his son Laertes in Shakespeare's *Hamlet* 'Neither a borrower nor a lender be.'[196]

One needs enough liquid to live but that means not too little and not too much. But eventually the finite amount is depleted. 'For dust thou art, and unto dust shalt thou return.' If drying is dying, then death is dust. The American slang idiom 'to bite the dust' reflects not only the convulsive act of a dying man whose mouth may touch the earth, but also the same wet-dry continuum which I have suggested underlies the whole evil-eye belief complex.

In the Judeo-Christian tradition, the after-life conception includes a solution to the problem of the imagined thirst of the dead. For heaven or paradise or the promised land is one which flows with milk and honey.[197] The phrase 'and the hills shall flow with milk'[198] strongly suggests that there may be an infantile prototype for this metaphor, namely, the initial postnatal breast-feeding constellation. In the idealised after-life, one is finally safe from the evil eye. Here there is plenty of milk and honey, enough for an eternity of replenishment. With unlimited liquid, one is free to enjoy life eternal. On the other hand, in hell, we have excessive heat — fire and water are presumably in opposition. And one thinks of the plight of the unfortunate Tantalus perpetually consumed by thirst he is unable to slake, as the waters cruelly recede whenever he bends down to drink.

In conclusion, it seems reasonable to argue that the wet-dry opposition is just as important as the hot-cold opposition which has been frequently studied by anthropologists and students of the history of medicine. Perhaps it is even more important. Classical humoural pathology in fact included all four distinctions: heat, dryness, moistness and cold.[199] In this connection, it is noteworthy that a reported native classification of foods in northern India included hot, cold, dry and wet.[200] If the wet-dry distinction does underlie the evil eye belief, then the distribution and age of the complex would tend to suggest that the wet-dry opposition is much older than its articulation among the ancient Greeks concerned with humoural pathology. Rather it would appear that humoural pathology formulations simply expressed a folk theory already in existence. One must keep in mind that all of the so-called humours were fluids and for that matter the term 'humour' itself comes from the Latin *umor* meaning fluid or moisture. It is even possible that the idea of an exceptionally dry sense of humour might imply that the normal state of humour was wet.

Foster has assumed that the wet-dry distinction has disappeared in Latin America. He asks, 'But why have the moist/dry qualities disappeared — apparently everywhere — in contemporary systems?' Foster answers his own question by suggesting that the moist-dry component so basic to classical humour pathology is less critical than the hot-cold distinction. 'Heat and cold, and not moistness or dryness, are the primary causes of illness', argues Foster, who is, of course, speaking only of conscious articulation of theories of illness causation.[201] If the wet-dry opposition is related to the evil eye belief complex, not to mention beliefs about the dead, one might take issue with both the idea that the wet-dry distinction has disappeared and the idea that it is less critical than the hot-cold dichotomy with respect to folk disease theory. On the contrary I believe there is ample evidence to support the notion that the opposition between wet and dry is a fundamental folk idea, albeit an unconscious one, in Indo-European and Semitic world view, a folk idea which is, metaphorically at any rate, a matter of life and death.

Notes

1. Rennell Rodd, *The Customs and Lore of Modern Greece* (Chicago, 1968), 160-1; cf. also W. Crooke, *The Popular Religion and Folklore of Northern India* (Delhi, 1968), II, 6.

2. cf. Edward Dodwell, *A Classical and Topographical Tour Through Greece* (London, 1819), II, 35-6.

3. John M. Roberts, 'Belief in the Evil Eye in World Perspective', *The Evil Eye*, ed. Clarence Moloney (New York, 1976), 229.

4. *ibid.*, 234.

5. V, Question 7.

6. St Basil, *Ascetical Works*, tr. Sister M. Monica Wagner (New York, 1950), 469-70.

7. Ibn Khaldûn, *The Muqaddimah*, tr. Franz Rosenthal (Princeton, 1967), 170-1.

8. e.g. William MacKenzie, *Gaelic Incantations, Charms and Blessings of the Hebrides* (Inverness, 1895); also José Cutiliero, *A Portuguese Rural Society* (Oxford, 1971), 274.

9. Nicola Valletta, *Cicilata sul Fascino, Volgarmente detto Jettatura* (Naples, 1787), 152.

10. Otto Jahn, *Über den Aberglauben des bösen Blicks bei den Alten* (Leipzig, 1855).

11. Henri Gaidoz, 'Jules Tuchmann', *Mélusine*, XI (1912), 148-51.

12. Arnold van Gennep, *The Semi-Scholars* (London, 1967), 32-6.

13. Edward Westermarck, *Ritual and Belief in Morocco* (London, 1926), 414-78.

14. Karl Meisen, 'Der böse Blick und anderer Schadenzauber in Glaube und Brauch der altern Völker und in frühchristlicher Zeit', *Rheinisches Jahrbuch für Volkskunde*, I (1950), 144-77; *idem*, 'Der böse Blick, das böse Wort und der Schadenzauber durch Berührung im Mittelalter und in der neueren Zeit', *Rheinisches Jahrbuch für Volkskunde*, III (1952), 169-225.

15. A. M. Hocart, 'The Mechanism of the Evil Eye', *Folk-Lore*, XLIX (1938), 156.

16. Brian Spooner, 'Anthropology and the Evil Eye', *The Evil Eye*, 281.

17. Richard Coss, 'Reflections on the Evil Eye', *Human Behaviour*, III (1974), 16-22.

18. Erik H. Erikson, *Toys and Reasons: Stages in the Ritualization of Experience* (New York, 1977), 58.

19. Frank J. MacHovec, 'The Evil Eye: Superstition or Hypnotic Phenomenon', *American Journal of Clinical Hypnosis*, XIX (1976), 74-9.

20. William G. Sumner, *Folkways* (New York, 1960), 434.

21. Frederick T. Elworthy, *The Evil Eye: The Origins and Practices of Superstition* (New York, 1958), 7; cf. also Ingrid Odelstierna, *Invidia, Invidiosus and Invidiam facere* (Uppsala, 1949), 72 n.1.

22. Spooner, 283.

23. *ibid.*

24. Valletta, 18-25; Jahn; A. Michaelis, 'Sarapis

Standing on a Xanthian Marble in the British Museum', *Journal of Hellenic Studies*, VI (1885), 287-318; Paul Wolters, 'Ein Apotropaion aus Baden im Aargau', *Bonner Jahrbücher*, CXVIII (1909), 257-74; S. Seligmann, *Der böse Blick und Verwandtes* (Berlin, 1910), 188-200; Elworthy, 149-54; Waldemar Deonna, *Le Symbolisme de l'Oeil* (Paris, 1965), 180-1.

25. J. Leite de Vasconcellos, *A Figa: Estudio de Etnografia Comparativa* (Porto, 1925), 92.

26. Filippo Valla, 'La Jettatura (Ocru malu) in Sardegna (Barbagia)', *Archivo per lo Studio delle Tradizione Popolari*, XIII (1894), 422n; Emilio Servadio, 'Die Angst vor dem bösen Blick', *Imago*, XXII (1936), 403 n.8.

27. Seligmann, I, 199; see also Servadio.

28. Roberts, 241, 258.

29. Rudolf Reiter, 'Zur Augensymbolik', *Internationale Zeitschrift für Ärztliche Psychoanalyse*, I (1913), 160.

30. Garfield Tourney and Dean J. Plasak, 'Evil Eye in Myth and Schizophrenia', *Psychiatric Quarterly*, XXVIII (1954), 489.

31. Géza Róheim, 'The Evil Eye', *American Imago*, IX (1952), 356.

32. Sigmund Freud, 'The "Uncanny" ', *Collected Papers* (New York, 1959), IV, 393.

33. Tourney and Plasak, 491.

34. Regina Dionisopoulos-Mass, 'The Evil Eye and Bewitchment in a Peasant Village', *The Evil Eye*, 46.

35. Margaret M. Hardie, 'The Evil Eye in Some Greek Villages of the Upper Haliakmon Valley in West Macedonia', *Journal of the Royal Anthropological Institute*, LIII (1923), 170.

36. Edgar Thurston, *Ethnographic Notes on Southern India* (Madras, 1907), 254.

37. cf. George M. Foster, 'Peasant Society and the Image of Limited Good', *American Anthropologist*, LXVII (1965).

38. Richard B. Onians, *The Origins of European Thought About the Body, the Mind, the Soul, the World, Time, and Fate* (Cambridge, 1951), 215, 256.

39. Foster (1965); Alvin W. Gouldner, *Enter Plato* (New York, 1965), 49-51.

40. Onians, 227.

41. Peter Browne, *A Discourse of Drinking Healths* (London, 1716), 19.

42. Claude Lévi-Strauss, *The Elementary Structures of Kinship* (Boston, 1969), 58-60.

43. MacKenzie, 39.

44. Edward Westermarck, 'The Magic Origin of Moorish Designs', *Journal of the Royal Anthropological Institute*, XXXIV (1904), 211; cf. also Edward S. Gifford, *The Evil Eye: Studies in the Folklore of Vision* (New York, 1958), 48-50.

45. Edward W. Lane, *An Account of the Manners and Customs of the Modern Egyptians* (London, 1895), 262.

46. Benjamin L. Gordon, 'Oculus Fascinus (Fascination, Evil Eye)', *Archives of Opthalmology*, XVII (1937), 306.

47. *ibid.*, 307.

48. George M. Foster, 'The Anatomy of Envy: A Study in Symbolic Behaviour', *Current Anthropology*, XIII (1972), 181.

49. *ibid.*

50. R. C. Maclagan, *Evil Eye in the Western Highlands* (London, 1902), 22-123.

51. Crooke, I, 2.

52. Hardie, 161.

53. Richard and Eva Blum, *The Dangerous Hour* (London, 1970), 146.

54. Howard F. Stein, 'Envy and Evil Eye among Slovak Americans', *Ethos*, II (1) (1974), 15-46.

55. A. Murgoci, 'The Evil Eye in Roumania, and its Antidotes', *Folk-Lore*, XXXIV (1923), 357.

56. Melanie Klein, *Envy and Gratitude: A Study of Unconscious Sources* (New York, 1957), 10, 29.

57. cf. Karl Fries, 'The Ethiopic Legend of Socinus and Ursula', *Actes de Huitième Congrès International des Orientalistes* (Leiden, 1891), II, 55-70; Moses Gaster, 'Two Thousand Years of a Charm Against the Child-Stealing Witch', *Folk-Lore*, XI (1900), 129-62; Hermann Gollancz, *The Book of Protection* (London, 1912); James A. Montgomery, *Aramaic Incantation Texts from Nippur* (Philadelphia, 1913),

259-62; Paul Pedrizet, *Negotium Perambulans in Tenebris* (Strasbourg, 1922); Alixa Naff, 'Belief in the Evil Eye among the Christian Syrian-Lebanese in America', *Journal of American Folklore*, LXXVIII, 46-51.

58. Moses Gaster, 139-42.

59. *ibid.*, 143-5; cf. also 147-8.

60. Pedrizet, 25.

61. cf. Matthieu Cassalis, 'The Dry and the Wet: A Semiological Analysis of Creation and Flood Myths', *Semiotica*, XVII (1976), 35-67.

62. Onians, 289.

63. cf. Motif E 80, *Water of Life*.

64. Motif D 11338.1.1, *Fountain of youth*.

65. E. Washburn Hopkins, 'The Fountain of Youth', *Journal of the American Oriental Society*, XXVI (1905), 55.

66. Onians, 212-4.

67. T. Canaan, 'Water and "The Water of Life" in Palestinian Superstition', *Journal of the Palestinian Oriental Society*, IX (1929), 59.

68. Onians, 285.

69. cf. Giuseppe Bellucci, 'Sul Bisogno di Dissetarsi Attributo All'Anima dei Morti', *Archivo per l'Antropologia e le Etnologia*, XXXIX (1909), 211-29; also esp. Waldemar Deonna, 'La soif des morts: Le mort musicien', *Revue de l'Histoire des Religions*, CXIX (1939), 53-77.

70. E. A. Wallis Budge, *The Liturgy of Funerary Offerings* (London, 1909), 34.

71. *ibid.*, 60, 156, 209.

72. *ibid.*, 147; cf. also 117, 129, 185.

73. *ibid.*, 46, 52.

74. Tourney and Plazak, 481.

75. Raphael Salillas, *La Fascinación en España* (Madrid, 1905), 44.

76. Tourney and Plazak, 488.

77. Erich Ebeling, 'Beschwörungen gegen den Feind und den bösen Blick aus dem Zweistromlande', *Archive Orientálni*, XVII (1949), 172-211.

78. Maurice Simon, *Berakoth (The Babylonian Talmud)* (London, 1948), 120 (20a), 340 (55b).

79. André Caquot and R. du Mesnil du Buisson, 'La seconde tablette ou "Petite amulette d'Arslan" d'Arslan-Tash', *Syria*, XLVIII (1971), 391-406.

80. Theodor H. Gaster, 'A Hang-up for Hang-ups. The Second Amuletic Plaque from Arslan Tash', *Bulletin of the American Schools of Oriental Research*, CCIX (1973), 18-26; but cf. Frank M. Cross, 'Leaves from an Epigraphist's Notebook', *Catholic Biblical Quarterly*, XXXVI (1974), 486-90.

81. Campbell Bonner, *Studies in Magical Amulets, Chiefly Graeco-Egyptian* (Ann Arbor, 1950), 213.

82. Alfred Bel, 'La Djâzya, Chanson Arabe', *Journal Asiatique*, I (10th series) (1950), 364.

83. J. E. Crombie, 'The Saliva Superstition', *The International Folk-Lore Congress, 1891; Papers and Transactions*, ed. Joseph and Alfred Nutt (London, 1892), 252.

84. cf. Onians, 233 n.5.

85. Ernest Jones, *Essays in Psycho-Analysis* (London, 1951), 63, 273.

86. G. Legman, *Rationale of the Dirty Joke* (New York, 1968), 584.

87. O. G. S. Crawford, *The Eye Goddess* (London, 1957), 41, 48, 96, 98; cf. also Deonna (1965), 64, and Joost A. M. Meerloo, *Intuition and the Evil Eye* (Wassenaar, 1971), 36.

88. Ernest Bornemann, *Sex in Volksmund* (Hamburg, 1971).

89. Tale Type 706B.

90. cf. Marjorie Williamson, 'Les Yeux Arrachés', *Philological Quarterly*, XI (1932), 149-62; Angel González Palencia, 'La Doncella Que Se Sacó Los Ojos', *Revista de la Biblioteca, Archivo y Museo*, IX (1932), 180-200, 272-94.

91. Albert Perry, *Tattoo* (New York, 1933), 136.

92. James Hornell, 'Survivals of the Use of Oculi in Modern Boats', *Journal of the Royal Anthropological Institute*, LIII (1923), 289-321; *idem*, 'Boat Oculi Survivals: Additional Records', *Journal of the Royal Anthropological Institute*, LXVIII (1938), 339-48.

93. For a discussion of blindness and castration as allomotifs, see Alan Dundes, 'From Etic to Emic Units in the Structural Study of Folk-

tales', *Journal of American Folklore*, LXXV (1962), 102.

94. Legman (1968), 611.

95. Alexandre Moret, *De Charactère Religieux de la Royauté Pharaonique* (Paris, 1902), 40-7; for the sun as a heavenly eye generally, see Otto Weinreich, 'Helios, Augen heiland', *Hessenische Blätter für Volkskunde*, VIII (1909), 168-73.

96. Moret, 47 n.2; cf. also Géza Róheim, *The Praise of the Gods and Other Essays* (New York, 1972), 162.

97. Moret, 48 n.1.

98. cf. Ernest Jones, *On the Nightmare* (New York, 1951), 233; G. Legman, *No Laughing Matter* (New York, 1975), 367.

99. John C. Lawson, *Modern Greek Folklore and Ancient Greek Religion* (Cambridge, 1910), 14; Robert A. Georges, 'Matiasma: Living Folk Belief', *Midwest Folklore*, XII (1962), 70.

100. Jones, *On the Nightmare*, 303.

101. W. Schwartz, 'Der (rothe) Sonnenphallos der Urzeit. Eine mythologisch-antropologische Untersschung', *Zeitschrift für Ethnologie* VI (1877), 167-88, 409-10; cf. also Jones, *On the Nightmare*, 278, 285.

102. Pierrette B. Rousseau, 'Contribution à l'étude de mauvais oeil en Corse', *Ethnopsychologie*, XXXI (1976), 6.

103. Ernest Jones, 'The Action of Suggestion in Psychotherapy', *Journal of Abnormal Psychology*, V (1910), 239.

104. Freud, 383-4.

105. Seligman, II, 28; Servadio, 405; Pedrizet, 31; Deonna (1965), 70.

106. Legman (1968), 241.

107. Shaykh Nefzawi, *The Perfumed Garden of the Shaykh Nefzawi*, tr. Richard F. Burton, ed. Alan H. Walton (London, 1963), 176.

108. Gifford, 81.

109. Canaan, 58.

110. (anon.), 'Chez les Wallons de Belgique', *Kryptadia*, VIII (1902), 1-148.

111. Alan Dundes, 'The Number Three in American Culture', *In Every Man His Way* (Englewood Cliffs, 1968), 420 n.1.

112. Legman (1975), 823.

113. *ibid.*, (1968), 585-6.

114. Weston La Barre, *They Shall Take Up Serpents* (Minneapolis, 1962), 61.

115. La Barre, 94; cf. Tale Type 285, *The Child and the Snake*, in which a snake drinks from the child's milk bottle.

116. cf. Tale Type 1137, *The Ogre Blinded*.

117. Westermarck (1926), I, 434-5; Yedida Stillman, 'The Evil Eye in Morocco', *Folklore Research Centre Studies*, ed. Dov Noy and Issachar Ben-Ami (Jerusalem, 1970), I, 90.

118. *ibid.*, 85.

119. Jean L. Comhaire, 'Oriental Versions of Polyphem's Myth', *Anthropological Quarterly*, XXXI (1958), 26.

120. Reiter, 161.

121. Motif F 531.1.1.1, *Giant with one eye in middle of forehead*.

122. Onians, 109-10, 234 n.6.

123. Naff, 49.

124. Seligmann, II, 183-4.

125.. James Napier, *Folk-Lore* (Paisley, 1879), 35.

126. Budge, 134-5, 255.

127. *ibid.*, 128, 245.

128. *ibid.*, 184.

129. Alexander H. Krappe, *Balor with the Evil Eye* (New York, 1927), 1-43.

130. *ibid.*, 4.

131. E. Douglas Van Buren, 'New Evidence Concerning an Eye-Divinity', *Iraq*, XVII (1955), 164, 169.

132. Wendy D. O'Flaherty, *Hindu Myths* (Baltimore, 1975), 137.

133. *idem*, 'The Symbolism of the Third Eye of Śiva in the Purānas', *Purāna*, XI (1969).

134. Westermarck (1926), I, 440.

135. Lawson, 9.

136. Westermarck (1926), I, 440; Lawson, 12-13.

137. Westermarck (1926), I, 459; Elworthy, 133.

138. Bonner, 97; cf. also 211.

139. Chester C. McCown, *The Testament of Solomon* (Leipzig, 1922), 8.

140. F.C.Conybeare, 'The Testament of Solomon', *The Jewish Quarterly Review*, XI (1899), 38.

141. Archer Taylor, *English Riddles from Oral Tradition* (Berkeley and Los Angeles, 1951); cf. riddles 1425-6, 1443-4, 'Hair Above, Hair Below'.

142. Leo J. Frachtenberg, 'Allusions to Witchcraft and Other Primitive Beliefs in the Zoroastrian Literature', *The Dastur Hoshang Memorial Volume* (Bombay, 1918), 421.

143. Meerloo, 54.

144. Gifford, 166.

145. *ibid.*, 66.

146. Gordon, 313.

147. Róheim (1952), 353.

148. Legman (1975), 653.

149. Jones, *On the Nightmare*, 120.

150. *ibid.*, 179.

151. Legman (1968), 356-60, for 'the unsatisfiable female'.

152. Nefzawi, 30.

153. Legman (1968), 403.

154. Legman (1975), 134.

155. John H. Weakland, 'Orality in Chinese Conceptions of Male Genital Sexuality', *Psychiatry*, XIX (1956), 241.

156. *ibid.*, 240.

157. *ibid.*, 241-2.

158. N. B. Dennys, *The Folk-Lore of China* (London, 1876), 49.

159. Seligmann, I, 43.

160. Leigh Minturn and John T. Hitchcock, *The Rājpūts of Khalapur, India* (New York, 1966), 74.

161. Alfred C. Kinsey, Wardell B. Pomeroy and Clyde E. Martin, *Sexual Behaviour in the Human Male* (Philadelphia, 1948), 297.

162. Motif F 547.1.1.

163. cf. La Barre, 89 n.

164. Naff, 50.

165. Guiseppe Pitrè, 'La Jettatura e il Malocchio', *Biblioteca delle Tradizione Populari Siciliane,* XVII (1889), 245; Barbara and Harris L. Kirshenblatt-Gimblett, 'The Evil Eye (The Good Eye) Einehore', *Alcheringa*, V (1973), 73.

166. cf. Elworthy, 138-41; Waldemar Deonna, *De Télesphore au 'moine beurre'* (Berchem-Brussels, 1955), 93-4; *idem* (1965), 180.

167. Emilio Magaldi, 'Di un particuloare ignorato e strano del culto della dea Fortuna', *Il Folklore Italiano*, VII (1932), 97; Deonna (1955), 94.

168. Seligmann, I, 302-3.

169. Géza Róheim, *Magic and Schizophrenia* (New York, 1955), 28-31.

170. *ibid.*, 25.

171. *ibid.*, 7.

172. Jones, *On the Nightmare*, 176.

173. Deonna (1965), 183.

174. G. P. Monger, 'Further Notes on Wedding Customs in Industry', *Folklore*, LXXXVI (1975), 50-61.

175. *ibid.*, 52.

176. *ibid.*, 56-7.

177. Arnold van Gennep, *Le Folklore du Dauphiné* (Paris, 1932), I, 161-2.

178. Monger, 58.

179. Jones, *Essays*, 22-109.

180. Tourney and Plazak, 491-2.

181. Legman (1975), 515.

182. *ibid.*, 822.

183. Luis Diego Cuscoy, 'Mal de Ojo, Amuletos, Ensalmos y Santiguadores en la Isla de Teneriffe', *Etnologia y Tradiciones Populares* (Saragossa, 1969), 502.

184. Maclagan, 30-1, 47.

185. *ibid.*, 69.

186. Frank J. Mather, 'The Evil Eye', *Century Magazine*, LXXX (1910), 42.

187. Gordon, 319.

188. Charles Edwardes, *Sardinia and the Sardes* (London, 1889), 326-7.

189. Gifford, 103.

190. Westermarck (1926), 426.

191. Pitrè, 247.

192. Alan Dundes, 'Folk Ideas as Units of Worldview', *Journal of American Folklore*, LXXXIV (1971), 93-103.

193. Naff. 49.

194. Minturn and Hitchcock, 111-2.

195. Morris L. and Natalie R. Haimowitz, 'The Evil Eye: Fear of Success', *Human Development*, ed. *idem* (New York, 1966), 677-85.

196. *Hamlet*, I, iii, 75.

197. *Genesis* 3:6; *Exodus* 33:3; *Jeremiah* 11:5, etc.

198. *Joel* 3:18.

199. cf. William W. Story, 'Roba di Roma: The Evil Eye and Other Superstitions', *Atlantic Monthly*, V (1860), 697; G. E. R. Lloyd, 'The Hot and the Cold, the Dry and the Wet in Greek Philosophy', *Journal of Hellenic Studies*, LXXXIV (1964), 567-93.

200. Minturn and Hitchcock, 73.

201. George M. Foster, 'Hippocrates' Latin American Legacy: 'Hot' and 'Cold' in Contemporary Folk Medicine', *Colloquio in Anthropology*, ed. R. K. Wetherington (Dallas, 1978), II.

Certain Laws of Folklore*

IONA AND PETER OPIE

MARY Douglas, referring to the widespread idea that primitive peoples are and always have been religious, once commented in her usual wise way: 'No discipline can hope to keep control over the popular uses of its work. But every now and again its assumptions need to be checked, not so much for the sake of the general public, who will always do what they like, but for the sake of the discipline itself.'[1]

Every folklorist is aware that investigations that are themselves concerned with popular beliefs are particularly vulnerable to popularisation; that the term 'folklore' itself embodies a misapprehension; and that the student who wishes to take up folklore as his subject needs first to be relieved of his preconceptions. It will be no surprise therefore when we say that our own observations give little support to the traditional image of tradition. Yet it is to be remembered, as Bacon noted, that there is superstition in avoiding superstition. And we must hope it will not become too apparent in what follows that we in our turn have been myth-led.

That the Way the Lore is Conveyed Determines its Nature

If we say that we have been able to monitor the transmission of oral lore over a course of five or six generations, and have done this in a period of little more than thirty years, some explanation may be necessary. We began our careers by making a study of nursery rhymes, those lullabies, knee-rides, jingles, and metrical histories that in the United States, in particular, are still referred to quaintly as the songs of Mother Goose. We found, after looking at their sources and histories, that one feature alone distinguished them from other traditional verse, and this was the manner in which they were now transmitted. We defined nursery rhymes as being the verses a mother or other adult customarily repeats for the entertainment or pacification of an infant. And here we may remark that the practice of men keeping alive the nursery tradition — whether as fathers, grandfathers, or strangers — long predates the introduction of Woman's Lib, even in this country. Thus Laetitia-Matilda Hawkins put on record that when she was small Oliver Goldsmith used to entertain her with that endlessly successful piece of nursery magic performed with two pieces of paper stuck on the forefingers, to the well-known recitation:

> Two little dicky birds sitting on a wall,
> One named Peter, one named Paul. . .

Only in the eighteenth century the imagery was not as sharp as it is today, and the birds were, for the benefit of rhyme, made to sit on a hill:

> There were two blackbirds sat upon a hill
> The one was nam'd Jack, the other nam'd Gill.[2]

When a person has a small child in his charge who trustingly imitates, or attempts to imitate, whatever words are spoken, there is a temptation

* This is an extended version of a paper originally published in *The Times Literary Supplement*'s Folklore Society Centenary issue on 14th July, 1978, and later read at the Centenary Conference.

The portion concerned is reprinted here by kind permission of the Editor, *The Times Literary Supplement*.

which some men find irresistible — referred to, for instance, by James Sully in 1884 — to teach the innocent to say words not ordinarily repeated in polite company. But in our early days as collectors we kept being given verses under the title of 'nursery rhymes' that certainly were traditional, and certainly were being orally transmitted, but just as certainly were not nursery rhymes as we understood them. They were not rhymes a normal mother would be eager to suckle her babes upon; nor were they the compositions of a delinquent father. They were rhymes that had a stridency and often a sauciness of their own:

Dirty Bill from Vinegar Hill,
Never had a bath and never will.

Good King Wenceslas
Knocked a bobby senseless
Right in the middle
Of Marks and Spencers.

Toorally oorally oorally oo,
They're wanting monkeys at the zoo.
I'd apply if I were you
And get a situation.

It was not long before we realised that the fundamental difference about these rhymes was the manner in which they were transmitted. Instead of being passed from adult to child, they were being passed from child to child, and ordinarily an adult knew little about them. It then occurred to us — this seems very obvious now — that since the term *nursery rhyme* referred not to the nature of the verse but to the environment in which it was now found, we might have been led into adopting as parochial a stance as people used to take when an international song such as 'Green grow the rushes, oh!' was termed a 'Somerset folksong,' simply because the recorder had heard it being sung by a yokel in Somerset. When we got down on hands and knees and stared the nursery rhymes in the face, we saw they were not juvenile rhymes but adult rhymes. They were verses which the adult preserved, and the adult chose to transmit. The true child rhymes were the ones in juvenile keeping, the ones which only a child would wish to utter, and then only in his own community:

My teacher's got a bunion,
A face like a pickled onion,

A nose like a squashed tomato,
And legs like matchsticks.

Further, we appreciated that not only did these two types of verse have different habitats, their life-styles were as unlike as those of civil servant and costermonger: the one seldom seen but apparently immovable, the other raucous on occasion but soon shifted. A nursery rhyme was likely to be learnt in infancy, and then stored in the recesses of the mind until the infant became a parent, and the verse was recalled for the squeaking pleasure of the next generation. Thereafter the rhyme might be forgotten again (as we ourselves have found) until the parent became a grandparent, and was again called upon to perform Jenny-come-trots that he, in turn, may have learnt from his own grandparents: a retransmission period of sixty, or seventy, or even eighty years.

With the schoolchild lore, however, the period before retransmission might be less than five minutes. A child, having learnt to his discomfort what not to say when consulted about the ancient bathers 'Adam and Eve and Nipmetight,' experiences an immediate urge to find another child, even greener than himself, upon whom to play the trick. And since in any one school where such rhymes and jokes circulate, a complete turnover of population takes place every five years or so, our claim to have been witness to the transmission of this lore through five or six generations will, we think, be upheld. In fact the amount of transmission and mutation we have seen amongst schoolchildren in thirty years is equivalent to the retransmission of nursery lore that takes place in a period of somewhere between 150 and 500 years.[3]

Here is not the place to enlarge on the respect for the community of childhood which might have been thought to follow the realisation that the young possess their own oral culture, rather than the exploitation which has in fact ensued. Yet even a folklorist may learn something from watching a small child grow up.

When an infant starts going to school at the age of five or even earlier, he has already absorbed one culture and is about to absorb another; and so different are these cultures that, in the way a convert seems unable to embrace the new faith without deriding the old, so will a small child assert his new-found independence of his home by actually making fun of the amusements that have hitherto been precious to him. He will learn to say: 'Mary had a little lamb and ate it with mint sauce,' and 'Humpty Dumpty fell off the wall and all the King's men had scrambled egg.' No amusement, for instance, could be more central to the English nursery tradition than the touching of each of a baby's toes in turn to the disposition:

This little pig went to market,
This little pig stayed at home,
This little pig had roast beef,
This little pig had none,
And this little pig went wee, wee, wee, all
    the way home.

But what happens in the playground? The other day we were button-holed by a nine-year-old: 'Shall I tell you a story? There were five pigs and one went into a pub and asked for a glass of milk; and the second and the third and the fourth pigs went into the pub, and each asked for a glass of milk, and the barman gave it to them. Then the fifth one went in and he asked: "Can I have six cokes, one can of lager, and twelve beers," and the barman said "What do you want all that for?" and this pig says "I'm the one who goes wee, wee, wee, all the way home".'

Now this is someone joking about nursery lore who at the beginning of the decade was not able even to talk; and it is someone who, although he does not yet realise it, in another six or seven years will be casting off this schoolchild culture (actually forgetting that it ever existed) as he becomes a senior teenager, and embraces the lore of the motorbike and mini-manliness. So, already, we find ourselves being led to one conclusion, that with oral transmission, as with other forms of communication, McLuhan is right, 'the medium is the message.' The way a piece of lore is passed on is as significant as what is passed on. To evaluate material properly a folklorist needs to know not only who imparted the piece of lore, and when, and where; but to whom and in what context.

If an item of worldly wisdom is being passed on from father to son the recorder will know it is intended to be taken seriously; if between old men its truth is unimportant compared with the need for it to confirm reputation; if it passes from maiden to maiden its purpose, possibly, is to enlarge wonder; and if from a youth to a youth it

will be repeated, perhaps, to win a reputation. The connotations of a riddle which one small child asks another, as we have heard —

What's long and thin,
Covered in skin,
Red in parts,
And goes in tarts?

Answer: rhubarb — are going to be very different indeed if the riddle is bandied between lovers.

That There is Diversity of Origin among Items of Similar Usage

Our own studies have touched upon only a minority, perhaps, of the forms of oral lore that exist. Yet whether we have been looking at nursery lore, schoolchild lore, folksongs and ballads, fairy tales, calendar customs, popular superstitions, or groundless rumours, we have continually been struck by the diversity of ages and sources of items whose usage today makes them appear to be related. Thus printed side-by-side in a tiny tot's playbook we may find 'Mary had a little lamb, its fleece was white as snow,' a composition for which the American authoress Sarah Josepha Hale was undoubtedly responsible; 'Baa, baa, black sheep, have you any wool?', a verse which was already nursery property in England 200 years ago; and a sheep-scoring jingle that may be so old it retains the sounds of numerals used before the English language was spoken:

Ono-ery, two-ery, ickery, Ann,
Phillisy, phollisy, Nicholas John,
Quever, quaver, Irish Mary,
Stickerum, stackerum, buck.

Or, another example:

Zinti, tinti, tethera, methera,
Bumfa, litera, hover, dover,
Dicket. . .

which may be compared with the numerals children still repeat in Cumbria when they are counting-out, or, as they now say, when they are 'dipping':

| Yan | sethera |
| tan | lethera |

tethera	hothera
methera	dothera
pimp	dick

All this is well known; and we have written about it many times.[4] No one with an ear for English poetry is going to mistake as a great Elizabethan ballad:

Mary had a little lamb,
    Its fleece was white as snow,
And everywhere that Mary went
    The lamb was sure to go.

On the other hand many a folklorist has been alerted to the possible antiquity of children's playtime gibberish; and has on occasion exercised his interpretative genius on a formula such as

Ena, meena, mona, mite,
Pasca, laura, bona, bite,
Eggs, butter, cheese, bread,
Stick, stock, stone dead.

The first two lines of this formula, it has been suggested, are 'a phonetic representation of the incantations performed by the Druids before the immolation of their victims.' While the line *Eggs, butter, cheese, bread* 'has reference to the fattening process to which the victims were subjected in anticipation of their immolation,' and *Stick, stock, stone dead* shows 'of course' (the words 'of course' should set off the alarm bells) that the manner of killing the victims was 'by beating them to death with sticks or stoning them with stones.'[5]

However much we may smile at the naivety of this particular interpretation (and its innocence will become the more apparent as we proceed), there are few of us who have not looked at these spell-like formulas and felt there must be something potent and mysterious in them, the way they appear to have been passed down for centuries, even though their significance is unknown to those who now repeat them. In 1888 Henry Carrington Bolton published an immense gathering of such verses, 'as used in many lands'; and he showed that the formula that was overwhelmingly the most popular in Britain and North America was that already quoted which begins 'One-ery, two-ery, ickery, Ann,' or 'One-ery, two-ery, ziccary, zan,' with the variation 'One-ery, two-ery, dickery, Davy.'[6] He was able to parade no less than eighty versions in his pages; and we were somewhat sur-

prised, therefore, when we carried out a survey in the 1960s among 10,000 children in England, Scotland, and Wales, and found that this formula was now unknown to them.

Many people, perhaps, would not have been surprised that a rhyme believed to have survived for a thousand years should disappear from memory in the course of a single lifetime. They would have considered it to be a sign of the times, have remembered that folklore consists of 'fast disappearing relics,' and felt it was wholly understandable that in the second half of the twentieth century children should discard such gibberish as outmoded. Indeed we ourselves might not have been surprised at the disappearance of the old formula, but for one fact; and this was that throughout the land, from Aberdeen to Anglesey, and in remote country places as much as in the cities, children were still conducting their counting-out with a piece of gibberish that was of equal absurdity, and seemingly of equal antiquity, yet it was a formula that was *unknown* to Bolton in the nineteenth century:

Eena meena macka racka
Air i domin acker
Chicka pocka, lollipopper,
Om, pom, push.

This replacement of one piece of gibberish by another of the same type and serving the same purpose, with nothing to recommend it — that the outsider could see — above the piece it had displaced, would seem inexplicable if we were not aware of the general laws that govern folklore. But before we suggest the reason for this replacement, it will be necessary to agree on exactly what folklore is, for unless we have firmly in mind what folklore is we cannot hope to understand its nature, and we will continue to be mystified by its manifestations.

That Folklore is Similar to Other Forms of Living Matter

When the Folklore Society was formed a hundred years ago the work of the folklorist was defined as being 'the study of survivals.' Our founding fathers laboured through the day, and argued into the night, under the conviction that folk tales, riddles, proverbial phrases, and even children's games (perhaps most of all children's games) contained survivals of our ancient past. Debates took place, remarkable both for their learning and their sophistication, which convinced the world that, for instance, folk tales preserve mythological conceptions, that children's diversions re-enact primitive institutions, that modern spiritualism was savage animism in a new dress, and that the belief in fairies stems from the memory of a vanished race. Tylor, whose *Primitive Culture* (1871) had been the catalyst that turned Thoms's ragbag of popular antiquities into data worthy of scientific investigation, held that the materials of folklore were to be valued 'as embodying early but quite real stages of philosophy among mankind.' In Richard Dorson's fine history of *The British Folklorists* we see our Society was formed 'to establish a science devoted to reconstructing the world view of prehistoric savages from the contemporary lore of peasants.' Despite the brave attempt of Sidney Hartland in 1885 to modify the view that folklore was 'limited to *survivals*, or to *archaic* beliefs and customs,' and the efforts of Moses Gaster to show that fairy tales were not uniformly ancient, the Society's first official handbook, published in 1890, continued to justify the Society's existence with the observation 'that within the circle of almost all human society, whether savage tribes or civilized countries, there exist old beliefs, old customs, old memories, which are relics of an unrecorded past. These very important facts introduce us to the study of what has conveniently been termed Folk-lore.' The work of the Society, it was believed, 'should continue until every scrap of Folk-lore is recorded in print.' In other words the materials of folklore were finite, in the way that, in theory, the materials of archaeology are finite. Folklore consisted, it seemed, of fossil bones from which, if properly identified, prehistoric monsters of thought could be reconstructed. And this analogy, unhappily, represents the popular view of folklore to this day.[7]

Twenty-five years ago, when one of us read a paper to the Royal Society of Arts to mark our Society's seventy-fifth anniversary, a definition of folklore was offered which met with some approval at the time, and which, being innocuous, will not jack up many eyebrows today. 'Folklore,' it was suggested, 'consists of all the knowledge traditionally passed on from one person to another which is not knowledge generally accepted or "officially" recognised.'[8]

The game of fivestones, we said, which one child taught another, was part of folklore; the game of fives, for which agreed rules have been laid down, was not. The legend of Robin Hood was of perennial interest to folklorists; the story of Robinson Crusoe was of none at all. Whether there was ever a real Robin Hood and whether there was ever a real Robinson Crusoe might be questions equally open to speculation, but the background in one case was tradition, in the other literature. The belief that warts could be cured by rubbing them with raw meat which was then buried in the ground was a part of folklore even though it was efficacious; the treatments prescribed under the National Health Service were not, no matter how unsuccessful. The rubbing of warts with raw meat was folklore because it was prescribed by charmers not by gentlemen with medical qualifications.

It is humbling to find, however, that although by this time we had conducted our first country-wide survey, we were still under the influence of the early writers. 'Folklorists' we continued, 'are interested in the sparks of an earlier thought and way of life glowing in a period when the unknown bonfire from which they come has long burnt itself out.' However glowing this description it is not one we would endorse today; not because the sparks have been extinguished, but because we know now that the bonfire itself is still burning merrily.

Folklore is not a phenomenon that is dying out or decaying or showing any signs of being in a decline. It is a force to be reckoned with, whether for good or evil, that possesses the characteristics of all living matter. Certainly it ages, and one part of it and then another may die off. But it is also capable of breeding; it grows, it spreads, it feeds on other matter, and it has the great quality essential for survival, the ability to adapt to changing circumstances. Only the young look at the world and believe that what they see around them today is what they will have to face tomorrow, that lessons once they have been learnt do not have to be relearnt. Folklore is not young; and it is as wily as a serpent.

That Customs are not Constant

It appears to us that folklore, despite being prescriptive, is in a perpetual state of transition. If we exclude from our inquiries those customs and rituals whose preservation does more credit to the enthusiasm of the spectators than the participants (tourists, as is well known, stultify the institutions they patronise), we may find tradition is ever on the outlook for novelty; and that this is so even on our best-established feast days.

Take Shrove Tuesday. Twenty-five years ago only one place, as far as we are aware, sported a pancake race on Shrove Tuesday: Olney in Buckinghamshire. Fifteen years ago we had records of six places that held pancake races. Today the pancake race is so commonplace on Shrove Tuesday it is taken for granted even on the cover of a children's comic (*Tammy*, 11th February, 1978). In our own village, where a race has been held for the past four years, the placards this year were headed, with a certain smugness, LISS ANNUAL PANCAKE RACE. (What might not George Laurence Gomme have deduced from this relic of early village life?) Yet 140 years ago even the making of pancakes seems to have been in a decline. William Holloway, who was familiar with our part of the country, spoke of 'Pan-cake-day' as being a provincialism for Shrove Tuesday, a day on which pancakes were, he said, 'formerly made' in most families.[9]

And take Mother's Day or Mothering Sunday. The regeneration of this day is so absurd a story of politics and quick assumptions it should be required reading for every apprentice folklorist. Sufficient here to remember that when the Folklore Society published its volume of 'Movable Feasts' in 1936, Mothering Sunday was found to be not merely movable but removable. Inquiries could produce not one instance of a mother being brought a gift by her children.[10] Yet today, forty-two years later, Mid-Lent Sunday has become, to quote *The Times*, 'the second most profitable event in the greetings card manufacturers' year' (4th March, 1978, 2/4).

And Easter. Has Easter ever looked back as a *popular* festival — in the south of England, that is — since an astute businessman named Cremer had the idea of opening up Easter eggs, and putting sweets or toys in them? And if that is felt to be too long ago, what of the arrival of the Easter hare, apparently from Germany, which now hides eggs in our gardens? To this day we are unclear how our children came to be brought up enjoying a custom we ourselves did not know when we were young.

And what is to be said of May Day, when this year a hundred workers at the Pirelli cable factory at Southampton went on strike in protest at being forced by their union and management to take, to quote *The Times* again (18th April, 1978, 4/1), their 'traditional holiday' on May Day? It was only this year May Day became a public holiday 'in celebration of British Labour'; and since the Government did not also decree how the day was to be spent it will be fascinating watching the way this further importation from the Continent develops. On the one hand the choice of the first of May for Labour Day is well-rooted, in that it goes back to a decision of the Second Socialist International in 1889. On the other hand the memory, or vision, of May Queens and maying, and the flouting of authority on this day, continues to be strong in England, though we need hardly mention that those who believe they are enacting the ways of old-tyme merrie England by dancing round a maypole clutching a ribbon, are deluding themselves almost as much as those who believe that Marxism under British control would not be repressive. The plaiting of ribbons around a maypole seems, in fact, to have been introduced to Britain at about the same time as the comrades in Paris were, less successfully, trying to marshal us in straight lines behind their banners.

But enough of this. The present age is known to be one of turmoil; and if the ordinary behaviour of folklore is to be determined it may be felt we should look at customs in a calmer period, such as the nineteenth century.

Recently we were given a children's race game entitled *The Game of Twelfth Night or Holydays and Customs,* in which the players see who can progress through the year the least distracted by seasonal junketings. This game was published in 1820, and the celebrations pictured on the race track are, naturally, those that were best known at the time. Yet eighty years later, at the end of the century, no more than half of these holidays and customs continued in anything but vestigial form. Thus the player landing on 30 January had to 'Pay

One' for King Charles I's martyrdom; on Easter Monday he had to 'Pay One' for Epping Hunt; on May Day 'Pay One to the Sweeps,' on Whit Monday he must 'Stop one turn' to take part in the ritual running or rolling downhill at Greenwich — a practice perhaps not one Thames-sider in a thousand would be aware of today — and on 6th September the player lost a turn if, like Pepys, he dawdled at Bartholomew Fair.

Even when the days shown on this board are still commemorated, the manner of celebration is likely to have changed. The player who landed on Christmas Day, for instance, was entitled to 'Take Two' for his dinner, but the dinner he was offered was rib of beef not turkey; and on Twelfth Night there was no nonsense about taking down Christmas cards (they had not yet been invented), the players had to sit around their Twelfth Cake and take part in a ritual for which we, like many another collector, possess the apparatus, but of which, nevertheless, no adequate account seems to have survived.

That the Survival of the Fittest means the Extinction of the Most Popular

In the old days, before folklorists appreciated that Darwin's message was addressed to them as well as everyone else, it was reasonable to speculate about the age or origin of a custom in the belief that it had been created whole. Today, when we are aware there are no ultimate answers, there are still problems we can examine with profit, and they are ones offering immensely richer rewards. We ask ourselves, for instance, why some practices disappear, while others seemingly as anachronistic continue, why some spread while others remain purely local, why some are taken seriously and others become a diversion. For many years now we have been giving attention to children's traditional games; and we find that not only do individual games rise or fall in popularity over the years, but that (this is something outsiders overlook) the make-up of the individual games may change, even though their names remain the same. And these changes may be brought about by the changes in the game's popularity. Thus a game which is in the ascendancy, which every child

wants to play as much as possible, tends to draw parts of other games into it. The playing of the game thus becomes more difficult, the rules more involved, the time required for the game's completion grows longer. Eventually the game may become such a monster it breaks up, leaving one or two residual amusements, or it may cease to be played altogether. Are games unique in faring in this way?

If we look at the history of the Epping Hunt we see that in 1829 — nine years after our race game was published — Thomas Hood 'striding in the steps of Strutt' knew the event would not last much longer. 'The Easter Chase will soon be numbered with the pastimes of past times: its dogs will have had their day, and its deer will be Fallow.' The reason, as he shows, was that the meeting had become *too popular*. Every butcher, baker, and idle spectator was now coming to see the sport, with the result that little sport took place to be seen.[11]

The history of Greenwich Fair, which was held at Easter as well as Whitsun, leads to a similar conclusion. In 1760, it is said, no fair existed: a single seller of gingerbread occupied the site. By the turn of the century, or thereabout, the crowds were such they supported even the presence of a circus. In 1838 no less than 200,000 persons were estimated to have descended on Greenwich for Easter Night; and even if descriptions did not exist the chaos can be imagined, as also the type of clientele. In 1857 *Punch* had no regrets that the fair had been stopped:

> . . .Greenwich town was upside down,
> Turned by a roaring mob;
> A crowded mass of human ass,
> Trull, ruffian, scoundrel, snob.[12]

The case of Bartholomew Fair is even more interesting because even better documented. In 1820, when our race game was published, the fair had been held for just on seven centuries (its charter had been granted by Henry I in 1133), but its end, too, was in sight; and the point we would make is that its end was due neither to a decline in popularity nor to the way the fair was conducted. When William Hone made his report on the entertainments provided in 1825 he remarked on the general excellence of the sideshows, the cleanliness of the animals, the friendliness of the showmen and freaks, and the good value (with one exception) that they offered the public. The trouble was not the fair itself but the people it attracted. At night mobs appeared from other districts who took advantage of the occasion, knocking at doors, assailing householders, committing offences against property, and rioting until three or four in the morning. That year, 1825, forty-five persons were charged with felonies, assaults, and other misdemeanours committed during the fair.[13] It all sounds very familiar. And the fact is that over and over again popular entertainments have had to be closed down because they have come to be attended too enthusiastically. Indeed it may be felt a folklorist is someone who should be able to predict trends and events. Only a romanticist, surely, lacking knowledge of both life and literature, would believe that a thousand young Mancunians could be delivered to Chelsea for the day and fighting *not* break out.

That Legends Feed on Their Own Commemoration

Enough authoritarian governments exist these days for us to know their habit of renaming streets and even cities in honour of current heroes, and of inserting new commemorations in the calendar. The date when the regime came into power will be celebrated; and there will perhaps also be an Army Day, a Freedom Day, and a day of fasting dedicated to some neighbouring territory which is coveted, and therefore in need of liberation. Traditional festivals, however, are not like this. If a festival is genuinely of the people the cause being commemorated is likely to be of little concern compared with its celebration; indeed the cause may be unknown to the celebrants, and a subject of dispute among the learned. Nobody supposes that because the people of Padstow romp a strange apparition through their streets on the first of May they are more concerned than their neighbours that summer should follow spring; or that the dancers of Abbots Bromley are more interested in achieving fertility than their contemporaries in Abbots Langley. What is honoured is not the origin of the celebration but its commemoration. Christmas, we are told, would scarcely be Christmas without plum pudding (and in confirmation

we hear of New Zealanders trying to do justice to suet in the heat of high summer); but we see all around us that Christmas can easily be Christmas without Christ. In short, the maintenance of a custom comes to be of more importance than its significance; and this is as much so with the young as with the elderly, as the grocer's boy Ralph is made to proclaim in *The Knight of the Burning Pestle*:

> And let it nere be said, for shame, that we
> the youths of London,
> Lay thrumming of our Caps at home, and
> left our custome vndone.[14]

Today no lad cares a hoot for the safety of James I and his parliament, or whether Guy Fawkes was the hero or, as now appears, the dupe in the conspiracy. Yet every boy continues to be interested in getting his hands on a half-dozen flash-bangs for 5th November. What is being remembered on this night is the previous year's celebration; and perhaps 'Bonfire Night' would not have become so big an occasion if the Gunpowder Plot had been discovered at another time of year. The early fathers of the Christian Church seem to have understood, like the International Socialists, that new customs grow strongest when grafted on indigenous roots; and it is noticeable that in English-speaking countries where Guy Fawkes Night is not celebrated, for instance in Eire and the United States, Hallowe'en remains a major festival.

Not only do legends feed on their own commemoration as, it is to be hoped, visitors to Winchester are now made aware when they are shown King Arthur's Round Table; but the folklorist needs to remember, as Dr Ellis Davidson showed in her Presidential Address in 1974, that if a tradition is particularly fantastic people like to be able to point to some natural feature or material object which proves to their satisfaction that the event really took place. The classic example, to our mind, if only in fiction, occurs when the canon tries to persuade Don Quixote that the books of chivalry are false, and that knights-errant never existed. Don Quixote replies:

> Why then, in my opinion, sir, it is yourself who are deranged and enchanted. . . To assert that there never was an Amadis in the

world nor any other of the knights-adventurers of whom so many records remain, is to say that the sun doth not enlighten, the frost produce cold, nor the earth yield sustenance. . . Who can deny the truth of the history of Peter of Provence and the fair Magalona since even to this day you may see in the king's armoury the very peg wherewith the valiant Peter steered the wooden horse that bore him through the air; which peg is somewhat larger than the pole of a coach; and near it lies the saddle of Babieca.[15]

Our own favourite present-day example occurs in the heart of London, within earshot of the Law Courts, and under Christian patronage. How many Londoners, let alone visitors from overseas, have not thrilled as they walked in the Strand and heard the bells of St Clement Danes chiming 'Oranges and Lemons.' Here, they may feel, the romance of their childhood is confirmed; and if this is what they want to feel there is probably no harm in it. Yet the reality is that when the bells were recast in 1958 and the mechanical peal installed, an extra bell had to be added so that 'Oranges and Lemons' could be played in the 'proper' key. Earlier the tune had to be modified to fit the bells. No evidence exists, as far as we know, that this church was the original of the nursery rhyme. The custom of having an annual service in which each child is given an orange or a lemon was started by the then rector in 1920.

That Today's Extraordinariness was probably also Yesterday's

Our theme so far has been that the appearance of stability is often deceptive. We will now look at the lore that the folklorist knows or suspects is old, but which is not recognised as such by those who come under its influence. Indeed here is a type of lore that would not survive unless it was thought to be new. Those adults, as well as children, who busy themselves collecting ring-pulls from drink-cans in the belief that riches are to be obtained from the accumulation of a million or so, are a case in point. They probably would not believe it, even if told, that they are the victims of a delusion that has often reoccurred; that before ring-pulls

the rumour was that a reward awaited those who could gather enought cigarette packets, and before cigarette packets it was bus tickets, and before bus tickets — more than a century ago — a fortune was said to await he who collected a million used postage stamps.

We all know that the two great preservatives of superstition are greed and anxiety; that anyone who claims the ability to spin straw into gold is assured of a following; and anyone able to arouse a specific fear which he himself is best able to mitigate will (whether his subject be demoniacal possession or constipation) receive both the gratitude and the savings of those with whom he comes into contact. However some continuations or reappearances of old fears are very subtle.

When we were at school we were taught that one of the immediate causes of the Indian Mutiny was that the cartridges for the Minié and Enfield rifles then in use were heavily greased. The story got around that the grease was pig's fat, and the sepoys believed that pig's fat was being used deliberately to make them unclean, since they had to bite off the cap of the cartridge to pour the powder into the barrel. Being British children, at the seat of Empire, we doubtless smiled at the naivety of the troops, and echoed the words of our elders that in India no story was too wild for belief if connected with religion.

The Indian Mutiny broke out in 1857. But we children were never told — since no one hitherto has pointed it out — that the story that aroused the sepoys was already current in Britain in a form only slightly more sophisticated. In 1840 Rowland Hill had introduced the penny post, with the condition that postage had to be prepaid. This was effected by the purchase either of a special envelope, or of an adhesive stamp. Contrary to expectations the official envelope (the notorious 'Mulready'), with its pretentious design showing Britannia sending news to all mankind, was laughed out of existence, which shows, incidentally, that the British in their days of power, were not always the tasteless chest-beaters their subsequent detractors like to portray. They opted for the beautifully designed but modest 'penny blacks,' as philatelists term them today, or 'Queen's heads' as people affectionately called them at the time.

There was however one snag. To make the stamp adhere to the envelope the glue had to be moistened, and the only suitable damp pad most people carry around with them is their tongue. At this time the normal adhesive was gum-arabic which was costly, and clearly was not the substance on the back of the Queen's heads. The story soon circulated that the glue was poisonous, that the most vile ingredients were employed in its manufacture, that human material was not excluded, and that those so rash as to lick the Queen's head were in danger of contracting cholera — a story scarcely made less believable by the Post Office's reluctance (or possibly inability) to divulge what in fact the substance was.

It may here be worth recording, if the absurdities of human history are within our province, that not long before the English man of letters was treating the glue like the plague, the Irish were rioting and committing arson in protest at its manufacture, since its constituent formed the chief part of their diet. The composition of the glue that Messrs Bacon & Petch were applying to the backs of the stamps was, of course, potato starch.

The scare about the glue on the backs of the postage stamps took place, as we have said, in the early 1840s. It will be remembered that until recently sponges were provided in post offices for moistening stamps; and as far as we are aware no further outcry has been raised about the glue's prescription. This does not mean however that the public has not been hugging its suspicions to its breast.

In January 1965 an underworld character known as Ginger Marks disappeared, apparently murdered, although his body has never been found. In October 1966 one of us had just finished writing a postcard in a Soho post office when the man next to us, filling in his football coupon, warned: 'Never lick a stamp.'

'Why not?' we asked.

'Never lick a stamp,' he repeated. 'You may be licking Ginger Marks.'

'How d'you mean, licking Ginger Marks?'

'Ah,' the man replied, 'he went into a glue factory, dinnen 'e? Everyone in south-east London knows that.'

That the Study of Folklore has Always Been in a State of Just-Beginning and Probably Always Will be

The Folklore Society has survived a hundred years without itself becoming a survival. The study of folklore, which started off in revolutionary fashion with a number of intellectual time-bombs which, in 1891, were — forgive the pun — effectively *diffused,* now proceeds safely, if prosaically, usually with the careful examination of some particular phenomenon, and often with splendid results. However, before we congratulate ourselves further, we might ask a final question. If, as we keep being told, nations live not so much by the realities as by their illusions; if, as Coleridge suggested, the greater part of mankind does not possess ideas but is possessed by them; and if the chief hinderance to our intellectual development is not so much what we do not know as what we think we already know, how comes it that folklore is not the most studied subject in the world?

To a folklorist every man is a capitalist, the inheritor of a treasury of formulated pleasures and prejudices, an inheritance so vast and commonplace that a lifetime is not long enough for him to recognise every assumption to which he is heir. We folklorists tend, therefore, to be like the old-time museum curators who were uninterested in anything from the past that was ordinary and snatched only at what was costly or extraordinary, with the result that our museums today are stuffed with examples of what was strange in the past, and with very little of what was typical.

Credulity, it appears to us, prospers in an age of disillusionment. The less capable people are of wonder the more ready they are to be beguiled by wonders. Like moths attracted to a flame, little men are fascinated by the mysterious and far-fetched; while, unhappily, a culture that becomes understandable and undemanding rapidly loses its appeal. The reason, incidentally, children gave up saying 'One-ery, two-ery, ickery Ann' in favour of 'Eena meena macka racka' was, we suspect, that versions of 'One-ery, two-ery, ickery, Ann' were coming to sound too much like ordinary English.

Yet the omens for the next hundred years of folklore-study are surely propitious. At long last the ghosts of Miss Moberly and Miss Jourdain have been laid, and men of culture who felt obliged to believe that something paranormal took place on an August afternoon at Versailles — since it was reported by two ladies of distinction — can now accept that there was a rational explanation.[16] Likewise, Dr Margaret Murray's covens are no longer likely to be given group-rates for excursions through our literature, when the existence of contemporary covens can be seen to be the product rather than the proof of her theories. And, just in time for our centenary, we have even had a correspondent in *Folklore*, an American, giving us as vivid a description as we could wish of how he himself has walked on fire, offering convincing testimony that Andrew Lang's prediction was correct: it would be found anyone could do it.[17]

The prime business of the folklorist is to identify and investigate what is known, not to make a marvel of what is unknown. We have only to look in our journal in recent years, for instance at the penetrating yet sympathetic account of the Fire Festival that takes place annually at Allendale in Northumberland on New Year's Eve, to see the shape that folklore studies are going to take.[18]

Nothing that we are saying, it must be emphasised, is being said to make little of life's essential mystery. A person would need to be remarkably insensitive to be unaware that there is more to this world than we shall ever know. But the strangeness of our existence is not diminished, rather the contrary, when we learn that each of us has the ability (given the courage) to walk on fire. And the story of man becomes even more intriguing when it is revealed that a seemingly ancient Northumbrian fire festival started only in the days of Queen Victoria. The fact is, that however many disguises we strip from the face of folklore, there is always likely to be another underneath. Indeed the study of folklore will probably still be in its infancy even when it is enabling Man to see with his own two eyes rather than continuing to allow him to be led by the nose.

Notes

1. Mary Douglas, 'Heathen Darkness, Modern Piety', *New Society* (12th March, 1970), 432.

2. Iona and Peter Opie, *The Oxford Dictionary of Nursery Rhymes* (Oxford, 1951), 147-8.

3. *idem, The Lore and Language of Schoolchildren* (Oxford, 1959), see esp. introductory Chap.

4. *idem, Children's Games in Street and Playground* (Oxford, 1969), 39-57.

5. It is almost unfair to give a single reference here, when statements like this are legion, but the particular words quoted are from *Notes and Queries,* 7th Series, IV (1887), 286.

6. Henry Carrington Bolton, *The Counting-Out Rhymes of Children* (London, 1888), 94-100.

7. See in particular E. Sidney Hartland, 'The Science of Folklore', *The Folk-Lore Journal,* III (1885), 117; Moses Gaster, 'The Modern Origin of Fairy Tales', *ibid.,* V (1887), 339-51; George Laurence Gomme, *The Handbook of Folklore* (London, 1890), 2; Richard M. Dorson, *The British Folklorists: A History* (London, 1968), esp. 200-25.

8. Peter Opie, 'The Collection of Folklore in England', *Journal of the Royal Society of Arts,* CI (1953), 697.

9. William Holloway, *A General Dictionary of Provincialisms* (Lewes, 1838), 124.

10. A. R. Wright, *British Calendar Customs: England* (London, 1936), I, 43-44.

11. Thomas Hood, 'The Epping Hunt', *Poetical Works* (London, n.d.), 310-25. The original date of publication was 1829. See also the advertisement to the second edition, reprinted in *Poetical Works*, 326.

12. 'Elegy on Greenwich Fair', *Punch,* XXXII (18th April, 1857), 157.

13. William Hone, 'Visit to Bartholomew Fair', *Every-Day Book* (London, 1826), 1167-1202. See also succeeding columns and Henry Morley, *Memoirs of Bartholomew Fair* (London, 1892).

14. Francis Beaumont, *The Knight of the Burning Pestle* (London, 1613) sig.I 2v.

15. Motteux's translation, first published 1700-03.

16. See Joan Evans, 'An End to *An Adventure*', *Encounter* (October, 1976), 33-47. This solving of the mystery of the Trianon is the more effective in that Dame Joan Evans, as the editor of the best-selling psychic classic, was a reluctant disbeliever. Full justice is not done, however, to the earlier work of Lucille Iremonger, *The Ghosts of Versailles*, (1957).

17. John Harmon McElroy, 'Fire Walking', *Folklore,* LXXXVIII (1977), 113-15.

18. Venetia Newall, 'The Allendale Fire Festival in Relation to its Contemporary Social Setting', *Folklore,* LXXXV (1974), 93-103.

From Illumination to Folksong; the Armed Snail, a Motif of Topsy-Turvy Land

ROGER PINON   Royal Belgian Folklore Commission

ONE of the most famous slanders against a European nation is the saying that *Itali sunt imbelles*, 'the Italians do not fight', meaning that when confronted with a battle they flee at the first opportunity.

The saying, which was revived during World War II, had already been quoted during the First World War, after the Caporetto battle. In fact it had been attributed long before, in 1860, to General Christophe de La Moricière, or to a minister de Lamoricière in 1849, and, apart from these two not very clearly differentiated personages, to Adolphe Thiers and a couple of other French politicians. But the first literary example of the French saying, *les Italiens ne se battent pas*, is to be found in a diplomatic letter by the famous French novelist Stendhal, alias Henri Beyle, in 1831. After a battle at Rimini on the 25th of March in that year he wrote: *Rovigo était exalté en quelque sorte par le petit combat de Rimini. Que l'on dise encore, s'écriait-on, que les Italiens ne se battent pas!* 'Rovigo was quite exalted by the little engagement at Rimini. Let people keep saying, they exclaimed, that the Italians do not fight!'[1]

Benedetto Croce,[2] the famous Italian philosopher, was first to recognise that the slander predated 1831, and that it is recorded in Germany as well as France. For the Germans, indeed, the Italians are *imbelles*, 'unfit for making war'. This idea arose, he says, in the sixteenth century, when the Italians did not oppose the Teutonic, French, and Spanish occupations. He also declares, and he is right, that this opinion was anticipated in the tale of the Lombard warrior trembling before an armed snail — hence the French proverbial saying *assaillir la limace*; 'to assail the slug' (see Appendix 1).

It is of immense importance to understand the origin and development of folk attitudes which are contemptuous of another nation, and are so deep-rooted as to be accepted automatically and regarded as unquestionable. I will therefore suggest a number of explanations which will help us to understand these attitudes.

1. An eleventh-century *Vita Hadriani*, which mentions Pope Hadrian II who summoned Charlemagne to fight the Lombard King Didier, refers to the latter as a panic-stricken coward.[3]

2. From this and several other similar texts we have the tale of the Lombard army struck with sudden terror, an eleventh-century motif which persisted until the end of the thirteenth century.[4]

3. From this motif, probably incorporating another showing a snail attacking an armed man, derives a twelfth-century Latin pseudo-Ovidian text entitled *De Lombardo et lumaca* (see Appendix 3).[5] John of Salisbury foreshadowed this in 1159, when he wrote to Thomas Becket that 'the French mock at the people of Emilia and Liguria' saying that when they are attacked by a tortoise, 'they write their wills, summon their neighbourhood and implore the assistance of armed soldiers' (see Appendix 2).[6]

4. Giovanni Villani's *Istorie fiorentine* of 1320 describes how the French laughed at the Lombards, saying that they were afraid of a slug or snail (see Appendix 1, no.8).[7] He adds, incidentally, that the French were afraid of the Viscontis' flag, which showed a coiled adder with a man in its jaws, easily confused with a snail from a distance.[8] In Froissart's Chronicles[9] something similar is mentioned, and Odofredo de Bolonia, possibly in the sixteenth century, notes that the French used

to insult the Italians with wall-graffiti of a slug or snail (see Appendix 2).[10]

Thus snail, slug and tortoise were indiscriminately used to caricature not only Lombards, Ligurians or Emilians, but also Italians in general.[11]

5. However, the fact that the satirical poem about the snail and the Lombard was written in Italy and not in France points to a different quarrel, between the Lombards and other Italians. Liudprando, bishop of Cremona in the tenth century, explains to Prince Niceforo Foca: 'We, Lombards, Saxons, Franks, Lorrainers, Bavarians, Suevians, and Burgundians disdain those Romans so much that, when we are angry, we say no more outrageous word to a personal enemy than "You Roman!" We understand under that word all possible lowness, cowardice, untruthfulness and vice.'[12] But this is part of an ancient quarrel between the Romans and Barbarians. Saint Eligius encountered it in the seventh century, when he was reproaching pagans from a country village near Noyon for persisting with their old traditions, and they insulted him: 'Never, you Roman, will you persuade us to renounce our old customs!' Many missionaries are said to have heard this same insult of 'Roman' from Germanic peoples.[13]

6. This attitude must certainly have provoked a retort, and indeed the word Lombard came to mean 'coward' and 'traitor'. Marguerite Zweifel[14] explored the semantic evolution of *Langobardus-Lombardus* brilliantly in 1921. The problem is to know whether the acquired meanings were attached to a tale already in existence, or on the contrary derived from the tale.[15]

Obviously the second hypothesis would be proved if documents showed that the snail symbolised cowardice before the tale came into existence. Unfortunately, despite the opinion of the German romanist Adolf Tobler,[16] the snail is never to my knowledge a symbol of cowardice. Of course a snail is slow, lumpish and ugly; it is also regarded as an ostentatious, mistrustful, and base animal, and much more, but if it is weak and insignificant, it is also stubborn. Sometimes its ambitions are unscrupulous, or resentful, so that it is used as a symbol of the vengeful, oppressed masses; and it is because of this implacability that it is the hero of the mocking tale already referred to.[17]

So it seems that the word Lombard was used to imply 'coward' before the tale was shifted onto the snail. Perhaps it replaced a tortoise, a suggestion which should be investigated.[18] Marguerite Zweifel correctly assumes a link between medieval literature and French and German denigration of Italian martial courage. Indeed there are numerous passages celebrating Charlemagne's victory over King Didier. What struck the epic poets was the strange fact that Lombardy was conquered without any great resistance from the King and his army. Four times they had refused to give battle, and then the battle at Pavia was drawn for a lengthy period. However, the *Chevalerie Ogier*, which dates from the end of the twelfth century, *Aimeri de Narbonne*, from the same period, and a few other texts, such as the *Roman de Thèbes* of 1150-1155, *Perceval* by Chrestien de Troyes, written between 1169 and 1188, a Provençal lay by Peire d'Alvernhe, predating 1173, and John of Salisbury before 1149, describe either the king or his army as cowards. One of them says that the troops broke into a rout at Pavia without any apparent reason. But the poets drew their matter from the *Vita Hadriani* already referred to, which sides with the Pope against Didier, probably for political reasons, since Papal policy led eventually to the re-establishment of the Roman Empire in Western Europe. The *Vita* makes the king a panic-stricken coward, whose army took to flight, and the author, a St Gall monk, describes him as seized four times by ascending bouts of restlessness, anxiety, fear, and panic: *aestuare coepit*, 'he begins to feel unquiet'; *mortisque desiderius*, 'wishing he were dead'; *frigido honor a frigidiori deferebatur populo*, 'an awestruck nation is dishonoured by one who was filled with an even greater terror'. *Pauli Diaconi continuatio tertia*, dating from the twelfth century, repeats the story of the Lombards' flight, and Godfrey of Viterbo, who died in 1190, says that 'when King Charlemagne attacks, the Ligurian party is put to flight, and Didier's army turns tail'.[19]

Of course these texts do not prove Didier's cowardice: they are too one-sided to be regarded as historical documents. On the contrary, history implies that his policy was to avoid war, and that the conflict was mainly political. Certainly Lombard soldiers were well thought of in the Middle Ages.

Marguerite Zweifel tells us that the motif of Lombard cowardice does not appear after the decline of this type of literature in the fourteenth century, though it had already become a stereotype, applied, for example, in *Aimeri de Narbonne* to Didier's successor, King Boniface. In fact, as Gaston Paris states in his *Histoire poétique de Charlemagne*, the Lombardy campaign had soon been forgotten, until it reappeared in the twelfth century as a piece of literary exotica.

7. Does this mean that literature had no effect on public opinion? Far from it. Jacques de Vitry's *Historia Occidentalis* refers to the fact that Lombard students were being insulted at the turn of the twelfth and thirteenth centuries as *imbelles*.[20] At the end of the fifteenth century Philippe de Commynes[21] reports that the French apparently refused the name of men to Italians, while Italians said that the French were more than men when entering their country, but less than women on leaving it. Similar gracious remarks were already current at the turn of the fourteenth and fifteenth centuries, as shown in a partisan poem, favouring the Burgundian cause during the Hundred Years' Wars: 'Qui vouldra la paix conquérir – Du roy de France et d'Angleterre, – Seize personnes fault conquérir, – Deux en fault de chaque terre: – Deux Bourguignons de pasience – Et deux Brettons de conscience; – Sans ordure deux Allemans – Et sans flatterie deux Normans; – Et fault sans orgueil deux Liégeois – Et sans trayson deux Engloys; – Et puis fault deux hardis Lombards, – Et sans insolence deux Picards; Et pour mettre la chose à fin, – Deux prud'homes de Limosin. – Hoigne qui groigne, – Vive Bourgoigne!'[22]

Each quality referred to has, of course, to be understood ironically: 'He who wants to achieve peace – And subdue the kings of France and England – Must conquer sixteen persons, – Two from each country: – Two Burgundians endowed with patience, – And two Bretons with a conscience; – Two Germans who are not filthy, – And two Normans who are not flatterers; – And two Liégeois who are not proud, – And two Englishmen without perfidy; – And then two bold Lombards, – And two Picards without impertinence; – And to put a good end to it, – Two men of integrity from Limousin. – Let him cry who grumbles, – Long live [the dukes of] Burgundy!'

A similar text from the end of the century stresses, by using a different introduction, that the qualities attributed to each nation are to be understood in reverse: *Recette pour guérir l'epydemie – Mais que l'on n'y croye mie*; 'Prescription for curing an epidemic – But don't believe in it'.[23] It claims that by mixing two Burgundians, two Bretons, two Germans, two Normans, two Lombards, two Picards, two Frenchmen, two Englishmen, two Flemings, two Limousins, crushing them in a mortar, and dipping one's bread in the mixture, a good cure-all against epidemics is achieved. *Cil est vray, nul n'y contredie*; 'This is true, let nobody contradict it'.

By the end of the fifteenth century, we find a French poem summarising the Lombards' supposed failings: they were *chiches, avares, jaloux, couards*; 'stingy, miserly, jealous, cowardly' – nearly the same list of adjectives as in Jacques de Vitry three centuries before, when he described them as 'miserly, malicious and unfit for making war'.[24]

An unfavourable opinion long persisted in western France as, for example, in a novel by Ernest Perochon published in 1936: *Criant contre ceux de l'abbaye voisine, ils les appelaient salauds, putiers, rufians, bougres, trafiquants, lombards, voleurs, regrattiers d'hosties*; 'Shouting at those from the neighbouring abbey, they called them dirty dogs, pimps, ruffians, pigs, traffickers, lombards, thieves, pedlars of the host'.[25]

This illustrates how long-lived was French disparagement of the Lombards. At one stage, in the sixteenth century, it was apparently also extended specifically to Piedmontese, as a passage from Remy Belleau, shows: *Et ce soldat, ce Piémontez – Retiré comme un limaçon*; 'and that soldier, that Piedmontese – Hidden away like a snail'.[26] But previous quotations prove that all Italians were included.

After all this situation is not new. Commenting upon John of Salisbury's joke (see Appendix 2), Marguerite Zweifel points out that it was created in a milieu where, instead of Latin, vulgar languages were used – presumably Italian or French. In the translations of the joke into Latin, Lombard is sometimes rendered by *Lombardus (Langobardus)*, sometimes by *Italus*. Indeed *Lombardus* means North Italian, as contrasted with *Romanus*. Emphasising this point, Giovanni Antonucci posits a Roman origin for the story of the snail and the Lombards.[27] The joke, in this case, would derive not from the Lombards' cowardice, but would hark back to the adventures of their king Alboin (561-573), who married the frigid Rosmunda. From this Antonucci argues that the tale originated in Roman curial and clerical circles, and later spread to France, where it was reinterpreted as we have seen.

The weakness of this suggestion is simply lack of positive evidence; no written source is quoted, and the lapse of time from the sixth to the twelfth century, when the joke receives its first textual mention, is too long to be plausible without any support. On the other hand, what would the snail really symbolise, should the hypothesis turn out to be true? Maybe the female sex organ, and indeed there is a very old symbolic link: for Plautus the Latin word *limax* meant a courtesan or a whore.[28]

8. Whatever may be the origin of the connection between *Lombard* and 'coward' or 'traitor', it is worth noting here that Erasmus knew the contempt many Europeans had for the Italian as a soldier, and refers to it in his *Adagia, Myconius calvus: Veluti si quis Scytham dicat eruditum, Italum bellacem, negociatorem integrum, militem pium, aut Poenum fidem*; 'it is as if someone said that the Scythian is learned, the Italian bellicose, a banker honest, a soldier pious, and a Phoenician trustworthy'.[29] But the protests of Lombard and Italian friends obliged him to delete the ironic use of his *Italus bellax* from subsequent editions. Rabelais, too, shares this opinion of the Italians, and in *Pantagruel*,[30] in the list of books in Saint Victor's library, there is one called *Poiltronismus rerum Italicarum, authore magistro Bruslefer* — a clear allusion to supposed Italian spinelessness.

Unlike Erasmus, Montaigne never had to eat his words on the Italians; it is true that he was in France, and he had taken the precaution of attributing his remarks on the Italian national psychology to a 'clever Italian': 'An Italian lord once remarked in my presence, to the disadvantage of his nation: That the Italians' subtlety and the vivacity of their conceptions were so great that they foresee dangers and accidents which the future may send to them from so far away that we must not find it strange if often in wartime they provided for their security even before having recognised the impending danger. . . .' (see Appendix 2).

9. I shall give only one other example of how this type of deprecation of the Italians has embedded itself very deeply in French popular opinion. In 1867, at a time when France and Italy were officially friends, Henri Carion wrote in his *Arména d'Jérôme Pleum'coq*, using the Picard dialect of French Hainault — more precisely of Berlaimont — that 'the Italians will certainly invent a machine to dig mouse-holes in which to take shelter when they see bullets on the way, or flashes of thunder, and they will not come out of them until they realise there is only one enemy left against ten of them'.[31]

10. The association of the Lombard motif and the snail does not prove the prior existence of the snail tale, but suggests their coexistence and mutual influence upon each other. According to Francesco Novati, an Italian philologist, the snail motif derives from miniatures; for Baist, a German romanist, it arose among itinerant minstrels. Both these see the attempt to slander Lombard soldiers as responsible for its diffusion, and date it from the beginning of the twelfth century.

The weakness of the first suggestion is evident. Illuminations or miniatures representing a confrontation between a snail and a man-at-arms all date from between 1284 and 1325; and of course none of them clearly shows that the soldier is a Lombard. As these portrayals date from a period at least one and a half centuries after the French story about the Lombards became widespread, it seems likely that the illuminations derive from the slander, not vice versa. There is another textual allusion to combat with a snail, in the *Roman de Renart* (1179):

Bien furent quatre cent vilain
Qui sont de moult tresmale estrace.
Chascuns porte baston ou mace
Ou flaël ou maçüe ou hache;
Bien combatront a la limace.

'They were no less than four hundred villeins — Who were of very rough extraction. — Each carried a stick or a mace — Or a flail or a club or an axe; — They will fight fiercely against the snail.'[32] But one must take into account that *Renart* (Reynaert) parodies feudal epics; therefore there is not necessarily any inconsistency with the suggestion already put forward, that snail and Lombard were connected from the start.

Now let us consider how the snail came to be associated with battle scenes in Gothic art. In the absence of further texts, we must now turn to the illuminations. The best authority on this subject is Lilian Randall, who dealt with the matter at some length in 'The Snail in Gothic Marginal Warfare'.[33] She examined over 70 marginal representations of the motif in 29 manuscripts, to which I have been able to add a few (see Appendix 4). Among these manuscripts, 26 at least date from 1284 to 1310 and 9 from 1310 to 1325. They include psalters, prayer-books, breviaries, pontificals, decretals, moral poem books and literary works such as *Lancelot du Lac* and *Tristram*, as well as pedagogical work.

The miniatures representing the armed, fighting snail appear along with many others, mostly belonging to the extensive domain of Topsy-Turvy Land. A notable feature is that drawings derived from literary themes, or relying on travesty, appear more frequently than those which are simply fantastic or grotesque.

The motif of the armed snail displays some variety. Frequently we have a 'knight armed with mace or sword confronting a snail whose horns are extended and often pointed like arrows. . .'; and commonly the 'adversary is a man in a short tunic, or occasionally nude, bearing an axe, spear, sword, or slingshot. In one instance a nude woman opposes the snail with spear and shield. Numerous scenes of a knight dropping his sword or kneeling submissively before his diminutive foe accentuate [the satire].' Sometimes women are shown begging a knight not to risk attacking the animal. The warrior may also be a monkey with a sword or cross-bow, or riding a horse with a spear in his hand, or a cat driving a snail away with a mouse's head; alternatively a dog, a drake, a ram, or even a hare may confront the snail. Not even this is a complete list: one can instance still more eccentric scenes, such as a man riding a snail and pursuing a stag, or a fox fleeing before a snail, both of which illustrate the topsy-turvy-land theme.

According to Lilian Randall, 'the predilection for the literary snail combat theme can be explained by the manifest current anti-Lombard sentiment; the rapid diffusion of the motif reflects the international character of the Lombards' pro-fessional activities [in finance]; and finally the concentration of the motif in late thirteenth and early fourteenth-century manuscripts mirrors the intense reaction to a current development which gradually lost its appeal along with its novelty. What better means for expressing popular opinion than by an amusing drawing in the margin of a manuscript which could be interpreted at will as a general representation of cowardice or as a specific allusion to Lombards, in some cases serving perhaps as a reminder of an object pawned or to be redeemed by the original owner of the manuscript.'[34]

The snail motif has also been carved in stone and wood. Formerly two reliefs were visible at Lyons cathedral, one representing a knight kneeling before a snail to obtain pardon, the other a man threatening a dog-headed snail with an axe.[35] At Dijon, in an arched window-panel at the front of the famous 'Maison du Miroir', a fully-armed knight was shown brandishing his sword before a gigantic, alarmingly behorned snail.[36] The same motif was later reproduced on a stone in the wall of the arch of Dijon castle entrance. In the thirteenth century a knight, dropping his weapons when confronted with a snail, was to be seen on the rood-screen at Chartres cathedral (see Appendix 4). In a stall at Barcelona cathedral, a carved snail appears on one side of a rosette, while on the other there is a knight: this may reflect our motif.[37] On a stall in Bristol cathedral, Violet Alford observed a scene dating from the fourteenth century, showing a snail near to a man with a whip or a slingshot, facing another man: he in turn is extending an arm in a gesture which may be interpreted as a movement of defence.[38] To be added to these carvings is a draughtsman representing a knight fighting against a snail, dating from 1320 and preserved at the British Museum: the animal is standing on a tower, while the knight is armed with a spear and carries a shield.[39]

Lilian Randall thinks that the iconographic theme disappeared after 1330, only to reappear in the fifteenth century, in the *Calendrier des Bergers*, as a method of ridiculing the rural militia which had recently been created.[40] It is indeed that century which gives us the *Très riches heures du duc de Berry*, the 'Maison du Miroir' in Dijon, a particular Flemish prayer-book with bearing on the present study, and the lawyer Bartoldo de

Brescia's manuscript (see Appendix 4, B, 2).

Let us examine particularly the *Grand Calendrier et Compost des Bergers, composé par le Berger de la Grand'-Montagne, fort utile et profitable à gens de tous estats, réformé selon le Calendrier de N.S. Père le pape Grégoire XIII* (1572-1585), which was published in 1633 in Lyons.[41] Though traceable, as we shall see, to 1488,[42] the *Débat des gens d'armes et d'une femme contre un lymasson* can here only be referenced to 1493; it is 'the debate of men-at-arms and a woman against a snail'. Both text and illustration are older, for they appear in a manuscript edition of the calendar illuminated by Antoine Vérard for King Charles VIII, who reigned from 1483 to 1498. Charles Nisard, who posits the precise date and provided the original evidence for the early example, rightly describes it as an attractive tale. The first personage is called the *Femme à Hardy Courage*, 'the Woman with a Bold Courage', because she is first to address the snail, standing threateningly, horns extended, at the top of a watch-tower on a fortified castle.[43] She is armed with a distaff, with which she threatens the snail, accusing it of ravaging the vines. Emboldened by her example, the men-at-arms, carrying broadswords or clubs, promise to assail the castle, despite the snail's menacing stance, and to eat the animal in a sauce which no Lombard ever tasted before. They tell it to draw its horns in, to which the snail responds that it will not be intimidated, that it carries its house on its back, a sign of power and foresight, and that it has neither flesh nor bones and is therefore inedible. It adds that its horns are like those of an ox, which it uses instead of cudgels — an excellent weapon with which to beat the besiegers. This paraphrases an iconographic subject appearing as early as the fourteenth century, in the *Missale Romanum* of Amiens illuminated by Pierre de Raimbaucourt (see Appendix 4, C, 2).[44] A warrior, armed with a slingshot and accompanied by his wife, who is holding a distaff, stand behind a shield planted in the ground, facing the onslaught of a snail.

This version of the armed snail motif survived through three centuries. But its ideological content came to differ from that in the Gothic illuminations of feudal-epic times: for now the snail is no longer the instrument through which an insult is directed at a knight, whether Italian or not, but the representative of the people in revolt against those who exploit them. In these various carvings, illuminations and other pictures, the snail, valiant against cringing warriors, and the very epitome of Topsy-Turvy Land, parallels the snail I have discussed in a previous study; insolent and rebellious, it characterises the discontent of the oppressed.

The transition between the two sets of illuminations is shown in a miniature from a manuscript edition of the *Jeu de Saint Nicolas*, which paints a knight attacking a hare and a snail simultaneously; he has, however, to be egged on by a woman armed with a distaff with which she prods him, while the two animals stand firm (see Appendix 4, A, 3). Evidently the role of the woman gradually developed, until she became the main protagonist.

Finally a word about the origin of the illuminations: with a few exceptions, they come from northern France, Flanders and England. Between 1284 and 1310, out of 22 manuscripts Lilian Randall observes that 11 are northern French, 7 Franco-Flemish, 4 English; from 1311 to 1325, 3 are Flemish, 3 English, 1 northern French. The Italian manuscripts came immediately after 1330, and seem to be only 2 or 3 in number.

We must now consider how the motif with which we are concerned achieved a popularity sufficient to make it widespread in European folklore. Ample evidence shows this to have been the case. First one must be clear that this popularity cannot possibly derive from the manuscripts or marginal miniatures. The number of people who saw them was certainly very restricted. On the contrary, the motif found a place in the manuscripts because it was a tale already known to those who read and possessed them. Considering the contents of the manuscripts, we can be sure that they were mainly clerics, that is to say cultured people who were associated with the more influential social classes of their period. This helps to explain how the miniatures derive from a mock fight between a Lombard and a snail, slug or tortoise. The adoption of the same motif by the folk involves an evolutionary process, via representations of the tale on paper, stone or wood, bringing it to the notice of ever lower echelons of society. In most cases, portrayals of this type were probably linked to specific problems.

The change of audience begins with the use of a snail as an important character in the *Roman de*

Renart. During the siege of Malpertuis, Reynaert (the fox) climbs the tower of his castle, recounts his exploits, praises the quality of the ramparts, and announces that he has gathered provisions for seven years. After six months he gets out of his castle one night and binds each of the animals to a tree, with the exception of Tardif, the snail. Tardif then frees all the prisoners, but he is so excited that he cuts a bit off each of their tails together with the rope which bound them. The snail is flag-bearer of the lion's army, and when the fox sees him, he tries to take refuge in his castle. The snail catches him by the feet, and brings him to the king; but before delivering the prisoner to the king's guards, he strikes him with his sword. In branch XI[45] (1195) the situation is inverted: Reynaert knocks him half senseless with a tambourine, takes his sword away and stabs him (see Appendix 5).[46]

Tardif was a character who acquired considerable prestige, and he is twice alluded to in the second part of the *Miracles de Nostre Dame* (see Appendix 5). It is possible that an illustration to the *Metamorphoses* by Ovid, done by the Nuremberg artist Jost Amman in 1574, recalls Tardif.[47] Alexander is sitting on a throne carried by an elephant; going ahead of him, a crane proclaims his virtues; next, a dwarf servant marches in a proud attitude, with an olive branch in one hand and leading a captive ostrich with the other; before them, a short warrior with an axe and a scimitar mounts the steps of a platform on which some kind of exotic animal is standing, blowing a horn to announce the return of the conqueror. A snail, on the main dais, seems to be reviewing the cortège.

In a book of emblems dated 1635, an illustration shows 'a man on an ass, preceded by a snail slowly ascending a hill towards a sphere at the top. Below a man holding a thong, galloping a stag towards a globe which represents the world. In the margin the inscription, *Da mihi froena timor; Da mihi calcar amor.* Signed: 'Ro[-bert] Vaughan fecit'. Here, too, there may have been an allusion to Tardif as a flag-bearer, but it is more probable that the snail is simply being used as a symbol of slowness.[48]

In a tale recorded by Charles Deulin from Condé in French Flanders, we find a twentieth-century allusion to Tardif: a small hunchback,

called Caracol, meaning snail, is victorious over a giant, to whom a beautiful girl was to have been delivered. In derision at the giant's defeat, Caracol sings the children's charm for snails: *Caracole, – bistécole, – montre tes cornes, cornes!*; 'Snail, push your horns out!'[49]

Reverting to the main stream of our discussion, we find the snail appearing in yet another role in the thirteenth century. It is now a character in those well-known improvisations, which were the first sign of a literary revolt against the established genres and their rules.[50] One of them goes as follows: *Un ours emplumés – fist semer uns blés – de Douvre à Wissent; – uns oignons pelez – estoit aprestés – de chanter devant, – qant sor un rouge olifant – vint uns limeçons armés – qui lor aloit escriant: – 'Fil a putain, sà venez! – Je versefie en dormant'*; 'A plumed bear – Had a corn-field sowed – From Dover to Wissant; – A peeled onion – Was prepared – To go ahead singing, – When on a red elephant – There came an armed snail – Who was riding and shouting: – "Whores' sons, come on! – I write poetry while sleeping".'

Another poem of the same kind says: *Quant uns limeçons armez – Hautemen Monjoie escrie. . .* 'When an armed snail [appears] – Montjoy loudly shouts. . .' Yet another example goes like this: *La feist tout craventer – Si ne fust uns limeçons – Qui la terre ot a garder – Qui commanda deux oiseaux – Quatre larrons trainer*; 'Everything would have been destroyed – Had there not been a snail – Who had to watch over the land – [And] who ordered two birds – To drag four thieves away'.

An English rhyme noted by James Halliwell-Phillipps is closely analogous to this: 'Sneel, snaul, – Robbers are coming to put down your wall! – Sneel, snaul, – Robbers are coming to steal your corn, – Coming at four o'clock in the morn'.[51] This situation is the reverse of the one in the *Compost des bergers*: the people become the snail's allies against its enemies. Fundamentally, though, the idea is the same, since the implication in each case is that the snail is very well armed. It can even be argued that the snail's role in a further doggerel derives from Tardif's position as a standard-bearer – a parody of a parody: *Uns lymeçons mande – Gent de huppelande – Sor deus syminiaus*; 'A snail summons – Some proper dandies – Seated upon two simonists. [?]' In fact the snail is not alone in epitomising warriorship in this type of parody; in another rhyme a butterfly takes up arms before daylight, to take part in some game: *Ne fust une pale-vole – Qui s'arma devant le jour – Por le gieu de la grimole....* This can be compared with an example from a different type of verse-lying-songs, in this instance one from Poitou: *Sur les ailes d'un papillon – J'allai faire la guerre*; 'On a butterfly's wings – I went and made war'.

In a lying-song published by Jacques Mangeant at Caen in 1615, Tardif kills a lion instead of making the fox prisoner.[52] This can possibly be traced to the fifteenth century: *J'ai veu un limasson en guerre – Qui jettoit un lion par terre – Et dessous lui s'assujettir*; 'I have seen a warring snail – Who was smiting the ground with a lion – And punishing it with him'. In a similar old German song, the date of which is unclear, a snail kills two lions: *Dô sach ich einen snecken – Zwêne lewen toeten*; 'There I saw a snail – Killing two lions'. This motif is clearly comparable with that in a rhyme by Philippe de Remi, Sire de Beaumanoir, written before 1280: *Li piés d'un sueron – Feri un lyon – Si k'il le navra*; 'A mite's foot – Hit a lion – So as to hurt him'.

The lying-song is more akin to the rhymes and doggerels discussed in the preceding section than to eighteenth-century nonsense poetry. The following song, apparently middle-Dutch, though the actual origin is obscure, depicts a *miles gloriosus* who owes something to the Lombard of earlier times:

Ende doen ic door dat wout reet, – daer moetet mi een slecke: – was ic niet een coene man? – Ic dorst mijn mest wel trecken! – [Refrain] Nu moghi horen, hoe coene dat ic si – op alle mijn ghelt! – Wie dat van mi hebben wil, – die come int velt! 'And as I was riding through that wood, – There I met a snail: – Was I not manly? – I dared to draw my knife! – [Refrain] Now you may hear how bold I am, – By all my wealth! – He who will get it from me, – Has but to come to the battle-field!'

Ende moete mi dan een velthoen, – ic dorst dat wel bedwinghen, – ende steke het dat hooft al door den tuin, – ic dorst daer wel over springhen! 'And then I met a partridge, – I dared to overcome it, – And as it fluttered hither and thither – I even dared jump over it!' *Ende waer ic dan ghewapent – van hoofden tot den voeten, – ende*

moete mi dan een vette capoen, – ic dorsten ooc wel groeten! 'And if I were armed from top to toe – And a fat capon should meet me, – I should certainly make bold to greet it!'[53]

The snail in lying-songs is shown eating, for example in those from Poitou: *Dans le feu je vis un limaçon – Qui mangeait de l'avoine*;[54] or from Ile-de-France: *Ce qui doit bien vous surprendre, – C'est que j'ai vu trois colimaçons – Manger vingt-quatre livres de viande – Et autant de bottes d'oignons.*[55] Alternatively, it is sometimes a heavy smoker, as at Hiberville (Quebec): *Un grand monstre de limace – Qui fumait comme un soldat*;[56] in the Gapençais, Nice, Brussels and Ile-de-France, on the other hand, it is putting on its trousers, this in a counting-out rhyme derived from a lying-song: *Un limaçon – Dans un flacon – Enfilait sa culotte.*[57] A German-Swiss rhyme has it kneading dough: *Wunder, Wunder über Wunder, – Wi di Schnegge chönnid chnete, – Das nimmt mi Wunder*,[58] while at Kempen in northern Belgium two snails prepare a threshing floor: *Daar waren twee slekken – De schurr aan't plekken; – Ei, dat graf mij wonder – Dat die slekken – Zoo kosten plekken...*[59] and in a Flemish lying-song noted in Wambeek two snails drag a cart full of manure: *Ik zag twee slekken 'nen mestwagen trekken – Wat mij zoo een wonder was – Wonder, ja wonder...*[60] A French poem says: *J'ai rencontré trois limaçons – Qui labouraient mon pré; – Venez tous voir! – Qui labouraient mon pré, – Ne venez pas!*,[61] a reference to ploughing, but in another from Quercy: *Y trobo soun qu'uno agasso – Qu'ambé la co dailhado un prat; – Lou limaou andé sas cournetos – Lou y tenio dé derrama*; '[The hare] finds there [in the church] nobody but a crow – Who was mowing a meadow with its tail; – The snail with its little horns – Was tossing the grass'.[62] In Picardy snails are of religious bent, being on their way to the offertory: *Et pi ches lémichons cornus – Qu'il alint à l'ofrande*,[63] and Ireland produces a rather eccentric reference: *Chonnaic mé an Pápa ag cardáil bharraigh Dia Luain, – Silide a' pardáil sráid Lunnainn le tuaigh....* 'I saw the Pope carding tow on Monday, – A snail paring a London street with a hatchet....'[64]

There are probably additional examples of the snail's Topsy-Turvy Land to be found in other lying-songs, a genre which is in fact widespread. I shall only remark here that in the Netherlands an echo of the Lombard soldier is to be found in the mention of his homeland in lying-songs from North Holland and Friesland. First in Dutch: *Koekeloere is mijn naam, – Ik wil gaan leren vrijen – In't land van Lombardijen – Toen hij in Lombardije kwam, – Raad eens wat hij daar vernam...* 'Tooreloore is my name, – I will go and learn courting – In the country of Lombardy. – And guess what he heard tell – When he arrived in Lombardy...';[65] and in Frisian: *Ik wil je wat fertellen, – Un lêgen, wat ik kan: – Ik sag 'n mölen flêgen, – De müller d'r agter an. – As ik in Lammerdiden kwam, – Sag ik dâr so'n grôt wunner an...* 'I will tell you something, – A lie which I know: – I saw a mill flying, – The miller behind it. – When I came to Lombardy, – I saw a great wonder....'[66] The term *Lombardije*, as used in the Dutch example, later became *Plompardije*, a joke name influenced by *plomp*, the same as English plump but with another meaning, that of 'thick' or 'dull-witted'. This is used in a Dutch proverb: *hij komt van Plompardije, niet van Scherpenisse*; 'he comes from numb-skull-land, not from the land of brains'.[67]

Freed from the anti-Lombard bias, the motif of the armed snail entered the field of drama in 1537 with an English play entitled *Thersites*. It is a new Latin adaptation of an earlier farce, also in Latin, by a Parisian writer, Jean Tissier de Ravisy (c.1470-1524). The earlier version was adapted from a piece of medieval Latin school literature. In *Thersites* events are given a more local and everyday slant: the *miles gloriosus*, Telemachus, wants to do battle with the Knights of the Round Table and aspires eventually to assail heaven. He is maltreated by Ulysses, but is then confronted by worms, who are routed by a farcical charm, provided by his mother. The simplicity of the play and its stylistic similarity to puppet drama make it very attractive, while the juxtaposition of popular and classical motifs is typical of the period.[68]

In Gascony we find that, in the seventeenth century, the armed snail has grown into an army.[69] Abbé d'Arquier of Saint-Clar-de-Lomagne wrote two poems in the Toulouse dialect, to which there is an anonymous sequel, in which snails are used to mock at the people of Lecton in the Gers department. The first poem is entitled *La Guérro deous limacs countro lous Leytouresses, siétge de la bilou lou 7 abriou 1689*; 'The war of the snails against the people of Lecton, and the siege of the town on the 7th of April 1689'. The inhabitants are warned that Huguenots are preparing an attack on their town; they make a sally and meet nothing but snails. The second poem deals with *La Metamorphoso dous higounaus en escargols dins le baloun de Leytouro*; 'The change of the Huguenots into snails in the valley of Lecton'. The snails are finally made prisoner and eaten with salt, pepper, oil and vinegar. The anonymous verse again pokes fun at Lecton's citizens, in a pretended answer to the preceding poems. These are said to have injured the town's good name, causing its inhabitants to be nicknamed *limacaires, estourdits, pauracs, rebaires*; 'snail-eaters, fools, timorous people, ribalds'.

The enlargement of one snail to gigantic proportions is worth considering alongside the appearance of an army of snails. This can first be seen in miniatures and paintings. At Avignon a knight fighting against an enormous snail is painted on the ceiling of a room in the Calvet Museum.[70] Similar literary treatment of the creature is found in Ogier's legend in the *Myreur des Histors* by Jean d'Outremeuse,[71] a Liégeois writer who lived from 1338 to 1400: *En chis pays at des si grans lymechons que dedens leurs esquargnes herbe(r) geroit bien unc d(i)estrier*; 'In this country there are snails so large that a war-horse could be concealed in each'. A similar contemporary reference comes from the *Travels* of Jean de Bourgogne, better known as John de Mandeville, who died in 1372: 'There ben also in that Contree a kynde of Snayles, that ben so grete that many persones may loggen hem in here Schelles, as men wolde done in a lityle Hous'. The same notion, slightly elaborated, occurs in the early fifteenth-century *Livre des Merveilles du Monde*: *dans l'île de Ceylan vivaient... des escargots géants, si grands que les hommes les habitaient et s'en nourrissaient comme des rats dans un fromage*; 'in the island of Ceylon were gigantic snails, so big that men dwelt within, feeding on them like rats in a cheese'.[72] Another early account speaks of a land situated 'between India and China', where snails are held to be 'the noblest flesh'. If a Franciscan contemporary of Mandeville's is taken literally, a sizeable banquet could have dined off the creature which he saw – *une lymace qui estoit si grande que ce estoit merveille. Elle estoit plus grande que le clochier de Saint Martin de Padue*; 'a snail which was so big that it was a marvel. It was bigger than the church tower of St Martin's at Padua'.[73] More prosaically, the world's largest non-aquatic snails, the biggest examples of which come from the tropics and the equatorial jungle, are only from four to eleven inches in length, according to habitat.[74] Equally mundanely, William Witney and Benjamin Smith suggest that the gigantic snail of early travellers' tales was simply a variant of the 'tortoise', or *testudo*, once used in warfare as a kind of collective helmet.[75]

The motif of the gigantic snail is also dealt with by Ubert Philippe de Villiers, lord of Blanchefort, in a burlesque poem entitled *Le Limas*, 'The Snail', which dates from 1564; it tells of a struggle between Silenus and an enormous snail, a battle which took place beside the river Yonne, at a place called Montbuvoys.[76]

Medieval legends are reported to speak of a gigantic snail protecting a marvellous castle, but I have never come across an actual example.[77] Ambroise Paré, a famous but credulous physician of the sixteenth century, describes an amphibious snail living on the banks of the Sarmatian Sea: it was as big as a barrel, with horns nearly as strong as those of a stag, ending with round, glistening points.[78]

The legend of gigantic snails seems to be paralleled in German-speaking Switzerland and Austria, with the song *D'Klosterfrau im Schneckehus – Het gmeint, si sig verborge; – Da kunnt der Pater Guardian – Und sait ere guete Morge*; 'The nun in the snail house – Thought she was hidden; – Then along came the Father Guardian – And said "Good morning" to her'. This rhyme is, however, connected with a specific tradition: wax nuns are actually put in snail shells and sold as souvenirs at Einsiedeln and other places of pilgrimage, and the rhyme is sometimes used as a jibe against monastic life (see Appendix 6).[79]

But let us return to the threatening snail, which appears in songs, rhymes and stories as an awe-inspiring figure, alarming particularly to children and the uneducated. A well-known tale in Luxemburg, Walloon-speaking Belgium and probably elsewhere, tells variously of a man, or a troop of peasants, who are terrified by one, three or seven snails crawling along a road, or on a bridge (see Appendix 7). A similar story occurs in a German-

language song found in Germany-proper as well as Luxemburg, Alsace, Lorraine, Switzerland and Austria, and also sung in Slovenia, In it three sailors are frightened by a snail, horns at the ready (see Appendix 8). Supposedly this parodies a Meistersinger's composition, or *Meistergesang*, loosely based on an earlier poem by Georg Hagen and written by the famous Hans Sachs of Nuremberg (1494-1576); it recounts how a hare is chased by nine Swabians.[80]

Bolte and Polivka mention a Scottish song, only the first line of which they quote: 'Four an' twenty Highlandmen chasing at a snail...' Obviously the reference is inadequate, and in fact, though the slight variation suggests the probability of a different source, this appears to be part of a nonsense song published in 1828 by Peter Buchan in *Ancient Ballads and Songs of the North of Scotland.*[81] The passage devoted to the snail, which consists of stanza 8 and part of 9, goes as follows:

Four and twenty Highlandmen chasing at a snail
Quo' the man to the joe, quo' the man to the joe!
'O, says the hindmost, weel take her by the tail'
Quo' the merry, merry man to the green joe!

The snail set up her horns like one humle cow...
'Fye, says the foremost, we're a' sticket now...

In the foregoing examples we probably in each case have an echo of something more serious, now reduced to a nonsense rhyme.

The following, which is suggestive of a similiar derivation, is from the Tyrol: *Einmal sein drei Schneider gewes'n, – Die habn an Schegg für an Bärn ang'sehn; – Als die Schnegg die Hörner ausstreckt, – Haben die Schneider das G'wehr niederg'legt; – Als die Schnegg kroch unter die Bank, – Da sagten die Schneider: Gott Lob und Dank!* 'Once there were three tailors, – Who mixed up a snail and a bear; – When the snail showed its horns, – They laid down their guns; – When the snail crept under the bench, – The tailors said: Praise and thanks be to God!'[82]

In Britain and America a similar rhyme says:

Four and twenty tailors
    Went to kill a snail,
The best man among them
    Durst not touch her tail;
She put out her horns
    like a little Kyloe cow,

Run, tailors, run
Or she'll kill you all e'en now.

The rhyme was first published in 1784, and a variant from Dorset (1844) has the snail roaring like a bull. Weavers are the protagonists in a version of 1871, and the bravest among them dies of fear, after treading on a snail's tail. In a still more recent example, 'Five and twenty tailors' are 'Riding on a snail', an image already noted, with one rider only, in thirteenth-century illuminations.[83] The Opies draw attention in their *Oxford Dictionary of Nursery Rhymes*, to the proverb 'Nine tailors make but one man', a version of which, dating from 1721, goes 'Four and twenty tailors cannot make a man', for me a clear allusion to the rhyme or song, or possibly to a tale from which they derive, the implication being that it was already in circulation at that time, and probably earlier.[84]

Only a few rhymes can be added to these. A murderous snail appears in a Limousin children's song from Mézières and Cognac-le-Froid: *Dô din! dô dan! – Qui ei mort? – Bertran. – Qui l'o tuat? – L'alima. – Qui o fat so caisso? – L'ôme d'Aisso. – Qui o fat soun crô? – L'ôme d'O. – Qui o dit sas prejeiras? – 'no troupo de bargeiras. – Qui o dit sous serviceis? – 'nos troupo de cheis*; 'Ding dong! ding dong! – Who is dead? – Bertrand. – Who killed him? – The slug. – Who made his coffin? – A man from Aixe. – Who made his cross? – John O'Bear. – Who said his prayers? – A troop of shepherdesses. – Who said mass for him? – A troop of dogs'.[85]

In Corrèze (France) the tale of the fighting snail is used by the rural people to mock at the simpletons. *Dziral lo gôgô ch'eï arme – Per ana battré loous limas. – Loous limas n'oount mai pougu, – Dziral lo gôgô ch'eï rendu*; 'Gerald Pudding has taken arms – To go and beat the snails. – The snails proved stronger, – Gerald Pudding has surrendered'.[86] A rather similar jibe is made at the expense of one, Nicolas Bajas, who has not used his sword for ten years. The joke is that then he had to draw it against little snails, who nonetheless forced him to retreat a step: *Nicolas Bajas avait une épée; – Y avait bien dix ans qu'il l'avait tirée, – Lorsque, le jour de la saint-Nicolas, – Il la tira sur de petits lumas. – Les petits lumas tirèrent leurs cornes; – Nicolas Bajas recula d'un pas.* This children's song was noted down at Montjean and Saint-Aubin-de-Luigné in Anjou.[87] Another, containing a similar motif, comes from the Bas-Maine, or Mayenne Department:

Le p'tit lumas a montré les cônes,
Monsieur Berton a r'culé pus d'eune aune,
En s'écriant: O mes amis!
Un p'tit lumas vient m'ôter la vie!

'The little snail has bared its horns, – Mr Berton has taken a good pace back, – Crying: O my friends! – A little snail is coming to make short of my life!'[88] So too in a 'little man' song from Provence: *Jean Pichoun vai dins un jardin – A chivau dessus un garri – A la guerr' es limaçouns, – Jean Pichoun! – N'en dariatz pa' 'n coou de poung*; 'Little John goes into a garden – Riding a pig – To make war on snails, – Little John! – He will not strike a blow'.[89]

The situation is rather different in a song noted by Bladé in Gascony. A little boy, Tricoutet, has been sent to market riding a snail; but the snail bucked, and Tricoutet got stamped upon: *Que l'èi mandat au marcat, – A chibau sur un limac. – Lou limac a reguinnat, – Tricoutet s'es esclahat.*[90]

Jules Mousseron, from Denain in Artois, uses the motif of encounter with a snail in one of his dialect poems, *Voyage autour d'eune cave*, 'A journey around a cellar': *Oui, dins l' grande forèt qu' l'in quite, – Il a vu un gros leumechon. – Cheule biète s'a mis à s' porswite... – I trane core, èl pauve garchon!* 'Yes, in the large forest which they are leaving, – He saw a big snail. – The beast has set off in his pursuit... – He is still trembling, the poor boy!'[91] A rhyme well-known in Luxemburg, Switzerland and Germany gives a truncated version of the same motif: *Schneck, Schneck, komm heraus, – Streck deine vier Hörner 'raus! – Es kommen zwei mit Spiessen – Die wollen dich erschiessen; – Es kommen zwei mit Stecken, – Die wollen dich erschrecken*; 'Snail, snail, come out, – Show your four horns! – Here come two men with pikes, – They intend to kill you; – Here come two men with sticks, – They intend to frighten you'.[92]

Sayings such as those which follow probably derive from rhymes or jokes like these. For example, in Cyrano de Bergerac (1615-1655), a braggart is called an *embrocheur de limas*, 'snail-spitter';[93] in the *Mazarinades* (1649) someone laughs at a sword with the words: 'Is it to kill snails or frogs?';[94] in Montauban a *sanno-limaous* or 'snail-bleeder' is a knife;[95] in Dutch a *slakken-steker* or *slakkenprikker* (a 'snail-sticker' or 'snail-pricker') is a bayonet; but in Maaseik a *slekken-steker* is a procrastinator (a person collecting snails on a skewer is indeed slow);[96] in Gâtinais the vine-growers were nicknamed *éborgneux de limas*, 'snail-blinders', there being a double entendre here involving the French word for a disbudder;[97] Noël du Fail (1547) mocks a hypocrite as follows: *ayant sa rapiere soubs le bras, en faisant du bon compaignon, disant quil ne la portoit pour faire mal, mais pour piquer les Limax*; 'having his rapier under his arm, playing the good companion [and] saying that he was not carrying it do any harm, but to prick slugs with'.[98] At Osse, in the Basse-Pyrénées department, the rudiments of a tale have been noted: 'You will vainly shout: "Snail, draw your lance, here is the king of France!" I shall answer: "Let him stay where he is!" Which means: I shall not do it in any case!'[99]

Turning to pictorial folk-art, among that which I consider the most beautiful is the decorative painting on beehive fronts in Slovenia. The pictures apparently stem from German tailor songs already discussed in this paper, the more certainly because of the Slovene version recorded in 1938-1939. The folk singer displayed a picture illustrating the song and showing three tailors frightened by a snail (see Appendix 8).

To conclude, perhaps I might mention that, as long ago as 1906, Jessie Weston, a distinguished early member of the Folklore Society, expressed the hope that someone would make a detailed study of the motifs of the armed snail and the snail under attack.[100] This is what I have attempted to do in the present paper, with reference specially to the problem of its origin, the relationship between its presence in high culture and in folk-lore, and its geographical location. I would also like to set forth my own observations regarding the role of the motif within narrative. Its forms were not sufficiently clearly defined by Stith Thompson,[101] and Gerald Thomas[102] was quite right in proposing a sharper distinction between the Land of Cokaygne[103] and Topsy-Turvy Land.[104] Indeed, 'the Schlaraffenland theme tends to unite impossible motifs about a "Land of Milk and Honey" or Earthly Paradise, a fantasy world in which every-thing is geared to the pleasurable', and 'in Topsy-Turvy Land (AT 1935) motifs tend to concentrate on a true reversal of normality'. All motifs described in this article pertain to the Topsy-Turvy Land theme, and I would like to draw attention to four categories:

1. The snail is assailed by one or several cowards, and stands up to them. Sometimes it is victorious, on other occasions it is beaten. We cannot always say for sure whether it is armed. Its assailants are knights on foot or on horseback, archers, soldiers, burghers, peasants, a woman. They attack separately or in groups of three or more, or, in one instance, four hundred peasants together, in another, the whole population of a town. Some-times they try to frighten their opponent by means of masks and other devices.[105] The snail, with its four horns at the ready, is called 'hardy'; its horns, in fact, constitute its weapons, to be compared with arrows, lances or sticks, and an analogy is drawn between them and those on a bull. Its shell is its house, sometimes imagined as of outsize proportions. This is never in the context of the snail being besieged, though the 'house' also serves as its refuge or shelter. The snail protects a castle, takes part in a tournament, stands sentry, has malefactors apprehended, and its army besieges a town. This form of the motif might be called 'the Lombard's attack'.

2. In the second version the snail appears as actively engaged in the confrontation, and un-wittingly spreads panic among ignorant cowards. Probably also very old, this form is notable for its jibes at the expense of tailors, who are generally three on the continent, and either twenty-four or twenty-five in Anglo-Saxon countries. On occasion tailors are replaced by weavers or peasants, and the motif sometimes, though by no means always, parodies a chase. It is a *beotianum* to which one might give the title 'The tailors' great fright'.

3. The snail is victorious over one or several lions. This is motif X.1345.1, with examples here from France and Germany.

4. The snail appears in animal epics as commander-in-chief or a courtier, though this form does not seem to exist in any folkloric versions. It is, how-ever, very early and can, perhaps, be linked to 'the Lombard's attack' (see 1, above).

As I have stressed several times, this motif, in its four forms, must be classed among the mass of amusing literature about Topsy-Turvy Land. It appears to be a medieval creation, and has been compared by the French folklorist A. Certeux[106] to the legend of St George. Indeed he sees in the *couteau de saint Georges*, the 'St George's knife', which appears in a few snail charms, a reference by way of parody to the saint's exploits.[107] This harks back to the events in Libya surrounding the dragon's death; it was first pinned to the ground with his lance, and St George then demanded the people's conversion to Christianity before using his sword to slay it. There are therefore major differences from the snail narratives, not least in that the saint, not the monster, does the killing, and Certeux's proposition thus seems unconvincing. The charms to which he alludes occur in a category of verse chiefly used nowadays for the amusement of children, and certainly taken seriously by few others. The knife referred to is an actual knife,

presented to a child on St George's Day (23rd April). In Lorraine, at Rosselange near Metz, snails on a spit are served on the nearest Sunday to this date, the occasion being called the *fête des escargots.*[108]

Any suggestion, therefore, that the snail motif derives in some way from the St George legend must be dismissed. Equally unlikely is any direct connection with a portrayal, on a romanesque capital in the church at Chaunay, of a knight fighting a basilisk. Local legend sees the knight as Frettard, a former Lord of Chaunay, and relates the creature to a snail; the scene portrayed supposedly symbolises the expulsion of the English from Loudun in 1350.[109] This is, of course, too late to have anything to do with the origin of the tale but, while wishing to be quite the reverse of unflattering to the English, I like the notion of concluding my paper with this little account from Chaunay, in which our cross-Channel neighbours are symbolised by something akin to a snail.

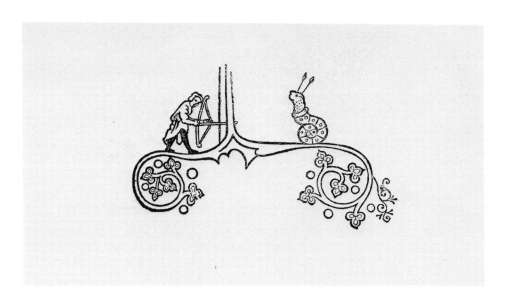

Plate 1. Illustration after a thirteenth-century manuscript, showing an archer aiming at a snail with its horns extended in the form of arrows.

Plate 2. Viennese manuscript illustration, showing a snail extending its horns and being attacked by soldiers carrying various weapons.

Plate 3. Snail confronting a soldier armed with a slingshot and protected by a shield, urged on by a woman with a distaff. From the Amiens *Missale Romanum*, dating from the fourteenth century.

Plate 4. Reynard carrying a snail in a wheelbarrow, probably in response to its menacing attitude. Drawn from the *Bréviaire du Saint-Sépulchre de Cambrai*, which dates from the late thirteenth or early fourteenth century. (See Appendix 4).

Plate 5. Scene of a knight fighting a snail, carved on a draughtsman. A fourteenth-century example in the British Museum (see Note 39). (*Photograph copyright: The British Museum*)

Plate 6. Illustration of *Le débat des gens d'armes et d'une femme contre un lymasson*, from the *Grand Compost du XVe siècle*. (See Note 41).

La fème a hardy couraige
Huy de ce lieu tresorde beste
q des vignes les bourgõs mènges
Sur arbre et sur buysson

As tout mãge iusqs aux brãches
De ma quenoille si tu tauances
Je te donray tel horion
Quon lentendra diey a nantes

Les gens darmes

Lymasson pour tes grans cornes
Le chasteau ne lairrons dassaillir
Et se pouons te ferons fouir
De ce beau lieu ou tu reposes
Oncques lombard ne te mangeat
A telle saulce que nous ferons
Si te mectrons en vng grant plat
Au popure noir et aux ongnons
Serre tes cornes si te prions
Et nous laisse entrer dedans
Autrement nous te assaillerons
De noz bastons qui sont trãchans

Le lymasson

Je suis de terrible fasson
Et si ne suis que lymasson
Ma maison porte sur mon dos
Et si ne suis de chair ne dos
Jay deux cornes dessus ma teste
Côme vng beuf quest grosse beste
De ma maison ie suis arme
Et de mes cornes embastonne
Se ces gens darmes la maprochent
Ilz en auront sur leurs caboches
Mais ie cuide quen bonne foy
Quilz treblent de grãt peur de moy

Plate 7. One version of the *Débat des gens d'armes et d'une femme*. (See also Plate 8).

La femme a hardy couraige
Huyde de ce lieu tresorde beste
qui des vignes les bourgons mages
Sur arbre et sur buysson

De tout mange iusques aux branches
De ma quenoille si tu tauances
Je te donray tel hourion
quon lentendra bien a nantes

Les gens darmes

Lymasson pour tes grans cornes
Le chasteau ne lairrons dassaillir
Et se pouons te ferons fouyr
De ce beau lieu ou tu reposes
Oncques sonibart ne te mangeat
A telle saulce que nous ferons
Si te mettrons en vng grant plat
Au poyure noir et aux ongnons
Serre tes cornes si te prions
Et nous laisse entrer dedans
Autrement nous te assaillerons
De noz bastons qui sont tranchans

Le lymasson

Je suys de terrible facon
Et si ne suys que lymasson
Ma maison porte sur mon dos
Et si ne suis de chair ne dos
Jay deux cornes dessus ma teste
Cōme vng beuf quest grosse beste
De ma maison ie suys arme
Et de mes cornes embastonne
Se ces gens darmes la maprochent
Ilz en auront sur leurs caboches
Mais ie cuide quen bonne foy
quilz treblent de grant peur de moy

Plate 8. Second version of the *Débat des gens d'armes et d'une femme*, after the MS. calendar illuminated by Antoine Vérard. (See Note 42).

Plate 9. Slovenian Beehive Front. See description in Appendix 8 (No. 6).

Plate 10. Slovenian Beehive Front. See description in Appendix 8 (No. 7).

Appendix 1

Assaillir la limace

See Adolf Tobler (*op. cit.* in Note 32), 101, continuing G. Baist's discussion (*op. cit.* in Note 39), 305. The French philogist A. Boucherie has made an attempt to explain it: *Peut-être [provient-elle] de quelque superstition italienne qui aurait considéré comme un présage fâcheux la rencontre d'un limaçon aux cornes allongées. Les signes d'inquiétude donnés par ceux qui se trouvaient ainsi en présence de la malencontreuse bestiole pouvaient être mal interprétés par des étrangers, par des Français surtout, naturellement moqueurs, et qui, ne connaissant ni ne pratiquant ce genre de superstition, devaient en rire et en faire un thème à 'gaberies'.* See *Revue des Langues romanes,* XXIX (1886), 94-5, especially note 1, in which Boucherie mentions that in Italy, according to a maid-servant he interviewed, a snail foretells good luck, and according to *Il Libro dei Sogni*, a snail (*lumacone*) means *carica onorifica; se mostra le corna: infideltà*, though I do not see the connection with the idiom under examination. He also draws attention to the fact that, in a folksong from Modena, a slug torments the damned souls in hell, but this seems equally irrelevant. Moreover, see Walter Benary: 'Zu "assaillir la limace" ', *Archiv für das Studium der neueren Sprachen und Litteraturen,* LXIV (124), 137-8, who additionally considers miniatures in the same connection. The relevant texts are as follows:

1. *Sone li sainz de la comune – Por ce que nus n'an i remaigne; – N'i a si mauvès qui ne praingne – Forche ou flaël ou pic ou mace; – Ains por assaillir la limace – N'ot an Lombardie tel noise* (Chrestien de Troyes, *Perceval le Gallois*, edited by Potvin at Mons, MS. H 5946: Tobler-Lommatzsch, lieferung 44, columns 468-9; twelfth century, between 1160-85). W. P. Ker mentions the last two lines in his review of Jessie L. Weston's *Legend of Sir Gawain. Studies upon its original scope and significance* (London, 1897): *Folk-Lore*, IV (3), 267: 'His (Chrestien de Troyes') story of Gawain is full of malice; for instance, in the humorous account of the rising of the town – mayor, échivins, and commune – against Gawain, to defend the honour of their lord, especially in the mock-heroic reference to the famous Lombard campaign against the snail'. See *Graal*, lines 7324-5.

2. *Vous venez droit de Lombardie, – Molt par avez la char hardie, – Que tué avez la lymache. – Fu che de pichois ou de mache – K'avez mort la beste cornue? – Molt seront lié de vo venue – Li baron et li bacheler. – Estes vos por chevalerie – Faire venus a cest tournoi* (Quoted from J. L. Weston and Joseph Bédier, 'Tristan Ménestrel. Extrait de la Continuation de Perceval par Gerbert [de Montreuil]), *Romania*, XXXV (1906), 528-9; thirteenth century.

3. *'Glouton,' dit Galien, 'se Dieu grant bien me face, – Ne prise pas un ail vostre faulce menace... – Pour vous ne fiüiray pour plain pié que je face. – Je ne suis pas Lombart qui fuit pour la lymaiche* (Edmund Stengel, *Galiens li Restorés*, final part of the Cheltenham *Guerin de Monglane* [Marburg, 1890], 307, 29).

4. *Li chapelains touz esgarez. ... – L'ostel douta plus et la place – Que li Lombarz ne fet limace* (M. de Méon, *Nouveau recueil de fabliaux et contes populaires* [Paris, 1808], II, 301, 260).

5. Keu mocks at Perceval and his miserable garb for a tournament: *Vous venez droit de Lombardie – Mo(u)lt par(t) avez la chair hardie – Que tüé avez la lymache. – Estes vos por chevalerie – Faire venus a cest tornoi?* (Chrestien de Troyes: *Conte du Graal*, quoted by Adolf Tobler [*op. cit.* in Note 32], 99).

6. ... *lo Lombart... non ausava intrar el cendier per la limassa que trazia ses corns...* (See Tobler, 101, after *Lexique roman*, IV, 75, s.v. limassa).

This attributes to the Lombards a trait mentioned in Monk Laurent's *Somme le roi*, dated 1279, when he speaks of the poltroon: *Cesti ressemble a celi qui n'ose entrer el sentier de bonne voie pour le limaçon qui li monstre ses cornes.* See Emile Mâle: *L'art religieux du XIIIE siècle en France. Etude sur l'iconographie du moyen âge et sur ses sources d'inspiration* (Paris, 1898), 167.

7. Ogier says to Adenet: *Ce sont Lombart; j'ai öi tesmoignier — qu'il ne valent en armes un denier* (Quoted by Tobler, from *Enfances Ogier*, 931).

8. *È da notare una favola che se dice e dipigne per dispetto degli Italiani in Francia: e' dicono ch'e' Lombardi hanno pauro della lumaccia, cioè lumaca* (Giovanni Villani, about 1320, quoted by Tobler; also by Francesco Novati [*op. cit.* in Note 6],

131); see also the Italian dictionary by Tommaseo-Bellini, III, 1295. The *Istorie fiorentine* by Giovanni Villani were published in Milan in 1802; see Book IX, Ch. 108, 4(c).

9. See also the quotation in the text from the *Roman de Renart*, lines 3466-70. This is taken from Tobler, 99-100, who further adds from lines 3419-20: *Et li clers (Gilain) a pris une mace — Qui fu hardiz comme limace.* This idea is repeated in lines 21705-6: *Un felon vilain, en riote — Plus hardi c'un limac escorne.*

10. The same idea is still living: in the dialect almanac, *El Carion d' Mons*, III (1874), 49, someone says: *C'ést pour mi come si tu crachwas par tére, — Vu qu' tu l' sés bé, j' n'é nié peur d'in lumeçon*: 'It is for me as if you were spitting on the ground, — Considering, as you well know, that I am not afraid of a slug'.

Appendix 2

Jibes at Lombards and Italians

First let us consider a few quotations from John of Salisbury's *Polycraticus sive de Nugis Curialium et Vestigiis philosophorum* (1159):

Aemilianos et Ligures Galli derident dicentes eos testamenta conficere, viciniam convocare, armorum implorare praesidia, si finibus eorum testudo immineat, quam oporteat oppugnare. Quod ex eo componitur, quod eos nunquam cuiuscumque certaminis cas invenit imparatos. Nostri vero quomodo ludibrii notas effugiunt, cum maiori tumultu et aegriori sollicitudine et ampliori sumptu solemne bellum credant bestiis indicendum?

(I, Ch.4, 10)

Quod ad istud orbem Romanum crede; memini me audisse Romanum pontificem solitum deridere Lumbardos, dicentem eos pilleum omnibus colloquentibus facere, eo quod in exordio dictionis beniuolentiam captent, et eorum cum quibis agitur, capita quodam commendationis demulceant oleo.

(VII, Ch.19, 682)

Regnante Rogero Siculo... Rodbertus iam dicti regis camellarius ... morum elegantia uenerabilis, eoque mirabilior in partibus illis quod inter Longobardos, quos parcissimos, ne auaros dicam, esse constat, faciebat sumptus immensos et gentis suae magnificentiam exhibebat; erat enim Anglicus natione.

(III, Ch.6, 487)

The following are translations of the second and third texts, one by Joseph B. Pike in *Frivolities of Courtiers and Footprints of Philosophers* (London, 1938), 168:

I remember having heard that the Roman Pontiff [Hadrian IV] was wont to deride the Lombards, saying that they took off their hats to all with whom they held discourse, with the idea of gaining their good will at the beginning of the discussion and of fattening their heads with oil of commendation [*Ps.* CXL.5], as it were.

the other by John Dickinson, in *The Statesman's Book of John of Salisbury* (New York, 1927), 296:

> When Roger of Sicily was king [in Apulia] ... Robert, the chancellor of the aforesaid king. . . was. . . respected for the elegance of his life, which was the more remarkable in those regions because among the Lombards, who are known to be the most frugal, not to say miserly, of men, he laid out great sums in sumptuous living and displayed the magnificence characteristic of his nation; for he was of English nationality.

From Odofredo de Bolonia: *Interpretatio in undecim primis Pandectarum libris* (Lugduni, MDL, *Digestio*, VI, I, 23, para.3, 238b):

> *Si pingeretur de vili materia ut faciunt ultramontani, [qui] pingunt limacem in vituperium Italicorum, vel scorpiones in vituperium Ultramontanorum in pariete de carbone, inconveniens esset quod paries caderet pictura.*

(*Digestio* XLI, *in postremo libro Pandectarum*, 43a):

> *Unde si pinx[er]it figuram domini nostri Iesu Christi vel figuram S. Marie, etc. et facit optimis coloribus, tunc tabula cedit picture. Secus, si pingeret de carbone vel de incausto vel de aliquo alio vilissimo colore ursum vel limacem, ut faciunt Gallici quando volunt deridere Italicos. Idem est si quis Italicus pingeret aliquem qui saporem pistaret vel qui faceret salsam viridem.*

From Michel Eyquem de Montaigne: *Essais*, 1580, II, Ch.11, 104 (the edition by Maurice Rat, Paris, 1941):

> *Un seigneur Italien tenoit une fois ce propos en ma presence, au desavantage de sa nation: Que la subtilité des Italiens et la vivacité de leurs conceptions estoit si grande qu'ils prevoyoyent les dangiers et accidens qui leur pouvoyent advenir, de si loin, qu'il ne falloit pas trouver estrange si on les voyoit souvent, à la guerre, prouvoir à leur seurté, voire avant que d'avoir reconneu le peril; que nous et les Espaignols, qui n'estions pas si fins, allions plus outre, et qu'il nous falloit voir à l'oeil et toucher à la main le dangier avant que de nous en effrayer, et que lors aussi nous n'avions plus de tenue; mais que les Allemans et les Souysses, plus grossiers et plus lourds, n'avoyent le sens de se raviser, à peine lors mesmes qu'ils estoyent accablez soubs les coups. Ce n'estoit à l'adventure que pour rire. . .*

Appendix 3

Ovidius De Lombardo et Lumaca

The text is to be found, published by A. Boucherie, in *Revue des Langues romanes* (1886), 96-7. The publisher recognises that he did not understand it completely. However here is a summary given by Lilian M. C. Randall [*op. cit.* in Note 8], 364:

> In this version a simple Lombard peasant is nonplussed at encountering a 'heavily armed' snail, horned and well fortified. While the gods encourage him to fight the beast with promises of great rewards, his wife, appalled by her husband's recklessness, pleads with him for her sake and the children's not to embark on such a dangerous mission, which neither Hercules, Achilles nor Hector would have dared undertake. Despite her entreaties, the peasant follows the gods' advice and destroys the monster with his spear. A suitable reward for this feat, says the author, must be decided upon by lawyers.

A prose version is to be found in two thirteenth-century manuals for students of the *stile epistolare* which are preserved in Vienna. Here is a copy of one of them:

> *Quidam Ytalus amico suo ut subveniat ei armata manu contra testudinem. – Cum grandia nobis incumbent negocio, si minoris*

potentie nos sentimus, confidenter ad eum accedimus, cuius manum nobis credimus adiutricem sata nostra cum hodie circuirem, accinctus gladio et munitus lancea, monstruosam et nimis terribilem inveni beluam prius incognitam et ad eius expavi continuo visionem. erat armata cornibus et tecta clypeo, quam et ipse monstrorum vastator Hercules absque vite formidine non videret. congelatum formidine me fuisse fateor; set non post multo tempore resumens animum, affectabam in beluam audacter irruere; set accepi consilium a deo scientie, ne tam

grande monstrum aggrederer inconsulte. inde est quod amorem tuum sollicito, mi care, cum multis precibus, ut ad bellum tam arduum et grandi plenum periculo summo mane sub ortu Luciferi mihi te prebeas adiutorem. scias quia multum nobis cedet ad gloriam, si de nova belua triumphare poterimus, a qua scio non mihi solummodo, sed toti mundo periculum imminere. verum quia tanti discriminis eventus est dubius. sumenda est eucharistia, ne, quod deus a nobis amoveat, a presentis vite [statu] decedamus inconfessi.

Appendix 4

Additions to Randall's list of miniatures showing armed snails

A. In France

1. At Douai: MS. no.171, psalter from between 1325 and 1346, executed by curate Thomas for Jean d'Aleshan, abbot of Gorleston; fo.211 a miniature represents a knight executing a brilliant passage of arms against a snail, while a herald riding on a legless cripple's back sounds a flourish for the tournament. As in the example from Chartres mentioned earlier, satirical intention against knights is apparent, a view for which there is considerable further evidence: in the MS. many other caricatures are to be seen showing disrespect for either kings, prelates, doctors or ladies. Besides there are other images of Topsy-Turvy Land, such as *des lièvres, dont l'un chevauche un lévrier, chass(a)nt un chien, . . . , un vieux roi. . . invectiv(ant) un fou qui, sans s'émouvoir, lui tire la langue et lui présente des arguments dont Abélard n'eût pu se prévaloir.* There is a caricature of a stag-hunt in fo.186; a hare is sounding the horn, while pursuing a hunter who runs away and another hare shoots an arrow at him. See Camille Enlart, 'La satire des moeurs dans l'Iconographie du Moyen Age', *Mercure de France*, 16 December, 1909, 629, and 1 January, 1910, 46-7; and Louis Maeterlinck, *Le genre satirique dans la peinture flamande* (Brussels, 1906), 55.

2. At Le Mans: MS. 2455, dating from the thirteenth century, representing a knight on horseback attacking a snail holding itself erect at the top of a leaf, the knight brandishing a broad sword. See A. Certeux, 'La formulette de l'escargot et quelques anciennes images', *Revue des Traditions populaires*, VII (1892), 508, quoting Eugène Hucher, *Le Saint-Graal, première branche des Romans de la Table ronde, publié d'après des textes et documents inédits* (Le Mans, 1878), illustration reproduced on the cover.

3. In Paris, Bibliothèque Nationale:
(a) Latin MS. 10.483, dominican breviary called *Bréviaire de Belleville*, dating from 1323, fo.42. It shows a frightened man facing a snail all four horns out. See abbé V. Leroquois, *Les bréviaires manuscrits des bibliothèques publiques de France* (Paris, 1934), II, 206.
(b) About 1400 the *Hours of the duke of Berry* give us another combat between a knight and a snail: the latter takes lance and shield away from its adversary. See Enlart, 629.
(c) A MS. telling the story of the Holy Grail, French stock, no.95. It shows a small archer taking aim at a snail, a scene depicted five times. See Maeterlinck, 56.
(d) Latin MS. no.22, fo.406 vo., at the bottom

across the margin; this is in a Bible prepared in Bologna for a canon at Maguelone shortly before 1284:

Vedesi dipinto un uomo ignudo che, copridosi con una rotella e brandendo una lunga spada, fa atto d'avventarsi contro un grosso lumacone il quale un po' al di sotto drizza verso di lui le corna minacciose.

From Paul Meyer, *Collection d'Héliogravures de l'Ecole des Chartres*, no.343, quoted in Novati, 149.

(e)   MS. no.1173 from the French stock, entitled *le Jeu de saint Nicolas*, fo.168. This shows a knight attacking both a snail and a hare:

Links ein Erdhügel, in dessen Innerem ein Hasenkopf sichtbar ist; auf dem Hügel sitzt, muschelartig zusammengerollt, die Hörner weit nach oben herausstreckend, eine Schnecke. Rechts davon ein Ritter zu Pferde . . . , mit eingelegter Lanze auf den Hasen zielend. In der Linken hält er den Schild, der in goldnem Feld ein rotes Kreuz zeigt. Hinter ihm steht eine Frau, die mit der Kunkel auf ihn einschlägt, und ihm zum Ueberfluss mit der Hand vor sich stösst, offenbar um ihn, den Aengstlichen anzuspornen.

A clerk living in Lombardy appears to be responsible for the text in its present form. See Benary, 137-8.

4. Paris, Bibliothèque de la Chambre des Députés: a book of Hours dating from the end of the fifteenth century, the work of a Flemish copyist and artist. The snail's adversary is a sort of 'wild man'. See Navati, 151.

B. In Italy

1. In a codex dating from 1325-1330, made in Genoa for the Saint Leonard Convent in Carignan, and kept at the university of that town; the combat against the snail is repeated six times with variations. See A. Neri, *Studî bibliografiche e letterarie* (Genoa, 1890), 8, quoted by Novati, 150. Randall says that the founder of that convent had a psalter book, which is at Cambrai, and had been acquired when he was provost at the Saint Donatien Church at Bruges from 1295 to 1304.

2. A miniature at the bottom of a page of a MS. copy of a work by jurisconsult Bartolomeo de Brescia shows a riding warrior who *tutto chiuso nell' armi, si scagliava, la lancia in resta, contro la lumaca ritta dinanzi a lui in segno di sfida.* This splendid miniature was Italian. See Novati, 150, who had examined the manuscript in a Milan antique shop.

C. Elsewhere

1. In Vienna: codex VIII.194 of the Rossiana library in Lainz-Vienna, dating from about 1284, from the San Michele Abbey at Bosco (same provenance as the Bologna bible), a miniature

Qui la scena è più complicata sull' appogio loro offerto dal fregio marginale si muovono tre figurine; due di esse in atto di colpire una grossa lumaca munita di quattro corna, assalendola simultaneamente davanti e di dietro con spada ed ascia; un terzo personaggio colla lancia in spalla accorre in aiuto dei valorosi compagni.

See Novati, 150, quoting Adolfo Venturi, *Storia dell' arte italiana* (Milan, 1904), III, 458, Fig.431, who says: . . . *uomini in arme, con lancia, martello e scure, s'avanzano timidamente verso una lumaca che sporge quattro cornetti fuor dal nicchio. . .*

2. In the Hague:

Plus curieuse est une miniature d'un Missale Romanum *du XIVe siècle, 'illuminatum per Petrum de Raimbaucourt', provenant d'Amiens et conservé à la Bibliothèque royale de La Haye (Ms. Y 400); nous y voyons un guerrier armé [d'une fronde], accompagné de sa femme tenant sa quenouille, soutenir à l'abri d'un bouclier planté en terre, l'assaut d'un limaçon, représentant cette fois le peuple. . .*

Maeterlinck, 56; see also Van Moerkerken (*op. cit.* in Note 44), 208 and illus.

3. In Luxemburg: MS. 80, Bibliothèque Nationale, fo.1, initial letter A, lower margin, entitled Alexander de Villa Dei: *Doctrinale Puerorum*, from the Abbey of Orval, late thirteenth- or early fourteenth-century:

Un seigneur part en guerre contre un escargot aussi grand que lui. Vêtu d'une robe bleue et de chausses noires collantes, il se protège avec son bouclier et brandit au-dessus de sa tête une énorme épée.

See Blanche Weicherding-Goergen, *Les Manuscrits à Peintures de la Bibliothèque Nationale de Luxembourg. Catalogue descriptif et critique* (Luxemburg, 1968), 68-9, pl.21.

Appendix 5

The Character of Tardif

It may be interesting to outline Tardif as he appears in the *Roman de Renart: Sire Tardif li limeçons* is the one who *lut par lui seul les .III. leçons* ('read alone the three lessons') of the Gospel at Dame Coupée's funeral (Lady Coupée is the hen who Reynaert has treacherously killed, a murder for which he is committed to trial) (lines 427-8). Tardif is also the flag-bearer who *porte l'ansaigne* and *bien les conduit par mi la plaigne* ('leads the army gallantly through the plain') (lines 1627-8). When Reynaert sees *l'ensegne qu'a vent ventelle – et voit que Tardis les cha(d)ele* ('the flag which is waving in the wind – and that Tardif is at their head') he runs away into his castle (lines 1631-2 drawn from other manuscripts than the basic one). *Mes dant Tardis li limeçons, – qui dut porter le confanon, – oublia Renart a lïer: – Cil cort les autres deslïer; – trait l'espee, si lor desnoe, – a chascun coupe de la coue* ('but Sir Tardif the snail, – who had to bear the gonfalon, – Reynaert forgot to bind: – Tardif runs and unbinds the others, – draws his sword, then unleashes them in such a way that he cuts a bit off their tails') (lines 1873-8). When Reynaert thinks he is safe, *a ce qu'il entre en sa tainiere – Tardis le saisi par derriere, – par mi les piez a soi le tire: – mout se contient bien comme sire* ('as he enters his lair – Tardif catches him from behind, – and draws him to himself by his feet: – he behaves very well as a lord') (lines 1887-90). Tardif calls the king, who hastens to him: *et dant Tardis, qui Renart tient, – parole au roi qui devant vient* ('and Sir Tardif, who holds Reynaert prisoner, – speaks to the approaching king') (lines 1893-4). When Reynaert has been tied up, *Tardis, qui porte la baniere, – li a donee une cropiere* ('Tardif, who bears the banner, – has given him a cut in the cruppers') (lines 1929-30).

In branch XVII (c.1200) the snail is again given the task of reading the religious service: this time it manages to say the whole response without mumbling or even much apparent effort, during the wake organised by the king around Reynaert, whom the court believes to be dead. In branch XI, dating from about 1195, Reynaert takes his revenge on his enemy Tardif: *d'un coup de tambourin, il assomme à demi Tardif, et lui prend son épée dont il le perce* (see lines 1523-1640). This quotation comes from Marc Boyon and Jean Frappier, *Le Roman de Renart* (Paris, 1939), 83 (branch XVII) and 74 (branch XI). The summary in the text of the article is inspired by Henry Carnoy, *Les Contes d'Animaux dans les Romans du Renard* (Paris, 1889), 69 (No. XXXVIII, after branch XX in the edition procured by M. D.-M. Méon, Paris, 1826). The quotations from branch I from Mario Roques, *Le Roman de Renart, première branche. Jugement de Renart. Siège de Maupertuis. Renart teinturier, éditée d'après le manuscrit de Cangé* (Paris, 1948).

According to Gaston Paris, *Mélanges de littérature française du Moyen Age* (Paris, 1912), 346-7, Tardif is present only in the branches which constitute the prototype of the Reynaert; an assertion which is not quite correct, since branch XX, which does not belong to that 'reconstruction', and appears in Méon's edition, II, 1-88, *Sire Tardis li Limaçons – Chanta por cele trois leçons, – Et Rooniax chanta li vers – Et il et Brichemers li Cers, – Et Brun li Ors dist l'oroi son – Que Diex gart l'ume de prison*. This of course restates a situation mentioned earlier, as it repeats the scene of Tardif at the head of the army and his capture of Reynaert. Lucien Foulet, *Le Roman de Renard* (Paris, 1914), 468, draws attention to the fact that the writer of branch XVII uses only characters from the previous branches, and all of them, in situations which are most often the repetition of scenes in which his predecessors had been most successful.

Here follows the text from the *Miracles de Nostre Dame*, prologue to book II, *Miracle de Notre-Dame de Sardenay*, quoted by M. Méon, I, v; *Romania*, XVII (1888), 429; John Flinn, *Le Roman de Renart dans la littérature française et dans les littératures étrangères au Moyen Age* (Toronto, 1963), 113 (with minor differences in the spelling from one text to another): *Plus delitant sont tuit li conte – A bonnes genz, par saint Omer, – Que de Renart ne de Romer – Ne de Tardiu le limeçon*. Méon considers this passage to be outside the Reynaert. Let me add that Flinn, quoting A.-E. Poquet, *Gautier de Coincy. Les Miracles de la Sainte Vierge* (Paris, 1857), gives another passage with Tardif: *Plus volentiers oent un conte, s'en leur conte, – Si com Tardius li limeçons – Lut et chanta les III. liçons – Seur la biere dame Coupee – Que Renard avoit escroupee, – Qu'il ne feroient, par Saint Gile, – Un bon serment d'une evangile.* Gauthier de Coincy was prior at Vic-sur-Aisne in Picardy, and died in 1236.

In *Le Dis d'Entendement* by Jean de Condé, written between 1340-5, *Tardif le limaçon, traditionnellement gonfanon, est devenu bouteiller et suit fidèlement les conseils de Renart* (Flinn, 350): *nul besoin d'xpliquer le rôle de Tardif, qui sert à Court-lent* (Flinn, 354).

In the same century, a text in the dialect of Metz in Lorraine quoted by Rolland (*op. cit.* in Note 35), 46, says that *Tardis li limesson sceit plus que le seirs ramez* ('Tardif the snail knows more than the antlered stag'). It is also possible that Gautier de Coincy harks back to Tardif's notoriety in the *Vie de Sainte Léocadie*, quoted here from La Curne de Ste-Palaye, *Dictionnaire historique de l'ancien language françois* (Paris, 1880), VII, limeçon: *Avoir fait bien par S. Fiacre – Tresorier et arcediacre – D'un crapoudel, d'un limeçon – Que ne set lire une leçon.*

The name Tardif itself has an onomatopoeic quality, as Charles Guerlin de Guer explains in the *Revue bimensuelle des Cours et Conférences*, XXX (15th June, 1929), 388. In old French *tardif* meant 'slow in one's movements', which is established in particular by the use of the word as a surname at Dijon as from 1280 and by various diminutives in the same sense used in the thirteenth and fourteenth centuries: see H. Carrez, 'Surnoms évoquant des infirmités', *Onoma*, I (1947), 43; and Albert Dauzat, *Dictionnaire étymologique des noms de famille et prénoms de France* (Paris, 1951), 563b. Compare too with a simile used in the *Lamenta* or *Lamentations* by Matheolus, alias Matheus, from Boulogne-sur-Mer, dating from before 1301: *Pour faire lever Pierrette: 'Je vois, je vois', ce dit souvent... – Tardive comme un limeçon'* ('To have Pierrette get up: – "Going, going' ' she keeps saying... – As slow as a slug".') From Ch.-V. Langlois, *La Vie en France au Moyen Age de la fin du XIIe au milieu du XIVe siècle d'après les moralistes du temps* (Paris, 1926), 255.

Appendix 6

D' Klosterfrau im Schneckehus

See Gertrud Züricher, *Kinderlieder der deutschen Schweiz* (Basel, 1926), 90 (No.1386), for Basel, Zurich and Winterthur, with additional versions from Zurich, Solothurn, Thurgau, Aarau; another variant, which is not so clear, is from Saint-Gall: *Chlosterfräuli, Schneckehüsli, – Meinst, i sei verborge? – Chonnt de Vater, fangt si Müsli, – Wünscht em guete Morge.* There is also a longer version in L. E. Rochholz, *Alemannisches Kinderlied und Kinderspiel aus der Schweiz* (Leipzig, 1857), 255, which is about a father-confessor, and the rhyme provides the snail with a more classical charm. Franz Magnus Böhme, *Deutsches Kinderlied und Kinderspiel* (Leipzig, 1924), 289 (No. 1415), records a similar rhyme from Salzburg which mocks at monastic life, but omits the reference to the snail's shell: *Dö Klostafrau en Gart'n-haus, – Dö glaubt, sö is vaboring: – Da kimt der Pater Guardian – Und wünscht iahr guat'n Moring.* Böhme confirms the light-hearted character of the rhyme, L. A. von Arnim and Clemens Brentano's version of which he republishes, 180 (No. 889). He posits an early origin for the examples with the snail's shell, a point which is, at best, debatable. A scenario proposed by Rochholz has a child playing the role of father-confessor, and asking permission to leave his cell to answer a question put by a Montpelier student. The question concerns that invaluable creature, the snail, but the whole notion seems fanciful and, to say the least, superfluous. Indeed an Austrian version from Innsbruck shows that we have to do with an old finger-rhyme adapted to other functions. It goes as follows: *Die Klosterfrau im Schneggehaus, – Die moant, sie sei verborg'n; – Da kimmt der Pater Guardian, – Wünscht iar an guat'n Morg'n. – 'Guten Morg'n, Pater Guardian!' – 'Guten Morg'n, Schwester Klara!. – 'Ich möchte gern beichten!' – 'Was haben Sie gethan?' – 'Ich habe einen Fisch gekauft – Und hab' ihn auf den Tisch gestellt. – Die Katz hat mir 'n gfressen.' – 'Was haben Sie gesagt?' – 'Du Dundersteufskatz!' – 'Des durfens nicht mehr sagen! – Zur heilsamen Buss, – Gebens mir einen Kuss!'* – See *Zeitschrift des Vereins für Volkskunde*, IV (1894), 199, where a difference of language – dialect at the beginning and *Hochdeutsch* in the rest – is noted; but this has no great importance, since versions of the rhyme are also known at Rotthalmünster (Niederbayern) and Straubing, where they are completely in High German (*ibid.* 438). A. Englert correctly asserts that the first four lines have a separate origin, and that another rhyme has become attached to them. Such a rhyme does indeed exist, in French, English, Dutch and German, without these lines (see my article, 'Théâtre des doigts, théâtre de marionnettes', *Bulletin de la Société royale Le Vieux-Liège*, VII (155) (1966), 102-103), a fact which supports his view. Adolf Tobler considers that the first rhyme concerns snail-breeding by the Capuchins in Germany; this too may be true, but needs clarification (see *Zeitschrift des Vereins für Volkskunde*, IV (1894), 439). Comparison with the following tale from the region of Campo in the Elba country quoted by Novati, 148-9, might be interesting:

Anni addietro de' Camposi giudiziosi erano occupati a seminar degli aghi, quando scorsero sopra un grosso cavolo una lumaca. Il loro stupore fu indescrivibile nel veder quel nuovo animaletto. Accordatisi coi preti e le donne del paese, presa con sè la lumaca, si misero processionalmente in viaggio verso Roma per chiedere al papa se la lumaca, chiusa nel suo guscio come in una nicchia, fosse un santo. E cammin facendo pregavano cosi:

S. *Spunta le corne: becco nun dè;*
P. *Gesù, Madonna aitaci: facci sapè che dè.*
S. *Butta la bava: vecchio nun dè;*
P. *Gesù, Madonna aitaci: facci sapè che dè.*
S. *Sta nella nicchia: ma santo nun dè;*
P. *Gesù, Madonna aitaci: facci sapè che dè.*
S. *Porta la mitra: vescovo nun dè;*
P. *Gesù, Madonna aitaci: facci sapè che dè.*

Finalmente arrivarono a Roma. Ad una finestra del palazzo papale videro un cardinale colla papalina rossa, e subito i Campesi gli rivolserola parola dicendo: 'O, quell'omo dalla coppola rossa, ci sarebbe il papa in casa? Chiamatelo subito gli dovemo fà vedè un santo novo!' Pochi minuti dopo il papa era loro davanti e con bella maniera chiedeva loro che cosa volessero. E quelli mostrandogli la lumaca: 'Volemo sapè che dè. Dev' esse un gran santo: che ne dite voi?'

Il papa, meravigliato che nel mondo vi fosse gente tanto scema, rispose risoluto: 'E un lumacone come voi!' I Campesi allora, allegri per il bel successo, se ne tornarono a casa, ripetendo per tutta la strada: 'D'era una lumachella: – Gesù, Madonna bella! – Ora pro me.'

Concerning wax figures in a snail shell, see *Zeitschrift des Vereins für Volkskunde*, IV (1894), 199: such souvenirs were to be bought in *Galanterläden*, and models of the snail and the nun were also used in hygrometers. See also Karl Meuli, 'Schneggehüsler, Blätzliböögg und Federchans', *Schweizer Volkskunde*, XXVIII (1) (1938), 1-10.

Appendix 7

Tales about frightened peasants or tailors

Here is the text collected by Adolphe Borgnet under his pseudonym Jérôme Pimpurniaux in his *Guide du Voyageur en Ardenne ou Excursions d'un Touriste belge en Belgique* (Brussels, 1857), II, 29-30:

Un habitant de Dahnen, sur l'Our [in the Grand duchy of Luxemburg] *venait de partir pour porter* [to the mill] *un sac de grain quand on le voit revenir sans charge, pâle, tremblant et les traits décomposés par la terreur. On s'empresse autour de lui. Que s'est-il passé? Il faut au malheureux quelque temps pour reprendre ses esprits. La parole enfin lui revient: il raconte, non sans frissonner encore, qu'il a rencontré au milieu du chemin un monstre dont il fait la description, et qui lui a barré le passage; à peine a-t-il eu le temps de jeter son sac à terre et de s'enfuir. Ce récit glace de frayeur les assistants, et de nouveau le Conseil communal se réunit pour délibérer. Il est décidé d'armer tous les hommes valides, avec des instruments tranchants ou contondants qu'ils sont le mieux habitués à manier, et le plus brave prend la tête de la colonne, armé d'un trident. On arrive à l'endroit désigné. Un magnifique escargot occupe le milieu de la route, et la troupe s'arrête à cet aspect. Le chef seul s'avance, mais avec précaution, et du bout de sa fourche touche la coquille du mystérieux animal. A ce contact l'escargot sort brusquement, déploie ses quatre 'cornes' et s'avance intrépidement contre ses adversaires. Ce ne peut être qu'un animal enchanté, un sorcier déguisé, et cette idée remplit d'effroi tous les coeurs. Un instant on hésite sur le parti à prendre; mais quand on entend le commandant s'écrier qu'il ne peut, avec les trois pointes de sa fourche, affronter la colère d'un monstre qui lui en présente quatre, l'irrésolution cesse et la déroute devient générale. La leçon avait été rude, et plutôt que de s'exposer de nouveau, on préféra laisser au diabolique escargot le chemin dont il avait pris possession, et l'on en contruisit à grands frais un nouveau, le même dont on use encore aujourd'hui.*

Joseph Hens at Vielsalm (Belgian Luxemburg) transcribed in *Wallonia*, XII (1904), 54-6 a long tale in Walloon dialect at the expense of the inhabitants of the *ban de Bastogne* (Bastogne region), ironically nicknamed *lès coupêres* or 'jolly good fellows'. The tale is composed of the snail motif + AT 1250 = J 2133.5 + AT 910G = J 163.1 (they lose the purchased wit and break down the oven into which the mouse representing the wit has run). This is the first motif:

On cinsî avût dès coupêres po vârlèts. I lès-èvoya â molin. Is d'vint passî l'êwe. Arivîs â pont, is trovint sîh, sèt' gros lumeçons â mitan dèl vôye. 'Qu'èst-ce çoula? Dji n' passe nin,' dit onk. – 'Fês tot doûs!' dit 'n-aute, 'dji m' va r'quî 'ne fotche.' Qwand qu'il ariva avou s' fotche, i vèya lès lumeçons qui lèvint leûs qwate cwènes vèrs lu. 'Dji n' passe nin nin pus,' d'hat-i, 'dji n'a qu' deûs dints, èt is 'n' ont qwate, sâvans-nos!'

A farmer had *compères* for men-servants. He sent them to the mill. They had to get over a river. Reaching the bridge, they found in the middle of the way six or seven big snails. 'What is that? I cannot get past!' one of them said. – 'Be cautious,' said another, 'I will go and fetch a fork.' When he arrived with his fork, he saw the snails drawing their four 'horns' out towards him. 'I cannot get past either,' he said, 'I have only two prongs to my fork, and they have four horns, let us run away!'

These tales and many similar ones generated songs and folk traditions, for example in rhymes or on signboards, of one episode or another. See e.g. Henri Gaidoz and Paul Sébillot, *Blason populaire de la France* (Paris, 1884), 328-9; one melody noted.

Appendix 8

Description of decorative paintings on Slovenian bee-hives

(For this information, and that on the same subject in the body of my paper, I am indebted to Niko Kuret and Milko Maticetov).

1. A man with a hat on, carrying a big laundry iron in the right hand and holding a kind of stick on the left shoulder seems to be chased by an enormous white snail; on the left a tree.

2. A tailor with his hat on, recognisable from his scissors and his laundry iron, flees before a big black snail. He seems to try to slacken the animal's pace by threatening it with his scissors, and calls out in Slovenian: 'If only I could escape!'

3. A white snail makes after a tailor with his hat on, carrying his laundry iron, and who has dropped his stick, while another tailor, also wearing his hat, has climbed into a tree and holds his iron at the end of his stick, as it were to drive the animal away. Dated 1902.

4. A grey snail, between two trees, makes after three men with their hats on; one is running with his stick in the left hand; another is going on all fours and has lost his scissors; the third is climbing into a tree. Dated 1866.

5. A big grey snail causes a tailor to run away; he has lost his hat and tries to defend himself with his stick; his two companions have lost their hats too; one is climbing into a tree in which the third has already found shelter and is brandishing his scissors as if he were opposing the animal, while the other is throwing his iron away.

6. A dark grey snail is attacking three men: a tailor who has lost his hat and taken refuge in a tree, from where he is brandishing his iron with his left hand and holding his scissors in the right; a second man, while attempting to join him, has also lost his hat and has fallen on his knees at the foot of the tree; the third man has picked up the hat belonging to the second and is proffering it to him, while preparing to take flight. Dated 1860.

7. Two tailors are working seated, one on a table and the other on a bench between the table and the wall; they look very much frightened by a big black snail entering the room; the former is brandishing his scissors, the other is holding his open

scissors towards the snail and threatening it with a stick. In the right hand corner a black cat is arching its back.

It is possible that the stick in these descriptions is a yard-stick; what is certain is that the bee-hive fronts listed here are connected with a folksong, the following version of which was recorded in 1938 at Filipove in the Batschka (Yugoslavia) in a German dialect. The market singer had illustrated the song with a drawing representing three tailors and a snail:

II. *Der erste sprach: Geh du voran.*
   Der zweite sprach: Ich trau mich nicht.

III. *Der dritte war wohl auch dabei,*
   Er sagt: Sie frisst uns alle drei.

IV. *Und als dis Schneck das Haus bewegt,*
   So haben die Schneider das Gewhr gestreckt.

V. Die Katze, *die hockt wohl auf dem Dach,*
   Die hat sich wohl zum Buckel gelabt.

Text from the Songbook of Jacob Keller at Filipove, tune from the same on 29 December, 1938; information supplied by the *Volksliedarchiv*, Freiburg im Breisgau (*Quelle zu landschaftlichen Volksliedern*, 37, No.19, DVA A170924); another version from Sotin collected in 1939 by the same collector, Helmut Bräutigam, has only four stanzas and a different chorus; see also Keller Fulop in *Volkslieder aus der Jugoslawischen Batschka* (1910). The following other versions of the same song are also known to the present writer:

1. From Luxemburg: see first stanza in Louis Pinck, *Verklingende Weisen. Lothringer Volkslieder* (Metz, 1933), III, 410, to be completed with the

French translation in Alfred Micha, *Chansons et Chansonniers* (Liège, 1924), 74-5.

2. From Alsace: Kurt Mündel, *Elsässische Volkslieder* (Strassburg, 1884), 211 (No.196).

3. From Lorraine: see Pinck, II (1928), 169-71 and 372; another notation from the same at the *Volksliedarchiv* (No.A93971; 11 stanzas, no melody, sung by Michel Klein, from Kreis Forbach); a further example from the same source, sent to *Volksliedarchiv* in 1931 (3 stanzas, with melody, sung by a performer from Kreis Diedenhofen-Ost).

4. From Swabia: Ernst Meier, *Schwäbische Volkslieder* (Berlin, 1855), 180 (No.86).

5. From the Rheinland: a version noted by Georg Schmidt in Kreis Prüm between 1926-8, now at the *Volksliedarchiv* (No.A126577; 6 stanzas and melody); another from the same collector (No. Q151810; 6 stanzas, melody).

6. From Zürcher Oberland: collected by F. Boller and published in *Schweizerisches Archiv für Volkskunde*, XI (1907), 60 (2 stanzas, melody).

7. From Oberösterreich: collected at Ried in 1929 by Professor Dr Avanzini: *Volksliedarchiv* (No. Q127584; 4 stanzas).

8. From unspecified German localities: see Marie Rehsener, 'Aus dem Leben der Gossensasser',

Zeitschrift des Vereins für Volkskunde, XV (1905), 56; see also Ludwig Erk, *Deutsche Liederhort.' Auswahl der vorsüglicheren deutschen Volkslieder, nach Wort und Weise aus der Vorzeit und Gegenwart gesammelt und erläutert* (Leipzig, 1856), III, 448 (No.187); in the edition published by Erk and Franz Magnus Böhme (Leipzig, 1894, and reprint of 1925 referred to here), II, 513 (No.1663). Song derived from L. A. von Arnim and Claus Brentano: *Des Knaben Wunderhorn*, I, 325 (cf. Erk, II, 395; the melody in Erk, I, 4, No.16 and No.187). In Arnim-Brentano is a stanza (VII) which was dropped by Erk-Böhme. The remarkable article by Monika Hasse, 'Das Schneiderlied', in the *Handbuch des Volksliedes* edited by Rolf Wilhelm Brednich, Lutz Röhrich and Wolfgang Suppan (Munich, 1973), I, 800-31; see esp. 818, a catalogue of 54 versions. At the end of the volume, illus. 25 reproduces a bee-hive from Slovenia, very similar to my illustration, Pl.19. The source is the same as mine, the *Slovenski Etnografski Muzej, Ljubljana*. Thanks to Niko Kuret and Milko Maticetov. I discovered in the small open-air museum of Skoja Loka a bee-hive house with one side decorated with the motif discussed here. In June 1965 I received from them the photographs the descriptions of which are given above, and for which I am deeply grateful, as I am also to the *Volksliedarchiv* for their assistance.

Appendix 9

Combat between snails and birds

The following Spanish tale, which dates from the fifteenth century, describes the defence put up by snails against the onslaught of merlins. The text, which is difficult, is taken from A. Paz y Melia, 'Libro de Cetreria de Evangelista y una Profecia del mismo, con Prologo, variantes, notes y glosarios', *Zeitschrift für romanische Philologie*, I (1877), 234-5:

> *Esmerejon es vna ave muy pequeña y es del plumaje del falcon: es muy corto de petrine tanto como de cuerpo: destros pocos*

ay y menos arran (or: *harán?*) *dellos los caçadores y cavsalo aver tan pocos por que presumen tanto de faser de su persona que acaban presto: ellos son grandes caracoleros y andan syenpre dos juntos por se ayudar y ponen tanta fuerça y descargan sobre al caracolar dando surtes al çielo y desçendiendo alos abismos que como los caracoles tengan los cuernos feroses conel desatyno que trahen se lançan el vno por el vn cuerno y el otro por el otro. Asy acaban los mas y*

105

los que quedan no tyenen ley con nadie, y luego se van: el remedio para que no se vayan es que te vayas tu antes del quel de ty, y asy no podra alanarse que se te fue (or: *y asy no podran dezir que se te fue*).

Summary: Merlins are few, not solely because of hunters, but more so because they are great snail-eaters; to do this, they always fly two by two, so that they can assist one another; they dive in full flight from the sky into the abysses where they see the snails, so that they can make a frontal attack on the ferocious defending horns of their opponents, as a result of which they are often speared; the surviving merlins become so daring that they forget all caution when approached by hunters.

G. Baist (*op. cit.* in Note 39) considers that, though the Spanish tale appears to have an independent origin, it unites almost every element in the French versions. It seems to me, however, that the fundamental situation, whereby a snail terrifies a coward or cowards, is absent.

Notes

1. Giuseppe Fumagalli, *Chi l' ha detto? Tesoro di Citazione italiane e straniere, di origine letteraria e storica, ordinate e annotate* (Milan, 1958), 603-5. In an Italian song circulated in 1860 and composed by Arnaldo Fusinato in opposition to *il Reverendo Padre Lamoricière, generale dell' Ordine...*, General Christophe de la Moricière is said to have harangued his soldiers as follows: *Che val se irrompono – Da tutti i lati – Quanti ha l'Italia – Armi ed armati? – Fuoco alla miccia – Avanti! Urrah! – Les Italiens – Ne se battent pas!* For the quotation from Stendhal, see 604-5.

2. 'La guerra italiana, l'esercito e il socialismo', *Pagina della guerra* (Naples, 1919), 220-9; quoted by Fumagalli, 605.

3. 'Vita Hadriani', *Liber Pontificalis*, I (31), ed. L. Duchesne (Paris, 1886), 184, covering the years 772-4; quoted in Marguerite Zweifel, *Untersuchung über die Bedeutungsentwicklung Langobardus-Lombardus* (Halle, 1921), 73. See also Rita Lejeune, *Recherches sur le Thème: Les Chansons de Geste et l'Histoire* (Liège, 1948), 65-83, on Charlemagne's policy in those years, directed against Autcharius, the protector of Carloman's widow and children, as much as Didier and his son Adalgise. Mgr. Duchesne says in his preface to the *Liber Pontificalis* (quoted in Lejeune, 56 n. 2): *L'influence du* Liber Pontificalis *sur la littérature historique du moyen âge est comparable à l'influence de la papauté dans le monde politique de son temps.* According to Joseph Bédier, *Légendes épiques*, the best-known part was the 'Vita Hadriani', a rich source of fables and legends. It is said to be nearly contemporary with the events it recounts; see Lejeune, 65.

4. Zweifel, 75-6.

5. cf. also Giuseppe Cocchiara, *Il Mondo alla Rovescia* (Turin, 1963), 200-1, esp. also the chapter on 'Il Lombardo e la lumaca singolar tenzone'.

6. cf. also Francesco Novati, *Attraverso il Medio Evo* (Bari, 1905), 120; Fumagalli, 606.

7. cf. also Novati, 131; Fumagalli, 607.

8. Lilian M. C. Randall, 'The Snail in Gothic Marginal Warfare', *Speculum* (1962), 363. A similar idea is expressed by Floribert Deprêtre, from Haine-Saint-Pierre in Walloon-speaking Belgium, in one of his dialect plays, *I n'a foc què Norè* (1931), 10: *Mi, dès lumeçons, dju d'ai dès cîns come dès coulwèves; dj'avoûs r'piqui dès salâdes, i n'in d'meure pus qu' lès tourèts*; 'I have slugs in my garden, as big as snakes; I had pricked out lettuce seedlings, and only their stems remain'.

9. Book IV, Chapter 20. Mentioned by Zweifel, 68.

10. cf. also Novati, 130.

11. *Testudo* in medieval Latin means both snail and tortoise; cf. H. Schuchardt in *Zeitschrift für romanische Philologie*, XXVI (1902), 324; also Emile Gachet in *Glossaire roman-latin du XVe siècle extrait de la Bibliotèque de la ville de Lille* (Brussels, 1846), 12, and Auguste Scheler, *ibid.* (Brussels, 1865), 30: *testudo* is translated as *limechon*.

12. Fumagalli, 605, referring to Pio Rajna's paper in a Florentine journal: 'Stulti sunt Romani; sapienti sunt Pajoàri', *Marzocco* (21st April, 1918).

13. Léon Van der Essen, *Le siècle des saints* (Brussels, 1943), 61-2, provides additional details.

14. Zweifel, *op. cit.*

15. *ibid.*, 69: *Ist nun aber das Primäre die Fabel, die sich auf ein bestimmtes Ereignis bezieht, oder aber war die Ansicht von der Feigheit der Lombards zuerst selbständig vorhanden, um sich erst nachträglich mit einem gegebenen Fabelstoff zu verbinden oder zur Erfindung einer Fabel Anlass zu geben?*

16. *ibid.*, 69-70, after Tobler (see Note 32, below): *Die Schnecke im altfranz.* [*war*] *besonders als feiges Tier bekannt. . . ; Furcht gegenüber diesem Tier bedeutete daher das äusserste, was an Feigheit gezeigt werden konnte.* cf. also Randall, 361; she describes *Ignavia* as represented in miniatures by a man dropping his sword when faced with a hare, while pusillanimity is typified by fear of a snail. The snail, of course, is simply used as accessory in a symbolic situation, whose actual reference is to the man's seeming cowardice. Emile Mâle compares this to *la Lâcheté à la Force* in similar scenes, but his view seems to me unacceptable; it is, after all, the man who is strong yet panic-stricken: see *L'art religieux du XIIIe siècle en France. Etude sur l'iconographie du moyen âge et sur ses sources d'inspiration* (Paris, 1898), 166-7.

17. Roger Pinon, 'La polysémie symbolique de la limace et de l'escargot dans le langage en Occident', *Mélanges de Philologie romane offerts à Charles Camproux* (Montpellier, 1978), II, 1055-74.

18. cf. Note 11. Hare, tortoise, hedgehog and snail seem to be interchangeable. See also Johannes Bolt and Georg Polívka, *Anmerkungen zu den Kinder- und Hausmärchen der Brüder Grimm* (Leipzig, 1913-32), III, 341-55 (No.187).

19. Zweifel, 74-5; Godfrey's Latin text says: *Rex ubi congreditur, Ligurum pars victa fugatur, – Sic Desiderii copia tergo dedit.*

20. *ibid.*, 66.

21. Gustave Charlier, *Commynes* (Brussels, 1945), 105: *Les Français les regardent de haut, jusqu' à leur refuser le nom d'hommes* (VII, 17). *Mais eux leur rendent mépris pour mépris, et disent, en manière de raillerie, qu'à leur descente des monts leurs voisins 'sont plus que*

des hommes, mais qu'à leur retraite ils sont moins que femmes* (VIII, 13).

22. cf. Erhard Lommatzsch, 'Kleinere Mitteilungen', *Archiv für das Studium der neueren Sprachen und Litteraturen*, LXVI (1912), 129, 454-5 n.1. The MS. is from The Hague, and dates from the end of the fourteenth or beginning of the fifteenth century.

23. 'Melusine', *Les rues et églises de Paris* (Paris, 1884-5), II, col. 285.

24. Iacobi de Vitriaco, *Libri due, quorum prior Orientalis . . . alter Occidentalis Historiae* (Duaci, 1597), II, 278-9: . . . *Lombardo avaros, malitiosos et imbelles . . .* ; for Antoine de Brueil le jeune, *Moyens très utiles et necessaires pour rendre le monde paisible et faire en brief revenir le Bon Temps* (Paris, 1615), stanza xv, line 121 ff.; A. de Montaiglon, *Recueil de poésies françaises des XVe et XVIe siècles* (Paris, 1856), IV, 139: . . . *Quand les Lombards ne seront plus – Chiches, avares, jaloux, couards, – Ne vous enquerez du sur plus, – Bon Temps viendra de toutes parts.*

25. P. Rézeau in *Revue des Langues Romanes*, CLXV-CLXVI (1978), 116. The novel from which the quotation comes dates from 1936.

26. Lommatzsch, 457; from *La Reconnue*, final scene.

27. Quoted here from Fumagalli, 607. Originally published in *Athenaeum* (1923), 184-208.

28. Pinon, *op. cit.* (see Note 17).

29. Fumagalli, 608 (s.v.).

30. Book II, Chapter 7.

31. *Lés-Italyins, eûs', il-invintront ène machine à fai dés trôs d' soris pou s' sauver d'dins quand is vèront ariver lés bales u bin lés-éclairs, èt is n'in sortiront foc qué quand i-gnara pus qu'un ènemi conte dîs'* (page 15).

32. Adolf Tobler and Erhard Lommatzsch, *Altfranzösisches Wörterbuch* (Wiesbaden), XLIV, col. 469; Adolf Tobler, 'Assaillir la limace', *Zeitschrift für romanische Philologie*, III (1879), 99.

33. Randall, 358-67.

34. *ibid.*, 366.

35. Eugène Rolland, *Faune populaire de la France* (Paris, 1909), XII, 45 (after Bégule, *Mono-*

graphie de la cathédrale de Lyon); quoted by Randall, 359.

36. Rolland, 45 (after Joseph Garnier in *Mémoires de la Commission des Antiquités de la Côte-d'Or*, XII (1833), 111 ff.); mentioned by Lommatzsch, 456. See also Henri Chabeuf, 'La Maison du Miroir ou des Chartreux à Dijon', *Revue de l'Art Chrétien*, XLII (1899), 112-8 and illus. According to Rolland, the townspeople considered the group with the knight and the snail to be an allusion to the local married men.

37. A. L. Meissner, 'Die bildlichen Darstellungen des Reineke Fuchs im Mittelalter', *Archiv für das Studium der neuren Sprachen und Litteraturen*, XXXV (65) (1881), 215.

38. *ibid.* I am also grateful to the late Miss Violet Alford for giving me the detailed description in 1966. The stall is the 24th from the altar, and the following is taken from a booklet on the cathedral: 'Man with whip urging on a snail with a bundle on its back. A second man in front. Supposed to represent the slowness of travel.' However a sculptured whip could easily be confused with a slingshot, besides which Miss Alford found that it was very difficult to examine the stall and see anything precise.

39. G. Baist in *Zeitschrift für romanische Philologie*, II (1878), 304. It was then on display in the British and Medieval Room at the British Museum, but has since been removed. The Curators kindly gave me access to it, and also provided the picture reproduced here, for both of which I am most grateful.

40. Novati, 132-3.

41. Charles Nisard, *Histoire des livres populaires et de la littérature de colportage* (Paris, 1864), I, 116-21; the 1854 edition varies slightly (pages 145-7, information which I owe to Lucien Gershel of Paris). The summarised text is to be found on pages 116-9 (see Plates 16 and 17, where the text as given in the manuscript is reproduced in full); cf. also A. Certeux, 'La formulette de l'escargot et quelques anciennes images', *Revue de Traditions populaires*, VII (1892), 511-3; Rolland, 44-5; Baist, 303-4.

42. For the date 1488 see Nisard, I, 83-5, quoting Brunet, *Manuel du Libraire*; cf. also C. Lenient, *La Satire en France au Moyen Age* (Paris, 1883), 225 n.1, who considers it to be the oldest French printed almanac. Lenient sees it as an imitation of Jehan de Brie's earlier *Vrai Régime et gouvernement des bergers et bergères* (1379), combined with the *Calendarium* by Regiomontanus or John Muller, and with another work by Pierre de Dacia, Rector of the University of Paris in about 1326; cf. also Tobler, quoting the *Ménagier de Paris* as edited by Jérôme Pichon in 1847 (II, 223 n.); at the same time there existed a *Calendrier des bergers* published by Guy Marchant, in which the illustration and the poem were to be found. But see P. Saintyves (Pierre Nourry), *L'astrologie populaire étudiée spécialement dans les doctrines et les traditions relatives à l'influence de la lune* (Paris, 1937), giving a list of the editions of the *Kalendrier* based chiefly on Brunet, with 1491 as the earliest instance. The relevant date in the 1488 (?) and 1493 editions is the same, 18th April; in 1493 there was a second printing, on 18th July: cf. Anatole Claudin, *Histoire de l'Imprimerie en France a XVe et au XVIe siècle* (Paris, 1900), I, 366. The 1493 edition is completely new and differs from that of 1491, which is the oldest known to Claudin. In the MS. copy of the *Kalendrier*, miniature and poem (see Plate 16) come at the end of the book. According to Saintyves, the *Kalendrier* was published from 1491 to 1791 under various titles, either in Paris, Lyons or Troyes. But the *Débat* is not reproduced in all editions.

43. In French the watch-tower is called an *échauguette*, and Nisard, followed by Baist and Certeux, suggests an etymological association between that word and *escargot*, a view which he develops in his *Curiosités de l'étymologie française* (Paris, 1863), 57-64; Littré in his Dictionary saw, perhaps more convincingly, nothing but a pun (see I (2), 1485, s.v., *escargot*). In fact *échauguette* is from Frankish, **skarwanta* + suffix *-ette*, and *escargot* is from Provençal, *escargol*, the origin of which is complex; see Oscar Bloch and Walther von Wartburg, *Dictionnaire étymologique de la langue française* (Paris, 1960). The pun is really quite amusing, considering that the snail is at the same time a watchman and a watch-tower.

44. See also Plate 12, and cf. Pieter Van Moerkerken, *De Satire in de Nederlandsche Kunst der*

Middeleeuwen (Amsterdam, 1904), who suggests that the miniature may be the illustration of a song examined later in the present text, and referenced under Note 53. In fact this seems rather unlikely, since the song is not drawn from the same manuscript.

45. The various sections of *Roman de Renart* are called branches by modern scholars, for this is the name given to them in the *Roman* itself.

46. Plate 13 shows Tardif and Reynaert, though the event depicted is not explained.

47. Thomas Wright, *Histoire de la Caricature et du Grotesque dans la littérature et dans l'art* (Paris, new edition, n.d.), 148-9 and illus.

48. A. M. Hind, *Engraving in England in the Sixteenth and Seventeenth Centuries*, ed. Margery Corbett and Michael Norton (Cambridge, 1964), III, 81.

49. Charles Deulin, *Contes du Roi Gambrinus* (Paris, n.d.), 241-76.

50. For the first text see *Lettres Romanes*, XVII (3) (1963), 286; Ariane de Félice, 'Les joutes de mensonges et les concours de vantardises dans le théâtre comique médiéval et le folklore français', *Actas do Congresso internacional de Etnografia* (Santo Tirso, 1963), II, 42; Octave Delepierre, *Macaroneana Ou Mélanges de Littérature macaronique des différents peuples de l'Europe* (Brighton, 1852), 23-4. For this text and others see Achille Jubinal, *Nouveau recueil des contes, dits et fabliaux et autres pièces inédites des XIIIe, XIVe et XVe siècles pour faire suite aux collections d'Aussy, Barbazan et Méon mis au jour pour la première fois* (Paris, 1842), II, 208-28, republished with improvements in the reading of the manuscript in question by Lambert C. Porter, *La fatrasie et le fatras. Essai sur la poésie irrationnelle en France au moyen âge* (Geneva-Paris, 1960), 109-36; see No.3, lines 8-11; 26, 10-11; 30, 7-11; 48, 4-6; 54, 1-11. A *fatrasie* consists of 11 lines on two rhymes, 5aabaab 7babab.

51. James O. Halliwell-Phillips, *Popular Rhymes and Nursery Tales* (London, 1849), 175.

52. Compare Tale Type 1930, which refers however to the Land of Cokayne instead of Topsy-Turvy Land. For the two songs quoted, see Jean-Baptiste Weckerlin, *L'ancienne Chan-*

son Populaire en France (Paris, 1887), 221 (stanza 1, lines 4-6), 511 (tune 22); O. L. B. Wolff, *Altfranzösische Volkslieder* (Leipzig, 1831), 25; Carl Müller-Fraureuth, *Die deutschen Lügendichtungen bis auf Münchhausen* (Halle, 1881), 88. See also John Meier and Erich Seemann, *Lesebuch des deutschen Volksliedes. Zweiter Teil: Individuallied und Lied der Gemeinschaft in ihren wechselseitigen Beziehungen* (Berlin, 1937), 71 (No.180B, lines 44-5; after Haupt-Hoffmann, *Altdeutsche Blätter*, I, 163-4). The motif of the snail subduing the lion is indexed X 1345.1 in Stith Thompson, *Motif Index of Folk Literature* (Bloomington, 1957), V, 530; a reference is provided to Bolte and Polivka where, however, I can find no trace of the motif.

On French *menteries*, see Patrice Coirault, *Formation de nos Chansons Folkloriques* (Paris, 1955), II, 194 n.5: in this work they are dated to the sixteenth century, a view not shared by P. L. Jacob, *Vaux-de-Vire d'olivier Basselin et de Jean Le Houx, suivis d'un choix d'anciens vaux-de-vire et d'anciennes chansons normandes tirées des manuscrits et des imprimés avec une notice préliminaire et des notes philologiques par A. Asselin, L. Dubois, Pluquet, Julien Traver et Charles Nodier* (Paris, 1858), 268 n.2, who suggests the fifteenth century; this is on the basis of a comparison with the famous lying song, *Compère, qu'as-tu vu?*, an old Norman version of which is said to be found in *La Friqvassee crotestylonnee* (Rouen, 1604), lines 537-8, a text which actually originates about a century earlier than the publication date. The same opinion is expressed in O. L. B. Wolff, 25, quoting Louis Dubois, *Vaux-de-vire d'Olivier Basselin* (Caen, 1821), but on the false assumption that the song under discussion belonged to the fifteenth century, though the manuscript containing it can actually be dated to the beginning of the sixteenth century.

53. Hoffmann von Fallersleben, *Niederländische Volkslieder* (Hannover, 1856), 243-4 (No. 132), from a Weimar MS. 1537, No.47; cf. *Weimarisches Jahrbuch für deutsche Sprache, Litteratur und Kunst*, I (1854), 119 (No.11). Pieter van Moerkerkan, *op. cit.*, commenting on Plate 3, suggests that it refers to the song discussed here, but in this he is wrong. Possibly he means that songs of similar content may have been inspired by the illumination.

54. II, 3; this was communicated to me by the late Jean Baucomont.

55. Eugène Rolland, *Rimes et jeux de l'Enfance* (Paris, 1883), 110 (No.4).

56. *La Patrie*, 26th July, 1942; an *enquête* by P'tite Mère (III, 3).

57. This was noted by the late Jean Baucomont; see also *Les comptines de langue française* (Paris, 1961), 267.

58. Gertrud Züricher, *Kinderlieder der deutschen Schweiz* (Basel, 1926), 88 (No.1339).

59. Theophiel Peeters, *Oudkempische Volksliederen en Dansen* (Brussels, 1952), III, 111.

60. Pol de Mont, 'Het lied van den boom, leugenliederen en -vertelsels', *Nederlandsch Museum* III (10-11) (1889), 243-5.

61. Claude Roy, *Trésor de la Poésie Populaire* (Paris, 1954), 51.

62. Froment de Beaurepaire in *La Tradition*, VI (1892), 292.

63. Henri Potz in *Revue des Etudes Rabelaisiennes*, V (1907), 153-4.

64. John B. Arthurs, 'A Tyrone Miscellany', *Ulster Folklife*, III (1) (1957), 44.

65. *Volkskunde*, VI (1893), 99.

66. *Zeitschrift des Vereins für Volkskunde*, II (1892), 324-5.

67. Auguste Cittée in *Volkskunde*, VI (1893), 99.

68. Wilhelm Creizenach, *Geschichte des neueren Dramas* (Halle, 1918), II, 60-1; III, 468; Alois Brandl, *Quellen des Weltlichen Dramas in England vor Shakespeare* (Strassburg, 1898), lxxi; Novati, 148, n.35.

69. Baist, 304, quoting F. T., *Poésies Gasconnes* (new edition, n.d.), II, 309-13, 315-20, 331 ff.

70. Jean Paul Clébert, *Bestiaire fabuleux* (Paris, 1971), 183a.

71. Jean Outremeuse, *Myreur des Histors*, III, 63; see also Jean Haust, 'Gloses liégeoises', IV (1946), 517 (quoting Jean d'Outremeuse, *La Geste de Liège*, line 11783). The philologist suggests that *esquangnes*, in the reading by the editor, Ad. Borgnet, should be *esquargnes*, 'shells'; this correction is already implicit in Louis Michel, *Les légendes épiques carolingiennes dans l'oeuvre de Jean d'Outremeuse* (Brussels, 1935), 92.

72. Reproduced in Clébert, 181.

73. Félice, 60, quoting Henri Cordier, *Le voyage du bienheureux Frère Odoric* (Paris, 1891), 188.

74. A press report in a Liégeois newspaper of 18-19 September, 1971, tells of giant snails a foot long in Florida, introduced illegally from Hawaii by a child: *Ces animaux, qui mangent des fleurs, des feuilles, des fruits et des légumes, peuvent aussi se rassasier de peinture, de stuc et défigurer les murs par des traces gluantes. Ils sont aussi un danger pour les tondeuses à gazon et leur goût de l'humidité peut les conduire à mettre hors de fonctionnement les conditionneurs d'air. Ces escargots n'ont même pas l'avantage d'être appréciés par les gourmets... Chaque escargot peut avoir six cents descendants par an. L'an passé au nord de Miami on en a dénombré quatorze mille.* Is this the new form of the tale of the gigantic snail?

It is also worth mentioning here the gigantification of a gnat in a Flemish lying song from Little-Brabant, given in Pol de Mont, 257 (IV), and n.56d: *En tot Brugge — zat een mugge — met haar' muil wijd open. — Zeven kwezels — en acht ezels — zijn er in gekropen*; 'And at Bruges — a gnat was sitting — with its mouth wide open. — Seven biggots — and eight asses — have crept into it'.

75. William Dwight Whitney, ed., *The Century Dictionary*, revised edition ed. Benjamin E. Smith (London, 1914), 5724.

76. A. Boucherie in *Revue des Langues romanes*, XXIX (1886), 95, n.1: the book itself was published by Nicolas Du Chemin, and is very rare. The description of the snail, with its warlike horns, derives from Ronsard's *Freslon*.

77. cf. E. E. Vanhées, *Arména berlaimontois*, (Berlaimont (Picardy), 1867), 49, for a modern version of the joke about defence *against* a snail: *Invintez un canon pou fai révernir tout d'un coup les quate fers in l'êr tous les lumechons d'êne rasiêre de blé*; 'Invent a canon which will make all the snails fall on their backs in a corn field'. Curiously enough the socialist Liégeois newspaper, *Le Monde du Travail* (27th July, 1972), printed a caricature showing a man aiming a bazooka at a snail with its horns out.

78. Ambroise Paré, *Des monstres et des prodiges*, 159, quoted in Clébert, 444; Paré cites Thevet; cf. also L. Charbonneau-Lassay, *La mystérieuse emblématique de Jésus-Christ. Le bestiaire du Christ* (Bruges, 1940), 929.

79. cf. also Claus and Liselotte Hansmann, *Viel köstlich Wachsgebild* (Munich, 1959), 18-19, and 2 illustrations.

80. Archer Taylor, *The Literary History of Meistergesang* (New York, 1937), 102. Georg Hagen's *Meistergesang* is entitled 'Der Krokodilfang im Predigerkloster'.

81. Bolte and Polivka, II, 559; Peter Buchan, *Ancient Ballads and Songs of the North of Scotland, hitherto unpublished* (Edinburgh, 1828), I, 259-60. The song, for which no source is given, was omitted from the 1873 edition of the same book. Bolte first published it in the *Zeitschrift des Vereins für Volkskunde*, IV (1894), 434, and it is said to predate that in which seven of nine Swabians chase a hare.

82. Anton Renk, 'Kinderreime aus Tirol', *Zeitschrift für österreichische Volkskunde*, II (1896), 101 (details from Patznaun).

83. Iona and Peter Opie, *The Oxford Dictionary of Nursery Rhymes* (London, 1951), 401-2; the earliest known mention (1784) is given in *The Oxford Dictionary of Quotations* (London, 1953), 366 (No.19). An American version, mentioned to me by Archer Taylor, is abridged: 'Four-and-twenty tailors went – A-hunting of a snail. – The bravest man amongst them – Durst not touch her tail'.

84. cf. Opie; a curious explanation of 'tailors' is to be found in William S. Baring-Gould and Cecil Baring-Gould, *The Annotated Mother Goose* (Cleveland and New York, 1967), 87, where it is suggested to be 'probably a corruption of "tellers", a teller being one stroke of the church bell at the time of a funeral.' This, however, seems implausible.

85. A. Goursaud, *La société rurale traditionelle en Limousin* (Paris, 1977), 376.

86. Rolland, *Rimes et jeux de l'Enfance*, 392-3.

87. A. -J. Verrier and J. Onillon, *Glossaire étymologique et historique des Patois et Parlers de l'Anjou* (Angers, 1908), I, 527b.

88. Georges Dottin, *Glossaire des Parlers du Bas-Maine (département de la Mayenne)* (Paris, 1899), 328a.

89. Damase Arbaud, *Chants populaires de la province* (Aix, 1864), II, 199-201 (stanza 1).

90. Jean-François Bladé, *Poésies populaires de la Gascogne* (Paris, 1882), II, 324-7 (iv).

91. Jules Mousseron, *Feuillets noircis* (Lille, 1907), 28 (stanza xv).

92. Maria, Kühn, *Alte deutsche Kinderlieder* (Königstein im Taunus, 1965), 122; Karl Mersch, *Die Luxemburger Kinderreime* (Luxemburg, 1884), 91; Richard Beitl, ed., *Wörterbuch der deutschen Volkskunde* (Stuttgart, 1955), 382; and for Switzerland, see Züricher, 89 (No.1365, collected in Basel, Bern, Aarau, Trogen), 448 (variant from Einseideln, where it introduces a charm).

93. Rolland, *Faune*, XII, 43; and cf. *Revue des Traditions populaires*, XXVI (1911), 113, after *Le Pédant joué* (1645), Act II, Scene 2.

94. Rolland, *Faune*, XII, 43, after *Recueil de pièces mazariniques parues en 1649* (Paris, 1650), 559.

95. Rolland, *Faune*, XII, 43-4.

96. Dr C. Kruyskamp, *Groot Woordenboek der Nederlandsche Taal* (The Hague, 1961), 1817; J. A. N. Knuttel, *Woordenboek der Nederlandsche Taal* (The Hague, 1936), XIV, 1547; M. Maasen and J. Goossens, *Limburgs Idioticon* (Tongeren, 1975), 232.

97. *Bulletin folklorique d'Ile-de-France*, III-IV (1945), 23.

98. Noël due Fail, *Propos rustiques suivis des Balivernes* (Paris, 1928), 74.

99. Rolland, *Faune*, XII, 44.

100. *Romania*, XXXV (1906), 529. It was Jessie L. Weston whose *From Ritual to Romance* (Cambridge, 1920) inspired the basic symbolism of T. S. Eliot's *The Waste Land*.

101. Antti Aarne and Stith Thompson, *The Types of the Folktale* (Helsinki, 1961), 517-8.

102. Gerald Thomas, *The Tall Tale and Philippe d'Alcripe* (St John's, 1977), 37-8.

103. On the Land of Cokayne, cf. Giuseppe Cocchiara, *Il Paese di Cuccagna* (Turin, 1956).

104. On Topsy-Turvy Land, cf. Giuseppe Coc-chiara, *Il Mondo alla Rovescia.*

105. The motif still survives; Dominique France, alias Julia Franz, from Auvelais in Walloon Belgium writes in a dialect fable entitled *Li crapaud èt l' bouledogue* ('The toad and the bulldog'): *Mins quand min.me avou l' tiésse qui t'as – Seûr qui t' fés peû auzès lumeçons;* 'Nonetheless with your head – You surely frighten slugs'. See *El Bourdon d' Châlèrwè èt co d'ayeurs*, VII (66) (1955), 30 (lines 28-9).

106. 'La formulette de l'escargot et quelques anciennes images', *Revue des Traditions populaires*, VII (1892), 507-14.

107. It is the *Couteau de saint Georges* in Brittany, Ile-de-France, Champagne, Lorraine; *grand couteau de saint Georges* in Franche-Comté; *petit couteau qu'on m'a donné à la saint-Georges* in Périgord. St George occurs in a few local versions in connection with the menaced snail's parents: behind Saint-Georges of St George's door in Lorraine; at St Peter's (not St George's) door in the Loire department; *darie chie Geoudje*, 'behind George's house', in the neighbourhood of Belfort. See Rolland, *Faune*, III, 202 and 204, and XII, 38; and Auguste Stöber, *Elsässisches Volksbüchlein* (Mulhouse, 1859), I, 193 (No. 423).

108. R. de Westphalen, *Petit Dictionnaire des Traditions populaires messines* (Metz, 1934), 243, quoted by Robert Wildhaber, 'Schneck-enzucht und Schneckenspeise', *Schweizerisches Archiv für Volkskunde*, XLVI (1950), 175.

109. *Bulletin de la Société de Mythologie Française*, II (1950), 12 and illus.; and R. F. in *Revue de Recherches ethnographiques*, X (5) (1976), 430-2.

Folklore and Advertising*

LUTZ RÖHRICH   University of Freiburg

IN its attempt to find new means and methods of praising consumer products, it was almost inevitable that the advertising industry would turn to folklore. The world of folklore, it is believed, has preserved the traditions and wisdom of the ages. Time-honoured and venerated items of folklore are thought to echo an earlier pre-industrial age, when the quality of products was known and cherished. In its use of such traditional items, the advertising industry has removed them from their original environment and shaped them for its own purposes. Not only has folklore had an influence upon advertising, but by the wide dissemination of traditional items, advertising has had its profound effect upon folklore.

I do not believe that advertising should be glorified or unduly praised, although I have an admiration for many of the clever and witty ideas expressed. There are also negative aspects to advertising, for instance the ever-increasing manipulation of man, who finds it harder and harder to cope with the increasingly refined techniques of the advertising industry. Advertising appeals mostly to unconscious drives and emotions, and thus the appeal is at the subconscious and/or emotional level. Decreasing ability to make rational judgements and increasing susceptibility are precariously balanced. The weaker the rational, conscious controls, the stronger the role played by unconscious and emotional drives.

There are diverse, often contrasting ways of attracting attention, usually unconsciously: the allusion to the familiar, often accompanied, however, by alienation and deviation from the norm; stimulating the imagination; attracting attention through repetition; appeals to basic drives all play and important role, especially sexual instincts. The association with sex is meant to make the products as attractive and desirable as possible.

But advertising is not limited to the appeal to sex-drives. All the drives and instincts are exploited: the drive for self-preservation, power and possessions, the drives of play, competion, the herd and imitative instincts are all played upon.

Though industrial production with its retail trade may appear to be diametrically opposed to traditional folklife, folklore and advertising have become inseparable. Both are, in an esthetic sense, popular rather than elitist, that is, questions of taste are governed in both instances by majority rule. An item becomes folklore, that is a part of popular tradition, only if it has mass appeal, and similarly only those items with mass appeal will sell. One accepts that which is familiar, simply because it is familiar; it need not be tested because it has, one assumes, been time-tested.

In advertising 'folklorism', that is elements which are based on traditions of folk culture, is widespread. For example there are:

1. Decorative items and implements of rustic origin, from timber-frame houses to regional costumes.
2. Explicit imitations of legends and folktales.
3. Allusions to superstitions in illustrations and text.
4. References to, and depiction of, folk customs.
5. The use of folk-speech in texts, proverbs and proverbial sayings, either directly, as an alienation device, or in parodied form.
6. Passages from folksongs and nursery rhymes.

* This is a much-shortened version of Professor Röhrich's paper, which originally included numerous illustrations the reproduction of which is unfortunately impossible in the present volume.

Among the effects achieved by the use of folk-lore in advertising is the association of nature with tradition. Folklorisms convince the consumer that there is nothing artificial in a natural product. They also conjure up associations with leisure and vacation time, carefree life in the country. Through the use of folklorisms, the product attains the aura of being 'home-made', and the social image of a rustic life-style is created. Folk-lorisms, above all, represent the traditional element in an advertisement. The recognition factor of something familiar is, in advertising, just as relevant as the appeal of something new. At least one element in the advertisement must be something to which the potential customer can relate; the remainder can be as modernistic as is desired. Man lives by his symbols, many of which have been formed in the past. Where can one locate better symbols of man's heritage that are readily recognised as such — at least unconsciously — than in folklore?

Folklore operates with that which is typical, and advertising wishes to introduce an item and make it as familiar and everyday as possible, so that it too will become something typical. In other words, advertising must discover those elements in a product which can themselves form tradition. Regardless of whether one wants to sell a political idea, a social programme, shoes, hats or apples, a purveyor must first of all seek to recognise the deeper significance which the product or services which he offers have for the public. It is not sufficient for the seller of hats to invent an advertising slogan which itself can become proverbial ('The man with a hat has a headstart', 'One can't go out anymore without a hat'); instead he must also give thought to the role hats have played in cultural history, he must discover the reasons for the unconscious resentment which many people have against hats and their cultural and social significance. The seller of textiles and fashions must give thought to the reasons for which, in most countries, women wear dresses and men trousers. When one purchases a pair of pants, a chair, a bed, a loaf of bread, a car or a tube of toothpaste, one is not just buying clothing, furniture, food or useful objects, one is acquiring to a great degree their inherent symbolic significance.

Advertising is most successful when it is able to activate collective norms. In all advertising there is invariably reference to a social imperative, to that indefinite 'they' by which all people regulate and measure their behaviour. Any advertising which tries to resist the norms deeply anchored in the public psyche is ill designed.

As I already stated, folklorisms represent the popular items in an advertisement. With the folk of folklorisms, the advertisement creates its own solidarity with the consumer. As a result the customer views the depiction of the ideal with less scepticism.

If I have given the impression that folklorisms are found in all advertisements, I wish to correct it. Only about 10-15 per cent of advertisements, can be analysed with reference to folklore. This frequency is, however, sufficient to justify devoting a detailed study to the topic. This paper was meant only as indication of a few of the possible staring points and directions for such a study.

GENERAL CONFERENCE PAPERS

Play

ROGER ABRAHAMS   University of Texas

OUR discipline commonly has differentiated implicitly between traditions of work and play by making a distinction between folklore and folklife. Because we have assumed that 'the folk' are a homogeneous group, usually pursuing an agrarian way of life, the distinction between work and play has not been pursued explicitly. We seem to have wanted to assume that somehow life among the folk is a seamless fabric, and that work and leisure activities reflect the same structures and practices — an assumption that I think has a good deal of validity to it.

However, because we have not made these implicit understandings and assumptions explicit, we have walked away from the opportunity to enter into the vibrant scholarly discussion of what constitutes play. Because so little of our professional efforts have gone into exploring how lore provides its special pleasures and illuminations, folklorists have added little to our understanding of what the state of playing is and means, or how humans operate when they engage in play. Yet there are certain facets of the process and products of playing that folklorists are in a unique position to explore, because we are used to dealing with such materials as they are acted on in recurrent situations, and often at times and places set aside for the playing. Furthermore, we have learned the usefulness of making cultural generalisations, both as such notions operate in different domains within one cultural community, and how any such insights may have application cross-culturally. There are those of us, of course, who argue that the products of man's creative instinct are infinitely more important than the creative process. Thus, philosophising is regarded as beyond our intellectual commitment, indeed antithetical to it, because it takes us so far away from our basic data — the texts of performance. Such an anti-philosophical position would maintain that analysis of the life of play eliminates the very heart of the play experience, just as explaining what is funny kills the humour in a joke.

To this argument one can only respond that by ignoring the theory of play (and work, for that matter), by not attempting to elicit the attitude of the players on what constitutes playing, what is good or beautiful about the experience or its product, we will miss the forest for the trees. I am not calling for an elaborate theory of play or creativity here so much as for an explanation of what our own theory may already be. That is, I will attempt to demonstrate that we already have a number of 'deep' (and therefore taken-for-granted), in-common and commonsensical notions about play; and that these notions are in fact at the centre of our means of communicating, celebrating, and especially having fun.

In all kinds of play, we are engaged with those special set-aside worlds in which rules and systems operate energetically yet effortlessly. This is because play invokes those fictions we are permitted to love most fully, for there is little to worry us within these worlds but the experience of experience itself — the expenditure of energy for the sake of celebrating our humanity, even when we do so in competition. As Paul Valéry observed, discussing the notion of culture itself:

> ... the whole system hangs upon the power of images and words... Under the names *foresight* and *tradition*, the future and the past, which are in fact only imaginary perspectives, dominate and control the system. The social world then seems to us as natural as Nature, although it is only held together by magic. Is it not, in truth, our enchanted

structure, a system founded . . . on obedience to words, the keeping of words, the power of images, the observance of customs and conventions — all of them pure fictions.

These fictions are the very stuff which enable life to be invested with meaning, inasmuch as they carry with them typical scripts or agendas, ways that we know in advance approximately what will happen. Further, each fiction restricts the moves and plays possible, for within the worlds invoked we must play by more restricted rules and more self-consciously modulated roles. The basic fiction of fictions, that invoked in all play, is that somehow playing is a liberating experience. Inasmuch as it does not demand a product or even the learning of a lesson, and inasmuch as no transformation of personal status is engineered with social consequences off the playing field, the stage, or the platform, play does in fact liberate us from the need to use our energies to produce or to proceed in life. On the other hand, entering into the play world in every other way is an extremely constricting experience. All play involves an intensification and coordination, but the price is the restriction of the number of roles one may play, as well as the repertoire of devices appropriate to that role. What I mean by this is that by tagging someone and saying 'You're it', one enters into a play world in which there are only two roles — it and the other — and the number of moves available to those playing is remarkably limited.

But playing involves much more than just games. In English, we seem to make a running distinction between three types of intensive activity all included in *play*: performance or entertainment; games and sports; and festivities and celebrations. To be sure, these are often found occurring in conjunction with each other, for the creation of a licensed play environment seems to invite the entire range of playful activities. Thus, in a festival, one often finds games and performances as part of the festivities. But while a performance is going on, there is little question that it is *a performance* and not a party or game or whatever. This is because someone (or ones) is playing the role of performer and holding up his behaviour to aesthetic scrutiny. Similarly, though there is much which can be described in performance terms in, say, of a game of tug-of-war or football, there is never a question as to whether it is a performance or a game, for the major focus of the play-event is on the competitive element, the *agon*. In addition, the further the event is set aside from the everyday flow of life, the greater the focus possible, and the more intensely focused the specific play events will be. This occurs because, among other things, there will be a greater investment of energy on the part of both players and onlookers (what Clifford Geertz adumbrates as 'deep play') and thus a strong sense of preparation and an ever greater need to play by the rules and within the boundaries.

In pursuit of our already existing implicit theory of play and celebration, I then posit three kinds of *pure* or *ideal* states of intense engagement, all of which are designated by us as *play* because they are: 'framed', having a sense of beginning and end, and reminders within the proceedings that what is happening is *just play*; 'stylised', made up of moves or behaviour which are in codes appropriate to the occasion (and only that kind of occasion), and which are repetitive and redundant and therefore predictable, and which involve a special dimension along which intensification occurs. The three types are: (1) *performance*, in which the stylised behaviour is under the control of designated performers or entertainers, who hold up their activity for aesthetic judgment, and who are therefore playing roles which differ from those of everyday life; (2) *games*, in which the action focusses on contest, and the roles played are therefore antagonistic, and play judged in terms of the involvement within the frame of competition and the furtherance of its flow; and (3) *festivities* or *celebrations*, in which the roles played are specially heightened and stylised versions of those played in the everyday, but the stylised behaviour is specific to the ceremony, the feast, the party. In the case of performance, the behaviour is judged in aesthetic terms primarily; in games by how it contributes to the process of competition; however, in what I have called celebrations (for want of a more precise term), the occasion is judged good or bad by how much *fun* is engendered, or how effective the intensified interactions are.

Examining the dimension *fun* casts some further light on the field of meaning of the playful. Fun is, in many of its uses, almost synonymous with play, especially with regard to describing the tone or state of being of an interaction. All play is supposed to involve some dimension of fun. Further, anything which is done *for fun* is marked as an essentially non-serious occasion — that is, the situation is not charged with driving toward a result other than the pure experience itself. Fun, like play, as a descriptive word is a way of marking the serious from the ludic — at least in the interactional sense that we do not have to assume responsibility for behaviour beyond the bounds of the situation. We need carry nothing but the by-products of exhilaration from the experience itself; if there are lessons to be learned, or products to be made, this has almost nothing to do with the fun of the occasion.

While fun has a kind of experiential consistency to it, we do distinguish between *having fun* and *making fun*. The former carries with it a sense of exhilaration for its own sake, while the latter makes a potential tendentious and aggressive dimension to fun-making occasions.

What all this means is that we do feel the need to contrast, from time to time, the expending of energy for productive purposes (in being *serious* or *working*), from those occasions when we seem to expend it for the experience itself. Thus, we feel called on to mark certain behaviour with 'but seriously . . .' and other as 'just for fun . . . .' I put it this way, because I want to emphasise that these are two motives and modalities that are commonly found intermingled as part of the same interactional occasion, and therefore in need of being directly referred to within the interaction itself whenever one wishes to switch interpretive frames. In everyday interactions, we assume that both seriousness and kidding can be carried on simultaneously — or at least we can switch back and forth without calling the nature of the occasion into question. However, the moment we enter into a play-frame, the 'for-fun' element becomes our primary mode of interpretation. Or, as Gregory Bateson notes, all behaviour within the play-frame carries the message 'This is play'. But as he pursues the subject, this message is meaningless as an interpretation screen without the accompanying question, 'Is it really play?' For play to be successful, for fun to be fun, there must be some attack mounted from within or without, which threatens to spill over, to take the play off the field and into the crowd, off the stage and into the audience.

From a folklorist's perspective, most of the occasions that we encounter with professional interest have this deeper and firmer framing going on, one which announces the entire experience is to be interpreted as fun and games, that is, playfully. The participants are *just* playing, *just* having fun. This *just*-ness carries the power of the disclaimer, a very large fiction which says that anything within this scene or event is not to be taken seriously (unless otherwise specified). It could be argued that just this framing technique and the master fiction it carries with it is the basis of culture, or to put it more confusingly, the fiction upon which all other fictions are predicated.

The introduction of the phrase 'just playing' or 'just kidding' is an indication that a shift of interpretive frame is called for in a conversational context. It is a minimal accounting procedure, a simple attempt to obtain license for reinterpretation. The obverse of this strategy would be to accuse someone of 'playing around' or 'playing with', thus using the play-frame not as a way around accountability but as an accusation of an inappropriate lack of seriousness. It is through such employment that we come to understand the terms as a means of establishing and maintaining behavioural boundaries, even while constantly readjusting interpretive frames and criteria of judgment.

In conversation, keeping open the possibility of shifting and adjusting such frames of interpretation is central to maintaining the openness on which interactional flow is predicated. But in the more intense and focussed occasions with which folklorists are used to dealing, the possibility of shifting frames becomes less and less viable, the greater the depth of play. Nonetheless, they must remain negotiable to a certain extent for, as noted, play does not succeed without the question remaining — 'is this serious?' Alternatively, we distinguish between *real* and *play* activities, and are thus able to call for an accounting in terms of authenticity as well as seriousness.

Thus, in an interlocking fashion, play is distinguished from real, everyday, serious work. In each case, the contrast leads to a slightly different field of meaning. But overlap occurs with regard to the sense of departure from the more various and mixed realms of interaction. Play then becomes the word which marks the onset of those special sets of patterned expectation which often go under the rubric of socio-fictions. Further, play is the fiction of fictions inasmuch as it is the concept-term that brings together all the ideal and sub-junctive constructs, the *as if*, as well as *what if*, words. Playing invokes the power of license or excuse just at the point where society would begin to impinge with its 'but seriously . . .' rules.

The paradox of playing is that playing subverts as it amplifies. It is our major fiction, but one which selectively undermines through parody, satire or some other ironic expression, while it underpins all of the other fictions by which we live. In this way we can, in any situation we call play, sense the presence of absent things doubly — in the fiction that gives place, substance, and meaning to the things, and in questioning the meaning at its moment of inception. This it does by *making fun* as well as *being fun*.

Miraculous Legends of Wartime

ISSACHER BEN-AMI   The Hebrew University, Jerusalem

THE Jews of Gola have lived through hundreds of years of incessant wars, battles and persecution and as a result have developed various defence mechanisms. With the creation of the State of Israel their struggle for the right to exist has taken a different form and this is demonstrated by their folklore. Traditional medicine, for example, is filled with customs and beliefs intended to preserve the patient from the enemy, prison, and other similar potential threats. In this context the folk saints of every nation who preserve the Jews from harm have an important role to play.

It is interesting to see the extent to which such customs, intended to preserve the life of the people in Gola, have persisted after the emigration of so many Jews to Israel and the ways in which they have altered. I propose in this study to concentrate mainly on one point: legends of folk saints which concern the defence and preservation of life.[1]

The legends which this study is based on were collected by my colleagues and myself: there are eighty-two.[2] The majority concern the Yom Kippur War, the struggle against terrorism, the War of Attrition, the Six-Day War, the Sinai Campaign, the War of Liberation, and the Second World War. I also include a few examples specifically connected with saving the life of Moroccan Jews, arising from an organised and armed attack against an entire settlement. The various motifs are classified into twenty-one groups and there are several examples of each one. These legends illustrate the diverse characteristics of the saint and of his relationship with his devotees. The link between the saint and his representative is maintained by dreams, and sometimes with the help of apparitions.

1. *The announcement that a war is about to begin.*

Three days before the Yom Kippur War, the saint tells his representative on earth that the War is about to begin. The announcement is made so that the devotee can plan the festive dinner held once a year in honour of the saint. The man wonders what he ought to do: should he tell the police? He finally decides not to, because no-one believes him. This motif is only to be found in Israel.

2. *The saints defend the frontiers.*

A woman dreams that she sees two saints during the night; both are armed. Visitors to a holy tomb note that the saint is not there: he is at the frontier guarding the soldiers. Each saint is responsible for a particular military area. Devotees used to dream about their saints, and this new function is a feature of the present situation in Israel.

3. *The saint defends soldiers and citizens.*

All the shells fired at Safed during the Six-Day War were sent back to Syria by the saint,[3] Rabbi Simon Bar-Johai. Some of the inhabitants of Ashquelon were unable to reach the shelters; they lit candles for the saint. Some dreamed that he was protecting them and helping them to take Gaza. Many saints in Israel help the soldiers. As one informant remarked: 'Do you think that we have strength? The strength belongs to God! The saints are helping us too!'

4. *The saint announces the approaching cease-fire.*

People are anxious about the progress of the Yom Kippur War. The saint, Rabbi Simon Bar-Johai, appears in a dream to a woman and tells her there will soon be a cease-fire.

5. *The saint warns his devotee before a coming alarm.*

During the War the saint wakes his devotee, says there will soon be an alarm and asks him to open the door of the shelter. It comes about just as he has said.

6. *The saint appears as an old man and saves soldiers at the front.*

Many stories describe an old man walking about at the front and rescuing soldiers. He tells them to leave their tank before it is destroyed and shows them where to find missing comrades. He often appears on a white horse, dressed in white. During the Six-Day War, Jerusalem Arabs thought old men were fighting against them.

7. *Invocation of the saint's help brings salvation.*

Faced with great danger, the soldier calls on the saint and is saved. In one case a shell fell nearby and the man was hurled into the air. Another soldier was saved in a car-crash. The wife of a soldier invokes the saint, lights candles, and her husband appears before her after two months of silence.

8. *Prayer and a direct appeal to the saint achieve miracles.*

Before the Six-Day War a man prays at the tomb of Rabbi Simon Bar-Johai that the Arabs will be defeated. He also asks the saint to order a taxi so that he can return to Jerusalem. His prayer is granted. A woman whose seven sons are at the front prays to the saint to return them safely to her; they all come back. Three are wounded. They tell her they are the only men who were saved. The people of Ashquelon pray to the saint and at once Gaza is taken.

9. *The saint heals the injured.*

A woman's son is seriously injured. The mother dreams that she sees the saint and her son recovers.

10. *The saint cares for prisoners-of war.*

Parents pray to the saint when their son is arrested or taken prisoner and he returns safely. In many cases the devotees make a vow and organise a dinner in honour of the saint.

11. *The saint announces approaching victory in a dream.*

The saint announces to a woman in a dream that victory is near and she tells her neighbours. Rabbi David Moshe's synagogue in Ashquelon miraculously glows with light and everyone knows that victory is at hand.

12. *Lives are saved during a terrorist attack.*

Terrorists attack a group of schoolchildren. One of them invokes the saint, who preserves her and helps her to escape.

13. *During the War Jews and Arabs visit the tomb of the saint.*

Jews and Arabs visit the tomb of the Prophet Elijah throughout the year. During the War they continue to visit the tomb, despite increasing tension.

14. *The saint defends Jews in the Diaspora against attack.*

Jewish communities and settlements have many legends of miraculous rescues performed either by the saint himself appearing on horseback or by means of rocks falling from the sky onto the enemy. In some examples pigeons put the enemy to flight. A Moslem fighting at the front in the Indo-Chinese conflict invokes a Jewish saint and is saved; each year he offers him a sacrifice. A Moslem tribe fighting another asks a Jewish saint for help and he saves them.

15. *A vow made during the War.*

Centuries ago, during one of the Israeli Wars, a man whose son was captured vowed to write down the whole of the Torah while standing in a pool, and he fulfilled his vow.

16. *The saint arranges an engagement in war-time.*

During the fighting the saint guides a young man to a young woman living in another town. The young man gives the saint's message to her family and the girl accepts him.

17. The use of amulets in war-time

Many soldiers wear a protective amulet in battle and the saint places one on the city walls to prevent the enemy from entering the Jewish quarter.

18. War-time fears

A soldier lies to his friends and says he thinks he is about to die. His friends tell him not to give way to Satan. The following night he is killed by a bullet, but his friends escape unharmed.

19. The saint as protector

Saint Lala Sulika saved a soldier's life while he was still a boy. Later when he was fighting in the army his car turned over three times but he was unhurt: the saint was still protecting him.

20. The saint sacrifices himself for the community

Moslems threaten to destroy the Jewish quarter but Rabbi David Abuhasera sacrifices himself to save his people.

21. The saint leaves Morocco

Many Moroccan Jews who settled in Israel dreamed that the saint left their homeland and came to Israel to protect them.

This research is based on legends illustrating the changes that occur in customs and art during war-time. But they only show one aspect of the phenomenon: personal and social factors must also be identified and evaluated. A distinction needs to be made between stories collected in war-time — or immediately before, or after — and those collected some while after, which have undergone considerable changes due to the altered situation.

The link, within the framework of the war-time situation, between the saint and the people he saves, as well as the expression of this attachment within a given homogeneous ethnic group,[4] enables us to comprehend this phenomenon in its entirety, though it may be possible to expand this on the basis of collected material.

The cult of the saint is undoubtedly strongest and most widespread within the Jewish Moroccan community. After five years of fieldwork we had collected the names of approximately five hundred

and sixty Moroccan saints, including twenty women.[5] Voinet refers to forty-five Jewish saints also venerated by Moslems, and thirty-one saints claimed by both Jews and Moslems. The cult of the saint is a universal phenomenon which still requires extensive research.[6]

Investigation into the existence and influence of the saints on their devotees needs to be conducted on two levels:

(1) Examination and comparison of the cult in Morocco and Israel.

(2) Examination of the phenomenon in the unusual conditions of war-time.

The cult as practised by the Jews of Morocco in their homeland served many functions. The custom of lying on the tombs of the righteous — a primitive observance in Jewry — was not in fact practised by the Hahams. There is no doubt that the very existence of such a widespread phenomenon among the Berbers and Arabs of North Africa[7] influenced local Jews, though Jewish influence on the cult of the saints was greater than that of the Moslems.[8]

Does the cult of saints in Morocco enable a persecuted national minority to feel that it is a Jewish entity in Israel? Does it represent an attempt to feel spiritually superior when faced with dire reality? Was it an attempt to escape from that reality, when the Jews spent a few weeks in an atmosphere of religious joy? Does the fact that the saints preserve the Jews and punish the oppressive Moslems serve as a form of physical insurance? It would seem that all these functions are indeed present. Moroccan Jews believe that many of their saints are buried in the homeland.[9] When they have all been located, the Messiah will come and save the Jews. This is the important role that Moroccan Jewry has taken on.

The focal point of the cult is the Hiloula of the saint. Seven days are spent near the tomb, praying, lighting candles, singing and dancing. A sacrifice is offered and this is a significant ceremony. The saint often finds a means of informing a devotee that his request has been granted — in a dream, through the appearance of a bird, or water flowing from the tomb. The sick lie on the gravestone and beg for a cure; women also observe this custom. In such an atmosphere, when it is expected that miracles will be performed, the blind do indeed begin to see and the lame walk. Moslems who attack Jews or deny the sanctity of the saint are punished and there are hundreds of legends which deal with this theme. Throughout the year the devotee petitions the saint about his problems and lights candles in honour of him each week or month.

When Moroccan Jews in economic or social difficulties emigrate to Israel the cult is less in evidence during the first years of integration. Hiloula was observed in private houses or synagogues. It was to the Holy Places in Israel[10] that people made a pilgrimage. When the conditions of Moroccan Jews began to improve, it was then that people mentioned the appearance of a saint in dreams and asked for the practice of Hiloula to be restored as it was in Morocco. The cult then gradually adapted to the new situation in Israel.

One assumes that the tension in Israel arising from the War and terrorist attacks was the most important factor in the renewal of the cult of the saint. Miraculous preservation of life among Moroccan Jews and other ethnic groups in Israel in the face of enemy hostility continued to be the most positive function of the saint. In the new country certain adaptations were made in keeping with the current situation. Thus, for example, the saints are armed. They allocate different parts of the country to one another, as in the army, and are manifested throughout the land of Israel, walking in the midst of the tanks and saving soldiers' lives. They appear in the Suez Canal and act according to present necessity.

The same conditions operate on the Golan Heights, where the saints return shells to the enemy, prevent them from exploding, or alter their mechanism. They even change the direction of enemy planes and cause them to crash.

As in Morocco, the saint appears in the form of an old man, usually dressed in white — the surest way to recognise him.[11] It is interesting to analyse this apparition, a well-known motif in Jewish folktales. In many instances in the past the Prophet Elijah appeared. Today it is nearly always a saint in the form of an old man and the question is: What is the significance of this change? The same phenomenon occurs in the Arab armies, who have reported the apparition of an old man appearing and promising to save them. The Egyptian Defence Minister sent a letter to the troops which contained the story of this old man. The Israeli journalist reporting this thought it was only propaganda. He did not understand that the same religious phenomenon was at work on both sides.

When we examine the age of the devotees during the War, we see that the phenomenon is not linked to any particular age group. Young and old are both involved. It seems the feeling that Israel would be redeemed reinforced the need for the saints as in Morocco. The intention was, and continues to be, to defend the Jewish people from danger that threatens from outside. The method has altered and adapted itself to the new situation.

Notes

1. See Issacher Ben-Ami, *Maase Nissim*; R. David Hashomer in *Le Judaisme Marocain, Etudes Ethno-Culturelles* (Jerusalem, 1975), 171-208; *Sefer Maase Nissim, ibid.*, 199-208; *Shevah Haim, ibid.*, 209-20; *Leheker Folklore Hamilhama, Motiv Hakedoshim* in Hakibbutz Hamenchad, *Sefer Dov Sadan* (Jerusalem, 1977), 87-104.

2. This collection was part of a research project 'The Tombs of Folk-saints in North African Jewry' under the auspices of the Folklore Research Centre. It will be published by the Ben Zir Institute Press.

3. When I visited the Grotto of Hatzor in Galilee on 4th November, 1973 I found a Jew there of Moroccan origin, sitting and reading the Bible. He told me the saint would not allow the falling shells to cause any destruction. See also E. Gellner, *Saints of the Atlas* (Chicago, 1969), 292-3.

4. The majority of the informants are of Moroccan origin and most of the saints referred to flourished in Morocco.

5. The first to write about this was L. Voinot, *Pélérinages Judéo-Musulmans du Maroc* (Paris, 1948).

6. See Richard P. Werbuer, ed., *Regional Cults* (London, 1977); *Les Pélérinages. Sources Orientales* (Paris, 1960); *Les Pélérinages de l'Antiquité Biblique et Classique a l'Occident Médiéval* (Paris, 1973); E. Westermarck, *Ritual and Belief in Morocco* (London, 1926); R. Roussel, *Les Pélérinages* (Paris, 1972); R. Oursel, *Pélérins du Moyen-Age* (Paris, 1078).

7. See E. Doutté, *Notes sur l'Islam Mafhrebin — Les Marabouts* (Paris, 1900); G. Drague, *Esquisse d'Histoire Religeuse du Maroc, Confreries et Zaouias* (Paris, 1951); E. Dermenghem, *Le Culte des Saints dans l'Islam Mafhrebin* (Paris, 1954); M. Morsy, *Les Ahangala, Examen Historique d'une Famille Maraboutique de l'Atlas Marocain au xviie Siècle, Recherches Mediterrainéennes*, Document V,
(Paris, 1972); P. Auge Koller, *Essai sur l'Esprit du Berbère Marocain* (Fribourg, 1949).

8. See my paper given at the Colloquium at Aix-en-Provence, November 1978, 'La Vénération des Saints chez les Juifs et les Musulmans' (in press).

9. Of the 560 saints buried in Morocco, 90 are from Israel, which includes those with the largest following.

10. For example, the tombs of Rabbi Simon Bar Yohai in Meron and Rabbi Meir Baal Hanes in Tiberias, the grotto of Elijah, the Wailing Wall, the tomb of Rachel, and others.

11. William A. Wilson referred to the same phenomenon in his lecture 'Mormon Folk Belief and the Arab-Israeli Conflict' at the World Congress of Jewish Studies in 1976 in Jerusalem: 'The story takes place in the Middle East sometime during the War for the Jews' independence. The story takes place during a battle between the Arabs and the Israelites. The Arabs were stocked with ammunition and the Israelites were not. The Israelites got all their tin-cans and stuff together to make as much noise as they could, so the Arabs wouldn't suspect they were running low on arms. They spaced their guns far apart between the noise. Oh they were worried. It was just a terrible situation. The Arabs came over and surrendered. The Israelites couldn't figure it out. Boy, I'd be shocked too. So they asked the Arabs why they had surrendered. The Arabs said a man in a white robe with a white beard appeared to them and advised them to give up. He said they would be crushed by the Israelites. He said the Israelites were too strong and the Arabs did not have a chance. It really puzzled the Israelites because they didn't know anything about the man. The man who advised them was one of the three Nephites. They could find no trace of him.'

Early Dance Phenomena and Possible Fish Imitation

SANDRA BILLINGTON   University of Cambridge

THE title of this paper may appear somewhat enigmatic. The reason is that I have deliberately omitted the name of the one dance out of which this study grew: the sixteenth-century English Morris. I have called examples of the dances 'phenomena' since they could not be described choreographically, rather, their lack of choreographic order is a fundamental feature. Two terms appear — the rout and the rey — and both may be names for similar wild activity. As the rey provides a complex subject in itself, I will, in the time available, limit myself to it. As far as I can discover there are five reference to a rey dance, all prior to 1550 and all in poetic works. There seems little doubt that the authors had some distinctive and strange custom in mind. Sometimes it is said that the performers wear a tattered dress, and sometimes it is said that they exhibit lawless behaviour.

Firstly, extracts from the works of John Skelton (c 1460-1529) provide a composite picture. He refers to the rey three times. Twice it is associated with running; once to describe the Scottish defeat in which the flight of the enemy included 'the ragged ray/ of Galloway.' And, the second time, in an argument (or flyting match) with a poet called Garnesche:

> Thou writest I should let thee go play:
> Go play thee, Garnesche, garnished gay . . .
> I cannot let [prevent] thee the knave to play
> To daunce the hay or run the ray:
> Thy fond [foolish] face cannot me fray
>   [frighten]

Thus the rey is an unidentified running activity which is included amongst others in the context of undignified and dishonest behaviour.

In the third quotation Skelton again calls the rey ragged. This passage is found in a poem written 'Against the Lutherans,' and is a more violent piece of invective. By a comparison with the dance, Skelton conveys how far outside the Churches laws Lutherans are:

> Ye stringed so Luther's Lute
> That ye dance all in a sute
> The heretics ragged ray
> That brings you out of the way
> Of holy Churches lay . . .

A *tattered* appearance is emphasised in the earlier lines:

> Helas ye wretches ye may be woe
> Thus to be laughed to scorn
> Thus tattered and thus torn!

And finally, mockery is included in the lines:

> Marked in your cradles
> To bear faggots for baubles.

I.e. instead of the fool's wooden bauble, they carry the timber for their own destruction.

Over a century earlier, Chaucer included the term 'rey' among the game activities recorded in the *Hous of Fame*. The narrator begins with foreign examples of love-stories, such as that of Dido and Eneas. Then an eagle with feathers of gold lifts him from the ground and takes him to complete his education by witnessing the activities of his own country and period. He is set down at the foot of a great hill, at the top of which he discovers the *Hous of Fame*, where songs and dances take place:

> Ther saugh I famous, olde and yonge
> Pypers of the Duche tongue
> To lerne love-daunces, springes,
> Reyes, and these straunge thinges.

There are no further details given of what the reys and love-dances are. They remain mysterious local customs, which Chaucer does not choose to elucidate. But the dress is described elsewhere in the poem. All the company appear to be wearing ribbons and fringes suspended from their clothes:

And many riban many frenges
Were on hir clothes trewely.

This is interesting, since it coincides with the dress of the period. In Chaucer's time a courtier might wear extravagant parti-colouring, with jagged edges and long tippets or streamers attached to the coat and sleeves, and a liripipe to the hood. Similar ornamentation fixed to a tight-fitting gown was the contemporary womens' dress.[1] One name for the elaborate jagged edges remained 'tatters,' as in Wyclif's comment that the earthly people had more liking for bodily decoration in 'sich knackynge and taterynge' than in hearing God's law.[2]

What is of further interest is that the same fashion of dress survives in 15th and 16th century illustrations of a wild and unidentified dance. The clearest example comes from the French MS of Michael Scot's *Liber Particularis*. Six male figures are shown leaping and cavorting round the figure of a woman dressed in tight-fitting gown with napkins or tippets from the sleeves. The men wave handkerchiefs and wear a number of appendages, with the result that their clothes look tattered. In a later illustration – The Betley May Game Window – depicting a dancing game, the lady has a liripipe and the two wildest dancers wear long streamers from their shoulders. Streamers or napkins and hanging sleeves were a part of the dress recorded in accounts of the sixteenth-century Morris dance. The Hereford dancers were said to wear *coates of the olde fashion, hie sleeves ... and hanging sleeves behind.* William Kemp's Morris dance to Norwich begins with an illustration showing Kemp wearing enormous single streamers, one from each shoulder. Further, Kemp's accompanying female dancer at Chelmsford asked to be dressed 'in the olde fashion with napkins on her armes.' All these dance costumes are based on the fashion which emerged two centuries earlier at Court. Since the later accounts read 'in the old fashion' it would appear that this was a deliberately maintained tradition, and the later dance was associated, at least in dress, with

some custom known to have taken place earlier.

There is a final reference to rey dancing, found in Alexander Barclay's *Eclogues*. In the opening dialogue, a shepherd, Corydon, makes a complaint on the misfortunes of being a countryman, much as do the shepherds in Mystery Play *Cycles*. Unlike the medieval situation, there is an alternative for Corydon. He can go to Court and there please some lord with his country talents, which we know became fashionable at the turn of the sixteenth-century; Corydon lists his abilities. He can wrestle, throw the caber, draw a bow, run and leap, and, he says:

I can daunce the ray, I can both pipe and sing.

Corydon's dancing ambitions would be related to some court fashion, and rey is the only one of his talents which is hard to define except by the other references, especially Skelton's: which would mean it was a lively, capering dance by men, wearing the appearance of tatters and possibly gaily-coloured clothes. Now it is strange that there is no evidence in court accounts for a dance called the rey becoming popular, only the Morris. Also, as the term Morris appears, rey disappears from literature, and the question which inevitably comes to mind is, were the two the same at some stage of the dance's evolution? Today's dance is believed to be based on ritual. Ribbons and handkerchiefs are still a fundamental part of present-day Morris, though no-one has found a ritualistic reason why. In 1903, Chambers thought there was no reason, nor historic antecedents. However, ribbons and handkerchiefs *were* found in sixteenth-century Morris dances and in various untitled illustrations, such as the Betley Window, and, a similar effect is described for the rey dance. Skelton implies that in the rey the tatters were intended as mockery, either by or towards the participants.

I should here like to postulate the theory that there could have been a ritualised game, which could also be used as an insult, and which involved the tail of the ray fish. I should suggest that this was a part of British, rather than Saxon customs, present in England before the second establishment of Christianity by St Augustine. It may be asked whether there is an example which can be produced towards proof, and the answer is yes, in connection with Augustine's own ill-reception in Dorset. The earliest account which mentions the ray specifically is that from William of Malmesbury, written about 1130. He relates that, after having converted the Saxon King and parts of the North of England, Augustine came south to Dorset. Here men gathered together:

> possessed with furious minds and shamefully in great injurious mood also fixed ray tails to his clothing, and pushed him about, pushed him before them, and turned him out.

In the 19th century, Sir Frederick Madden noticed that when the historian, John Hutchins, included Malmesbury's story in a History of Dorset, he deliberately changed the fish tails into those of cows, adding in a note '*Racharum*, i.e. *Vaccarum* or cows.' The same deliberate emendation can be found in Wm. Dugdale's *Monasticon*. It is important to point these out, since such reputable works help to establish a false origin. The result seems to be that all references to tails in Sword and Morris dances and Mumming games are assumed to be animal tails, whereas it is clear that the fish tail could also have been used.

Bede does not mention the fish tail insult. He tells, however, of a dispute between Augustine and the British Bishops, which fits chronologically with Malmesbury's *History*. The Bishops from Wales arranged to meet Augustine in the West of England, to discuss whether the Britons would forgo their heretical customs. The Britons had already decided that should Augustine show humility and rise to meet them, they would follow his advice. However, Augustine remained seated, the Bishops were enraged, they set him down as a proud man and strove to contradict everything he said. Although it seems unlikely that the Bishops themselves would have insulted Augustine with the tails, it is not a far step for the people to have shown their repudiation by a heretical British custom. Bede, who was writing for the established Church, omits the tail story, as does the twelfth-century historian Geoffrey of Monmouth, when he was writing for the established Monarchy. However, Geoffrey also wrote a Welsh version of his History and this includes the tail incident. This suggests that the ray story might have been better understood and appreciated among the Celts. Madden again points out that a subsequent English translation of the Welsh text, mistranslates the ray tails, and his changed them to 'tails of beasts.'

Between Bede and Malmsbury comes an Anglo-Norman chronicler called Goscelin. He is aware of the tail insult and calls the appendages the long parts of fish. He says that the incident *fama est*, suggesting knowledge of it had spread by word of mouth. Of the *quamdam villam*, 'a certain village' in Dorset, he says:

> The impious people, blinded by darkness, were unwilling to hear the life-giving gospel, but indulged in a very tempest of practical jokes and insults.

After Malmesbury, the most famous survival of the story is that in Layamon's *Brut*, written about 1200. Two texts exist, in which alternative readings are given for the place where the insult occurred. In the earlier MS it is Dorchester, and in the later it is Rochester. Madden has made a composite translation of both, which reads that Augustine:

> came to Dorchester (or Rochester). There he found the worst men that dwelt in the land. He taught them Christianity and they grinned at him, and they approached, and took tails of rays and hanged them on his cope on each side, and then ran beside him with their foul scorns.

This follows Malmesbury. However, instead of saying that Augustine bore this humbly and gladly, Layamon agrees with Goscelin in inserting an unlikely story of magical revenge:

> Saint Augustine became exceeding wroth, and he proceded five miles from Dorchester (or Rochester) and called toward God that he should avenge him of the cursed folk who had dishonoured him. Our Lord heard him and sent his vengeance on the wretched folk that hanged the rays tails on the clerks. The tails came on them, therefore they all bare tails. Disgraced was the race for *muggles* they had: and in each company among the king and his knights men call them *mugglings*, and every free man speaketh foul of them; and in foreign lands for the same deed . . . many a good man's son who dwelt far from them is called base.

From the localised insult in Goscelin, a reputation has arisen that the whole of the now English race is tailed. Robert of Brunne in his *History of England*, written two centuries later, laments the fact. But at the same time he applies the term of abuse to the British monks who quarrelled with Augustine. They eventually fought the Saxons and were slain:

Monk and heremite ilk a tail.

Again this leads one to wonder whether it could have been the Britons who originated the story through the nature of their abuse to Augustine. It would seem that the story common to many accounts and the extended story of making men tailed in revenge, came from an observation of customs. Goscelin almost says as much: 'The people indulged in a tempest of practical jokes,' of which hanging fish tails on people was one. Therefore, it seems fairly certain that while animal tails were used in folk games, there was also a custom of attaching ray tails to one's clothes and hindquarters. It is no wonder Goscelin used the word *ludibriorum,* or unseemly jesting, to describe such behaviour, since it could provoke mutual amusement, as well as being a means of mockery. A sixteenth-century description of the tail of *Raia miraletus* leads one critic to conclude that the thorny spines would themselves provide means of attachment to clothing; this itself could provide a form of amusement, in the way that children play at trying to shake off burrs today. The tails would stream out as the wearers shook them, and look like ribbons or streamers or tattered dress, if they ran, leaped or danced. And, of course, the long appendages, combined with leaping and running are features found in the story of the insult in Layamon, ray dancing, and the dress and activity depicted in unnamed illustrations such as that of Michael Scot. It is interesting to note the care and exactness of the details given by Layamon. His offenders, running beside Augustine, are said to attach the tails so that they:

hangede on his cape · on elchere halue.

That is, they hung from his cope on either side, from each shoulder or arm, just as was the fashion at Court in the late fourteenth century, and as the wild dancers in the illustrations are also dressed. The illustration of Scot is of particular interest, because the appendages on two of the dancers look fibrous and spiny enough to be fish cartilege. It seems curious that Layamon should give such careful design to the perpetration of what was an insult. It leads to the conclusion that his descrip-

tion was more than accidental, especially as the later positioning of the streamers in Kemp's dance repeats exactly Layamon's own positioning.

In the Betley and Michael Scot illustrations, a tail is depicted on the fool character, which, according to Layamon, was a 'muggle'. It is interesting that the etymology of 'Muggle' and 'Mugglings' leads back to fish. Stratman's definition of tails, and therefore, 'the tailed ones,' will not suffice, since Stratman cites Layamon as his earliest example, and there are tenth century translations of 'mugil' as either pike or mullet. Thomas Wright, too, states that 'mugil' meant mullet fish, and today *Mugilidae* is the generic name for the mullet and related fish. It would seem, therefore, that mugglings did not mean 'the tailed ones,' but was more likely to have meant 'the fish ones.' When Bishop Isidore, in the sixth century, described the fish, *mugilis,* in his *Etymology,* he stated that the name was given to fish which are extremely agile and which, when they feel themselves caught, leap over the net, so that they are seen to fly. Therefore, mugglings would seem to have more specifically meant 'the leaping fish ones.' The choice of this term in Layamon and its etymology supports other fish associations in the insulting jest. Also it adds the possibility of leaping and somersaulting to the running mentioned by Layamon. Moreover, the mullet have rays which suspend from their mouths. These are of sufficient length and flexibility to have been used in the mocking and scourging, and these could explain the adoption of the name, muggle, rather than ray as a name for the tailed men. Again, the mullet section of the *mugil* family are brightly coloured, and the most common variety on English shores is the striped mullet, which is pink and yellow when in the water, and bright red and purple when prepared for cooking. These are the colours which predominate in early illustrations of parti-colouring, such as in the famous illustration in the Bodleian (MS. Bodley 264, f. 84v), in which a group of men, holding hands and wearing particoloured dress of predominantly red, pink and yellow, perform an antic dance. The same colours reappear in the late fourteenth-century fashion described by Chaucer and accurately reproduced by Doreen Yarwood in her work on Medieval costume.

What I am here suggesting is that fish in general, and the ray and mullet in particular, could have

131

influenced dance behaviour. A folklorist's argument against such imitation might be that primitive man only identified himself with forms of food he relied on. However, this would seem to be an argument *for* such fish imitation, since for early settlers, Britons and Saxons, fish was basic to their diet, and Isidore claims that the flesh of the mullet was considered a delicacy. As a species it is a lively, gregarious, intelligent fish, which wanders into lagoons and rivers, since it adapts well to both sea and fresh water. It could well have been that the arrival of swarms of brightly coloured and edible fish in the fresh water of large river mouths, such as the Thames and the Severn, provoked excitement and possibly gave rise to an imitative ritual. Although a rising shoal of men in bright colours and streamers, swarming through the English countryside, may seem a naive correlation with the arrival of fish, it is perhaps no more unlikely than dressing in animal skins, especially if one considers the excellent and gratuitous supplement to the diet which the fish would supply. Some such tradition would accord with the few details which survive of a rey dance.

If I were then asked what this had to do with the Morris of today, I would answer, probably very little except for the dress. Both R.K. Schofield and Douglas Kennedy have observed that today's dance need not be identical with what has preceded it. Schofield in particular presented today's Royton Morris as one example of recorded change. He says the dance

> has undergone such a marked evolution in the life-time of the present team that its members distinguish their own method of dancing as 'new style' and still remember the 'old style' dance.[3]

There is, perhaps, one early record of change. In the Draper's Accounts for 1541, in an assessment of their contribution to the Midsummer Watch, 5s is said to have been paid to 'John Lymyr, bow-string maker . . . and his company of 7 morris dancers and their minstrel . . . *so that they be well trimmed after the gorgeous fashion*'[4] (my italics).

There could have been many such points of evolution, and it is possible that rey was a country name, or an earlier name, for what became the sixteenth-century Morris. This would imply that

Morris, or Moorish, was used by Court observers adjectivally, because its wildness and heathen associations reminded sophisticated onlookers of the Moorish dances they had seen. Kennedy made the observation regarding the word, blackamoor, that:

> two or three centuries ago the word negro for a black man was not current usage. A black man was a blackamoor.[5]

'Black-a-moor' is specifically adjectival: consciously comparing black faces with the Moorish complexion. A similar form of comparison could account for the word Morris. The question which arises is why, if, according to Chaucer, reyes were popular at Court in the fourteenth century, should it have been another century before we hear of them in greater detail and with the changed name? One answer could be that the Wars of the Roses and with France made such activity appear a useless frivolity. In war-time, any 'rising' of men would be dangerous, even in a game. Also, it could be, as has been suggested by others, that some new step was introduced in the fifteenth century.

However, it does seem that the parallels between the rey, unnamed illustrations and the sixteenth-century Morris, are striking. Further, whereas the origin of the Morris is a constant puzzle, the rey is one dance which has not yet been considered. As well as being an intriguing activity in itself, it is worth looking at in relation to the more famous dance. Although there appear to be no present day survivals of named Morris dancing along the south coast, one stronghold lies between the upper reaches of the Thames and Severn. This is particularly interesting in view of the mullet fishes' predilection for wandering upstream. The arrival *inland* of shoals of brightly coloured, lively and good-tasting fish might be more likely to cause excitement and imitive ritual than the same arrival actually on the coast where fishing was the normal livelihood. Finally, the fact that the mullet tend to come to England during the summer months could coincide with the fact that Morris dancing is usually a Whit or summer custom. The arrival of the fish could have heralded the arrival of summer.

One hopes that more factual evidence may come to light. Alan Smith has raised interesting questions to which I have not as yet found the answer. One is that the colloquial name today for the ray fish in the U.S.A. is 'devil fish'. As much American idiom descends from seventeenth-century English, there might have been an earlier English usage. A similar query arises over the derogatory term 'cheap skate'. Fish themselves are symbolic of jokes. One knows the terms in the North of England 'codding someone on'. And the very fact of something being fishy immediately makes it suspect as a practical joke. Possibly the iconography of the skate in medieval paintings such as those of Bosch might also throw some light.[6] These interesting lines of enquiry remain to be explored.

Much of what I have tried to piece together in this paper seems to have been previously overlooked because of numerous Church prohibitions against animal disguise. Any possible fish imitation does not seem to have provoked such out right condemnation. According to Chaucer the 'rey' was simply a 'straunge' thing which went on in the countryside and which most writers ignored. Only Goscelin refers to playing with fish tails as one of the unseemly games which went on in Dorsetshire. It is not surprising therefore that later antiquarians were puzzled by reference to *caudas racharum* (ray tails), and could only explain them as scribal errors for animal tails. I hope I have at least shown that this was not so, and that ray tails were used for scourging and mocking purposes, and, along with the rays of the mullet, they might well have served as streamers in a high spirited running dance called the rey, whose origins were gradually forgotten as it was absorbed into the games and dances which blossomed in the sixteenth century.

Notes

1. See Doreen Yarwood, *English Costume,* (London, 1952).

2. *O.E.D.*

3. 'The evolution of the Morris dance', *English Dance and Song*, II (5) (May 1938), 81.

4. Malone Society *Collections* (Oxford, 1954), III, 33.

5. *English Folk Dancing* (London, 1964), 49.

6. The suggestion has been made by Jacqueline Simpson.

Volk or Proletariat? Folklore and Agitprop

PHILIP BRADY   **University of London**

THE title of this paper may seem to be making uneasy couples out of ill-suited partners. *Volk* is vaguely all-embracing enough to mean much, or little, or nothing at all; *Proletariat* is more sharply focussed, it is definable, relatively modern, polemical. Agitprop — topical, political, seemingly as short-lived as the issues it confronts[1] — seems remote from the world of folklore. My aim in bringing these two disparate worlds together is to find the old within the new, continuity within discontinuity, the *Volk*, so to speak, within the *Proletariat*.

Agitprop can embrace many contexts and many forms. I shall concentrate on one context and one form. The context is Germany during the period of the Weimar Republic.[2] The form is a literary, dramatic form: playlets and sketches written, often as a group enterprise, to serve a specific, non-literary, political purpose, a purpose which is invariably left-wing and usually Communist.[3] The Agitprop play is by nature unambiguous, that is, it resolves doubts and urges unequivocal commitment to a revolutionary cause. The amibguity — and ultimately, in fact, the interest for the folklorist — lies in the modes and forms adopted in pursuit of the goal. A quotation from a Marxist critic, Bruno Frei, writing in 1929, unintentionally highlights this ambiguity. Frei is reviewing a performance by an Agitprop troupe:

Draussen in den Arbeiterbezirken ist ein Gedanke Wirklichkeit geworden, der zu den besten Traditionen volkstümlicher Kunst in einem merkwürdigen Verwandtschaftsverhältnis steht. Volkstümlich, im besten und tiefsten Sinne des Wortes, ist das Komödiespielen aus dem Leben für das Leben. Es ist nicht gerade die Passion Christi, die das österlich erbaute Volk an das Leid des Lamms mahnt. Nein, es sind die Helden des politischen Theaters, die hier zu einem Rüpelspiel . . . verzerrt und verzogen ersheinen. Und wenn man nachdenkt, ist es doch ein Passionspiel.[4]

What Frei has seen he has found new, exciting, and yet it acquires definition, stature even, through comparison with popular religious drama, to which it is seen to be related. Frei is, in other words, playing with the idea of an unplanned encounter between *Volk*, here construed as the begetter and recipient of Passion-plays, and *Proletariat*. Looking back in the 1930s Bertolt Brecht is more precise than Frei about the creative fruits of this encounter:

Die sogenannte Agitpropkunst, über die nicht besten Nasen gerümpft werden, war eine Fundgrube neuartiger künstlerischer Mittel und Ausdrucksarten. In ihr tauchten längst vergessene grossartige Elemente echt volkstümlicher Kunstepochen auf, den neuen gesellschaftlichen Zwecken kühn zugeschnitten. Waghalsige Abkürzungen und Komprimierungen, schöne Vereinfachungen; da gab es oft eine erstaunliche Eleganz und Prägnanz.[5]

The encounter between a vaguely discerned *Volk*, seen as a reservoir of traditional forms, and the *Proletariat*, whose interests were more clearly defined, is not unusual, nor is it accidental. There is indeed an interplay of accident and design. On the one hand affinities in form and matter between an Agitprop playlet and popular drama may be unintended, on the other hand there may be an element of calculation. Explicit encouragement — this is the element of calculation — was given by critics and theorists of the extreme Left to writers and performers, encouragement to revive and renew old forms of popular culture, exploiting the durable strength of these forms while stripping away what were seen as suffocating irrelevancies which had come with age. The theorists could underpin their revivalist enterprise with Lenin's dictum that Revolution is revolutionary and evolutionary, that is to say it makes new but it also renews, it has at once discontinuity and continuity.[6] What has come to be called in familiar jargon the dialectic of continuity and discontinuity may well interest the political theorist inasmuch as it produces a variety of tensions. For the student of literature and, indeed, of folklore, the interest lies in the kind of continuity which can be discerned at the grassroots of political agitation.

How far a tradition is kept alive — and in what proportion — by both external and internal pressures is a question familiar to students of folklore. And it is clear that the renewal, whether conscious or unconscious, of popular forms as a vehicle for effective propaganda, is by no means unique to the Agitprop of the 1920s. The very title, for example, of Wolfgang Brückner's authoritative handbook — *Volkserzählung und Reformation*[7] — suggests at once the interaction of tradition and actuality at a far earlier time of revolution. And students of Reformation pamphlet-literature know that traditional medieval and pre-medieval forms of dialogue-encounter were recharged to serve as weapons in that particular war of words.[8] Again — less remote in time — a recent collection of so-called Berlin Street-Corner Literature,[9] the pamphlets of the years 1848-9, shows that the propagandist in the mid-nineteenth century, when he wrote a dramatic sketch, was presenting what the editors call 'archetypal topoi of plot and argument'. If we move forwards from the 1920s instead of backwards we again find a similar reliance on established modes, a similar sense of continuity. And it may be explicit. The most renowned German Agitprop troupe of recent years — Floh de Cologne — claimed in an article published in East Germany in 1973: 'We regard our way of playing as a parallel to that of the Agitprop troupes of the 1920s. With them, as with us, old, popular forms are being utilised again.'[10]

The case for drawing special attention to 1920s

Agitprop cannot, in other words, rest on any alleged uniqueness in this process of revival and renewal. What is, however, distinctive is that the theory and practice of renewal — the translation, so to speak, from *Volk* into *Proletariat* — is so well documented.

If the documents revealed only party-hacks making vague gestures in the direction of folk-tradition they would hold little interest for the folklorist. In fact they reveal writers who were closely and pragmatically familiar with the world whose modes they sought to revive. An example illustrates this. In 1930 Kurt Kläber, a man best known for his prose-writing, exhorts his fellow-writers to learn from popular theatre.[11] His case is a familiar one — we need, he asserts, rustic farces ('bäuerliche Schwänke') in the Hans Sachs manner, we need brief impromptu playlets. This, too, might be no more than a token gesture, but Kläber's views are rooted in experience and this he describes:

> Seit ungefähr sechs Jahren betrachten die katholischen Laienspielverbände das gesamte Land als ihre Spieldomäne. Ich habe sie in der Eifel gesehen, in den bayrischen Bergen, in den Königsberger Grenzgebieten, in Pommern bei den Bauern, im Vogtland, in Nieder- und Oberschlesien auf jedem kleinen Nest, und was sie da leisten, ist wirklich erstaunlich. Legion sind alle Jahre ihre Aufführungen, Aufführungen vom armen Mann, der gerade wegen seiner Armut einmal aller Segnungen des Himmels teilhaftig werden wird, Aufführungen vom guten Knecht, der einmal die beste Ackerstelle im Jenseits bekommt . . .
>
> Lacht nicht über die Beispiele. Sie wirken auf bäuerliche Gemüter. Diese Laienspieler sind auch keine schlechten Spieler. Sie spielen sogar mit einer seltenen Inbrunst und Hingabe. Noch etwas ist dabei zu berücksichtigen. Ihre Figuren. Sie zeigen ja nicht nur den armen Mann. Sie zeigen auch den Reichen. Der Arme ist dieser und jener Arme aus dem Dorfe, oder der und der müde und geschundene Landarbeiter. Der Reiche aber der Gutsbesitzer, Schnauzbart usw., aus unserem Karikaturenkabinett. Der Arme wird dann vom heiligen Lazarus in den

Himmel geholt, der Gutsbesitzer aber von einem schrecklichen Teufel in die Hölle. Man kann ihn dort sogar braten sehen und stöhnen hören. Lacht wieder nicht. Das gefällt den Bauern, den Knechten. Gefällt ihnen genau so gut, als wenn ein Rotfrontkämpfer in unseren Stücken auftritt, den Gutsbesitzer am Kragen nimmt und ihn in eine Ecke wirft.

Kläber's closeness to the facts of experience and observation supplies the thrust to his argument. The facts are those of a living popular tradition. They might equally be the facts of a less easily observable tradition – thus a dramatist of the time, Friedrich Wolf, based his own energetic efforts on behalf of Agitprop theatre not on plays seen in villages but on what, in 1933, he claimed to have been ten years' close study of sixteenth-century popular theatre.[12]

It is fruitless to conjecture how far the words of influential figures such as Wolf or Kläber affected the efforts of those who wrote Agitprop plays. Certainly the question peculiarly relevant to Agitprop-writing is whether the critic, the cultural policy-maker, the ideologist, is a key figure bridging the gap between folk tradition and proletarian forms. The risk, of course, is that, in asking the question, we are presupposing the gap, suggesting that popular forms inhabited a realm from which a proletarian Agitprop-troupe was by very nature excluded.[13] An element of guidance, from those well-versed in the historic arts of popular drama and of propaganda, may be assumed, even if it cannot be measured, guidance which came through active collaboration. On the other hand the creative independence of Agitprop-troupes, if equally imponderable, seems to have impressed observers. Béla Balász, a renowned critic in his day, put this view very strongly in an article in one of the most reputable of weekly journals, *Die Weltbühne*. If anything, Balász stresses the new growth at the expense of the old roots:

Nun, in der Arbeitertheater-Bewegung ist eine neue Kunstform entstanden. Und zwar eine neue Volksdichtung. Denn die Arbeiter schreiben sich, improvisieren sich ihre Stücke selber. Sie übernehmen sie voneinander, ändern sie um, kennen keine Urheber und kein Urheberrecht. Arbeitertheater ist die Volksdichtung des klassenbewussten Proletariats.[14]

In the face both of so many imponderables and of the less ambiguous chorus of exhortation and acclaim, it is worth surveying, however sketchily, the evidence from the texts themselves of the survival of popular forms. Plentiful, if neglected, evidence comes from the records of audience-reaction. It seems plain that audience-participation meant not simple empathy but a vociferous taking-of-sides. In the most general terms this is a strategy which reminds us of an early form of popular theatre: the late fifteenth-century Shrovetide-play, unlike its successors in the genre, was non-mimetic in aim and invited the audience to attend a dispute or a mock-trial between sharply opposed standpoints. The Agitprop-playlet of the 1920s, if it did not encourage the balanced weighing-up of conflicting views, at least seems to have provoked a degree of raucous involvement over pros and cons.[15] In such a case audience-response helps define the form.

Not all Agitprop plays – to turn from audience to text – are built around a conflict of views; all are, however, and this is not the least important aspect for the folklorist, non-mimetic in character. Béla Balász, in the article already quoted, summarised this:

Da wird nicht das Elend des Proletariats naturgetreu dargestellt. Für den Proleten ist das nämlich keine Sensation. Er interessiert sich für die konkreten Einzelheiten seiner Not ganz und gar nicht . . . In diesen Szenen gibt es keinen persönlichen Charakter und kein persönliches Schicksal.

Not, as another observer puts it, 'naturalistic long-windedness' was the vital ingredient of Agitprop, but 'three-minute pictures'.[16] Such pictures, such brevity, simplify in the interests of effective propaganda. The result is stylised, formalised, a return, it might be said, to some of the ritual first-principles of drama. It might also be said that such brevity makes it easier to detect affinities of plot or of form. The worker who deliberately plays ignorance,[17] hearing the threat of '*Beschlagnahme*' (confiscation) as a promise of '*Schlagsahne*' (whipped cream), is an Eulenspiegal, whilst his final address to the audience – *'Das Spiel ist aus! der Sinn ist klar . . .'* (Our play is done, the sense is plain), exploits a stereotype of moralising peroration familiar from popular drama. In another playlet[18] it is the simple possibilities of animal symbolism which are pursued when a street-seller enters, pulling animals out of his bag (a monkey which somersaults – the Reichstag parties; a piglet squealing with hunger – the gentry). And it is allegory of a familiar kind which produces World Capital, *Weltkapital*, dressed in the shape of a giant money-bag and wearing a top-hat.[19] When the deposed exploiters and tyrants troop symmetrically in and speak in turn of their sins the playlet is relying on what students of early drama know as Revueform.[20] When, in the same play, culprits are brought in by a circus ringmaster or their heads form targets in a fairground booth we are even nearer to a popular mode.

This kind of writing has hitherto attracted more attention from historians of proletarian-revolutionary literature than from students of popular tradition. This is explained perhaps by the fact that the texts have been treated as documents of a class-struggle conducted in words. But, like so much propaganda, and certainly like that earlier propaganda of the 1520s, this is a struggle conducted in part through pictures. Worldcapital in his top-hat is, of course, a picture, but the visual component in Agitprop extends beyond the allegorical figures illustrating a technical argument. Here, perhaps, in the elucidation of the visual character of propaganda, the folklorist may be better able to document the affinities. He may, for instance, be able to place in a tradition of pictorial motifs the stage directions to a play entitled *Worker, Peasant and Spartakus* (a title itself reminiscent of the pamphlet dialogues of the Reformation). One notes the overriding visual contrast, the crossroads, the stereotype encounter which opens the action:

Ort der Handlung: Kreuzweg auf freier Anhöhe. Rings Wiesen und Felder. Rechts im Hintergrund ein Dorf. Links werden die Kamine, Türme und Kuppel einer fernen Stadt sichtbar. Am Kreuzweg auf einem Meilenstein sitzt müde und niedergeschlagen ein Arbeiter. Von rechts kommt ein Bauer, die Sense über der Schulter.[21]

When, later in the same playlet, there occurs an obvious piece of stylised symbolic knockabout when Aristocrat, Capitalist and Cleric seize a worker and throw him to the ground only to find that Spartacus like Robin Hood springs to the rescue, it is perhaps the folklorist who behind the unequivocal appeal of such a scene to the *Proletariat* can discern the durable presence of the *Volk* and its concerns.

It may perhaps be easier to glimpse the tradition to which such stylised visual effects might belong than actually to document the connections. It is certainly easy, however, to see that, if this is in fact the renewal of traditional motifs, then it is being carried out in a far more oblique way than in works written not *by* workers for propaganda ends but *for* workers for amusement. These plays, written for worker-actors and published in series, are, for all their guise of topicality, remote from Agitprop. They are, however, a fruitful and unexplored source of comparison because they show a different, less authentic kind of *Volk – Proletariat* encounter. The *Arbeitstheater* publisher Alfred Jahn produced, for example, a series of short plays in the late 1920s in pamphlet-form allegedly by a certain Hans von Sachsen.[22] The texts, besides being in format very close to their nineteenth-century models, bear titles which echo their forbear:

Tod und Teufel suchen wieder Stellung. Ein kurzweiliges Stücklein mit Musik; Die Himmelfahrt der Schieber.

Woodcuts adorn the title-pages – in one case a clergyman is disguised as a Devil and courting a woman, a situation straight out of the Shrovetide repertoire. Such playlets hint at topicality but are primarily designed as pastiche exercises in an old-time mode. Their audience and that of the Agitprop-plays must have overlapped to a marked degree. The proletarian, it seems, had an appetite for tradition, which he received in the old-fashioned fancy-dress of a Hans Sachs pastiche or in the far less overt traditionalism of Agitprop.

The Agitprop play, for all its debts to tradition, never runs the danger of offering such an indulgent escape into folksiness. The danger is a different one and it was much commented on by faithful but critical supporters. The risk was that an appeal via familiar motifs and images would yield 'Schablone', routine formula, stereotype, or 'Schematismus.'[23] An anonymous commentator, writing in 1932, saw the danger inherent in those very simplifications which so many admired:

> Viele Truppen glaubten, dass sie die gesellschaftliche Macht des Kapitalismus mit all seinen vielfältigen Beziehungen und Verflechtungen darstellen können, wenn sie einen Mann auftreten lassen, der einen Zylinderhut aufhat, ein Schild mit der Aufschrift 'Kapital' umgehängt, und der sagt: 'Ich beute aus'.[24]

The danger, it must be admitted, was not avoided.

The emergence of stereotypes and schematic forms is clearly of interest to the student of popular literature. The particular interest of Agitprop writing is that we can see the stereotypes emerge in the hands of people who were acutely aware of their audience and who were often in fact markedly flexible and non-schematic in their response to that audience. The final shape of a playlet was often achieved by a process of trial and error in which popular reception on the spot was crucial. A member of a Dresden troupe (the Red Rats) which produced perhaps the most successful Agitprop play, *Trotz alledem*, has this to say about their work:

> Man kann von dramaturgischen Regeln sprechen, die sich aus den Erfahrungen hinsichtlich der Wirkung auf die Zuschauer ergaben. Keiner von uns hatte Dramaturgie studiert oder sich nur oberflächlich mit ihr befasst. Wir fanden aber schon nach den ersten erfolgreichen Auftritten heraus, an welche Stelle die einzelnen Nummern zu setzen sind . . . Wir bemühten uns zu zeigen, wie die Gegner der Arbeiterklasse wirklich sind und hinter welchen Maskierungen sie ihr wahres Gesicht verbergen. Das erforderte, mit Distanz zu spielen . . . Hieraus erklärt sich auch unsere betonte Maskenmacherei. Wir schufen durch sie eine bewusste Distanz zu allem Negativen, gegen das wir zu Felde zogen.[25]

That mixture of sophistication and simple audience-appeal is characteristic. And the tangled mixture of artfulness and spontaneity that results deserves a closer look. A set of simple instructions for Agitprop-troupes published in their principal organ, *Das rote Sprachrohr*, in 1929, gives us clear directions where we might start looking, where we might begin to disentangle the tangle. Many a troupe, the writer complains, has had to contend with a self-appointed joker among its members:

> Dabei war ein Genosse, der gewissermassen den 'Dummer August' spielte, der den grossten Blödsinn sagte, denn er wollte nur, dass die Zuschauer lachten. Das ist natürlich grundverkehrt. Es ist falsch, wenn man solche Witze reisst und nicht versteht, sie politisch zu würzen . . .[26]

And there follows advice of a different kind, advice to use verse — easy to learn, if more difficult to write.

It is the student of literature who might look with interest at the verses which followed from that last instruction. The folklorist, on the other hand, might wish to know whether that troublesome, irrepressible comrade still managed to play the fool. And what kind of a fool he played.

Notes

1. On the twin functions of Agitation and Propaganda, combined in Agitprop, see Lenin, *What is to be done?*, Section III, B.

2. The specific context, revolutionary-proletarian literature and literary politics, is discussed by Rob Burns, 'Theory and organisation of revolutionary working-class literature in the Weimar Republic', *Culture and Society in the Weimar Republic*, ed. K. Bullivant (Manchester, 1977), 122-49.

3. Agitprop became — on the Russian model — a Communist-party responsibility in Germany from 1927 with its own coordinating administration, the *Zentralagitprop*. See Gudrun Klatt, *Arbeiterklasse und Theater* (Berlin, 1975), 7 ff. The texts themselves have been collected in L. Hoffmann and D. Hoffmann-Ostwald, *Deutsches Arbeitertheater 1918-1933*, 2 vols (Berlin, 1977; first edition 1961). A selection also in G. Heintz, ed., *Texte der proletarisch-revolutionären Literatur Deutschlands 1919-1933* (Stuttgart, 1974).

4. Hoffmann, II, 160. Translations of this and other quotations in German follow these notes.

5. *Gesammelte Werke*, Edition Suhrkamp (Frankfurt am Main, 1967), XIX, 329.

6. The principal source of the doctrine was seen as *On Proletarian Culture* (1920). The discussion is traced by W. Fähnders and M. Rector, *Linksradikalismus und Literatur: Untersuchungen zur Geschichte der sozialistischen Literatur in der Weimarer Republik* (Reinbek, 1974), II, 54 ff.

7. Wolfgang Brückner, *Volkserzählung und Reformation* (Berlin, 1974).

8. Maurice Gravier, *Luther et l'opinion publique* (Paris, 1942), 168 ff.

9. G. Albert *et al., Berliner Strasseneckenliteratur 1848-9* (Stuttgart, 1977).

10. *Forum*, IX (1973), 5. Recent examples of Agitprop-theatre in West Germany are collected in A. Hübner, ed., *Strassentheater* (Frankfurt am Main, 1970). American examples are in H. Lesnick, ed., *Guerilla Street Theater* (New York, 1973).

11. Hoffmann, II, 35.

12. Letter to *Internationales Theater* of 21st August 1933, quoted in Klatt, 47.

13. On the possible continuities between folk-tradition and proletarian culture see especially the work of Wolfgang Steinitz, for example 'Arbeiterlied und Volkslied', *Deutsches Jahrbuch für Volkskunde*, XII (1966), 1-14.

14. Hoffmann, II, 119-20.

15. The particularly vigorous response of German audiences to Agitprop-theatre was vividly described by a Russian visitor, Michael Kolzow, writing in the German-language Moscow periodical *Internationales Theater* (Hoffmann, II, 232 ff).

16. Hoffmann, II, 125.

17. *Die RFB-Pauke* (Hoffmann, II, 182 ff).

18. *Ausverkauf der Dawes-Republik* (Hoffmann, I, 192 ff).

19. *Russlands Tag* (Hoffmann, I, 56 ff).

20. *Für die Sowjetmacht* (Hoffmann, II, 209).

21. Hoffmann, I, 77. The play itself is by Edwin Hoernle.

22. The texts, which have not been reprinted, are in the Theatersammlung Rainer Theobald, Munich.

23. On the nature of these stereotypes see in particular the critical retrospective account of Agitprop-theatre in *Das Rote Sprachrohr*,

itself the principal vehicle for publication of play-texts (Hoffmann, II, 282 ff)

24. Hoffmann, II, 345.

25. Hoffmann, II, 363.

26. Hoffmann, II, 70.

Translations

[p.135, 'Draussen. . .'] Out in the working-class-districts an idea is becoming a reality, an idea which is related in a remarkable way to the best traditions of popular art. Popular in the best and most profound sense of the word is this play-acting drawn from life and played for the sake of life. It is not exactly Christ's Passion, reminding the flock at its Easter devotions of the suffering of the Lamb of God. No, it's the central figures of political theatre, who are appearing, distorted and travestied, in a crude knockabout. And yet, if we think about it, it is still a Passion Play.

[p.135. 'Die sogenannte. . .'] So-called Agitprop-art, at which many inferior noses are turned up, was a treasure-trove of new artistic techniques and forms of expression. Long-forgotten, impressive elements from periods of genuine popular art appeared, boldly adapted to fit new social goals. There were daring abbreviations and acts of compression, there were beautiful simplifications; and there was often an astonishing elegance and expressive power.

[p.136, 'Seit ungefähr. . .'] For about the last six years Catholic amateur-theatre organisations have regarded the entire country as their territory. I have seen them in the Eifel, in the Bavarian mountains, in the frontier regions around Königsberg, on farms in Pomerania, in the Vogtland, in every tiny village in Lower and Upper Silesia — and what they achieve is truly amazing. Year in year out their performances are legion, plays about the poor man who finally achieves heavenly bliss precisely by virtue of his poverty, plays about the good servant, who finally gets the best plot in Heaven. . .

Don't laugh at these examples. They work on the minds of the country-folk. And these amateur actors are not bad actors. They perform in fact with a strange intensity and devotion. And something else is worth noting. The characters. They

don't depict just the poor man. They also show the rich man. The poor man is a typical village-man or a typical weary, oppressed farm-worker. But the rich man is a loud-mouthed landowner straight out of caricature. The poor man is taken up into Heaven by Lazarus, the landowner, however, is dragged down to Hell by a fearful devil. There you can even see him being roasted and you can hear him groaning. Again don't laugh. This pleases farm-workers and servants. It pleases them just as much as when a Red-Front-Fighter in one of our plays comes in, seizes a landowner by the scruff of the neck and tosses him into a corner.

[p.137, 'Nun, in der. . .'] In the workers'-theatre-movement a new art-form has in fact emerged. It is indeed a new folk-literature. For the workers are writing and improvising their own plays. They take each other's plays and adapt them, they have no copyright-owners, no copyright-law. Workers' theatre is the folk-literature of the class-conscious proletariat.

[p.137. 'Da wird. . .'] The suffering of the proletariat is not depicted in a life-like manner. That, after all, would not be of sensational interest to the proletarian. He is not in the least interested in the concrete details of his poverty. . . In these scenes there is no individual character, no individual fate.

[p.138, 'Ort der Handlung. . .'] Scene: a cross-roads on the brow of a hill. All around fields and meadows. To the right in the background a village. To the left the chimneys, towers and domes of a distant town can be seen. At the crossing, sitting on a milestone, a worker, tired and dejected. Enter from right a farmworker, a scythe over his shoulder.

[p.139, 'Viele Truppen. . .'] Many troupes thought that they could depict the social might of capitalism with all its complex workings and interactions simply by having a man enter in a top-hat, a placard with the word 'Capital' round his neck, who then says, 'I exploit people.'

[p.139, 'Man kann. . .'] One can speak of dramatic rules which grow out of experiencing one's effect on the audience. None of us had studied drama, not even superficially. Yet we soon found out after our first successful appearances where to place the individual items. . . We tried hard to show how the enemies of the working-class really are and how they hide their true face behind various masks. That meant playing in a distanced manner. . . And this explains our own emphasis on masks. Through them we created a conscious distance from all those negative features against which we were campaigning.

[p.139, 'Dabei war. . .'] There was a comrade, who, so to speak, played the silly ass, saying the most idiotic things just because he wanted to make the audience laugh. That of course is absolutely wrong. It is wrong to crack jokes if you don't know how to spice them with politics. . .

Some Unpleasant Characters among British Fairies

KATHARINE BRIGGS

EVEN the Good Fairies — The Seelie Court as they are called in the Scottish Lowlands[1] — can make themselves formidable to mortals if they are displeased. People feel, or used to feel, that they have to walk carefully with them. There are stringent laws of etiquette to be observed even with the 'Good Neighbours' who are on the whole well-disposed towards humans, who are responsible for the fertility of crops and stock, who sometimes perform active services for favoured individuals and occasionally give valuable gifts. I am putting this in the present tense, though most of it should be in the past, because in a few Celtic areas of these Islands there are still living fairy beliefs. They are most lively in Ireland. For instance in *Hereditas*, the collection of essays presented to Professor O Duillearga in 1975, Professor Reidar Christiansen cited an instance as late as 1959, when a new road being built at Torglas in County Mayo had to be re-routed because a fairy palace lay on its course.[2] Again D. A. MacManus in *The Middle Kingdom*[3] gives an example which was brought to his attention as late as 1935 of four children who died one after the other, and whose death was ascribed to the father of the family having extended his house westward over a neighbouring field so that he had inadvertently built across a fairy road. This was an easy thing to do because the fairy roads were invisible, like birds' migration routes. A fifth child had sickened, but the heart-broken father, on the advice of a Wise Woman, had hastily pulled down the building and the child had at once recovered. These 'Good Neighbours', for all their benevolent disposition, were indeed a nasty lot of people to annoy.

There is no humbug about 'The Unseelie Court', however. They appear to be wholly malevolent, concentrated on harassing, terrifying, injuring, and finally totally exterminating the human race. The Unseelie Host in the Highlands were called 'the Sluagh', the Host of the Unforgiven Dead. Alexander Carmichael gives an account of 'the Sluagh' in the notes to Volume II of his *Carmina Gadelica,*[4] and he repeats a part of this in his evidence given to Evans Wentz in *Fairy Faith in Celtic Countries:*[5] *Sluagh,* 'the host', the spirit world. The 'hosts' are the spirits of mortals who have died. The people have many stories on this subject. According to one informant, the spirits fly about in great clouds, up and down the face of the world like starlings, and come back to the scenes of their earthly transgressions. No soul of them is without the clouds of earth dimming the brightness of the works of God, nor can any win heaven till satisfaction is made for the sins of earth. In bad nights, the hosts shelter themselves behind little russet docken stems and little yellow ragwort stalks. They fight battles in the air, as men do on the earth. They may be heard and seen on clear frosty nights, advancing and retreating and advancing, against one another. After a battle, as I was told in Barra, their crimson blood may be seen staining rocks and stones. The blood of the hosts is the beautiful red 'crotal' of the rocks melted by the frost. These spirits used to kill cats and dogs, sheep and cattle, with their unerring venomous darts. They commanded men to follow them, and men obeyed, having no alternative.

'It was these men of earth who slew and maimed at the bidding of their spirit-masters, who in return ill-treated them in a most pitiless manner. They would be rolling and dragging and trouncing them in mud and mire and pools.' So his informant said, and continued: 'There is less faith now, and people see less, for seeing is of faith. God grant to thee, and to me, my dear, the faith of the great Son of the lovely Mary.' 'This', says Carmichael, 'is the substance of a graphic account of the "Sluagh" given to me in Uist by a bright old woman, endowed with many natural gifts and possessed of much old lore'. He goes on to tell of two men who were carried off from time to time by 'the hosts', and of their sufferings under the 'infliction'. There is also a story of a daughter of a King of France who was carried off by 'the host', and left dying on the little island of Heistamel, off Benbecula. Before she died, she told the people about the lands to which she had been carried and all the hardships she had suffered.[6]

These Sluagh and others of the same kind in different parts of the country are the evil ones among the Trooping Fairies, the Devil and his Dandy Dogs, the Yeth Hounds, the Gabriel Ratchets, the Cwn Annwn of Wales; these are creatures of ill-omen which hunt in packs. There are other species of evil fairies which are collectively described but which act, not as packs, but as individuals. The Duergar of the North Country belong to this class. They were the Black Dwarfs of England, as sinister as the Black Dwarfs of Germany or Scandinavia. *Northumberland Words* tersely describes them as 'the worst and most malicious of fairies'.[7] The Border Redcaps might be classed among the Duergar. They were accustomed to inhabit old Peel Towers, where cruel and murderous deeds had been done. They wore rusty-looking red caps and it was their delight to re-dye them in the blood of any benighted traveller who was unfortunate enough to take refuge in one of these half-ruined towers. Dunters and Powries were something of the same nature, but less murderous than the Redcaps. A characteristic story of a Duergar is told in Grice's *Folk-Tales of the North Country.*[8] Unfortunately the source is not given. A stranger, making his way across the Simonside Hills of Northumberland towards Rothbury, found himself astray as twilight was falling and did not know which landmarks to follow. The footpath was treacherous, and, as it grew darker, he thought that his only hope of safety was to shelter under a rock he saw just ahead of him. Just as he reached it, he saw beyond him a faint light, and felt his way stumbling towards it. When he reached it, he saw in front of him a little stone hut, such as shepherds build for shelter in the hills. The door was unlocked and there was a small fire burning on the rough hearth. There was

a stone on each side of it; to the right was a pile of kindling and, to the left, two great logs. The traveller seated himself full of relief and joy, on the right-hand stone, revived the fire with a small supply of kindling and began to warm his frozen hands and feet. In a minute he heard footsteps outside, the door burst open, and a strange figure came in. He was a dwarf, no higher than the man's knee, but very broad and strong. He wore a coat of lambskin, shoes and breeches of moleskins, and a high hat made of green moss with a pheasant's feather stuck in it. He scowled at the traveller, stumped over to the right-hand stone and perched on it, but said nothing. The traveller said nothing either, for he guessed that this was one of the Duergars of the mountain, and they were said to be dangerous. So the two sat and stared at each other, and it grew bitterly cold as the fire sank low. At length the traveller reached for some of the brushwood and revived the fire. The Duergar glared at him more fiercely than ever. The kindling did not last long, and the Duergar, with a grin, reached out for one of the great logs. It was longer than his leg and twice as thick, but he broke it like a twig and fed the fire. They sat opposite each other while the fire blazed up and died down. The dwarf signed to the traveller to put on the second log, but the traveller made no move. He thought there was a trap somewhere. They sat for hours, but at length a faint light showed through the tiny window and gradually strengthened, till in the distance the traveller heard the far-away crowing of a cock. At the sound the Duergar vanished, and so did the hut and the fire. The two stones were left, the topmost pinnacles of two great stacks of rock. If the traveller had moved one step to lift the log he would have fallen into the deep ravine, and there would have been nothing left of him but broken bones.

There are other creatures as sinister, the Nursery Bogies, frightening figures, invented to keep children under control. Awd Goggie,[9] the guardian of the gooseberry bushes and Melsh Dick[10] of the Nut Trees, Peg Powler,[11] whose suds frighten children from rapid water, or Nelly Long-Arms[12] who keeps them from weedy pools. Goblins and Bogles and that nasty spirit, Rawhead-and-Bloody-Bones, mentioned by Reginald Scot and Samuel Johnson. The name was sometimes shortened to Tommy Rawhead, and Ruth Tongue, the Somerset folklorist knew it in childhood as 'Bloody-Bones'.[13] It lived in a cupboard under the stairs. 'If you were heroic enough', she says, 'to peep through a crack you saw a creature, with blood running down his face, seated, waiting on a pile of raw bones that had belonged to children who told lies or said bad words. If you peeped through the keyhole at him, he got you anyway'.

These Nursery Goblins, however, were obviously cautionary figures, and were not likely to frighten anyone over eight years old. The Celtic imagination could do better than this. We have, for instance, the *Fachan* in both Gaelic and Irish Folklore. J. F. Campbell gives us a description of a *Fachan* in his *Popular Tales*, with an illustration thrown in for good measure, with one hand out of his chest, one leg out of his haunch and one eye out of the front of his head. Later on he says: 'Ugly was the make of the Fachin; there was one hand out of the ridge of his chest, and one tuft out of the top of his head. It were easier to take a mountain from the root than to bend that tuft.'[14]

Douglas Hyde, in the Preface to *Beside the Fire*, gives an even more vivid and detailed description of the monster:

> And Iollann was not long at this, until he saw the devilish misformed element, and the fierce and horrible spectre, and the gloomy disgusting enemy, and the morose unlovely churl; and this is how he was: he held a very thick iron flail-club in his skinny hand, and twenty chains out of it, and fifty apples on each chain of them, and a venomous spell on each great apple of them, and a girdle of the skins of deer and roebuck around the thing that was his body, and one eye in the forehead of his black-faced countenance, and one bare, hard, very hairy hand coming out of his chest, and one veiny, thick-soled leg supporting him, and a close, firm, dark blue mantle of twisted hard-thick feathers, protecting his body, and surely he was more like unto devil than to man.[15]

One cannot usually say of the Irish folk tales that they fail from under-statement.

There are dozens more unpleasant, many of them water spirits. We might set aside the mermaids, because they differed so much in character. Some of them were murderous wreckers, some of them were carniverous blood drinkers, like the one from whom the Young Laird of Lorntie was barely rescued by the quickness and perception of his man. As the two rode away from the loch the mermaid rose from the water and chanted with unearthly fury:

> Lorntie, Lorntie, wert na for thy man
> I had garred thy life bluid skirl in my pan![16]

There are others, however, who are unselfishly solicitous about the health of pining maidens, or can make and keep friendship with earthly friends. So let us set mermaids aside.

There are plenty of others, however, who are wholly sinister. The Fideal was a Highland water spirit who haunted Loch na Fideil at Gairloch. She was supposed to lure men into the water and drown them. She was finally destroyed by a champion named Ewen, who lost his life in the battle.[17] In England there are two spirits very like her, Peg Powler of the Tees, and Jenny Greenteeth, who haunts the Lancashire streams. W. Henderson describes them in his *Folk-Lore of the Northern Counties*:

> The river Tees has its spirit, called Peg Powler, a sort of Lorelei, with green tresses, and an insatiable desire for human life, as has Jenny Greenteeth of Lancashire streams. Both are said to lure people to their subaqueous haunts, and then drown or devour them. The foam or froth often seen floating on the higher portions of the Tees in large masses, is called 'Peg Powler's suds'; the finer, less sponge-like froth is called 'Peg Powler's cream'.[18]

There are many other ferocious water spirits, of which the various forms of the water-horse, the Kelpie, the Cabyll Ustey, and so forth, is one of the most striking. The water-bull is comparatively harmless, and even a welcome addition to a mortal herd, but it is always the object of the water-horse to decoy human beings under the water, tear them to pieces and devour them, leaving only the liver to float ashore in the morning. Sometimes it assumes the form of a pretty little horse, which allows itself to be mounted and then dashes into the water to devour its victim at leisure. Its skin is adhesive, so that the rider cannot leap off its back. Others of the water-horses assume human forms and court maidens who are walking alone by the lochside. They can be detected by the sand and sea-shells in their hair, but the discovery often comes too late.[19]

Notes

1. A literary reference. See J. M. McPherson, *Primitive Beliefs in the North-East of Scotland* (London, 1929), 98.
2. Reidar T. Christiansen, 'Some notes on the fairies and the Fairy Faith', *Hereditas,* ed. Bo Almqvist *et al* (Dublin, 1975), 102.
3. D. A. McManus, *The Middle Kingdom* (London, 1959), 103-5.
4. Alexander Carmichael, *Carmina Gadelica* (Edinburgh, 1928), II, 357-8.
5. Evans Wentz, *Fairy Faith in Celtic Countries* (London, 1911), 85.
6. Carmichael, II, 358.
7. See Oliver Heslop, *Northumberland Words* (London, 1892), 257. *The Oxford English Dictionary* (Oxford, 1971), I, 814, lists Duerch, Duergh, Duerwe and Duery as obsolete forms of dwarf.
8. F. Grice, *Folk Tales of the North Country* (London, 1944), 130-3.
9. E. M. Wright, *Rustic Speech and Folk-Lore* (London, 1913), 198.
10. *ibid.*
11. W. Henderson, *Folk-Lore of the Northern Counties* (London, 1879), 265.
12. Wright, 198-9.
13. R. L. Tongue, *Somerset Folklore* (London, 1965), 123.
14. J. F. Campbell, *Popular Tales of the West Highlands* (Paisley, 1898), IV, 298.
15. Douglas Hyde, *Beside the Fire* (London, 1890), xxi.
16. R. Chambers, *Popular Rhymes of Scotland* (London, 1870), 332.
17. D. A. Mackenzie, *Scottish Folk-Lore and Folk Life* (London, 1935), 235-6.
18. Henderson, 265.
19. Mackenzie, 237-8.

Some Aspects of the Otherworld

ALAN BRUFORD   **University of Edinburgh**

IT is not necessary to imagine that supernatural beings inhabit some other region or dimension than our own. It is characteristic of fairy legends that the fairies are depicted as living quite close to human dwellings, though perhaps they more often haunt hills and uncultivated ground than the ground under our own feet. It is quite possible to tell how they appeared in such or such a place, and not speculate about where they went when they vanished, or simply assume that they were still there, though invisible, and I think it may be fair to say that this is the usual situation in English, and possibly Welsh, belief. On the other hand, the underlying assumption in Irish and Scottish legends is often that outlined by early Irish pseudo-historians describing the euhemerised *Tuatha Dé Danann*: that they live underground, with specific centres in natural hills, prehistoric chamber-tombs or ruined forts, and also have dwellings, such as the 'Land of Promise', overseas. Though the *Tuatha Dé Danann* are represented by historians as previous inhabitants of Ireland, conquered by the Gaels, and though people believed to be dead may actually be living with them, the main clue to their nature is the fact that the names of their leaders are often undoubtedly those of pagan Celtic deities. The fairies of modern Irish and Scottish Gaelic tradition share most of the characteristics of the *Tuatha Dé Danann*, and are usually called by a name containing the element, *sidh*, whose basic meaning in Old Irish is this same fairy other-world which I want to consider. So it seems likely that behind present-day notions of the otherworld there lies some sort of paradise — an Olympus for the gods, Elysian Fields for the notable dead, or more probably, judging by some classical accounts of Celtic beliefs, a combination of the two not very unlike the Christian Heaven — whose two

elements, the nearby subterranean world and the overseas isles of the blessed, may reflect two stages of belief, or the sort of hierarchy of fertility gods and more aristocratic deities postulated by Dumézil.

The overseas otherworld, in fact, does not play a large part in recent legends, though it probably lies behind tales of mysterious islands to the West, shrouded in perpetual mist or appearing only once in seven years, but the more plebeian underground version is still well remembered. The man in Yell about a hundred years ago, who got a sudden pain in his ankle when passing a great recumbent stone, and went back there to pour a libation of fish-soup to the fairy he said had struck him,[1] was by that date considered eccentric enough to be remembered for it, but another century earlier might have been normal enough: in the eighteenth century small sacrifices, generally of milk, to underground fertility spirits or household spirits were common in many country areas.[2] Practically every parish in the Highlands had its own fairy hill, where offer-ings might be made, and the most widespread of Scottish migratory fairy legends might be located — the story of the two men fetching drink for some celebration, who heard music and saw the hill open and the fairies dancing inside: one went in to join them and the door closed on him. A year later his companion found the door open again and managed to drag him away from the dance, which he was still footing vigorously, in spite of the heavy keg of whisky strapped on his back, and he complained that he might at least have been left long enough to finish dancing one reel.[3] I do not know of exact parallels to this outside Scotland, including the Northern Isles, as well as the Gaelic area: much the same story is reported from Wales,[4] but significantly without the underground setting — the dance takes place in the open air and the dancers simply vanish. On the other hand, at least one other tale of underground fairies seems to be known over a good part of Europe, if not further afield — that where a visitor appears and asks a householder to move the site of a drain, or the like, which is discharging into the top of the visitor's house, or in a Scottish variant a stake to tether a cow which has been driven through his roof.[5] But perhaps this belongs more with those medieval tales of ships sailing through the air, than with the Gaelic fairy underworld.

In some cases the pagan otherworld seems to overlap with Christian notions of the next world. In the legend just mentioned, the man dancing in the fairy hill is usually rescued after a year or less, but sometimes he has to wait until he is let out and finds, like Rip van Winkle, that so long has passed that most people have forgotten that he ever existed.[6] Orcadians indeed claim that Washington Irving got the basis of the Rip van Winkle story from his parents, who had emigrated from Orkney, and, in view of the rarity of fairy legends in the New World, there may be something in this. There is an overlap here with the so-called 'Don Juan' legend (Tale Type 470A), a fairly rare international folktale: in traditional versions the hero usually invites the skull, rather than the statue of a dead man, to share some feast with him, and when the owner's ghost has carried him off to the other world, he returns beiefly to tell of the sights which he has seen there. Gaelic versions seem to follow the tradition of the early Irish 'Vision' tales in concentrating on the Christian rewards and punishments of the next world. In Shetland, where the tale seems to have been well known at one time, these are usually not mentioned at all; the ending is just like that in the fairy-hill story — when the hero realises what has happened, he simply crumbles into dust, and, according to one version, is swept up, along with the ashes of the fire, by the woman who is tidying the house where his wedding party was once held — and there is little to show that this is a Christian, rather than a fairy, legend. In fact one isolated Shetland community, at least, seems to have dealt with this by splitting the tale into two versions; a short warning legend in which a skull answers a young man, who invites it to his wedding with a verse reminding him of his own mortality, and,

shortly after, the man dies; and a longer version with the visit to the other world and return.[7]

Another legend from the same district, 'The Three Yells', begins like the alternative version of Tale Type 470, with two close friends one of whom dies. The survivor dreams three nights running that his friend wants him to come at midnight on horseback to a notorious haunt of the trows, or fairies, nearby. He does not, however, carry him away to the otherworld, but gives him a more prosaic warning that his wife is carrying on with another man. The living man must now get away home as fast as he can, before he hears the third of the yells of the title — in fact he is just riding straight through the door as he hears it, and he survives, but the pony, whose hindquarters were still outside, dies.[8] It appears here that the fairies are the guardians of the gateway to the next world — both departments of it: there is no suggestion that the good neighbour is returning from Hell rather than Heaven. A local legend from North Ronaldsay in Orkney has the same implication. A young man there is said to have consulted a witch about some way to see his dead wife again, and been told to go to a cave below a cairn at the north end of the island on the night of the full moon, read a few verses from the Bible and throw in a black cat, and his wife would appear. But 'the fairy folk' would hold on to her and try to stop her, unless he could beat them off with a thick oaken staff. He succeeded, and had every night of the full moon with her, presumably as long as the supply of black cats lasted.[9] But, again, the fairies are guardians of the gate, as no doubt they were in pagan times.

It is difficult, however, to construct any sort of consistent belief about the otherworld from surviving legends. Normally hours in the otherworld correspond to years in this world, an idea which has probably come into Christian tales such as the Don Juan legend, or the tale of the monk who remains rapt for years, listening to a heavenly bird (Tale Type 471A), from Old Irish concepts originally applying to the pagan paradise. On the other hand, there are tales where a visit to the otherworld takes little or no time: no doubt this is based on the experience of dreams, but in one Shetland tale it appears that the fairies themselves can control time — a fiddler setting out to play at a mortal wedding, is asked to play at a fairy one, and is given a guarantee that, though he plays all evening, he will still be in time for his original appointment.[10] The fairy bride, incidentally, proves to be a mortal woman, who recently dropped dead. In this tale, as in the legend of the midwife to the fairies and others, the mortal is strictly warned not to touch fairy food or drink; but, in this case, an exception can be made for any brought by the fairy man who invited him to the feast. In the fairly widespread legend of the two men who wish for food or drink from the fairy hill, the one who takes what is offered to him actually gets a blessing, and it is the one who refuses to eat or drink who is cursed.[11] The point here is not, I think, that the food has become harmless by being brought out of the otherworld into this — in other instances, fairy food, like fairy money and artefacts, turns into leaves or toad-stools in such circumstances, though in some tales a cup may be brought home safely if the drink in it is thrown away. The point is that the one who refuses the drink is the one who made the rash wish in the first place, and then compounds the felony by rejecting what he wished for, through fear: the fairies act as a nemesis on such rash wishers in other tales, for instance on the house-wife who wants help with her work and then cannot get rid of her helpers,[12] and evidently the taboo on wishing takes precedence over the taboo on fairy food, and allows the rules of common courtesy to operate.

My last example is slightly different: it is chosen to show just how ill-defined the limits of the otherworld are. It is a variant of the story listed in *The Types of the Irish Folktale* as AT Tale Type 241B, and also known in various forms in Gaelic Scotland, about the man who could not take his turn at telling stories in a house he was visiting and had some experience, usually horrific, in the course of that night, after which his host was able to tell him: '*Now* you have a story to tell!' In this version[13] the storyteller is Bessie Whyte, a Scots-speaking traveller, now living in Montrose:

This is away back donkeys' years ago; it was on a farm, ye see, an every year they used tae have a competition — the farmer had — whoever could tell the biggest lie would get a guinea o a prize. So all the cottar folk (ye know, a farm was jist like a wee town at one time, wi all the cottar hooses) . . . they all told their stories an told their stories. But they had a cattleman there . . . an he was jist a stupid lump, ye ken, he kent nothing, an jist goin aboot wi his boots aa dung and sleepin in the bothy, an he really kent nothin — an he says, 'What aboot you?'

He says, 'Ye ken fine I cannae tell stories, I dinnae ken nothing tae tell.'

'Aw come on,' he says, 'ye could tell us something.'

He says, 'No,' he says — but the farmer, ye see, he hed the Black Art, an he said tae him, 'Well, A'll tell ye whit tae do. Go doon tae the river,' he says, 'an clean my boat oot,' he says, 'A havenae been an used it since last summer,' he says. 'Clean it oot, and when ye come back ye'll maybe be able tae tell us a story.'

So doon he goes, an he gets intae the boat an he's balin oot the water, because it — some water had gotten in it. . . But this boat takes off wi him, ye see? The boat takes off wi him, and . . . goes on an on. But half-way across this stretch o water he looks doon at himsel, an in place o this big auld tackety boots covered wi dung there wis dainty wee shoes; silk stockins; nice skirt! Well he seen this, an then he looks ower intae the water an there's the face o a beautiful girl showin back at him. He says, 'That's funny,' he says. 'That's queer, that!'

But anyway he wis nearin the other side by this time, an as he neared the other side he — or she — wis trying tae get in tae the edge, when there wis a young man came along, an he waded intae the water an pulls the boat in, and lifted her out o the water. And they got to know each ither, and they fell in love, an got married, and they had two o a family.

So — aw, there a few years and they come back doon this way again, and as they're walkin along wi the bairns rinnin in front o them, she says, 'Look, there's the little boat that I came here in!' She says, 'I must go doon an see it.' So she ran doon tae the boat, an she jumps intae it tae have a right look, and she says, 'The baler's still here an everything.' But the boat, it starts off wi her again! And right away across, an then half-way across the water she looks doon, and there's this auld tackety boots, all dirty dung; cord troosers; and this auld jacket, moleskin jacket. And, 'Oh my God,' he says, 'whit's this? Whit's this?'

Then he landed right back at where he'd started aff, at this farm, an he's howlin an greetin an pullin his hair an tearin himsel; an he comes rinnin up tae the farm, an howlin an greetin — an the farmer says tae him, 'Whit's the matter wi ye?'

He says, 'Whit's the matter? Dinnae speak tae me. It's ma man an ma bairns, ma man an ma bairns,' he says, 'dinnae speak tae me!'

He says, 'What are ye speakin aboot?'

He says, 'Ma man an ma bairns! Oh, dinnae speak.'

'Ach, sit doon,' the farmer says, 'an tell us aboot it.'

Now when he'd left they'd on a pot o sowens. (I don't know — you'll no ken whit sowens is — it's an aald Scotch [dish] — *you'll* ken whit sowens is.) An the sowens an the pot were still on when he came back. The farmer says, 'Well tell us then.'

So he sat and related that story tae them, ye see, an the farmer says, 'Very good!' he says. 'That's the biggest lie 'at's been told the night, so you get the prize!'

But he'd — the farmer had put the Black Art on him so that he'd imagined he'd been away for years an had a family an everything: actually he was only awa aboot half an 'oor. Ye see? It was jist that he'd done that tae him.

I think this story may have come from Argyll through Bessie's mother, who was from a Gaelic-speaking tinker family from that side of the country: certainly we have an earlier recording in Gaelic from the Ross of Mull,[14] without the sex-change element, but with the marriage and children. The otherworld across the water is there, firmly identified as Donegal in Ireland, and a mysterious boat carries the hero, who has been sent out to repair the byre, there from Uisken in Mull. In both versions the host at the storytelling is clearly behind the whole thing: this is true of most versions of 'The Man who had no Story', but in other cases the scene is often a strange dwelling, where a traveller spends the night, and it seems to be implied that the host himself, like the beings encountered in the nocturnal adventure, is a fairy, or at any rate someone not of this world. Here the house is in an ordinary community, and the host is a mortal with some power of hypnotism or magic — what Bessie calls a 'Black Laird', a magician-farmer. We need not bother to look here for an otherworld reflecting pagan beliefs: but still it seems to me that this tale of virtual reincarnation is worth setting beside other stories of a visit to the otherworld — the basic idea is the same, but, because the story itself, rather than any beliefs reflected in it, is the essential here, the concept has been carried as far as it can go, without overstraining the imagination of a country audience, in something resembling folk science-fiction.

In fact we may have to reckon with this approach in other fairy legends. As Otto Blehr has pointed out[15] in the context of Norwegian super-natural legends and memorates, the beliefs may be governed by the stories, just as much as the stories are by the beliefs, and sometimes the course of the story may be decided, as it generally is in inter-national wonder-tales, by literary criteria — the need for a logically satisfying plot or a happy end, or indeed a delight in paradox: in that last tale, the main point of the otherworld is its sheer otherness. Again, legends may be influenced by memorate elements, 'true' experiences of a story-teller, which may derive from dreams or, for all we know, from those phenomena arising from more complex psychological experiences. Once some-thing has got into a story it is part of belief, as long and as far as that story is told and believed. Since there are no longer priests, druids, or even official storytellers, to codify beliefs about the fairies and their world — and traditional communities are not, I hope, going to pay too much heed to folklorists' or antiquaries' attempts at codification — the beliefs must needs depend mainly on the stories, and we need not expect to find a consistent body of belief anywhere.

We may, in fact, be thankful for the richness of what we do have. Beliefs about the otherworld have survived the coming of more 'advanced' religions, perhaps because most such religions approve of stories which stress the illusory nature, not only of the fairies' world, but of our own as set beside it. We may still find a value in them, apart from mere entertainment: they intensified that sense of living in a dangerous and incomprehensible world which Victorian rationalism and twentieth-century materialism tried to take away from us, and the many today who dabble in ESP or witchcraft, faith healing or UFOlogy, science fantasy or science fact, are trying to recapture.

Notes

1. *Tocher*, XXVIII, 203-4.

2. See for instance J. G. Campbell, *Superstitions of the Scottish Highlands* (Glasgow, 1900), 184-8; G. F. Black, *County Folklore III ... Orkney and Shetland Islands* (London, 1903), 20, 47.

3. Printed versions include James MacDougall, *Folk Tales and Fairy Lore* (Edinburgh, 1910), 162-7 (repr. *Highland Fairy Legends* (Ipswich, 1978), 28-30); J. F. Campbell, *Popular Tales of the West Highlands* vol.2 (Paisley, 1890), 65, 74; J. G. Campbell, 61-3; *Celtic Review*, V, 169; *Folk-Lore*, XI, 442-3; *Transactions of the Gaelic Society of Inverness*, XXVI, 57-9; XXIX, 272-4; and at least 30 others, in print, MS. or recordings.

4. Wirt Sikes, *British Goblins* (London, 1880, repr. Wakefield, 1973), 70-9.

5. J. F. Campbell, 49; J. G. Campbell, 13; *Tocher*, XXVIII, 197. The version with a drain seems better known in Galloway and Northern Ireland than Northern Scotland, but is also common as far away as Finland (catalogued in *FF Communications*, CLXXXII, 123-4, Nos M76, 342).

6. J. G. Campbell, 64-5; *Tocher*, XXVI, 104-5.

7. Published by Calum Maclean in *Scottish Studies*, I (1957), 65-9; *Shetland Folk Book*, III (1957), 65-7; another North Highland version like the first is in *Folk-Lore Journal*, VI (1888), 183-5. Since writing this paper I have discovered variants in Gaelic much like the Shetland ones: thus, in the version from Barra referred to by Calum Maclean (Irish Folklore Commission MS. 1028, 468-78); the hero goes into a hill, where he hears beautiful music after encountering the skull, is given food there, and reappears, without further adventures, many years later; in a version from Lady Evelyn Stewart-Murray's Perthshire MS. collection, No.205, a skull invited to dinner comes as an old man, and would have eaten his hosts out of house and home, if not given a bannock with a cross on it.

8. *Tocher*, XXVIII, 217.

9. Quoted from SA 1967/112 B3; also published by the informant's sister, Mary A. Scott, *Island Saga* (Aberdeen [1968]), 155-6.

10. *Tocher*, XXVIII, 202-3.

11. J. F. Campbell, 79; *Tocher*, XX, 132-5; XXV, 14-15; cf. R. H. Cromek, *Remains of Nithsdale and Galloway Song* (repr. Paisley, 1880), 241-2, where the motif of the rash wish is *not* present.

12. Much anthologised from the version in Lord Archibald Campbell's *Waifs and Strays of Celtic Tradition*, vol.1 (London, 1889), 56-69.

13. SA 1973/162/4, recorded by Peter Cooke and Linda Headlee on their first visit to Bessie Whyte: the story is quite unrehearsed, but, even, so, something of Bessie's quality as a storyteller comes through, and several of those who heard the tape remarked on it. For more information on Bessie Whyte see *Tocher*, XXIII, *passim*.

14. SA 1953/102/2, recorded by Calum Maclean from Duncan Cameron, Leob.

15. Most recently expressed in a paper summarised in *NIF Newsletter*, II (1978), 10.

Social Function and Traditional Scottish Rhymes

DAVID BUCHAN   University of Stirling

TRADITIONAL rhymes have been most often considered by folklorists in the context of child-lore. They occupied, however, an important place in the lives of the adult community in a traditional culture, and deserve rather more attention than they have received in the past. In generic surveys of folksay — to adopt a handy term for language in tradition — one will find discussion of the proverb and its associated forms as distinguished by Archer Taylor, and the riddle, with the hetero-geneous area of 'rhymes, miscellaneous' bringing up the rear. If, that is, they appear at all; in the large and useful *Folklore and Folklife* of recent years they attract no mention. Brunvand points out that 'these bits of fluid folklore are highly elusive and have not been systematically collected or arranged on a large scale in the United States' and limits his discussion of specifically adult rhymes to three varieties of what he calls work rhymes.[1] To my knowledge no systematic cover-age of adult rhymes exists for Britain either. Recent folksay scholarship has underlined the importance of considering context and function for a full understanding of the proverbial genres, and in this paper I propose to examine some aspects of function and traditional rhymes in Scotland with a view to gaining a clearer perspec-tive on this somewhat amorphous area of folksay, itself a generic division yet to receive a proper taxonomy.

Like all varieties of folklore, rhymes perform functions which collectively work towards 'main-taining the stability of culture'; these we can call the general cultural functions.[2] They — to use Bascom's convenient fourfold distinction — first of all provide entertainment; this derives from both the aesthetic features of the form — assonance, alliteration, euphony, rhythm, rhyming itself —

and the wit or humour of the content, often made sharper by the form's compression. Second, they can validate the culture, though this may not be a major function. Again, they help maintain con-formity to accepted patterns of social behaviour. For example, a community may typify the characters of women whose washday is other than Monday by the following:

> Her it washes on Monanday
> Gets a' the ook t' dry.
> Her it washes on Tyesday
> Is nae far bye.
> Her it washes on Wednesday,
> She is a dainty dame.
> Her it washes on Feersday
> Is muckle t' the same.
> Her it washes on Friday
> Hiz little skeel indeed.
> Her it washes on Satterday,
> It's jist a dud for need.[3]

There are many examples of rhymes exercising such social controls. Finally, they educate, by carrying the lore of the tribe from generation to generation. They carry not only attitudes to, but also the facts of, such large areas of human knowl-edge as history, geography, law, medicine, belief, and occupational lore.

This attractive topic merits further study, but it is not the present concern. As Bascom points out, the functions of the individual genres of folk-lore 'are to some extent distinctive and must be analysed separately' from the general functions shared by all the genres.[4] These functions — of rhymes as a separate generic category — do con-stitute the concern. Now Patrick Mullen in an excellent article on 'Legend and Belief' has shown that 'function and classification of legend are interrelated problems and cannot be studied separately.'[5] If the interrelatedness of function and classification were also to hold good for rhyme, then it could be that an examination of the functions served by rhyme in a social context could lead to an understanding of the distinctive kinds of rhyme and hence perhaps to a taxonomic scheme for these distinctive kinds.

Rhyming, the device, appears of course in other folk literature genres, such as folksong and folk drama, and this is hardly surprising, given the way rhyming functions to heighten, intensify, distance, sharpen, or make memorable, pithy, amusing, the subject presented. Rhyme, the form, occurs in folk narrative and the proverb and the riddle. There is in fact an overlapping zone between rhyme and proverb and rhyme and folksong: a proverb may be in rhyming form and a lullaby, for example, may be sung, crooned, chanted, or recited. The concern here, however, is with the distinctive sub-genres of rhyme which can be isolated by virtue of their social function, and these, though they can be largely separated from the literature genres, necessarily involve practices relating to folk belief and folk custom.

On the basis of the Scottish material one can distinguish eight general categories for the distinctive sub-genres. In general terms the earlier categories involve belief and the latter ones custom. The first category consists of rhymes relating to specific forms of folk belief which involve a practice or luck-connected activity and whose functions are to ensure the success of the practice or to mark the importance of the activity. There are six sub-genres here: the charm, the cure, the divination, the omen, the safeguard, the prohibition. The second category consists of other rhymes involving belief, whose overt functions are to attempt expression of the unknowable or to avoid expression of the sacred. The first function is that of the prophecy rhyme, which could well be held to belong to the cultural function rhymes concerned with the transmission of knowledge, but which I would include because it can often serve, as in 'Betide, betide, whate'er betide, / Haig shall be Haig of Bermersyde,'[6] such social purposes as reassurance or reinforcement of group pride. The second overt function − to avoid expression of the sacred − is that of the psalmody rhyme, which may be a sub-genre peculiar to Scot-

land. These seem to be of nineteenth-century currency and derive from ministers' fearing what irreverent midweek choirs and singing classes might do to the sacred words of the psalms and decreeing that the singers at psalmody rehearsals use innocuous verbal substitutes. This rather rebounded on the ministers since many of these substitutes developed an inappropriately hilarious secularity and, indeed, a popular life of their own. One is still widely quoted as a short comic poem: 'There was a Presbyterian cat' or 'auld Seceder cat' depending on one's denomination. The tune of 'Bangor', for instance, was served by this couplet:

The high, high notes of Bangor's tune are
  very hard to raise
And trying hard to reach them gars the lasses
  burst their stays.[7]

In both these sub-genres the overt belief function may be superseded in practice by other, more earthbound functions.

The third category comprises rhymes of beneficent purpose, whose function is to invoke good fortune on an occasion or undertaking. The sub-genres here are the blessing, the prayer, the grace, and the toast. In Lowland Scotland, in contrast to Highland Scotland, the blessing and the prayer have been only infrequently recorded. In the Northeast, in fact, prayer became associated with its obverse, for 'prayers' was the common term for curses, and the Lord's Prayer, recited backwards, was necessary for the reestin, or stopping, of a mill wheel, or beast, or person.[8] Parody prayers also exist, as do comic graces for after, as well as before, a meal.

In the fourth category are rhymes of malificent or unfriendly purpose, whose function is to cause harm or annoyance or laughter. The sub-genres in this category consist of the curse, the taunt, and the blason populaire. The function of the last, the blason populaire, can be difficult to determine, since it depends upon context, as Dr John Widdowson showed in a recent conference paper: it could be used directly as a taunt by one group against another or it could serve, within one group only, to provoke amusement or a sense of group solidarity.

With this last category, after the curse, we have moved away from belief to sub-genres more concerned, broadly speaking, with custom. Category five consists of rhymes whose function is to mark or facilitate an act of social interaction. Here there are rhymes of situation, and rhymes of conversation. Of the first kind is the rhyme that is said when a practical joke is played, or the rhyme of reparation, which was publicly recited at the church door as an act of penance for scandal-mongering. It takes two forms depending on whether the object of slander is a woman or a man; here is that for a man:

> First I ca'd him honest man —
> Twas true indeed
> Syne I ca'd him *thief's face* —
> Fause tongue, ye lee'd.[9]

Conversation rhymes convey formalised reactions within what would nowadays be called intra-personal relations, where the formalisation, by its distancing, serves to reduce possible tension or friction. There are rhymes conveying incredulity, if hoaxing is suspected, and faint praise, and dislike of unwelcome advice, and reproach to someone who, having formerly shunned his acquaintance, now requests assistance, or someone who, having given a thing, now asks for it back again. This, perhaps the most fascinating of the sub-genres, overlaps of course with those proverbial rhymes which fulfil the more general cultural function of maintaining conformity to accepted patterns of behaviour. A special group of social interaction rhymes is that of rhymes used to children.

The sixth category contains rhymes whose function is to mark or facilitate a commercial transaction. The first sub-genre is the oath, often, though not always, connected with sealing a bargain, as still today in childlore:

> I trapse my word abune my breath,
> I've touched cauld airn afore ye!
> (Here the boot tackets are touched.)[10]

There is an interesting parallel here to the apotropaic use of 'cauld airn' among fishermen if a taboo word happens to be used at sea. The second sub-genre is the well-known one of the vendor's cry. An unusual example comes from Forfar, chanted line by line by an itinerant cobbler's son, his wife, and the cobbler himself:

The boy	: My father mends bellises;
Wife	: It's true 'at the lad does say;
Cobbler	: And I'm the boy 'at can dae it,
	Wi my tiddy-fal-lal-de-lal-lay.[11]

The seventh category consists of rhymes whose function is, quite specifically, amusement. Narrative rhymes figure here, as do nonsense rhymes, though frequently what appear to be nonsense rhymes turn out to have belonged to other sub-genres, such as the next one, the tongue twister, designed to test both the tongue's dexterity and its rapidity. There may in fact be two varities here, one emphasising the first and the other the second:

> Kittok sat in pepper pock
> pikel pepper Kittok[12]

and

> Rob Low's lum reeks,
> Roond about the chimley cheeks,
> Wi' a pair o' blue breeks.[13]

The eighth and final and widely inclusive category contains rhymes relating to folk custom whose function is integral to the event. Division into sub-genres here follows the basic threefold classification of folk custom into periodic custom rhymes, rites of passage rhymes, and occasional custom rhymes. The first group includes, for example, the standard Hogmanay rhyme:

> Rise up, guidwife, an' shak' yer feathers,
> Dinna think that we are beggars;
> We are guid folks come to play,
> Rise up an' gie's oor Hogmanay.
> Hogmanay, Trol-lol-lay.[14]

The second group is already well represented in the baptismal and wedding toasts but also includes such rhymes as those spoken at the saining of a corpse. The third, occasional custom rhymes, has this one for a house warming:

> Braw . . . stands . . . oor . . . hoose!
>   Fair fa' the biggin' o't;
> Cheese and bannocks oor door-cheeks,
>   Pancakes the riggin' o't![15]

Or this one to start a horse race:

> Bel-horses, Bel-horses, Beware o' the day,
> One o'clock, two o'clock, Three and away![16]

These, then, are the twenty-six sub-genres of rhyme distinguishable from the Scottish evidence on the basis of social function. Many traditional rhymes would of course be classified under cultural function where they would be arranged largely by the kinds of knowledge they carry. The distinction between cultural and social function is obviously a far from precise one, but in essence the one is concerned with the transmission of knowledge, the other with the performing of a habitual practice. In fact, the underlying concept for the material discussed has been that of rhyme as verbal practice in a social context. What Mullen found for legend, that function and classification are interrelated, holds true here too, where analysis of the contextual functions reveals the distinctive sub-genres of rhyme. The classification scheme inevitably is not ideal: there is the usual over-lapping of sub-genres, and the problem of the recalcitrant item.

How, for example, does one classify the rhyme chanted at the rider of a piebald horse because such a person was believed to know the cure for the whooping-cough:

> Man wi the piety horse,
> What's gude for the kink host?[17]

This classification, however, does give some definition to the amorphous area of 'rhymes, miscellaneous'. Moreover, since many of these sub-genres have manifestations in prose form too, this scheme may also cover non-rhyming material of traditional language and contribute towards the much needed taxonomy of folksay as a whole. And finally, a look at the social function of these Scottish rhymes does indicate the extent to which they permeated the lives of the adult traditional community.[18]

Notes

1. Jan Harold Brunvand, *The Study of American Folklore: An Introduction* (New York, 1968), 61, 69-71.

2. William Bascom, 'Four Functions of Folklore', *The Study of Folklore*, ed. Alan Dundes (Englewood Cliffs, 1965), 297.

3. Walter Gregor, *Notes on the Folk-Lore of the North-East of Scotland* (London, 1881), 177.

4. Bascom, 296.

5. *Journal of American Folklore*, LXXXIV (1971), 413.

6. Eve Blantyre Simpson, *Folk Lore in Lowland Scotland* (London, 1908), 176.

7. Alan Reid, 'Psalmody Rhymes', *Miscellanea of the Rymour Club*, I (Edinburgh, 1906-1911), 38.

8. Gregor, 35, 183, 216.

9. Robert Chambers, *Popular Rhymes of Scotland* (Edinburgh, 1870), 382.

10. Bruce J. Home, 'Edinburgh Rhymes', *Miscellanea of the Rymour Club*, I (1906-1911), 168.

11. *Miscellanea of the Rymour Club*, I (1906-1911), 238.

12. Erskine Beveridge, ed., *Fergusson's Scottish Proverbs* (Edinburgh, 1924), 71.

13. *Miscellanea of the Rymour Club*, I (1906-1911), 176.

14. M. M. Banks, *British Calendar Customs: Scotland*, II (London, 1939), 46.

15. Jessie Patrick Findlay, 'Folk-Rhymes and Proverbs of Fife', *Transactions of the Rymour Club*, III (Edinburgh, 1928), 136.

16. *Miscellanea of the Rymour Club*, I (1906-1911), 238.

17. James Napier, *Folk Lore in the West of Scotland* (Paisley, 1879), 96.

18. This paper is a prelininary sketch of the topic which will be dealt with in greater detail at a later date.

The Colbeck Legend in English Tradition of the Twelfth and Thirteenth Centuries

MICHAEL CHESNUTT   University of Copenhagen

THE medieval religious legend of the dancers of Colbek is found in three distinct early redactions, of which two are cast in the form of a first-person narrative purporting to derive from one of the participants in the famous dance.[1] It is generally agreed that the origin of the legend should be sought in an outbreak of St Vitus' dance (*chorea*) or some similar convulsive disorder, and that this outbreak actually occurred at Colbek (Kölbigk) in East Saxony in the first quarter of the eleventh century; the probable historicity of the event is confirmed by a reference in the works of the monastic chronicler Lambert of Hersfeld, who records that a certain man named Ruthart, who had participated in the 'famous dance' at Colbek, was cured after twenty-three years of suffering and entered the service of St Wigbert. This cure is piously counted as one of the miracles with which God consoled the brethren of Hersfeld for the destruction of their monastery by fire in the year 1038.[2]

The luckless victims of the outbreak of *chorea* would appear to have been driven into exile, carrying with them some kind of written record of the mishap which had befallen them, and from this record derives the textual tradition of the three early redactions. The authorship, content, and successive revisions of the original record, have been the subject of much scholarly debate: Baesecke, for example, assumed that the original record already had the character of a miracle and argued that it might have been composed by Thietmar of Merseburg, while Ernst Erich Metzner, the author of the most recent and also the most detailed discussion of the subject, considers that miraculous features were not present in the original record, that the latter was written not by Thietmar but by the lesser-known Arnold of Halberstadt,

and that the legendary embroidery of the extant redactions is due to a revision of the original record carried out at the monastery of Korvey.[3] On its continued journey westwards the text — now in the form of the archetype of the extant early redactions — reached the vicinity of Cologne, where it was subjected to further revisions by a redactor familiar with an analogous tale found in the writings of St Augustine;[4] this secondary version employed for the first time the form of a first-person narrative, and it was presumably compiled for the benefit of a band of vagrants who claimed, whether truly or otherwise, to have been among those who were expelled from Colbek. It is the version thus produced which lies behind the numerous variants of the legend in medieval chronicles and collections of *exempla.*

The most popular offshoot of the version just described was the redaction claiming to be the reminiscences of a certain Othbert, who had been furnished with a written account of his experiences authorised by Pilgrim (Peregrinus), bishop of Cologne, 1021-36. The oldest witness to this redaction is the *Gesta regum Anglorum* of William of Malmesbury,[5] in which the Colbek legend is treated as an event of the year 1012. The *Gesta regum Anglorum* can be dated to the first half of the twelfth century; from the end of the same century and the beginning of the following we have groups of German and French transcriptions of the Othbert redaction in a slightly fuller form than that given by William of Malmesbury. The most influential factor in the dissemination of the redaction was not, however, its inclusion in these relatively early sources, but its later adaptation by Vincent of Beauvais for his *Speculum historiale* (1244), from which it passed into the international narrative repertoire of the preaching friars. Vincent's source, as he clearly indicates in his text, was the English historian of the previous century.

Of greatest interest from an English point of view is the second of the two early redactions which use the first-person form, namely that claiming to report the experiences of Theoderic, who like Othbert received a testimonial from a bishop of the church – in this case no less distinguished a figure than Bruno, bishop of Toul, 1027-48, later known as Pope Leo IX. The Latin text of the Theoderic redaction appears in an autograph copy by the Anglo-French historian Orderic Vitalis (second quarter of the twelfth century) and in four English manuscripts of the twelfth, thirteenth and fourteenth centuries; a fifth English manuscript, now lost, is attested by the sixteenth-century author, Nicolas Harpsfield, who quoted from it in his English ecclesiastical history.[6] Apart from Verrier, who argued unconvincingly that Orderic Vitalis wrote the Theoderic redaction in France, no-one has seriously questioned its dating in the eleventh century and its English provenance.[7] The latter is strongly supported by the fact that Theoderic is said ultimately to have been released from his sufferings at the tomb of St Edith at Wilton, near Salisbury, which provides an obvious parallel to the cure of Ruthart, as reported by Lambert of Hersfeld. In two of the surviving English manuscripts of the Latin text, the Theoderic redaction is incorporated into the *Vita S. Edithe* of the Flemish monk Goscelin,[8] who emigrated to England some years before the Norman Conquest and attained a high reputation as a hagiographer in his adopted country: William of Malmesbury called him second to none, after Bede, in extolling the merits of English saints.[9] The extant form of the Theoderic redaction may have been composed as part of the *Vita* of St Edith, or more probably – as Metzner has argued – as an independent work, which was later included in the *Vita*. That Goscelin was its author would at all events seem to be indisputable. On the other hand, the text itself indicates in its concluding lines that another, evidently vernacular version of Theoderic's story, was made at Wilton immediately after his cure: in the words of Bodleian Library MS Fairfax 17, *Hec in presencia Brichtive ipsius loci abbatisse declarata et patriis literis sunt mandata*, which is not likely to be a reference to an earlier work by Goscelin himself, but rather to a notice (or *procès-verbal*, as Wilmart calls it) in Anglo-Saxon.[10]

The Theoderic redaction circulated in England in manuscript form as late as the fifteenth century, when it was consulted by the anonymous author of a verse life of St Edith in Middle English.[11] It had also been paraphrased in Middle English verse at the beginning of the previous century, as part of the *Handlyng Synne* of Robert Mannyng of Brunne,[12] a canon of the Gilbertine house of Sempringham in Lincolnshire who, according to his own account, commenced work on this important book in the year 1303:

> For lewde men y vndyr-toke
> On englyssh tunge to make þys boke.
> . . .
> Of Brunnewake yn Kesteuene,
> Syxe myle be-syde Sympryngham euene,
> Y dwelled yn þe pryorye
> Fyftene ȝere yn cumpanye
> . . .
> Dane Felyp was mayster þat tyme
> Þ at y began þys englyssh ryme.
> Þe ȝeres of grace fyl þan to be
> A þousynd & þre hundred & þre
> (EETS edition, lines 43-76).

Robert Mannyng's 'englyssh ryme' is a kind of popular devotional handbook intended to assist penitents in the systematic examination of their consciences;[13] it is based on an anonymous Anglo-Norman text entitled *Le Manuel des Pechiez*, which was composed c.1270 and is one of numerous English religious writings inspired by the educational reforms decreed at the Fourth Lateran Council.[14] Among the many *exempla* included in the *Manuel* is a summary in a few lines of the Othbert redaction of the Colbek legend. When Robert Mannyng made his Middle English paraphrase, he did not content himself with this very paltry account of the famous dance but turned instead to a copy of the Theoderic redaction, which he apparently had at his disposal. Concrete evidence for the availability of such a copy in Lincolnshire is afforded already in the previous century by the Fairfax manuscript, which originally belonged to the Cistercian abbey at Louth Park.[15] The instances where the Fairfax manuscript exhibits distinctive readings do not, however, point to this manuscript having been that actually used by Robert:

(1) *Fairfax* At ille patrio precepto paret arreptamque manu sororem trahebat (Schröder 128/58-60).

Rawl. (Vita S. Edithe) It ille patrio precepto, arreptamque manu sororem trahebat (Wilmart 288/25-289/1).

Handlyng Synne Aȝone wende weyl for to spede; Vn-to þe karolle asswyþe he ȝede; hys systyr by þe arme he hente . . .
(lines 9097-99).

(2) *Fairfax* 'En pater, ait, suscipe . . .' (128/67).

Rawl. 'En pater, suscipe . . .' (289/8-9).

Handlyng Synne 'loke, fadyr,' he seyd, 'and haue hyt here . . .' (line 9111).

(3) *Fairfax* Sepultum membrum invenitur sequenti die summotenus proiectum (128/70-71).

Rawl. Sepultum membrum inuenit sequenti die summotenus proiectum (289/12-13).

Handlyng Synne þe nexte day, þe arme of Aue, he fonde hyt lyggyng aboue þe graue
(lines 9125-26)

There is nevertheless a chronological and geographical likelihood that Robert Mannyng's Latin exemplar was of similar provenance to the Fairfax manuscript.

Whereas the Othbert redaction, as already mentioned, attained very wide currency in Europe, owing to its employment by Vincent of Beauvais, the Theoderic redaction seems to have constituted a distinctly insular branch of the tradition, enjoying little influence beyond the ambience of St Edith's shrine at Wilton, and those other parts of England to which copies of the text may have been carried by preachers and pilgrims. It is accordingly rather surprising to find that the only two European variants of the Colbek legend which can be associated with the Theoderic redaction come from places as remote as South Germany and Sweden. The first of these two variants occurs in the *Liber constructionis* of the monastery of St Blasien in the Black Forest;[16] the compilation referred to by this title is preserved in St Paul im Lavanttal (Austria), Stiftsbibliothek MS 25.3.8a of the beginning of the fifteenth century, but its variant of the Colbek legend would seem to belong to the internal tradition of the monastery and to have been originally recorded in writing at least two centuries earlier. The miraculous dance is here presented as one of the remarkable sights seen by the pilgrim Iring, who had spent a long life wandering around the world and ended his days at St Blasien, where he died, probably in the year 1190.

The version in the *Liber constructionis* informs us that Iring had seen the accursed dancers on no less than five separate visits to a certain island *in extremis partibus occidentis sita ad septentrionalem plagam* (Book III, ch.25 *ad init.*). In view of the immediately preceding context, where it is stated that Iring had travelled in Britain and Ireland and had reached *occidentalia littora Brittanniae insulae oceani* (Book III, ch.23), it seems reasonable to identify the scene of the miraculous dance with the Hebrides or the Orkneys. The latter are referred to unambiguously as the scene of the dance in the variant of the legend which survives in Uppsala, Universitetsbiblioteket MS C 528 (Codex Bildstenianus) as part of a supplement to the *Old Swedish Legendary*,[17] a work of which the main part is usually dated on internal evidence to the second half of the thirteenth century.[18] This Swedish vernacular text has falsely identified St Magnus the martyr — who appears in the three early redactions of the Colbek legend as the saint to whom the local church is dedicated, and who responds to the priest's angry call for vengeance upon the dancers, who have sacrilegiously disturbed the Christmas Mass — with the later Norse saint Magnús Erlendsson, Earl of the Orkneys, who was murdered in 1115 or 1116 and canonised in 1135;[19] it has also confounded Magnús Erlendsson with Magnús the Good, illegitimate son of St Óláf Haraldsson and King of Norway in the second quarter of the eleventh century.

Dag Strömbäck has argued that the *Old Swedish Legendary* was following the literary model of the Theoderic redaction, not only with regard to the basic outline of the legend, but also with regard to the frame tale concerning Theoderic's cure at Wilton:[20] the originally continental narrative, having first been converted into a miracle of the English saint Edith, was then attracted by the identity of names into the cycle of miracles associated with St Magnús Erlendsson. The evidence

160

of the Iring version, which shows that the Colbek legend had been relocalised in the Scottish islands already in the twelfth century, would point to the transformation of the legend at this early date into a miracle of the Orcadian Magnús, though the *Liber constructionis* admittedly mentions neither the saint nor the scene of the action by name. The *Old Swedish Legendary* would thus preserve the literary form of the Theoderic redaction as adapted to the cult of the Norse saint, while the Iring version, which contains various secondary elements, would be a record of some oral retelling which Iring had heard during a visit to the British Isles.[21]

Strömbäck emphasises that not one whole sentence in the Iring version displays formal correspondence to a sentence of similar content in the three early redactions of the Colbek legend, and expresses it as his considered opinion that the Iring version reflects what he calls *en fri och fantasifull muntlig tradition.*[22] Meier has nevertheless demonstrated a number of verbal parallels between the Iring version and one or more of the early redactions,[23] and the implications of these and other points of textual agreement have been reconsidered by Metzner in his recent book. The conclusion there reached is that the Iring version and that of the *Old Swedish Legendary* go back to a common written source which circulated in Scandinavia as early as the eleventh or twelfth centuries. This source, which is presumed to have been in Latin, was in Metzner's opinion a reflex, not of Goscelin's extant redaction, but of the lost account of Theoderic's cure, said to have been composed in *patriis literis*: it thus preserved elements of the archetype, which were suppressed or changed in the version of Goscelin, who likewise drew on the lost account, but perhaps treated his materials with more stylistic freedom than the writer of the postulated Scandinavian text.[24]

None of the positions adopted by these three scholars is entirely satisfactory. Meier takes it for granted that Iring *folgt ... mündlicher Tradition* but makes the reservation that *trotz alledem scheint durch die Darstellung noch die frühere schriftliche Quelle durch;*[25] Strömbäck minimises the significance of the verbal similarities identified by Meier; and Metzner fails to explain how readings closely reflecting the Latin archetype could occur in a Scandinavian text supposed to be a

reflex of an account written in Anglo-Saxon. It seems to be a rather desperate expedient when Metzner attempts to resolve this last-mentioned difficulty by conceding that the lost account in *patriis literis* may have been 'partly' written in Latin.[26] Nor is the coherence of Metzner's argument increased by his efforts to explain a peculiarity of the Iring version as a misunderstanding on Iring's part of a Norse word used by an oral informant.[27] This informant would have been providing Iring with a paraphrase of the Latin story found in the supposed Scandinavian written text; but such a method of transmission would apparently not have prevented verbal reminiscences of the Latin story from appearing at third hand in our extant record, which a monk of St Blasien later produced on the basis of Iring's recital or dictation.

One of the main questions on which Metzner takes issue with Strömbäck is the existence of the legend in oral tradition in Britain in the twelfth century.[28] Strömbäck regards the Iring version as proof of such oral dissemination, while Metzner regards it as a derivative of his postulated Scandinavian source of the eleventh or twelfth century. Metzner's arguments are not of sufficient weight to invalidate the theory of Strömbäck: quite apart from the improbability of his explanation of the genesis of the Iring version, his evidence for the dependence of the *Old Swedish Legendary* on a source antecedent to Goscelin does not stand up to critical scrutiny.[29] Strömbäck's position does, however, require modification with respect to the 'oral' status of the Iring redaction. The text in the *Liber constructionis* cannot depend on oral tradition alone but must be the work of a scribe who had access to one or more literary versions of the legend, and who was influenced by these in his choice of language, when he wrote down the variant ascribed to the aged pilgrim (or copied it into the *Liber constructionis* from a previously existing transcript, which is perhaps the more likely alternative in view of Mone's demonstration that the extant text is taken over from an older exemplar).[30] This explanation is essentially a clarification of Meier's view, with the emphasis shifted from the oral report to its subsequent written transmission; it agrees with what we know of the practice of medieval scribes, who recorded popular tales and *exempla*, which were in simultaneous oral and literary circulation. It may be noted here that Toul in Lorraine, the ostensible place of origin of the Theoderic redaction, is not much more than 200 kilometres distant from St Blasien, and that the traffic up the Rhine valley would have exposed the monastery to cultural influences emanating from the region of Cologne, where the archetype of all three early redactions is believed to have been carried shortly after its composition. It is therefore possible, and even probable, that the legend was familiar to the brethren of St Blasien from sources other than Iring. At the same time, there is no reason to doubt that Iring was responsible for some important secondary features, such as the localisation in the Northern Isles, and that these features reflect the story as Iring had heard it in Britain. This does not, however, by any means prove that Iring actually encountered his variant of the tradition in the Orkneys, or even that it originated there, though this is what at first sight might be inferred from the record handed down by the monks of St Blasien. On the countrary, the transference of the legend of Edith to the new Northern saint is a device which would naturally have suggested itself to a twelfth-century English cleric like *magister Rodbert* (Robert of Cricklade?), who composed the lost Latin *Vita* of St Magnús Erlendsson.[31] Iring could have heard the story in England just as well as in Scotland; and the Latin exemplar of the version in the *Old Swedish Legendary*, which is believed to be a compilation of Dominican provenance, could have been obtained in England by a Swedish monk, who had visited his order's *studium generale* at Oxford.[32] While all such explanations must necessarily remain within the realm of speculation, an explanation which is naturally compatible with the history of the religious foundations known, or likely to have been responsible, for the transmission of the existing texts is in my view much to be preferred to that offered by Metzner, who would connect his postulated Scandinavian text of the Colbek legend with the family of Sveinn Estridsson and with Anglo-Danish cultural exchanges in the mid-eleventh century.[33]

It is interesting, in view of what has been said, to note that Robert Mannyng occasionally expresses himself in terms that might indicate awareness of an oral tradition parallel to his literary sources. As Kunz already remarked in 1913, Robert seems to treat the tale as a report of something which had happened in England, whereas Goscelin's redaction only localises the cure of Theoderic in that country.[34] It should have been evident from such names as Colbek, Merswynde, Wybessyne and Aзone, not to mention the participation of the Emperoure Henry (EETS edition, lines 9018, 9028, 9092, 9159 etc.), that the sacrilegious dance did not take place in England, but the latter is what Robert unmistakably asserts in his introduction:

> But for to leue, yn cherche to daunce,
> Y shal зow telle a ful grete chaunce
> . . .
> And fyl þys chaunce yn þys londe,
> Yn Ingland, as y vndyrstonde;
> Yn a kynges tyme þat hyght Edward,
> Fyl þys chaunce þat was so hard
> (lines 9007-14).

The 'hard chaunce' of line 9014 cannot refer to the cure of Theoderic at Wilton, and it is difficult to believe that this divergence from the Latin source could have been the result of mere carelessness on the part of an intelligent and well-read author, such as Robert undoubtedly was. Rather it would seem that he had *bona fide* reasons for believing in the English origin of the tale. Towards the conclusion he complains that the Colbek legend is relatively little known in England:

> Pys at þe court of Rome þey wyte,
> And yn þe kronykeles hyt ys wryte,
> Yn many stedys be-зounde þe see,
> More þan ys yn þys cuntre;
> Parfor men seye, an weyl ys trowed,
> 'Þe nere þe cherche, þe fyrþer fro God'
> (lines 9237-42).

The first line probably echoes Goscelin's opening sentence *Romanus orbis nouit et hodierna iuuentus recolit homines noua inquietudine corporum diuinitus percussos* etc.,[35] while the second may be an exaggeration based on the (admittedly false) source reference prefixed to the story in the *Manuel des Pechiez*. The author of the *Manuel* tells us that he borrowed the legend from the so-called *Itinerarium Clementis*:

> En le itineraire de seint Clement,
> Qu fu de si beal document,
> Vne cunte de mult grant pité

Encuntre tiels auum troué
(EETS edition, lines 6931-34).

This manifestly impossible statement, which is omitted or altered in some manuscripts,[36] can be ascribed with Schröder to the casual insertion of the Othbert redaction into some vacant space in a copy of the *Itinerarium*,[37] but it may nevertheless have been regarded by Robert Mannyng as sufficient grounds for accusing his compatriots of indifference to what should have been a source of national pride. This is clearly the implication of the proverb quoted in line 9242. What Robert seems to be saying is that the 'hard chaunce' is better known abroad than in England *where it happened*; but, as always, those who are nearest to something pay least regard to it.

One of the more curious passages in Robert's paraphrase is that in which he describes the curse called down on the dancers. Here he writes that the priest prayed:

> Þat swych a veniaunce were on hem sent
> Are þey oute of þat stedé were went,
> Þat þey myȝt euer, ryȝt so wende
> Vnto þat tyme tweluemonth ende:
> (Yn þe latyne þat y fonde þore,
> he seyþ nat 'tweluemonth,' but 'euermore.')
> He cursed hem þere alsaume
> As þey karoled on here gaume
>
> (lines 9079-86).

The 'latyne' of the Theoderic redaction does not, however, say unambiguously that the priest prayed that they might dance for 'euermore': the words of his prayer, as put into his mouth by Goscelin, were *Ab isto . . . officio ex Dei nutu amodo non cessetis*,[38] where the adverb *amodo* need only be taken to mean 'until further notice' or the like. One of the distinctive features of the Iring version is precisely that the miraculous dance, which ceases a year after its commencement in the three early redactions, has been turned into a dance *which is never to end* — according to the *Liber constructionis*, it had already been going on for 300 years when Iring saw it. Robert Mannyng's tendentious translation of the Latin word *amodo* may therefore betray the unconscious influence of a variant tradition which he had heard; and similarly, if he thought that the miraculous dance took place in the British Isles and not in Germany, his belief may have been due, not so much to pious nationalism, as to his acquaintance with a parallel oral tradition resembling the Iring version. In the introduction to *Handlyng Synne*, we are told that the work was compiled from both literary and oral sources:

> Talys shalt þou fynde þerynne,
> And chauncys þat haþ happed for synne;
> Meruelys, some as y fonde wrytyn,
> And oþter þat haue be seyn & wetyn;
> None ben þare-yn, more ne lesse,
> But þat y founde wryte, or had wytnesse
>
> (lines 131-136).

On the evidence furnished by Robert Mannyng, we must reckon with the distinct possibility that oral variants of the Colbek legend were in circulation in England as late as the beginning of the fourteenth century.

Notes

1. The fundamental study of these three redactions is by Edward Schröder, 'Die Tänzer von Kölbigk: ein Mirakel des 11. Jahrhunderts', *Zeitschrift für Kirchengeschichte*, XVII (1-2) (1896), 94-164. For the most recent supplementary studies see Karl-Heinz Borck, 'Der Tanz zu Kölbigk', *Beiträge zur Geschichte der deutschen Sprache und Literatur*, LXXVI (1954/55), 241-320, and Metzner, *Zur frühesten Geschichte der europäischen Balladendichtung* (note 3 below). Numerous variants of the legend are listed in Frederic C. Tubach, *Index Exemplorum: a handbook of medieval religious tales*, FF Communications, CCIV (Helsinki, 1969), No.1419; cf. also Stith Thompson, *Motif-Index of Folk-Literature*, revised edition (Copenhagen, 1955-58), motif C 94.1.1, and Johannes Bolte (ed.), *Johannes Pauli: Schimpf und Ernst* (Berlin, 1924), No. 388 and notes.

2. Oswald Holder-Egger (ed.), *Lamperti monachi Hersfeldensis opera*, Monumenta Germaniae historica, Scriptores rerum germanicarum in usum scholarum ... recusi, 38 (Hannover/Leipzig, 1894), 350-1. Cf. Schröder, 94-5, and Borck, 305 and note 1. For the incidence of *chorea* in medieval Germany, see Alfred Martin, 'Geschichte der Tanzkrankheit in Deutschland', *Zeitschrift des Vereins für Volkskunde*, XXIV (1914), 255-39.

3. See Georg Baesecke, 'Der Kölbigker Tanz: philologisch und literarisch', *Zeitschrift für deutsches Altertum*, LXXVIII (1941), 1-36, rpt. in: Werner Schröder (ed.), *Georg Baesecke: Kleinere Schriften zur althochdeutschen Sprache und Literatur* (Bern/München, 1966), 249-84; and Ernst Erich Metzner, 'Zur frühesten Geschichte der europäischen Balladendichtung: der Tanz in Kölbigk', *Frankfurter Beiträge zur Germanistik*, XIV (Frankfurt am Main, 1972), esp. 54-70, 110-12 and 149-54.

4. *De civitate Dei*, XXII, 8 and Sermon 322 (the story of Paulus and Palladia of Caesarea). Cf. *Patrologia latina*, XLI (Paris, 1861), 769-71; *ibid.*, XXXVIII (1865), 1443-45; Schröder, 144-46.

5. William Stubbs (ed.), *Willelmi Malmesbiriensis monachi De gestis regum Anglorum libri quinque* (...), Rolls Series, XC (London, 1887-89), I, 203-4. Cf. Schröder, 99, and Metzner, 84-5.

6. Richard Gibbons, (ed.), *Historia anglicana ecclesiastica* (Douai, 1662), 205-6; cf. Schröder, 124.

7. See Paul Verrier, 'La plus vieille citation de carole', *Romania*, LVIII (1932), 380-421, and the violently polemical reply by Schröder, 'Das Tanzlied von Kölbigk', *Nachrichten der Gesellschaft der Wissenschaften zu Göttingen* (Berlin, 1933), 355-72.

8. André Wilmart, 'La Légende de Ste Édith en prose et vers par le moine Goscelin', *Analecta bollandiana*, LVI (1938), 5-101 and 265-307.

9. Stubbs, II, 389; cf. Wilmart, 6-7.

10. For the quotation in the text see Schröder, 130/158-9. Bodleian MS Rawlinson C 938 of the *Vita S. Edithe* has the variant reading: '... in presencia memorate abbatisse Brihgtiue declarata ...' (Wilmart, 292/11-12). Cf. also Wilmart, 292, n.3, and Metzner 42, n.20.

11. Edited from British Library MS Cotton Faustina B III by C. Horstmann, *S. Editha sive Chronicon Vilodunense* (Heilbronn, 1883).

12. Frederick J. Furnivall (ed.), *Roberd of Brunnè's Handlyng Synne* . . . *with the French treatise on which it is founded, Le Manuel des Pechiez* . . . *printed for the Roxburghe Club* (London, 1862). Republished as *Robert of Brunne's 'Handlyng Synne'* . . . *with those parts of the Anglo-French treatise on which it was founded* (. . .), Early English Text Society, Original series, CXIX and CXXIII (London, 1901-03), quoted below as 'EETS edition'. — For the life of the author see Ruth Crosby, 'Robert Mannyng of Brunne: a new biography', *PMLA*, LVII (1942), 15-28.

13. cf. D. W. Robertson, 'The cultural tradition of *Handlyng Synne*', *Speculum*, XXII (1947), 162-85.

14. See the study by E. J. Arnould, *Le Manuel des péchés: étude de littérature religieuse anglo-normande* (Paris, 1940).

15. cf. Schröder, 125 and n.1.

16. F. J. Mone (ed.), 'Der *liber constructionis monasterii ad s. Blasium*', in *Quellensammlung der badischen Landesgeschichte*, IV (1) (Karlsruhe, 1867), 76-142. This edition is based on a late transcript of the original manuscript, which Mone wrongly believed to have been destroyed in 1768; the text of the legend (Mone, 115) is reprinted from a collation with the original manuscript in John Meier's article 'Das Tanzlied der Tänzer von Kölbigk', *Schweizerisches Archiv für Volkskunde*, XXXIII (1934), 152-65.

17. George Stephens (ed.), *Ett forn-svenskt legendarium*, Samlingar utgivna av Svenska fornskrift-sällskapet, VII (1-2) (Stockholm, 1847-58), II, 875-80: 'Sagan om den helige Magnus, jarl på Orkenöarne'.

18. Valter Jansson, *Fornsvenska legendariet: handskrifter och språk*, Nordiska texter och undersökningar, IV (Stockholm/Copenhagen, 1934), 2-4; on the supplement concerning Nordic saints, see 13-15.

19. cf. the article 'Magnús' in *Kulturhistorisk leksikon for nordisk middelalder*, XI (Copenhagen, 1966), 221-22 and literature there cited.

20. Dag Strömbäck, 'Den underbara årsdansen', in K. G. Ljunggren a.o. (eds), *Festskrift till Jöran Sahlgren 8.4.1944* (Lund, 1944), 431-46; *Arkiv för nordisk filologi*, LIX (1944), 111-26, rpt. in Strömbäck, *Folklore och filologi*, Acta Academiae regiae Gustavi Adolphi, XLVIII (Uppsala, 1970), 54-69. Cf. Strömbäck, 'Kölbigk och Hårga I: en sägenhistorisk undersökning', *Arv*, XVII (1961), 27-8.

21. 'Det är . . . ingenting som förbjuder oss att antaga att kort före mitten eller i varje fall vid mitten av 1100-talet dansundret kan ha förknippats med den helige Magnus av Orkneyöarna och införlivats i mirakelberättelserna om honom, ehuru ingenting därom finnes anfört i Orkneyinga saga eller andra källor om Magnus. I så fall skulle vår fornsvenska version vara en direkt avläggare till en dylik efter Magnus jarl anpassad och snarast i England eller Skottland uppkommen redaktion av Theoderik-relationen.' Moreover: 'förhandenvaron av en relation i England eller Skottland, som faktiskt knutit dansundret till någon av öarna i väster, stödjes också av Iring av S:t Blasien-versionen. Ty denna torde vara en genom predikanters förkunnelse under senare hälften av 1100-talet uppkommen muntlig sägen om dansundret, en sägen som Iring av S:t Blasien hört någonstädes under sina färder på de Brittiska öarna och som knappast kan ha utgått från någon annan relation än den som förbundit dansundret med Orkneyöarnas helige jarl' (Strömbäck [1944, rpt. 1970], 68-9).

22. *ibid.*, 67.

23. Meier, 157.

24. Metzner, 85-101.

25. Meier, 157.

26. cf. the stemma in Metzner, 154, where the lost account is classified as an 'ae., *möglicherweise teilweise* lat. Redaktion' (my italics).

27. Metzner, 89-90.

28. *ibid.*, 93. Here Metzner polemicises *inter alia* against a position which Strömbäck never adopted, viz. that the lost vernacular account from Wilton did *not* contain the frame tale about Theoderic's cure. This error is evidently due to a misunderstanding of Strömbäck's Swedish text.

29. For this evidence see Metzner, 96-100.

30. Mone, 79 and nn. on 112-13 and 115.

31. For this *Vita* see Gudbrand Vigfusson and G. W. Dasent, *Icelandic sagas and other historical documents*, Rolls Series, LXXXVIII (London, 1887-94), I, 237 and III, 239, and the discussion in Einar Ól. Sveinsson, *Sagnaritun Oddaverja*, Studia islandica, I (Reykjavík, 1937), 19-34.

32. cf. Jansson, 4-5.

33. Metzner, 101 n.190, 184 n.120.

34. Alfred Kunz, *Robert Mannyng of Brunne's Handlyng Synne verglichen mit der anglonormannischen Vorlage . . .* (diss. Königsberg, 1913), 51.

35. Wilmart, 285/17-286/1; for the echo of St Augustine in this sentence see Wilmart's note.

36. Arnould, 164-5.

37. Schröder, 99.

38. Wilmart, 288/18-19.

166

Fox Hunting; A Form of Traditional Behaviour Providing Social Cohesiveness*

MANUEL DANNEMANN   University of Chile

IN traditional Chilean culture, fox-hunting is a sport with a strong communal element. The main purpose of this short paper is to clarify its significance and importance.

We know from both oral and written sources that, during the second half of the 19th century, members of the Valparaiso British colony — in the central littoral — introduced fox-hounds as a means of continuing one of their favourite pastimes. But all the hills and ravines were unsuitable for the usual type of fox-hunt: riders could not cover the vast distances involved, nor could they jump all the obstacles in the rough terrain, so unlike the hedges of the English countryside.

The breeding of fox-hounds was well established in Chile early in this century, and has continued to flourish. Today the sport occurs in an area extending from Choapa to Osorno, from north to south, and covering eight of Chile's twelve regions, with significant concentrations in Casablanca, the fifth region, and Melipilla, in the metropolitan area. There are a large number of packs in both these regions, and a great deal of hunting takes place, usually on Sundays during the Chilean winter months of June, July and August, when the ground is damp and it is easier to pick up the scent and spoor of the fox; the ground is also softer for the hounds' feet.

Chilean fox-hound owners come from a wide range of social, economic and educational backgrounds. They include wealthy landowners enjoying a high standard of living, small farmers, and even farm-hands employed by the landowners. But, in spite of this, the hounds are bred, trained and looked after in much the same way, the only noticeable difference being that the well-to-do may own more than one pack, and can cover greater distances than those with more limited means.

There is only one variety of fox-hound in Chile today, the result of crossing the breed first introduced from England with those brought more recently from the United States, and also, to some extent, from France. None have been imported recently. Foxes hunted in Chile belong to two different types: *culpeo,* which is a large breed with reddish fur (*Ducicyon culpaeus*), and *chilla,* which is smaller and has greyish fur (*Ducicyon griseus*).

All fox-hunts follow the same basic pattern. For the huntsmen the excitement begins the moment they get up, while it is still dark. Sometimes they need to rise long before dawn, if they have to travel several miles on horseback to reach the place where the dogs are released. The same degree of excitement continues after the hunt is over, when it is usual to hold a party out-of-doors. This function, which complements the hunt itself, sometimes continues until dusk.

We have seen that, whether they follow the hunt on foot or on horseback, the topography of the Chilean countryside prevents the huntsmen from coming too near. They watch from nearby hill-tops and, when the dogs disappear in the distance or into a ravine, an important form of communication between man and dog comes into play. The owner can distinguish the bark of each hound and hence is able to follow what is happening, even though it may be hidden from view.

Once the dogs are released none of the huntsmen makes any attempt to control or guide them in a particular direction. The main attraction consists in watching the dogs at work. Only the

* Full summary.

167

huntsman known as the *punteador* or *picador,* who looks after the pack, is allowed to be present, if this is in fact feasible, when the hounds are preparing to kill the fox. His job is to prevent it going to earth and also to ensure that the hounds do not tear its pelt; he needs to be a good walker.

The various stages of the hunt are:

1. *Largar los porros:* the release of the hounds.
2. *El campeo:* searching for the scent.
3. *Caer a la huella:* locating the fox.
4. *La levantada del zorro:* tracing the scent.
5. *La carrera:* the pursuit of the fox.
6. *La pillada:* the death of the fox.

If the pack is a good one, they last approximately two to three hours.

Of course fox-hunting in Chile is a means of preventing the damage that the animal does, especially to new-born lambs. But its particular significance derives from the fact that it is a traditional sport, which brings together owners of hounds — the hunters *par excellence* — and the amateurs who do not possess any, but take part and are often just as knowledgeable. This sense of participation is reflected in the party that follows, which includes a barbecue with salads, and local wine. Outstanding moments of the hunt are once again relived, special stories are told, and proverbs are quoted. Some of the stories bear the hallmark of the true folktale. Here is one:

The hunter hears a very tired, panting, fox approach. The hounds are chasing it. He hides behind a tree and, as the fox passes, he throws his jacket over it, but the animal escapes through one of the sleeves. The hunter bemoans his loss: 'I should have tied up the sleeves!'

A spot beside a house or farm, or not far away, is selected for the party, and the women may come and perform traditional songs and dances. This is the only time when they join in, for they seldom follow the actual hunt.

Fox-hunting provides an opportunity to take part in a tradition. Since the sport was introduced into Chile it has been transformed. It unites the participants in a common purpose, and they regard the sport as truly their own. For them it is authentic and they do not worry about whether or not it is an old tradition. Amateurs who join in find themselves part of a group, sharing in a custom which enjoys a considerable appeal in many parts of the country.

Bibliography

William Scarth Dixon, *Fox-Hunting in the Twentieth Century* (London, 1925).

Charles Frederick a. o., *Fox-Hunting* (London, 1930).

Charles Hillman, *Old-Timers, British and American, in Chile* (Santiago, n.d.).

Benjamín Vicuña Mackenna, *Historia de Valparaíso*, 2 Vols (Santiago, 1936).

Folklore and Folly

H. R. ELLIS DAVIDSON   **University of Cambridge**

MUCH interest has been shown in the figures of the Fool and the Trickster. In her pioneer study on the Fool in 1935, Enid Welsford showed the importance of this character in both social life and literature.[1] As for the Trickster, Paul Radin realised the major part which he plays in the myths and legends of many cultures, and recent work by Professor Gifford has further emphasised his importance in mythology.[2] The possibilities of these characters both in popular tales and in sophisticated literature are immense; it is a far cry from the Fool in Lear to the dancing figure with his bladder in the Morris, or from Dionysius in the Underworld in *The Frogs* of Aristophanes[3] to the crude pranks of Brer Rabbit. But what I want to consider today, in a brief introduction to a very large subject, is the part played in folklore by Folly in general. I will begin by quoting from Roger Abrahams, writing on the Life Cycle as applied to Folk Plays in Britain in *Folklore* in 1970:[4]

> We have tended to underline the heroic combats because they provide us with such a clear message of continuing fertility, that is, of conflict, death, and regenesis. But this had led us to neglect what are (both qualitatively and quantitatively) the most important figures and actions of the mumming plays — clowning.

He also makes another point: namely that the licensed festival occasions at which the plays are performed are times which call for the bringing of luck, when 'license is permitted to free the vital energies of the community, but these energies are channeled into a closed world of play.'

My attention was caught by this, because it echoes conclusions reached in my own work on pre-Christian religion in northern Europe. Luck is a basic concept in ceremonies connected with the great gods; for instance, we have the appeal to chance in the drawing of lots for the sacrifice of men or animals, and the use of ritual, amulet or symbol to evoke the protection of the powers against dangers threatening individual or community. We have also the seeking for luck in its more positive aspects: the ability of the luck-bringer, the lucky person, the man under the protection, to sustain life, to ensure survival in battle and on dangerous journeys, to bring fish into fiords and lead hunters to their prey, to enable herds to increase and healthy children to be born. This is a powerful motive behind the conducting of rites and festivals. The actual pattern of performance will vary according to the needs of the community, and will tend to be at the turning points of the year, and at public holidays when men can come together, as also at times of tension, need and danger.[5]

But why should clowning play so important a part in these luck-bringing rituals? That this has been so from early times seems well established. There is a famous passage from Athenaeus, often quoted by those discussing the origins of Greek Comedy, which describes certain rites in the theatre in the second century B.C. and earlier, when the phallus was brought in on a pole.[6] It includes a reference to the Ithyphalli, wearing drunkards' masks, wreaths of flowers and what sound like women's robes, who enter the theatre and call on the audience to make way for the phallus: 'The god, erect and in full vigour, will pass through the midst,' they proclaim. The Phallophori are also mentioned, who accompany the bearer of the phallus, a figure smeared with soot. These wear wreaths and masks of flowers and leaves, and are wrapped in cloaks; they come in by several entrances, declaring in their song to Bacchus that their words are new, never before uttered, and they run up to various members of the audience and ridicule them. Francis Cornford likened such bands of satirical performers, raising laughter by their attacks on their victims, to the French Guilds of Fools in the fifteenth century. It seems that such performers developed out of the simple rustic type of phallic procession, but, as Cornford says, personal satire and abuse are not in any way dramatic; 'they involve no germ out of which a drama could grow.'[7]

In the same way, those studying the so-called Mummers' plays have been puzzled by the fact that these are not really dramatic at all; the fights between characters suggest some kind of action, but much of the material is separate from this, and a number of stock characters seem to be quite unconnected with it, figures such as Big Head, Beelzebub, the Man-Woman, Jack and his family, and the Sweeper. They usually appear in the Quête, the section leading up to a request for a reward: 'Music, dance and song, helped by patter,' says Chambers, 'often turn it into something like a revue.'[8] Fooling is an essential part of the performance whenever the plays appear, but it is difficult to study, because it must be largely extempore, like the songs to Bacchus, and consequently ephemeral and elusive, depending on gestures, pantomime, local jests, crude double entendre, and the instinctive immediate reaction to the audience. While the literary level of the texts is abysmal, it is the liveliness and feeling of spontaneity within the formal setting which makes the plays effective; it is as though the lame speeches and unintelligent literary borrowings are pegs on which to hang the real business of the ritual: rapid exchange, insults, conflict, satire and nonsense talk, the topsy-turvyism which involves audience as well as actors. The plays have lasted within small communities, in spite of competition from more finished forms of entertainment, because they provide one type of setting for the fooling which seems to serve a perennial human need.

A paper by Alex Helm, 'In comes I, St George', published in *Folklore* in 1965, offers us several clues.[9] He pointed out how misleading the word 'play' is, since when a producer attempts to turn the Mummers' entertainment into a true drama,

making the characters distinctive, the results are disastrous. He then gives an account of the presentation of the Cheshire Souling play from Antrobus by the boys of the Approved School where he taught. The standard of intelligence was low, and they seemed hardly capable of memorising, and yet, he says, when

> ... the producer gave them their heads within the limits of what he had seen at Antrobus, the results were, to us, surprising.

The boys learned the nonsense text without difficulty; the disguises kept them from being self-conscious, and though the staff were somewhat bewildered, 'looking for something which did not exist, namely, a sense of theatre', the school was utterly caught up in the spirit of the performance, becoming unwitting participants when the Wild Horse appeared:

> The antics of this horse were known, or appeared to be known, instinctively by performers and audience boys alike. Without rehearsal, the horse performed as we had seen the traditional equivalent at Antrobus: it sat on knees in the audience... it attempted to kick the Driver, chattered its jaws in an attempt to bite and so on. It was a completely natural effort which appeared to grow out of the boys themselves.

Clowning then, within a satisfactory traditional framework, seems to come naturally to young and old. The occasion may not be a play: both the Mummers' entertainment and also the ritual performances of animal figures like the Hobby-horses fit easily into the overall pattern of the House Visit, the coming of a company to bring luck. A band, or bands, of people in some kind of disguise visits house or village; they ask for food or money, sometimes entertain or indulge in competitive play with their hosts. They bring luck with them, even if unconsciously. Alex Helm mentions performances by the Mummers put on to raise money for November 5th, but adds that even this blatantly mercenary motive did not obscure the underlying ceremony, and he also points out that in the Abbots Bromley area there are farmers who consider it lucky if the Horn Dancers visit their farms and unlucky if they do not. Indeed, the desire for gifts or money is not a degenerate feature of the visit, but forms a basic part of the ceremony. There must be a fair exchange; luck is not given as a charity, but must be earned by participation. Carsten Bregenhøj, in an important study of House-visiting on Agersø, a remote island in Denmark,[10] claims that the visit is like a gift, and demands a gift in return. This does not mean that the gifts are polite, conventional ones. He mentions how, on New Year's Eve, the door would be opened and a clay pot full of dry ashes knocked into the room, so that it was filled with dust. The householders would try and catch the culprit, but not to punish him; if caught, he and his gang would be given food and drink. There is much boisterous fooling of this kind in Scandinavian Christmas customs: glass may be put over the top of the chimney, to make it smoke, or a wagon taken to pieces and put up on the roof. In such cases, the family must guess which neighbour is responsible; if they cannot catch him at his work, they will then go to the house of the supposed trickster at night to carry out a return piece of fooling. This type of behaviour, Bregenhøj claims, is an extended part of Christmas mumming.

The man in animal disguise also fits into the pattern. The famous Padstow Red 'Oss performs in the open, perambulating through the town in his dance, but the Blue 'Oss, followed by locals rather than tourists, can be seen visiting houses in the section of the town near the harbour, wherever there are old people unable to get out. They greet him enthusiastically at the door ('Lovely to see you,' I heard one old lady say) and put something in his collecting box. There may also be violence and antagonism between visitors and householders, as Herbert Halpert, G. M. Story and other contributors have shown in their collection of detailed studies of House Visiting in Newfoundland,[11] where present-day janneys (the disguised mummers) may so terrify women and children that people are genuinely afraid of meeting them out of doors. Halpert also quotes an illuminating account written by Samuel Breck, who lived at Boston, Mass., in the eighteenth century:[12]

I forget on what holiday it was that the Anticks, another exploded remnant of colonial manners, used to perambulate the town. They have ceased to do it now, but I remember them as late as 1782. They were a set of the lowest blackguards, who, disguised in filthy clothes and ofttimes with masked faces, went from house to house in large companies ... and would demean themselves with great insolence. I have seen them at my father's, when his assembled friends were at cards, take possession of a table, seat themselves on rich furniture, and proceed to handle the cards, to the great annoyance of the company. The only way to get rid of them was to give them money, and listen patiently to a foolish dialogue between two or more of them. One of them would cry out, 'Ladies and gentlemen sitting by the fire, put your hands in your pockets and give us our desire.' When this was done, and they had received some money, a kind of acting took place. One fellow was knocked down and lay sprawling on the carpet, while another bellowed out,

> See, there he lies,
> But ere he dies
> A doctor must be had.

He calls for a doctor, who soon appears, and enacts the part so well that the wounded man revives. In this way they would continue for half an hour, and it happened not infrequently that the house would be filled by another gang when these had departed. There was no refusing admittance. Custom had licensed these vagabonds to enter even by force any place they chose. What should we say to such intruders now? Our manners would not brook such usage a moment.

Similarly in Wales we have the visits of the Mari Lwyd, a truly terrifying monster, whose head is a horse's skull with chattering jaws, carried on a pole by a bearer hidden under a blanket, so that it is tall enough to peer into upstairs windows or be pushed round the door.[13] Here there is a verse dialogue as a formalised conflict between those inside and those demanding admittance, a confrontation and exchange of impromptu verses, such as can be recognised as a popular ritual used for ceremonial occasions such as weddings in many parts of the world.[14] It has left its mark on much medieval literature, for instance in the mythological poems of the Icelandic Poetic Edda. Clowning cannot be separated from conflict, invective and abuse, which in a small community can be merciless in its effectiveness, often resulting in real and not simulated violence. Sean O'Sullivan has some splendid examples in the games formerly played at Irish wakes; activities known as Sconcing, Scogging and Jibbing meant deliberate mockery directed at some unfortunate individual, which had to be endured:[15]

> Resentment at some jibe only made matters worse; the best policy for the recipient of the mockery was to take it in good part and hope that it would shortly be over.

This was exactly the experience, it seems, of the victims of the clowns accompanying the phallus in ancient Greece, and of the suffering gentry in Boston. The mockery in the Irish games might be helped by formal pantomime: Making a Stack, for a young couple intending to be married (with appropriate comments), or Selling the Old Cow, in which the organiser pretended to divide up the carcase among those present (with questions, generally of a coarse and unpleasant kind, to the recipients). There has always been an element of the earthy and disgusting in clowning, and yet as Willeford commented in his study of the fool,[16] 'the value of foolish obscenity is not simple but complex.'

In the case of the Wake games, one disadvantage which no doubt led to bad feeling was the lack of disguise. Luck-bringers proper are masked, or have their faces covered or disguised in some way, wear loose clothes, so that their sex cannot be recognised, and speak in assumed voices, such as the high-pitched squeak caused by intake of breath, as used in Newfoundland,[17] while, like the Doctor in the Mummers' Play, they declare that they come from some obscure place far away, out of this world, as it were. When disguised they may behave in an uninhibited manner foreign to their normal code. Clyde Williams gives an instance of two very respectable middle-aged women in Newfoundland who used considerable freedom of language and gesture towards the men in the house they visited; this seemed to cause no embarrassment or resentment, and once the disguise is off, janneys revert to normal behaviour.[18] Where funeral games are concerned, it is obvious that both laughter and anger may have a valuable part to play; as Willeford says;[19]

> In many societies, merrymaking after a funeral is sanctioned. The laughter is then mirthful rather than a shocked reaction to horror, and it is institutionalised rather than purely spontaneous ... it probably serves the purpose of putting death at a distance and asserting the continuation of life.

The clown, with whitened face like a mask, and loose clothes, disguising his figure, or the man in animal disguise under the skirts of the Hobby Horse, or the mummer in his costume of ribbons or torn paper, becomes an anonymous figure. He can do and say what a friend or acquaintance dare not. He can escape for a while from the restrictions of ordinary living, not only the moral restrictions of society, but also the physical restrictions of our mortality. He is knocked down, to bounce up again in a mock resurrection. After one such blow, Willeford notes, 'Harlequin once picked his brains out and ate them with relish, suffering only an increase of stupidity.'[19] In the same way, Radin's Trickster feasts on portions of his own anatomy. The clown is freed from the bounds of convention and reason, and also from his own sexual instincts; the Trickster packs up his penis in a box,[20] while clowns among the Zuñi have theirs tied up with cotton, and can be looked at naked, since, it is said, 'they are just like children'; Willeford notes that the mythical forbears of these clowns are claimed to have been without the fruit of sex, although they were in direct contact with the generative powers of nature.[21]

No taboo is too sacred for the clown to break. A small but significant example is the development of the figure of Peeping Tom in the Godiva legend, for revered though she undoubtedly is in Coventry, the joke of the man who tried to catch sight of her naked never dies.[22] I suspect that he first came into the legend as a local jest (he is not included in the earliest versions), and when the figure of Godiva on her horse became a leading attraction in the procession at the Show Fair, Tom was seen there too; an early nineteenth century pamphlet[23] describes him as a Merry Andrew, diverting the populace with his profane conceits; he was pulled along in his little house on a wagon behind Godiva, popping his head in and out of the window with lewd gestures, we are told, to amuse the crowd. A later pamphlet-writer, disapproving of such vulgarity, gives the information that one of these clowns was taken ill immediately after his performance and died 'in a most shocking manner', intimidating others from 'carrying on the burlesque.'[24] Clowning shocks and disgusts as surely as it delights, and folklore records are a long catalogue of attempted suppression of the rough and the vulgar when, as Samuel Breck put it, 'Our manners will no longer brook such usage.'

The language of folly is a study in itself, and I can only mention it briefly here, although it was this aspect which started me on the present line of study. Songs and the use of verse dialogue are two important headings, but there are many more. Much of it, as I have noted, is oral and ephemeral, the meaning lost once the moment has passed and the atmosphere dissipated. Great writers like Aristophanes and Shakespeare capture something of it for us, giving it significance and enduring literary quality, but even here we are painfully limited by changing fashions in jokes, seeking for the point of a rude remark through pages of learned commentary. At certain periods oral exchanges have been cultivated to reach considerable heights of ingenuity and wit. While working on the twelfth century Danish historian Saxo Grammaticus, who wrote in Latin[25] – the last place, one would think, to find folly – I have been fascinated by one of his characters, Erik the Eloquent (Ericus Disertus). He is a young Norwegian who receives a supernatural gift through eating a special meal prepared from snakes – the gift of quick-wittedness; the donor in Saxo's unknown source may well have been Odin himself, god of magic and inspiration and giver of luck. Erik came to the Danish court to serve the young king, who was under the control of as nasty a gang of bully boys as can be found in medieval literature, and they gave him a rough welcome. But he proved too much for them all. He showed himself a master of invective, overcoming the bully who met him with shouted insults by countering them with proverbial sayings, which struck home, until the bully retreated roaring with baffled fury. He capped obscene verses with an old woman who was their acknowledged expert, and outdid her easily. He proved a brilliant riddle-maker, bewildering the king with an account of his journey which sounds like nonsense, but abounds with clues like those of a modern crossword puzzle of the more complicated kind. He played the fool with a piece of ice, pretending that it was a rich gift for the king, and causing someone to drop it in the fire before the trick was discovered; he also outdid opponents at various rough types of horseplay, like pulling a skin from under someone's feet, or hauling one's opponent on to the fire. He used a horse's skull on a pole as a means of calling down a curse on his opponents. He got his own way at home and abroad by ingenious tricks of the kind remembered in folktales, and in the end he became the king's chief adviser and ambassador, bringing him such good fortune and renown that he became a truly great ruler; indeed Saxo uses Erik as a model for his patron Absalon, the gifted Archbishop of Lund, righthand man of King Valdemar the Great. Erik is in no accepted sense a fool, and never pretends to be one; he gets his own way by verbal dexterity and quickness of wit, but in his extraordinary achievements we get a cross-section of the type of wit and folly admired in twelfth century Denmark. And, to take us back to the point where we began, he is undoubtedly a luck-bringer, deriving his gifts from supernatural powers. Erik has made me realise how much there is in folly which merits serious study.

174

Notes

1. E. Welsford, *The Fool, his Social and Literary History* (London, 1935).

2. P. Radin, *The Trickster: a Study in American Indian Mythology* (London, 1956); 'Iconographical Notes towards a Definition of the Medieval Fool', *Journal of the Warburg and Courtauld Institute*, XXXVII (1974), 336-42. See also Professor Gilford's paper in the present volume.

3. In an essay included in Radin's study of the Trickster (see note 2, above), Karl Kerenyi points out, on page 179, that both Heracles and Dionysius act as Tricksters in Greek myth and drama.

4. R. D. Abrahams, 'British West Indian Folk Drama and the "Life Cycle" Problem', *Folklore*, LXXXI (1970), 243; cf. H. Halpert and G. M. Story, eds., *Christmas Mumming in Newfoundland* (Toronto, 1969), 60.

5. There has been a controversy here between E. T. Kirby ('The Origins of the Mummers' play', *Journal of American Folklore*, LXXXIV [1971], 275-88) who emphasises resemblances between the play and the performances of the shaman, and C. Cawte (*ibid.*, LXXXV [1972], 375-6) who thinks the main emphasis should be put on its connection with seasonal festivals. See also Kirby's reply (*ibid.*, LXXXVI [1973], 282-5). It seems possible to resolve these two opposed points of view without much difficulty, if the emphasis is placed on the bringing of luck; in a predominantly agricultural society, the seasonal festivals would be the times when this was particularly needed.

6. F. M. Cornford, *The Origin of Attic Comedy* (Cambridge, 1934), 41 ff. Athenaeus quotes from Sosibios of Laconia (c. 300 B.C.) and Semos of Delos (first century B.C. or earlier); cf. Sir Arthur Pickard-Cambridge, *Dithyramb, Tragedy and Comedy* (Oxford, 1933), 70.

7. Cornford, 47.

8. E. K. Chambers, *The English Folk-Play* (Oxford, 1933), 70.

9. A. Helm, 'In Comes I, St George', *Folklore*, LXXVI (1965), 118-36. See esp. 126 ff. Cf. R. J. E. Tiddy, *The Mummers' Play* (Oxford, 1923), 89.

10. C. Bregenhøj, *Helligtrekongersløb på Agersø; Dansk Folkemindesamling* 3 (Copenhagen, 1974); see esp. 109 ff.

11. Halpert and Story, *op. cit.* (note 4).

12. *ibid.*, 52-3. Taken from H. E. Scudder, ed., *Recollections of Samuel Breck, with passages from his Note-Books (1771-1862)* (Philadelphia, 1877), 35-6. See also Kittredge, *Journal of American Folklore*, XXII (1909), 394.

13. T. M. Owen, *Welsh Folk Customs* (Cardiff, 1974), 49 ff; C. Cawte, *Ritual Animal Disguise* (London, 1978), 96 ff.

14. H. M. and N. K. Chadwick, *The Growth of Literature*, Vols II and III (Cambridge, 1936 and 1940). Cf. also my 'Insults and Riddles in the Edda Poems', (see note 25, below).

15. S. Ó Súilleabháin, *Irish Wake Amusements* (Cork, 1967), 56 ff.

16. W. Willeford, *The Fool and his Sceptre* (London, 1969), 126.

17. Halpert and Story, 40, 110, 211 n.6.

18. *ibid.*, 213-14 and 132.

19. Willeford, 89.

20. Radin, 38.

21. Willeford, 127. He quotes from R. L. Bunzel, 'Zuñi Katcinas', *Bureau of American Ethnology Annual Report*, XLVII, 1929-30 (Washington D.C., 1932), 946-8.

22. H. R. Ellis Davidson, 'The Legend of Lady Godiva', *Folklore*, LXXX (1969), 107 ff, esp. 116 ff for Peeping Tom.

23. W. Reader, *Origin and Description of Coventry Show Fair* (Coventry, 1830).

24. Thomas Burbidge, *A Brief Account of the Origin and Mode of conducting the Show Fair* (Coventry, n.d.).

25. *Saxo Grammaticus: The History of the Danes Books I-IX*, translated by Peter Fisher and edited with a commentary by H. R. Ellis Davidson, 2 vols, (Cambridge, 1979-80). I have discussed some of the characteristics of Erik the Eloquent in a paper, *Insults and Riddles in the Edda Poems*, to be published in a volume of the University of Manitoba Icelandic Studies.

The Future of Folklore

INDRA DEVA   Ravishankar University

THIS paper is an attempt to bring out briefly the
new possibilities that exist now for the growth of
folklore and folk culture in the underdeveloped or
developing countries of today. It is well known
that in the earlier phases of the modern era,
industrialisation and urbanisation had a devastating impact on the folklore and folk culture of the
countries that were the first to embark on the path
of modernisation. However, the modern forces of
today are not the same as they were in the
eighteenth and nineteenth centuries. The nature of
technological, economic, political and ideological
forces has undergone a basic change. Their interaction with the vigorous streams of folklore and
folk culture in the developing countries of today,
may therefore lead to very different consequences.
Through an interaction with these mellowed down
and sophisticated modern forces, folklore and folk
culture in these countries may find entirely new
lines of evolution and growth.

The whole context of the interaction of folk
culture with modern forces stands transformed.
Even if the developing countries wished to follow
the same path as that taken by those who were the
first to industrialise themselves, they would find it
blocked in many ways. But they have certain new
options open to them which were not and are still
not available, even to the most advanced countries.
They have vigorous folk traditions which have
vitality enough to imbibe new elements and bring
forth new forms; and the peculiar cross-currents of
contemporary social change have brought these
traditions face to face with modern forces, which
have reached great maturity. Thus the stage is set
for the ushering in of a new civilisation which need
not be a mere artificial synthesis but may possess
emergent qualities. We shall try to examine how
far such a possibility really exists.

When we think of the processes of modernisation
in the developing countries of today, it would be
wrong to take a static view of what constitutes the
modern. Besides referring to certain attributes of
society and culture which cannot but be dynamic,
the term itself has a temporal reference. A dictionary meaning of modern is 'of present or recent
times'. Etymologically also the word is derived
from a latin root which means 'just now'. It is
obvious then that the content of what is regarded
as modern is likely to vary from time to time.

This is the more so because, after the decline of
medievalism, the rate of social change has been
generally high. What was considered to be modern
in the eighteenth and nineteenth centuries is not
so regarded in the latter half of the twentieth
century. As we know, in the eighteenth and nineteenth centuries, individualism, *laissez-faire*, competition and unlimited acquisitiveness were taken
to be the essence of modernity. Today, however,
these are considered to be outmoded by many.
Also in technology and items of everyday use,
things which were regarded as modern a hundred
years back can no more be considered to be so.
Many machines, industrial processes and their
products which were, till recently, thought to be
glorious contributions of the modern age, are now
looked upon with suspicion as sources of, for
example, atmospheric pollution, constituting a
threat to the very existence of humanity.

In view of this, when we consider the problems
of modernisation in underdeveloped countries we
have to be clear in our mind what type of
modernity we are thinking of. The idea that, when
we talk about underdeveloped countries it should
be sufficient to make use of the older concepts, is
extremely dubious. In fact some of the underdeveloped countries of today may be more recep-

tive to mid-twentieth century values, institutions and technology than they would have been to comparable trends in the eighteenth and nineteenth centuries. In such matters, they may show a greater tolerance than those countries which broke away from medievalism earlier.

It may be pointed out, for instance, that even though today the limitations of individualism, *laissez-faire* and perpetual competition are widely recognised, the countries of Western Europe and North America, which have built up a high level of prosperity based on these principles, find it extremely difficult to give them up or even restrict them within reasonable limits. These values and the institutional and cultural elements based on them have become so firmly entrenched that it is difficult to dislodge them. On the other hand, in the underdeveloped countries, these eighteenth and nineteenth-century values have not as yet found a strong foothold among the masses. They can therefore be more easily replaced by institutional and attitudinal patterns based on ideas of cooperation, security and the collective good.

Similarly, there has been a considerable shift in the nature of technology and its products. The earlier period of industrialisation gave rise to gigantic factories operated by the power of coal and steam. It also brought about a split between objects of utility and beauty, a phase which Lewis Mumford has called the paleotechnic age.[1] But, as he has pointed out, this is being replaced by what he calls the neotechnic era. In this latter era, with the discovery of new sources of power like electricity and petroleum, industries can be diffused over a wide area. Machines become smaller and are not the monsters they were in the paleotechnic era, attempts are made to bridge the gulf between utility and beauty. As Mumford himself pointed out, this new phase has more in common with the premodern, eotechnic phase than the paleotechnic phase of modernisation.[2] It is possible that the underdeveloped countries which have not yet developed paleotechnic industry may be more willing to adopt neotechnic machines and the way of life based on them than the countries which became industrialised earlier and have developed vast structures of paleotechnic industrial culture. The underdeveloped countries still preserve to a considerable extent the folk blending of utilitarian and aesthetic aspects in objects and activities.

Modern technological, economic and cultural forces, as they exist in the latter half of the twentieth century, appear to be less hostile to some traditional, institutional and cultural patterns than the nascent forces of modernism were in the eighteenth and nineteenth centuries. The more recent ideas, which detest the alienation of work and life, utility and beauty, which look down on the rat-race inspired by the goal of maximising personal pecuniary profit, and which emphasise the need for emotional and social security are far less antithetical to the traditional values and attitudes prevailing in the underdeveloped countries than those ideas of early modernity, which regarded all traditional elements as backward and reprehensible.

The fact that the underdeveloped countries of today face up to these new forces which are basically different from the forces of early modernity, opens up unforeseen possibilities.

Apart from the transformation of the forces of modernisation, the pace and pattern of sociocultural change in developing countries seem to increase the chances of the emergence of a new synthesis. While the stream of folk culture and folklore remains fairly vigorous in these countries, certain sections of their population and some aspects of life are undergoing change at a tremendously fast rate. The urban élite in the developing countries has passed through, in the course of the last one hundred years or so, sociocultural eras and movements which took several centuries to germinate and grow in the countries of Western Europe and North America. Countries like India have witnessed their renaissance, reformation, age of reason, rise of romanticism, experiments with democracy and socioeconomic planning — all in the span of one century. Literary and artistic movements have been similarly compressed.

This naturally leads to a lot of overlapping. Long before one cultural era has declined or vanished, a number of successive forms enter the arena. In India, for example, while the centuries-old mystical songs of Kabir have not lost their appeal among the rural folk and even among substantial parts of the urban population, the latest ideas and ideologies of the contemporary world are seriously discussed by certain influential, though relatively small sections of the people. Many developing countries are large and diversified.

Their social structures have been greatly stratified and differentiated. Various sections in the population thus exhibit wide contrasts in their inclination and aptitude to the adoption of new ideas. But this tendency is not confined to the larger groups. Not infrequently, within the same family, some members are ultra-modern in outlook, while others remain firmly tied to tradition. In fact even individuals tend to have in their personalties elements derived from vastly diverse sociocultural eras. In the case of those engaged in modern occupations in developing countries, sociologists have reported a wide gap between their behaviour patterns in places of work and in the home. This is not surprising, as a whole generation of men and women exists which has witnessed within its lifetime the rise and fall of a number of cultural patterns. Usually one historical era covers several generations; but in the developing countries today one generation encompasses several eras.

This contemporaneity of culture and values that are sociologically non-contemporary creates serious problems for groups as well as individuals. But it also opens up possibilities of unprecedented combinations and the emergence of new patterns.

Folk culture and folklore in developing countries like India have certainly been influenced by modern forces, but they have not as yet lost their vigour. While some genres of folklore show signs of decline, the trend, as a whole, seems to have enough vitality not only to sustain itself but also to imbibe new elements. References to modern objects, events and experiences find their way into folklore through the usual process of reworking traditional items, the composition of new pieces, and even the emergence of new types.

The existing oral tradition of the folk shows signs of both continuity and growth. No celebration of a birth or marriage is conceivable without the singing of folksongs appropriate to the particular ceremony. Calendar festivals, too, are celebrated with the telling of particular tales and the singing of special songs traditionally used for the purpose. In fact, without these, the ritual would not be considered complete. Market-place conversation and bargaining, as well as gossip and quarrels, particularly among women, are, even today, rich in traditional proverbs. Putting riddles to each other is still a favourite pastime. Large crowds assemble to listen to the singing of epic lays. And one can,

even now, find singers of epic lays who can still compose in the true style of heroic poetry.

A large majority of the population in a country like India remain active bearers of traditional folk genres. In rural areas almost everyone sings. In towns and cities women of all classes sing in unison at least on special occasions like weddings and child-birth. Other folk forms can also be seen to have a comparable circulation among large sections of the people.

While assessing the impact of modern social forces on folk literature, care has to be taken in identifying genuine pieces. Due to the popularity of folk forms in developing countries, certain pieces are composed and propogated by individuals and groups who do not really belong to the folk. It must be noted that references to modern objects occur in songs which are genuine folk songs by any standards. They are transmitted through oral tradition and subjected to continued reworking by the folk, who are still predominantly unlettered. The nature of references to modern elements testifies to the folk outlook of the people who have introduced them. Thus, in well known Avadhi folksongs, the railway train is compared to the co-wife who takes away the husband. This image, drawn from the railway train, is a testimony to the vigour of folk tradition in countries like India. It is remarkable that noted folklorists have expressed the view that images drawn from the railway train in folksongs are rather 'forced'. Such views seem to be based on the experience of folk traditions which do not now have the vitality required for creating new images. But in countries where the tradition of folklore is vigorous, one can find a large number of appealing and natural images drawn from modern objects.

The decline of village handicrafts, as a result of competition from factory-made goods, failure of crops due to the vagaries of nature, and the increasing pressure of population on the land, compel large numbers of villagers to seek employment in the cities. The testimony of folk literature, as well as field surveys in industrial centres, show that it is dire economic necessity, rather than the attraction of city life, which is primarily responsible for this emigration. In India, and countries similarly placed, such emigration is predominantly selective. The emigrant is usually an able-bodied male and, while he goes out to earn in big cities

179

like Calcutta and Bombay, he leaves behind part of his family, particularly women folk and aged parents, in the villages. This causes serious anxiety both to the emigrants and those members of the family who are left behind. Folk literature, especially in the regions from which such migration has been heavy, has not failed to respond to this situation. In fact the impact of this emigration has been so deep that it has given rise to some new genres. In the Bhojpuri area a new folk opera, *Bidesia*, emerged and gained wide popularity. It deals primarily with the temptation and torments to which an emigrant and his wife are subjected.

On the whole it would be far from correct to say that the folk tradition itself is on the verge of extinction. If some of the traditional types are declining, certain other folk forms like the *Bidesia* opera, which are more relevant to the contemporary experience of the folk, are emerging. The stream of folk culture still has enough vitality to absorb and integrate new elements. It has not become a vestige or a mere survival.[3]

In the light of the above analysis it is clear that we find in the developing countries today a grouping of new forces. Sophisticated, contemporary forces are interacting with folk traditions which have sufficient vigour to bring forth new forms. The forces of modernisation which crushed the same elements in European countries in the eighteenth century were very different from modern forces as we find them today.

In the eighteenth and nineteenth centuries when coal was the only source of power, industries had to be concentrated around coal mines. This created gigantic industrial centres and villages were turned into markets for insipid mass produced goods, and into suppliers of cheap labour and raw materials. This is not unavoidable now. Electric power can be taken to villages and small-sized labour-intensive industries can be set up. These industries need not employ outmoded technology. On the contrary they can make good use of the most modern developments, like those in the field of electronics, which have made possible reduction in the size of machines to an unprecedented degree. In view of the scarcity of capital and abundance of unemployed labour in the developing countries, it will be far more economical to keep the machines labour intensive.[4]

Thus it is no longer necessary to uproot people from the countryside on a large scale to create industrialisation. The settled life of the folk in which there is traditionally a balance between agriculture and industry can be given a new dimension by imaginative use of the most sophisticated technology for human ends.

The ideological elements too are not so hostile now to the folk way of life as they were in the early phase of modernity. The limitations of rationalism are widely recognised. Numerous ideological movements emphasise the value of cooperation and security. This is not to say that the modern élite are returning to the values of the folk communities. They, however, do not harbour that self-righteous indignation which impelled their predecessors to combat and suppress traditional folk values. Under these changed material and ideological circumstances, it is not impossible that folk forms find certain avenues of survival and growth. Of course, we cannot expect them to remain just as they have been traditionally. They will have to raise themselves to a new level by interacting with contemporary modern elements.

If there is any chance of such interaction it is much more hopeful in the newly developing countries than in the highly developed parts of the world, which set out on the path of modernisation several centuries ago. It seems that in those countries the attraction towards folk forms is likely to remain rather romantic; for nascent forces of eighteenth and nineteenth-century industrialisation and modernity have already destroyed much of their folk patterns long ago. This is also borne out by the experience of the collectors of various folk genres. Cecil. J. Sharp said that the twentieth-century collector of English folksongs is a hundred years too late; 'The English ballad is moribund; its account well-nigh closed.'[5] The Society of Antiquaries of Newcastle-upon-Tyne had reached a similar conclusion in 1855 when they set about the collection of Northumbrian ballads and recorded in their first report that they were 'half-a-century too late'. Robert Graves says that in England the ballad proper gradually ceased to be composed after Tudor times.[6]

Only the future can tell whether the folk traditions in the developing countries will really be able to attain a new level by harnessing the technological, economic and ideological resources made available by the closing decades of the twentieth century. A number of factors, however, exist which should deter us from rejecting such a possibility out of hand. The peculiar pattern of social change, with much overlapping of different cultural eras, has brought vigorous folk traditions in close proximity to modern forces which have attained a high degree of maturity. These countries may therefore chart out a new course in their march towards modernity. This is all the more likely because many of the ways taken by the countries, which were the first to industrialise and modernise themselves, are no longer open to the newly-developing countries. It is well known, for instance, that the industrial revolution in Western Europe was made possible largely with the help of the capital acquired through the exploitation of colonies. To the newly-developing countries of today neither colonies nor virgin lands are available. Due to the prevailing ideas regarding welfare of labour it is no longer possible for these countries to accumulate capital, even by the exploitation of their inland labour, as in the western countries during the eighteenth and nineteenth centuries. But the developing countries have an abundance of unemployed labour, though the capital available is very scarce. Thus, in addition to factors already considered, those countries are being compelled by circumstances to think in terms of labour-intensive small-scale industries.

It is not necessary for us to agree with the unilinear view that all cultures must necessarily pass through the same successive stages of evolution. The long strides of socio-economic change in the developing countries of today may permit the by-passing of some of the earlier stages of large-scale industrialisation. These countries face a unique challenge, and it is not impossible that this may evoke a magnificent response and lead to the growth of a new civilisation. Folk culture is marked by a balance between considerations of beauty and utility. For the folk craftsman, work is not alienated from life and the objects produced by him have both utilitarian and aesthetic aspects. In folk society the artist is not a special kind of man, every man is a special kind of artist.

If the developing countries of today succeed in building up such a civilisation, they may have achieved a type of society which many sensitive thinkers in the most advanced countries sincerely cherish. In this sense, the countries which have lagged behind may be able to take a step which has been eluding those more advanced. This may look rather surprising but such turns in the course of social change are not unknown to history. In fact I have ventured to put forward elsewhere a general hypothesis to this effect.[7] This general hypothesis about the course of social change has received considerable recognition by noted sociologists like Paul F. Lazarsfeld, and it seems applicable also to the prospects of growth of folk culture to a new level in developing countries.[8]

Notes

1. Lewis Mumford, *Technics and Civilisation* (London, 1947).

2. Mumford, 212.

3. Indra Deva, 'Modern Social forces in Indian folk songs', *Diogenes*, XV (1956), 48-64; *idem, Sociology of Bhojpuri folk-literature* (Lucknow, 1958); *idem*, 'The changing pattern of rural society and culture: significance of the rural-urban nexus', *Trends of socio-economic change in India, 1871-1961*, ed. M. K. Chaturvedi (Simla, 1969), 162-75; *idem*, 'Folklore studies: a trend report', *A Survey of Research in Sociology and Social Anthropology* (Bombay, 1972), 197-239.

4. Gunnar Myrdal, *Asian Drama* (London, 1968), II, 1207-40.

5. Cecil J. Sharp, *The English Folk Song: Some Conclusions* (London, 1907), 102.

6. Robert Graves, *The English Ballad* (London, 1927), 22.

7. Indra Deva, 'The Course of Social Change: a Hypothesis', *Diogenes*, LVI (1966), 74-91.

8. Paul F. Lazarsfeld, 'Sociology', *Main Trends of Research in Social and Human Sciences*, I (1970), 87.

The Cunning Folk in English and Hungarian Witch Trials

TEKLA DÖMÖTÖR   University of Budapest

THE title of the paper seems to indicate that I am going to deal with purely historical material. However, this is not the case, since in Hungary some categories of magicians mentioned in the trials were still active around 1900 and the memory of their activities is still very much alive in Hungarian rural tradition.

The enormous number of texts relating to witch trials not only informs us about the so-called witch-craze of the sixteenth, seventeenth and eighteenth centuries, but provides insight into the folk religion of European peoples, as well. There is for example a common tendency in the trials to differentiate witches from the cunning folk. For the prosecutors, all magical practices seemed dangerous, whereas the accused and the witnesses were often able to make a clear distinction between witches and other kinds of magical practitioners.

When I refer to the cunning folk, I have in mind the definition by Alan Macfarlane who states that 'the cunning folk were magical practitioneers who possessed "cunning" or knowledge or who could heal animals, detect witches and find lost property.'

The Hungarian term for magical practitioners is *tudományos*, which is similar to the English term. The verb *tud* means to know something, to be able to do something. *Tudományos* might be a noun or an adjective, and denotes a person who possesses some extraordinary knowledge or power.

The first problem I consider is whether it is worthwhile to compare English and Hungarian cunning folk without examining the same categories in other countries as well. There has certainly never been any direct contact between the witches or the wise men of England and Hungary. Still, both countries were far from what is considered to be the main area of the witch-craze during the period of legal witch-hunting, centred on the Alpine countries. Therefore, the similarities are not to be considered as the consequences of any direct influence, but must be attributed to the fact that the chief elements in the witch-craze were imported and not indigenous. I find the English trials much more similar to the Hungarian ones than, for example, those in Switzerland and Bavaria.

Little is known abroad about Hungarian witch-trials, because the published texts are in Hungarian. Three volumes contain information about nine hundred trials, and a fourth volume will follow very soon. In Hungary there were relatively few death warrants, with the exception of the trials in Szeged, which became notorious all over Europe.

In this paper I will not discuss the witches themselves, but the other magical practitioners. Scientists were so fascinated and horrified by the prominent features of witch trials that they paid little attention to the cunning folk. Let me mention here that in Hungarian folk belief the term 'white magic' has no equivalent at all, and is used only by scholars.

The most important point here is to find out whether the authorities themselves made a distinction between the cunning folk and the witches. Both witches and the cunning folk could be concerned with sickness, mental and physical. In Hungarian trials it is sometimes difficult to decide who is the bewitcher and who is the healer, since very often a person can only be healed by the same person who bewitched him.

Witch trials started later and lasted longer in Hungary than in England. During the seventeenth century persons who claimed that they had magic power, but did not use it for evil purposes, were often acquitted. In the eighteenth century, however, this excuse was no longer accepted and any sort of magical activity was considered suspicious.

In Hungary no mention is made of the category called in English 'witch doctors'. On the other hand, the accused persons very often defended themselves by stating that they were not witches but *táltos* and it is well known that a *táltos* is the enemy of the witches. It is not easy to find a good English translation for this word. The *táltos* are generally considered by scholars to be the direct descendants of the former Hungarian *Shamans*. The name itself occurs in medieval sources and until the twentieth century people existed whom others called *táltos*, or who called themselves by this name. During the last two centuries their main function was to fight a duel, and to fight against hail and storm, but according to earlier documents they also, among other activities, detected lost property or treasure buried in the ground and they sang devilish songs. All *táltos* were considered to be enemies of witches.

Let us quote some examples of the behaviour of the *táltos* as described in trials. At one held in 1725, in Debrecen, the wife of András Bartha, on trial for witchcraft, defends herself by saying that she is a *táltos* and so is her daughter. She learned the art of healing from her brother, but her quality of *táltos* was decided while she was still unborn. Her daughter was born with two teeth. This motif always recurs in Hungarian *táltos* tradition and in the Shamanistic tradition of Finno-Ugric peoples, as well; Shamans often have a surplus bone or are born with teeth. Mrs Bartha also declared that the *táltos* can fly like birds and fight in the sky.

Táltos are also mentioned in other Debrecen trials. As early as 1626, an accused person states that she is a *táltos*, and her helper is a dragon. She has nothing to do with the devil and she never bewitched anybody. The committee acquitted her.

In 1711 there is another trial in Debrecen when the *táltos* question is considered. The witnesses mention several facts about a *táltos*-woman. She could smell money hidden in the cellar by putting bread and salt on a plate and turning the bread on a needle. This woman also seemed to be a fortune-teller. She prophesied that Germans and Hungarians would fight in Debrecen. After that, the 'pagans' – that is the Turks – would set fire to the city. Considering the history of Debrecen at this period, these prophecies were likely to be fulfilled, because such disturbances took place repeatedly.

Another witness mentioned that the accused woman had learned the art of finding treasure from the Turks. She also used to look through her nail after spitting on it. Still other witnesses mentioned the same facts with similar details. However, the most important part of each confession was that the woman had foretold war and found hidden treasure. She was not sentenced to death but branded. In a witch trial in 1702 a man was even referred to as 'the Prince of the *táltos*'.

Of course, the *táltos* term is not confined to the Debrecen trials. In Békés County, a *táltos* man is accused of singing devilish songs beside a 'pagan' bonfire. In 1708, in Ugocsa County, the accused woman states that she used to be a *táltos* and could cure the sick, but the Tartars bewitched her, and since then, she can only use half her healing powers. In the witch trials of western Hungary, the *táltos* were often mentioned, but seldom tried.

Prophecy was another activity where it was difficult to decide whether the accused person used black or white magic. To return again to Debrecen, in 1681 a man was accused of frightening the townsfolk by saying that he would destroy the city. In the same year, a woman was accused of being a fortune-teller able to read from the stars and the moon and of having had illicit intercourse with the Turks. She was burnt at the stake.

Other persons were accused of interfering with the weather or the crops. Tampering with the weather could be either for good or evil purposes. Interfering with the crops was always considered evil. In one of the most famous trials in Szeged, a company of male and female witches were accused of having sold rain to the Turks for money. The accused persons admitted to this, but defended themselves by stating that they bought back the rain later. In several trials the witnesses mention that the defendants collect the dew and sell it, together with the fertility of the soil.

Similar charges occur in a great number of trials in other parts of Hungary, too. In 1648, in Borsod County, a woman was accused of conjuring hail dropped by the horse of a wandering scholar – in Hungarian *garaboncia diák*. She could also make corn rusty on St George's Eve. This woman was sentenced to death.

In 1648, in a Transdanubian trial, a group of

people were again accused of making corn rusty on St George's Eve and of conjuring hail. The names show that the accused were of German origin. A special Hungarian phenomenon is the duel of magicians: healers, *táltos*, midwives and witches all fight one another.

To summarise: fortune-telling, healing, finding treasure or lost or stolen goods might be the result of using white or black magic. But if there was proof that the accused caused the illness or death of a person or valuable animal, this was considered to be evidence of sorcery and black magic.

In England the situation was similar. Let me cite a few examples concerning magical influence on the weather. To quote Keith Thomas' study, *Religion and the Decline of Magic*: 'Meteorologists denied that evil spirits were responsible for tempests, but many contemporaries were less certain. "It is a common opinion," wrote an Essex clergyman in 1587, "when there are mighty winds and thunders with terrible lightnings that the Devil is abroad."' We hear about English witches who caused a storm at sea by stirring water in a small pond. Of course, in England, causing a storm at sea was highly dangerous. As Hungary is a country far from the sea, witches were accused of conjuring hail, which could destroy the crops and disperse the cattle, or of causing a drought which meant disaster for the rural population. In the same way, in various European countries, witches were said to bring about that kind of meteorological disorder which was most dangerous for the population.

Let me return now to the problem of bewitching and healing. In most trials the defendants were accused of causing sickness or death. In a few cases they admitted to this, and the verdict was accordingly very severe. The admission of the defendant might have different reasons. Some confessed under torture. Others admitted murder because of a bad conscience, as it was probable that some of the accused really were murderers, usually poisoners. Most of the defendants, however, deny bewitching or murdering anybody, but not that they looked after sick people. Considering that the rural population in Hungary had scarcely any medical aid or facilities during the Turkish occupation, specialists were certainly needed for healing people and animals, and there was also need of midwives.

So there were quite a lot of healers in Hungarian villages whose training was rather dubious. If the sick person died during the treatment, it was possible for the family to accuse the healer of witchcraft, because in this way they could avoid payment. The fate of the healers depended upon the confessions of witnesses. To be a healer in this period was rather dangerous, but if there was real need, the community produced people willing to undertake the task, even if it involved a certain risk.

It is very difficult at present to make statistical comparisons between English and Hungarian witch trials. Certainly, most of the witches were female and most of the cunning folk were male. But as we have seen in the foregoing, there were exceptions.

In Hungary quite a number of witches and midwives are supposed to be able to bewitch a newborn child, or take away the mother's milk. Of course these are all women. But the leaders of the so-called covens are generally men. For example in the Szeged trials mentioned earlier, most defendants were female, but the leader was a very rich citizen of Szeged. The cunning folk in Hungary might be men or women. In England the term cunning folk generally refers to men, but the borderline between white and black magic is equally ambiguous, whether men or women are involved.

When the Empress Maria Theresa in Vienna put an end to the Hungarian witch trials, genuine folk belief reasserted itself. In the nineteenth century rural tradition freed itself from those characteristics which became part of the trials through the influence of the learned classes. It is only in epic tradition, occuring chiefly in legends, that witches remained the concubines of the devil and flew to the Witches' Sabbath. The simple village-witch could bewitch young children or animals, take away milk from the cow, and destroy true love, but she did few other evil deeds. Other kinds of magical practitioners continued to exist; the *táltos*, the wandering scholar, the healer, women who could talk to the dead, those who could find lost property, and so on. But an examination of their activities during the nineteenth and twentieth centuries would lead me very far from the main topic of this paper.

Sometimes the technical expertise of the witches and cunning folk is also mentioned.

Hungarian witches frequently bound their victims by making knots, thus inflicting on them sickness, death, impotence, or other evils. The objects found in the homes of the accused are often described by witnesses, and sometimes decide the outcome of the trial. For those who read today about the witch trials, these are only proofs of the incredible poverty of the Hungarian countryside. Neither witches nor the cunning folk in Hungary had any special technical aids: they used straw, animal bones, plants, stones, whips, scissors, needles, household items or consecrated objects, for both white or black magic. Salt, coal, under-clothes, the possessions of a man who had been hanged and hangman's rope seemed to be valued by all those who practised any kind of magic.

In one case, the witnesses enumerate the following objects found in the possession of two coachmen, who were supposed to have magic power: the right hand of a dead man, a purse made out of the clothing of a man cut down from the gallows and also part of his male organ, a human skull, some wires and chains, morsels from a cake, a branch of hazel. The coachmen had to pay a fine and were sentenced to one hundred strokes.

The texts published in the three Hungarian volumes refer to trials where the accused were simple citizens or serfs. Of course, there were also a few witch-accusations against the nobility, but in these cases the legal procedure was somewhat different and the records of the trials are not to be found in our public archives. In these trials, the situation is generally clear. Either the family wanted to obtain property by declaring one of its members a witch, or, in other cases, the accused person was evidently insane. But of course, we find cunning men only occasionally among the aristocracy or the upper classes, with the exception of a few scholars who were thought to get their knowledge from the devil.

The most interesting fact that emerges from Hungarian witch-hunting is that Catholics and Protestants disagreed about nearly everything, but had one point in common — that witches existed and must be exterminated. Both Catholics and Protestants also believed in the magic power of cunning men. Sometimes the trials mention the religion of the accused, but often we find no reference at all to this.

The defendants were always asked about their connection with the Devil, the Witches' Sabbath and so on. But in their answers and in the testimonies of the witnesses, the Evil One plays a minor role. Only under torture do the accused confess to having seen the Devil. Even if they do not deny sorcery, they speak only in stereotypes about the 'Mass of Witches' *et alia*.

One of the most interesting points in Hungarian witch trials is the complete lack of iconography. We have no contemporary illustrations of the trials, witches, devils, sorcery or the cunning folk, contrary to other European countries, where paintings and etchings frequently showed this interesting topic and represented witches and cunning folk with considerable imagination.

To sum up: both judges and accused seemed to believe in white and black magic, but death warrants were only signed when the practice of black magic could be proved. This is the more interesting in that during the sixteenth century, certain Calvinistic synods in Hungary more or less denied the existence of magic power and considered sorcery directed by the Devil himself to be pure nonsense. So, during the seventeenth century, ideas about witchcraft were more backward than in the sixteenth century. The lower classes of course, believed in both black and white magic before the trials, and went on believing in them after the end of the witch-hunt too. Cunning folk played as great a part in rural life as the witches themselves, or even greater, and we can still find some survivors of their profession in Hungarian villages of today.

Bibliography

Norman Cohn, *Europe's Inner Demons* (London, 1975).

Vilmos Diószegi, ed., *Glaubenswelt und Folklore der sibirischen Völker* (Budapest, 1963).

Tekla Dömötör, 'Die Hebamme als Hexe', *Probleme der Sagenforschung*, ed. Lutz Röhrich (Freiburg im Breisgau, 1973).

Mary Douglas, ed., *Witchcraft Confessions and Accusations* (London, 1970).

Andor Komáromy, *Magyarországi boszorkányperek oklevéltára* (Budapest, 1910).

Alan Macfarlaine, *Witchcraft in Tudor and Stuart England* (London, 1970).

Venetia Newall, ed., *The Witch Figure* (London, 1973).

János Reizner, *Szeged története*, Vols I and IV (Szeged, 1899/1900).

Géza Róheim, *Hungarian and Vogul Mythology* (New York, 1954).

Ferenc Schram, *Magyarországi boszorkányperek, 1529-1763*, 2 vols (Budapest, 1970).

Keith Thomas, *Religion and the Decline of Magic* (London, 1971).

H. R. Trevor-Roper, *The European Witch-Craze of the 16th and 17th Centuries* (Harmondsworth, 1969).

The Persian 'Passion Play'

L. P. ELWELL-SUTTON   University of Edinburgh

I HAVE entitled this paper 'The Persian Passion Play', and the term is not misleading, even though the context and nature of the subject differs in many respects from the medieval European performance to which that term is usually applied. The common element is the theme of the conflict of life and death, light and darkness, the self-sacrifice of the individual for the salvation of the community, the ultimate defeat of evil by good. In the case of the Iranian version, the sources are certainly not Christian, they are probably not even Islamic; though the setting and characters are based on an historical episode in the history of Islam, they draw inspiration rather from a combination of Zoroastrian themes and traditional folkloric elements.

What is misleading is perhaps to speak of *the* Persian passion play. This is to give the impression that there is one accepted text or set of texts, whereas there is in fact not only a cycle of more than a hundred subjects, some of which ostensibly have little to do with the central episode, but also widely differing versions from different parts of the geographical area in which they occur.

The central episode in question is the one that led to the first major split in the young Islamic faith. When the Prophet Mohammad died in 632 A.D., ten years after the Hijra or Emigration from Mecca to Medina that is taken as the beginning of the Islamic era, the question of his successor was unclear. On the one hand there was the traditional Arab democratic view, which was that leaders should be elected by the community. Opposed to this were the advocates of hereditary succession, whose case was hampered by the absence of a male heir — the Prophet's three sons all died in infancy; in the face of this dilemma they gave their support to Mohammad's son-in-law Ali, husband of his daughter Fatima. The upholders of democracy carried the day so far as the first four successors or Caliphs were concerned, Ali himself eventually being chosen in 656. His tenure of office was not without its ups and downs, and when in 661 he was assassinated — the same fate had attended two of his three predecessors — the Caliphate was seized by his rival Mo'awiya, who established his capital at Damascus. Sporadic opposition was carried on by the Shi'a or Party of Ali, a name that subsequently attached itself to the whole body of followers of this sect of Islam, until 680, when by an ironic twist Hosein, son of Ali and Fatima, challenged the testament of Mo'awiya under which the latter's son Yazid was to initiate an hereditary line of Caliphs, the Omayyads. Hosein, with a small band of family and followers, marched against the Syrian army, only to be surrounded on the plain of Kerbela, not far from the later city of Baghdad, the men massacred, and the women carried off to slavery in Damascus. The horror of this episode, the villainy of the vanquishers and the heroism of their victims, the sufferings the latter underwent in the scorching heat of the desert, cut off deliberately by their enemies even from the water of the nearby Euphrates, and above all the thought of their close relationship to the Founder of the Faith, has caught the imagination of Moslems everywhere, even among the Sunni majority.

Nevertheless the Shi'at Ali was long to remain, with occasional exceptions, the party of opposition in Islam, developing, in the absence of political power, the doctrinal and mystical aspects of the faith. As the representative of the downtrodden, it gained some popularity in the non-Arab areas of the Islamic world, particularly in Iran, where the legitimacy of the movement was enhanced by the belief that Hosein had married Shahrbanu, the daughter of the last Sasanian ruler of Iran. Finally, at the beginning of the sixteenth century, the Safavid dynasty in Iran established Shi'ism as the official faith. It was from this time that the commemoration of the tragedy of Kerbela, of which we find occasional mention in the history of earlier periods, became an accepted part of everyday life in Iran. Even today popular street-corner and market-place entertainment generally has a religious colouring. The strong man invokes Ali, Hasan and Hosein; the snake-charmer purports to control his performers through the magic power of these same names. Of a more specifically religious nature is the *rouze-khani*, at which the story of Kerbela is recited, often with the aid of a vividly coloured representation of the scene. But most characteristic is the *ta'ziya* or mourning ceremony, which takes place on the anniversary of the events of Kerbela. This certainly dates back to a time long prior to the Safavids, but it was not described or depicted in detail until European travellers began to visit Iran during the sixteenth and seventeenth centuries. One of the first of these was the German Adam Olearius, who was there with a diplomatic mission from the Duke of Holstein in 1635, and whose illustration of a *ta'ziya* procession does not differ greatly from the kind of procession that may occasionally be seen at the present day.

At some stage these processions, which were accompanied by recited accounts of the martyrdom of Hosein and his family, developed into dramatised representations of the story. While there is no precise record of this taking place, an eyewitness account by the English traveller William Fancklyn, who saw performances in Shiraz in 1786, describes what sounds like a transitional phase. Certainly by the middle of the nineteenth century, when the eccentric diplomat Comte de Gobineau gathered the material for his classic study of religion in Persia, the *ta'ziya* performances had reached a peak of elaboration and sophistication. But thereafter, the spread of education, the widening influence of European culture, and the political upheavals of the early twentieth century, all combined to produce stagnation and decline in this form of popular ritual. Finally, under the reforming Reza Shah, the performances and processions were banned as

symbols of the traditional and conservative society from which the modern Iran was trying to escape. In recent years, as part of the general revival of interest in the traditional folk culture of Iran, the *ta'ziya* performances have been resuscitated, and are now regularly performed, and even televised, under official patronage. Although there is an element of self-consciousness about this, as well as of tourist appeal, it is noteworthy not only that the time-honoured texts and techniques have survived, but that there is also a marked degree of audience participation, a fact which suggests that the religious and ritual aspects are not yet dead.

I said at the beginning that not one, but many Persian passion plays exist. One problem is that, apart even from the fact that the texts have survived only in the memories of the performers, it was not the practice to preserve complete written acting scripts, but rather to provide each actor with his own lines and cues. From these it would be possible to construct full texts, and over the years this has been done to an increasing extent. One of the earliest collections was that made by the Russian scholar Chodzko: thirty-three texts now in the Bibliothèque Nationale in Paris, five of which were translated by Chodzko and published in 1852, and the full texts of which are now in course of publication in Iran. Gobineau's texts, seven of which he summarised in French in 1865, are unfortunately lost, as are those of the thirty-seven plays translated into English by Sir Lewis Pelly in 1879. Wilhelm Litten published facsimile texts of fifteen plays in 1929, and one or two other single texts have been published in Europe from time to time. An extremely important collection of over a thousand manuscripts made by the Italian Minister in Iran, Enrico Cerulli, during the 'thirties and deposited in the Vatican Library, have not so far been published or even very carefully examined. During the past thirty or forty years a number of *ta'ziyas* have been published in Iran in popular, vigorously illustrated, 'chapbook' form, as have other traditional poems and folk-epics, both religious and non-religious. More recently Iranian scholars have turned their attention to the subject, and have produced a number of collections. All this is helping to give a more accurate overall view of the *ta'ziya* cycle.

The subjects of the plays — which vary in length, but in performance usually last between one and two hours — may be divided into several categories. At the heart of the cycle are those depicting the events of Kerbela — the heroic martyrdom of Hosein's sons, brothers and followers, the tragic story of the marriage of Hosein's nephew Qasem to his daughter Fatima on the field of Kerbela and his subsequent death in battle, the martyrdom of Hosein himself, the flight of his widow, the Persian princess Shahrbanu. In the second category are the events immediately following the field of Kerbela — the captivity of Hosein's womenfolk and children, the conversion and martyrdom of various figures, including members of the Syrian army, a Frankish ambassador, a Christian maiden. Yet another category deals with earlier episodes in the history of Islam — the death of the Prophet Mohammad, of his son Ibrahim and of his daughter Fatima, wife of Ali and mother of Hosein, the martyrdom of Ali and of his elder son Hasan, the usurpation of the Caliphate by Abu Bakr — or later ones, including the martyrdom of the sixth, seventh and eighth Imams, Ja'far Sadeq, Musa Kazem, Ali Reza, descendants of Hosein. Next the settings move backwards in time — the sacrifice of Ishmael by Abraham, the story of Joseph and his brethren, of Solomon and the Queen of Sheba — or forwards to the conqueror Tamerlane, a mythical Christian king Qaniya, and even an episode depicting the Day of Resurrection. Finally, mention must be made of a whole series of plays performed by women only, and of a group of 'comic' *ta'ziyas* generally used as curtain-raisers, A typical example tells the story of a demon: Ali used one of his own hairs to bind the creature's thumbs. The captive then found that, despite appeals to Adam, Solomon and Mohammad, only Ali's son, Hosein, could release him.

The sources of these texts have not been traced in detail, but one fact is noticeable, that the language and style, contrary to expectations, is almost entirely literary. Not only are they wholly in verse, but the verse-metres are those of the classical literature, and not of popular poetry. This leads one to assume that much of the material is drawn from literary sources, probably the same as those used for the *rouze-khani* referred to earlier. This is not to exclude the probability that the language may sometimes be colloquialised during the actual performance, though there is no evidence that this happens to any great extent.

Traditionally the *ta'ziya* plays are performed during the Moslem month of Moharram, the anniversary of the battle of Kerbela, or during the following month, or on the anniversary of the death of Ali, or indeed on any other religious anniversary. Since the Moslem calendar is lunar, the performances are not tied to any particular season of the solar year. The place of performance, or Hoseiniya, may range from the splendid Takye-e Doulat, built during the latter half of the nineteenth century and demolished some fifty years ago, to a bare open space in a village, usually covered by an awning. Often the awning is elaborately decorated with symbolic figures. In the centre of the space is a low platform or group of platforms, on which the principal action takes place. The performance is 'in the round', the audience being seated on all four sides, one side being reserved for the women. Preliminary music of a martial kind is provided by a wind and percussion band, while other musicians at the side of the acting area accompany the action with appropriately varied rhythms.

The actors come from many walks of life. Some are full-time performers, belonging to groups who travel from place to place, giving performances all the year round. Others only participate during the two sacred months, and for the rest of the year are engaged in secular occupations. In the villages the performers are normally amateurs. In all cases the roles are likely to be hereditary, and there are stories of individuals becoming so identified with particular characters, especially the villainous ones, that they come to assume these roles even in their daily lives.

Characterisation is not in general very subtle. The good are good, and the bad detestable. This is further underlined in performance by the fact that the former wear sober costumes of black or green, while the villains are garbed in red or yellow. The good characters sing their roles, while the bad speak theirs. Women's parts are normally played by boys, though on occasion a major female role may be played by an adult male. No actresses participate in these plays, apart from the women's plays already mentioned, in which there are of course no men, but since the female characters are normally veiled, this does not present any problem. In any case, strict realism is not the aim. Indeed it has been suggested that there are sound religious grounds for not making the performances too authentic. Though the Iranians have never paid too much attention to the conventional Islamic ban on the representation of human figures in art, nevertheless it is probably felt that no effort should be made to convince the audience that they are watching anything but actors performing roles in a well-known story — the Brechtian *Verfremdungs-Effekt*, in fact, though probably not influenced, as Brecht was, by the Chinese theatre. Another contribution to this alienation effect is the practice, particularly among the younger and less experienced actors, of carrying their scripts with them, while the producer remains on the scene throughout, cuing the actors and helping them when they get into difficulties. The same disregard for realism is carried through in the setting and properties. A bowl of water represents the Euphrates, the burning of a camp by setting fire to a single tent, a vision of Hell by blackened figures leaping through flames; wooden heads raised on poles depict a massacre, a masked face and blood-stained robe the ghost of a martyr. Costumes are often detailed and accurate, at any rate where oriental figures are concerned. The Frankish ambassador, on the other hand, is likely to be depicted with a collar and tie. Masks are not normally used, unless to represent wild beasts and monsters — a lion or a demon. Riding beasts however, such as horses and camels, are often brought on to the stage.

As suggested earlier, in spite of the intrusion of tourism and the media, the *ta'ziya* still retains much of its original function as a ritual rather than a spectacle. Audience participation is involved even before the performance, when each member is invited to dab his face and hands with rosewater in a symbolic purification gesture, while, even though the stories told are as well known to the spectators as our biblical stories to an earlier generation, the emotional tension is built up as the tragic tale unfolds. The women begin to wail and lament, and high points of drama are accompanied by a rhythmic beating of breasts.

The history of the Persian passion play is almost at an end. A period of a bare two centuries has seen its birth, flowering, brilliant zenith, slow decline under the pressures of the industrial age, and final fossilisation as a museum piece. Unlike the medieval plays of Europe, it never gave rise to a theatrical tradition. The secular theatre is now developing in Iran, but its sources have so far been European. Nevertheless it is still perhaps possible to end this paper on a question-mark: given the new-found interest in the *ta'ziya*, will the playwrights and producers of Iran be tempted to look to it as a source of inspiration?

The Theme of Twins in Relation to that of the Trickster in Latin American Mythology and Folklore

DOUGLAS GIFFORD   University of St Andrews

Gemini . . . l'image de toutes les oppositions intérieures et extérieures, contraires ou complimentaires, relatives ou absolues, qui se resolvent dans une tension créatrice. . .
(Dictionnaire des Symbols)

THE theme of twins in folktales and myths has fascinated story-tellers and poets in all ages.[1] This of course is partly explained by the aura of abnormality that surrounds any such phenomenon, for it suggests a relationship with the supernatural that provides an excellent motif for the myth-ologiser. In this short paper I take two European-inspired tales from Argentina and Peru, as proto-types of two aspects of the treatment accorded to the twin-myth. By comparing them with Amer-indian and other areas of treatment I hope to show that there may be an earlier stage of development where the two figures are in fact only one.

Students of folklore and mythology have for long been concerned with the archetype of the twin: the Dioscuri, Romulus and Remus, and the very large number of Christian twin saints and heroes, all these testify to a persistent legendary tradition. I should add at this juncture that the term *twin* is not generally used in the literal sense in current folktales, but that it usually includes ordinary brothers and close friends.

The two prototype tales I wish to discuss initially either stress the similarity and closeness of the two protagonists, or the reverse. In the last case their dissimilarity and antipathy towards one another is usually brought out in a comic vein.

Here is an Argentinian folktale from the first class:

Pedro and Juan are two brothers, and one day they go out to *rodar la tierra*. They see a beautiful bird and catch it. It turns into a princess. All three continue on their way. When they rest by the roadside, Juan and the princess go to sleep, but Pedro remains awake. A bird appears and warns him against three things which will constitute dangers for them: these mean that the princess must not drink or eat. They must also be on guard against a seven-headed serpent in a house at which they will arrive. Pedro, forewarned in this way, avoids all dangers. However, there is another warning: if he divulges how he was told about the dangers, he will turn to stone. But his behaviour has been so strange in the eyes of the other two that he is forced to tell them what happened. Soon he has turned into a statue. Juan and the princess now marry, and have an infant son. One day, a paper appears at the base of Pedro's statue telling Juan that if he is to bring his brother back to life he must kill his child and bathe the statue in its blood. Juan decides that brotherly love must come before all things, and duly kills his son. The stone Pedro is bathed in his blood, and comes to life again. As soon as this happens, the now resurrected Pedro puts the infant's head back on him and he too is brought back to life.[2]

This tale deals with brotherly devotion. In other variants of the story, the brother who breaks the taboo is turned into a leper, but the same solution is found. In all versions the event of resurrection is the climax of the tale.

The other prototype tale, from Peru, is comic, dealing with the antipathy between the two brothers:

Once there were two brothers: one is rich and hardworking, the other poor and idle. The idle tries to borrow money from the rich, but is sent packing. He wanders into the wood to collect firewood to sell. There he catches two rabbits, and, keeping them alive, takes them home and asks his wife to prepare a supper for his rich brother. He takes one rabbit with him and goes to the brother's house. 'Come to supper,' he says. The rich brother says yes, and the other says 'I'll let my wife know,' and releases the rabbit. 'He'll go off and tell her,' he explains. When they get to idle brother's house, the guest sees a rabbit and imagines it to be the same one. 'What a clever rabbit — sell it me!' he begs. The idle brother, after much humming and hawing, agrees to part with it for a very large sum. The rich brother soon finds out he has been tricked, and comes storming back to his brother's house. When idle brother sees him coming he gets his wife to tie a bag of red dye to her belt, and to fall over and pretend to die when rich brother hits or pushes her. Idle brother now hides. Rich brother enters in a rage, knocks over the wife, who falls as if dead, squeezing a liberal amount of red dye everywhere. Idle brother now appears from hiding and starts to play a drum over the 'body' of his wife. She comes to, bit by bit, as arranged, and is soon hale and hearty once more. Of course rich brother begs to be allowed to buy the drum, and once more a large sum changes hands. Rich brother goes off with the drum, gets home, kills his wife and starts to play the drum over. Of course nothing happens, for the drum is no more magical than the rabbit. Rich brother now traps idle brother, puts him in a sack and makes off to a cliff in order to throw him into the sea. On the way he stops for *chicha*. Idle brother seizes on a passing shepherd and puts him in the sack instead. Rich brother comes out from his *chicha*-drinking and heaves the sack into the sea. Idle brother remains with the shepherd's flock. Some time later he is met by rich brother. On being asked what he is doing, he tells him: 'When you threw me over the cliff I fell into the water and there were hundreds of animals there. I gathered them up and now I've become rich.' Rich brother now begs to be put into a sack and thrown into the sea. This is done, and so rich brother perishes.[3]

This type of tale deliberately travesties both magical and supernatural themes, as well as that of resurrection. The disparity between the two brothers, and the antipathy between them, provides a tricker-and-tricked plot full of humour.

Both these tales are well documented in medieval literature:[4] antecedents include the tales of Amicus and Amelius and Ai Tolysy and the second story possibly owes a lot to the miracle traditions of divine or holy pairs who wander through the world.[5] But in both prototypes the action turns on the fact that the two brothers or friends are dissimilar: one can understand the magical language of birds, the other cannot; one is clever, the other stupid. This essential dissimilarity may stem from the ancient belief, still prevalent today in many cultures, that twins cannot share the same father, for one man can only engender one child. In many twin legends one brother is son of a supernatural being or spirit, the other of a mortal one. Castor and Pollux provide an example, with Pollux as son of Zeus. Medieval legends also illustrate this, as for instance that of the Cid, who was believed to be the twin brother of a miller's son. His father fell in love with the miller's wife, and she conceived by him the same night as she did by her husband. The dissimilarity between the infant Cid and his miller twin is brought out in the legend: the Cidling plays at knights and soldiers with wooden lances and make-believe horses, while the small miller plays with ploughs and clay oxen.[6]

Keeping this theme of dissimilarity in mind, I now turn to Amerindian mythology. Here the theme of twins is very prevalent. In one myth, cited by Métraux, the wife of the culture hero or creator god is killed by jaguars, who find in her womb a pair of twins. Saving these, they bring them up, but, once grown to maturity, the twins discover, generally from another animal, who the murderers of their mother are. They take revenge on the jaguars, and after killing them perform many miraculous deeds, finally climbing up into the sky on a chain of arrows and becoming the sun and moon.[7] As to the characters of the twins themselves, however, these are nearly always dissimilar. Sometimes the clever brother is the sun and his stupid twin the moon. But in many adventures the clever twin is rescued by the stupid one. Keri, the Bakairi god, is burnt in a great fire and brought back to life again by being blown on by his brother. Nanderiquey, the more intelligent of another pair of twins, is also rescued and brought back to life by his brother.[8]

Whether the many similarities between Amerindian tales and European counterparts are due to the contiguity of one civilisation with another, it is difficult to say. What is very probable, however, is that there are many pre-Columban features still extant in Amerindian mythology. To my mind, one of these features shows that, in addition to the many twin pairs in indigenous myth, there are single gods who are dualistic in nature. Makunaima, the Carib god, unites in his one person traits of both creator and trickster: at times he is friend of mankind, and at others a stupid practical joker, often worsted in his undertakings and having to be rescued. Here then are the characteristics of twins within the one figure. One well-known 'dual' character is Wadjungkaga, the trickster god of the Winnebago tribe.[9] Radin says of him that 'this two-fold function of benefactor and buffoon . . . is the outstanding characteristic of the overwhelming majority of trickster heroes wherever they are encountered in aboriginal America.'[10]

How do the two traits of one person then pass through myth or folktale to become two characters? Wadjungkaga provides an interesting clue in letting the two sides of his ambiguity come into conflict with *each other*. Here is his story:

> Once upon a time there was a village in which there lived a chief who was preparing to take his tribe on a warpath. Warriors were told to obtain material with which to build a fire for the preparatory feast. Four large deer were brought, prepared, and placed on the fire. Then the feast took place, but at the end of it, Wadjungkaga suddenly left the company and went to his own hut. After a long time some of the warriors went to see what he was doing and were horrified to find him co-habiting with a woman. The warriors return to the feast and tell the others, where-

upon they all go home. For a taboo has been broken — that no chief preparing for a warpath should indulge in sexual relations with a woman. But this happens twice more, and the warriors become more and more disillusioned with their chief. Finally however they set off on their warpath. But after a very short distance Wadjungkaga brings his canoe to land and breaks it to pieces, shouting 'It is I who am going to fight! You cannot fight!' His warriors think him a wicked man, and many now abandon him. A few follow him, however. He goes on breaking taboo after taboo and soon is left completely alone. By now he is looked on as a complete fool, and is utterly desocialised.

Wandering on by himself, he meets an old water-buffalo, and kills it. What follows is significant, for the ambiguities which have become apparent in his character are now manifested. While he is skinning the buffalo with his right hand:

> Suddenly his left arm grabbed the buffalo. 'Give that back to me, it is mine! Stop that or I'll use my knife on you!' So spoke the right arm. 'I'll cut you to pieces, that's what I'll do,' continued the right arm. Thereupon the left arm released its hold. Shortly after, the left arm again grabbed hold of the right arm. This time it grabbed hold of its wrist just at the moment that the right arm had commenced to skin the buffalo. Again and again this was repeated. In that manner did Trickster make both his arms quarrel. That quarrel soon turned into a vicious fight and the left arm was badly cut up. 'Oh! Oh! Why did I do this? Why have I done this? I have made myself suffer!' The left arm was indeed bleeding profusely.[11]

Now this is a humourous incident and designed to make an audience laugh, but it is quite clear at the same time that here is an attempt to personalise two different and warring parts of Trickster into two characters in a story. The episode ties in naturally with the paradoxes that go before it: a chief about to go on the most important of all enterprises deliberately breaks the very rules and taboos which protect the wellbeing and success of that enterprise. Yet, as has been pointed out by C. G. Jung, it is only when Trickster has thoroughly cut himself off from all his social ties that he can in fact help his tribe, for he becomes a divine being. At the end of the myth he goes first into the ocean and finally up to the heavens. Jung connects him with the saviour figure:

Anyone who belongs to a sphere of culture that seeks the perfect state somewhere in the past must feel very queerly indeed when confronted with the figure of the Trickster. He is a forerunner of the saviour, and, like him, God, Man and animal at once. He is both subhuman and superhuman, a bestial and a divine being, whose chief and most alarming characteristic is his unconsciousness . . . the trickster is a primitive 'cosmic' being of a *divine-animal* nature, on the one hand superior to man because of his superhuman qualities, and on the other inferior to him because of his unreason and unconsciousness . . .[12]

His behaviour to mortals, then is ambiguous and paradoxical and results within folklore in the personification of his attributes.

Outside Latin America both Trickster and Twin can be found in almost every culture, even if not to such a wide extent. It might be useful to consider one or two other examples of the benefactor-buffoon figure in another context. The field I shall take is that of Jewish folklore, for the best example of the progenitor of the twin comes — to my mind — from the conception of demonic figures. In the exegetical literature surrounding Old Testament studies, from the second century A.D. onwards, we learn of such demons as Ashmedai or Samael.[13] These are patently trickster figures and connect with the myth of twins. For Samael fathered Cain, while Adam fathered Abel: Eve bears both brothers. Ashmedai is an ambiguous figure; tricking Solomon out of his kingdom, he takes his place on the throne for a period, but horrifies everyone by breaking the most sacred taboos, sleeping with his mother and with the women of the harem during their menstrual periods. Yet Ashmedai is also benevolent and compassionate, as is convincingly and deliberately shown earlier in the legend.[14]

Even the attributes of God the Father himself become personalised, as can be seen in the legend of the Creation. In a fourth-century narrative we get: 'In the hour when the Holy One, blessed be He, came to create the first man, the ministering angels formed themselves into parties and companies. Some said "let him be created," others "let him not be created" . . . Kindness said "let him be created, for he is a bestower of loving-kindness." Truth said "let him not be created, for he is falsehood." Justice said "let him be created, for he deals justly." Peace said "let him not be created, for he is wholly quarrelsome." '[15] Does this account reflect a folk-belief that the Creator Himself had had doubts as to whether to create Man or not?

To return to our two European-inspired folk-tales, the one showing devotion, the other comic antipathy, we have seen how within the action of these tales the element of paradox presents itself. For even as in Amerindian mythology Makunaima has to be rescued by his less intelligent brother, so the hard-working and rich brother is tricked by his 'stupid' and poor counterpart. Things do not work out as one expects them to, just as in the case of the trickster himself. The stronger becomes the weaker, the weaker rescues the stronger.[16]

There is one further point of interest which may relate the theme of the twins to literature. The archetype itself in myth or folklore lends colour to one literary device — that of dialogue. Do not the twins represent dialogue in folkloric form? The many miraculous legends of the Middle Ages based on two saintly men walking together over the face of the earth, one superior to the other, provide many dialogues and actions resulting from them.[17] These characters seem to represent, as do those in our Argentinian and Peruvian folktales, two poles, a positive and a negative, between which a spark is continually passing. The spark depends on the dissimilarity of their natures and characters but at the same time on their closeness: they attract and repel each other at the same time. In Spanish literature this formula has seldom been used with more success than in Don Quixote and Sancho Panza.

One final myth neatly expresses the division of the divine into two. It comes from the Yamana Indians of Tierra del Fuego. The culture hero Yoálox has married and becomes the father of a son. The baby cries incessantly and drives his father to distraction. He tries building another hut for himself, but he can still hear his son crying even louder. 'Sulkily one day he again entered the hut where his little son was lying. With both hands he grabbed him under his armpits, lifted him up, stared sharply into his face and roared: "Will you stop screaming!" This very instant the little boy split right down the middle, so that Yoálox now had two sons. They did not cry, though. They were the first humans.'[18]

Notes

1. Numerous works relating to this subject can be cited, of which the following are a few: M. Deren, *Divine Horsemen. The Living Gods of Haiti* (London, 1953); L. A. Deubner, *Kosmas und Damian* (Leipzig/Berlin, 1907); F. J. Dölger, 'Dioskuri. Das Riesenschiff des Apostol Paulus und seine Schutzgötter', *Antike und Christentum*, VI (1950), 276-85; P. Ehrenreich, *Die Mythen und Legenden der Südamerikanishcen Urvölker* (Berlin, 1905); H. Grégoire, *Saints jumeaux et dieux cavaliers* (Paris, 1905); M. Gusinde, 'Das Bruderpaar in der Südamerikanischen Mythologie', *Internationaler Amerikanisten Kongress XXIII*, 1928 (New York, 1930), 687-98; J. R. Harris, *The Dioscuri in the Christian Legends* (London, 1903); *idem, The Cult of the Heavenly Twins* (Cambridge, 1906); K. Jaisle, *Die Dioskuren als Retter zur See bei Griechen und Römern und ihr Fortleben in Christlichen Legenden* (Tübingen, 1907); A. H. Krappe, 'The Legend of Amicus and Amelius', *Modern Language Review*, XVIII (1923), 152-61; *idem*, 'Spanish Twin Cults', *Studi e materiali di storia delle religione*, VIII (1932), 1-22; E. M. Loeb, 'The Twin Cult in the Old and the New World', *Miscellanea Paul Rivet* (Mexico, 1968), I, 154-74; A. Métraux, 'Twin Heroes in South American Mythology', *Journal of American Folklore*, LIX (1946), 114-23; D. Ward, *The Divine Twins. An Indo-European Myth in Germanic Tradition* (Berkeley/Los Angeles, 1968); *idem*, 'An Indo-European Mythological Theme in Germanic Tradition', *Indo-European and Indo-Europeans*, ed. Cardona, Hoenigswald and Senn (Philadelphia, 1970), 405-20.

2. S. Chertudi, *Cuentos folklóricos de la Argentina*, 1a serie (Buenos Aires, 1960), 94-6 (*El Cuento de los hermanitos*). Two of the episodes are listed in Aarne-Thompson, Tale Type 303. This version comes from Catamarca. For another Argentinian variant, see the story of Guillermo and Tomás in M. R. Lida de Malkiel, *El Cuento popular hispano-americano y la literatura* (Buenos Aires, 1941), 79 ff.

3. 'Les deux frères', *Amérindia*, II (1977), 146-60 (from Jalca, Peru; published by G. Taylor). I am grateful to Rosaleen Howard and Leslie Hoggarth for pointing out the similarity between this tale-type and the 'Rabbit and Fox' (Ecuador), or the 'Mouse and Fox' tales (Peru).

4. Krappe (1923), 152-61; *idem, The Science of Folklore* (London, 1930), 207 ff., for a general historical account.

5. Ward (1968), 67, suggests that the heavenly visitors, Christ (or God) and St Peter, may in folklore be related to the theme of the Heavenly Twins. Hans Sachs (1494-1576) provides other early examples of tales of this type; see e.g., *Vier Meister Stücke von Hans Sachs* (Leipzig, 1918), or W. Leighton, tr., *Merry Tales and Three Shrovetide Plays by Hans Sachs* (London, 1910).

6. S. Armistead, 'Two Rival Traditions concerning the Parentage of the Cid' (cited in Ward [1968], 23).

7. Métraux, 119; R. Karsten, *Indian Tribes of the Gran Chaco* (Helsinki, 1932), 78-9, speaks of Indian beliefs concerning twins; cf. also N. Yampey, 'El mito de los gemelos en la cultura indo-americana', *Revista del Ateneo paraguayo*, II (1966), 143-60.

8. Métraux, 115. Nanderiquey is a god in Apocuva-Guarani mythology.

9. P. Radin, *The Trickster* (New York, 1972), with commentaries by K. Kerényi and C. G. Jung.

10. *ibid.*, 124.

11. *ibid.*, 8.

12. *ibid.*, 203.

13. For an excellent study, see L. Jung, *Fallen Angels in Jewish, Christian and Mohammedan Literature* (New York, 1974).

14. *ibid.*, 85. Ashmedai shows much tenderness of heart when he sees a wedding party enjoying

itself; he weeps because he knows that the husband is to die in three days time. He shows equal compassion towards a blind man who has strayed from his path.

15. *ibid.*, 45. The legend goes on to mention that God then took Truth and cast it to the ground. The minstering angels then pleaded for Truth and asked for it to come up from the earth. This is interesting in the light of the myth of the Tree of Knowledge of Good and Evil.

16. A full discussion of the arch-trickster figure of Spanish folklore, Pedro de Urdemalas, is impossible here, but a very large number of Latin-American folktales choose him as protagonist. See, in the Argentine, A. Carrizo, *Historia del Folklore Argentino* (Buenos Aires, 1953); also P. Bustamente, *Girón de Historia, leyendas* (Buenos Aires, 1922), which has a chapter entitled Pedro Ordimán (cited in Carrizo, 124). In Chile, see Y. Pino Saavedra, *Cuentos folklóricos de Chile*, 3 vols (Santiago, 1960-63), which provides good source material. In Spain, see A. Espinosa, *Cuentos populares españoles recogidos de la tradición oral de España* (Madrid, 1946), which remains a standard work.

17. For a good example of these, see A. Stacpoole, 'Hugo of Cluny and the Hildebrandtine miracle tradition', *Revue Bénédictine*, 1967, 341 ff.

18. J. Wilbert, ed., *Folk Literature of the Yamana Indians. Martin Gusinde's Collection of Yamana Narratives* (Berkeley/Los Angeles, 1977), 48.

The Folk Artist in Yemenite Jewish Society in Yemen and Israel

OLGA GOLDBERG-MULKIEWICZ   The Hebrew University, Jerusalem

THE Yemenite Jews are descendants of the most ancient Jewish diaspora. It is true that no historical sources demonstrating the authenticity of the traditions concerning the beginnings of Jewish settlement in Yemen are available, but evidence suggests that Jews were already in the region during the period of the Second Temple.[1] Perhaps modern archeological research will confirm the legends prevalent among the Yemenite Jewish community, which relate that the first group of Jewish immigrants came to Yemen in the tenth century B.C. as the result of contacts established between the Queen of Sheba and King Solomon.[2] The legends tell us that Solomon sent a group of Jews to Yemen, including several teachers for the son he had by the Queen of Sheba, and a large contingent of silversmiths. These craftsmen brought gifts from Solomon, and they were enjoined to remain at the court and supply the Queen of Sheba with jewellery.

But, setting aside the oral folk tradition, which as we know can only in very rare cases be taken by historians as a credible source, we know from research that the Yemenite community was of all Jewish societies the most outstanding in its originality. It was isolated from frequent contact with other Jewish groups, and its members were little influenced by the surrounding non-Jewish culture. Evidence for this phenomenon can be found in all the elements of Yemenite Jewish culture, in speech, pronunciation, social norms, crafts, costume and so on.[3] The silversmiths artistic production confirms the tradition concerning the antiquity of their settlement, and the isolation of their culture. Their style, and some of their technical solutions in making jewellery are associated by some researchers with the Greco-Roman period,[4] and they continued in these old forms almost unchanged until the first half of the present century.

Undoubtedly jewellery was a Jewish craft in Yemen even before the introduction of Islam, with its strong prohibition on work in gold and silver. This ban only strengthened the position of the Jewish silversmiths in the area, and in fact the Jews were the only silversmiths in Yemen up to 1949-50, the period of their mass emigration to Israel. Their position as silversmiths was so unique that in the fifties the local government asked some of them to stay on for a while in order to teach their craft to some Arab artisans.

The craft of the silversmith was quite common in Yemen. There was always a big demand for jewellery among the population; both Arab and Jewish women had a great ·deal which was the traditional gift on all occasions.[5] As we will see later, its function was not only to announce the economic status of the wearer, but above all to protect her from evil, and to express her social position. There was also a strong demand for decorated weapons. The Jews were on the whole forbidden to produce arms, and obviously to wear them, but they were allowed to ornament them.

The social and economic position of the silversmiths was generally very high, and there were several reasons for this. The occupation was usually hereditary, and the craftsmen came from the richest and most influential familites, for it was impossible to work in the craft without having some initial capital. However, the esteem attaching to silversmiths was due mainly to non economic causes. First of all the position was connected with the magical function ascribed to jewellery. Manufacture of a piece of jewellery required not only technical skills, but considerable kabbalistic expertise, in order to adapt the piece to the particular needs of the customer, his way of life, social position and so on. Thus the silversmith had to be a scholar first, and a craftsman second. Lack of kabbalistic erudition could lead to fatal results. The craftsman had to consult his books for a proper interpretation, and only after that could he start to prepare the piece. Often he had to write the correct amulet and place it in the ornament. The significance of, for instance, a necklace was in its magical or social functions, not in the originality of the design. In principle there were only a few traditional and strictly determined forms of jewellery, one for each occasion, and the craftsmen continually repeated these forms exclusively. They worked according to established models and a fixed iconography. The beauty of the product lay in its precision and not necessarily in the pattern itself, which was generally the same, or at least approximated to the traditional one. Craftsmen spent many hours working on a piece, and this time was not calculated in its price. The form of the jewellery, especially the number of leaves, beads and other details, and their shape had a special magical significance.[6] When we examine a piece of traditional Yemenite jewellery we always note the occurrence of the same number of motif details and the same symbols. For instance, the fertility symbol, a small pendant in the form of a fish or an ear of wheat, a small 'rattler', known to be very efficient against the evil eye, red coral, which has the same function, and so on, are constantly repeated.

A silversmith famous in the community was a man who could produce very meticulous jewellery, but, more important, who was known as a learned sage. The community appreciated his technical skills, but valued his erudition even more. It was also known in the community that to be a silversmith meant to have the time and ability to discuss philosophical and religious problems with other craftsmen or other learned men whom the silversmiths might meet during their wanderings when looking for orders. Not all silversmiths in Yemen travelled from place to place, but many of them did and they were known as the men bringing new problems to discuss. The community did not esteem the silversmiths only because of their wealth as such, for intellectual skills were always uppermost in the Yemenite hierarchy of evaluation, as regards both craftsmen and other members of the community.

There were two important waves of immigration from Yemen to Israel, both relevant to our study.

The first group arrived in Palestine in the last decade of the nineteenth century and the beginning of the twentieth, and the second mass immigration, of the whole Yemenite Jewish community, took place in the years 1949-50. The first group settled mainly in Jerusalem and its vicinity, and of course included several silversmiths. They experienced great difficulty in finding exployment in the local economy, for there was no need for their products. But at that time a workshop for goldsmiths had been set up in the newly established Academy of Fine Arts in Jerusalem (Bezalel), and a group of about forty-five Yemenite Jewish silversmiths started to work there. The aim of the workshop was to create a new style mainly based on traditional Yemenite work, to give the craftsmen an opportunity to pursue their art, and to provide them with a livelihood.[7] Production was of course chiefly for export. Living until then in extremely precarious conditions, and having no experience of the modern world, the silversmiths were very happy to be able to work and earn a living, but the divergences between their condition in Yemen and in Jerusalem were striking.

First of all they surrendered their social position as scholar-craftsmen, and became only artisans. They lost the close contact between themselves and their customers, for they were receiving anonymous orders for large numbers of exactly the same piece. Jewellery produced for an unknown customer could obviously not incorporate magical components. In the new workshop they had to produce not only according to the specifications of an impersonal commercial order, but also to employ new forms. The workshop at Bezalel made not only jewellery, but also other types of metalwork, chiefly objects connected with traditional Jewish religious life, like the candlesticks used every Friday during the Sabbath-eve meal; *seder* plates — the special ritual plate used on Passover eve, one of the most important Jewish festivals; Hanukkah lamps — the special lamps with eight burners, and so on. All these things were very different in style from those traditionally used by the Jews in Yemen, and the production was strange to them. There was also a significant change in working conditions. Used to small groups of craftsmen, debating the Bible and problems of Jewish philosophy while they worked, the Yemenites found themselves in one large noisy workshop, where it was impossible to concentrate. They nevertheless made some efforts to introduce intellectual values to the workshop. For instance they launched the custom of writing poems for festive occasions. These poems were traditional in form, but with secular and contemporary contents. They referred to events in the Academy, the return of the director, the opening of a new workshop and so on. The poems always stress their composers' satisfaction in working and earning their living.

Bezalel's intention was to create a new style. The Yemenite Jewish craftsmen, accustomed to the perpetual repetition of traditional forms and designs, had to work according to new patterns, very often created by the artistic directors of the school. They used traditional techniques, but also had to learn new ones. There was another new factor as well. In Yemen the time consumed in production was not very important, but here the silversmiths realised that the chief aim was to produce a large number of pieces and the time taken by the work was one of the important factors in the whole process.

However the Bezalel workshop represents only a relatively short period in the history of Yemenite silversmith work in Israel. On the eve of the first world war the school was closed and the silversmiths could not continue their profession. Most of them became builders, stonemasons and traders. Only a few found employment in other workshops, and even fewer were able to open their own establishments, using the experience they had acquired in Bezalel. In most cases these workshops still exist. Their work is of course based on modern techniques, but the style is mainly traditional, contrasting with what had come to be known as the Bezalel style.

The second large wave of immigration from Yemen to Israel, in the 1950s also included a large group of silversmiths. The same phenomenon occurred — it was impossible to absorb them according to their skills. Most of them were sent through the reception centres to new villages, where in due course they became farmers and chicken breeders. Those who got houses in small towns started to look for new jobs, but a small group continued and is continuing today in the craft. Here we can observe two trends. One group works for the larger shops, or in indiviudal workshops, and concentrates on developing its technical skills.

They do not much care for the traditional forms, and their production is based on the demands of the anonymous customer. They have studied jewellery types of other ethnic groups in Israel, and according to the situation of the market, they can produce jewellery in Moroccan or other styles. Generally speaking, they do not mix different styles, their productions are rather simple, with less ornamentation, and they omit types that require much labour.

But a small group of silversmiths still exist who work mostly for the Jewish community of Yemenite descent. They continue not only in their traditional work, but also in their traditional way of life. As many silversmiths used to do in Yemen, they wander from one settlement to another looking for commissions. In this way they come close to their customers and can make jewellery according to all the traditional rules. The customer usually does not specify the symbols, since they are not known to him, and the silversmith enjoys his full confidence in this respect. The economic situation of these craftsmen is not very good, but they always insist in working in this way as they experience great satisfaction and the work is more interesting. Wandering through the settlements they gather not only orders for jewellery, but have many opportunities of meeting interesting people, the old and the learned. They discuss religious problems with them, and this gives them a sense of the richness of life. In the settlements which they visit they are welcome and attractive guests. They are well entertained, the people talk to them about their problems, and ask for advice. They have become a sort of institution, and they feel very much at ease in this situation. Their production, as I have remarked, is based mainly on the traditional patterns, but it is simpler, and very far from the precision of the old forms.

The third group of silversmiths — the biggest — do not work as craftsmen. They have become farmers, and their economic situation is quite good, but there are a few, who, as they say, cannot be chicken-breeders only. They have no workshops, and no means of working in metal, or any economic need to do so, but they still find it very difficult to get accustomed to the new way of life. They remain very close to their traditional customs, spending all their free time reading the Bible and studying, but this activity does not give them the special status that they had before. However they have found a way to exploit the knowledge they had acquired as silversmiths in Yemen by preparing amulets for members of the community. In doing this they use the same books, they work in their traditional way and preserve their status as learned men, who can prepare preventive measures against evil. Some of them are so famous that members of other ethnic groups also come to them, to ask for help.

In this last example we can discern an important moment in the process of rapid change which has taken place in the new and very different situation. Let us be clear that we are dealing with a very specific type of craft. To be a good craftsman in traditional Yemenite society meant to combine technical and artistic skills with intellectual prowess. Only a learned silversmith could work in this craft and attain a high position in society. In the new Israeli situation all the circumstances combine to force the craftsmen to change their attitude to their work, but they have not been able to reconcile themselves to this, and have always made great efforts to preserve the intellectual values connected with their craft. We can observe this process in all the stages that we have discussed above. For example the Bezalel workers wrote poems. Equally the present day traditional craftsmen wander from one settlement to another, even though they have no real economic need to look for orders, since they can get them at home. Nevertheless the close contact with their customers gives them the feeling of supplementing their craft with intellectual values. And lastly — the craftsmen who cannot continue their manual work develop those elements of the craft which require intellectual efforts only.

Notes

1. S. D. Goitein, *Studies in Islamic History and Institutions* (Leiden, 1966), 329-50; H. Z. Hirschberg, *Israel ba-Arav* (Tel-Aviv, 1946); M. Zadoc, *Yehudei Teiman Toledoteiha ve-Orot Heyyeihem* (Tel-Aviv, 1967).

2. J. Halevy, 'Voyage au Nedjran', *Bulletin de la Société de Géographie de Paris,* VI (1873), 22.

3. E. Brauer, *Ethnologie der Jemenitischen Juden* (Heidelberg, 1934); J. Kafah, *Halikhot Teiman* (Jerusalem, 1969); S. Morag, *Ha—Iwrith she-b Peh Yehudei Teiman* (Jerusalem, 1963); J. N. Levi, *M-Tsfunoth Yehudei Teiman* (Tel-Aviv/ Jaffa, 1962); J. Ratzaby, ed., *Bo'i Teiman* ([Israel], 1947).

4. M. Narkiss, *The Artcraft of Yemenite Jews* (Jerusalem, 1949), 9-13 (in Hebrew).

5. Ratzaby, 145.

6. Levi, 47, 56-62; A. Lantzet, 'Tashbukh Lulu — Ateret ha-Kala ha-Yehudit mi-Zana', *Sefer Harel,* 1962, 176-82.

7. B. Schatz, *Bezalel* (Jerusalem, 1910).

Culturally-Based Science; The Potential for Traditional People, Science and Folklore

RAYNA GREEN   American Association for the Advancement of Science

FOR the past three years, I have been the Director of the Project on Native Americans in Science for the American Association for the Advancement of Science in Washington, D.C. Well might folklorists wonder what one of their profession could do for a scientific professional organisation or why that organisation would want a folklorist. The Association is known primarily as the publisher of *Science*, the distinguished weekly that reports science research and news to over 130,000 readers in the natural and social sciences. Moreover, the AAAS is either renowned or notorious, depending on whom one asks, for its commitments to public discussion of science policy. So what is a nice folklorist like me doing in an organisation like that? Actually, the Association has long supported various activities in the social sciences, and in 1968, it published Alan Lomax' *Folk Song Style and Culture*. So the connections with modern folkloristics are clearly there, if muted. Yet AAAS established my project for reasons somewhat different than those which usually govern its work in the social sciences. A major reason for the Association's commitment of effort and money was the Board's long term interest – as expressed through its Office of Opportunities in Science – to reverse the under-representation of women, minorities and the handicapped in the scientific and technical professions. The Board's perception of the dramatically low numbers of American Indians in scientific fields thus led them to establish a special project and to search for an Indian project director trained in the natural or applied social sciences.

Thus, as an Indian applied social scientist, I filled some job requirements neatly. It was, however, the second mandate of the Project that made someone with training in cultural analysis an imperative as Director. In January, 1975, the AAAS Board led by Margaret Mead, passed an important resolution. They stated: 'Be it resolved that the Board and Council of the Association: (a) formally recognize the contributions made by Native Americans in their own traditions of inquiry to the various fields of science, engineering and medicine and; (b) encourage and support the development and growth of natural and social science programs in which traditional Native American approaches and contributions to science, engineering and medicine are the subject of serious study and research.' Thus, however applied and Indian I might be, my training in folkloristics is especially appropriate for some of the tasks I've had to carry out under the auspices of the Project. I would like, in this paper, to suggest that the second mandate of the Project – that of encouraging and supporting the serious study of culturally-based science – should be taken more seriously by many traditional peoples besides American Indians, by scientists, by educators, and by folklorists and anthropologists. In short, I would like to demonstrate here that the seeming incongruity in what I do at AAAS is not incongruous at all, but natural and needed, for traditional people, for scientists and for social scientists trained in the analysis of traditional cultures.

Continuing into a fourth year, the Project has gone far in fulfilling both its mandates, the first – that of working to increase the pool of Indians in scientific fields – admittedly the most pressing; the second – that of supporting culturally-based science – the steady and presently growing thread binding the whole together. In yearly seminars on culturally-based science research and its applications to education and economic development; in speeches I make throughout the year; in meetings on mathematics and science education; in a forthcoming volume on the topic; and in projects this office assists, the second mandate of the Board is being fulfilled insofar as AAAS is concerned. However, the enormous needs felt by traditional peoples for this kind of support and the enormous benefits we at AAAS feel would accrue to all involved in such work prompt me to make an argument for the further involvement of a range of people. Thus, in this paper I would like to show why AAAS 'encourages the serious study' of culturally-based science by demonstrating the benefits to all involved through both the application of knowledge gained to the resolution of problems in educational, health and economic development and to the discipline and practice of biology, medicine, psychology, psychiatry, botany, agriculture, economics, linguistics, astronomy, mathematics, pharmacy, biochemistry, education, anthropology and folklore.

First, however, some definitions and guidelines will be set forth in order to clarify what this essay can and cannot do. The term, 'culturally-based science', is a non-academic way of saying 'ethnoscience', and it encompasses, as does 'ethnoscience', both substance and method. I am not constrained here, however, to offer a defense of ethnoscience as a field of study or as a methodology since the field has long since demonstrated its utility in the analysis of cultural materials. I am here simply assuming the worth of ethnoscience in general and am more concerned to illuminate specific contributions the applications of ethnoscientific or culturally-based scientific knowledge may make. Neither am I concerned to develop elaborate distinctions between 'non-Western science' and 'science' as those trained in a Western, rationalist system understand it. I am assuming the worth, utility and appropriateness of both. In fact, I am assuming that they are both forms of 'culturally-based science', and that each form has something to offer the other. So, this essay speaks of ethnoscience, in Clara Sue Kidwell's terms, as 'the attempt to comprehend scientific knowledge and scientific systems from the perspective of the group rather than from a single perspective, as that of Western, Anglo or European culture', unless, of course, the group in question is from a Western, Anglo or European origin. Further, this essay speaks of 'science' in the broadest sense, as human

attempts to explain material phenomenon and of 'group' in the broadest sense, as any group retaining a shared world view and shared forms of expressive behaviour. I will argue that 'science' is not the exclusive property of any group and that every group has a 'science' based on observation, experiment and tradition, whether the 'science' is called 'belief' or 'hypothesis'; whether 'science' is imparted traditionally through 'shamans' or 'books', whether scientific knowledge is developed through 'experiment' or 'trial-and-error observation', and whether knowledge is organised into a 'systematic body' or diffused throughout the range of cultural expression and behaviour. In other words, Western scientists' beliefs in black holes and charmed quarks; suburban white English-speaking teenager's belief that Coca-Cola is an effective spermicide; and the Navajo tribal belief that exposure to red ants causes bladder trouble are here treated as one and the same insofar as they represent part of the body of scientific knowledge for each group. Contrasts made between them below are not qualitative, but descriptive, each contrast attempting to show the manner in which the particular form of science operates and how and where it can be useful in specific contexts of dysfunctional as a 'universal'.

The definitions given above may help to illuminate the reasons for AAAS' involvement in developing the needed pool of American Indian scientific professionals as well as the needs for the development of culturally-based science. The pool of Native Americans in the scientific professions is tiny, including no more than 40 at the Ph.D. level in the natural sciences and about the same number in the social sciences. Even discounting Ph.Ds, the number working in educational or applied contexts, in industry for example, is still quite small. A number of analyses, including my own study of two years ago, have determined that the lack of Indian participation in science is as much due to an alienation from the traditions of Western science as from lack of access to science education, bad training in science or any of the other reasons conventionally given for 'minority' exclusion from scientific professionalism. Contrary to the general insistence of Western scientists that science is not culture bound and that it produces good, many native people feel that science and scientists are thoroughly Western, rather than 'universal', and that science is negative. They insist that the practice of Western science trains alien, unfeeling people who bring environmental and human damage in their wake. More importantly, they perceive themselves as among the increasing numbers of endangered species for which they hold scientists responsible. With good evidence on their side, Native people fear the Westernisation, and consequent alienation from their communities, of tribal members who become 'scientists' in the Western manner. They fear that Western science is the antithesis of traditional religious belief – a fear expressed by many Christian traditionalists – and that Natives trained in a Western tradition will lose their respect for 'the old ways'. Whether or not their perceptions are 'correct', their feelings do affect the career decisions of many young Native people, and those who do choose scientific training are well aware of the censure and suspicion which will attend their choice. Regrettably, many Western-trained scientists reinforce Native fears by describing Native tradition (i.e. science) as 'old wive's tales', 'primitive belief', 'myth' and 'folklore', and young Native students are told to 'give up' their old ideas in order to 'free their minds for the universal, objective truths' of science.

Yet Native people in America, like other regional or ethnic minority folk, know full well that their ability to survive depends on their attainment of self-determination, and that self-determination is in turn dependent on control of their own human and natural resources. For many land-based Indians who are rich in oil, timber, coal, uranium, molybdenum and that most precious resource, water, the dilemma is greatly exacerbated. What they have is needed and desired by the outside world, and, again with good evidence on their side, they cannot depend on outsiders to act in their best interests when it concerns exploitation of their resources. Whatever one's political feelings toward Indians, or, for that matter, Arabs, their analysis is understandable. Even if, like many communities, they did not own exploitable resources, they know the importance of a general science literacy in a world increasingly dependent on technology and increasingly short of the kinds of natural resources needed for survival. Mayors of small, rural towns and big cities; town, tribal and community council members; miners in coal mines; truck drivers; homeowners and hunter-gatherers – all must decide wisely about the allocation of precious resources for future survival. Likewise, they must make sensible decisions about maintaining good health. Thus, no matter who and where one is, access to who and what will operate in one's best interest is essential for suvival. For Native American people, and others, such an understanding means producing Native scientists trained in a Western system and committed to Native communities. But how may they resolve the paradox and train Indians who remain Indian, yet who have the skills that Western scientific training offers?

The resolution the tribes seek lies in their increasing insistence that learning is a two-way street, and their means of addressing the paradox increasingly lies in the development of culturally-based science and science education. As many people all over the world have begun to seek and investigate environmentally appropriate technologies, Native peoples have begun to investigate culturally appropriate science. In so doing, they have had to face yet other problems as onerous as the old ones, yet many tribes and individuals have begun to act vigorously to implement projects and programmes in culturally-based science. Either through direct assistance to these programmes or through other forms of indirect support, a network of those working in the field has been created, and the spin-off of information from one project to another can now be felt in new developments from individual programmes. Essentially, two kinds of approaches have been developed to match the needs in the diverse communities. One approach evolves out of tribal and community education efforts and the other out of efforts directed at health and economic development. The one depends largely on the work of non-professionals (i.e. educators and students) to develop the body of knowledge and the other depends on the cooperative and interdependent team of professionals (i.e. scientists, social scientists, traditional healers and health professionals). Both kinds of projects have immediate applications to education, economic development, health improvement and professional development for the tribes, and both involve entire communities in league with sympathetic, trustworthy, interested 'outsiders' strictly accountable to the tribe. And both strive to integrate the seeking of knowledge (research) with the uses of knowledge (application) into a traditionally holistic system where world view and its institutionalised manifestations (i.e. religion, education, personal and interpersonal behaviour) are themselves integrated. Further, both approaches operate from a perspective which insists on the value of every institution and individual in the community with regard to the development and use of knowledge, rather than from a perspective which values people called 'scientists' and 'scholars' and institutions called 'schools', which hold a monopoly on the development and dissemination of knowledge.

In the first kind of effort, one of the Indian community colleges has implemented a programme of general science and specialist pre-professional education in which traditional healers, herbalists, medicine men and women are present in every science class offered by the college. All science majors are also 'apprenticed' to a traditionalist during the course of their continuing professional education. These traditionalists are there, like their compatriots in the reservation clinics, to teach native science in tandem with Western science rather than to conflict with it. The students are thus encouraged to learn the best of both systems and to put both to use, when and where appropriate. Other students in the nearby tribal high school, have worked with a curriculum development group hired by the tribe − including Native and non-native educators − to prepare a bilingual and bicultural science and maths curriculum for Grades One through Twelve. Senior students at another high school nearby have prepared an extensive analysis of traditional area ecosystem management, partly to develop science materials for their school and partly to give to the tribe for its consideration in its new agriculture programme. In North Dakota, Indian teachers worked with a white English-speaking geologist to develop a general science curriculum based on the traditional world views and sites of area tribes, and this system is being used in tribal schools. And one of the regional universities in Brazil now trains science educators in Native systems so that they can teach Indians in a system that includes and respects Native science. In the foregoing projects, three goals are apparent: one the development of culturally-appropriate knowledge for science education; another the documentation of knowl-

edge which can be pursued further in tribal health and economic development; and another, the development of a new form of cultural reinforcement for Native people who require professional encouragement toward the sciences.

The second approach tribes use is both more applicable to the immediate resolution of pressing economic and health problems as well as to the general thrust of this essay. Based on the same principles as the educational projects and even utilising data collected in those programmes, this approach is more specific in its immediate or future potentials for application. Every scholar will have some familiarity with this area of application, even if only in the most marginal knowledge about the development of native plant substances into quinine, digitalis and mescaline. Most social scientists would surely be familiar with the interests psychiatrists have had in native forms of healing. But I suspect that few would really know how little systematic research has been undertaken on how few native plant materials, medicines and healing techniques. This real lack of attention to these substances and techniques, in spite of the dramatic success of ones which have entered into the Western repertoire, focuses on a rationale for paying attention, as well as underscoring the difficulties of undertaking such work. Once again, example serves to illustrate both what is being done along with the problems of doing it.

Two tribes, one in California, the other in Montana, developed what they believe to be as complete a documentation of Native plants and their uses as possible, given the large number of traditional healers, herbalists and agriculturalists who have died or no longer practice their craft. Having developed the knowledge into curriculum materials for the schools, both tribes now wish to undertake a secondary phase of scientific analysis for the materials to determine any medicinal and nutritional values. They want to assess, based on hard data, which native plants are likely candidates for cultivation and for commercial medicinal development. In each instance, they have two concerns: the low nutritional status of a people converted to welfare diets of processed foods and the low economic status of peoples with little possibility of industrial development on reservation. To do this assessment, they require the assistance of nutritionists, biochemists, economic botanists, pharmaceutical analysts and developers, and agricultural development specialists. Yet, based on their past experiences with both social scientists and corporations, they fear exploitation with little or no return to tribal members. They fear insensitivity from scientists who will want access to all material, no matter how sacred or private. And they know full well that the chance of retaining scientists, who are both skilled in their fields and culturally sensitive, is small. Another project, undertaken by an Indian junior college science faculty, involves using students in the collection and biochemical analysis of plant materials once used by the now absent native populations of the area. Without traditional herbalists and healers, or perhaps anthropologists and archaeologists to assist in reconstruction, the team does not have the expertise to complete a pharmacopoeia or suggest applications based on traditional medicines, since any efficacy some medicines may have had probably depended on various combinations of substances rather than single herbs alone. In each instance given above, some key component necessary to a complete analysis and potential application is missing, whether the missing component involves needed, trustworthy people operating in a predictable and trustworthy situation or missing human links in the analytical chain.

The same tribe which initiated the 'medicine man in the classroom' programme has begun to act on a comprehensive plan involving complete teams of data collectors, analysts and applications specialists — some Native, some non-Native — all under the governance of strict rules concerning access to and use of the materials. This tribe has assembled anthropologists of all kinds, traditional healers, herbalists and diagnosticians, religious leaders, science educators, medical personnel, Indian and non-Indian teachers, Indian students and community members and Indian and non-Indian scientists to work on the initial production of a native anatomical dictionary and ethnomedical encyclopedia. This project has been accompanied, or rather preceded, by years of tribal attention to these materials and the consequent use of these materials in their schools. This project, as with every effort the tribe undertakes involving its traditonal knowledge, is governed by rules concerning the collection,

analysis, description, storage, and application of the material, and tribal and non-tribal members work under committee and contractual oversight as to who does what with which materials. The 'rules' follow traditional guidelines concerning who should know and receive certain materials and new rules have been developed to accommodate a concern for the involvement of 'outsiders' as well as for new uses to which the material might be put. The tribe plans second stages of biophysical analysis for some material — probably undertaken in the tribal college with scientists on contract to the tribe — and a third stage of applications to the tribe's new agricultural programme, to a new Indian medical school curriculum, and further, to tribal educational systems. Such cooperative team efforts are being undertaken all over the world, primarily for the benefit of 'traditional' peoples, but in a final analysis, for the benefit of all humanity. The mass cultivation of the Asian winged bean for cheaply, quickly produced, high protein diet supplements; the development of new applications for theories based on South American Indian models of population and genetic management; the 'rediscovery' of native slash-and-burn techniques for high yield and quick reforestation in Indian and commercial timber operations; the new utilisation of traditional fish conservation methods for the growth of Indian commercial hatchery operations; the cultivation of native species instead of worthless, imported ones in reclamation of coal-stripped land; the application of native architectural principles to reduction of materials cost and energy waste in contemporary building; the cultivation of native plants to create 200 new products, including precious oil and rubber substitutes — all have evolved out of team efforts inspired by traditional peoples and their traditional scientific knowledge.

In all the lists of how team approaches can operate and the benefit that such projects can bring, I would be remiss if I did not point out that the people who undertake these tasks have more than simple economic and physical benefits at heart. Certainly, economic development linked to tradition makes good sense, especially when introduced to people who have never before undertaken such development. Those who have seen Western introductions of high technology programmes fail in lesser developed countries will be persuaded of the sense that such an alternative effort makes. More importantly to traditional peoples, however, such projects make a major contribution to the spiritual and cultural strength of the people while, at the same time, they contribute to their physical well-being. In this instance, reinforcement of traditional scientific tradition accrues to reinforcement of religious tradition, or where religious tradition is not so closely linked to scientific knowledge, a general strengthening of the cultural framework can be affected in ways not usually possible with the customary forms of 'cultural revival'. For an enquiry into modes and content of scientific knowledge is potentially more profound than enquiries into the visible manifestations of cultural behaviour in the verbal, visual and kinesic arts. Those are the manifestations of 'culture' usually 'preserved' by traditional people and certainly the ones usually 'studied' by scholars. Those more obscure, less visible, less accessible forms of cultural behaviour suffer from both community and scholarly neglect, and they are more likely to disappear, with the deaths of older people, than pots, songs and dances. Unless transferred onto pots or into songs and dances – an occurrence which does happen and which offers a role for folklorists of which I will later speak – these ideas, concepts and forms of knowledge are too connected to the frailer human vessel. Yet these ideas are intimately connected with the most profound forms of life, with language, for example, and with the most sacred, most private and most individually held beliefs. Knowledge of such materials is often restricted to certain types of people, by virtue of family, clan or gender membership, and in some instances, may not be passed on if the appropriate person does not exist or refuses to learn the tradition. Thus access to these materials is difficult, requiring either a perseverance or 'natural' entrance that most outsiders and some insiders never have or gain. But traditional peoples must make the decisions regarding their needs and pursue them, using a team approach which distinguishes who can do which task. The motive must be to discover the widest range of benefits that this kind of research and its practical application can offer, whether educational, economic, physical or spiritual.

I am concerned, however, beyond an analysis of the benefits of culturally-based science for any group who has the knowledge to build on, to suggest the benefits of participation in its research and application to 'outsiders' who possess skills needed for the projects. Certainly, most scientists, no matter what their field of specialisation, would wish good economic, physical and cultural health to other humans, and certainly, the motivation for some into science is the desire to make positive contributions to humanity. Just as certainly, there have been scientists who undertook work in communities because they felt that work would bring them personal gain, and we are all familiar with the results of such motivations. Yet, however convincing and conventional the arguments may be for charitable involvement in work, I am not going to argue that such worthy intentions are reason enough for scientists' involvement. Traditional communities know, as well as they know the results of self-interest, the hazards of accepting 'good deeds' from 'sympathetic' outsiders, and they know that the best results come when, in good faith, all parties benefit in some positive way from their efforts. I would now like to consider those benefits, some obvious, some not so obvious, for the natural and social sciences in general and for folklore in particular.

The obvious argument for any scientists' or folklorists' involvement in culturally-based science is for the 'contributions to knowledge' this kind of study can make. Indisputably, there have been and would be major contributions. But I could never, with good conscience, recommend that such a goal – that is, the increase of non-native or native knowledge – would suffice as a sole reason for involvement. For many traditional communities, the seeking of knowledge is admirable; the piling up of knowledge for its own sake is both peculiar and dangerous; knowledge is specific, not general, and meant to be put to use in specific contexts. Such an increase in the body of knowledge would then violate the understandings of most communities about the uses to which knowledge is put. Moreover, even in non-traditional terms, such a goal is the most unimaginative reason for the expenditure of effort, when change of the discipline is as much a possibility as additions to it. It is in such change that more knowledge is inevitably put to its best and most creative uses.

For the natural sciences, work in culturally-based science could make more than a mere cliché out of science's admitted need to 'humanise' itself. By definition, culturally-based science is a 'humanised' science, and to undertake it requires considerations never made even in the concerns for regulation of research with human and animal substances. Those concerns generally revolve around cost-benefit analyses, for example the relative danger versus the relative virtue of a particular drug, and the potential of research for physical harm to those creatures involved in experiments. If making judgements based on religious and cultural considerations would humanise a science too sure of its universality and objectivity, then culturally-based science holds the key.

Many would also say of the natural sciences that their very obsession with objectivity is the key to their inhumanity, and that a counter influence, to be found in non-Western, non-rationalist traditions, would multiply the maximum benefits of science. Perhaps the rewards of having alternative systems of scientific knowledge and enquiry available will have to wait for a dramatic demonstration, a discovery in Western terms, made by someone capable of operating in both traditions. In the absence of that dramatic event, however, culturally-based science can both bring a new kind of knowledge – a knowledge which changes the scientific disciplines – and humanise those disciplines simultaneously.

For folklore – a discipline which already thinks of itself as humanised – the arguments will have to be different and more extensive than for those in the sciences. Obviously too, much of what will be said about folklore could apply to those most culturally-based of the social sciences, anthropology and linguistics, as well. But here the contributions to a study of culturally-based science have to make their basis of concern the discipline and practice of folklore – some of the unmended flaws and predilections in the theory and practice of the discipline, and some of the impacts changes in the discipline might have on those the discipline most impacts on, the folk. I refer here both to the continuing folkloristic passion for romanticism and primitivism which characterises even the most sophisticated of folklore theory and to the effects application of certain popular theories actually have on those human beings that folklorists call their informants.

I would insist that a careful and monitored participation in culturally-based science would force folklorists into the mainstream of the applied social sciences from which they have excluded themselves and in so doing, would further force them to codify professional ethics for the practice of applied folklore. Further, I would suggest that such changes would affect the other areas of folkloristic research, and would work toward dissolution of the parochialism, narrowness and theoretical regressivism that continues to hamper the discipline's progress and recognition. Current definitions of applied activities in the field rarely move beyond the term as relevant to the production of anything but folk festivals and curriculum materials. The range of activities defined under the term applied, as it is used in anthropology, have continued to elude folkloristics, and that resistance to a broadening of participation in applications derives in turn from the burdens imposed by narrow definitions of what folklorists do with the material they call 'folklore'. The resistance of folklorists to the genuinely varied fields of specialisation and activities possible in the fields of applied folklore mirrors their resistance to a codification of ethics, a codification common to every other applied field.

Since most of those who need and want culturally-based science demand ethics in practice, folklorists would be forced to respond by obeying, if not developing, the rules. My view is that resistance to the development of ethical codes stems, not from inherent insensitivity or callousness, but from a failure to perceive how ethical codes can be applied to folklore. Placed in that light, as well as in the context of folklorists' limited experience with a range of applications, their failures seem both understandable and remediable. I want to insist here that culturally-based scientific development offers, not only an exciting means of making human and scholarly contributions, but a measurable way of rectifying some problems in the discipline. Participation in applications and the consequent necessary development of ethics then seems a major contribution to the discipline.

But there are other disciplinary problems which participation in culturally-based science projects might remedy. However quaint and narrow text-centred folkloristics might have been or continues to be, the current theoretical passion for performance-centred theory reinforces the limits of folkloristic application. Performance-centred theory consigns traditional materials to the domains of art and artistry, and thus prevents folklorists from dealing effectively in an applied context with materials whose major function and potential application is not artistic. Consider, for example, a Navajo healing ceremony and the components of it that folklorists regard as their proper domain. Such a ceremony, called a 'sing' in the vernacular, may consist of many parts including dry or sand paintings, sung and/or spoken chants, prayers and invocations, and the administering of medicinal compounds by a 'singer'. Conventional folkloristic study used to focus on the texts, symbols, and medicinal recipes. Contextual and performance theory forced a welcome refocusing on those items only in the context of the event itself, its place in the life of the patient, the 'singer' and others in the culture, and the transmissions of these events within the culture. Thus, the performer, the performance event, the structure and role of that event — all would be the appropriate concern of a modern folklorist. Others, interested in the cultural and psychiatric workings and well-being of those affected by this event, would concern themselves with the functions the ceremony had. But very few would be interested in applying their skills in event analysis to a further analysis of the tangible parts of that event which might have functions beyond the vaguely cultural and the specifically psychiatric realms of behaviour.

Most folklorists, in fact, would shy away from examining either the scientific bases for the efficacy of medicinal materials, such a study being neither in their realm of expertise nor appropriate to their definitions of folklore. They might wonder if a particular medicine was effective, and some would even attribute to it real values, whether physical or psychiatric. But, like most anthropologists, being enjoined by the restraints of cultural relativism to accept native beliefs, they would eschew examination of the merits or demerits of the native systems. Most would not want to make further enquiries into the efficacy of herbs, lest they appear either to question the validity of traditional systems, or prove its invalidity. The result of cultural relativism thus restricts folkloristic attentions to the utterance of beliefs rather than

turning their attentions to an investigation of how that belief might contain scientific knowledge of potential value. If they document such knowledge at all, it is recorded simply as the expressive record of belief — the 'One Thousand Chinese Herbal Recipes' approach to folklore — or as evidence of the cultural typology into which the group fits — the 'Group X: Witchcraft, Power and Culture Change' approach to folklore. Thus the humanity and niceness which makes folklorists think of themselves as unlike scientists and which makes them believe they don't need a code of ethics also consigns much of what they uncover to the arts-and-crafts midden pile.

The very language folklorists and others use, in spite of many attempts to reform terminology and taxonomy toward less culturally prescriptive words, helps in consigning traditional science to the anthropological trash heap. Beliefs, customs and myths are not the stuff of science in the Western world, and few attempts at ethnoscientific definition by group have rid folklorists' vocabularies of those words. A participation in culturally-based scientific research and application, however, would necessarily change folkloristic perspective on those materials that give the discipline so much trouble in definition and terminology. Instead of myths and so forth, folklorists would study traditional science and the various forms of scientific enquiry and practice. They would document important scientific knowledge rather than insignificant or wrong beliefs and customs. Folklorists would study potentially useful scientific contributions instead of psychologically profound but incomprehensible myths. And if the products of traditional scientific enquiry are science, then those who produced and practiced such knowledge would be scientists, scholars, linguists, physicians and colleagues instead of witchdoctors, medicine men, shamans and astrologers. In short, the study of culturally-based science offers the profession a way to stop demeaning the materials, the subjects and the practitioners of the discipline. It represents an opportunity to accept the seriousness, validity and utility of what they know and what we study.

If folklore is such a flawed discipline, I hear professionals saying, what then could it offer traditional cultures in culturally-based scientific studies. But it has much to offer. The curious thing is that, with respect to the very materials and systems involved in culturally-based studies, folklore's very problems as a discipline can also be its virtues. The first major contribution possible involves folklore's absorption with texts, with artifacts, with discrete expressive items. Folklorists have always analysed texts for their reflection of cultural content, but once they have noted the existence and content of the material, little further analysis has taken place. Traditional texts have rarely been used, for example, to develop a body of knowledge about native astronomical systems, but rather as examples of the group's beliefs in astronomical systems, one group oriented toward the sun, the other toward the moon and so forth. And then sun or moon symbols could be pointed out on pottery or in pictographs to demonstrate the power of that symbol for the culture. Rarely, however, as in a recent case, has analysis produced documentary records of sixteenth-century supernovae observed and recorded by native peoples and that documentation used to explain other celestial events important to astrophysics and thus to weather and catastrophe prediction. Rarely have the pottery or painted pictographs of dead and living peoples been used, as they were recently, to reconstruct maps of old irrigation canals now put to use in a contemporary farm irrigation project. Rarely have folklorists helped to recover, as they did recently, numbering systems from chants and beadwork in order to teach native mathematics in the school system. But folklorists and some anthropologists are the only scholars trained to examine these materials and to break them down into discrete and significant parts. They are trained to take texts, pots, pictures and designs apart, to develop taxonomies and make lists, without getting lost in cultural descriptions of the whole. They are trained to follow up information gained in one interview with information gained elsewhere. And they are trained to look at and where scientists never look — at those artistic, expressive materials that are the antithesis of science and the essence of culturally-based science.

It should now be clear why folklorists both can and ought to work in this branch of science and why scientists should be interested in this branch of folklore. It should, I hope, be clear why traditional peoples with scientific knowledge to document would want both kinds of scientists involved along with their scientists. All can make major contributions to the fields of study and to the people they represent, as well as to mankind in general. In redefining the terms under which some scholarly disciplines operate and in directing efforts toward real and profound applications of knowledge for human benefit, a scholarly mission is redefined as well for a greater good. The development of the new field of culturally-based science can have wider benefits for a wider number of people than either the older, narrower definitions of science as it stood alone in Western terms or the older definitions of culture as cultures stood alone in terms no Westerner could understand. The Board of the American Association for the Advancement of Science saw its commitment to culturally-based Native science as the other side of a two-way street. I see it as a bridge — for traditional peoples, for scientists, for social scientists — for the merging of useful knowledge, rather than for the continuing separation of it into mutually incomprehensible categories.

A Century of the Study of Folklore of Archeological Sites, and Prospects for the Future

L. V. GRINSELL, O.B.E.   City Museum, Bristol (retired)

THE study of the popular beliefs and legends relating to archaeological sites in Britain began long before the word *folklore* was coined in 1846, or the Folklore Society was established in 1878. References to the subject occur for example in the writings of John Aubrey,[1] William Stukeley,[2] Rev. W. C. Borlase,[3] T. Stephens,[4] R. Perrott,[5] and Thomas Wright,[6] in most instances in connection with megalithic sites.

The attitudes of earlier investigators have however varied. Writing of the Borestone, an Early Christian monument in Perthshire, an author in the *Statistical Account of Scotland* (1791-9) observed: 'there are many traditions and legends connected with this stone, but they are too absurd to be committed to writing'.[7] In 1834 W. J. Thoms, whose influence later contributed to the founding of the Folklore Society, wrote:

How many an antiquary, who has travelled miles to see a druidical monument, has cried 'Pish' — at the legend, with which his peasant guide would illustrate it, when reflection would have told him, that under the garb of fiction the truth of history is frequently con- concealed.[8]

In 1862 John Thurnam, a distinguished and far-sighted archaeologist of his day, wrote:

It is only necessary to add that the story of Wayland and his Smithy shows the import- ance, in connexion with the history of ancient pagan beliefs of our country, of col- lecting and putting on record all local tra- ditions — wherever found and however idle they may appear — before the progress of modern education and enlightenment shall have entirely eradicated them.[9]

When the Folklore Society was founded in 1878 it was believed by many of its leading promoters, including Sir Laurence Gomme and E. B. Tylor, that it would be possible to fill out some of the details of the life of prehistoric man from the lore of the contemporary peasant. So also Edward Clodd observed, 'we have but to scratch the rustic to find the barbarian underneath'.[10] Thus the first published List of Members contained the names of notable archaeologists including (Sir) A. W. Franks, (Sir) John Lubbock, William Pengelly, and (Sir) John Evans, whose son (Sir) Arthur contributed to vol. VI of *Folk-lore* a masterly paper on 'The Roll-right Stones and their Folk-lore'.[11] Even O. G. S. Crawford wrote in his *Long Barrows of the Cots-wolds* that 'it is one of the objects of these researches to discover evidence of the beliefs and rituals of the makers (of the stone circles and long barrows) . . . The best clues are in the customs and traditions which have been recorded about indi-vidual monuments. But the passing of three or four thousand years and the disturbing influence of at least five invasions have both wrought much havoc'.[12]

When I began by own study of the folklore of archaeological sites in about 1930, I was partly influenced by this belief in the utility of folklore to the prehistorian. My present belief is that the study of folklore relating to prehistoric sites con-tributes little or nothing to our knowledge of those who built them; but may and sometimes does contribute materially to our knowledge of their later history. In many instances megalithic monu-ments were Christianised by having a cross carved or placed on them. In some instances, traditional attribution of Iron Age hill-forts to the Civil Wars resulted from their re-use during the period of those wars. Apart from this, the subject is worthy of study in its own right as a kind of oral literature possessing elements of considerable charm.

In 1912 Albany Major, Secretary of the Earthworks Committee of the Congress of Archaeological Societies, appealed to the Folklore Society to put on record the folklore of ancient earthworks; but nothing material resulted from this suggestion.[13] Some years afterwards a useful paper on the folklore of Aberdeenshire stone circles came from the pen of James Ritchie.[14] The legendary history of Stonehenge was the subject of papers by Laura Hibbard Loomis[15] and Stuart Piggott.[16]

The year 1934 was marked in the history of our subject by the publication of the first volume of the *Corpus du Folklore Préhistorique en France et dans les Colonies Françaises,* edited and largely written by Emile Nourry under the pseudonym Pierre Saintyves. The work as a whole is in three volumes, comprising 1,540 pages in all, of which 300 pages deal with flint arrowheads, stone axeheads and other implements, and the rest with the folklore of megalithic sites.[17] It was, incidentally, the year when I joined the Folklore Society, and at one of the first meetings I attended, I had the pleasure of meeting Lady Alice Gomme, widow of the Society's first Secretary Sir Laurence Gomme. Largely inspired by the work of Pierre Saintyves and his collaborators, a project was set on foot, under the auspices of this Society and with support from the Prehistoric Society, to record the folklore of prehistoric remains.[18] Launched in December 1939 its timing could scarcely have been more unfortunate. None the less, Dr Edith M. Guest collected material from Cumberland, Westmorland, Northumberland and Durham until her death in 1942; material from the Newbury region was published by H. J. E. Peake;[19] a useful paper on the folklore of the megaliths in the Medway valley in Kent was published the same year.[20] A card catalogue of material from the other English counties was compiled by 1941, when further work was deferred until after the War. Apart from occasional incursions into parts of the subject,[21] it was not until retirement in April 1972 that it became possible to assemble the material from the British Isles for publication, in a volume which appeared in 1976.[22] The Welsh part of the inventory was prepared with assistance from Mr Arthur Ap Gwyn, Dr G. M. Ashton, Robin Gwyndaf,

Dr E. D. Jones and Mr Donald Moore, and the Scottish part with the assistance of Dr Alan Bruford of the School of Scottish Studies and various Scottish prehistorians.

The resulting inventory showed that nearly all the material collected falls under a couple of dozen headings: a stone cult embodying healing and other virtues; Christianisation; attribution to the Devil; heathenism; a solar cult; giants; fairies; ghosts; Arthurian tradition; Ossianic and Irish traditions; other medieval traditions including Sir Bevis of Hampton, Jack o'Kent, Michael Scot, and Robin Hood; historical personages and events; assemblies and calendar customs; building legends; petrifaction, usually for wrongdoing; movement of stones; stones supposedly immovable; number mysticism; countless stones; fear of retribution for disturbing an antiquity; buried treasure (sometimes guarded by a dragon); and folk etymology.

For various reasons Ireland was omitted from this survey. Until recently the bulk of the Irish material has been successfully excluded from most English readers by being published in Irish; but, apart from that, the sheer quantity of folklore attached to prehistoric sites in Ireland is such that it can best be handled by those resident in Ireland as a whole-time job extending over several years.

For the rest, outstanding tasks include:

(i) examination of the literature in Welsh, Gaelic and Manx for folklore published only in those languages.

(ii) preparation of an inventory of folklore relating to Roman and later sites down to the Norman Conquest and, if possible, to the end of the medieval period, say 1540. Until that has been done, the folklore of prehistoric sites cannot be studied in chronological perspective.

(iii) preparation of an inventory of folklore relating to natural phenomena resembling prehistoric sites, such as unusually shaped rock outcrops, for the purpose of comparative study.

(iv) a study of the use made of folklore in works of fiction, including children's fiction, which may contribute to our knowledge of how legends sometimes adapt themselves to external influences.

(v) the recording of folklore heard by archaeologists in the course of fieldwork or during their excavations. Ideally, each archaeological excavation should have a recorder of folklore.

The British material has to be considered in the context of Western Europe as a whole. For France, the comprehensive, but somewhat uneven *Corpus du Folklore Préhistorique,* is now being supplemented and given better order in the folklore sections of the *Inventaire des Mégalithes de la France* (1963 onwards), published by the Centre National des Recherches Scientifiques, and by other publications, including the various volumes of *Contributions au Folklore des Provinces de France* (1935 to date), and some important studies with distribution maps, mostly by J. Cartraud, in the *Bulletin de la Société de Mythologie Française* since 1956. Of unusual importance is a paper by Roger Agache,[23] explaining his procedure of examining the local legends before arranging his flying programme for the aerial photography of archaeological sites. A field called Champ de la Danse, containing vegetation rings, known locally as Ronds de Fées, was shown to contain a group of prehistoric round barrows. In a popular, but reliable and well illustrated form, there are the *Guides Noires* (editions Tchou) in the series *La France Mystérieuse,* of which the volumes on Brittany, the Val de Loire, and Corsica are particularly informative on the folklore of ancient sites.

The Iberian Peninsula has megalithic monuments whose folklore is the subject of a paper by Amades,[24] which indicates the scope of the subject, and the Portuguese material was covered by Leite de Vasconcellos.[25] The monuments of the Talayotic culture in Majorca have associated folklore which has been studied by Llompart.[26] In Sardinia, the nuraghi, giants' tombs and other prehistoric sites have folklore which has been exhaustively studied by Losengo and by Enrica Delitala.[27]

To conclude: four points need emphasis. The first is the similarity of folklore motifs relating, for example, to megalithic monuments in all the areas passed under review, although there are, of course, regional variations such as legends of Gargantua, peculiar to certain parts of France. The second is the element of chance: whether a prehistoric site has attracted any folklore. A broad generalisation, to which there are many exceptions, is that the commoner a particular type of prehistoric site is in a given area, the less likely it is to have attracted folklore, because it is taken for granted. On the other hand, an unusual feature in a locality tends to call for explanation and so to generate folklore. The point can be illustrated by the folklore of the Beedon round barrow in Berkshire, and Wick Barrow in West Somerset, both in areas where such objects are uncommon; yet in the counties of Dorset and Wiltshire where barrows can be counted in their thousands, very few have any recorded folklore. What is equally striking is that a major monument, such as the West Kennet long barrow, appears to have no recorded traditions. The third point is that a good deal of forgotten folklore survives fossilised in local names such as the Cock Crow Stone, the Giant's Grave, Robin Hood's Butts, and many others. The fourth point is that a large proportion, perhaps more than half, of the recorded traditions are now being kept alive, if at all, only by their existence in publications, or by their occasional revival on broadcasting or television programmes, or in the more reliable works of fiction. It is difficult to find any areas in Western Europe so remote and secluded as to have escaped the influence of the popular media.

Notes

1. John Aubrey, *Monumenta Britannica* c. 1690. (Edited facsimile, Sherborne, 1980).

2. William Stukeley, *Stonehenge: a Temple Restor'd to the British Druids* (London, 1740); *idem, Abury: a Temple of the British Druids* (London, 1743).

3. W. C. Borlase, *Antiquities of Cornwall* (London, 1754).

4. T. Stephens, 'On the names of cromlechau', *Archaeologia Cambrensis,* 3rd Series, II (1856), 99-109.

5. R. Perrott, 'On . . . stones called dancers in northern Gaul and Brittany', *Archaeologia Cambrensis,* 3rd Series, IV (1858), 388-96.

6. Thomas Wright, 'On the legend of Wayland Smith', *Journal of the British Archaeological Association*, XVI (1860), 50-58; *idem*, 'On the local legends of Shropshire', *Collectanea Archaeologica,* I (1862), 50-66.

7. Sir John Sinclair, *Statistical Account of Scotland,* 21 vols (1791-9).

8. W. J. Thoms, ed., *Lays and Legends of France* (London, 1834), vi, n.

9. John Thurnam, 'On Wayland's Smithy . . . ', *Wiltshire Archaeological Magazine,* VII (1862), 321-33.

10. R. M. Dorson, *The British Folklorists: a History* (London, 1968), 250.

11. Sir Arthur Evans, 'The Rollright Stones and their Folklore', *Folk-lore,* VI (1895), 5-50.

12. O. G. S. Crawford, *Long Barrows of the Cotswolds* (Gloucester, 1925).

13. Albany Major, 'The folklore of earthworks', *Folk-lore,* XXIII (1912), 115.

14. James Ritchie, 'Folklore of the Aberdeenshire stone circles', *Proceedings of the Society of Antiquaries of Scotland,* LX (1926), 304-13.

15. Laura H. Loomis, 'Geoffrey of Monmouth and Stonehenge', *Publications of the Modern Language Association of America,* XLV (1930), 400-15.

16. Stuart Piggott, 'The sources of Geoffrey of Monmouth: the Stonehenge story', *Antiquity,* XV (1941), 305-19.

17. Pierre Saintyves, *Corpus du Folklore Préhistorique en France et dans les Colonies Françaises,* 3 vols (Paris, 1934-6).

18. L. V. Grinsell, 'Scheme for recording the folklore of prehistoric remains', *Folk-lore,* L (1939), 323-32.

19. H. J. E. Peake, 'The folklore of prehistoric remains in the Newbury district', *Transactions of the Newbury District Field Club,* VIII (1946), 250-4.

20. J. H. Evans, 'Notes on the folklore . . . of the Kentish megaliths', *Folk-lore,* LVII (1946), 36-43.

21. L. V. Grinsell, 'Early funerary superstitions in Britain', *Folk-lore,* LXIV (1953), 271-81; *idem*, 'The ferryman and his fee', *Folk-lore,* LXVIII (1957), 257-69; *idem*, 'Barrow treasure in fact, tradition and legislation', *Folk-lore,* LXXVIII (1967), 1-38.

22. *idem, Folklore of Prehistoric Sites in Britain* (Newton Abbot, 1976).

23. Roger Agache, 'Vues aériennes et folklore de cropmarks circulaires au nord d' Amiens. Les "ronds de fées du champ de la danse",' *Bulletin de la Société préhistorique française*, LVIII (1961), 224-36.

24. Juan Amades, 'Mitologia megalitica', *Ampurias,* III (1941), 113-34.

25. José Leite de Vasconcellos, *Tradicoes populares de Portugal* (Lisbon, 1882); *idem*, *Religioes de Lusitania* (Lisbon, 1897), I, 289-93.

26. G. Llompart, 'Nomenclatura popular de la cultura de los talayots en Mallorca', *Revista de Dialectologia y Tradiciones Populares,* XVI (l960), 288-94.

27. Enrica Delitala, 'Materiali per lo studio degli esseri fantastici del mondo tradizionale sardo', *Studi Sardi,* XXIII (1975 [1974]), 306-54; R. Losengo, *Folklore della terra de delle pietre in Sardegna* (Unpublished thesis, University of Cagliari, 1960-61); *idem*, 'Le janus sarde', *Atti del Convegno di Studi religiose sardi,* Vol 2 (Padua, 1963), 269-84; *idem*, 'La pietrificazione punitiva nella tradizione orale sarda', *Bolletino del repertorio e del atlante demonologico sardo,* Vol. 2 (Cagliari, 1967), 13-26.

The Welsh Folk-Narrative Tradition

ROBIN GWYNDAF   Welsh Folk Museum

SINCE the Middle Ages, which gave us the classic tales of the *Mabinogion*,[1] Wales has not seen professional storytellers with a large repertoire of long *Märchen, Novelle* and heroic tales. Yet, up to the beginning of the twentieth century, the role of the ordinary storyteller in the Welsh community was an important one. He was the active folk narrative tradition-bearer, who kept the old and the new tales and traditions alive by telling them to others. He would usually have a ready audience. Those were the days when the community not only had to create its own culture and entertainment, but also when the magic of folklore delighted and sustained the spirit of man.

By today there has been a change. Many people believe that they have less need for magic and, consequently, belief in the supernatural has diminished. There is less leisure and more haste. Much of our culture is ready-made. In areas where the Welsh language has died, a great wealth of legends and traditions have died with it. There has been a weakening of the Welsh pastoral way of life and a movement towards urbanisation. In some districts there has been a gradual breakdown of communal life and traditional channels of transmission, and in many rural areas depopulation and the disappearance of old, deeply-rooted families with strong kinship connections have greatly affected the continuity of the narrative tradition.

And yet, when all is said, we still have in Wales many passive and active folk-narrative tradition-bearers: men and women who still remember the tales and who are prepared to tell them again – if we are prepared to listen with sympathy and understanding. There are also new channels of transmission, such as the radio, the television and the telephone. Although many of these people do not themselves believe in the supernatural elements of the tales, they will recite them with sincerity and reverence. Their attitude is that of the Carmarthenshire man who confessed:

> I cannot tell how the truth may be,
> I say the tale as 'twas said to me.[2]

These then are the people who have been recorded by the Welsh Folk Museum since 1964, with the emphasis on the Welsh-speaking areas of the country.[3] The purpose of the work is to make as complete a survey as possible of Welsh folk narratives, from very early times to the present day, and to record as much information as possible about the social background to their recitation.

The term 'folk narratives' is here used to mean the traditional prose tales, legends (*Memorates*), jokes and anecdotes which have formed part of the cultural inheritance of the people of Wales from very early times to the present day. The narratives are traditional in the sense that most of them have a long history and were transmitted mainly, though not exclusively, by oral means, in the words of the old chronicler: *iocunde et memoriter* – with joy and by word of mouth.[4]

Today the passive folk-narrative tradition-bearers, at least, are decreasing, and when they die their tales and traditions die too. They must be recorded now, for their like will not be heard again. The words of the countryman, quoted in a seventeenth-century English tract, are even truer today:

> We old men are old chronicles, and when our tongues go they are not clocks to tell only the time present, but large books unclasped; and our speeches, like leaves turned over and over, discover wonders that are long since past.[5]

And we in Wales today could well add our own remarks to those of the countryman: to make these silent, self-taught, cultured people speak is our challenge; to listen to them is our privilege; to record, study and present their tales and traditions is our most rewarding duty.

In order to understand the nature of the Welsh folk narrative tradition we could refer to three fairly distinct streams.

1. *Magic and the belief in the supernatural*

Civilisations may disappear, man's beliefs may change, but his innermost desires remain the same through the ages. And one of his most constant aims was to avoid the routine and certainty of this world and escape into the enchanting world of the unknown. Man in Wales was no exception. Especially when 'chance and circumstances [were] not fully controlled by knowledge',[6] he too resorted to magic.

Today, few tales of magic (*Märchen*) remain in current Welsh oral tradition, and these are usually very much shortened versions. Even so, they give us a brief glimpse of the ever-present atmosphere of wonder, which was so characteristic of the medieval world. For example, the tale of the monk of Maes-glas, Clwyd, who listened to the nightingale's song, and when he returned to his monastery found it in ruins, and all his fellow monks dead for many years[7] — the same motif of the supernatural passage of time as we find in the tale of Branwen, in the *Mabinogion*, where the Birds of Rhiannon sing a most beautiful song for seven years to the seven men at Harlech, or, indeed, in the Second Epistle of Saint Peter: '... one day is with the Lord as a thousand years and a thousand years is as one day.'[8]

But if there is a shortage in Wales of long international wonder tales, there is no shortage of brief local legends (*Sagen*) and *Memorates* illustrating man's belief in the supernatural: fairies, the devil, ghosts, apparitions, and so forth. Many of the *Memorates* are first-hand experiences, related in the first person singular. They belong mainly to what we could term the individual or family tradition.[9] But the vast majority of the *Memorates* have by now become stereotyped, and the content is more schematic and impersonal. They correspond to the *Sagen* in form and style and are well on the way to developing into local-belief legends and becoming part of the collective tradition of the community.

2. *History and tradition*

Medieval storytellers and poets in many countries were expected to be well-versed in the history, traditions and genealogy of their people; for example, the Teutonic *scop*, the Irish *fili* and the Welsh *pencerdd*.[10] In many countries the same also applies to post-medieval storytellers and poets. It is true, for example, of the Irish *seanchai*[11] and, to a lesser extent, of the Welsh storyteller. In Wales, as elsewhere, the link between the present and the past was a very real one. Folk memory made people conscious of a long and vivid history.

In the *Trioedd Cerdd*, 'the poetic or song triads', we read the following words: *Tri pheth a beir y gerddawr vot yn amyl: kyvarwyddyt ystoryeau, a barddoniaeth a hengerdd* ('three things that give amplitude to a poet: knowledge of histories, the poetic art and old verse').[12] *Ystoryeau* in this context, to quote Rachel Bromwich, means 'the national inheritance of ancient traditions.'[13] The word is a late borrowing from the Latin *historia*, and the repertoire of a number of cultured tradition-bearers in Wales today, men who often combine the two roles of local historian and poet, is a remarkable reminder of the eleventh century triad.

This 'national inheritance of ancient traditions' includes:

(i) Legends and traditions relating to remarkable or famous local characters and pseudo-historical characters.

(ii) Legends and traditions relating to remarkable local events and pseudo-historical events.

(iii) Legends and traditions relating to place-names and physical features, such as stones, lakes and caves, many of which are onomastic.

A number of the legends in this category are local legends in the sense of, to quote Lauri Honko, 'a legend attached to a certain place'. They could be referred to as 'district legends' to distinguish them from the other meaning of a local legend, 'a legend of limited distribution'.[14] The majority of the legends and traditions are very brief and of fragmentary character. Many of them are not much more than a statement, without any such narrative characteristics as a plot.

One recurring element in these narratives is the close interrelationship which exists between history and tradition, fact and fiction. The description of an eighteenth-century horrific murder may be a fact, but is the irremovable blood-stain on the wall merely a folk belief?

3. *Humour*

Narratives illustrating the Welshman's humour may be sub-divided into four main groups:

(i) Humorous stories, white-lie tales and jokes, generally known throughout Wales, with similar versions in other countries. Many of these form cycles and the same story may be told about different characters.

(ii) Humorous stories and anecdotes, based mainly upon humour of speech (wit), which reflect the interests, work and personality of a certain social group; for example the miners of South Wales or the quarrymen of North Wales.

(iii) Humorous anecdotes relating to well-known local characters. In studying these anecdotes which, to quote William Bascom, may be referred to as a 'sub-type of the legend, or a proto-legend',[15] one question which should be asked is whether or not there is any justification in regarding them as an independent prose narrative genre? Admittedly it is difficult at times to pin-point clearly defined narrative items in the midst of a mass of reminiscent material, but in my opinion these anecdotes can and should be regarded as a separate genre. One or more of the following three main criteria were used in deciding whether or not to classify a certain item of narrative as an anecdote. Firstly: has the anecdote been retold so frequently as to acquire some of the characteristics of the style and form of verbal art? Secondly: is the anecdote an independent item and able to stand apart from the other reminiscent material about the character? Thirdly: is there a possibility that these self-supporting anecdotes (on account of their style, form and interesting content) will become stereotyped and attached to other characters within or even outside the locality? In other words is it

possible for these anecdotes to form cycles and develop into humorous tales or jokes on similar lines as *Memorates* develop into local legends (*Sagen*)? This is most likely to happen with those humorous anecdotes based upon wit, in which the all-important element is the quick answer — the catch-phrase — at the end, rather than on the actual character who utters it.[16]

(iv) Humorous anecdotes relating to untoward local incidents, referred to in Welsh as *troeon trwstan*, which literally means awkward or clumsy incidents. These are brief, lively descriptions of some unfortunate and usually humorous incidents which have occurred to certain members of the community during the narrator's lifetime or shortly before. Some of the anecdotes describe a deliberate incident. For example, a group of young people lock the door of a house and block the chimney during a Knitting Evening. Other anecdotes describe unintentional incidents. For example, a man sleeps on a bridge wall and falls into the water. But the element common to both types of incident is that someone hears about it and retells it to others, until it spreads like a rumour and becomes the common knowledge of the whole community, much to the delight of its members. Anecdotes relating to untoward incidents are characteristic of small, closely-knit communities, in which the participant is generally known to every-one, and in which those who narrate the incident can do so in an atmosphere of non-malicious leg-pulling, without, except on rare occasions, fear of any ill-feeling.

Often, simply retelling the incident was not thought to be sufficient. An active local bard would always be ready to recreate the whole incident in verse, and to do so dramatically in true comedy fashion. The poems, composed in a simple style and in well-known metres, were easily remembered and soon became part of the community's entertainment. Wales is a country renowned for this type of special incidental verse. However, one question which should be considered is, to what extent was verse included primarily for mnemonic purposes, and to what extent was it included to supplement, as it were, the apparent formless, fragmentary character of the anecdote?

*   *   *

220

I have discussed briefly the three main streams in the Welsh folk-narrative tradition — with its emphasis on *Memorates*, socio-historical local legends, traditions, jokes and anecdotes. I should now like to mention four fairly general points that would further help us to understand the nature of this tradition, especially in relation to its vitality and continuity:

1. *The human need which had created the numerous channels of transmission*

Most communities were, to a very great extent, self-supporting and they had to create not only their own work, but also their own culture and entertainment.

2. *The favourable conditions that were responsible for maintaining channels of transmission*

Generally speaking Wales was a nation of small, closely-knit communities, in which there was constant reciprocity between individuals, affecting the swiftness with which any new story or anecdote spread from person to person. We should also mention the leisurely atmosphere of most kinds of work. We can compare, for example, how forestry workers in the twenties of this century would recite stories when they were paid on a daily basis, but had no time for this later, when they were on piece-work.

3. *Storytelling was only one aspect of the people's entertainment and was an integral part of a more general activity*

This included: local gossip; reciting and singing of *penillion telyn* (harp stanzas), incidental verse, ballads and folk-songs, and the playing of games.

4. *The informal and unconscious nature of story-telling occasions*

Members of the Welsh community rarely met specifically to tell stories. Wherever and whenever two or more people met in a happy, leisurely atmosphere, storytelling would be a natural and spontaneous outcome of such meetings. Stories were recited during worktime as well as during leisure hours. This point is made by the poet John Davies (Taliesin Hiraethog) in a Welsh essay entitled *Hen Draddodiadau* ('old traditions')[17] in which he refers to the period around the middle of the nineteenth century. This is a translation of the opening paragraph:

> Cerrigydrudion is the highest and most remote parish in Denbighshire. Its coarse-grass hills and heathery mountain pastures are full of interest to the antiquarian. Every mound and hillock, every brook and river are full of old traditions of days gone by, and its rural inhabitants on long winter nights have much delight in reciting the tales and folklore that belongs to this land. When the writer was a young boy, shepherding his father's sheep along the banks of the river Alwen and Llyn Dau Ychen ('the lake of the two sources'), he and his fellow shepherds spent many a happy hour reciting these tales while sitting on a small heap of rushes to keep the sheep from wandering on early summer days.

If storytelling was an informal and unconscious activity in the nineteenth century, it became even more so during the twentieth. Indeed, by today storytelling has become an organic part of the joy of everyday conversation, and it supplies man's everlasting need for a good laugh and to escape, however briefly, from the routine and monotony of life. It is as if the Welsh folktale has completed a full cycle. From the ordinary, everyday speech of the people, the imagination and skill of a gifted narrator and the communal need for entertainment and escapism to the world of wonder, it developed in the Middle Ages into the *Märchen* and *Novelle* motifs and types. By today the emphasis is on the simpler joke and anecdote, which once again closely resembles the everyday speech of the people. The close affinity between tale and speech is further demonstrated by the Irish, Cornish and Welsh words for tale (*scéal*, *wethl* and *chwedl*), which are believed to be derived from an Indo-European stem *sequ*, meaning 'to speak'. And of course, we are reminded of the Latin term *sequor* and the German *Sagen*. We are reminded also of the South Wales word for 'to speak', namely *wilia*, a term which derives from *chwedleua*, 'to tell a tale'.

To illustrate this shift from the *Märchen* to the *Sagen*, and from the *Novelle* to the joke and anecdote, I will relate one story which my father used to recite to us children on the farm in the rural district of Uwchaled, North Wales, during the nineteen forties: 'The story of the Two Brothers: Bob and Jack':

> Bob wanted to become a Parson and one day he goes to see the Bishop of Llanelwy (St Asaph). The Bishop asks him three questions: 'How deep is the sea?' 'How much am I worth in this oak chair?' 'What am I thinking?' Bob has no answer to any of these questions, so the Bishop tells him to return in one week's time. Bob goes home and tells the story to his brother Jack. 'Oh, don't you worry, Bob bach,' says Jack, 'I'll go to see the Bishop next week.' So Jack goes. 'First question,' says the Bishop, 'How deep is the sea?' *Ergyd carreg, Syr,* Jack answers ('as far as a stone will travel'). 'Very good,' says the Bishop. 'Second question: what am I worth in this oak chair?' 'Twenty-nine pence, Sir, because Jesus Christ was only worth thirty pence.' 'Very good, indeed,' says the Bishop. 'Third question: what am I thinking?' 'Well, Sir,' says Jack, 'you think that I am my brother Bob!'

My father told this narrative mainly as a brief, humorous story to make us children laugh. He had heard it from a neighbouring farmer. But many of the readers will know that this story is but a shortened version of a much older and longer international tale (A.T. 922) generally referred to as 'The King and the Abbot'.[18] According to Walter Anderson the tale could be of Jewish origin, dating from perhaps the seventh century, and possibly brought to Europe by the Crusaders.[19] The story could well have been recited in the medieval courts of the princes and gentry of Wales.

In studying Welsh folk narratives we notice, therefore, a remarkable continuity of tradition from very early times to the present day. The reason for this continuity is because the tradition was, and to a great extent still is, a living tradition. From time to time, therefore, the function of the narratives altered, but their actual content remained almost unchanged.

No living folk-narrative tradition is static. It develops as the mind of man develops; it changes as the nature of society changes. This explains why so many of the Welsh legends survived the eighteenth and nineteenth-century Religious Revivals.

A study of the morphology of Welsh folk-narratives shows, not only how a number of old motifs may be combined in one tale, but also how these old motifs may be adapted to a new environment in a later period. For example, the legends about the Devil (usually in the form of a gentleman) playing cards on a bridge with a champion card-player[20] contain at least two very old, pre-Christian motifs: the cloven-footed Devil and the wheel of fire.[21] But the form of these legends is late. They were told for didactic reasons — as part of the prejudice against card-playing during the last century.

*   *   *

Those, then, are four points to be borne in mind when considering the vitality and continuity of the Welsh folk-narrative tradition. Let me briefly now mention at least four particular aspects of study, which are important if we are to fully understand the nature of this tradition.

1. *The origin, growth and distribution of Welsh folk narratives*

One should consider, for example, which narratives represent Wales as being once part of the continents of Europe and Asia; Wales as part of the Celtic countries; Wales as part of Britain, and Wales as, more or less, an independent unit.[22]

2. *The nature of their oral transmission, morphology, structure, form, style — a study of folk-narratives as a living art*

The following questions arise from this; how a folk-narrative changes by being transmitted orally from one person and district to the other?; to what extent a folk-narrative tradition-bearer is also a tradition creator, supplying his own additions and corrections?; what is the influence of faulty memory?; how can the recording of an informant under different conditions or after the lapse of some years teach as much about the nature of a storyteller's memory?; to whom did the storyteller recite his stories, and on what occasion?; what role was played by the audience?; was it a passive or an active role?; which narratives, once part of the oral tradition, were later recorded in manuscript or print but have now returned into oral tradition? It is said that Wales during the eighteenth and nineteenth centuries became one of the most literate nations in Europe, and the question of the influence of booklore on folklore is most relevant.[23]

3. *Use, meaning and function of the narrative*

Many of the narratives are based on pre-Christian folk beliefs, but what world do these folk beliefs represent?; which narratives were recited for didactic reasons?; which narratives were merely retold for entertainment?; and which narratives express man's desire to 'avoid the routine and certainty of this world and escape into the enchanting world of the unknown'?

4. *What factors determine the nature and extent of a tradition-bearer's folk-narrative repertoire in the Welsh community today?*

On the one hand this question could be considered from the point of view of the influence of the cultural and social environment on the narrator's repertoire, and, on the other hand, it could be considered from the point of view of the influence of the individual himself on the formation and nature of his own repertoire; for example his personality and character, intellect, memory, knowledge, interests, place of abode and work.[24]

*   *   *

Now that we have had a glimpse of the nature of the Welsh folk-narrative tradition and, having mentioned also a few aspects of its study, one could well ask: what is the value today of collecting and studying Welsh folk-narratives, indeed the folk-narratives of any country? My answer, briefly, would be threefold.

Firstly, they deserve our attention because of their aesthetic qualities. Many of the tales and legends are minor works of art, great in their sincerity of purpose, vividness of characterisation, and simplicity of style and form.

Secondly, an understanding of the storyteller's role in the community and of the function of his narratives will help us to better understand the nature of the whole community.

And thirdly, the more we study folk narratives, the closer we come to an understanding of the nature of human culture and of life itself. We are given a glimpse of the development of man's mind and culture through the centuries until the present day. The one great essential of any folk-narrative collector is a sympathetic attitude towards his subject. It is so easy for us today to regard our forefathers' tales as merely entertainment, and the old motifs as merely superstitions. But we must always remember that to them these tales and motifs were an intrinsic part of man's belief. They had meaning which people accepted with reverence. We are reminded that the Latin word *historia* not only gave us the Welsh word *ystoreau*, 'histories', but that it also gave us the Welsh word *ystyr*, 'meaning'. We are reminded too that the early Welsh word for storyteller was *y cyfarwydd*, 'the familiar one'. His task was *cyfarwyddo*, 'to direct'. It is believed that the Welsh word *gweled*, 'to see', and the Irish word *fili* (gen. *filed*) both derive from the same Indo-European stem. The Welsh *cyfarwydd*, like the Irish *fili*, was a poet – a visionary, an interpreter – the one who helped his people to 'see' – to visualise the invisible, to give meaning to the meaningless.

To us today, this meaning is often a magic one. But we must always remember that to our forefathers there was meaning in the magic. The folklorist's task, indeed his privilege, is to endeavour to understand this meaning. His efforts will not be in vain, because, as the Irish proverb says:

> *Is buaine port ná glór na n-éan,*
> *Is buaine focal ná toice an tsaoil*

– 'a tune is more lasting than the song of birds, and a word is more lasting than the wealth of the world'.[25]

Notes

1. See *The Mabinogion*, translated with an introduction by Gwyn Jones and Thomas Jones (London, 1948). See also Thomas Parry, *A History of Welsh Literature*, translated from the Welsh by H. Idris Bell (Oxford, 1955).

2. W. Howells, *Cambrian Superstitions, Comprising Ghosts, Omens, Witchcraft, Traditions, etc.* (Tipton, 1831), 144.

3. During 1964-78 approximately 1,100 tapes (550 hours) were recorded.

4. Quoted in E. K. Wells, *The Ballad Tree — A Study of British and American Ballads, their Folklore, Verse and Music* (London, 1950), 8.

5. Quoted in George Ewart Evans, *Ask the Fellows who Cut the Hay* (London, 1966), 4.

6. A reference to Branislaw Malinowski's theory of magic, quoted in Gustav Jahoda, *The Psychology of Superstition* (London, 1969), 127-8.

7. Type A.T. 471 A.

8. Chapter 3, verse 8.

9. See Juha Pentikäinen, 'Depth Research', *Acta Ethnographica*, XXI (1972), 127-151.

10. See Karl Julius Holzknecht, *Literary Patronage in the Middle Ages* (Philadelphia, 1923), 21-2, and J. E. Caerwyn Williams, *Y Storïwr Gwyddeleg a'i Chwedlau* (The Irish Storyteller and his Tales) (Cardiff, 1972), 15.

11. See J. H. Delargy, *The Gaelic Story-Teller*, The Sir John Rhys Memorial Lecture, 1945 (London, 1946).

12. As recorded in the *Llyfr Coch Hergest* version of the *dwned* (grammar), attributed to Einion Offeiriad.

13. *Trioedd Ynys Prydein. The Welsh Triads* (Cardiff, 1961), lxxi.

14. 'Genre Analysis in Folkloristics and Comparative Religion', *Temenos*, III (1968), 63.

15. 'The Forms of Folklore: Prose Narratives', *Journal of American Folklore*, LXXVIII (1965), 5.

16. This, and the following two paragraphs is, in part, a quotation from my article 'The Prose Narrative Repertoire of a Passive Tradition Bearer in a Welsh Rural Community: Genre Analysis and Formation', *Folk Narrative Research*, special volume (XX) of *Studia Fennica*, (Helsinki, 1976), 283-93.

17. MS. *Ty'n Pant*, 113, at present in the author's possession.

18. In England the story is retold in the well-known ballad 'King John and the Abbot of Canterbury'. See ballad No. 45 in Francis James Child, *The English and Scottish Popular Ballads*, Vol. 1 (New York, 1965), 403-14.

19. See *Kaiser und Abt: die Geschichte eines Schwanks*, F.F. Communications, No. 42 (Helsinki, 1923).

20. Type No. 3015 in Reider Th. Christiansen, *The Migratory Legends. A Proposed List of Types with a Systematic Catalogue of the Norwegian Variants*, F.F. Communications, No. 175 (Helsinki, 1958).

21. Motif Nos G303.4.5.3.1. and E421.3.1. in Stith Thompson, *Motif-Index of Folk-Literature*, Vols 3 and 2, F.F. Communications (Copenhagen, 1956).

22. See Kenneth Jackson, 'The Folk-tale in Gaelic Scotland', *The Proceedings of the Scottish Anthropological and Folklore Society*, IV (3) (1952), 123-40, and, Thomas Jones, 'Y Stori Werin yng Nghymru' (the folktale in Wales), *Transactions of the Honourable Society of Cymmrodorion*, Part 1 (1970), 16-32.

23. See H. J. Chaytor, *From Script to Print* (Cambridge, 1950).

24. For a discussion of this question, see my article 'The Prose Narrative Repertoire of a Passive Tradition Bearer . . .' (referred to in Note 16, above), 287-92.

25. I am very grateful to my colleage John Williams-Davies for reading this paper in manuscript form and for his kind suggestions.

Supernatural Sanctions and the Legend

HERBERT HALPERT   Memorial University of Newfoundland

MYTHOLOGISTS, anthropologists and students of religion have long been aware that most cultures use legends about supernatural punishments to support the belief systems which govern both social and individual behaviour. Only a few American or English folklorists have shown much interest in investigating legends in which supernatural sanctions either prescribe man's behaviour toward supernatural beings or define a moral code which controls man's behaviour both towards the divine and towards his fellow men.

In this paper I propose to survey the articles and studies in English that consider aspects of supernatural sanctions and legends, supplementing them with further references and observations. I shall also comment on a number of printed sources that would be useful for the study of religious legends about supernatural sanctions, and offer some suggestions for future work on supernatural sanctions in other kinds of legends.

In 1942, Grace Partridge Smith, an American folklorist, studied the European parallels of a popular American humourous tale in which a man disguised himself as a ghost by donning a white bedsheet, to frighten another man. Instead of accomplishing this, the prankster was himself frightened by his imitative pet monkey, which had followed him covered with a towel or pillow case. Smith adduced half a dozen European parallels, including one from Wales, demonstrating that the American tale was an attenuated version of a widespread legend in which a practical joker, disguised as a ghost or devil, finds himself pursued by a real ghost or devil. The joker is so frightened by this experience that he becomes seriously ill, or even dies of the shock. In some versions he is severely injured by the supernatural being.

As Smith points out, these legends demonstrate the existence of a strong taboo against imitating supernatural beings. Breaking this taboo calls up the beings who are mocked, and they punish the mockers. The didactic function of such legends is obvious.

In the years since Smith's pioneering article appeared in *Southern Folklore Quarterly*,[1] other versions of the tale she had studied, 'Run, — Big 'Fraid, Little 'Fraid 'll catch you!' have been published in America.[2] In some of these, as in the European parallels, the trickster becomes ill or even dies from fright. Although the imitative-monkey tale apparently has not yet been reported from Great Britain, there are at least half a dozen British parallels of the related tale, 'Run, White Devil, or the Black one will catch you!'[3] for which Smith only gave a text from Wales. In this group, as in the other European legends, the ghost/devil imitator is frightened and becomes ill, or loses his sanity; in one version he is carried off by the Devil and never seen again. There are other English and American legends of ghost or devil imitators, many of which have similar serious consequences for the ones attempting to play such practical jokes.[4]

In 1959 another American scholar, Barbara Allen Woods, published a study of international devil lore entitled *The Devil in Dog-Form*, a work which is a major contribution to the investigation of supernatural legendry. The section on 'The Devil and Evil-Doers' in her chapter on 'The Spirit of Evil',[5] discusses a number of legend categories in which the Devil appears when certain taboos are broken, ranging from being outdoors at forbidden hours to taking part in forbidden activities such as card-playing, fiddling, dancing, etc. The Devil's appearance at these times, as well as when he is named or called up by swearing, is accepted by legend narrators as a clear indication that the activities are evil.

A third major discussion of stories which show the potentially dangerous relationship between man and supernatural beings deals with Norwegian legends, but for the most part could apply with little change to British, Irish and American narratives. Ronald Grambo's 'Guilt and Punishment in Norwegian Legends', published in *Fabula* in 1970,[6] discusses the punishments meted out to man by a variety of supernatural beings: the devil, ghosts, fairies, witches — that is, persons with supernatural powers — mermaids and domestic spirits. The punishments, as Grambo points out, are for infractions of various taboos. The sum of these taboos, though Grambo does not phrase it thus, amounts to a code of behaviour that man is required to follow to avoid punishment by the supernatural world.

Grambo has also made an important contribution in attempting to analyse the function in Norwegian rural culture of each of the legend categories presented. Such analyses I regard as essential for further investigation of the significance of related legends.

In the hundred years of official folklore collection and study in England, and for at least ninety years in the United States, legends about supernatural figures — ghosts, fairies, the devil and witches — have been collected in large numbers. Some few categories have been studied comparatively. So far as I know, the only serious attempt to investigate the role of such legends and their attendant beliefs in English culture has been made not by a folklorists, but by an historian, Keith Thomas. I shall refer later, in another connection, to his important book, *Religion and the Decline of Magic*.[7] Here I will note only that Thomas has had to adopt anthropological theories to develop his insights on English folkloristic topics. This is a clear indication of the regrettable paucity of theoretical discussion of the supernatural legend by English and American folklorists.

Neither Woods nor Grambo makes any reference to the very useful concept of a 'Traditional Code of Right and Wrong', which, to the best of my knowledge, was first proposed in English in 1942 by Seán Ó Súilleabháin in *A Handbook of Irish Folklore*.[8] It is unfortunate that the concept has not been more widely used by folklorists. So far as I know, even Irish legend scholars had not referred to it in articles in English until Ó Súilleabháin himself did so in 1974.

Perhaps one thing that has delayed the recognition of the significance of this concept is the form in which it is presented. As Ó Súilleabháin points out, it is merely 'a suggestive list' of commands and prohibitions, presented in 18 subsections each with a title in boldface heading. The first six titles are on religious topics, with questions under Sacrilege; Interference with Holy Places, Holy Persons, and Holy Things; Profanation of the Sabbath; and Desecration of Holy Wells. The next three sub-sections deal with the fairy world. All other supernatural figures are lumped together in the tenth sub-section: Interference with Supernatural Beings. The remaining eight sub-sections, broader in scope, present: Molestation of Dumb Creatures; Keeping Late House; Forbidden Speech; Mocking and Mimicry; Practical Jokes; Murder; Dishonesty; and Other Wrong Deeds.

It should be remembered that Ó Súilleabháin prepared this listing with Irish fieldworkers in mind and that the topics and suggested questions reflect the collected materials in the Archive of the Irish Folklore Commission. He mentions that hundreds of commands and prohibitions are scattered throughout the *Handbook*, but unfortunately he did not include a list of cross-references to other sections.

This 'traditional code of right and wrong' is basic for further investigations. It covers the sanctions governing man's behaviour toward supernatural beings, towards the divine, and toward his fellow human beings. I shall try to show, however, that additional topics may have to be given emphasis to make this code more useful for studying the British-American tradition. To begin, let me compare the categories included in two articles by Ó Súilleabháin and myself on the same topic and then describe one category of American legend material apparently not found or at least not emphasised in the Irish tradition.

In Ó Súilleabháin's first article on the traditional code, 'Nemesis Follows Wrong Acts', published in *Arv* in 1974,[9] he is concerned with 'certain aspects of the traditional code of proper behaviour, as illustrated by Irish folk-lore — those which deal with certain wrong acts or words which bring punishment on those who are responsible for them.' His citations include about thirty reports from the Irish Folklore Commission Archive manuscripts, more than half a dozen personal communications from folklore collectors for the Commission, and other references from printed sources. In nearly all examples the punishment for wrongdoing is a serious bodily defect in the new-born child or children of the wrongdoer. Most of the legends are summarised under six categories: A. The Baby without a mouth. B. Child born with pig's (or other animal's) head. C. Child born without limbs. D. Multiple deformity of children. E. Other results of wrong behaviour. F. Multiple births as punishment.

In 1958 I contributed a short article, 'Legends of the Cursed Child', to a *Festschrift* which had only a limited circulation; the paper was also published in a small state journal, the *New York Folklore Quarterly*.[10] Since I unfortunately neglected to secure offprints to send to colleagues, the article dropped into obscurity; Ó Súilleabháin could hardly have been expected to know of its existence. My paper was based on a much smaller body of legends and memorates than Ó Súillea-bháin's, and with a wider geographical distribution. The nine previously printed texts I discussed included one each from the Isle of Skye and Shropshire, two from Ireland, one from Ontario, Canada, one from Illinois and three from New York state. There were six American reports from oral tradition: one each from Indiana, Illinois and North Carolina, and three from Kentucky.

Like Ó Súilleabháin's texts, those I used were stories in which wrongdoing was punished by birth defects in the child or children of the wrongdoer. Four or five of the stories parallel examples in Ó Súilleabháin's first two categories. In the Isle of Skye Gaelic tale, a rich woman who had mocked her poor sister's newborn child by saying a mouth should come where there was food, herself had a child born without a mouth.[11] In a New York text a rich woman, who referred to a beggar woman and her children as a sow and her brood, had a child born with a pig's foot instead of a hand. In an Ontario version, a woman who refused help to a beggar woman with the same slurring remark, had a child born with a pig's head.[12] In an Illinois story a rich woman who sat admiring her cows but did not help her overworked servant was punished by having a child with a cow's head.

In my article I emphasised the several kinds of misdeeds and the punishments which resulted; for example, refusal to give help to a pedlar with a withered arm brought about a child with a defective arm; cruelty to a woman with a club-foot led to a child born with a club-foot; and mockery of an idiot child in church brought to parents the punishment of three idiot children. I also presented several stories in which rejecting God's will, either by not wanting a child, or by sacrilegiously saying one would rather have three blind sons than more daughters, brought as divine retribution an ailing child, and three blind sons. Finally, a man who cursed God at an outdoor baptism and mockingly crucified a turtle, had a child that looked and acted like a turtle.

In concluding I suggested, without realising that Ó Súilleabháin had anticipated me in the *Handbook*, that my group of stories might be used 'to define what folk tradition would regard as a moral code.' But I added that in defining such a code one should also consider the positive qualities that are admired by the folk in other traditional tales and songs.

Obviously it would be unwise to suggest that the themes in my article that differ from those in Ó Súilleabháin's are not found in the Irish tradition. It would be safer to say that one might expect different cultural emphases in Ireland and the United States. Such a difference is illustrated in legends of the Devil-Child.

In the section on 'Devils' in the *Handbook*, Ó Súilleabháin refers to only one Devil-Child theme: 'devil's son (by human mother) becomes a priest.'[13] Nor is there any mention of Devil-Child stories in Ó Súilleabháin's survey of 'some of the . . . types of Devil tales, of the *Sagen* variety.'[14]

In sharp contrast is the rich development of the Devil-Child theme in North America. I am restricting my discussion to stories in which a child is born with some of the physical characteristics of the Devil as a symbol of, or punishment for, the behaviour of one or both parents.

The birth of a Devil Child has been reported in stories from at least a dozen Canadian provinces and American states. In a few versions the child is born a devil because of the general wickedness of one or both parents. More commonly the devil child is the result of a specific action, as in the following examples:

1. A woman refuses to give a gypsy food and is cursed.

2. A wicked family runs a preacher out of their house. He predicts that their child will be a devil.

3. A minister earns the money to build his church in a crap game.

4. A man gets married without confessing some terrible deed in his past. (The deed is not specified).

5a. A woman with many children says that if she has another, she hopes it will be the devil.

5b. A man with many daughters says he'd rather have a devil than another daughter.

There is one popular theme found in what I call Catholic and Protestant forms. The Catholic versions involve a holy picture. A woman refuses to buy a holy picture, saying she would rather have a devil in the house. Alternatively, an atheistic husband tears down a picture of the Holy Virgin making a similar remark.

In the Protestant form of the story, a Bible replaces the holy picture. In the most common version, a woman refuses a Bible-seller, saying she would rather have a devil in the house than a Bible. Sometimes she also throws the Bible in the fire. In a variant form, a woman throws the Bible or some other religious book in the fire without making the standard remark, but the result is always the same: a devil baby is born.[15]

The relationship of these Devil-Child stories to what I called the Cursed Child legends is clear. In North America the two traditions flourish side by side. At least from present information, in Ireland the Devil-Child appears to be of minor significance as a form of supernatural punishment.

Let me complete this survey of published studies by citing two important articles that stress the theme of religious supernatural sanctions. In Wayland D. Hand's careful examination of 'Deformity, Disease and Physical Ailment as Divine Retribution', published in a *Festschrift* in 1972,[16] he presents examples from his unmatched assemblage of North American folk beliefs and legends. He extends his study both by citations from European folk belief materials and by full Biblical references. Hand also demonstrates that many non-Christian world cultures share related beliefs about the inevitable divine retribution for infractions of the moral code.

The second major contribution on the theme of religious supernatural sanctions was published in 1976 in *Béaloideas*. It is Pádraig Ó Héalaí's 'Moral Values in Irish Religious Tales',[17] which is an exhaustive survey of many categories of the religious legends of Ireland, based on the manuscripts in the Archive of the Department of Irish Folklore, University College, Dublin.

In effect, this study is a full treatment of nearly all of the six religious topics that make up the first third of Ó Súilleabháin's 'Traditional Code . . .' in the *Handbook*. Ó Héalaí includes, of course, the many legends that deal with punishments for infractions of the Traditional Code. He also includes legends that show the religious rewards people secure for following a positive code of correct behaviour. Highest on the list of virtuous acts is generosity to the poor, but there are others. Thus his article includes that combination of positive and negative sanctions which I had suggested was needed to determine a folk moral code. It serves as a useful model for the area of Catholic religious legend. It will take further investigation in English and American folk legends to determine how well the model will serve for Protestant religious tradition. Hand's article will be valuable in suggesting aspects of religious legends that might repay additional exploration.

In attempting to describe comprehensively a 'Traditional Code of Right and Wrong' it will be necessary to examine many other categories of Anglo-American legend. The obvious first step would be a careful search of the many legends abstracted in Baughman's *Motif-Index*. Since the *Index* is easily available, I shall not attempt to point out the many categories in that compilation which have appropriate materials for constructing or deducing a code. Instead I shall comment on a number of printed sources that would be of importance for any extensive study of legends about supernatural religious sanctions.

In his article 'Nemesis Follows Wrong Acts' Ó Súilleabháin gives some printed references showing that legends about the pig-faced child had been localised about a Mrs Steevens, whose money founded a hospital in Dublin.[18] He also remarks[19] that he could not find any of the types of legends discussed in his article in the index of medieval exempla compiled by Tubach.[20] Ó Héalaí, on the other hand, mentions that he found in Tubach many exempla parallels to the Irish religious tales presented in his collection.[21]

It is probable that there are parallels to many of the religious tales demonstrating supernatural sanctions, particularly those concerning the devil, blasphemy, sacrilege, and monster children, in the rich literature on Remarkable Providences that appeared in sixteenth- and seventeenth-century England and America. Thomas has an admirable discussion of the topic of 'Providence', with full bibliographical references, in the fourth chapter of his *Religion and the Decline of Magic*, referred to earlier. The subsections on 'Cautionary tales' and 'Sacrilege' as well as part of the following subsection[22] are especially pertinent. Having pointed out the extent of the literary compilations of anecdotes about God's judgments, Thomas suggests that these 'were intended to reinforce some existing moral code.' In other words, these were memorates and legends about religious supernatural sanctions.

Nor did such printed cautionary stories circulate only in books. The subtitle to Rollins's *The Pack of Autolycus*,[23] a compilation of seventeenth-century broadside ballads, includes such subjects as 'Monstrous Births, . . . Judgments of God, and other Prodigious and Fearful Happenings . . .'

Similar stories also appeared in prose tracts and broadsides. W. B. Gerish reprinted a seventeenth-century tract, *The Mowing Devil*,[24] with some interesting parallels which I shall comment on below. Hindley republished a nineteenth-century broadside entitled 'Wonderful, Just & Terrible Judgment on a Blasphemer'.[25] Undoubtedly broadside specialists could point out other prose ephemera of the same character.

Stories of the same nature and apparent purpose are also found in newspapers. In 1926 A. S. Macmillan[26] reprinted about half a dozen news reports from eighteenth- and nineteenth-century West Country newspapers. In these accounts persons who used blasphemy, or who swore false oaths, suffered either death or the same bodily deformities mentioned in their oaths.

Even a specialised publication like the *Hertfordshire Archeological Notes and Queries* published supposedly local stories about the consequence of impious remarks. Three of these were reprinted by W. B. Gerish in his introduction to *The Mowing Devil*, mentioned above. Among other interesting observations, Gerish suggests: 'Other counties doubtless possess equally rich stores of these judgments on impiety and false swearing . . .' In addition Gerish gives the full titles of two other seventeenth-century pamphlets in which, as in the tract he reprints, someone blasphemously calls upon the Devil, only to have him appear with fearful consequences to the blasphemer.

Let me return for a moment to Thomas's discussion of Providences, in which he comments: 'In many respects nineteenth-century Evangelicals and sectarians had as literal a faith in the doctrine of divine providence as any to be found in the age of Cromwell or Baxter.'[27] An interesting demonstration of the correctness of this observation may be found in the autobiographies of nineteenth-century American Methodist itinerant preachers. A good sampling and analysis of the legends and other folklore in these circuit-riders' reminiscences is in a doctoral dissertation by Donald E. Byrnes, Jr., published in 1975.[28] Part II of this study, entitled 'Remarkable Providences', has many stories of both negative and positive sanctions. Chapter 2, 'Remarkable Judgments', includes a variety of stories about punishments. Other chapters include examples of the literal fulfillment of pious prayers, and so on. This is an important work for the study of religious legends.

Apart from the Methodist autobiographies, most nineteenth-century compilations of religious anecdotes are pretty thin stuff. Quite by accident I secured one far superior to the majority, entitled *Touching Incidents and Remarkable Answers to Prayers*,[29] containing stories related by more than twenty-four clergymen, including Martin Luther, John Knox, George Fox, John Wesley, and a number of preachers of the late nineteenth century. The book is a curious mixture. There are a number of 'Touching Incidents', best classified as 'tear jerkers'. There are a few stories of visions of hell, a pattern found in medieval exempla, and a couple of dramatic death-bed scenes of sinners who put off repentance until it was too late, but stories of remarkable answers to prayer predominate. Here we have modern versions of Remarkable Providences, and it is particularly worth observing that they are examples of miraculous rewards for true religious faith.

The last work that I shall mention because of its importance to students of supernatural religious sanctions is perhaps the most unexpected one. It is a twentieth-century series of five volumes called *Uncle Arthur's Bedtime Stories*,[30] written, of course, for children. Every story, we are told, 'contains some uplifting, character-building lesson.' The Lesson Indexes in the volumes are the equivalent of the topic classifications of some medieval exempla collections. In some respects this set is a collection of modern exempla.

Scattered throughout the five volumes are a large number of memorates — we are assured that all of the stories are true experiences — of which about sixty-five are miraculous answers to prayer, much like those in *Touching Incidents* . . . , discussed above. One story of especial interest to me, because it is related to certain Newfoundland religious traditions, describes how prayer saved a Bible in a burning house, and left it completely unmarked by fire.

In summary, the belief in Remarkable Providences has existed over more than four centuries in England and America, and has produced, as this survey of printed sources suggests, a large body of religious memorates and legends that is available for future religious legend research. Most of this, I fear, will have the usual limitations of much archive and library material, a paucity of information on the social context and functions of these stories, but such extensive materials will amply repay investigation and analysis.

In conclusion, it is not difficult to suggest a number of other legend patterns found in North America, and occasionally in England, in which supernatural sanctions are demonstrated. I find of special interest the stories of symbolic markings of supernatural origin, such as 'the face on the window' supposedly printed there by lightning, and marks that emerge on tombstones.

Such legends may be variously interpreted as judgment or vindication. This variation applies also to the many tree and plant legends in which guilt or innocence are symbolised. A tree that grows from a grave may be explained as a sign that the person buried there was innocent of a crime of which he had been accused, or conversely that he was guilty and had gone to hell. Less subject to varied explanations is a story pattern reported from both Kentucky and Pennsylvania-German traditions, in which the leaves of a vine, bush, or tree growing from a grave have verses on them; I have difficulty in visualising this. The verse says that the sinful person buried there, who died from a sudden accident, was not damned because he had repented 'between the saddle and the ground'. Sometimes the words name the hitherto unrevealed murderer of the grave inhabitant.

On the other hand, sometimes a legendary explanation or interpretation is lacking just when one would expect it. I have assembled a number of English references, from folklore journals and other regional sources, to trees that grew either from a murderer's gallows, or from a stake driven through a suicide's body. For not one of these reports is there any explanatory comment, though it is difficult to believe that there are no further explanations in terms of the traditional moral code.

Some of the foregoing legend types, in which guilt, innocence, reward and punishment are symbolised, do not seem to be included in Ó Súilleabháin's *Handbook* questions, but this is no proof that they are not represented in the Archive of the Department of Irish Folklore. While we await with interest further publications based on materials in that Archive, English and American folklorists might profitably investigate whether a 'Traditional Code of Right and Wrong' based on Anglo-American legends would differ to any great extent from the Irish model outlined by Ó Súilleabháin.

Fieldwork on various aspects of this broad topic would be highly desirable, with collectors bearing in mind the need to secure, along with the narratives, data on the social context and functions of these stories of supernatural sanctions. In spite of, or perhaps because of, the fact that these legends are of great importance in the thoughts and emotions of informants, I have a strong conviction that many people would be able and willing to comment on the implications of such stories.

No doubt collectors will find that the most dramatic tales deal with supernatural retribution for wrongdoing, but as I pointed out in my earlier paper, a moral code should be defined positively as well as negatively. We must learn as much as we can about the rewards to individuals who behave 'properly' towards the supernatural world, towards the divine, and towards their fellows. Since many of these stories are not church-inspired exempla, I would expect the rewards, like the punishments, to be on this earth.

Notes

1. Grace Partridge Smith, 'The European Origins of an Illinois Tale', *Southern Folklore Quarterly*, VI (1942), 89-94.

2. Ernest W. Baughman, *Type and Motif-Index of the Folktales of England and North America* (The Hague, 1966), Type 1676A, 'Big 'Fraid and Little 'Fraid', and Motif K1682.1 (same title).

3. See Baughman, K1682.1(a), for an Ontario, Canada, version. Some British versions are listed under Type 1676A in the Tale-Type Index in Katharine M. Briggs, *A Dictionary of British Folk-Tales in the English Language* (London, 1971), Part B 1 (Folk Legends), xxxi.

4. Baughman, K1682.1(b)-K1682.1(f); Briggs, xxx-xxxi, Types 1676 and 1676A (variant).

5. Barbara Allen Woods, *The Devil in Dog Form. A Partial Type-Index of Devil Legends* (Berkeley and Los Angeles, 1959), 63-84.

6. Ronald Grambo, 'Guilt as Punishment in Norwegian Legends', *Fabula*, XI (1970), 253-70.

7. Keith Thomas, *Religion and the Decline of Magic* (London, 1971).

8. Seán Ó Súilleabháin, *A Handbook of Irish Folklore* (Dublin, 1942, reprinted at Hatboro, 1963), 434-8.

9. *idem*, 'Nemesis Follows Wrong Acts', *Arv*, XXIX-XXX (1973-74), 36-49.

10. Herbert Halpert, 'Legends of the Cursed Child', *Whatever Makes Papa Laugh*, ed. Warren S. Walker (Cooperstown, 1958), and (same title) in *New York Folklore Quarterly*, XIV (1958), 233-41.

11. Kenneth Jackson, 'The Folktale in Gaelic Scotland', *Proceedings of the Scottish Anthropological and Folklore Society*, IV (3) (1952), 127; *idem*, 'The Baby without a Mouth', *Béaloideas*, XXXIX-XLI (1971-73), 157-64; Ó Súilleabháin (1973-74), 36-7 (Category A); Baughman, Q552(a).

12. Baughman, Q522(b)-Q552(d); cf. Ó Súilleabháin (1973-74), 37-44 (Category B).

13. Ó Súilleabháin (1942), 433-6 (the citation is on 444). For a version of this see Jeremiah Curtin, *Irish Folk-Tales*, ed. Seámus Ó Duilearga (Dublin, 1943), 75-84.

14. Seán Ó Súilleabháin, 'The Devil in Irish Folk Narrative', *Volksüberlieferung*, ed. Fritz Harkort *et al.* (Göttingen, 1968), 275-86.

15. For references to some of the motifs discussed. see Baughman, G303.25.21*, 'Woman bears devil child', and the sub-divisions under that motif. Baughman does not refer to two other motifs in Thompson that are appropriate for Devil-Child stories: see Stith Thompson, *Motif-Index of Folk Literature*, 6 vols (Bloomington, 1955-58), Motif S223.0.1, 'Robert the Devil', and Motif S223.2, 'Mother curses her unborn child'. A major source on the socio-psychological impact of the modern Devil-Child legends is the article by Jane Addams, 'The Devil Baby at Hull House', *Atlantic Monthly*, CXVIII (Oct. 1916), 441-51.

16. Wayland D. Hand, 'Deformity, Disease and Physical Ailment as Divine Retribution', *Festschrift Matthias Zender: Studien zur Volkskultur, Sprache und Landesgeschichte*, ed. Edith Ennen and Günter Wiegelmann (Bonn, 1972), 519-25.

17. Pádraig Ó Héalaí, 'Moral Values in Irish Religious Tales', *Béaloideas*, XLII-XLIV (1974-76), 176-212.

18. Ó Súilleabháin (1973-74), 38-40.

19. *ibid.*, 49.

20. F. C. Tubach, *Index Exemplorum: A Handbook of Medieval Religious Tales* (Helsinki, 1969).

21. Ó Héalaí, 176.

22. Thomas, 89-110.

23. Hyder Edward Rollins, ed., *The Pack of Autolycus, or Strange and Terrible News of Ghosts, Apparitions, Monstrous Births, Showers of Wheat, Judgements of God, and Other Prodigious and Fearful Happenings as Told in Broadside Ballads of the Years 1624-1693* (1927, reprint Washington and London, 1969).

24. W. B. Gerish, ed., *The Mowing Devil, or Strange News Out of Hertfordshire, 1678.*

With an Introductory Setting Forth Other Examples of Judgements on Impiety and False Swearing (Bishop's Stortford, 1913).

25. Charles Hindley, *Curiosities of Street Literature* (1871; reprint London, 1966), 24.

26. A. S. Macmillan, 'Impious Prayers', *Word-Lore*, I (1926), 59-62.

27. Thomas, 110.

28. Donald E. Byrne, Jr., *No Foot of Land: Folklore of American Methodist Itinerants* (Metuchen, 1975).

29. S. B. Shaw, *Touching Incidents and Remarkable Answers to Prayer* (Grand Rapids, 1893).

30. Arthur S. Maxwell, *Uncle Arthur's Bedtime Stories*, 5 vols (Washington, 1950: earlier edition 1941). I am indebted to my friend and former secretary, Winnie Martin, for calling my attention to these books and lending them to me.

Some Typical Spanish Traditions*

MARÍA LUISA HERRERA   Museo Nacional del Pueblo Espanol, Madrid

THIS paper will consider a few customs from various parts of Spain, selected because of their widely differing origins and characteristics. Some show the influence of the intense religious fervour which has characterised the Spanish people throughout their history. Others demonstrate how a pagan ancestral rite can develop into the simple popular feast that it has become today. The paper will also comment on customs which are the disappearing relics of historic events that once transformed the nation's life. Mention will also be made of ceremonies which form a part of every-day life: a declaration of love, a wedding, and the funeral of a child.

The fundamental significance of two traditions selected for consideration derives from Catholic belief in the Communion of Saints, and the concept of personal sacrifice as an instrument of redemption Both customs are not only deeply ascetic, but full of pathos. They lack any spectacular festive setting, springing, as they do, from a tragic awareness of the life of the spirit and the duty of Christians to help one another achieve happy and everlasting life.

The first of these traditions is observed in the village of La Alberca, in the province of Salamanca, an area noted for its conservative customs and the elaborate dress of its womenfolk. Medieval features can be discerned in its architecture and in the narrowness and singularity of the streets and squares. Every day at sun-set a woman referred to as 'the hand-maiden of the souls' leads a procession round the village, in fulfilment of a solemn vow. Accompanied by anyone wishing to join her, she walks through the village streets, ringing a small bell and knocking on the doors of the houses, inviting everyone to join her in prayer for the souls of the departed and the repentance of sinners.

The second tradition, which is still observed at Valverde de la Vera — in Cáceres, in the same part of Spain — is called *los empalados*. The participants are penitents, performing a vow to walk in prayer along the *Via Crucis* (the Way of the Cross) through the village streets. They are lonely figures, walking in an attitude of solemn penitence, with outstretched, cross-like arms tied to wood, which is carried on the shoulders. A companion walks in front, ringing a little bell — a signal to passers-by to give way. These solitary, mortified penitents present a striking contrast to the ostentation, lights and pompous show so typical of Holy Week processions in other parts of Spain.

The origins of the next tradition are remote. It is associated with fire and purificatory rituals. Today it has developed into a popular festival known as 'Passing over the Fire', which is held on St John's Eve in Castille, at S. Pedro Manrique, near Soria, in the north central plateau region. Most of the local men observe this old custom, which involves walking barefoot across live coals, spread out like a carpet, 2 by 3 metres in area, and 15 centimetres high. They carry another man on their shoulders and the weight of their burden helps to crush the live coals, which are trodden with brisk, firm steps.

This festival was thought to be the continuation of an ancient rite, which prefaced an act of sun-worship. It is supposed that, later, it was transformed into a purificatory ritual involving the use of fire, and that those who took part did so in a frame of mind which was both superstitious and penitential. With the coming of Christianity, it became both a penance and an act beseeching mercy and benefits. Subsequently it developed, as

* Summary of the commentary accompanying a film shown by Señora Herrera.

an eminent scholar has recently pointed out, into a kind of sport, with psychological and pathological overtones, performed by men hoping to become local heroes. Today it is nothing more than an entertainment, though it must be stressed that participants need to be very courageous.

There is a similar custom in parts of India, and in Haiti. Contemporary Spanish accounts from the time of the Mexican Conquest refer to the natives of Yucatan passing over fire to ward off evil. Classical authors like Virgil and the elder Pliny refer to an analogous rite performed in honour of the goddess Feronia. In a recent book entitled *Ritos y Mitos equivocos* (Madrid, 1974), the distinguished Spanish scholar Professor Caro Baroja discusses a similar tradition still practised in Bulgari, a village in the part of Bulgaria that used to be ancient Thrace. On the local Patron Saint's Day members of a brotherhood, known as the *nestinari*, dance barefoot on live coals, carrying an icon and led by a woman called the *nuna*. The similarity of all these customs is explained if we examine their ancient historic origins in terms of an ancestral rite.

The conflict between Moors and Christians, that devastated Spain for eight centuries, left its mark in the form of festivals, known as 'Moors and Christians', that are held in different parts of the country, and even in Spanish-America. These amusements are best known in eastern Spain, an area where Saracen influence was strongest — though this has not prevented Christians from celebrating their victory over the medieval invader with the greatest enthusiasm. They have certain significant features in common: the use of flares; groups of Moorish and Christian warriors marching to their own bands; mock fights involving salvos of gun-powder, flashes, and rockets; finally, an assault on a specially constructed fortress, which is always conquered by the Christian army, with the help of the local Patron Saint.

An opulent display by these different groups — filás, as they are called — is typical of such festivals. Each group consists of 12 or 14 warriors, and they can be either Moors or Christians. They vie with one another to see who can produce the most luxurious and original costumes, appear to the best advantage on parade, and present their mock battles in the most lavish manner.

As far as every-day customs are concerned, there are two rather unusual observances, which come under the general heading of courtship and wedding traditions. The first involves the use of gun-powder as a declaration of love. Sometimes the shot is aimed through the girl's window, or, even more dangerously, at her feet when she is walking down the street: it is an act expressing devoted homage. This custom is well-known in eastern Spain and in the Balearic Isles. Moslem influence in these parts provides the explanation, for Spanish Moslems were the first to introduce gun-powder into the country, and it is still popular.

Another custom connected with love and marriage is known as 'The Apple Dance', and it is typical of certain villages in western Spain. After the religious ceremony is over, the bride must dance with any guest who gives her a coin. She sticks the piece of money into an apple, which already has a knife thrust into it. Then she dances, holding the knife, and this has to be done very carefully because, if the coin drops out of the apple before the dance is over, it must be handed back to the donor. In La Armuña (Salamanca) the bride must use her teeth to remove the coin from between the teeth of the man who has invited her to dance. In the province of Burgos she carries a pipe for tasting wine and invites her partners to drink from it as a gesture of thanks for their gifts.

By way of conclusion, I should like to mention another, rather unusual Spanish custom, the Funeral Dance of Jijona in Alicante. For local people the death of a child is a time to rejoice — or at any rate for those who are not its close relatives — because they believe that the innocent soul has gone straight to eternal glory. The dance is performed inside the house, in front of the body and it is not clear whether it is meant to celebrate the child's entry into heaven, or to lessen the grief of the parents. Some villages in Cataluña perform the dance in the village square immediately after the burial and the weeping parents must join in. There is a similar custom in some Spanish-American countries, for instance, Colombia and Venezuela.

Oppositions and Contrasts in Folklore

BENGT HOLBEK   University of Copenhagen

WHEN I received the invitation to participate in the International Centenary Conference of the Folklore Society, the first idea that occurred to me was that it would be appropriate to present some observations on a subject that I had noticed long ago but had never yet found the time to investigate. The subject was 'England in Danish folklore'. England has played a role in Danish song and narrative for centuries. The earliest instance is found in a manuscript from the early thirteenth century called *Gesta Danorum*, The Deeds of the Danes. We read in that book how a certain Hamlet, prince of Denmark, went to England to visit the royal court, where he won fame and riches as well as the king's daughter. Hamlet is only the first in a long succession of Danish heroes, who have crossed the North Sea to visit the land of opportunity. England must have possessed an inexhaustible supply of princesses in those times.

When the recording of ballads began in the sixteenth century, new examples of the heroic journey to England were added to the tale of Hamlet's exploits, and further examples — hundreds of them — were added when our folktales were recorded from the 1850s onwards. It would be a simple task, demanding only patience and energy, to collect all this material in a monograph. I might perhaps trace the concept of the heroic journey to a foreign court through various medieval sagas and epic songs directly back to Beowulf, who advised the Danish king Hrothgar to let his son Hrethric visit the court of his homeland: 'Foreign countries are most profitably visited by one who is himself of merit,' as Beowulf says. The monograph might be embellished with accounts of the Danish conquest of England in the Viking Age, ending with a glorious description of the might of king Canute the Great, conveniently disregarding that his realm crumbled to pieces at his death). I might then conclude that recollections of the marvellous deeds of our forefathers had sunk down to the level of the common folk, there to be treasured in tales and songs through the centuries, right down to our own time, as a living proof of the continuity and coherence of our ancient culture. And how could I be proved wrong? Nearly all the members of the supposed chain of tradition-bearers have vanished without a trace, but that does not in itself invalidate the hypothesis.

The idea of writing such a monograph has been on my mind for many years, but I never got around to doing it, and as I took it out for examination again last year, I found that it had grown stale. What had happened to it?

Such a title as 'England in Danish folklore' has countless precedents — 'The magical shot as an aetiology of disease in Danish folk belief' for example. What such studies have in common is, fundamentally, the conception of folklore as a more or less uniform mass of information. We dive into our endless archives, search our bookshelves labelled 'folklore', and come up with evidence concerning a specific subject. If the evidence is not already separated from its sources, the so-called folk, in the collections of material which we consult, then the separation is performed by our approach.

The question that did not even occur to me when I conceived the idea of such a monograph twenty years ago was the following: are we justified in conceiving of folklore as such an undifferentiated mass of information? Later studies have led me to think that this is not the case, and the aim of this paper is to demonstrate why. I shall give three examples. The first example has to do with proverbs. A decade ago I published, together with a Scandinavian philologist, an anthology of Danish proverbs. We divided the task between us in such a manner that he took responsibility for the written sources from the fourteenth century onwards, whereas I went through the proverbs taken down from oral tradition. This proved a fortunate division of labour. His material and mine turned out to differ considerably, not in the sense that the historical texts were proverbs and those from oral tradition were not, or the other way around: both text groups were as genuine as could be wished for; but they differed in another sense, which is best illustrated by means of a few quotations. The written sources provide us with such wisdom as the following: He is good who is good in God's eyes; The old should be honoured, the young should be taught; Merciless masters are far from God; Wisdom grows with age; A child must crawl before it can walk; Don't quarrel with your judge, and so on. All these texts are taken from a medieval collection that was undoubtedly used in schools and has provided material for many later authors of schoolbooks. When I was a boy, I too copied proverbs from this collection in what was supposed to be fine handwriting. In this way an endless succession of schoolchildren have been taught obedience, patience, respect, diligence, thrift, and similar virtues.

Some of these proverbs have, of course, seeped into oral tradition; every collection of oral repertoires of proverbs provides examples, and it would be impossible to determine now which proverbs were originally oral and which were not. But very many proverbs have been in daily use, which no schoolmaster in his right mind would have his pupils put on paper, not even in the finest handwriting. Quite a number of them are drastic and rude. I shall give a few examples: Money is a traveller, and shame upon him who keeps it back; Brothers may be of one blood, they are seldom of one mind; You can lick my arse for a long time before you reach my heart; It is easy to clench your fists in your pockets; Great are my master's commands, but greater the commands of my bowels; These are hard times, the master must make his own children, he can't afford to pay someone to make them for him; and so on, and so forth. I should like to quote many more of these proverbs, but the difference is no doubt already clear. These proverbs are not a means of instruction or indoctrination. There bleak realism, their irony, and their rebellious temper show that they are weapons with which to overcome the hardships and frustrations of difficult life-conditions. I have of course selected particularly illustrative examples, but it would be hard to deny that a division of our proverbs by sources brings out differences in attitude – and in style, but that is not apparent in a translation – so remarkable as to question our habit of considering the proverbs as one genre.

My next example concerns customs connected with the life cycle: baptism, wedding, and burial customs. Traditional studies of Danish folklore emphasise the most impressive features of traditional rural life. Much attention has been paid to these customs, just as we have careful records of the most prominent artistic expressions: ballads, folktales, folk music, etc. Similarly, our museums have very good collections of clothes worn on festive occasions, of hand-carved wooden implements and kitchen utensils, preserved and exhibited in beautifully restored farm houses. Adding these elements together, we can construct an enchanting picture of traditional rural life; and that, indeed, is what we find in many studies of Danish folk culture.

The museum people have long ago discovered the fallacies of this idyllic picture of traditional country life. They are aware of the unimpressive trivialities of daily life that have been omitted, but their problem is that the material remains of the rural proletarian culture have largely perished. We tend to forget that there was such a proletariat, but the fact is that it outnumbered the farmers in nineteenth century Denmark. Their cottages are mostly gone, however; their clothes, furniture, kitchen utensils, and agricultural implements, such as they were, have only been preserved to a small extent. At the time when they might have been collected they were considered worthless and uninteresting. It would not be easy to document today how a farm-labourer might live even towards the end of the nineteenth century, whereas the living conditions of the more prosperous farmers can be documented in detail.

Is it relevant for the folklorist that there was such an economic and social distinction between farmers and proletariate? It certainly is. Celebrations of festive events in the life-cycle are well documented for farmers, but one can search our archives and books for a long time before turning up a description of how a farm-labourer married a smallholder's daughter, or of how a pauper was buried. The same is true of other customs connected in one way or another with possession of the means of production. On the other hand, ballads and tales recorded among farmers, or examples of farmers playing traditional music are equally hard to find. The poor had little to celebrate, and no means of celebrating, but they spent much time and energy on developing such means of artistic expression as were accessible to them, whereas the better situated farmers, at least in the best documented period after about 1850, tended to look down upon such matters. We may speculate why this was so, and some hypotheses might be advanced, but time does not permit it now. At this point we must content ourselves with the observation that the idyllic image of traditional country life which we find in many folkloristic studies is best characterised as unreliable patchworth. The 'folk' culture that we like to theorise about has been constructed by ourselves on the basis of material from different classes of people.

My final example is taken from the field of folktale study in which I am engaged at the moment. I started out with the preconception that of folktales were the property of the much-discussed folk, and then had to accept that as far as this material was concerned, the 'folk' meant the old rural proletariat from whom more than 90 per cent of our folktales have come. But that was not all. My attention soon centered on the enormous collections of Evald Tang Kristensen. He was an active collector for more than forty years and covered large parts of our country, mostly on foot. He recorded all kinds of folklore, indiscriminately, and also noted much information about his informants. It may be estimated that they numbered close to 8,000 all told, an incredible feat when we remember that he also worked as a teacher during the first twenty years of his field-work besides publishing about fifty large collections of folklore, as well as a journal and innumerable articles. He used several methods to get into contact with good informants, and there is no doubt that he covered the ground well. When he had located a satisfactory source he would often remain for days, or pay repeated visits. He frequently notes in his field-diary how he stayed with an informant until he had pumped him dry, as he puts it. If what we customarily call 'Danish folklore' really existed, we might safely neglect what accidental differences could be observed between his informants. But they exhibit strongly individual characteristics at close inspection; the traditional folkloristic notion that the anonymous common people had a common culture must have been created at the writing desks. In Tang Kristensen's material we find what any modern fieldworker will confirm: that common people differ markedly amongst themselves. One informant is an expert on local legends and knows any number of stories about ghosts and revenants; another scoffs at his credulity. One likes bawdy tales; another finds them sinful. One is a fine fiddle-player, but does not know a single ballad; and so on. As for folktales we learn that in forty years of intensive fieldwork, Tang Kristensen found no more than about 170 narrators from whom he could record more than just a couple of tales and anecdotes — only about two per cent of his informants. If we take into account the endless numbers of people he contacted without being able to record anything at all, we must conclude that the so-called folktales were told by far less than one per cent of the folk. And there is more. A careful analysis discloses remarkable differences between male and female repertoires. A certain series of tale types are preferred by women and seldom told by men, whereas the opposite is the case with another series. The picture becomes even clearer if we disregard the informants of whom we know that their sole source was a person of the opposite sex. There are other differences too, but we cannot discuss them all. One interesting point, though: almost two thirds of Tank Kristensen's folktale narrators were men; almost two thirds of his ballad-singers were women. Are we, then, really justified in speaking of folktales, folksongs, etc.? The word folk implies much more than the sources will account for.

Thus our conception of folklore as an undifferentiated mass of information crumbles when we turn our attention from the material itself to its sources. We find that literary sources must be kept carefully apart from oral ones, because they belong to a different part of the population and serve different purposes, even if their form resembles that of their oral counterparts. We find that there are important class differences within the traditional rural population, with different economic, social, and cultural characteristics. And we find, finally, that sexual and individual differences turn out to be much more marked than our all-inclusive concept of 'folklore' has led us to expect. We must begin to ask ourselves how much of our proud building of folkloristics has been built on sand.

My reasoning has been based on a few examples, of course, and examples prove nothing. They do indicate, however, that a study like 'England in Danish folklore' would in all probability be misleading if we disregarded what I have pointed out here. The question then arises what benefit may be expected from a study of the matter, bearing these facts in mind. We may just consider it briefly.

A few facts become apparent from a cursory examination of the material. England is not the only possible goal of the heroic journeys of Danish heroes. In many cases the foreign kingdom is not named or is manifestly not one to be found on a map of the kind produced nowadays — maps are not what they used to be. Otherwise the most commonly mentioned places are England, Holland, and Spain in records from Jutland, and Norway in some cases. In records from the Danish islands we find not infrequently mention of Austria, Turkey, Arabia, and India. I do not know how to explain this distribution, and I have not examined enough material to guarantee that it is not accidental. But if my preliminary observations hold, I would not try to trace the position of England, Holland, and Spain in folktales from Jutland back to the Viking Age. The narrators were unlikely to know such early history. They would know, on the other hand, that the main trade-routes by sea went to those countries, and it is highly probable that the folktales had changed little since the eighteenth century, when it was still forbidden for the adult men to leave their own parish without written permission from the parson; the reason was that they had to be available for villein service and military duties. Many of them fled abroad in those times. When one's only prospects were a life in poverty and bondage, and drafting for military service meant ten, or even twenty years, of hardship and misery, the risks of flight into the unknown perhaps did not appear to be worse. I think that England appeared to those people, the immediate ancestors of our proletarian narrators and singers, as a land of opportunity and hope. It is consistent with this line of thought that America has taken the place of England in at least one late Norwegian folktale. The same might have happened in Denmark. The prospects of leaving the country were poorer on the Danish islands, and that may be why the tales and songs from those regions dream of more fantastic, less attainable places, known from chapbooks and similar escapist literature. But note: I have not said that this is how the question *should* be answered, only that it is the kind of answer that presents itself as a possibility, when attention shifts from folklore as material to folklore as expressions of the dreams and needs fears and hopes of many different individuals.

Turkey Buzzard Tales of the Ecuadorean Quichua

ROSALEEN HOWARD   University of St Andrews

THE tales discussed in this paper were collected in 1976 in the Quichua language from Indian inhabitants of small agricultural communities which surround the Ecuadorean town of Cañar, in the province of that name. The town stands at 3000 metres above sea-level, 2.5° S., and has a population of about 8000. This urban population comprises Spanish-speaking *mestizos*, forming a sharp cultural and linguistic contrast with the rural dwellers. The dividing line between Indian and *mestizo* culture forms an area of much social tension, some of which is expressed in the tales found among the Quichua-speaking group. Some of these can conveniently be grouped as Turkey Buzzard tales.

The Ecuadorean Turkey Buzzard (*Cathartos burroviana Cass*) is a carrion-eating bird, not unlike a small vulture in appearance. It is a common feature of the landscape in the Cañar area, often to be seen wheeling in the sky above the marshy infertile moorlands or *páramo*. These lie some 4000 metres above sea-level, are uninhabited, and used by the Indians solely for the herding of cattle and sheep and the cultivation of hardy tubers. This zone has an important role to play as the ecological setting for many of the tales.

The Turkey Buzzard tales are a group of six texts collected in three different communities, reflecting a popular belief, widespread in the area, that unmarried women or men are likely to be captured by the bird, married to it, and then devoured alive. They provide an interesting illustration of the interdependent relationship which exists between popular belief and folktale, a relationship also studied in connection with other Tale Types from Cañar. As a general rule it has been found that while local belief can account for features of certain tales, belief and tale can usually be separated for the purposes of analysis. Informants themselves would make this distinction clear: for example, local belief accounts for the idea of a 'hill father' (*urcu yaya*) that inhabits the hills of the area and to whom it is said that sacrifice of newly-born infants was once made. Separate, yet obviously related on a metaphorical level, is Tale 1 of this collection, where a woman carrying her child over a certain hill is abducted by its *urcu yaya*, and agrees to the latter becoming the baby's godfather.

In the case of the Turkey Buzzard tales, however, it was found that belief and tale were so firmly interconnected that all informants queried about the former, would automatically illustrate it with his or her own version of the narrative. For this reason these stories seemed to be the most actively functional group of narratives to be found. They follow certain traditional narrative patterns, which act as vehicles for the literary expression of social and moral preoccupations. Informants' unfailing familiarity with them, and the consistency in their construction from one version to the other, are due, it would seem, to the active role performed by the didactic content. They are also of curiosity in that they appear to be the only set of tales involving specifically the Turkey Buzzard as protagonist to be found among Indian groups in Highland Ecuador.

The tales have been divided into two groups according to the narrative pattern they follow. By 'narrative pattern' is meant the sequence of episodes as it can be traced by following the linear development of the plot. In grouping tales together under one such 'pattern' or 'type' the underlying meaning of actions for the subsequent course of the narrative is taken into account, but those actions are not reduced to the level of 'functions' in the Proppian mode, as this would obscure the identity of the protagonist — the Turkey Buzzard — with its specifically local associations. This is to say that, while Propp's methods, and the theories of his later exponents were helpful, the highly individualistic internal structure and regional cultural significance of these tales do not allow for a rigid application of external theoretical models.

The first of the two groups of tales is that which follows the pattern of a widespread Andean Tale Type which can be labelled 'The Condor and the Shepherd Girl', and which relates how a young girl pasturing the sheep is abducted by a condor in handsome human form and taken to live in his cave. Before the connections between this and the Turkey Buzzard tales can be discussed, we must look at the outline of variant versions of the latter. (See Fig. I).

We can then compare the pattern followed by these with that of versions of 'The Condor and the Shepherd Girl' from other parts of Ecuador, and also with two typical versions of that tale from S. Peru (see Figs. II & III). In broad outline, the pattern is an overall one: a single girl, away from her familiar surroundings, meets and is seduced by a bird lover who takes on human form for the purpose of courtship. She is taken, willingly or by a trick, to the cave-dwelling of the latter, from which she attempts to escape, successfully or not. An animal or bird mediates between her and her parents and reestablishes contact between them either before or after her death.

The differences between the three sets of texts are also helpful for our understanding of the Cañar versions in the wider context. We can notice immediately the contrast in the 'Initial Situation' of those tales where the buzzard is the protagonist, and those where the condor fills the role. The girl's attendance at Mass on her own, and her refusal of the suitors she meets there, would appear to belong to a more acculturated realm of associations than that to which the girl out pasturing her sheep in the hills belongs. The 'attendance at Mass' motif is reminiscent of another Cañar tale in which the heroine's abduction, this time by the Rainbow, is triggered off by an 'Initial Situation', in which she spends too much time in the hills pasturing the sheep, thereby neglecting to attend Mass. The implication that Catholic duty is being underrated by

overattention to Indian tasks gives us a clue to the logical processes by which acculturation in narrative takes place. In the Cañar Buzzard tale, however, there is an inversion of the situation: attendance, not neglect, of Mass leads to the subsequent events. Is it that Catholic duty has now been overrated? Probably not; the moral message of the tale focusses on social, not religious behaviour. The 'attendance at Mass' motif has surely lost semantic value, but provides merely a convenient, realistic prop: it is after all at Mass that potential husbands are to be found.

Other dissimilarities in the outer content of the tales in Pattern 1 may be explained in terms of transformation. The shift from humming-bird as intermediary in the Peruvian Condor texts, to dog in the Ecuadorean Condor and Buzzard texts, is an example. This appears to be a result of a process of rationalisation, perhaps akin to that of acculturation. It is more reasonable to expect the shepherd girl to be assisted by a dog than by a humming-bird. By the time we reach the Cañar texts, the 'shepherding' theme has disappeared, but the company of a dog on a journey is no less realistic a touch.

Of course the outstanding transformation to be accounted for is that which allows for the buzzard in the Cañar tales to play the role elsewhere filled by the condor. This instance is not simply a matter of a shift in surface structure that does not alter the internal meaning or 'function' of the actor in question. The investigations included much questioning on the moral preoccupations reflected in these stories, and the concern that those who did not marry would be devoured by a non-human spouse were quite emphatically connected with the Turkey Buzzard, while no reference was found to the condor in this region. So the peculiarity can be explained if we recall that in the 'Condor' tales (both Ecuadorean and Peruvian), virtually no explicit didactic element is found, while in connection with the buzzard, the moral message is practically the tales' *raison d'être*. It would seem therefore, to come back to the original point about the interrelationship between belief and tale, that the Cañar texts are indeed an example of the way in which an already existing, traditional, narrative framework can be used for the expression of specifically local beliefs.

This theory, that in the Turkey Buzzard tales

FIGURE I (Pattern 1)

TURKEY BUZZARD TALES: CAÑAR

		(1) (key text)	(2)	(3)	(4)	(5)	(6)
INITIAL SITUATION		Single girl goes to Mass; ignores all suitors	⟶	⟶	(girl's family lives in 'Jerusalem')	⟶	⟶
Episode I	MOVE I	Meets finely-dressed young man (buzzard)	⟶	⟶	(appears at house-building)	⟶	⟶
II	MOVE I	Buzzard-man (BM) builds house rapidly	X X X X	⟶	⟶	⟶	⟶
III	MOVE I	BM fetches thatching; devours a mule	⟶	X X X X	(fetches wood, cane and straw succesively)	X X X X	X X X X
IV	MOVE I	BM weaves poncho rapidly	⟶	X X X X	X X X X	⟶	⟶
V	MOVE I	BM tames wild bull	X X X X	X X X X	X X X X	X X X X	X X X X
VI	MOVE I	Wedding	⟶	⟶	⟶	(at door of church; won't enter)	⟶
VII	MOVE II	BM suggests visit to his family	(flies her on his back)	⟶	⟶	⟶	⟶
VIII	MOVE II	food prepared for in-laws	⟶	⟶	⟶	⟶	⟶
IX	MOVE II	arrive at Buzzard's cave	⟶	⟶	⟶	⟶	X X X X
X	MOVE II	Buzzard mother-in-law warns girl	⟶	⟶	(mother-in-law called 'mother of devil')	⟶	X X X X
XI	MOVE II	warning unheeded; girl devoured	⟶	⟶	⟶	⟶	devoured before end of journey
XII	MOVE III	dog informs parents	⟶	⟶	⟶	⟶	⟶
XIII	MOVE III	parents collect remains	⟶	⟶	⟶	⟶	⟶
XIV	MOVE III	burial of heroine	revives from blood placed in pot	X X X X	(parents place cross at spot where died)	priest blesses remains; re-form into body for burial	X X X X
MORAL MESSAGE?		punishment for being choosy & delaying marriage	X X X X	⟶	⟶	⟶	⟶

FIGURE II (Pattern 1)
'THE CONDOR & THE SHEPHERD GIRL': ECUADOR

(1) CHIBULEO (key text) (2) SALASACA (3) SALASACA (4) IMBABURA

		(1) CHIBULEO (key text)	(2) SALASACA	(3) SALASACA	(4) IMBABURA
INITIAL SITUATION		girl pasturing sheep (wants to marry man in high position)	⟶	girl enjoys silence of hills; bathes in condor's pool	⟶
Episode I	MOVE I	condor as handsome man talks to her	⟶	⟶	⟶
II		by trick condor carries her to cave in cliff	⟶	⟶	⟶
III	MOVE II	dog leads parents to her	⟶	X X X X	⟶
IV		parents rescue girl	⟶	X X X X	⟶
V		girl covered in feathers	X X X X	girl gives birth to feathered child	covered in hair
VI		parents hide her in pot	⟶	X X X X	priest helps remove hair
VII	MOVE III	condor breaks pot; takes her away for good	⟶	girl dies; condor sad	hair removed; girl safe
MORAL MESSAGE?		Ambition punished	X X X X	X X X X	X X X X

FIGURE III (Pattern 1)
'THE CONDOR & THE SHEPHERD GIRL': S. PERU

(1) Coll. Argüedas (key text)   (2) Coll. Mitchell

		(1) Coll. Argüedas (key text)	(2) Coll. Mitchell
INITIAL SITUATION		girl pasturing sheep	⟶
Episode I	MOVE I	condor appears as handsome man	⟶
II		regular meetings ensue	X X X X
III		girl conceives child	(after arrival in cave)
IV		girl goes with condor	(tricked into going)
V		discovers his identity too late	⟶
VI		only raw meat in cave	⟶
VII	MOVE II	humming-bird informs parents	⟶
VIII		humming-bird tricks condor; girl escapes	⟶
IX	MOVE III	condor pursues her	⟶
X		humming-bird overcomes condor in fight	X X X X
XI		condor comes to girl's house	⟶
XII		condor drowns in boiling water	⟶
MORAL MESSAGE?		X X X X	X X X X

we have a sort of fusion between localised belief and a narrative pattern derived from a wider tradition, is supported by the fact that the same belief and its associated preoccupations are to be found expressed in tales from the area of an apparently different pattern. This second pattern will be considered now. The analysis of tales in this section will differ somewhat from those in Pattern 1, in that no comparative texts from other parts of the Andes will be included, and it will be restricted to the evidence found in the Cañar material itself. For the outline of the two Cañar Turkey Buzzard tales now to be discussed, it is necessary to refer to Figures IV and V.

FIGURE IV (Pattern 2)

THE TWO BROTHERS AND THE TURKEY BUZZARDS (A)

INITIAL SITUATION		there are two unmarried brothers (B1 & B2)
Episode I	MOVE I	they die one after the other
II		the second to die (B2) rejoins the first (B1)
III		B2 goes to call B1's wife, 'Mama Andrea', who is gathering tubers in ravine
IV		finds only an old female buzzard whom he curses
V	II	returns to B1 who is alarmed
VI		buzzards come & devour B2
VII	III	next evening they vomit what they have eaten and B2 revives from vomit
VIII		B2 returns home & marries, learning from B1's fate
MORAL MESSAGE?		punishment for not marrying

FIGURE V (Pattern 2)

THE TWO BROTHERS AND THE TURKEY BUZZARDS (B)

INITIAL SITUATION		there are two unmarried brothers (B1 & B2)
Episode I	MOVE I	B1 dies and B2 sets out fo find him
II		B2 arrives at a roadside crucifix where a white man directs him to a ravine
III		meets buzzard-woman (BW) 'Mama Andrea' who then goes to fetch tubers
IV		B2 is sent to fetch mule whose eye he accidentally wounds with whip
V		B2 returns home to BW's house where he is given cooked tubers to eat
VI		they go to sleep in separate rooms
VII	MOVE II	B2 hears cries in the night
VIII		B2 awakens to find B1 devoured by BW, only bones remain
IX		B2 takes B1's bones & returns to road where crucifix is
X	MOVE III	arriving on crucifix road B1 revives from bones
XI		B1 warns B2 he must marry
XII		B2 returns home where finds his *comadre* has wounded eye
XIII	IV	B2 marries but dies after one year
MORAL MESSAGE?		punishment for not marrying

While these two tales seek to convey a moral message similar to that of the Pattern 1 group, they appear to belong to a different narrative type. The two most outstanding aspects in which they differ are, firstly, in the marriage of the hero to the buzzard taking place *after* death, instead of constituting the episode that leads *to* death. This factor does away with the need for the Turkey Buzzard to take on human form in order to entice the erring human into marriage, which gave the Pattern 1 texts such a close affinity with the 'Condor and Shepherd Girl' tales. Secondly, in Pattern 2 the function of hero is split equally between two brothers, whose roles are interdependent and complementary. It is necessary for B1 to die, in order that B2 may follow him into death, observe his fate, and escape a wiser man. The argument that these two tales belong to a different Pattern or Type group is supported by the existence of other tales in the Cañar material, of dissimilar outer content, but whose narrative structure ties in very closely with that of these Pattern 2 tales. To illustrate this, it is necessary to look at the outline of Tale 9 of the collection as an example. (See Fig. VI).

FIGURE VI (Pattern 2)
'THE TWO FRIENDS AND THE DEVIL'

INITIAL SITUATION		two friends (F1 & F2) are bathing in a river
Episode I	MOVE I	F1 dies; F2 survives
II		F2 sets out in search of F1
III		on the road he meets a *mestizo* landowner who takes him to his *hacienda*
IV	MOVE II	in the *hacienda* (hell) F1 is found suspended above a cauldron
V		F1 gives F2 advice on how to escape the *mestizo* (devil)
VI		F2 follows advice successfully
VII	III	F1 returns home having learnt from F2's fate
MORAL MESSAGE?		not explicit

This tale, of course, can only be fully appreciated in the context of the many devil narratives found in Cañar, whose treatment is beyond the scope of this paper. What is interesting for the moment is the similarity in structure of the tales, whereby a 'split hero', two brothers or friends, separated by death, play out a sequence of episodes where they depend on each other for the development of the action. The comparison is close with Mama Andrea (see Fig. V), where the intervention of a *mestizo* landowner, who guides the hero, is placed at a structurally identical point in the sequence of episodes. Such a figure in Cañar folktales, incidentally, may represent either side of the same coin: devil or deity.

While these tales do follow two narrative patterns distinct from each other, a rigid dividing line between them should not be drawn. The resuscitation of the heroine from a drop of her own blood in Fig. I, for example, might be considered structurally equivalent to the hero's revival from vomit in Fig. IV, or revival from bones in Fig. V. The revival from vomit may be a transformation deriving from empirical observation of the Turkey Buzzard's real-life habits. He is known to vomit up his food in order to lighten himself before taking flight.* The revival from bones in Fig. V, on the other hand, is embedded in differ-

* Garcilaso de la Vega, *Royal Commentaries of the Incas* (London, 1869), II, 390. Translation published by the Hakluyt Society.

ent narrative pattern to that in which the episode in Fig. I was found, and further study suggested that there might be influence here from other Tale Patterns belonging to the Cañar material.

There exists a tale which could be described as an Indian version of Thompson Type 327A 'Hansel and Gretel': here the brother is devoured by a cannibalistic old woman, and his sister escapes carrying his bones. On the road she meets a *mestizo* landowner, who tells her to turn away her head, while he makes her brother whole again. Because she breaks the prohibition, the brother is re-formed as a dog instead of a human being. The hero's revival from bones in Fig. V is, perhaps, a borrowing due to similarities in the narrative pattern of the two stories at a particular point, and encouraged by the existence of 'resuscitation' of this kind elsewhere in the Turkey Buzzard tradition.

There remains a final aspect of oral tradition surrounding the Turkey Buzzard in Cañar, and in examining it we shall see the tales in a broader perspective, one that no longer demands their separation according to Type or Pattern group. In a wider context, the Turkey Buzzard is considered to be an 'agent of the devil'. We have already had a hint of this in Fig. I (4), where the buzzard mother-in-law is referred to as 'mother of the devil'. The same label attaches to the cannibalistic old woman figure of another group of Cañar tales, to which reference has just been made. In some versions of that tale she is found in company with her numerous devil offspring. So a 'family likeness' between the buzzard and the devil suggests itself, and the chain of associations set up at this level develops still further.

An aetiological tale from the area tells how the Turkey Buzzard was cursed by God and condemned to eating raw meat for disobeying orders. References made in the context of the Cañar devil narratives also support the argument: in one tale the chief devil uses a quill pen of Turkey Buzzard feathers with which to note down sins; elsewhere, an unfaithful wife is threatened by a flock of birds, which circles threateningly overhead; not long afterwards, she is abducted by the devil.

This analysis of tales involving the Turkey Buzzard has led to various conclusions. Firstly, they follow two main trends in narrative pattern: one of widespread, traditional origin, the other of apparently local derivation, more usually employed for stories involving encounters with the devil. Both patterns served as vehicles for the expression in narrative form of certain local beliefs. The super-imposition of these beliefs upon the pattern, particularly in the case of Pattern 1, seemed to have given rise to certain acculturative processes. Although there is no historical evidence, it seems that these tales are more modern in their creation than the Condor tales, whose didactic element is minimal.

It was not always advisable to adhere to a rigid classification along the lines of 'Pattern groups': knowledge of tales of other Types from the area suggested extra affinities of minor structural importance. As far as Pattern 2 tales are concerned, one final note should be made. Their structural connection with devil narratives probably derives from the wider association between the two figures discovered by studying narrative contexts in which the two were juxtaposed. One might conclude that what began as a connection at an external level — devil and buzzard belong to the same 'other world' — became a connection at an internal level — devil narrative and buzzard narrative share the same structure.

The Thomas Rymer Ballad and the Urashima Legend

HIROKO IKEDA   University of Hawaii at Manoa

THERE is an important cycle of folk narrative concerning the visit to the other world. The other world can be fairyland, the land of the dead, Paradise, Hell, the sea world or the sky world. The cycle consists of the following elements:

(1) The hero is invited, induced or persuaded to visit the other world by its inhabitant, or by someone who is familiar with the place, and accompanied by that person.

(2) On the way the hero witnesses strange or unusual sights, and these are explained by his companion.

(3) The guide/companion may advise the hero what to ask for as parting gifts.

(4) He arrives and stays in the other world. Sometimes there are time-differences between the two worlds. The hero may become homesick.

(5) The gifts from the other world are of a supernatural nature: magic objects, magic animals, a supernatural wife and various others. Because of the gifts the hero, upon return, excels in life, becoming a poet-prophet, a ruler, or a wealthy man.

Various combinations of the above elements form the cycle of Tale Type 470, which is one of the oldest tale types throughout the world. The pattern has been adopted into literary works such as Dante's *Divine Comedy,* Paul Bunyan's *Pilgrim's Progress,* Dickens's *Christmas Carol,* and Maeterlink's *The Blue Bird.*

The ballad 'Thomas Rymer' also falls into this category. The hero is thought to have been Thomas of Erceldoune, now Earlstoune, in Scotland. He lived in the thirteenth century (1220-97), and many prophetic poems and gnomic verses are supposedly his work. One such romance relates his visit as a young man to the land of fairies, and tells of his receiving the gift of prophecy from the fairy queen. The plot of the ballad is no different from the romance.

It begins with Thomas, idle and lying on a river bank, when he sees the fairy queen — 'a lady bright come riding down by the Eildon Tree'. They converse, fall in love, and leave for fairyland, where he agrees to serve her for seven years. On the way, they ride rapidly and first come to a desert, where the fairy queen shows Thomas 'three different roads', one narrow, one broad, and one 'bonny'. The last leads them to fairyland. In the fourteenth stanza Thomas is warned by the fairy queen against uttering words in Elfland when they get there. Still, for many days and nights they travel in the dark, wading through the waters. They hear in the distance the thunderous roar of the sea. They wade through the river of blood, for blood shed on earth is supposed to run through the springs of fairyland. This suggests that in the popular mind fairyland is situated in the lower strata of the earth. Finally they come to a 'garden green', and there the queen gives Thomas an apple, which endows him with the gifts of poetry and prophecy. This particular version consists of 20 stanzas, and the above episodes occupy 19 stanzas. Only one stanza, the 20th and the last, tells us that Thomas was not seen on earth till seven years were gone.

As contrasted with the 'Thomas Rymer' ballad, Japanese analogues are in the form of a cluster of sub-types belonging to a cycle. In the title of this paper I have listed only the Urashima legend, but I did so because it is the best known among the sub-types.

The eighth century record entitled the *Fudoki*

recounts a story, which is said to have happened in A.D. 478. The hero Urashima is a young fisherman, who goes to sea alone in a small boat. He catches a five-coloured turtle in mid-ocean, which turns into a beautiful princess. They fall in love and go down to the sea world to live together. At the palace gate she tells him to wait, while she explains the matter to her parents. He sees, first seven, and then eight children, come to the gate and play. When the princess comes back to get him, she explains that those children are the Pleiades and the Bull. After three years in the sea world, Urashima develops a strong desire to visit his home. He is given a little box to take along on his journey home, and is warned never to open it if he wishes to come back to the sea world. When he is back in his village, he discovers that he has been away many centuries. He does not recognise the place or know a soul. In desperation he opens the forbidden box, which causes him to age instantly and die.

Another eighth century tale belonging to this cycle is the story of the 'Lost Fish Hook', and the distribution pattern of its variants is scattered throughout the Pacific (Japan, the North-west coast of the United States, the Palau Islands). This story has caught the attention of many scholars in the past. The hero's going to the sea world is to search for a lost fish-hook. There he marries the Sea King's daughter, but after three years he suddenly remembers the reason why he is there, and tells the King of the lost fish-hook. All the fish are summoned, and the hook is recovered. The couple come back to this world with many marvellous gifts from the King, such as magic jewels to control the tide, and the hero becomes the ruler of Japan, making use of these treasures. He is one of the ancestors of the Imperial family. When the time comes for his wife to give birth to a child, she forbids her husband to look into the room where she is confined. He breaks this taboo and finds that his wife has taken the form of a huge crocodile, as she gives birth to a human heir. Because of the broken taboo, he loses his wife.

The above two stories end with the separation of the couple. This is the 'Forgotten Fiancée' motif, which I shall explain later.

The third story of the visit to the sea world is supposed to have happened in the tenth century. Abe-no-Seimei died in A.D. 1005, at the age of 83 or 84. He was a famous court diviner and sooth-sayer. Many legends are told about him, including the one that his mother was a fox of Shinoda Forest, and his visit to the sea world in his child-hood. What he received from the Sea King as a parting gift was a power to understand animal languages, and this accounts for his becoming a respected court soothsayer later, an exact analogue of the ballad of 'Thomas Rymer'.

Depending on the kinds of gifts, there are more variants of the visit to the sea world, but another sub-type of Type 470, which is the visit to the land of the dead, can now be considered. The visit to Hell or Paradise is very well-known in the West, but it is also a firmly established Buddhist story.

In the collection of Buddhist anecdotes entitled *Nippon Ryōiki*, compiled in A.D. 822, there are 116 tales of Buddhist miracles, and twelve of these are of this type. Another collection of Buddhist and secular tales compiled in the eleventh century, the *Konjaku Monogatari*, consists of over a thousand tales, and over 80 are of this type. There is no doubt that these Buddhist tales are derived from Chinese and Indian originals. A story in the *Ryōiki*, (v.3:23) goes as follows:

A man erects a family temple with the cooperation of his clansmen and starts to live there, making a vow to copy a Buddhist sutra. However, he is accused of a certain crime, and is murdered by those clansmen in the third month of A.D. 774. His family, in anticipation of a murder trial, does not cremate the body, but places it in a tempor-ary tomb. After five days, the man revives and tells his experience:

'When I died, five messengers came and accompanied me to where there was a steep hill. From its top could be seen three forked roads. One was wide and straight. The next was untrodden and poorly maintained. The third was overgrown with weeds. At the fork was the king of the land of the dead. Pointing to the wide road, he ordered the messengers to take me through it. At the end of the road was a huge cauldron, which was steam-ing and boiling over, and the sound was like thunderous waves. The messengers picked me up and threw me into the cauldron. All of a sudden the boiling water cooled and the cauldron cracked and broke into four pieces.

This was because I had died before fulfilling the austere vow of copying the sutra. I was returned to accomplish the vow. I came through the same wide road as before, down the same steep hill, and suddenly realised that I was restored to life. In spite of my devotion to the Buddha, the punishment of being murdered was brought on me, because I had made free use of the temple property for my own ends.'

Now I have introduced the necessary material for my discussion. In the ballad, the visit of the hero was to the land of fairies, and in Japan heroes visit various other worlds. There are no fairies in Japan, but the motifs pertaining to them are almost all present in terms of the actions of indigenous supernatural beings. For example, Japanese foxes in their difficult childbirth ask for human midwives' help, and their payments like fairies' gifts fade away.

Stith Thompson's *Motif Index,* in its F 'Marvel' section, assigns different motif numbers to the actions of fairies, leprechauns, trolls, brownies, elves, etc., but their actions are very often identical. Thus motifs are unnecessarily duplicated, bearing many different numbers. These motifs should be re-arranged into one set, covering actions, or antics, of supernatural beings in general.

In the ballad of 'Thomas Rymer', he sees the fairy queen 'come riding down by the Eildon Tree', when he 'lay on Huntlie bank'. In Japan there are several methods of seeing supernatural beings when they are among us in this world, so as not to become victims of their mischief, but to be able to deal with them on an equal basis. In the first place there are certain haunts of those beings. The discreet will avoid such places, even during the day. In the second place, applying one's own saliva to one's eyebrows will give extraordinary vision, enabling one to see them through their disguise, or even if they have made themselves invisible. To look backwards through one's parted legs is another method, and to squat or lie on the ground, making one's eye-level low, and look over grass-blades, is yet another.

Huntlie bank is situated along the river Leader, not far from Earlstoune, and locally there is the belief that the fairies often gather here. I do not know if the Eildon Tree still stands, but it must have had a unique feature to hear a name, and it is known that, after Thomas came back from fairyland, it was under this tree that he gave his prophecies.

Comparing 'Thomas Rymer' and the Japanese counterparts, we see that both have the guide explaining three unusual roads. The land of the dead is supposed to be beyond a river, in the Orient and elsewhere, like the Styx in Greek myth, and so is the land of fairies. For days Thomas and the fairy queen wade through rivers in absolute darkness, and: 'they saw neither sun nor moon, but they heard the roaring of the sea'. As to the analogue of the gift of prophecy, I have already mentioned this above.

One important element in the visits to the other world is that very often the hero becomes homesick after a while, as in the Urashima legend and the 'Lost Fish Hook' story. He is permitted to go home, but with some sort of taboo attached. If the taboo is not violated, he is able to come back to his wife. However, there is no taboo which goes unbroken. Thus, the hero and his supernatural wife are separated by death, distance or forgetfulness. In other words, some forms of Type 470 will take as their ending 'the Forgotten Fiancée', motif F2001, in which Walter Anderson was interested in his later years, and which I have treated in my other papers.

At the beginning of this paper, I introduced the term 'cycle', and used it throughout. It is a cluster of types and sub-types which share themes and motifs, the beginning and/or ending sections. Along with the already established concepts of types and motifs, I should like to see this 'cycle' accepted in the analysis of folk literature.

For some years I have been engaged in the comparative study of ballads with Japanese material. The purpose is twofold: to introduce the Japanese material to the West, and the ballad material to Japan.

The Axis Mundi and the Phallus; Some Unrecognised East-West Parallels

JOHN IRWIN   Victoria and Albert Museum (retired)

WITH the growth of antiquarianism in the nineteenth century and its extension to early Christian monuments, it came to be known that a number of those traditionally worshipped as 'Crosses' were in fact nothing recognisably of the kind. So far from any clear relationship to the Cross Ecclesiastical, some had the obvious appearance of phallic symbols.

How did the Cross and phallus ever get mixed up? To most Victorians, phallic worship was a sign of 'lower' religion alien and even antithetical to their own ideas of what Christianity stood for. So it is not surprising that when public attention was drawn to the existence of such 'Crosses', they often disappeared soon afterwards from the sites where they had been reported.[1] No doubt the agents of their disappearance hoped that all memory of them would be forgotten, and in most cases it probably was. But there were exceptions, and one of them is reproduced in Plate 11.

In spite of the attempted destruction and burial of this 'Cross' in 1840, it was unexpectedly dug up a few decades later by roadbuilders working near its original site, which was the market crossroads at Langholm, Dumfriesshire. This rediscovery happened just in time for elderly citizens of the town to be able to explain the original setting and local traditions associated with it. Known to them as the 'Mercat [Market] Cross', it was said to have served as the focus of all important civic events, including the announcement of royal and other proclamations of communal concern.[2] It was then carefully pieced together and re-erected in the compound of the Langholm Library, a private trust founded by the great engineer Thomas Telford who had been a native of the district, where it still stands today.

The only cross associated with this object is one engraved on the top, and there is no evidence to tell if this engraving is contemporary with the monument or a later addition. Whatever the facts in this particular case, it is possible to cite other phallus-like stones standing at crossroads in Scotland that have no cross of any kind associated with them. The example at Plate 12 stands at Clackmannan, near Stirling. The drawing was published by J. W. Small in 1900,[3] but the author makes no reference to its meaning. He does, however, draw attention to the fact that the medieval 'Market Cross' standing nearby is itself without any kind of cruciform. It is now for us to note that the shaft of the medieval monument is octagonal in the centre and square at the base – exactly as in the case of the Langholm 'Market Cross' which we recognise as phallic. At Clackmannan, there is no doubt that the phallic stone is older than the medieval monument and almost certainly pre-Christian, because the stone (*clack*) gives the name to the place which is known to have been a royal seat as far back as Pictish times.[4]

There is no reason to suppose that phallic posts or pillars were not once common in Britain as we know they were on the continent. In Scandinavia, many survive up to the present day (Plate 13). They are known as *bautas*, and in Norway more particularly as *pighellen*, literally 'penis-stone'. In ancient Greece they were called *herms*, described by Pausanias (VI.26.3) as 'nothing but the male organ of generation erect on a pedestal'; however, in classical times they were already being frowned upon and gradually replaced by humanised images of the chthonic god who took the name Hermes. Phallic stones were also common in the Near East where they belonged to a class of sacred erections called *massebas*. Recently, archaeologists have traced the prototype of the *masseba* as far back as

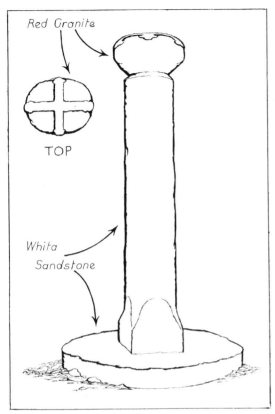

Plate 11. Drawing of the Langholm 'cross' (see Note 2). On the left, the cross emblem incised on top of the stone and, to the right, the entire 'cross', showing the phallus-shaft of white sandstone, surmounted by red granite bearing the cross emblem. (*Drawing: Margaret Hall*).

Plate 12. Medieval 'Market Cross' and (right) phallic stone at Clackmannan, near Stirling (after J. W. Small; see Note 3).

the seventh millennium B.C. in Jericho.[5]

When Pope Gregory issued his famous sixth-century directive to emissaries bound for Britain not to destroy pagan shrines but to adapt them for Christian worship, he was realistic enough to warn them that they could not expect to banish pagan associations in one step.[6] There is much evidence to suggest that phallic worship was among the rites that persisted in some areas and for many centuries after nominal conversion to Christianity, although, as might be expected, our evidence for this is mainly in the form of injunctions aimed at suppressing such rites. Professor K. P. Wentersdorf has

introduced me to an interesting case recorded in the *Chronicon de Lanercost*. As late as the twelfth century A.D., a priest at Inverkeithing in Fifeshire celebrated Easter by marshalling the young girls of his parish and making them dance round a phallic post to the accompaniment of obscene language. Here we recognise a religious rite probably once universal, still performed as a Spring rite in India up to the present day in the thinly disguised form of the Holi Festival. The *Chronicon de Lanercost* adds two interesting details: when the respectably married parishioners were scandalised, their protests had the effect of driving the priest to ever

Plate 13. Phallic stone (*bauta*), Denmark (after T. Vanngaard; see Notes 9 and 10).

Plate 14. Twelfth-century Romanesque granite phallus with cross ornamentation, in Tømmerby Church, north Jutland (after T. Vanngaard; see Notes 9 and 10).

greater excess; on the other hand we are told that so highly did they hold in regard his office that he never lost their respect.[7]

In Denmark, which was not Christianised until the tenth century A.D., the Church's toleration of such rites extended to the acceptance of phallic symbols within the church itself. A remarkable example is the phallus in Plate 23 which remains to the present day within the Romanesque church at Tømmerby in northern Jutland. It even has carved in relief on its shaft an image of what appears to be a conventionalised image of Christ Incarnate on the Cross. In depicting this image, the artist seems to have been influenced by very ancient resurrection and Key-of-Life symbols that circulated widely in the pagan world.[8] Danish

authorities are convinced that this phallic monument is contemporary with the twelfth-century foundation of the church. In the opinion of Dr Thorkil Vanggaard who first published the monolith,[9] it can be taken with other Danish evidence, including a baptismal font with phallic ornament, to prove that 'phallic symbolism was carried over from the Frey cult of pre-Christian times into the cult of fully-blooming twelfth-century Christianity in Denmark.'[10] Once again, we should note that the shaft of the Danish phallus, like the 'Market Crosses' we have seen in Scotland, is octagonal in the centre, and square where it enters the ground. Is it pure accident, do you suppose, that the same convention characterises the Indian sacred phallus or Śiva-liṅga, symbol of the god Śiva? In its monu-

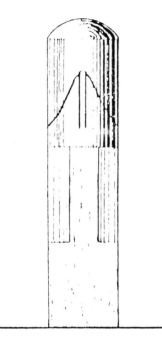

Plate 15. Drawing of a typical medieval Śiva-liṅga (after T. G. Rao; see Note 11).

mental form it is known as *sthāvara-liṅga*,[11] a drawing of which is shown here in Plate 15.

In this paper our main interest is not simply to record pagan survivals as was the concern of pioneer scholars in the field, like Eugene Goblet d'Alviella. Our aim is to re-examine such survivals in terms of their original metaphysical meaning, which the 'historical' religions like Christianity and Hinduism inherited from prehistory. It has been reluctance even to explore these deeper connections that accounts for the weakness of modern archaeological interpretation, notwithstanding astonishing technological advances.

For the next stage, let us forget the phallic aspect of our subject and think of the cult-objects we have been discussing under their common denominator as different kinds of sacred pillar or post. We shall see that most ancient sacred pillars the world over have many other features in common. For instance, they are everywhere com-

monly sited at crossroads. These crossroads were usually the location of annual fairs or festivals; they marked the spot at which proclamations were made, and where justice was administered; they commonly witnessed the swearing of oaths, and constituted the local market-place where weights and measures and other commercial procedures were controlled for the benefit of the community as a whole. In most parts of the world, the rite of worship is known to have been by clockwise circumambulation, in Celtic known as *deasil*, in Latin, *dextratio*, in Sanskrit *pradakṣiṇa* – all words with root-meaning of 'the right' and implying circumambulation with the venerated object on the worshipper's right. Traditionally, the principle time of worship was at sunrise during the annual festival.[12]

Concentrating for the moment on the Indian evidence, we find that one of the principle beliefs surrounding pillar-worship from earliest times is the mythical axis of the world, and that the sun unites with its summit daily when it reaches its zenith. At this moment, the sun and the pillar are conceived as a metaphysical unity: the pillar is the sun, and the sun is the pillar, say the ancient texts. In art, this identification is symbolised by a sun-wheel (*cakra*) at the summit (Plate 16).

The same symbolism recurs in many other parts of the world, including Europe and the Americas, so this might be the moment to ask if it has any bearing on the fact that all the earliest Christian cult-crosses were not crucifixes but wheel-crosses, such as we see in Plate 17? Association between the wheel-cross and the sun is explicit in Anglo-Saxon poems like *The Dream of the Rood, Elene,* and *Daniel.* Although in these poems the overall emphasis of the religious message is on Crucifixion rather than Resurrection, thus reversing the emphasis of the teaching of the early Christian Fathers, the instrument of Christ's death is described in solar terms as 'blazing', 'the brightest of all beacons', 'drenched in gold', 'wound round with light', and so on.

In this context we should take full account of the fact that there is nothing in the Greek version of the New Testament to say that Christ was crucified or that the instrument of his agony and death was a cross. The Epistles, which are earlier than the Gospels, tell us only that Jesus was 'hanged on a tree'. The word rendered in the

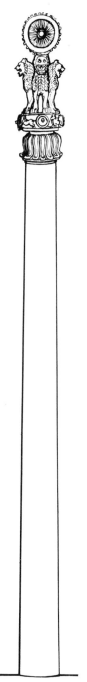

Plate 16. Artist's reconstruction of the Aśokan Pillar at Sarnath, north India. The pillar dates from the third century B.C.

Plate 17. The 'Gosforth Cross' or Rood, from Gosforth in Northumberland (eighth century; see *Archaeological Journal*, XL [1883]).

Gospels in Latin as *crux* and in English as 'cross' is the Greek word *stauros*, which in pre-Christian Greek literature denoted, not 'cross', but 'stake' or 'post' — in other words, a single piece of upright timber without crosspiece.

A point of special relevance, in my opinion, is that Greek *stauros* derives from the same Indo-Aryan root that gave to the Vedic language *skambha*, and to Sanskrit, *stambha* — both words used in the religious context to denote the *cosmic* pillar or metaphysical axis of the universe. In the earliest Indian texts, *skambha* is used exclusively with this metaphysical meaning; the later term *stambha*, was applied to pillars in their material form erected for worship. The Indo-Aryan root from which all these words derived had the meaning, 'make firm' or 'fix'. What is even more important to us, the ultimate associations of *stauros*, *skambha*, and *stambha* were not merely cosmic but more specifically cosmogonic. Since this comes out most clearly in the Indian evidence, this is the moment to explain in outline the facts of the earliest Indian cosmogony as now revealed to us by the latest research in Vedic scholarship.[13]

Before the world began there was only Chaos, without life or any of the dualities which constitute our organised universe, such as heaven and earth, good and evil, fire and water, male and female, and so on. This Chaos was visualised as Water, constituting the Cosmic Ocean. The first stage in the Creation was when a clod of earth floated to the surface of the Waters, to be tossed about on the waves. This clod I shall call, for clarity of exposition, by my own term Primordial Mound. The second stage began with the birth of Indra, when heaven and earth were still compacted within the Primordial Mound, and when the latter was guarded by Vṛtra, a serpent-personification of the idea of 'obstruction' or 'resistence'. Whereas Vṛtra's role was to obstruct or lock up the waters within the Mound, Indra's demiurgic act was to kill the serpent and release the waters. At the same time, he separated heaven and earth and released the sun from the waters, thereby creating time and the seasons and all the basic dualities like night and day, fire and water, and so on. The vacuum between earth and heaven was filled by space, which expanded horizontally to give birth to the Four Quarters.

The instrument used by Indra to separate heaven and earth was also used by him as a peg to fix the Primordial Mound to the bottom of the cosmic ocean, thereby providing the stability needed for the Mound to expand into our universe. This instrument was commonly visualised as a pillar — sacred archetype of every ritual pillar, post, pole or standard — which was mystically identified with the cosmic tree from which it was ritually fashioned. From this it followed that every ritual object of this kind had to be of wood. When sacred pillars were later copied in permanent materials like stone or metal, this meant that the significance of the original rite had already been partly forgotten.

The above summarised version of the Indian cosmogony is mainly based on the evidence of the Ṛgveda as interpreted by F. B. J. Kuiper and other modern specialists in this field. The special importance of the Vedas in this connection is that they provide the earliest well-documented cosmogony known to us. Moreover, the basic pattern of this cosmogony seems to have been widely if not universally shared in the prehistoric world. For instance, the Cosmic Waters, the Primordial Mound, the Separation of Heaven and Earth, and the release of the Sun from the Waters to start the cosmic life-cycle can be traced wherever evidence of the earliest cosmogonies survives, and this includes all regions which later became Christianised. The hypothesis on which I am working is that these apparently universal elements of prehistoric cosmogony have roots going back at least as far as the neolithic revolution in Western Asia. However, whatever the truth on this score, there is abundant proof that pillar- and cross-worship was widespread if not universal in areas later Christianised. The early Christian Fathers, unlike many later leaders of the Established Church, went out of their way to emphasise the continuity of this rite.[14] *O Crux, splendidor cunctis astris, mundo celebris, hominibus multum amabilis, Sanctior universis*, says the York breviary, at a much later date. Even more to the point is the famous passage in Sermon VI for Holy Week, variously attributed to St Hippolytus and Pseudo-Crysostom:

> This Tree [the Cross], vast as heaven itself, rises from the earth to the heavens, a plant immortal, set firm in the midst of heaven and earth, fulcrum of the universe, it towers to the highest heavens and spans with its all-

embracing arms the boundless gulf of space between... With its foot planted firmly on the earth, it towers up to the highest heavens and spans with its all-embracing arms the boundless gulf of space between...

While this description is still fresh in memory, it is fitting to recall similar words describing the cosmic pillar in Indian hymns at least a thousand years earlier. For instance, of *skambha* – which we have already mentioned as deriving from the same Indo-Aryan root as Greek *stauros*, rendered in our English version of the New Testament as 'cross' – it is said in *Atharva-veda* X.7. that it is the 'fulcrum of the universe' and of the whole of existence (verses 3 and 35), both separating and uniting heaven and earth, penetrating all the cosmic regions, including the waters below the earth, the earth itself, the atmosphere, and the celestial spheres (verses 8, 30 and 41), containing within itself everything that is sacred. In Vedic ritual, *skambha* is materialised as a post or pillar (*yūpa*) which had to be fashioned from the trunk of a sacred tree. Even after being made into a pillar it is addressed as Vanaspati, 'Lord of the Forest', and while it is being erected, the priest declaims as follows: 'With thy top thou has touched the heavens, with thy middle thou hast filled the air; with thy foot thou hast steadied the earth', and so on.[15]

Now where does the phallus come into all this? In India, the answer is clear. It is associated with the germination of life at the creation. Heaven and earth, after their initial separation, then came together again as the archetypal bridal pair. The cosmic pillar in the form of a phallus is therefore symbolic of the Axis Mundi in its *uniting*, as distinct from separating, role. At the folklore level, it is the symbol of the generative organ with which Father Heaven inseminates Mother Earth.

The above conception of phallus as Axis Mundi persists widely in Indian fertility rites up to the present day. One instance of this recently came to my notice when touring northern Bihar. I saw that most of the irrigation ponds had a large wooden pillar standing in the centre, and when I asked the reason I was told that this was 'ancient custom'. It transpired that when a pond was dug, or renewed, it was consecrated by the rite of erecting a pillar in the water as symbol of the act of insemination.

Pillars standing in water I also noticed to be the central theme of paintings on the walls of marriage pavilions in the same region, especially in Mithila District. These paintings were not made for decoration in our modern sense but as part of the marriage ritual itself, because every human marriage is considered to be a repetition of the archetypal divine marriage. 'I am Heaven, thou art Earth,' says the bridegroom to bride in the Hindu marriage ceremony. In short, re-enactment of the primodial act of creation at the wedding is thought to ensure the fecundity of the union.

Going back to the Vedas which represent the other end of Indian tradition, Kuiper has drawn attention to the fact that the notion of 'standing erect' was synonymous with Life.[16] For instance, it is said of the personification of Vitality in *Rgveda* III.61.3: 'Thou standest erect as symbol of Life.' Parallels have been noted in other religions – for instance, in connection with the Israelite *massēba* and the Egyptian *djed*-pillar, both symbolic of life and resurrection. A. K. Coomaraswamy, remarking upon the emphasis and repetition of the word 'erect' in the ceremony of raising a *yūpa*, has used this to explain why, in Indian depiction of *lingam-yoni*, the phallus stands head upwards in the vulva in what is strictly speaking an unnatural position.[17]

With these associations in mind it might be worth reconsidering the meaning of *Atharva-veda* X.7.41., where the Axis Mundi as *Skambha* is described in terms expressing the visual image of a pillar rising out of the cosmic waters in the form of *vetasam hiranyayam*, 'golden reed or bamboo'. Although *vetasa* means 'reed' or 'bamboo', its derivative *vaitasa* (literally made of reed) is used very clearly in *Rgveda* IV.58.5. in the sense of 'penis'. There is no proof that the *Atharva-veda* passage was intended to carry a phallic overtone, but it does not seem unlikely, seeing that later Hindu mythology exactly expresses this phallic association in the well-known legend of the origin of the Śiva-liṅgam.[18]

Is all this a far cry from the early Christian cult-cross? I do not think so. In the first place it should be remembered that although in retrospect we talk about a *cross*-cult, the people who carved and erected these monuments never did. They called them 'Roods'. Why? The standard works of reference do not tell us. I have been unable to find a single mention of 'Rood', except in the later association of 'rood-screen', in works like Eadie's *Ecclesiastical Encyclopaedia,* or the *Oxford Dictionary of Christian Church Architecture,* or the twelve monumental volumes of the *Encyclopaedia of Religion and Ethics.* Even the *Oxford English Dictionary* omits any reference to 'rood' in its early English usage.

Of course, it should now be obvious that one reason why a 'Rood' was not called a 'Cross' is because the early type was never in any accurate or meaningful sense a *cross:* it was an image of a tree, the Tree of Life, which was only later and in a mythical way identified with the instrument of Christ's torture. But is there not possible significance in the fact — so far neglected by etymologists and lexigrophers discussing English 'rood' — that the German and Dutch words *rute* and *roede,* with the primary meaning wooden 'rod' or 'pole', have always had the secondary meaning 'penis'?

The history of the early Christian cross-cult has always been surrounded with problems. One result of this paper may be to extend rather than reduce them. Yet, even that may prove to have been worth doing if it stimulates fresh thinking on a subject so important in the art traditions of both East and West, and at the same time helps to throw fresh light on the unity within the diversity of human culture.

Notes

1. Cases of the disappearance of phallic-like Crosses are reported by T. F. G. and H. Dexter, *Cornish Crosses* (London, 1938), *passim.*

2. J. and R. Hyslop, *Langholm as it was: A History of Langholm and Eskdale from Earliest Times* (Dumfries, 1912), 418-20. The drawing of the Langholm 'Cross' published by these authors is inaccurate in some important details and should be ignored. Mr Robert B. Chenciner, who brought this monument to my attention, also kindly supplied the photograph from which Margaret Hall's drawing in Plate 11 is taken.

3. J. W. Small, *Scottish Market Crosses* (Stirling, 1900), Pl. 32. The stone had been previously drawn and published by Peter Miller, 'Standing Stones of Alloa and Clackmanan', *Proceedings of the Society of Antiquaries of Scotland*, XXIII (1889), 159-60. Neither of the authors acknowledged the phallic symbolism, which we must now regard as fortunate.

4. Miller, *op. cit.*; W. C. Mackenzie, *Scottish Place-names* (London, 1931), 65.

5. Kathleen M. Kenyon, 'Jericho and its setting in Near Eastern history', *Antiquity*, XXX (1965), 185-6.

6. *Nam duris mentibus simul omnia abscidere impossible esse non dubium est...*; Bede, *Historia Ecclesiastica*, Liber I, Cap. XXX.

7. *Chronicon de Lanercost, 1201-1346,* edited by J. Stevenson and published by the Bannatyne Club (Glasgow, 1839), 109, kindly brought to my attention by Professor Karl P. Wentersdorf, of Xavier University, Cincinnati, Ohio.

8. These images were discussed by Count Goblet d'Alviella, 'Des Symboles qui ont influencé la Représentation figurée des Pierres coniques chez les Sémites', *Revue de l'Histoire des Religions*, XX (1889), 135-50.

9. Thorkil Vanggaard, *Phallos, a Symbol and its History in the Male World* (London, 1972), 84, and Pl. 11. I am especially grateful to Dr W. M. S. Russell for first bringing this book to my notice.

10. Quoted from a letter written to me by the author, dated 23/8/1979. I am also most grateful to Dr Vangaard for Plates 13 and 14, illustrating the present paper.

11. For illustrations and authoritative discussion of the Śiva-liṅgam, see T. A. G. Rao, *Elements of Hindu Iconography* (Madras, 1914-15), II, part 1, 75-102, esp. Pl. VI. Plate 15 in the present volume is based on Plate VIII in Rao, II, part 2.

12. Here I presented slides of photographs taken at Lauriya-Nandangarh, north Bihar (India), in January, 1976, showing the famous Aśokan lion-pillar under worship at dawn, at the time of the annual fair held at the site. So-called Aśokan pillars are generally believed to have been erected by king Aśoka (272-231 B.C.) to advertise his edicts which in most cases are engraved on the shafts. Many of their sites have been identified as ancient crossroads, and worship of the pillars is known to have been by clockwise circumambulation. For fuller discussion, see my articles, ' "Aśokan" Pillars: a re-assessment of the evidence', *Burlington Magazine,* CXV (1973), 706-20; CXVI (1974), 712-27; CXVII (1975), 631-43; CXVIII

(1976), 734-53. For West European evidence of the worship of the so-called 'Market Cross' at dawn, see Count Goblet d'Alviella, 'Les Perrons de la Wallonie', *Bulletin de l'Académie royale de Belgique*, Classe des Lettres, XI (1913), 374-5.

13. I refer in particular to the works of Professor W. Norman Brown and F. B. J. Kuiper, so far confined to specialist journals. For bibliography and discussion see my article, Part IV, 'Symbolism', in the series mentioned in Note 12 above (1976), 738 ff.

14. For instance, Justin Martyr, *Apologia*, I, 55, and Tertullian, *Apologeticus*, 16, 6-8. Echoes of the pre-Christian phallic associations of the Cross are traceable even in post-Augustinian sermons. 'Through the sign of the Cross you are conceived in the womb of your holy Mother, the Church'. (Quoted by H. Rahner, *Greek Myths and Christian Mysteries*, London, 1963, p.78). In other words, it is by the procreative power of the Cross that the Church is here said to be fructified.

15. See Śatapatha Brāhmana III.7.1. 14. For slightly variant translation, see J. Eggeling, *Sacred Books of the East*, vol.XXVI, 1885, 171.

16. F. B. J. Kuiper, 'The Ancient Indian Verbal Conquest', *Indo-Iranian Journal*, IV (1960), 232.

17. A. K. Coomaraswamy, 'The Inverted Tree', *Quarterly Journal of the Mythic Society of Bangalore*, XXIX (1938), Note 65.

18. For a summary of the myth of the Origin of the Śiva-*lingam*, see Heinrich Zimmer, *Myths and Symbols in Indian Art and Civilization* (Princeton, 1946), 138 ff. The association between cosmic pillar and phallus is explicit in Mağābhārata X.17.8 ff. where Śiva pulls off his own penis and sets it up as a sacred pillar (*stambha*).

Perspectives in the Study of Eating Behaviour

MICHAEL OWEN JONES   The University of California, Los Angeles

'NUTRITION as a biological process is more fundamental than sex', reads the first sentence of Audrey
Richards' book *Hunger and Work in a Savage Tribe,*
first published in England in 1932 and printed
again in America in 1948.[1] Her mentor Malinowski
was enthusiastic about the book, writing in the
preface, 'After reading it, my conviction deepened
that society is not animated by one obsessive
force, that of sex.'[2] His statement is noteworthy,
if for no other reason than that he had recently
published four books dealing largely with sexual
behaviour in savage society. Though two of his
books even had 'sex' on the title page, Malinowski
was to contend in his preface to Richards' study of
the cultural aspects of food and eating: 'Among
the Melanesians whom I studied, the most important motive in the life of the community and in
the interests of the individual is food, not sex.'[3]
And further he notes, regarding Richards' book:
'In having written the first scientific memoir on
the subject of the sociology and psychology of
nutrition, she reaps the reward of pioneering
achievement. No serious anthropologist can afford
to neglect the present study, which opens new
prospects and dictates new questions in field-
work.'[4] Forty years later, in his article 'The Study
of Contemporary Foodways in American Folklife
Research', Jay Anderson was to contend that
Richards' work, 'a pioneer study', had served as
'an important influence on students of American
folk foodways. . .'[5]

I mention these matters for several reasons.
First, as an American folklorist, interested in
eating behaviour, who is attending the Centenary
Conference of the Folklore Society, I feel that
acknowledgment should be given to British researchers whose works have affected me and some
other American investigators. Second, the subject

of foodways is indeed important, though still
generally neglected in folkloristics, for it is unique
in the range of related phenomena and their
centrality in peoples' lives. Third, Richards' book
on food and eating in savage society as culturally-
determined behaviour presaged an era of research
informed by one of the major perspectives in
foodways study, which is the topic of my paper. I
would point out now that the recent work of yet
another British researcher, Mary Douglas, suggests
some of the elements of a second major perspective
which is imerging. Her remarks, on deciphering a
meal by members of her own middle-class family
in England, appeared in *Daedalus* in 1972, exactly
four decades after Richards' study was published.[6]

To return to the subject of Richards' book, it
should be noted that her study was intended to
complement and supplement Malinowski's research,
not to supplant it. Indeed, Richards sets forth her
pronouncements within a conceptual framework
taught her by Malinowski, among others, differing
from her mentor's position in her focus on food-
getting, rather than reproduction, as a – or perhaps
the – primary biological need of human beings
serving as the locus of culture perpetuating society,
at least among savages.

Like Malinowski, she began with the assumption
of the fundamental unity of social institutions;
while she assumed that shared sentiments bound
together members of a group, she puzzled over
what those attitudes, in the main, concerned:
reproduction, food, shelter? Malinowski had emphasised procreation; Richards concluded food-
getting. Why food? Because it is both a 'more
primary and recurrent physical want', for the
impulse to seek food recurs regularly and cannot
be long inhibited or repressed. As a constant
necessity, food-getting, rather than some other

260

biological need, determined the nature of social groupings and their activities.[7] Having decided that nutrition was primary in shaping the social institutions which were unified into a whole, Richards sought to illustrate her thesis. 'I want to examine the human relationships of a primitive society as determined by nutritional needs,' she writes, 'showing how hunger shapes the sentiments which bind together the members of each social group.'[8] The choice of a savage tribe in part depended on her assumption that its simplicity and the insecurity of the food supply would enable her to 'see the situation more clearly',[9] for she supposed that the nature of, and conditions of life in, a contemporary savage society more fully approximated to man's earliest existence.

Though principally a functional analysis of how food is used to symbolise certain social relationships in a primitive tribe, maintaining cohesion and thus perpetuating that society, Richards' study is grounded on her notions of a 'nutritional system' and how it must have developed initially. The individual is driven by hunger, she contends, which renders food-getting a compelling urge, investing it with a meaning and value unique among human activities. The most basic social relationship is that involving mother and child, which is also physiological. Hence, the family is held together by the object of procuring food. Within the structure of the family and its food-centered activities, the child learns who will provide sustenance and with whom and how it must be shared. Families are linked together in 'ties of reciprocity' to form a larger social system, facilitating the food quest and regulating the ownership and distribution of food resources. Once this system has been established, the individual's behaviour, through the family initially, is determined in regard to diet and manner of eating by social customs and group sentiments.[10] In primitive conditions, therefore, writes Richards, 'food itself becomes symbolic of the human relationships which it brings into being'.[11]

'Food As a Symbol' is the title of the concluding chapter of Richards' book. Other researchers after Richards — whether directly influenced by her study or not — also have been concerned about the apparent emotional and social significance of food and about the extranutritional meanings sometimes attributed to food, its preparation, distribution, and consumption. Numerous individuals have con-

sidered the possible correlation between childhood feeding experiences and adult interpersonal relations, often assuming that the behaviour patterns are crystallised into institutionalised attitudes toward food, reinforcing existing systems of belief, economic distribution, and child-rearing practices.[12] Others have been intrigued by the meanings and social functions of food sharing, assuming that communal eating is a cohesive act uniting members of a social unit, which they then illustrate by referring to selected behaviour of their subjects. Food as a status symbol, food as a badge of group identity, and food as a vehicle for socialising behaviour are topics of great interest, the treatment of which has been based on the assumption that the subjects constitute a relatively homogeneous group, whose sentiments are shared by its members.[13] How food preferences and aversions are generated, why consistencies and continuities in eating behaviour exist, and how to change food habits are questions that have occupied yet other investigators, who seem to assume that they are dealing with cultural artifacts surviving in a historical context.[14] As survivals within culture, aspects of human subsistence have been regarded principally as indexes to ways of life in the past and to psychical states and socio-cultural processes.

Something of a departure from the general tendency to exclude from consideration the researcher's own behaviour and to avoid studying eating *per se*, however, is the article 'Deciphering a Meal' by Mary Douglas.[15] She assumes, as Richards had assumed, that the 'taking of food', like sex, while biological, is principally a cultural phenomenon; that food communicates to others much about patterns of social relations; and that a family relies on symbolic structures pervasive within a wider social system. In essence, like Richards, she begins with an assumption of the fundamental unity of culture binding together members of a group. But the data base differs. Early in her essay Douglas presents a 'humble and trivial case' of eating behaviour,[16] that of the main food categories used in her own home as she became aware of them one evening when her attempts to serve soup as a 'meal' met with strenuous objections. The second half of her article concerns, however, as did her book *Purity and Danger: An Analysis of Concepts of Pollution and Taboo*,[17] a 'more serious example',[18] that of the Jewish meal governed by the

Mosaic dietary rules. Her premise, which relates these to seemingly disparate instances, is that a meal is an ordered system which, because it represents all the ordered systems associated with it, arouses strong emotions when that category is threatened.[19] But, while considering her own family's behaviour, Douglas began to realise that the meaning of a meal is not fixed; rather, meanings are enriched through time, for eating is an on-going human experience. 'Each meal carries something of the meaning of the other meals,' she writes,[20] which leads her to consider the structure of a particular kind of meal in her own home.

Studies, principally of savages and other rural and cultural isolates, make it clear that nutrition is a fundamental — if not the primary — biological need in human beings, generating such a wide range of activities as food production, storage, processing, distribution, preparation, service, and consumption, as well as waste disposal, cleaning, and reordering with tools and techniques appropriate to each activity. Furthermore, it is apparent that sometimes some food-related experiences earlier in life affect present behaviour and attitudes, that various aspects of subsistence may be social in nature, and that food often acquires a meaning and significance beyond simple bodily nourishment, which may change through time. What remains to be established, however, on the basis of clues provided by Richards, Douglas, and others, is the character of eating *per se,* that makes these things possible for all human beings.

That food, its preparation, service, and consumption, serve all human beings as a basis of interaction and a vehicle of communication, a source of associations and symbolic structures, and a locus of consistencies and continuities in behaviour results from the fact that eating is:

1. a biological need which is recurrent and insistent;

2. always an individual act, but often also a social activity;

3. a physiological and an intellectual experience.

As a biological need that is insistent and compelling, and which, as Richards suggests, cannot be successfully inhibited or repressed beyond a limited period of time, eating has an immediacy and primacy unique among human concerns and endeavours. The physiological function of eating is met frequently and regularly, and therefore each instance of eating is both similar to and different from every past occasion of eating; as a consequence, there are continuities as well as unique features in eating-related behaviour. Eating is an experience common to all human beings and therefore readily comprehensible and frequently the subject of attention; hence, food-sharing is a fundamental human act, whether food and drink are distributed to strangers, offered to friends, or used as the basis of, as well as the justification for, more general social contacts.

Eating is often associated with other people and activities. It may be either the focus of interaction, or only incidental to it, and the rationale for assembling together, or simply the outcome; but as a social experience, eating embraces identities as well as rights and responsibilities deemed appropriate to those designations, thus establishing social relations among participants in the event. Experiencing food with others results in a transference to food — its preparation, service, and consumption — of assessments and valuations of those experiences, as well as the association of food with selected identities, events, values, and behaviour. Because food is a perceptible phenomenon, unique in the number of senses affected and in the intensity of affect, which is realised by each human being, the quantity and quality of food are assumed to manifest intangible conditions and results, including relative wealth, status, sophistication, and attitudes toward others. Recognising that food and food-centred activities may be considered symbolic, might be taken as manifestations of latent or intangible phenomena, and could serve as a vehicle of communication encoding messages for others to decipher, human beings sometimes take pains to inform others that the food or the circumstance should not be conceived of as an expression of values, attitudes, or identities; and other human beings sometimes ignore or discount one or another of the multiple 'messages' that might be inferred from the food, its preparation, service, and consumption, as well as its quantity and quality.

While often a social activity, eating is always a singular act. Because it is idiosyncratic, unique attitudes and behaviour are generated. Despite a shared identity, one person does not always eat what another eats, or in the same way; though in the company of each other, people who share food do not always feel a sense of community; and, while engaged in the same kind of activity at the same time and in the same place, participants do not always interpret the event in the same way. As a personal experience, eating produces in one a wide range of physical sensations and intellectual states, which themselves are an important aspect of the event, determining one's reactions and responses to this event and to subsequent events.

Whatever else characterises eating, the act of consuming food is first and foremost a physiological and an intellectual experience — unique in the range and intensity of effect — that is on-going, at once familiar and also novel. In providing pleasures and satisfactions personally and immediately, food can enliven social relations, enrich spiritual affairs, and enhance an individual's sense of well-being; it can be used to threaten, reward, cajole, or punish and in other ways control behaviour. Abstinence can be uplifting, and the denial of food by others devastating. Eating as a continuous experience in the lives of human beings results in the generation of preferences and dislikes, and even disgust and aversion, which, however, are subject to change through time with new experiences and the reassessment of self, previous events and relationships with others. Because food affects so many senses and produces such a broad spectrum of states, the timing and the manner of preparation, service, and consumption of food assume special importance, resulting in the development of skills, values, and criteria for evaluating these activities.

Each of these postulates — that eating is a biological need which is recurrent and insistent; eating is always an individual act, but often also a social activity; and eating is a physiological and an intellectual experience — whether taken severally or in combination, provides the basis for creating a new perspective in the study of eating behaviour appropriate to such recurrent problems in folkloristics as the ways in which aspects of behaviour are generated, the reasons for continuities and consistencies in behaviour, and the consequences of behaviour as a mode of human expression. These questions need not be limited to selected subjects, as in the past, but can be addressed to all human beings, including ourselves. And when answering these questions, it might even seem that 'dining out' one night a week, eating TV dinners, and attending banquets at meetings of professional organisations are as 'traditional' as is serving turkey at Thanksgiving . . . or taking tea at four o'clock . . .

Notes

1. Audrey I. Richards, *Hunger and Work in a Savage Tribe* (Glencoe, Ill., 1948), 1.

2. Bronislaw Malinowski, 'Preface', in *Hunger and Work in a Savage Tribe*, xii.

3. *ibid.*, xv.

4. *ibid.*, x.

5. Jay Allan Anderson, 'The Study of Contemporary Foodways in American Folklife Research', *Keystone Folklore Quarterly*, XVI (4) (1971), 156, 157.

6. Mary Douglas, 'Deciphering a Meal', *Daedalus*, CI (1972), 61-81.

7. Richards, 1.

8. *ibid.*, 23.

9. *ibid.*, 213.

10. *ibid.*, 212; see also 20-30.

11. *ibid.*, 213.

12. See, for example, Richard L. Currier, 'The Hot-Cold Syndrome and Symbolic Balance in Mexican and Spanish-American Folk Medicine', *Ethnology*, V (1966), 251-61; Yehudi A. Cohen, *Social Structure and Personality: A Case Book* (New York, 1961), 312-50; Cora DuBois, 'Attitudes Toward Food and Hunger in Alor', *Language, Culture and Personality: Essays in Honor of Edward Sapir*, ed. L. Spier, A. I. Hallowell, and S. Newmann (Menasha, 1941), 272-81; Dorothy N. Shack, 'Nutritional Processes and Personality Development among the Gurage of Ethiopia', *Ethnology*, VIII (3) (1969), 292-300.

13. John W. Bennett, 'Food and Social Status in a Rural Society', *American Sociological Review*, XIII (1943), 561-8; Charles W. Joyner, 'Soul Food and the Sambo Stereotype: Folklore from the Slave Narrative Collection', *Keystone Folklore Quarterly*, XVI (1971), 171-8; Roger L. Welsch, '"We Are What We Eat": Omaha Food As Symbol', *Keystone Folklore Quarterly*, XVI (1971), 165-70; Hortense Powdermaker, 'Feasts in New Ireland: The Social Function of Eating', *American Anthropologist*, XXXIV (1932), 236-47; Harriet Bruce Moore, 'The Meaning of Food', *American Journal of Clinical Nutrition*, V (1957), 77-82; Octavio Paz, 'Eroticism and Gastrosophy', *Daedalus*, CI (4) (1972), 67-85; James H. Bossard, 'Family Table Talk — An Area for Sociological Study', *American Sociological Review*, XVIII (1943), 295-301.

14. Frederick J. Simoons, *Eat Not This Flesh: Food Avoidances in the Old World* (Madison, 1961); A. Angyal, 'Disgust and Related Aversions', *Journal of Abnormal and Social Psychology*, XXXVI (1941), 393-412; Roy N. Dorcus, 'Food Habits: Their Origin and Control', *American Dietetic Association Journal*, XVIII (1942), 738-40; Gregory Gizelis, 'Foodways Acculturation in the Greek Community of Philadelphia', *Pennsylvania Folklife*, XX (2) (1970-71), 9-15; Sam Hilliard, 'Hog Meat and Corn Pone: Food Habits in the Ante-Bellum South', *Proceedings of the American Philosophical Society*, CXIII (1969), 1-13; Jitsuichic Masuoka, 'Changing Food Habits of the Japanese in Hawaii', *American Sociological Review*, X (1945), 759-65; Toni F. Fratto, 'Cooking in Red and White', *Pennsylvania Folklife*, XIX (1970), 2-15; Marjorie Sackett, 'Folk Recipes As a Measure of Intercultural Penetration', *Journal of American Folklore*, LXXXV (335) (1972), 77-81; Margaret Mead,

'The Problem of Changing Food Habits', *The Problem of Changing Food Habits*, National Research Council Bulletin, Number 108 (1943); Kurt Lewin, 'Forces Behind Food Habits and Methods of Change', *The Problem of Changing Food Habits*, National Research Council Bulletin, Number 108 (1943).

15. Douglas, 61-81.

16. *ibid.*, 61.

17. Mary Douglas, *Purity and Danger: An Analysis of Concepts of Pollution and Taboo* (London, 1966).

18. Douglas, 'Deciphering', 70.

19. *ibid.*, 80.

20. *ibid.*, 69.

The Social as a Folklore Category*

MÁRIA KOSOVÁ   **Institute of Ethnology, Bratislava**

THIS paper is based on a consideration of the situation which has characterised the humanities for the last 20 years, and is a feature of any common approach to the sciences and humanities. It is particularly noticeable in the choice of research methods employed, and in conceptions of the universe as an ordered system and as a part of semiotics. The theoretical and methodological basis of this paper is derived from research into the general theory of systems, and signs, otherwise known as semiotics.

In contemporary science, efforts have been made to discover the laws of organisation operating on every level of reality. It is therefore necessary to look at phenomena and their related systems as a unity, and not as a conglomeration of different parts. They must be considered, not out of context, but against as broad a background as possible.

For the investigation of social events, it is necessary to extend the number of categories and models used, and also to broaden the scope of scientific analysis. This is why inter-disciplinary research is increasingly used as a model. It involves a simultaneous approach, utilising many specialised branches of contemporary methods of scientific analysis. Examples are the methods used in mathematics and formal logic, literary theory, linguistics, ethnology, folklore, sociology, and, by way of contrast, grammar, used in consideration of the biological process.

In the present analysis of folklore phenomena, it has proved useful to apply the model of the open system, borrowed from the general theory of systems. In this sense folklore, an artistic expression which is simultaneously traditional and innovatory, is considered as an open system, which functions and exists within the relationships and changes of its component parts.

From the standpoint of semiotics, man's activity, regardless of biological need, can be understood in terms of symbols. Semiotics provides us with another method of scientific analysis, which helps to answer questions about the organisation of phenomena, i.e. in what way a particular system of signs is manifested within the artistic expression of a world-view. If we want to know what a work of art is stating, we must find out how the statement is formed. By using instruments of scientific analysis, we can begin to analyse the social as a phenomenon in narrative folklore and, presumably, in folk culture as a whole.

I understand social characteristics by relating them to the whole, and I use the expression 'social' to create a paradigm. I investigate the way the concept of the social fact — a term coined by the French sociologist Mauss — functions in narrative folklore, how it developed in historical terms, and what forms it takes. This approach underlines the social importance of folklore phenomena, and at the same time conceives of it as socially conditioned. Since its inception, folklore has been a means of humanising mankind, and increased sociability is a concrete embodiment of this phenomenon. Folklore has always been inherent in society, and has shared the fate of mankind; that is why social phenomena are so noticeable in all the different genres of folklore.

We must consider social phenomena in terms of their historical development. This historic aspect operates on two levels: one is embodied in folklore and is fundamental to it; the other, in relation to

*   Full summary.

266

the texts, is conveyed to us by the collector. Here I have in mind some stylised folklore collections from a period beginning with the end of the eighteenth century, and extending through to the first half of the nineteenth century, and also social phenomena in the material currently being collected by field-workers.

Social relations in narrative folklore can be studied with the help of three basic categories, which occur in epic works: action, characters, and milieu. They can also be regarded, in semiotic terms, as extended categories, whereby the work of the narrator can be studied. By using these three categories, the social is distinguished as a phenomenon by its completeness, because it is determined by the social structure of those who create and transmit folklore. The phenomenon of social consciousness, which is by nature collective, is the most important.

As regards the category of action, the social occurs as a phenomenon in folklore texts within the introductory situation, e.g. 'Once upon a time, there was a poor man'; 'Once upon a time there was a poor widow, who lived with her daughter.' This is followed by a declaration of intention, e.g. 'The poor man cannot make a living for his family and decides to kill himself in despair'; or: 'The poor father is old. He can no longer take care of his sons and sends them into the world, to live on their own.' Their fate is then acted out.

Action in narrative folklore is based on characters, who enact it and convey the social relationships which occur (as has been convincingly proved by Propp). The functions of the characters are disclosed through their different characteristics, which enable them to enact certain actions, and which also give rise to social tensions among them.

The social in terms of milieu takes a very specific form. The symbolic world of narrative folklore, especially within the fairy tale, is unnatural, e.g. mountains and towns under a magic spell; mountains of gold, silver, and diamond; a glass castle; a dragon's nest; houses of the sun and moon, and so on. Here it is the story-teller who creates the human dimension. This is also true of legend, especially belief legend. The role of the story-teller in relation to his text can be seen by the way in which he makes the environment of a particular fairy tale, or legend, familiar to his audience.

By analysing folklore texts using systems theory and semiotic theory, it is possible to establish categories within which the phenomenon of the social functions. Some of these fundamental categories are:

Binary opposition, where the world of the mighty rich is contrasted with that of the helpless poor.

Opposition within the very notion of the social itself:

1. Poverty as a social evil, which forces people to leave their environment for the unknown world, and consequently drives them to despair.

2. Membership of a social group comprising the poor and helpless as a positive phenomenon which signifies: nobility of mind, wisdom, beauty, unusual strength and courage.

Opposition within the paradigm itself — bad king versus positive hero, the son of a peasant.

Contrast is set against opposition, and expresses the relationship between structurally related syntagmatic units: e.g. the relationship between brother and sister, husband and wife.

Equivalents:	all the variable features of the social are equivalent to its stable structure.
Similarity:	describing characters and their milieu by approximating to the social milieu of the audience.
Dissimilarity:	the opposite of the above.
Transformation:	this concerns the milieu, as well as the characters.
Substitution:	replacement of characters by others from a different social level.
Suppression:	suppression of certain signified elements.
Combination:	re-arrangement of relationships.
Mutation:	the transfer of elements from other structures.
Expansion:	extension of the elements.
Reduction:	reduction in scope.

Translation:	transference of the major units into action and milieu; transfer of the action to a folk milieu.
Selection:	selection from the component parts of the paradigm, giving priority to the social aspects.

The methods of analysis listed above, which are presented in semiotic terminology, relate to the text. But several relate to the role of the story-teller (and, incidentally, to the singer, traditional carver, painter, and embroiderer). The story-teller and his audience together create the amount of the social which occurs in narrative folklore, and, in a broader sense, this is true of the creators of folk culture as a whole.

By utilising sign and system procedures in our analysis, we can see that the social as a phenomenon functions as an integral part of works of folklore: that is to say, it unifies folklore activity within a given ethnic community. Social consciousness in its most basic form is characteristic of all folklore. It differentiates one ethnic community from another.

Within the process of integration, the following factors are very important: (1) space, (2) time. Less stress is laid on social aspects in nineteenth-century reproductions than in texts recorded in this century. Within the process of differentiation, distinctions occur, though, at the same time, the phenomenon of the social in neighbouring cultures is emphasised, e.g. the differences between Slovak and Hungarian folklore.

Social motivation in works of folklore is also apparent on another level — the symbolic and non-symbolic levels of the text. Research has, to some extent, shown that a member of a traditional community was in the past more aware of the symbolic level which exists in a folklore text, within its deep structure. Modern readers of folk-lore texts, especially the new editions — and I am thinking particularly of younger readers — view the phenomenon of the social in non-symbolic terms, i.e. they see only the story as it stands. Social motivation is evident in narratives taken directly from life, particularly reminiscences.

To conclude, as the humanities, including folk-lore, draw increasingly on techniques used in the sciences, a new view is emerging regarding the deep structure in works of folklore, and the ways in which they are created and function. I am aware that the theories considered here often lead to a considerable degree of abstraction, and I do not regard them as the final answer, but rather as useful tools for more exactly determining the intuitive knowledge of the subject of this investigation.

Festive Functions of Hungarian Pottery

MÁRIA KRESZ   Néprajzi Museum, Budapest

IN folk art festive functions and everyday functions are not in contradiction, but are part of a gradual scale from the simplest undecorated shapes to the most sophisticated richly decorated objects. Most majestic are the large wine jugs, mostly glazed green, which were used by certain communities, their decoration and inscription expressing the character of the specific community. Best known are wine jugs of various guilds; more rare are those belonging to village leaders. Jugs for communion wine, owned by Calvinist Churches, are also of significance.

The oldest dated example of these community jugs was made in 1680 and is from western Hungary. At the bottom of its two handles are serpents, a feature that occurs also on wine jugs of later periods. The earliest large wine jug inscribed by its maker, a certain Stephanus Brenner, is dated 1732 and originates in Transylvania. Several similar jugs are known to have been made by the same potter for various guilds of craftsmen. In the guild-system the young journey-man was accepted after he had made his masterpiece and he had to invite all the masters to a dinner, providing the food and drink himself. On such occasions wine was poured from large jugs decorated with the insignia of the craft, the names of the leading members of the corporation inscribed on their sides. On a jug dated 1758, belonging to the boot-makers of the town of Ozora in southern Transdanubia, a crafts-man is represented in yellow clothing, surrounded by a laurel-wreath, a Renaissance motif. It is striking how this figure resembles a stove tile from the royal castle of Buda, representing King Matthias Corvinus, and made in the fifteenth century. The green glaze of large wine jugs and their applied relief decoration is very similar to stove tiles of the fifthteenth century, later popular throughout the country. Though Renaissance culture was destroyed by the Ottoman Turks, artisans living in country towns remained true to tradition three hundred years later.

Guild jugs are often decorated with religious symbols, and yet the inscription can include very profane lines. Thus, a famous jug belonging to weavers in a village not far from Lake Balaton, dated 1750, has the following verse:

> Let your poor throat swallow,
> and your purse get hollow. . .

Similar in style is another jug, also the property of the weavers, dated 1770, and from the same region, which includes part of a loom and the bust of Queen Maria Theresia. A large jug with double handles, also from the Balaton region, with a crucifix on one side and bootmakers' tools on the other, is another example of a profane inscription giving us an idea of the merry spirit of the craftsmen:

> Here's nothing,
> here's something,
> fellow don't sing,
> here's for drinking!

Even fishermen had their own corporation, like those of Keszthely on Lake Balaton. The jug, dated 1774, shows a fisherman standing in his boat, holding a harpoon; a fish is under the boat. Noteworthy are two tiny figures on each side of the main decoration, tiny nude women. Wine jugs very often have anthropomorphic features as decoration.

All sorts of guilds had community jugs and potters made fine jugs for their own corporations. Ják, a village on the western border noted for its church in Romanesque style with the twelve apostles around the entrance, still has potters working today and celebrating the festival of their patron saints, the apostles Philip and Jacob, whom they regard as members of their own profession. On that day potters and members of their family attend the 'potters' mass' and then have a drink. One of their jugs is dated 1835 and includes the figure of a potter and his wheel; their other jug has three masks on its sides. Young members of the guild could form a corporation with their own wine-jug, like the journeymen of Debrecen, decorating their jug with designs of flowers and birds.

The leaders of a village community often feasted together and sometimes had a common jug for the purpose. 'Long live the Judge and the Jury' reads the inscription on a jug of 1744 decorated with a yellow bird, from a village close to Lake Balaton. The inscription on a bottle, dated 1764, is 'Kjrálybiró' or 'Royal Judge' and there is a wonderful 'tree of life' and two peacocks on each side; it derives from the most distant eastern region of Transylvania.

Large wine jugs were made to order for Protestant churches. The centre of the Calvinist religion, Debrecen, was a place where they might be ordered, possibly in pairs, like those belonging to the church of Báránd, dated 1793. A green jug, with yellow fruit on its lid, was made in Nagyszalonta, in 1828, commissioned by husband and wife. A large jug for the church of Vári, dated 1838, has wonderful flowers in relief on its sides. Sometimes the church would be given a jug that had been originally used by a guild and was then passed on to the church. A late example, dated 1902, proves that such jugs were commissioned even during this century. An instance is known of Hungarian Calvinists living in Saskatchewan, Canada, who in their new home Békevár — 'Fortress of Peace' — ordered a jug for their church in Hungary inscribed in their native language.

Pottery, therefore, could express the sentiments of a community, a guild, a village, a church — the celebration taking the form of communion, or simple feasting and drinking.

One of the best-known shapes in Hungarian pottery are man-headed wine-jugs very similar to English Tobies, called 'Miska'-jugs. The finest were made in the early nineteenth century by outstanding potters of Mezócsát and Tiszafüred. Apart from the human head and the jacket with its row of buttons, the serpent on the belly of the figure is a striking feature. The back of the jug is beautifully decorated and the inscription is placed below the handle. Though Hungarian museums have a fine collection of 'Miska'-jugs, little was known of their function until recently. Among the pious Catholics of Mezókövesd there was a custom of commemorating the dead called 'Feeding the poor'. Twelve beggars were invited to a feast when 'blessed' wine was poured out of a man-headed jug, while the ballad of St Elisabeth of Hungary was sung. Then the name of each deceased relative was recited and the gathering of beggars would sing and pray for their souls. The man-headed wine-jug was therefore not regarded as a joke, but was taken very seriously as part of a pious rite in honour of the ancestors.

Most extraordinary anthropomorphic jugs come from the northern part of Hungary, especially from a village of minor nobility called Nemes-Radnót. These jugs were used at weddings and on the jug is a bed with a couple sitting on it. There is a point during the festivities when the relatives of the bride's family come to the house of the bridegroom and the bride offers all the guests wine or brandy as a gift from her family, the drink being intended to unite the two families. After this rite the 'dance of the bride' follows, and dancing continues till the candles go out. Earthernware chandeliers were made to match the jugs. So the jugs were most appropriative for the occasion, the nuptial night, though certainly they are extremely rare.

A wedding is in any case a festive occasion for using pottery and in some places a whole kilnfull was ordered for use on the wedding table. Guests were expected to bring their own knives, forks and spoons; if they forgot they might be given a plate with this design. The best man had his wine in a round flask, but for brandy each man would have a small flattened flask, his individual personal property, inscribed with his name. These flat flasks were greatly favoured in the Hungarian Plain and were often gifts for friends, inscribed with good wishes — or a curse for him who dared to steal it. Sometimes brandy-bottles were made in the figure of a man, a woman, or even an animal. Guests invited to weddings brought presents of food, chickens to cook in the preparation of broth. Ribbon-like doughnuts were served on open-work dishes. If a potter was invited to a wedding, his present would be his own ware, a large jar for flour, or a very large dish to hang on the wall.

After a birth, godmothers would bring food to the young mother in festive pots, more ornate than the ones in which food is carried to the field, pottery in this case expressing the relationship of one woman to another. This relationship has already begun before the mother's marriage. If two young girls want to become close friends, a gift of a plateful of sweetmeats is carried with a flask of brandy in the middle, and a rhyme is recited:

Heart sends to heart,
Let our friendship last . . .

Years later, when the two girls are married, they ask each other to be godmother. A little dish, collected in the village Piliny, northern Hungary, and dated 1788, has a tiny brandy-jug in the middle and extremely fine decoration and colouring suitable to express the occasion.

It is with these festive wine-jugs that we wish to greet the festive centenary of The Folklore Society, ten years older than the Hungarian Néprajzi Társaság.

Some Continuities between Oral and Written Literature

MARY ELLEN LEWIS   Indiana University

LITERATURE, whether transmitted orally or in writing, derives from culture, is produced by cultural beings, and reflects to some extent cultural concerns. It seems natural then, that all literatures share attributes, though differences, largely resulting from the means of communication, have been stressed and surely do exist. However, an artist of words, whether verbalising or writing as a vehicle of artistry, draws from culture in surface, as well as in depth.

In studying folklore, meant here specifically to denote oral literature,[1] and its relationship with written literature, much stress has been placed on surface similarities in content, on the overt use of folklore in, or transformation of folklore, into written literature.

Some study, however, has provided glimpses of depth relationships,[2] focusing on folklore's oral literary dimension, both in contrast to, and in comparison with, written literature. Both are rooted in culture and derive from it, changing as culture changes. Both seek to communicate, drawing from culture not only specific content — such as the surface detail, long stressed by students of folklore in literature — but general themes, ways of telling stories, strategies of communication; both are performances, are created and performed by individuals for individuals; both the oral and written redactor — the users of extant cultural creative materials — stand in similar relationships to the received tradition.

It is probably only through the study of depth similarities and continuities that we will be able to discover the fundamental relationships between oral and written literatures, such as those suggested already in genre,[3] in theme, style, and especially structure;[4] this approach will undoubtedly place less emphasis on the individual work as isolate, being essentially comparative in scope.

While much attention has been drawn to the differences between oral and written literature, considerable work has generally suggested that all literatures share many attributes. And this position is by no means revolutionary. The early work of Jolles on *Einfache Formen* implied an unconscious literary 'ideal', actualised in both oral and written form. Archer Taylor's 1948 paper[5] concluded that, while oral literature differed from written in terms of media and aesthetic, both shared materials, strategies, and styles. But his suggestions have not been followed up.

Much work, even that which has stressed similarity, has often implied that oral literature, derived from a homogeneous culture, is of the past or of the contemporary peasant and primitive. Oral literature is static. By contrast, written literature is 'civilization's', reflecting a heterogeneous, educated culture. Written literature is seen as changing, as developing. Just as much written literature has perished — the foci and themes, the ways of communicating, having today no audience, much oral literature no longer circulates, no longer adequately answering its audience's need. These two literatures are not mutually exclusive: the oral does not cease when one learns to read and write; in fact, the two exist simultaneously, sometimes shared by the same individual, sometimes not.[6] They are coexistent, different and yet similar. The study of surface similarity, particularly in content, has pointed this out. Depth study of various rhetorical devices such as style[7] and strategy further supports the suggestion that oral and written literatures share many things. Inevitably one is dealing here with content, or aspects of content; but the focus is not on the content *per se*, but with the ways it is communicated, the styles and strategies.

Max Lüthi in several provocative papers[8] has pointed out the stylistic characteristics of the European folk *Märchen* — its emphasis on one-dimensional, stereotyped characters; on clear, bright colours; on bold, straight geometric descriptions; its use of repetition; its isolation of characters, in general its penchant for pushing things to extremes — qualities which are evident in various works of written literature: Charles Dickens' *Hard Times* is a case in point.[9] The sharply drawn characters, with one-dimensional attributes, exemplified in such names as Gradgrind, Bounderby, McChoakumchild, and Harthouse; the use of distinct colours and bold architectural descriptions such as 'A great square house, with a heavy portico darkening the principal window ... A calculated, cast up, balanced, and proved house. Six windows on this side of the door, six on that side; a total of twelve in this wing, a total of twelve in the other wing; four-and-twenty carried over to the back wings. A lawn and garden and an infant avenue, all ruled straight like a botanical account book',[10] further suggest Dickens' use of a fairy-tale style. Bounderby's repeated disclaimers, protesting his humble origins, and the artificial isolation from his mother, show as well remarkable parallels with the *Märchen* style described by Lüthi. That Dickens was aware of fairy tales, perhaps through oral tradition but certainly through written, is demonstrable; he corresponded with Hans Christian Andersen and wrote elsewhere that the imaginative fantasy found in fairy tales was an essential ingredient in life: 'In an utilitarian age, of all other times, it is a matter of grave importance that Fairy tales should be respected ... every one who has considered the subject knows full well that a nation without fancy, without some romance, never did, never can, never will, hold a great place under the sun.'[11]

The world that Dickens describes using these qualities is, however, far from imaginative; it is removed from fantasy in its harsh reduction of humanity, in its denial of the inner person. In fact, Dickens' use of these stylistic features is surely ironic; for the *Märchen*-like style might lull readers into certain expectations, but the world created is in sharp contrast to the fantasy usually a part of the *Märchen* in oral form.

Lüthi also, through contrast with the *Märchen*, points out legend qualities — more fully rounded characters, earth-toned colours, caves rather than palaces — which are found in portions of *Hard Times*, especially when looking at the events surrounding Stephen Blackpool, whose name itself suggests depth, and whose expressive conversations indicate a multiplicity of emotion, of inner consideration. The haze-like descriptions of the workers' environment, the cave-like quality of their dwellings and the shaft into which Stephen falls, may well exemplify such qualities. Louisa, herself, takes steps to move from the *Märchen* world to the legend wholeness, as she recognises the necessity for emotion, for self-knowledge.

It would be overstating the evidence to assert that Dickens' use of these stylistic elements was overtly and frankly conscious; rather it seems safer to suggest that these stylistic techniques exist and existed, are codes to the audiences which cue, which elicit certain expectations. Thus, such stylistic devices are one kind of cultural tool available to the artist in words — whether spoken or printed — and suggest one possible point of similarity of all literature, regardless of its media of communication. Identifying these points of stylistic similarity aids in the explication of the particular work, in addition to serving as an example of an oral-written literary parallel.

Undoubtedly the style of the *Märchen* derives partly from its fictive, symbolic form. The legend, by contrast, is typified by possibility, by plausibility; thus its style is more realistic.[12] Unlike the symbolic and fictive *Märchen*, the question of belief is central to the folk legend, necessitating the audience's participatory response, whether of belief, denial, or ambivalence. When told in a receptive, natural context, the folk legend is invariably cumulatively built by the initiator-teller and the audience, for the essential content, as with other genres, such as the *Märchen* in its natural, oral environment, is known to all, or most, hearers. But the communication of the legend is not as distanced a performance as that of the *Märchen*. As a result, its telling may be a corporate activity, involving all present in the offering of alternate details, in the wonder at and acceptance of the event by the believer, in the debunking by the sceptic, and in the denial by the non-believer. This participatory quality, resulting from multiple response to the legend narrative's belief core, has been discussed by Linda Dégh and Andrew Vázsonyi in several papers,[13] particularly one denoting this aspect of the legend as the dialectic of the legend. The dialectic quality of early oral dialogue is most widely known in the Socratian context. In the oral milieu it continues and thrives as an important aspect of the communication of the folk legend. Localisation and personalisation contribute to the veracity of the account; variation questions its central truth.

Widespread in current, as well as past, oral legend exchanges, the dialectic strategy is also used in written literature, sometimes within a work and sometimes between a work and the reader/audience, attesting again to rhetorical similarities of all literature.

Nathaniel Hawthorne's short story 'The Great Carbuncle', offers an example of the use of dialectics of the legend in written literature, adding another element from the legend exchange in oral tradition, a visit to the locale described, to ascertain the narrative's verity or test its reliability.[14] Hawthorne makes use of this by describing seven characters in search of the carbuncle, and an eighth, the cynic, eager to disprove its existence. All were motivated by accounts of a great stone, that is the legend, elsewhere spelled out by Hawthorne:

> Gem, of such immense size as to be seen shining miles away, hangs from a rock over a clear, deep lake, high up among the hills. They who had once beheld its splendor were inthralled with an unutterable yearning to possess it. But a spirit guarded that inestimable jewel, and bewildered the adventurer with a dark mist from the enchanted lake. Thus life was worn away in the vain search for all unearthly treasure. On this theme methinks I could frame a tale with a deep moral.[15]

The reader meets the characters at a forced overnight retreat where the searchers are only minimally cooperative as each, with the exception of a young couple who share the same goal, is engrossed in the search for individual aggrandisement. Drawn together reluctantly, members of the group share accounts of their initial encounter with the legend, which provides the reader with a cumulatively built account of the legend itself:

> Beneath the shelter of one hut, in the bright blaze of the same fire, sat this varied group of adventurers, all so intent upon a single object, that, of whatever else they began to speak, their closing words were sure to be illuminated with the Great Carbuncle. Several related the circumstances that brought them thither. One had listened to a traveller's tale of this marvellous stone in his own distant country, and had immediately been seized with such a thirst for beholding it as could only be quenched in its intensest lustre. Another, so long ago as when the famous Captain Smith visited these coasts, had seen it blazing far at sea, and had felt no rest in all the intervening years till now that he took up the search. A third, being encamped on a hunting expedition full forty miles south of the White Mountains, awoke at midnight, and beheld the Great Carbuncle gleaming like a meteor, so that the shadows of the trees fell backward from it. They spoke of the innumerable attempts which had been made to reach the spot, and of the singular fatality which had hitherto withheld success from all adventurers, though it might seem so easy to follow to its source a light that overpowered the moon, and almost matched the sun. It was observable that each smiled scornfully at the madness of every other in anticipating better fortune than the past, yet nourished a scarcely hidden conviction that he would himself be the favored one. As if to allay their too sanguine hopes, they recurred to the Indian traditions that a spirit kept watch about the gem, and bewildered those who sought it either by removing it from peak to peak of the higher hills, or by calling up a mist from the enchanted lake over which it hung. But these tales were deemed unworthy of credit, all professing to believe that the search had been baffled by want of sagacity or perseverance in the adventurers, or such other causes as might naturally obstruct the passage to any given point among the intricacies of forest, valley, and mountain.[16]

Then they individually present their own private and selfish reasons for the search. The legend and its potential meaning to the participants, if achieved, are worked out in dialectic fashion, returned to again in the conclusion, as Hawthorne provides continuing alternate visions or versions:

Matthew and his bride spent many peaceful years, and were fond of telling the legend of the Great Carbuncle. The tale, however, towards the close of their lengthened lives, did not meet with the full credence that had been accorded to it by those who remembered the ancient lustre of the gem. For it is affirmed that, from the hour when two mortals had shown themselves so simply wise as to reject a jewel which would have dimmed all earthly things, its splendor waned. When other pilgrims reached the cliff, they found only an opaque stone, with particles of mica glittering on its surface. There is also a tradition that, as the youthful pair departed, the gem was loosened from the forehead of the cliff, and fell into the enchanted lake, and that, at noontide, the Seeker's form may still be seen to bend over its quenchless gleam.

Some few believe that this inestimable stone is blazing as of old, and say that they have caught its radiance, like a flash of summer lightning, far down the valley of the Saco. And be it owned that, many a mile from the Crystal Hills, I saw a wondrous light around their summits, and was lured, by the faith of poesy, to be the latest pilgrim of the GREAT CARBUNCLE.[17]

The actual search for the treasured stone continues after the night's delay with its discussion of the legend and its potential meaning to the participants. Matthew and Hannah, the recently married couple, find the jewel just when they have given up the search; they realise the folly of their initial desire to have the carbuncle as their own to light their humble cabin. Continuing the alternate presentation, paralleling the earlier dialectic response to the legend, Hawthorne describes the results of the search for the other characters: several took with them what they erroneously thought was the carbuncle; one died and became as if stone on viewing the jewel; the cynic, when stripped of the glasses which limited and coloured his vision, was blinded by a single glimpse which proved beyond doubt the existence of the carbuncle he had so denied.

Hawthorne, of course, does more than recreate a legend and the alternate responses to the belief at its core. He imbued his story with the 'deep moral' which was his reason, no doubt, for using the legend at all, in pointing out the positive value of believing in something greater than self. The great carbuncle became his vehicle for doing so. The dialectic response among the characters, both to the legend core and in differing goals and expectations, draws readers into the work as well. Hawthorne's sympathy, and thus the readers', is focused on Hannah and Matthew, whose mutual love and joint search, success, and re-entry into life are meant to represent the optimal response to such mysteries of life. An oral technique becomes a powerful means of influencing a readership, illustrating again the continuities in communicative strategies between oral and written literatures.

These several examples have been meant to suggest but one level of similarity, beyond surface content, between oral and written narrative literature. And this level of similarity is predicated on the assumption that all literatures are fundamentally communicative events, which seek to create response: one way of doing so is by employing a variety of shared rhetorical devices. In presenting general information to affirm the depth, in addition to surface or content, relationships of all literatures, this paper has secondarily sought to add another dimension to the study of selected literary works by presenting explanations for individual author's employment of various communicative techniques in order to enhance the analysts' ability to describe what an author is about and the means employed, which may, in many instances, expand the possible meanings of any given work.

It has been widely assumed, especially by students of written literature, that folk or oral literature is not only static but in essence conservative, repetitive, and unchanging. By contrast, great written literature, chosen by the Academy for scrutiny, is dynamic, innovative, and infinitely varaible. This latter is probably a postulated aesthetic ideal; for few works, few authors, break radically with the past: themes recur; structural patterns reappear; styles repeat. So do basic strategies of communication, rhetorical devices. Detailed examination, on both the surface and depth levels, indicates, to be sure, that literatures are different; but, likewise, that in some ways they are very much alike. Perceiving this, working to discover the points of similarity, students of both oral and written literature can collaborate. The results may tell us much that we need and want to know about the literary arts as 'equipment for living'.[18]

Notes

1. Father Ong, among others, has pointed out the fallacy inherent in the term *oral literature*, because *literature* implies writing. I follow and accept the statement of Robert Kellogg ('Oral Literature', *New Literary History*, V [1973], 56): 'because instances of oral and written literature can and do share a fictive, making, creating aspect, it is possible now to use the word *literature* about them both.'

2. See such authors and works as Max Lüthi, 'Parallel Themes in Folk Narrative and Art Literature', *Journal of the Folklore Institute*, IV (1967), 3-16; *idem*, 'Aspects of the Märchen and the Legend', *Genre*, II (1969), 162-78; and Roger Abrahams, 'Folklore and Literature as Performance', *Journal of the Folklore Institute*, IX (1972), 75-94.

3. See the work of Andre Jolles on *Einfache Formen*, summarised in English by Robert Scholes in *Structuralism in Literature* (New Haven, 1974), 42-50.

4. See Campbell, Propp, Olrik, Lévi-Strauss, Bremond, and Gremais. Again Scholes' survey provides an introductory summary.

5. 'Folklore and the Student of Literature', *The Pacific Spectator*, II (1948), 216-23, reprinted in Alan Dundes, *The Study of Folklore* (Englewood Cliffs, 1965), 34-42.

6. See Ong as well as the various works of Marshall McLuhan.

7. See Sandra D. K. Stahl, 'Style in Written and Oral Narrative', *Folklore Preprint Series* (Bloomington, 1975), for a discussion of some surface stylistic devices which are, however, different.

8. See Note 2.

9. My attention to folklore and *Hard Times* was drawn by Susan Cooper in a seminar paper, which focused on the structural parallels of *Hard Times* with aspects of Propp's *Morphology of the Folktale*.

10. Charles Dickens, *Hard Times* (New York, 1961), 19.

11. Charles Dickens, 'Frauds on the Fairies', *Household Words*, VIII (October 1, 1853), 97.

12. See Max Lüthi, *Once Upon a Time* (New York, 1970), Chapter 6.

13. Linda Dégh and Andrew Vázsonyi, 'The Crack on The Red Goblet or Truth and Modern Legend', *Folklore in the Modern World*, ed. Richard M. Dorson (The Hague, 1978); *idem*, 'Legend and Belief', *Genre*, IV (1971), 281-304.

14. See Linda Dégh, 'The Haunted Bridges Near Avon and Danville and Their Role in Legend Formation', *Indiana Folklore*, II (1969), 54-89 for an example.

15. Nathaniel Hawthorne, *The Complete Works of Nathaniel Hawthorne* (Boston, 1909), II, 482-3.

16. *ibid.*, I, 176-7.

17. *ibid.*, I, 191.

18. I have shamelessly borrowed this phrase from Kenneth Burke. See his essay, 'Literature as Equipment for Living', *The Philosophy of Literary Form* (New York, 1957), 253-62.

277

A Commentary on the Presidential Address of W. H. D. Rouse in 1905*

DEMETRIOS LOUKATOS   University of Jannina

WILLIAM Henry Denham Rouse was a distinguished member of the Folklore Society, whose work was well-known to foreign scholars. His research into early Greek folklore is of the utmost importance. He joined the Folklore Society in 1891 and, after contributing various articles to *Folklore*,[1] was elected President and held office from 1905-1906. A classical scholar, who developed an early interest in ethnology, Rouse was involved in comparative philology and worked in the field of Indo-Germanic languages. He also taught Greek and Latin at Perse School, Cambridge.

Rouse was greatly interested in Greek culture, and in 1902 he published a book entitled *Greek Votive Offerings*.[2] Two years later he travelled to Greece to do research. He went to the Dodecanese in the south-east Aegean, and stayed on Kos, Hippocrates' island, where he discovered the importance of modern Greek folklore and language for any study of ancient Greek culture and language. A local scholar, Jacob Zarraftis, helped him to collect material. We know this, thanks to Richard Dawkins' obituary of Rouse, published in *Folklore* in 1951.[3] Dawkins was another English scholar working in the field of modern Greek language and folklore. He, too, was a prominent member of the Folklore Society, and later served as its President. The rich collections which Zarraftis made for Rouse were deposited in the library of the Classics Faculty in Cambridge, in 1951 and, if they still exist, English and foreign folklorists can consult them there. The island of Kos is particularly interesting because it is typical not only of the Dodecanese but also of Crete, Cyprus, the Cyclades, and the earlier Greek populations of Asia Minor.

The Greek Journal *Laographia*[4] has published many of Zarraftis' collections of folklore,[5] and Dawkins included many of the tales in his book *Forty-five Stories from the Dodecanese*,[6] in which he also discusses Zarraftis and his friendship with Rouse.

And so it was that, filled with impressions obtained at first-hand, Rouse decided to make Greek folklore, including research and study programmes, the subject of his 1905 Presidential Address.[7] His paper is filled with affection and admiration for the modern Greek people, whose folklore, culture and language he regarded as on a par with that of the ancients.

He begins with a short survey of European folklore, and admits that, in spite of the efforts of contemporary European folklorists, there is a danger that culture and traditions may disappear, for 'wherever there is education, the national culture of the folk is destroyed.'[8] Indeed Rouse could be regarded as the forerunner of present interest in the necessity for urgent anthropological research. He had already said in 1905 that 'in all countries which are called civilised, the present generations will probably be the last when such collection is possible.'[9] However he was reassured that in Europe 'there are still two districts which are a rich crop ready for the reaper; the Slavonic area and Greece.'[10]

Rouse makes a clear distinction between free Greece (the Kingdom of Greece) and the area still under Turkish rule. With that impersonal scientific detachment of the scholar who sometimes ignores political factors when studying a particular problem, Rouse thought the occupied area the more interesting, since the Turks kept their Greek

* Full summary.

districts completely isolated. Free Greece, on the other hand, had experienced many changes because 'it was overrun with schoolmasters and politicians, who unfortunately despised the popular language and all its works.'[11]

Fortunately for Greek unity, most of the remaining provinces were soon freed, in 1912 and 1913, and the inevitable schoolmasters and politicians did little harm either to the older generation, to those with a modern outlook, or to the refugees that came from Asia Minor and Thrace during the period 1922-23.[12] The biggest blow was to come later, with World War and the development of technology, especially in the field of communications. Besides, there were always good local scholars, who were fond of the popular language, as Rouse himself points out: 'There is already collected a great mass of material for modern Greece. The local patriotism of people is intense and nearly every considerable place has found its historian, who often gives notes on the dialects . . . legends and tales or ballads. Some of these collections . . . such as those of Epirus . . . of Cyprus . . . of Chios . . . of Crete . . . are full and good.'[13]

The urge to write about local history and folklore was ever present in Greece, and it intensified during the period 1922-23. This was when the refugees arrived and, feeling homesick as refugees always do, they founded associations, published books and journals, established archives, and tried to preserve customs, texts, traditional costume, dances, music, and anything[14] that could be put into a museum collection. It is interesting that this movement inspired local people to try and do the same for their own areas.[15]

Of course Rouse was right when he wrote in 1905 that: 'there was much work to be done in Greece', and that 'there were still many places which were quite virgin soil', and 'as a rule, compilers didn't use a scientific method, and didn't always care for accuracy.' He lived long enough to see the rapid changes that took place in Greece and to know that Greek folklorists were interested in scientific methods and systematic research. When the Folklore Society celebrated its 50th anniversary, Richard Dawkins referred enthusiastically to the progress that had been made. He said: 'The study of folklore in Greece has in recent years made great progress.' Apart

from the 'great multitude of Greek folklorists', he singles out for special mention Nicholas Politis and his magazine *Laographia*.[16]

In fact the Hellenic Folklore Society, which was founded in 1909 in Athens, with Nicholas Politis as its President, is about to celebrate its 70th anniversary. The same year saw the first issue of *Laographia*, which was to become an excellent tool for the study of traditional material. Rouse at once wrote review articles in *Folklore*, welcoming the new Journal ('we give a cordial welcome to this magazine') and he says of Politis: 'Critical and scientific enquirers are few in Greece, but we may hope that their number will grow. One of them certainly is the veteran Politis (he was then 59 years old), who is really the founder of Greek folklore study.'[17] He is optimistic about research and the future of the Society: 'The list of members covers a large part of the Greek world and, if each searches his own district, there will be no lack of matter to fill dozens of volumes.'[18]

Rouse spoke prophetic words. In 1928 Dawkins referred to 9 'substantial volumes' of *Laographia*. By the time Rouse had died in 1950, there were 13; now there will soon be 31. Contributors to the journal, edited by Politis, and later by Kyriakidis and Megas, organised research programmes. Today *Laographia* is well-known in libraries throughout the world.

There were other scientific achievements, and Rouse must have welcomed them. The Folklore Archives were founded in 1918, under the auspices of the Academy of Athens. In 1939 the first Annual Report was published, and today it runs to 24 volumes. Scholars work in the Archives (subsequently renamed the Centre for Greek Folklore Studies) preparing comparative studies along the lines proposed by Rouse. The Annual Report also publishes a detailed bibliography of Greek studies and foreign work which deals with Greek folklore. It covers the period from 1800 to the present day. After the Second World War the Director, G. Megas, sent detailed questionnaires to every teacher in Greece, and they produced a wealth of material. Collections of folklore are officially recognised and rewarded by the Academy of Athens. Local folklore conferences are often held, and folklore is taught at the universities of Athens, Thesalonika and Jannina, as well as in teachers training colleges.

Specialised studies have been written about

different folklore genres, and collections have been made. Politis wrote about proverbs and traditions in two books published in 1899 and 1904.[19] Oddly enough, Rouse does not refer to them, though Dawkins wrote reviews. Songs were published in systematic collections by Politis in 1914, Petropoulos in 1958-59, and the Academy of Athens in 1962 and 1968. This was in addition to the earlier well-known collections by Fauriel in 1824-25, and Passow in 1860.[20] Tales were printed in many important collections, including three compiled by Dawkins.[21]

Traditional house-types have been studied by both folklorists and architects, and agricultural, pastoral and maritime studies have been made. Good books have been written on popular cults, notably *Greek Calendar Customs* by Megas. I should also like to mention two surveys of Greek folklore. The first, *Hellenic Laography* (1923 & 1965), is by Stilpon Kyriakidis. The second, *Introduction to Hellenic Laography* (1977), I wrote myself.

If all the studies and collections of Greek folklore could be translated into one of the major international languages, what a benefit to international folklore studies that would be. Fortunately, in the last few years young Greeks have been studying abroad, and foreign scholars working on ethnological, sociological and economic projects are coming to Greece to study traditional society and the traditional way of life in our villages and cities. These scholars, who use the new ethnological methods current in France, England, America and the Soviet Union, have introduced them into folklore research and provided it with an anthropological orientation.[22]

The danger that traditional elements may disappear from modern life is of course a hazard in Greece too. Dawkins pointed this out in 1928: 'Old customs tend to disappear, all the more as Greeks are people avid of change, and thus the collector of folklore is often gathering up scraps.'[23] Nevertheless, when one sees how tradition has disappeared in other countries, there is no doubt that Greece, with its great wealth of material from both land and sea, is still in a privileged position, as Rouse observed in 1911: 'There is no part of Europe so rich, as are the Greek lands, in traditional lore of all sorts.'[24]

There was something else which Rouse rightly regarded as detrimental to the progress of the Greek people and their traditional vivacity: the scholars' insistence on using purist language in imitation of ancient Greek, and their contempt for the popular language and all that it entails. Happily this obstacle has now been overcome. Since 1917 the Greek government has been discussing the best way to tackle the problem and, when the dictatorship was overthrown, the popular language was recognised by law as the official tongue. And so it was that the state finally adopted what society, literature and folklore had recognised many years ago.

Now I would like to discuss the important comments which Rouse made about Greek folklorists and other European folklore scholars preparing comparative studies utilising the lore of antiquity. Rouse wrote in 1905: 'Greece offers to the student of folklore one great advantage: he is able to trace a great deal of myth and custom to an earlier source.'[25] He continues: 'Greek antiquity is, to a great extent, known; and where it is neglected in modern Greece, we have evidence to show how far oral tradition can be trusted and what changes may occur by its means ... The acknowledged facts are of so great a value, that it is a wonder they have never been gathered and compared.'[26] 'In the meanwhile,' he notes, 'a great quantity of fresh material has been published' and that is why 'the attention of classical scholars ought to be directed to this field of research.' But 'unfortunately,' he adds, 'there is hardly anyone in England who thinks modern Greek to be worthy of serious study.'[27]

Rouse's belief that modern Greek folklore and language are essential for a fuller knowledge of the ancient world is shared by Greek and non-Greek scholars, who had reached the same conclusion long before his article was published.[28] It also paved the way for this research method in England, for it inspired outstanding scholars like Lawson,[29] Halliday,[30] Rose,[31] and above all Dawkins, to follow in his footsteps. And they have given us so much, with their work and their use of the comparative method.

In Greece Richard Dawkins is regarded as an outstanding folklorist. From 1902 until his death in 1955 his published work was concerned with modern Greek language and folklore. He began it with a description of a wooden olive-press on the island of Karpathos (it was published in the Annual Report of the British School of Athens in 1902) and ended with a review of my own *Proverbs from Kephalonia* in 1954 in *Folklore*, and I am very moved when I remember this great honour which he did me. And so, by means of his various studies and collections of tales, he crossed Greece, symbolically speaking, from east to west, from the Hellespont and Asia Minor to Cyprus and Crete.

After Rouse's address in 1905, his student and successor, Dawkins, followed in his teacher's footsteps, continuing the comparative study of Greek culture. *The Modern Carnival in Thrace and the Cult of Dionysus*,[32] published in 1906, and his remarks in a later study, *Modern Greek Folktales*, published in 1953, are typical of his approach: 'These folktales of today do suggest one very real inheritance from the ancient world, and that is the character of the Greeks themselves.'[33] He was fond of Greece and held the post of Director of the British School of Athens; later he became an honorary fellow of the Hellenic Folklore Society. He could also speak and write the Greek language. We loved him too. It is not by chance that, apart from the official obituary by Halliday, published in *Folklore* in 1955, another contributor of Greek origin, Robert Georges, wrote ten years later, describing Dawkins' life and work in loving detail.[34]

I have discussed Dawkins' work at some length because I see him as the disciple and successor of Rouse. The student writing an obituary of his teacher, as I mentioned earlier, reflects this continuity. And, indeed, Greek folklorists regard them both as being of equal importance. In his 1905 Presidential Address, Rouse quoted examples of comparative study of ancient and modern Greek culture from the point of view of an objective classical scholar.[35] Dawkins, and English and Greek scholars, followed him, while at the same time paying due attention to recent developments in sociology.

The scientific work of British scholars is always of importance and the work of the Folklore Society, from its foundation in 1878 to the present day, has provided us in Greece with fine examples of organisation and editorial work. As President of the Hellenic Society of Laographia, I honour the memory of two Hellenist Presidents of the Folklore Society, and I bring greetings and good wishes from the Greek folklorists for a long and productive future.

Notes

1. See *Folklore*, Vol.VII (1896), Vol.X (1899), Vol.XV (1904), Vol.XVI (1905), Vol.XIX (1908), Vol.XXII (1911), *et al.*

2. Rouse made valuable contributions to the 'Loeb Classical Library', including an admirable translation of the ancient Greek text *Dionysiaca* by Nonnos.

3. *Folklore*, Vol.LXII (1951), 269-70. I wish to express thanks to my colleague, Dr Venetia Newall, who sent me a copy of the obituary, which provided additional information about Rouse's scientific activities.

4. *Laographia*, Vol.XIII (1951).

5. R. M. Dawkins, *Tragoudia tōn Dodekanesōn* (Songs of the Dodecanese); in *Laographia*, Vol.XIII (1951), 33-99, with commentary in English, texts in modern Greek. See also Jacob Zarraftis, *Folklore of Kos*, ed. D. B. Oeconomidis, *Laographia*, Vol.XIII (1951), 285-339 (in Greek).

6. Edited and translated from the manuscripts of Jacob Zarraftis; Cambridge, 1950.

7. See *Folklore*, Vol.XVI (1905), 14-26.

8. *ibid.*, 16.

9. *ibid.*

10. *ibid.*

11. *ibid.*

12. During the period 1912-13 wars of national liberation were fought in Macedonia and Epirus. In 1920 Thrace and part of Asia Minor were liberated, but in 1922 the Greek populations of Asia Minor and eastern Thrace were expelled by the Turks, and in 1923 the Greek and Turkish populations remaining in the two countries were exchanged.

13. *Folklore*, Vol.XVI (1905), 17.

14. I would like to mention the Societies of Pontus (1928), Thrace (1928), Asia Minor (1938), and the Centre for Studies of Asia Minor (1930-48) organised by O. M. Merliez along ethnological lines and which included a younger generation of researchers among its collaborators.

15. See D. Loukatos, 'État actuel des études folkloriques en Grèce', *Actes du IIe Congrès International des Études du Sud-Est Europeen*, Athènes, Mai 1970, (Athens, 1972), 551-82.

16. 'The Recent Study of Folklore in Greece', *Papers and Transactions of the Jubilee Congress of the Folklore Society* (London, 1930), 121-37.

17. *Folklore*, Vol.XXII (1911), 248-9.

18. *ibid.*, 250.

19. N. G. Politis, *Studies of the Life and Language of the Hellenic People* (in two parts). I. *Paroemiae*, Vols 1-4 (Athens, 1899-1902); II. *Paradoseis*, Vols 1-2 (Athens, 1904) (in Greek).

20. The modern Swiss Hellenist, Samuel Baud-Bovey, introduced Greek songs to the international public through his studies (as Fauriel and Garnett and Abbott had earlier, through their translation). He wrote many papers, both philological and musicological, on the songs of the Dodecanese (1935-36), the songs of the 1821 war (1949, 1954), Byzantine epic poetry (1938) and Greek verse in general.

21. There are comprehensive bibliographies in: R. M. Dawkins, *Forty-five Stories from the Dodecanese* (Cambridge, 1950); *idem, Modern Greek Folktales* (Oxford, 1953); *idem, More Greek Folktales* (Oxford, 1955). See also: D. Loukatos, *Neoellenika Laographika Keimena* (Modern Greek Folk-texts) (Athens, 1957); and Antti Aarne & Stith Thompson, *The Types of the Folktale* (Helsinki, 1964).

22. Examples are: E. Friedl, *Vasilika: A Village in Modern Greece* (New York, 1962); J. K. Campbell, *Honour, Family and Patronage in a Greek Mountain Community* (Oxford, 1964); Georges Kavadias, *Pasteurs, Nomades Méditerannéens. Les Saracatsans de Grèce* (Paris, 1965); Juliet du Bonlay, *Portrait of a Greek Mountain Village* (Oxford, 1974); M. Dimen and E. Friedl, ed., *Regional Variation in Modern Greece and Cyprus: toward a perspective on the Ethnography of Greece* (New York, 1976). Additional bibliographical information about more recent socio-anthropological studies can be found in the bulletins: *A News-letter of Modern Greek* (New Hampton, N.Y.) and *Mandatoros* in *Modern Greek Studies* (University of Birmingham), both founded in 1972.

23. *Papers and Transactions of the Jubilee Congress of the Folklore Society.*

24. *Folklore*, Vol.XXII (1911), 248.

25. *Folklore*, Vol.XVI (1905), 17.

26. Rouse mentions as 'the only work of the kind', Bernhard Schmidt, *Das Volksleben der Neugriechen und das Hellenische Alterthum* (1871), which he does not regard as satisfactory. Also of interest in this connection are the following works, all published prior to 1905: Kurt Wachmuth, *Das alte Griechenland im neuen* (Bonn, 1864); Lucy M. J. Garnett, *Greek Folk-Poesy: Folk-verse and Folk-Prose* (London, 1896); G. F. Abbott, *Macedonian Folklore* (Cambridge, 1903), which was reviewed by Rouse in *The Classical Review*, Vol.XVII (1903), 472.

27. *Folklore*, Vol.XVI (1905), 18.

28. For example, E. Bybilakis, *Neugriechisches Leben vergliechen mit dem altgriechischen* (Berlin, 1840), and G. Loukas, *Philologikae Episkepseisiin Cyprus* (Philological Research in Cyprus) (Athens, 1874). Greek authors and studies from the period prior to Rouse' Presidential Address are referred to by Dawkins in 'The Recent Study of Folklore in Greece', in *Papers and Transactions of the Folklore Society* (London, 1930), 121-37.

29. J. C. Lawson, *Modern Greek Folklore and Ancient Greek Religion* (Cambridge, 1910; reprint 1964).

30. W. R. Halliday, *Folklore Studies, Ancient and Modern* (London, 1924).

31. H. J. Rose (1883-1961) collaborated with Rouse for the Loeb Classical Library series. He was Professor of Ancient Greek at the University of St Andrews and author of *Primitive Culture in Greece* (London, 1925), *Ancient Greek Religion* (London, 1946), *Handbook of Greek Mythology* (London, 1958), *Religion in Greece and Rome* (1959), and collaborated with P. Argenti on *The Folklore of Chios* (Cambridge, 1949), 2 vols. (See *Laographia*, Vol.XIII [1951], 396-405.)

32. See *Journal of Hellenic Studies*, Vol.XXVI (1906), 191-206.

33. Richard Dawkins, *Modern Greek Folktales*, xxxii.

34. Robert A. Georges, 'Richard Dawkins: A Commemorative Essay on the Tenth Anniversary of His Death', *Folklore*, Vol.LXXVI (1965), 202-12.

35. See Rouse' Presidential Address in *Folklore*, Vol.XVI (1905), esp. 20-25.

Beliefs and Customs associated with Dress in Ireland

BRID MAHON   University College, Dublin

IN the early 1940s the Irish Folklore Commission (later to become the Department of Irish Folklore in University College, Dublin) issued a questionnaire on dress to some 500 correspondents and helpers throughout Ireland. In all four thousand one hundred and twenty pages of information were received, and these are now bound in fourteen volumes. The information in this short paper is gleaned from those replies — as well as from the general collections in our archives.

Beliefs and customs associated with the wearing of dress in Ireland are widespread, covering as they do, the whole span of a man's life from his birth to his death. In addition there is a multitude of beliefs associated with everyday living.

It was considered unlucky to throw an old shoe down the road after the man of the house on his way to a fair. A spider found crawling on your clothes meant you would get new wearing apparel. Spiders were considered unlucky. If you burnt a hole in the front of a garment while the moon was full, it meant good luck, but if the hole was in the back of the garment, ill luck would follow. If a cricket was injured in a strange house, it would revenge itself by destroying the clothes of the person responsible. If you put a shirt or a shift on inside out, you should leave it so for the day. If you went astray on a journey, you should turn your coat inside out so that the fairies would not steal you away.

There were widespread beliefs connected with various festivals. A ribbon left on a bush or on a window ledge on St Brigid's night, February 1st, could cure toothache or headache. It was said that the holy Brigid walked the roads of Ireland on this, her night. In Tipperary; in the Thurles district, a ribbon was measured and put through a window. After a time it was taken in again. If it had grown longer, it was a sign of a prosperous year ahead; if shorter, it was a sign of a bad year. A wedding tie hung on a bush on May Eve cured a headache. A cloth dipped in the blood of a bird or animal killed on Martinmas, November 10th, cured pains and aches, or a piece of flannel might be left on a bush on this night with the same result.

In Co. Cavan a story is told of a woman who sees a crock of gold beside ragwort or rag weed and ties her garter to the plant to mark the spot. But, when she returns, every bush in the field is tied with a garter and so she never finds the gold. There are many versions of this story told in the south east and north west of the country. In marriage divinations a shirt or garter was commonly used to foretell the future. On Hallowee'n a young unmarried girl would place three knots in her garter, and at each knot recited the following incantation:

> This knot, this knot, this knot I see
> The thing I never saw yet
> To see my love in his array
> And what he walks in every day
>
> This night may I in my dreams see
> And if my love be clad in green
> His love for me it is well seen
> And if my love be clad in grey
> His love for me is far away
> And if my love be clad in blue
> His love for me is very true

In Co. Wexford there is a custom known as 'galloping for the garter': 'On the occasion of a marriage, a pair of garters were given to the person who was first home from the place where the pair were married. The race was on horseback. It was a great honour to get the garters. Sometimes the race was run in a field, specially selected. The last race I saw here was won by a certain Billy Brennan. He had a wonderful horse. He owed eleven years' rent and the landlord said he would forego the rent if Billy would give him the horse. But Billy would not part.'

A common belief was that a river or stream running between fields, farms or townlands, had magical qualities, and could be used to cure ailments or to foretell the future. If a young man washed his shirt in boundary water against the stream and hung it over a chair in front of the fire to dry, he would dream of a young woman turning his shirt. This young woman would be his future wife. Likewise, if a girl washed her shift, she would see her future husband.

Another belief connected with marriage was that if a knot was tied in a handkerchief at a certain point in the marriage ceremony, the marriage would be childless, and so remain until the person who had tied the knot untied it.

One account from Co. Mayo related: 'If an educated person ties a knot in a silk handkerchief at a certain part of the ceremony, when the priest says a certain word, the newly-weds will have no family. They say it was done to a young woman in the parish, and she had no family for a long time. But the one who tied the knot must have loosened it again, for now there are two girls in it.'

In many areas it was the custom for the local 'go boys', as they were called, to dress up in women's clothes and appear as uninvited guests at the wedding feast, where they were well received. They made sure to give the bride a round of swinging in the half-sets in the wedding dance that followed. They were said to be the life and soul of the party. The same boys went around on St Stephen's night to hunt the wren.

In the north-west of the country it was the custom for the bride to borrow her wedding dress — and indeed in many places it was common to borrow the christening robe and a cradle for the first-born. Often a bride did not get a new outfit for her wedding. The custom was that the husband bought his wife a new outfit immediately after marriage. This was especially so in the case of a match or made marriage. The newly-weds did not go to church on the Sunday following the wedding, but waited until the second Sunday when the new bride appeared in all her finery, sometimes accompanied by her bridesmaids. This was known as *Domhnach an Bhun Bealaigh* or 'Rising out Sunday'. An account from Co. Longford says: 'Shortly after the wedding it was the custom for the husband to take his wife into town and buy her a new outfit, coat, hat, shoes, stockings, etc., the splendour of the outfit depending on the purse and generosity of the husband. Very often it was the only outfit a woman ever got. The second Sunday following the marriage, the bride would appear in all her finery. The custom is still carried out, but now the groom buys the outfit on the honeymoon.'

Colour played an important part in people's lives. Red was a lucky colour, a protection against the fairies, who might otherwise take the child away and leave a changeling in its place. Often a baby was wrapped in red flannel to be taken to the church for christening. A child would wear a red petticoat, or waistcoat, or have a red thread or piece of red ribbon sewn into its clothes as a protection against the fairies or against blinking — the evil eye. This was common all over the country. In Co. Wexford a red bead was tied around a child's neck to cure diseases of the blood.

If red was lucky, green was not, and this prejudice was widespread. In Donegal it was said that red, or a mixture of red and any colour except green, was lucky. In Co. Cavan they said that a person with an 'O' or a 'Mac' before his name should not wear green. The same belief was recorded in Galway.

Sayings about green include: green for grief; if you wear green you'll wear black; a person never wore green without grief following. In Co. Roscommon it was held that the fairies were jealous of those who wore green because it was their colour. In Leitrim it was said: No-one should wear green to a wedding because it would bring grief before the year was out. And there is a tradition that the nineteenth century Irish leader, Charles Stewart Parnell, once said, 'The reason Ireland is so unfortunate is because green is the national colour.'

In Glencolmcille in Co. Donegal they wouldn't wear green, and if a Catholic wore orange he was called *Albanach Buidhe,* meaning Orange Presbytarian. In Co. Cavan orange was not worn because it was a Protestant colour. Children could not be got to wear orange lest they be called Orangemen, or Billy's pets.

Colour, too, played an important part in the bride's outfit. A popular saying went:

Married in blue, you're sure to rue
Married in grey, you'll go far away
Married in yellow, ashamed of your fellow
Married in brown, you'll live out of town
Married in white, you'll be alright
Married in red, you'll wish yourself dead
Married in green, not fit to be seen.

It was generally accepted that the bride should wear, something old, something new, something borrowed and something blue.

All over Ireland up to the end of the nineteenth century, the married status was marked by the acquisition of the hooded cloak. One informant in Co. Monaghan summed it up neatly: 'A woman got a new cloak when she married, wore it until she died, and then handed it down to her eldest daughter.' The last hooded cloak in this parish was made around 1880. Under the hood of the cloak the married woman wore a white frilled cap. Only in a few instances are there accounts of single women wearing the cap. On the Inishowen peninsula in Co. Donegal it was said, 'There was no distinction between married and single', and in Belclare, south of Tuam, Co. Galway, one informant said, 'On reaching the age of sixty spinsters also wore the white frilled cap.' Presumably at that ripe age they were accepted as the equal of their married sisters.

Generally speaking the year in Ireland was divided into two seasons – 1st May and 1st November, and these were the accepted times for buying new clothes. However, in parts of Galway it was customary to get new clothes for Easter Day: *Bia is deoch faoi Nodlag is éadach nua faoi Caisg.* – Food and drink for Christmas and new clothes for Easter.'

It was considered unlucky to change your clothes on May Day and a popular saying in northern counties went: 'Change not your clout till May is out.' Children who wore shoes in the winter generally put them aside on May 1st. New clothes should always be worn first to Mass, never to a wake or funeral. Holy water was sprinkled on new clothes, and in Co. Galway they said: 'If a person could not go to Mass, he should pull a thread of the new garment, give it to a neighbour to dip in the holy water font outside the church.

When the neighbour returned from church, he must first make the sign of the cross on the person to whom the new garment belongs, then rub the garment all over with the thread.'

Another custom was to put a pinch of salt in the pocket of a suit or new dress to keep away bad luck. New clothes were always shown off to neighbours, especially by children, who went from house to house, sometimes getting a hansel for the pocket, a penny or an egg. The good wishes ran to a pattern all over the country: 'Well to wear and soon to tear and may the bushes have their share.' Adults were expected to treat their neighbours and were given such broad hints as: 'Well to wear and many's the better, for the beverage you're the debtor,' and 'Well to wear and pay the beverage.' In Tipperary they said, 'We'll wet it tonight,' meaning they would all adjourn to a public house to celebrate. Incidentally, here the same custom was observed when the blacksmith put the first pair of shoes on the colt.

However much a girl or a woman might admire a new garment, she should never be the first to say so. A man or boy should always make the first wish. In Galway: 'Lucky for a man to be the first to say "Well to wear" unlucky if a woman says it first.' In Sligo: 'Considered unlucky for a woman to say it first. The wish is always made by the male sex, never the female.' In Donegal: 'No-one should say, "Well wear" until the man of the house says it first.' Westmeath: 'Considered unlucky for a female to express these good wishes. Women usually refrained, until a man offered his congratulations.' And so it was in almost every parish and townland.

But if new clothes were lavishly praised and celebrated, there was a strong prejudice against second-hand clothes. In most parts of the country people either said that they never bought second-hand clothes, or that they were afraid of them. Even in areas like the Kilkenny-Carlow border, where old clothes – called Cant or Canty clothes – were sold extensively at marts and fairs, there was a lingering objection: 'You wouldn't know who was wearing them.' In Galway 'they would not buy second-hand clothes for fear of some horrid disease,' and, to prove the point, they recounted how, in a place near Tuam, in that County, some villagers once bought second-hand cast-offs belonging to fever patients, and as a result half of the village died. No doubt the resistance to the practice, which seemed to survive in both town and country well into the present century, had its roots in the plagues and famines of the preceeding centuries, when, too often, disease was transmitted by rats and vermin, and when hygiene was at a premium.

One story from Muskerry in Co. Cork, recorded in 1937, explains why some people have good clothes, and others are obliged to make do with shabby ones:

'Long ago when Adam and Eve were in paradise, they had a large family. Now on a certain day God decided to pay them a visit and when Eve heard this she dressed half of her children in good clothes, but there was nothing left for the remainder but rags. She wondered what was best to do, and in the end locked the six ragged children in a shed behind the house. When God arrived and saw the children wearing good, clean clothes he was pleased. He didn't see the ragged ones at all. Ever since that day some people have fine clean clothes, like the gentry, doctors, teachers and so on while other have the leavings, like farmers and beggars.'

If clothes were important to the living, they were equally so to the dead. According to tradition a dead person would go naked in the next world, unless his clothes were given away to a needy neighbour, who was required to wear them to Mass for three Sundays in a row, and to pray for the soul of the dead.

There are hundreds of stories telling of the dire results of breaking the custom.

From Kells, Co. Meath, we have the tale of two sisters, who lived together for many years. The elder died and the younger, being of a miserly disposition, refused to part. From then on she was constantly haunted by her sister's ghost. One night she ventured to ask the spirit what was troubling her, and got the reply: 'Not even a handkerchief has been given away for my soul.' Of course the sister lost no time in disposing of the clothes of the dead and from then on the ghostly visits ceased.

From Tipperary we have the account of a school-teacher called Mrs Bourke, who died and was laid out by a neighbour, Mrs White. Mrs White was given the skirt, cloak and bonnet belonging to the corpse but, as she had never worn anything grander in her life than a shawl, she hadn't the courage to dress up in Mrs Bourke's finery. Mrs Bourke's ghost duly appeared with the plea: 'Glory be Mrs White why don't you wear my clothes to Mass?' Mrs White promised she would, but again her courage failed her, and again the ghost appeared. This happened three times and in the end Mrs White went to Mass dressed up in Mrs Bourke's finery and from then on Mrs Bourke's spirit was at rest.

On no account should clothes of the dead be put into pawn or kept under lock and key, the reason being that the shade in the next world might require his clothes while suffering purgatory, and if they were not freely available, he would be forced to go naked.

From Stradbally in Leix comes the story of a woman who sold her dead brother's coat and was haunted by the ghost complaining that, as the garment had been sold, it no longer belonged to him and he needed it. She bought the coat back, and the ghost was happy once more.

Another account from the same district tells of a man called Cooney, who stole the shirt off a corpse carried ashore by the tide. From that day on the ghost was frequently seen calling out: 'Cooney, Cooney, give me back my shirt! The north wind blows and the cold is coming.'

In Ireland traditions about the dead and the fairies, or Good People as they are known, appear to be inextricably mixed. People who tell stories about them are not always clear as to whether fairies or the dead are being spoken of.

A common belief was that the dead could be seen in the company of the fairies, often playing a game of football. One such account from Whitechurch in Co. Waterford tells of a miserly man, who locked up his dead brother's clothes in a trunk. Shortly after, the wise woman of the district reported that she had witnessed a football match between two fairy hosts, and that the dead man was quite naked among the players. When she related the story, with appropriate comments, the miser was so shamed that he unlocked the trunk, and distributed his dead brother's clothes. And, of course, shortly after, the wise woman reported that she had once again seen the Good People at play, but that now the dead man was fully and respectably dressed.

Not only were new clothes given away and worn for the dead, but new ones were made if the old were too shabby, and it was essential that they should be finished and the tailor paid, before the soul drew his last breath. In Co. Kildare a man appeared to his brother the night after the burial, asking that the tailor be made to hurry on with the suit he had started and not finished. 'I'm perished minding the church gates these cold nights in my skin,' he said peevishly.

The belief was that the last person to die became the gate-keeper and, unless and until his clothes were given away and prayers offered for his soul, he was compelled to remain at the cemetry gate, naked and shivering, if necessary for evermore.

The Didactic Story in Old Yiddish Folk Literature*

J. J. MAITLIS

IN this paper I shall confine myself to the prose tale in Old Yiddish folk literature and I shall concentrate on the exemplary story; there will be no attempt at classification.

The Old Yiddish story, the Ma'aseh, is essentially didactic in character; its purpose is to teach and edify. Its distinctive feature is that it maintained a close link with the Jewish religion and can be regarded as a manifestation of Jewish tradition and the Jewish way of life. It follows the established pattern of the Hebrew Ma'aseh, applied to a diversity of narrative material and traditional lore.

The term Ma'aseh denotes folktale, story, legend, traditional lore, parable and anecdote. It also signifies action, *res gestae* – as in the *Gesta Romanorum* – based on some credible event, whether historical or concerning illustrious personalities of the past. Such stories were intended to point a moral, raise the spirits, and strengthen the bonds of faith from within.

Old Yiddish literature is also rich in etiological tales explaining the origin or importance of some custom, practice or folk belief. I should like to mention two examples: 'The corpse and the torn sleeve', and 'Rabbi Akiva redeems the sinner from Hell'. The moral of the first is that God requires the pure heart of man; the second expounds the origin and importance of *Kaddish,* the mourners' prayer, using a variety of Aarne-Thompson motifs – return from the dead, punishment of the sinner in hell, and salvation through prayer. The moral is placed at the end of the tale in the traditional way.

The Old Yiddish tale can be traced back to literary traditions like the Aggadah and medieval ethical treatises; there is also the oral lore, constantly told and retold, elaborated and moulded, often with some changes and new elements added to the plot.

The popular Ma'aseh ranges from a single incident or narrative motif to a more elaborate, composite story-structure (the German *Kettenmärchen*) with a complex plot. It goes without saying that many widespread international motifs and narratives occur in Old Yiddish story-telling, often reworked, with elements substituted and adapted to suit Jewish taste and religious outlook. Jewish folk literature, like any other, contains much that is borrowed from the outside world. But Jews did not merely borrow: they repaid the debt handsomely with their own lore and exemplary narratives. Indeed they are the great folklore intermediaries, the transmitters of valuable narrative material from East to West. At all events stories and legends became judaized: they were clad in Jewish garb, absorbed Jewish characteristics and were given Jewish colouring. I feel that Jewish traditional folklore, the process of diffusion and adaptation, its style and technique, deserves further comprehensive study by the student of folklore.

Old Yiddish Ma'aseh material has been preserved in manuscript and in later printed story collections. I should like to single out for mention the famous *Ma'aseh Buch,* a great repository of Old Yiddish stories, printed for the first time in Basel in 1602, and revised and reprinted many times subsequently. It became one of the most popular folk books during a didactic age. Its primary purpose was to edify and to use its illustrative stories to teach a moral lesson. The *Ma'aseh Buch* contains current medieval lore, legends and oral traditions concerning the lives and deeds of prominent Jewish

* Summary

personalities during the Middle Ages. The compiler could not ignore the prevailing popular trend and he included in his pious book a number of light and amusing stories, in the style of the *fabliaux*, for the entertainment and delight of his readers. But, whatever the origin and source of a story, it was modified and adapted to serve a Jewish didactic purpose, with a moral dictum at the end.

The Hanging of Calvin Logsdon

LYNWOOD MONTELL   Western Kentucky University

THE setting for this study in oral folk history is centered on the Valley of the Three Forks of the Wolf River, located in north-central Tennessee's Upper Cumberland region about twelve miles north of Jamestown, county seat of Fentress County. Here Calvin Logsdon[1] was hanged three times on 5th April, 1872 for an alleged triple murder that occurred on 19th November, 1868. The story has crystallised into legend and has assumed proportions of a regional saga told in at least four counties in Tennessee and in three adjacent Kentucky counties.[2] Nashville newspapers picked up the story once the Logsdon trial entered the Tennessee Supreme Court, and the trial briefs are intact. Two kinds of written corroborative evidence — court records and newspaper accounts — make it possible to examine a rather old oral tradition in context. Further, the published diary of the Methodist circuit riding preacher, who attended Logsdon during his last hours, is available. All the ingredients necessary for a study in folklore and history are present.

The Logsdon story begins and ends in oral tradition; the other sources do not address themselves to the entire story. The courts were concerned only with the details of the crime, the Nashville newspapers mainly covered Supreme Court proceedings, and the diary describes the death scene.

James Calvin Logsdon drifted into Fentress County from Scott County and settled near the Forbus community. He was the product of a broken home; his mother resided in Scott or Campbell County while the father lived in Houstonville, Kentucky near Danville.[3] Later it will be demonstrated that the father's location and personal influence on Cal figured prominently in the Logsdon story on two different occasions.

Cal may have been a close neighbour of a widower Burr,[4] who had two daughters, Jane and Eliza. Most likely, however, Cal lived in the house with the Burrs.[5] The relationship between the Burrs and Logsdon is clouded, but it is probable that he was a resident hired hand who worked for a daily wage of twenty-five cents plus room and board. Such an arrangement was common throughout the Upper Cumberland region until the early 1940s, by which time the wages had escalated to fifty cents. The Burr sisters were pleasantly attractive and their father, while not a well-to-do farmer, adequately provided for their needs.

Not far from the Burrs was the Possum Trot community, where Catherine Outcast,[6] forty-six, resided along with her daughter, Lucy Outcast, twenty-seven, and Lucy's two illegitimate sons, James, eight, and W.B., four.[7] One informant claimed that both women were 'seeing men',[8] but oral tradition does not otherwise attest to the character of Catherine, the older woman. Lucy, however, is still referred to variously as a trollop, prostitute, trash, and whore. The Outcast house, a double fireplace log structure,[9] was regularly frequented by men who sought Lucy's favours.[10] This arrangement had gone on for at least nine years, as James was eight years old when his brother, mother, and grandmother were murdered. Oral tradition holds that a frequent visitor in the Outcast house was Mr Burr, who was in love with Lucy and had announced his intentions, at least to his two daughters, to marry her. Burr and Lucy were engaged and were planning 'to get married just shortly after the murder happened, perhaps within a week or so', according to Mrs. C. E. Toney. Thoughts of their father being married to a woman of such low character incensed Jane and Eliza.[11]

The sisters persuaded Cal Logsdon to accompany them and to do the actual killing. J. D. Lowrey noted that Logsdon was even paid to kill the Outcasts: 'They thought their father was going to marry one of them, so [the Burr sisters] give him forty dollars to kill them.' Mrs Toney painted the picture in more graphic terms and opened up the possibility that Cal had help in the crime: 'Jane just said, "Now, listen Cal, my father is going to marry that notorious thing, and you're going with us and we're going to kill her." ' Logsdon and the Burrs went to the Outcast home one night in November, 1868.[12] According to Mrs Toney they first killed Lucy, then proceeded to attack her mother: 'The old lady was carding wool in the corner by her fireplace in the lamp light... "I never harmed you folks in my life," she said, "Don't hit me." But they killed her with a shovel.' They also killed the younger child.

The gory murder details prompted the Nashville *Republican Banner* to describe the event as 'the most fiendish deed of blood ever perpetuated within the borders of Tennessee'.[13] Court hearings and trial proceedings recorded the gruesome story of the triple murders in sordid detail. Certain men, who were called upon to take depositions, provided graphic eye-witness descriptions of the mutilated bodies. The following deposition by J. W. Storie is typical:

> Early on Friday morning when we found the bodies, W. B. Outcast was lying by the back door, Catherine Outcast was also found lying, and in the back of the house Lucy Outcast was lying struck five times with something similar to a shovel on the head and side of her neck. Her head was cut open and her brains run out... There was an axe in the house that was bloody. I saw where an axe had struck the house over where Lucy Outcast was found lying. The strikes were made by a person that is left handed... The axe had blood, brains, and hair on the blade and handle. Also a shovel but it had been used in the fire before we examined it.

Oral traditional accounts list the murder weapons but do not vividly describe the mangled bodies. Mrs Toney did, however, offer an explicit account of the initial discovery of the boy's corpse:

> Jane's father went on Sunday morning to see this girl, Lucy, that he was going to

marry... Said the little boy's hair was sticking out through the crack under the door.

> And the old man thought he's got up while the others were getting breakfast and laid down there and went to sleep. He retch down here and pulled the little fellow's hair — but he never moved.[14] Pulled his hair two or three times; still he didn't move. Then he thought something was wrong. He went in and there they were — dead!

Oral tradition, court records, and newspaper accounts all testify that James Outcast, eight, survived the slaughter. Court testimony claimed that James recovered after lying in a state of insensibility for two days, but offered no information as to his whereabouts during that time. Oral tradition offers an explanation but is divided in its opinion. Ed Moody, J. D. Lowrey, and Ona Barton claimed that the boy was hit in the head with a hatchet but was not killed. Their versions help to verify the claim of insensibility mentioned in the court records. Lowrey additionally stated that the lad hid from his assailant by 'crawling up in the fireplace'.[15] Ona Barton claimed that when the boy was stunned he fell backwards into the feather-bed and laid there for three days. He survived only because of the warmth provided by the feathers.[16] Fred Johnson recalled the boy's survival in much the same terms: 'How come that child to live, back then they had featherbeds and that child was buried in a featherbed. It was cold, snowy weather. It just sunk down in it — a warm place.'[17] Lonnie Barton, grandson of Ona Barton and present during the interview with Johnson and Crouch, echoed his grandmother's sentiments that 'it was three days before they ever found the child. That's the way I've always heard it.'

Cal Logsdon left the scene of the crime and headed for Kentucky. Oral traditions and the court briefs attest to his destination. Jefferson Evans, who gave a deposition, seemingly tried to cover for Cal.[18] Evans claimed that on the morning prior to the murders Logsdon headed for 'Green River, Kentucky, where his father lived.' Evans and his brother supposedly 'walked with him to the mill' and watched him go out of sight. Logsdon was wearing two six-shooters. Evans testified that en route to the mill the three had seen 'the two Outcast boys playing by the door, and Catherine was standing in the door'. James Pennycuff, who lived twenty miles to the north in Clinton County, Kentucky, gave a deposition that he 'saw the defendant on Thursday evening about dark'. At that encounter, Logsdon pretended to be George Choate, the son of Jim Choate of Scott County. Choate [actually Logsdon], who was described as wearing two five-shooters, told Pennycuff of the murders. Choate claimed that 'Cal Logsdon and William Reagor' were being sought for the crime, and noted that 'Logsdon was a cowardly fellow. . .'

Informant Daily Crouch offered the following account of the capture:

Fred's [Fred Johnson, another informant] daddy kept a scrapbook. One Sunday afternoon we was talking about the murder. He went to the house and came back with that scrapbook.

He said what tripped Logsdon up, he went on and he was crossing the Cumberland River on a ferry... He was leaving the country; going up in Kentucky... He asked the ferryman if he'd heard of this killing over here. Otherwise, he would have gone scot free; 'cause there was no witnesses except that little boy.

Fred Johnson added, 'See, the bodies hadn't been found at that time when he asked that on the ferry at Burkesville. Nobody knew it.' To that informant Crouch replied, 'Now, that seems to be the general deduction. . . The testimony of the ferryman clinched the whole deal.'[19]

Informant J. D. Lowrey claimed that Logsdon attempted the river crossing at Rowena, not Burkesville.

I don't know what time it was of a night that it happened, but he crossed the Cumberland River at Rowena and he told the ferryman that somebody had killed the women that night, and the neighbours didn't know it at the time.[20]

A vigilante committee under the leadership of Edgar Miles went, in the words of Miles, 'four miles above Houstonville, Kentucky and arrested Logsdon at his father's house'. Miles further testified by deposition that Logsdon told his mother to

give him some clothes. 'All were dirty,' Miles claimed, 'except for one pair of drawers. He had on a very dirty shirt. I could have worn a shirt two months and it would not have been dirtier than his.'[21]

Logsdon was tried three times in the circuit courts of Scott, Overton, and Fentress Counties. Each time the guilty verdict was appealed to the Tennessee Supreme Court where the decisions of the lower courts were twice overturned but finally upheld.

The first trial commenced in Jamestown, Fentress County, November 30, 1868. Logsdon immediately petitioned for a change of venue on the grounds that he 'could not safely go to trial at the present term of the court'.[22] The trial was moved to adjacent Scott County. His lawyer appealed the case to the Supreme Court on the grounds that the murder did not occur in Scott County. The trial was repeated in neighbouring Overton County, where the accused was convicted principally on the testimony of the young Outcast survivor,[23] and again the Supreme Court ruled in favour of Logsdon because of an unspecified technicality, despite an attempted jailbreak by Logsdon during his confinement there. The trial was returned to Fentress where he was convicted for the third time. The Supreme Court affirmed the conviction this time and James Calvin Logsdon was slated to be hanged.[24]

Following the pronouncement that the accused should be hanged, Logsdon made no statement when asked if he had anything to say. A few hours later, however, he penned the following statement to the members of the Supreme Court:

To the Honorable Supreme Court in Session:
I state that from the fact that I am laboring under severe cold I could not bear the sentence passed upon me by your honors, and on the desire to say to the Court I am innocent of the charge. I left the neighborhood of the unfortunate occurence [sic] on Tuesday, two days before it is charged the murder was perpetuated. I desire to say this much to the court and shall die if die I must free from any stain of blood on me for I could have had no motives to kill the parties, neither do I know who did kill them. I was a stranger in the country. Someone did the

killing and it was an easy matter to single me, a stranger out. And [,] in their conspiracy [,] to move the proof on me.

Tennessee's Governor Brown visited the Nashville jail in response to this and several other messages from Logsdon begging the Governor to come and hear what he had to say. The interview with Logsdon lasted half an hour. Governor Brown told Logsdon that he had not had time to examine the papers in the case, but that Logsdon had been afforded three trials by jury and three hearings by the Supreme Court. There was no doubt as to his guilt that would leave room for Executive clemency. Firmly advising the condemned man to 'cherish no vain hope of pardon or commutation of his sentence, the Governor impressed upon Logsdon the importance of preparing to meet his fate'.[25] The prisoner was scheduled to die by hanging in Jamestown on 5th April, 1872.[26]

Logsdon left for Fentress County on the steamer 'Ella Hughes' on 23rd March, 1872 in custody of Thomas C. Martin, who was Sheriff of the Supreme Court, and two deputies. Once the 'Hughes' was under steam and en route northward, it became evident that among the passengers on board was Logsdon's father and a sizeable number of 'friends', most of whom lived in Kentucky where Logsdon's father resided. There was no mistaking the fact that plans had been made to facilitate Logsdon's escape. The fact that he had been taken out of the jail in Livingston by his father and a large party of friends during his confinement there increased the suspicions of the three officers in charge of the prisoner. Sheriff Martin somehow sent word ahead that he needed additional deputies.

Logsdon's behaviour and attitude was at first cheerful, even playful, for he was confident of escape at the opportune time. But when Sheriff Martin's requested additional deputies came on board the boat, perhaps at Carthage about fifty miles up the river, Logdon's countenance fell. For the first time, Sheriff Martin reported, Logsdon realised that he was doomed to die.

The prisoner was removed from the steamer at the frontier town of Celina about 1.00 a.m. For the remainder of the night Logsdon was escorted in great discomfort overland to Jamestown about forty miles eastward into the hinterland. His hands were bound behind him, he was placed astraddle a horse without the benefit of a saddle, and the horse was led at a fast pace the entire distance. They did not stop for refreshments or rest. Despite the fact that Logsdon 'had been so long confined in prison he bore it well', according to Sheriff Martin.[27]

Logsdon was placed in jail at Jamestown awaiting the day of his execution. He was in the custody of Sheriff J. C. Taylor of Fentress County. At this point oral tradition again picks the story up and continues it through the hanging, through a flood predicted by Logsdon to prove his innocence, and described the ghostly phenomenon which Jane Burr purportedly saw every night for the rest of her life, presumably as positive proof that it was she who did the killings for which Cal Logsdon paid with his life.

The hanging of Logsdon is recounted in vivid fashion in oral tradition by informants whose grandparents were present at the event. Oral traditional accounts were cross-fertilised in 1896 with the appearance in print of the diary of the Reverend A. B. Wright, the Methodist circuit rider who baptised Logsdon during his final days of confinement, preached the final sermon proceeding the execution, and was present when Logsdon was finally pronounced dead. The diary, published as *The Autobiography of Reverend A. B. Wright*, was known by all of the informants interviewed, and read by some. It is possible to separate original oral traditions from Wright's printed account and from subsequent oral tradition spawned by Wright's book, but the distinction is virtually impossible when it comes to identifying the hymns sung during the final hours.

Oral sources agree with Reverend Wright that Logsdon rode to his hanging on an ox-drawn two-wheel cart, which hauled his coffin as well. Gladys Williams of Wolf River Valley claimed that Henry Pyles rode on the casket with Logsdon. A contingency followed alongside and behind the cart singing the old hymn 'O Come Angel Band, Come and around me stand; O bear me away on your snowy wings, To my immortal home.'[28]

Logsdon's funeral was preached by Reverend Wright on the topic, 'Whoso sheddeth man's blood, by man shall his blood be shed'.[29] The doomed man sat listening on his coffin, awaiting his execution, when the service was over. When the crowd began the hymn 'I would not live always; I ask not to stay', most of those gathered close by broke down emotionally and could not continue. Logsdon chided them in gentle fashion, then led the rest of the song himself.[30]

Logsdon was taken to the gallows, located on the spot in Jamestown now occupied by a poultry-processing plant, and the noose was placed around his neck. At that instant Logsdon again reaffirmed his innocence and concluded by uttering a rain promise to those within earshot: 'To prove I'm innocent, there'll be three days and three nights rain if you kill me. And tomorrow will be the biggest tide [flood] that was ever on the Obey River... If it don't rain, I'll be guilty.'[31]

The hangman's rope broke twice during the execution and Logsdon, whose photograph depicts an exceptionally large and muscular neck, plumeted to the ground both times. Dennis Crockett, informant, noted, 'Some of them says that the first fall broke his neck, but I don't know how they knowed.'[32] Daily Crouch recalled the grim event from the account repeatedly told to him by an eye-witness:

> He was hanged in 1872, the year my daddy was born... Uncle Jack Pyle was there the day he was hanged. He was a guard hired to keep people back...
> Uncle Jack told me many times setting here on this [store] porch that two ropes broke that they knotted around. Evidentally they didn't know exactly how. He said Logsdon kept saying, 'Boys, let me go!'
> Said they strung him up with the third rope and that time it did the job.[33]

J. D. Lowrey filled in the details surrounding the third and successful attempt:

> He broke the rope twice at the hanging. There was an old Civil War captain there. The Old Captain [Tinker Dave Beatty] said, 'Get a withe[34] the next time...' Some of them said, they guessed he had hung people during the War with withes.[35]

Logsdon took twenty-seven minutes to die. During this traumatic period of time women screamed and cried, and numerous witnesses fainted.[36] Fred Johnson had been told the 'women fell all over that hill up there... like they saw a shot'.[37]

The man who did the hanging was Sheriff J. C. Taylor.[38] Sheriff Taylor reputedly exonerated Logsdon in his own mind when the rope broke the first time. Informant Mrs C. E. Toney, whose husband was a nephew of Sheriff Taylor, had heard it said many times that the Sheriff claimed, 'That man wasn't guilty or the rope wouldn't have broke.' Mrs Toney went on to say, 'And it broke twice! Well if it had broke one more time, they wouldn't of had to hang him, see.'[39]

It is common knowledge that Sheriff Taylor supposedly said that he would resign his office before he would ever perform another hanging.

It will be recalled that Logsdon uttered a flood pronouncement on the Obey River area in the event they hanged an innocent man. Many of those interviewed for this study knew of the promise and, on the basis of their grandparents' eyewitness testimonies, claimed that the rain came in unheard of quantity. Elvin Byrd of Clinton County, Kentucky testified:

> Mama said that grandpa said that none of them didn't hardly get away from down there 'til it clouded up and started raining. It rained three days and three nights, and they called it the Logsdon Tide.

Although most informants referred to the deluge as a tide, Flossie Crocket and Daily Crouch said that old-timers originally called it the Logsdon Flood, and Ona Barton claimed that it was once called the Logsdon Fresh.

Whatever the term was, the meaning was clear to these mountain people: Logsdon had promised enough water and then some in the Obey River Channel to float log rafts down stream to Celina. Ample water was extremely important to these people, for all too often their logs had been left stranded in the stream channel when the water receded too rapidly. Fred Johnson exclaimed of the Logsdon Tide, 'The Obey River really got wild!'[40]

Flossie Crockett's version of the flood promise mentions heaven and hell as a part of Logsdon's final words prior to his death. There is no mention of his innocence or guilt although the implications are present:

> And they asked Logsdon when they went to hang him if they was any last words he wanted to say. And he told them if he went

to heaven they'd have a tide, and if he went to hell, the people would have a drought.

And Granny said when they started home it commenced raining, and the next morning there's some big sycamores that's marked on Wolf River[41] where they marked on it 'The Logsdon Tide' and they said the river was out of banks. . .

Granny said before they got home it went to pouring rain on them and said it rained all night. And said the next morning all the neighbors and everybody went to the river to see how big it was, and some of them marked these big trees along the river. And she said, 'That was the marks of the Logsdon Tide.'

Said he said they'd be a tide, and they was![42]

Daily Crouch and Mrs C. E. Toney were more reserved regarding the quantity of rain which fell following the hanging. Mrs Toney said simply, 'It rained, but they wasn't no flood.'[43] Crouch stated, 'Well, it just set in to raining at the time. After it warmed up and the rains came, they called it the Logsdon Tide.'[44]

Until I interviewed Mrs Toney, I considered Logsdon guilty of the crimes for which he was hanged. Now, I am not so sure either of his guilt or of his innocence. Mrs Toney's testimony contains details which cannot be substantiated; neither can they be readily discounted. Her account, in part, is as follows:

Years after that my mother's father married this girl [Jane Burr] they said the one that killed these people. These two girls, Jane and Louisa Burr, turned state's evidence against Logsdon at trial. They hung him in place of the girls. . .

Jane's father was going to marry this [Outcast] girl, but Jane wasn't going to let him take that girl. . . They didn't believe in that.

And so they [Cal and the two Burr sisters] went. . . and killed them. . .

Years after that, my mother's father [James Short] from Calfkiller Creek [in White County] married this Jane. . . They always said Jane did it. . . The family feels that Jane did the killing. Jane Burr Short

raised my mother. . . Well, Mother said that anytime that Jane got out of the house on a real dark night somebody would raise up in front of her. She said there were two of them ghostly beings. And Jane could see them. She said, 'Why, I could put my hand on their head.'

And Mother said, 'Now, Jane, you don't see such as that.'

She said, 'All Right. . ., I want you to go out with me tonight and I'll show them to you.'

Well, Mother said they went out between the house and the barn that night, and it was just black; you couldn't see a thing.

And she said Jane said, 'Now there they are.' My Mother's name was Amanda. Said, 'Mandy, don't you see them there?' . . . . . .

Mother said, 'I couldn't see a thing in the world.' She said, 'No, Jane, and you don't see them either!'

'Yes,' she said, 'I do.' Said, 'I could lay my hand on their head — but they don't have a head.'

And she saw that all of her life! Until she died! She thought they was the two she had killed.

My mother told her a-many a-time, 'Jane, you just as sure killed them two women as sure as you're standing here.'

· 'Aw,' she'd say, 'You little fool, I didn't do it.'

. . . Mother said Cal Logsdon was a clear man.

While the oral folk history which undergirds the Logsdon story is itself a part and parcel of folklore, it can readily be discerned that the Logsdon legend complex had captured five identifiable universal folklore motifs, and affords a strong example of the law of repetition in legend composition. Chief among the motifs are Cf. A1017.3, 'Flood caused by curse', *E422.1.1 'Headless revenant', E422.1.1 (b), 'Headless woman, appearance only', F511.0.1 'Headless person', and S31, 'Cruel stepmother'. Motifs such as these add colour and embellishmental detail to the legend process, and make a good story even better. Countless retellings crystallised the form of certain legend segments of the Logsdon story into fixed narrative frames. Universal motifs, telescoping and patterning coloured the story to the extent that it is hard to imagine the initial skeletal historical account before the embellishmental details were added. We do not yet understand why people added ornamentation to the legend process, but we do know that they did. This was and is a part of the folk historical process.

The figure three looms paramount throughout the Logsdon legend from beginning to end. Three people were initially charged for the murder of three persons. The lone survivor escaped by hiding three days. Logsdon was tried for murder three times in three different counties and was sentenced to death three times. He took the case to the Supreme Court three times, stayed in jail three years, was escorted up river by three guards, and because the rope broke twice, he was hanged three times.[45] Just before the first attempt to hang him Logsdon pronounced a rain prediction, calling for rain for three days and three nights. Finally, he took twenty-seven minutes, a multiple of three (3x3x3), to die.

Folklorists have long taken note of the frequent occurence of three-fold repetition in oral tradition. Axel Olrik in particular called attention to the repetitive use of three as a means of producing emphasis. This is what he called the Law of Repetition, and pointed out that three appears in *Märchen,* myths, and local legends with incredible frequency.[46]

The Nashville *Republican Banner* painted word pictures of Logsdon as an ignorant hillcountry bumkin who knew not how to spell his own name, and as a murderous beast who committed the grossest crime in Tennessee's history. There is implied evidence[47] that even the folk around Jamestown initially looked upon Logsdon in a similar vein. There is no way to determine to what extent newspaper accounts were influenced by public sentiment. Nashville newspapers probably did not influence public sentiment in and around Jamestown at all due to the great distance from Nashville. And Jamestown itself had no newspaper during the period 1868-1872.

The grassroots sympathy manifested on Logsdon's behalf upon his return to Jamestown to be hanged was both a reaction to the lengthy trial and prison ordeal he had undergone and the torturous horseback trip to which he had been subjected. Public opinion favoured the underdog.

And after his prediction of a flood came true, public sympathy turned to a sense of awe. Here was a man with God on his side — an innocent victim whose supernatural promise of rain had been fulfilled.[48] Here was a man whose story was worthy of oral continuance.

Two questions of a historical nature also call for analysis: First, who actually killed the three Outcasts? Second, did a flood really occur at the event of Logsdon's death? I support the notion that the Outcasts were murdered by Logsdon and his two female conspirators, Jane and Eliza Burr. These three were originally charged with the murder, and internal evidence contained within the narratives themselves corroborate the notion that Logsdon had help. The fact that the two women jointly turned State's evidence on Logsdon does not free them of the actual guilt for the crime. And, according to oral testimonies, not long after the murders took place, one of the Burrs asked the eight-year-old survivor, 'Who hit you?' He responded, 'You ought to know, you were there.'[49] There is little reason to exonerate Logsdon of the murders on the other hand. J. D. Lowrey pointed out, 'They had Logsdon in the lineup several times, and the little boy [the survivor] never failed to pick him out. He [Logsdon] wanted to kill the little boy, but the little boy wouldn't come near him when they went to hang him.'[50]

The fact that one informant's mother placed all the guilt on Jane and not on her sister Eliza, or Cal, is not very helpful either. For, in this instance, Jane later became the stepmother of the informant's mother. Not only did Jane reputedly see ghosts of the murdered women for the rest of her life as the result of a guilt complex, she was also a mean, heartless woman who despised little children.[51] The cruel stepmother motif is universally common in folklore. The fact that it appears here in an historical legend context rather than in a folktale should not detract from the folkloric patterning which is present. Even Logsdon's mother does not escape a finger of guilt being pointed at her, because she condoned and even sanctioned her son's childhood thievery. Tradition has it that Logsdon testified on the gallows, 'The first thing I ever stole was eggs, and I took them home and my mother cooked them.'[52]

Logically, there are two possibilities regarding the actuality of the flood-producing rain — either it occurred or it did not. Nothing is written to confirm that it did,[53] and official weather bureau records do not reach back to 1872. The only written eye-witness account of the hanging is contained in Reverend Wright's autobiography, and the flood is not mentioned by him. If for a moment we can assume that the rain occurred, Reverend Wright may have omitted mention of it for two reasons. First, he did not hear Logsdon's final words. This is unlikely, however, since he was with the condemned man during his last hours of confinement and preached the final sermon at the site of the hanging. Second, Reverend Wright refused to mention the prediction because he was a minister, and to most conservative, evangelical mountain preachers then and now, a prophecy of such magnitude as the one pronounced by Logsdon may be the work of Satan.

Oral evidence strongly contends that the rain did occur. First, the grandparents of virtually all of the informants were present at the hanging. There is no reason to doubt their presence. There were thus numerous relatives and other personal acquaintances of the informants present. At least ninety per cent of the informants verified the rain on the basis of eye-witness testimonies told to them personally. Second, the lapse of time between 1872, when the hanging occurred, and the early childhoods of the informants was only thirty-five years. If the flood-tide was the product of someone's imagination, the neatly crystallised fabrication is not likely to have so quickly won such popular acceptance over such a widespread geographical area. Third, among the informants who attested to the rain were the widow of Sheriff J. C. Taylor's nephew and the grand-nephew of Sheriff Taylor. Fourth, the Logsdon Tide is identified strongly with particular places and actions within the Obey-Wolf River Valleys. It is these affiliations that provide informants with emotional ties to history, thus affording stimuli to hard core narrative resiliency. Two examples should suffice: Informant Charlie Bertram, a 75-year-old storekeeper in the Chestnut Grove Community of neighbouring Wayne County, Kentucky, points to two large present-day gulleys in that community, which were created by the rains caused by Logsdon's hanging:

I've heard him [grandfather Elzie Bertram] tell it different times that them two gulleys here both washed out the day that they hung Logsdon. And Logsdon said — and this is grandaddy's tale — he said, 'you'll see that you are hanging the wrong man'. Said, 'They'll come a flood today.' And that evening, this one [gulley] up here at Skooger's [one-quarter mile away] washed out, and then that one on the other side up there. Grandaddy said 'There never was gulleys there 'til that night. . . That was called the Logsdon Flood.'

Mrs. Ona Barton provided the second example of the importance of place/action in the crystallisation of oral traditional historical narratives:

This Old Woman lived up here at the foot of Jamestown Mountain where the rock quarry is now, there at the edge of Wolf River Valley. She heard this young man — the mail carrier — ride up. He was carrying the mail from Jamestown down through Wolf River country.

She run out and told him that the Valley was flooded, that he would be drowned if he didn't turn around. He said, 'But the mail has got to go through,' and turned to ride off.

She forcibly pulled him from the horse. It was the awfulest time anybody'd ever seen! Why that young fellow would have drowned! The Logsdon Tide was all over Wolf River Valley, just a few yards ahead of him. His horse would have gone right into that water and he would have drowned.

Fifth, a proverbial comparison grew out of the Logsdon legend. Cordell Dishman and Charlie Bertram, both life-long residents of the Chestnut Grove community of Wayne County, Kentucky, located some twenty-five miles from the scene of the hanging, knew of the older local practice of comparing all big rains with the Logsdon-produced deluge. Dishman recalled, 'I remember when I was growing up and it would come a big rain, they'd say, "This is almost as big as the Logsdon Flood." It wasn't as big, though, you see.' Sixth, the flood itself may not have taken place within the three days prescribed by Logsdon. Eight oral testimonies claim that the flood occurred immediately. The others note that it rained and subsequent flooding occurred, but they are unspecific as to when. One person stated that the flooding occurred in the spring. It may thus be that heavy rains produced flooding a few weeks after the hanging and Logsdon's curse was recalled at that time. This theory would explain why the rain prophecy did not get into Reverend Wright's diary. While the truth may never be known, we do have in the composite Logsdon legend a fine example of the significance of place/action association in the creation of an historical legend. Of equal importance is the illustrated folk practice of compressing events by removing blocks of intervening time so as to bring two separate events into direct contact and association. This is referred to as telescoping, a not uncommon practice which, in this instance, provides a fantastic ending to the Logsdon story and an appropriate beginning to the process of legend embellishment — and legend sustenance. Without the rain prophecy and attendant narratives, the Logsden story likely would have ended at the gallows.

Notes

1. Logsdon spelled his name with a 'd'. He was tried and hanged, however, as Calvin Logston. His gravemarker in Jamestown, Tennessee reads 'Cal Logston Hanged 1872'.

2. A total of twenty-one informants were interviewed from these seven counties. Eleven of these persons lived in Fentress County, Tennessee, where the murders occurred.

3. Oral tradition holds that the mother lived in Scott County at the time of the murders, and *The Autobiography of The Reverend A. B. Wright* (Jamestown, Tenn., 1896) implies that she resided there when she was baptised. At the time of the hanging she was in Campbell County, Tennessee. See Note 21. Court records testify that the father lived in Kentucky.

4. Burr is a pseudonym designed to protect the identities of living descendants. The surname pseudonym is used consistently throughout this study. First names are real.

5. Mrs C. E. Toney, Allardt, Tennessee, 16th March, 1978.

6. Outcast is a pseudonym and is used for the same purpose and in the same manner as described in Note 4.

7. Mrs C. E. Toney, 16th March, 1978; Avo Rains, Moodyville, Tennessee, 5th January, 1978. According to the deposition taken from J. W. Storie, Lucy also had an infant child. That child was not mentioned by informants.

8. Rains, 5th January, 1978.

9. Daily Crouch, Forbus, Tennessee, 16th November, 1977; Fred Johnson, Forbus, Tennessee, 16th November, 1977; Toney, 16th March, 1978; Rains, 5th January, 1978.

10. Toney, 16th March, 1978.

11. Toney, 16th March, 1978; Lonnie Barton, Forbus, Tennessee, 16th November, 1977; J. D. Lowrey, Edd Moody, and Flossie Crockett, all of Moodyville, Tennessee, 16th November, 1977.

12. There is no agreement as to which night the murders were actually committed. Wednesday, Friday, and Saturday were suggested by oral informants. Even the Supreme Court hearings indicated 19th November and 20th November, 1868. Logsdon himself indicates that it was Thursday; see his letter to the Supreme Court, page 293-4.

13. Nashville *Republican Banner*, 22nd February, 1872.

14. Ona Barton, Forbus, Tennessee, 16th November, 1977, also recalled that the boy's hair was seen under the door: 'The little dead boy was found because his hair was sticking out from under the door.'

15. Lowrey's daughter, Flossie Crockett, who was also present at the interview, knew the traditional account of the killing and offered the same information as her father. Avo Rains, 5th January, 1978, also claimed that the boy hid in the fireplace.

16. 16th November, 1977. Daily Crouch, had heard that Logsdon thought the boy was dead, but that the lad later revived and identified the killer.

17. 16th November, 1977. Johnson and Daily Crouch both felt that the murder weapon was an axe.

18. Virtually all informants claimed that the two women who employed Logsdon to kill the Outcasts were Evanses not Burrs. I do not place any credence in the claim that they were Evanses, since the Burr sisters were officially implicated, but am not yet prepared to offer an explanation for the confusion.

19. Crouch and Johnson, 16th November, 1977.

20. 16th November, 1977. Lowrey's daughter repeated her father's account almost verbatim. Rowena is located upriver from Burkesville. Both are about the same distance overland from the scene of the murder. If Logsdon were headed for his father's residence, Rowena would have been the logical site of the crossing.

21. It is interesting to speculate as to the truthfulness of Miles' statement regarding the mother. She was living in Campbell County, Tennessee, according to a newspaper report, just prior to his execution. See Nashville *Republican Banner*, 6th April, 1872.

22. Tennessee Supreme Court hearings.

23. When James Outcast took the witness stand, the Judge asked him if he knew what happened to little boys who lied. The lad responded, 'Yes, the booger man will get me.' 'Who told you this,' the Judge asked. 'My mother,' said the little boy.

24. Hogue, *History of Fentress County*, 112. Several of the informants stated that Logsdon had three trials, but none knew the specifics regarding the locations of the trials.

25. Nashville *Republican Banner*, 24th March, 1872. There is no mention in oral tradition of the Governor's visit to Logsdon.

26. *ibid.*

27. Upon returning to Nashville, Martin gave to the Nashville *Republican Banner* an account of the trip upriver and overland to Jamestown to deliver his prisoner. Oral tradition around Jamestown did not pick up on the story of Logsdon's journey from Nashville to Jamestown.

28. The only clear-cut case of the song's title retained through oral tradition came from Lucinda Byrd, Albany, Clinton County, Kentucky, 6th March, 1976.

29. Recorded only in *The Autobiography of The Reverend A. B. Wright*, 97.

30. Oral knowledge regarding the second hymn seemingly all stems from oral traditions derived from the *Autobiography*.

31. Elvin Byrd, Speck Community, Clinton County, Kentucky, 27th February, 1976.

32. 16th November, 1977.

33. *ibid.*

34. The informant described a withe as 'a hickory sprout. You can twist it and beat it and it'll be almost like a rope and stronger than a rope.'

35. 16th November, 1977.

36. Avo Rains, 5th January, 1978, and numerous others.

37. 16th November, 1977.

38. Fred Johnson, 16th November, 1977; Earl Taylor, the great-nephew of Sheriff Taylor, Allardt, Tennessee, 18th March, 1978; Mrs C. E. Toney, Allardt, Tennessee, 18th March, 1978; Ona Barton, letter to Montell, 10th January, 1978.

39. 18th March, 1978.

40. 16th November, 1977.

41. Jamestown is located on the fluvial divide between the Obey and Wolf Rivers. Persons in attendance at the hanging came from both valleys.

42. 16th November, 1977.

43. 18th March, 1978.

44. 16th November, 1977.

45. While Logsdon's triple hanging was recorded in Ripley's 'Believe it or Not', there is at least one other instance of a criminal who was hanged three times. In January 1885, 20-year-old John Lee of Babbacombe, near Torquay, England, was placed on the scaffold three times within the space of an hour, and each time the trap doors failed to drop. Lee was reprieved but went on to serve twenty-two years in prison. See Mark Kidel, 'The Man They Could Not Hang', *The Listener*, 6th February, 1975.

46. Alan Dundes, *The Study of Folklore* (Englewood Cliffs, 1965), 132-3; see esp. 133, Note

4, where several early studies of threefold repetition are mentioned, including Olrik's, many of which were published in non-folklore journals.

47. Miles' testament (see Note 21), page 6.

48. William F. Allen *et al.*, *Slave Songs of the United States* (1867; reprint, New York, 1951), 21-22, quotes a source as saying that a baptismal was only good when it rained. 'If the Lord was pleased with those who had been "in the wilderness" he would send rain.' *The Frank C. Brown Collection of North Carolina Folklore* notes that in the folk belief of both whites and blacks in the South, and also internationally, rain is a sign of God's approval. One belief reads, 'Blessed are the dead that it rains on.' Annotation provided courtesy of Dr Venetia J. Newall, letter to Lynwood Montell, 30th October, 1978.

49. Ona Barton, 16th November, 1977.

50. 16th November, 1977.

51. Mrs C. E. Toney, 18th March, 1978.

52. Mrs Iva Stephens, Red Hill Community, Fentress County, Tennessee, as told to Mrs Ona Barton, 15th September, 1978.

53. Subsequent research in published legend materials may reveal that the flood prediction is a part of universal folk legendry, and follows patterning prescribed for migratory legends. Until such evidence is found, however, it must be assumed that this portion of the legend was spawned by the actual event of Logsdon's hanging.

The Embroidery and Costume Collections of the Jewish Historical Museum, Belgrade

VIDOSAVA NEDOMAČKI   Jewish Historical Museum, Belgrade

IN the mosaic of the many nations, nationalities and ethnic groups living on the territory of Yugoslavia, the Jews who began to settle there as far back as the end of the ancient era have their place, too. Through centuries, despite assimilatory trends and processes, they treasured and cultivated their traditional customs, languages, songs, proverbs, tales, costumes, and the specific design of their synagogue architecture, as well as the ornamentation of their synagogue interiors and Torah scrolls with embroidered fabrics. The form of Jewish tombstones in Yugoslavia also possesses specific traditional features.

The first Jewish settlers who came to the area of what is today Yugoslavia some 2,000 years ago, were undoubtedly wearing such clothes as they used to wear in their homeland, ancient Palestine – that is the type of clothing in use in areas under strong Hellenistic influence. The basic parts of this clothing were a *hiton* and a *himation*, and essentially it did not differ too much from traditional Jewish clothing: a simple shirt to the ankles, or a shorter one covering the knees only, with long or short sleeves (*ketonet*), woven from wool or flax, but never from a combination of the two, and a mantle of rectangular shape, cut out for the purpose from a piece of fabric (*simla*). It was mandatory to have long fringes (*tzitzit, tzitziot*) at the angles of the clothing. Although such fringes can be seen on old Assyrian and Byzantine clothing as well, clear religious symbolic meaning as to their making and wearing is given only in Jewish written sources (Numbers, 15:38-40; Deuteronomy, 22:12).

The extent to which Jewish clothing was already influenced by other eastern peoples in the ancient homeland is clear from certain passages in the Old Testament objecting to the trend (Leviti-cus, 18:3; Ezekiel, 16:10, 13-18; Isaiah, 3:18-23; Zephaniah, 1:8; Joshua, 7:21), in particular the images on the walls of the Dura Europos synagogue dating from the middle of the third century A.D.

The Jewish dispersion brought about an even greater variety of national influences to which Jewish customs and costumes were exposed in the new environments. These influences become more noticeable at the end of the eighteenth century and during the nineteenth, when the doors of the ghettoes burst open, and the Jews were granted civil rights. However, it is true that the Jews tended to accept such influences if their ethnic identity and the basic values of their faith were not affected.

As both Ashkenazi and Sephardi Jews lived in Yugoslavia, the Ashkenazi from the beginning of the twelfth century and the Sephardi from the end of the fifteenth century, the traits of these two ethnic groups are to be found within the cultural heritage of our Jewish community. It is thus greatly enriched, in terms of the language of the texts – in addition to Hebrew, the Judeo-Spanish Ladino and Judeo-German Yiddish – as well as in terms of the songs, poems, tales, prayers, religious and festive rites, style of clothing and shape of synagogue ornaments.

The clothing of Ashkenazi and Sephardi Jews living on the territory of what is today Yugoslavia had the same variety of ornamentation as that of other city dwellers. But all the same, if we look at the style of their clothing, three main groups emerge. Those who lived in areas which were for centuries under Turkish rule (Macedonia, Serbia, Bosnia and Herzegovina) would fall in the first group, those along the Adriatic coast where Italian influence was strong would be in the second, while those north of the Sava and Danube where they were exposed to the influence of the countries of Central and Eastern Europe would fall in the third group.

The Sephardim, who after their expulsion from Spain and Portugal started their arduous migration by going first to Italy and thence to Dalmatia and other western parts of Yugoslav territory, maintained the style of clothing of the Iberian and Italian peninsulas for a long time. Those who first went to Greece and Turkey and then, after a few decades, in the sixteenth century started to arrive in the Yugslav areas under Turkish rule, were exposed to a completely different cultural influence and had rapidly to adjust their appearance in some measure to their new environment in order to survive. For generations they came to Yugoslav areas dressed like Turkish city-dwellers. They had, however, to observe those rules which imposed certain restrictions upon non-moslems – on Christians and Jews – denying them the right to wear turbans, fezes and clothing of certain colours. The turban of a Jew had to be yellow, the fez dark blue, while his clothing could be of any colour but green. In Bosnia and Herzegovina this style of clothing lasted longer than in other parts of the country. Sephardi women, for instance, used to wear, until the end of the first World War, a long embroidered dress called *anteriya*, and a special type of cap, called the *tokado*. This *tokado* had a line of small ducats, called *frontera*, strung on it, giving the impression of golden braid around the edge. Tradition demanded that the women hide their hair, and to meet this demand long fringes reaching to the shoulders were sewn below the back part of the *tokado*. These fringes were called *purchul* and served as a substitute for the woman's hair, hidden under the cap. Widows did not wear *fronteras*, while young girls wore only small *tokas* with ducats sewn on in line around, but not so close together as on the women's *tokados*; sometimes, in fact, they had only one large ducat on their caps. On Saturdays and holidays the *anteriyas* and dresses of the women had richer embroidered ornamentation.

Between the two World Wars only older women still wore *tokados*. On special occasions, on holidays and family celebrations, they also wore their ornamented *anteriyas*.

The cut of Sephardi men's clothing scarcely differed from that of Turkish city-dwellers. Older Sephardim wore the fez until the end of World War II, although in all other respects they adopted European styles of dress much earlier.

Examples of clothing and embroidered fabric from the Jews in Macedonia (Bitola, Skopje) show some differences from the clothing in Bosnia and Herzegovina, due to the influence of Macedonian folklore and the clothing styles of the Salonikan Jews.

In Belgrade and other cities of Serbia proper, where Sephardi and Ashkenazi Jews lived side by side and where the influence of both the Balkans and Central Europe was felt, all the characteristic traits of both ethnic groups were present. The style of dress and the shape and ornamentation of synagogue fabrics illustrates this.

In addition to long ceremonial dresses – *anteriyas* – bodices, belts, shoes and slippers were also ornamented with embroidery, as well as many types of capes and kerchiefs. Men had to wear small caps (*kipa, kepele, la kapika*), which were sometimes embroidered. They also wore a ritual covering (*tallith*) made of white wool or silk fabric, with black or blue woven stripes at the edges. This cover which was sometimes as narrow as a scarf, always had a decorative strip (*atarah*) around the neck and fringes (*tzitziot*) at the corners, but in Bosnia it also had embroidered square-shaped appliqué at the corners and the *tzitziot* were run through these.

Where traditional customs were maintained men, starting from their childhood, wore over their shirts a so-called *tallith katan* – rectangular fabric with an aperture for the head so that it could be put on. At the corners it always had fringes, which hung beneath the vest or jacket, and sometimes it was decorated with embroidery.

As to the small ornamental examples, the most popular was the bag for *tallith, tefillin* and payerbook, and it might be that the prayer-book binding was also embroidered. Newly-weds, and engaged couples would usually give each other these bags and prayer-books. Towels used by women for the ritual bath, especially for the bride, were also ornamented with embroidery.

For use in the synagogue, Yugoslav Jews embroidered the curtains of the Torah Ark (*parchet*), the drapery above the curtains (*kaporet*), the covers for the reader's desk, and the Torah mantles. The Ashkenazi Jews made an embroidered mantle for their Torah scroll, the *meil*, shaped like a longish pillow-case, with one of the narrow ends open so that it could be put on the scroll. The other narrow end had two small slips in its seam for the upper ends of the two poles, around which the scroll was rolled, to pass through. *Meils* of this type were made mostly of velvet and embroidered with gilded or silver thread wound around yarn.

The Sephardim made a small trapezoid-like mantle for their Torah scrolls, its upper narrow end sewn to an inserted oval-shaped piece of cardboard, covered with fabric. The lower end of the mantle fell freely along the scroll. The cardboard insert had two holes through which the upper ends of the poles passed. The mantle was often made of brocade and usually had no embroidery or text on it. Only its edges were ornamented with fringes, as was the oval inset.

In some cases, however, the Ashkenazi Torah mantles also have a solid oval inset with holes for the poles in their upper parts. These mantles were intended for use in both Ashkenazi and Sephardi synagogues; this is evident from the names of the donors embroidered on them.

Ribbons for Torah scrolls (*mapa*) which serve to keep the scrolls rolled tight under the mantle are also sometimes embroidered. In certain areas these ribbons are made from the diapers of new-born boys and have a wide variety of motifs, reflecting situations which the boy will find himself in during his life. Particular importance is given to the boy's study of the Torah, and to the colourful scene when he gets married. All these scenes have captions with explanations in which good wishes are expressed for the happiness of the new-born boy. The embroidery is usually made (sometimes even painted) by the mother or the older sister of the new-born infant in whose name the ribbon is presented to the synagogue. Special long embroidered ribbons were prepared for Simhat Torah, as on that holiday all the Torah scrolls are displayed. Baldachins (*hupa*) under which marriage ceremonies are performed in synagogues, are also embroidered.

As to the ceremonies at home, there was hardly a family which would not have its own Shabbath bread-cover and a cover for Pesach-bread (*matzoth*); this last was sometimes a napkin, and sometimes a bag with three divisions. It is a traditional custom to donate to happy new mothers a nicely embroidered bedspread which was later often remade and used as a curtain (*parokhet*) in synagogues. If the embroidered ornamentation on the *parokhet* is distributed evenly and symmetrically, as one sees on a carpet spread horizontally, it is clear that it was transformed from an embroidered bedspread. Floral ornamentation is nearly always used on the fabric, while the text of dedication, or a simple monogram, was subsequently embroidered between the mofits on the bedspread itself or sometimes on an additional piece of fabric. Sometimes we may find only rings sewn on the bedspread to hang them up as in the case of a *parokhet*. On a *parokhet* made specially for use in the synagogue, the ornamentation is embroidered in a way that can be seen when the curtain is in a vertical position. In addition to decorative elements, symbolic motifs suitable for the purpose are also embroidered, while a special space, usually medallion-shaped, is reserved for texts relating to the donor.

The style, the symbolic meaning of the motifs, the type of fabric, the quality of embroidery and the language of the embroidered text reflect the variety of cultural influences and socio-economic conditions in which the Yugoslav Jews lived for centuries. This variety is evident in the style which was influenced by the East, the West and local non-Jewish folklore, in the preservation of traditional Jewish symbolism and shapes of objects and in the way the general decorative elements were accepted, to a greater or lesser extent. Whether a sumptuous or a modest piece of embroidery was produced depended, as a rule, on economic conditions. Even if there is almost nothing in the style, the selection of the fabric or the type of embroidery, which could be said to be specifically characteristic of the Jewish craftsmen's work, the choice of motifs and their symbolism, the shape and the use of specific pieces of embroidered fabrics surely have such qualities.

Compositions with human figures can usually be found on ribbons for Torah scrolls, in scenes conveying situations in various phases of human life, as well as on *matzot* covers decorated with scenes with which the Haggadah for Pesach is illustrated, and on other decorated household fabrics as well. Of animals it is the lion which is usually represented; in fact two rampant lions always appear together, either facing each other or in opposed positions. Originally the lion was the symbol of the tribe of Judah but, as time passed, it was assigned the role of protector of the Tablets of the Law and of the Torah scrolls. The figures of the pigeon, lamb and fish also possess symbolic meaning in keeping with the texts of the Old Testament; this is also true of the hybrid figures of *heruvim*, the biblical protectors of the Ark of the Covenant.

As to objects with symbolic meaning: the Ark of the Covenant, the Tablets of the Law, the seven-branched candelabrum (*menorah*), the ram's horn (*shofar*) and the Torah crown (*keter Torah*) can be found on embroidered fabrics. Architectural motifs include the sky-line of Jerusalem, the temple in Jerusalem by itself, its portal, its entrance, and the pillars of Jahim and Boaz which stand in front of the entrance. One of the motifs on fabrics which decorate the Sukkoth booth is the Tabernacle — *Sukkah*. Two hands, symbolising the priests of Jerusalem (*kohanim*) and the six-pointed 'star' (*Magen David*), also appear on embroidered fabrics.

Various fruits, grapevines or bunches of grapes, pomegranates (*rimonim*), and a lime-like citrus fruit (*etrog*) are embroidered as symbols of fertility, and the palm branch (*lulav*) is a plant which serves the same purpose. On the synagogue curtains (*parokhets*) in front of the Torah shrine, and on the Torah scrolls' mantles, the most frequent mofits are the crown held by two rampant lions, the Ark of the Covenant, the Tablets of the Law, the portal of the Jerusalem Temple and the Jahim and Boaz pillars. Various decorative elements are often added to all these motifs.

Shabbath bread-covers are usually embroidered with a braided loaf of bread (*challa*) and two Shabbath candelabras. *Matzot* covers are often embroidered with the motif of the table, as prepared for the festive Seder dinner on the eve of Pesach and the dish with the traditional food, but we will probably only find a piece of *matzot*, the ceremonial wineglass, or sometimes the book describing Israel's bondage in and flight from Egypt — the *Haggadah shel Pesach*, with some scenes from the same book depicted.

The embroidered texts on various fabrics relate to the donors, the synagogues which the fabric was donated to, the place and date of the donation, and also contain a great number of blessings. Unfortunately, it is hardly ever possible to establish who a given embroidery was made by. The technique of the embroideries is of different kinds. Sephardi clothing — various *anteriyas* and bodices — were ornamented mostly by a special *terziya* technique, i.e. ornamentation achieved by sewing on gold, silver, silk or cotton braids of various widths and thicknesses.

For use in the synagogue embroidery generally employed thin gilded copper thread, gilded silver thread, or pure silver thread wound around silk yarn. For certain details only narrow gilded or silver wire was used. Some pieces which have been preserved are embroidered with multi-coloured silk yarn or with a combination of both types of yarn and also with wool. Various gilded or copper tinsel, pearls, and fringes were also used for ornamentation.

Many motifs were prepared using appliqué. This technique was generally used to make the Torah crown, the Tablets of the Covenant and the Lions. These are embroidered in high relief on a separate piece of fabric which is sewn to the Ark curtain or the Torah mantle. The other motifs, especially the donor's text, were made using a relief type of embroidery, either laid over a rough basic embroidery prepared with yarn, or over a cardboard pattern matching the ornamental model.

The small number of Yugoslav Jews who survived the Nazi occupation still maintain some of their ancient traditions, but generally speaking the preservation of the Jewish cultural heritage is today the task of the Jewish Historical Museum in Belgrade, which was established by the Federation of Jewish Communities in Yugoslavia in 1948. In addition to historical, art and ethnological collections, a collection of embroidered fabrics and costumes is also preserved there. This collection contains fine examples of traditional Sephardi costumes and different richly embroidered curtains for the Torah Ark, mantles for Torah scrolls, various covers for the reader's desk in synagogues, bread-covers used on holidays, napkins, bags for prayer-books, and prayer-book bindings.

Smaller collections still exist in several Jewish communities in Yugoslavia: in Dubrovnik (the oldest preserved collection), Sarajevo and Zagreb, — in the Museum of the Jews from Bosnia and

Herzegovina in Sarajevo, and in the Museum of Art and Craft in Zagreb. Single examples exist in synagogues which are still functioning, and are in private possession. Nearly all the extant pieces were damaged during the last war, either intentionally by the Nazis, or because of inadequate conditions in the places where they were hidden.

The Jewish Historical Museum in Belgrade organised in April 1978 the first exhibition of Jewish embroideries and costumes in Yugoslavia. As a result it was possible to identify their basic characteristics and encourage further study.

The Black Outsider; Racist Images in Britain

VENETIA NEWALL   University of London

THE eminent psychologist David Stafford-Clark once remarked: 'Any community, of any size, which makes differences of ethnic origin a reason for unkindness, let alone anything worse, is uncivilized. There are no civilized communities by this definition.'[1] Nearly three hundred years ago, the author of *Robinson Crusoe*, Daniel Defoe, wrote a satirical poem, which he called *The True-Born Englishman*. It was in defence of no less a person than the king himself, who had been subjected to 'lampoons and invectives' and 'insulted by insolent pedants and ballad-making poets for ... being a foreigner.'[2] William III was Dutch and the poem is a telling indictment of the racial prejudice of the time. If a white-skinned head of state could be subjected to such abuse, it is hardly surprising that ordinary citizens of different ethnic origin, especially those easily identifiable because of a different physical appearance, were not spared. The traditional reasons for this phenomenon are interesting, if unpleasant, and we shall briefly consider a few of them here.

Early misconceptions about the continent of Africa were a prime source of prejudice. In the fifteenth and sixteenth centuries, when the leading European maritime powers were developing contacts with West Africa, exciting travellers' tales found willing readers.[3] Indeed, Mandeville's largely fictional *Travels*, describing the fabulous Kingdom of Prester John, was circulating in manuscript earlier, from the middle of the fourteenth century.[4] Most of these accounts were both fanciful and inaccurate. One of the most influential was Richard Hakluyt's *Principall Navigations, Voiages and Discoveries of the English Nation* of 1589. While resident in Paris, as chaplain to the British Ambassador, Hakluyt heard that the British were noted for 'their sluggish security'. He accordingly resolved to devote the rest of his life to collecting and publishing accounts of the English explorations.[5] The travellers' tales which he gathered together contain numerous errors and distortions. George Best, who sailed with Martin Frobisher, states the traditional view that blackness was a divine punishment, the result of Noah's curse on his son Ham, for disobedience.[6] Richard Eden's account of Benin exaggerates nature, animal life and the weather: 'hote showres of rain ... scorching windes ... they seeme at certaine times to live ... in fornaces, and in manner already halfe way in Purgatorie or hell ... streames of water ... falling out of the aire into the sea, and ... some of these are as bigge as the great pillars of Churches ... Some faine that these should be the cataracts of heaven, which were all opened at Noes floud.'[7]

Such descriptions were not new but now, for the first time, they were recounted by English travellers, which gave them an added sense of freshness and importance. 'The myths of Africa,' writes James Walvin, 'were to prove more influential than its truths.'[8] Recently, two African students at Cambridge wrote in their College magazine criticising the wild stories that circulate about animals and excessive heat. 'A number of people believe that Africa is ... swarming with snakes, lions, leopards, crocodiles.' According to one story some people were 'playing tennis when snakes issued suddenly from the bush, swallowed the balls, and disappeared... It is so hot that only wood can be used in making bridges, for metal will melt under the blazing sun... A careless African woman ... dropped her basket. By the time she had finished picking up the other things ... some broken eggs ... had become cooked... A young missionary going ... to West Africa for the first time ... was very pleased to be going to the only place in Nigeria where a piano exists for any length of time.' She thought the strings would melt.[9]

The work of the Elizabethan Hakluyt 'gave a great impetus to discovery and colonization.'[10] Three centuries later, during another period of travel and overseas expansion, the Victorians were to send home inaccurate accounts of a somewhat different nature. Many who travelled in Africa and reported back to the learned societies had little, if any, grasp of local languages, a study which did not develop sufficiently to alter the low opinion, shared by most Victorians, of indigenous culture, whose functioning they did not properly understand. Those who pointed out the skill of Africans in learning other languages under great adversity — in, for instance, the West Indies and the United States — were very much in a minority. Most white travellers were not interested and, as both Tylor and Pitt-Rivers pointed out, the profusion of local languages made them difficult to master.[11] During the 1890s the eminent philologist Max Müller was to stress the importance, when writing about indigenous peoples, of living amongst them and learning their languages. But for many years to come this remained nothing but an ideal.[12] It was, of course, much easier to provide straightforward descriptions of dress, housing, food, implements, and other aspects of material culture, than to comcomprehend patterns of thought and belief.

Commercial involvement in slavery created the need for an ideological system justifying the brutal treatment of other human beings. There was thus a practical need to fabricate examples of the supposed inferiority of black races.[13] The fundamental basis for this thinking was provided by Edward Long, an abusive Jamaican planter. His book *History of Jamaica*, published in 1774, sets out to erect a pseudo-intellectual justification for racism.[14] It was influential during the eighteenth century, but his concept of racial gradation, expressed in the term 'Chain of Being', had already been challenged by the classification systems of Linnaeus, which were descriptive rather than hierarchical.[15]

The caricature of the African, promoted by the planters, was taken up by writers like Carlyle and Trollope.[16] In 1849 Carlyle published an offensive document, *Discourse on the Nigger Question*, which effectively put an end to his friendship with John Stuart Mill, the liberal philosopher. Mill refuted it the following year, but Carlyle had become notable by then and his essay merely underlined the established caricature.

There was in Victorian times a tendency, still by no means expunged, to generalise about the African character. Few observers looked to social explanations for unfamiliar patterns of behaviour and morality — arising from specific demographic factors in the case of West Indian slave society, and from African tribal society, whose rich and varied nature was not perfectly understood. Slave morality was of course a natural result of frightful plantation conditions. An imbalance between the sexes and frequent movement between properties made stable relationships almost impossible. Nor should one overlook the sexually exploitive behaviour of some slave owners towards their slaves, who were, of course, chattels and obliged to do as they were told. Complaints about the misuse of negro women by European men were published by The Society for the Propagation of the Gospel.[17]

In popular tradition a definite connection came to be established between blackness and heightened sexuality. Nineteenth-century sensibility had been shocked by African nudity which, ignoring the climatic element, it associated with immodesty and lack of sexual restraint.[18] Walvin, commenting on the more robust outlook of Elizabethan times, observes that female nakedness: 'apparently offended what few sensitivities the English seamen possessed.'[19] Parts of the human body not exposed to the public gaze in cooler lands occasioned comment: 'Divers of the women have such exceedingly long breasts that some of them will lay the same upon the ground and lie downe by them.'[20] Similar tall stories had the men equally well-endowed. Richard Jobson wrote of the Mandingo in 1623 that they were 'furnist with such members as are after a sort burthensome unto them.'[21] Shakespeare's play *Othello*, which is rich in sexual imagery, contains all the subconscious racial tensions and fears of the period. But the genius of the author, so much in advance of his day, endows the portagonist with characteristics traditionally singled out as associated primarily with the white man, and Othello's excesses, in the form of jealousy, are no more extreme or unrealistic than those of other tragic heroes like Lear and Macbeth.[22]

'Many of these racial attitudes,' writes Christine Bolt, 'remain to disturb the present.'[23] The sexual traditions are especially persistent. Both black and white informants thought that black women have larger breasts. West Indian female informants also thought that nursing black mothers were able to give more milk.[24] Contraceptives, it is said, are a white invention intended to keep down the black population, and therefore should be avoided.[25] A West Indian girl, whose father works for British Rail, recorded for me the common belief that 'British Rail puts something into their tea, but it only affects the black ones.'[26] Blacks themselves have sometimes taken up and adopted the image of sexual potency. Various Jamaican informants explain that it is not because black men are more generously endowed by nature, but because they are more skilled, and eat more pepper.[27] *Powerman* is a Nigerian variant of the American comic strip, *Superman*. In one episode Powerman captures an arsonist and is surrounded by admiring women: 'You are our hero, Powerman! Take one of us and enjoy your reward.' 'One of you? I am Powerman! I will take you all!'[28]

Animalisation is another important category of racial image. An elderly Jamaican informant reacted strongly to a television commercial of a well-known brand of tea. It showed the chimpanzee tea-party in London Zoo: 'You know that puts me right off that tea. I am not going to buy monkey tea.'[29] Blacks taunted with supposed simian characteristics − although many simians actually have white skin − respond in the same style. The insulting white is nothing but a pork, or pig.[30] And the English in general are too fond of dogs. Never accept a lift from a white man, young girls are warned, because he loves his dog so much that he probably sleeps with it, and will expect you to do the same.[31] This belief was especially prevalent at the beginning of the 1960s, during the earlier stage of immigration from the West Indies.

Many informants reject Darwinism, which one woman dismissed as 'rubbish', and its concomitant, the theory of evolution. There is, of course, a practical objection to Darwinism, which is plain to anyone who has suffered from racial prejudice. A misuse of Darwin's theory is referred to, but a disagreeable ideology termed 'Social Darwinism' lay behind the notions of Houston Stewart Chamberlain and many still more extreme precur-

sors of the Nazis. A folk element enters into the legends perpetuated by writers of this sort, who attach outmoded dogmas and deep instinctive fears to a spurious type of scientific theory, backed neither by logical investigation, nor by commonplace, everyday observation.[32]

The traditional negative associations of black in our culture are too well known to be given again here.[33] They are listed at some length in the *Oxford Dictionary* and *Roget's Thesaurus*. The equation of black with evil was engrained in Christian teaching for centuries,[34] and by Victorian times it was closely connected with sin, dirt, night, ugliness and death.[35] The identification of beauty and colour reaches its height in the ethnocentrism of Oliver Goldsmith: 'Of all the colours by which mankind is diversified, it is easy to perceive that ours is not only the most beautiful to the eye, but the most advantageous. The fair complexion seems, if I may so express it, as a transparent covering to the soul.'[36] It was left to the Rev James Ramsay to point out that the soul is: 'a simple substance, not to be distinguished by black, brown or fair.'[37]

Black children are often strongly aware of colour. Little Jason, aged six, who has known me since he was a baby, looked at me recently and said: 'You are white. Why?' His cousin Andrew, who is now a little older, once wondered whether I was a ghost. Black children in English schools, especially West Indians, often want to be white, a distressing expression of adult racial attitudes. Andrew said: 'I want your face', that presumably being the most striking feature of whiteness that had occurred to him.[38]

In my view an effective means of combating patterned, traditional, racialist, prejudiced thinking lies in humour. Various positive educational efforts in this direction have been taken by the media. The jokes, which are often told by black comedians, take the negative images and utilise them in a positive function, to undermine and attack racism by creating laughter and good nature, and relieving tension in a socially acceptable form.[39] 'I used to work down the mines. But they fired me . . . because they could never find me.'[40] 'I used to work in the Post Office. I was a black-mailer.'[41] 'I know a man who's so prejudiced, he won't even let his wife watch colour television.'[42]

Telly is what we often call television in England. It is also the name of the famous bald actor who plays Kojak. 'A white man went to the barber and asked for a Telly hairdo, so the barber shaved his head and charged £2.00. The white man left and bumped into a black friend, who admired his new hair-style. "Well," said the white man, "the barber shop is just down there and it only costs £2.00." So the black man went along to the barber and also asked for a Telly hairdo. After shaving his scalp, the barber charged £3.00. "That's not right," said the black man; "my white friend was in earlier today and you charged £2.00." "Well," said the barber, "colour telly is more expensive." '[43] 'Three men died at the same time and went to the gates of Heaven. Two were white, one was black. They're met by the Angel Gabriel, who says, "There's no discrimination here, but you have to pass a spelling test before you can come in." He says to the first white man, "Can you spell God?" He says "G – O – D." Gabriel says "Fine! Come inside!" He says to the second white man: "Can you spell Jesus?" He says "J – E – S – U – S." Gabriel says: "Fine! Come inside!" Then he says to the black man, "Now you'll find no discrimination here. No discrimination whatsoever. Can you spell Chrysanthemum?" '[44]

I have recently collected another version of the modern legend about a packet of biscuits, which has been in circulation for the last three years or so. In my version a motorist buys a cup of tea and a packet of biscuits, and sits at a table occupied by a West Indian. As he drinks the tea and eats his biscuits, the West Indian also helps himself to the biscuits. Whenever he takes a biscuit, his uninvited companion does the same, until there is only one left. At this point the West Indian smiles pleasantly, breaks the remaining biscuit in two halves, eats one of them, and leaves. The Englishman is furious. What confounded cheek! He then discovers that his own packet of biscuits is still in his pocket. The venue alters in the different versions, and sometimes the stranger is a Pakistani or an African, but the basic structure, theme, and dénouement are the same. My version comes from Wolverhampton, an area with a high imigrant population, where Enoch Powell, high priest of racial consciousness, was Member of Parliament. It has been suggested that the legend concerns: 'the patient and indeed saintly character of the often despised and rejected'.[45]

E. B. Tylor, father of British anthropology and founder-member of the Folklore Society, helped to demonstrate 'that man ... is always and everywhere the same unhappy fellow, whatever the colour of his hair or skin.'[46] However it has to be admitted that the concept of survivals used by Tylor, Frazer and others to explain anachronistic elements in social life as relics of past states of society, did not assist acceptance of the African as an equal. It is perhaps of more positive interest to the folklorist in this connection that material culture played a crucial role in the campaign of Thomas Clarkson, a leading abolitionist, to end slavery. Clarkson boarded a ship, which had recently traded with Africa, and was shown one or two pieces of cloth: 'Here new feelings arose ... when I considered that persons of so much apparent ingenuity, and capable of such beautiful work as the Africans, should be made slaves.' When he first met William Pitt, Clarkson says, the Prime Minister was unwilling to accept his remarks about the 'genius and abilities' of the African peoples. By showing the artefacts he had collected, Clarkson convinced Pitt.[47]

In conclusion, scholarship does not exist in a vacuum and folklore has a continuing role of importance to play. The first Annual Report of the Folklore Society in 1879 stated one of its objects as printing folklore of the colonies and foreign countries.[48] One hundred years later we continue to cherish this ideal of international co-operation in folklore, which this Conference represents. If we could pool our knowledge and understanding of racial problems through our familiarity with the related folklore and traditional patterns of prejudice, what a positive step this would be in contributing towards the achievement of the international family of man. It was the late and much lamented Fran Utley who wrote:'[The] modern folklorists' need for both international stimulus and discussion, and international data ... makes them perhaps the best transcenders of boundaries of all kinds.'[49]

Notes

1. Introductory remarks made before a paper by D. I. Brough on 'Prejudice Affecting Relationships Between Ethnic Groups in the United Kingdom', read to the Royal Society of Arts on February 2nd 1971. David Stafford-Clark was in the Chair.

2. Daniel Defoe, *Works* (London, 1843; 1st edn. 1701), III, 3.

3. James Walvin, *Black & White* (London, 1973), 16.

4. *idem*, 4-5; *idem, The Black Presence* (London, 1971), 20; *The Travels of Sir John Mandeville* (London, 1900), 178-84; the account dates from mid-fourteenth century.

5. Sir Paul Harvey, ed., *The Oxford Companion to English Literature* (Oxford, 1960), 347.

6. Walvin, *Black & White*, 20; Richard Hakluyt, *The Principal Navigations, Voyages, Traffiques & Discoveries of the English Nation* (Glasgow, 1904; reissue of 2nd edn., 1598-1600), VIII, 264.

7. Hakluyt, VI, 170-1; Walvin, *Black & White*, 18.

8. *ibid.*, 18-28.

9. Quoted in Kenneth Little, *Negroes in Britain* (London, 1972), 281.

10. Harvey, 348.

11. E. B. Tylor, *Anthropology: an Introduction to the Study of Man & Civilisation* (London, 1881), 152; A. Lane-Fox Pitt-Rivers, *The Evolution of Culture & Other Essays* (Oxford, 1906), 13; Christine Bolt, *Victorian Attitudes to Race* (London, 1971), 14-15, 143.

12. *Journal of the Anthropological Institute of Great Britain & Ireland*, XXI (1892), 187.

13. Charles Husband, 'Racism in Society and the Mass Media: A Critical Interaction', *White Media and Black Britain*, ed. Charles Husband (London, 1975), 22.

14. Edward Long, *History of Jamaica*, 3 vols (London, 1774). Long (1734-1813) lived in Jamaica for 12 years.

15. Walvin, *Black & White*, 163; Anthony J. Barker, *The African Link* (London, 1978), 42, 45, 55.

16. Anthony Trollope, *The West Indies & the Spanish Main* (London, 1859); Thomas Carlyle, *Occasional Discourse Upon the Nigger Question* (London, 1853); Walvin, *The Black Presence*, 30, 115-117; *idem, Black & White*, 166.

17. *Abstracts of the Proceedings of the Society for the Propagation of the Gospel in Foreign Parts* (1768), 65-6; Barker, 126; Walvin, *Black & White*, 162; Bolt, 142.

18. *ibid.*, 134-6; Barker, 121.

19. Walvin, *Black & White*, 22.

20. 'William Towerson's first voyage, 1555', Hakluyt, VI, 184, 187.

21. Quoted in Winthrop Jordan, *White over Black* (Baltimore, 1969), 13; see also Walvin, *Black & White*, 162.

22. *Othello*, I.i. and passim; Husband, 21; Walvin, *Black & White*, 26; Barker, 121.

23. Bolt, 218.

24. F.M.F., September 1973.

25. *Race Today*, V (7) (1973), 209.

26. F.M.F., March 1975.

27. Jennifer James, 1975.

28. Quoted in *Oui*, VII (2) (1978), 23.

29. G.F., January 1973.

30. F.M.F., April 1975 and various informants.

31. F.M.F., July 1973.

32. Venetia Newall, 'Black Britain: The Jamaicans & Their Folklore', *Folklore*, LXXXVI (1975), 29.

33. Little, 252, note 1.

34. Barker, 44.

35. Bolt, 131.

36. Oliver Goldsmith, *History of the Earth* (London, 1774), II, 77, 232.

37. Quoted by Walvin, *The Black Presence*, 30. Ramsay was active in the anti-slavery movement from 1780-1800.

38. January 1975; see also Husband, 70.

39. Husband, 33.

40. Ken Irwin, ed., *The Comedians* (London, 1972), 132. Told by black comedian Sammy Thomas.

41. *ibid.*

42. *ibid.*, 68. Told by black comedian Jos White.

43. F.M.F., 1976.

44. Irwin, 55. Told by black comedian Charlie Williams.

45. Told by the Bursar of Tettenhall College, Wolverhampton, to Richard Wheeler, 1978. See also Alan Smith, 'Letter', *Folklore*, LXXXVI (1975), 139.

46. *Anthropological Essays Presented to Edward Burnett Tylor in Honour of his 75th Birthday, October 2nd 1907* (London, 1907), 6; Bolt, 153.

47. *ibid.*, 119, 229.

48. *The Folklore Record*, II (1879), 5.

49. Francis L. Utley, 'Oral Genres as a Bridge to Written Literature', *Folklore Genres*, ed. Dan Ben-Amos (Austin, 1976), 6.

Time in Folk-Narrative

W. F. H. NICOLAISEN   State University of New York, Binghamton

THE eminent Swiss folklorist Max Lüthi, to whom I wish to dedicate my small contribution to the centenary celebrations of the Folklore Society, has on several occasions said wise things about the major characteristics of the different folk-narrative genres. Among these chief qualities, the treatment of, or attitude towards time, has, in my view, been a particularly felicitous means of distinguishing especially legend and folktale proper, and I have used Lüthi's statements in this respect, in my teaching, ever since I first became aware of them. 'The fairy tale [i.e. the *Märchen*],' says Lüthi, 'portrays an imperishable world ... The local legend and the saint's legend, however, do exactly the opposite, they make us especially aware of the passage of time and cessation of things.'[1] Lüthi's favourite illustration in this regard is the story of the sleeper, and he delights in contrasting a local Swiss legend with Tale Type AT410 'Sleeping Beauty':

> When, in the local legend from Wallis, the prior collapses the moment he learns that he has slept without noticing it for 308 years, it is as if he suddenly becomes aware of the passage of time and in one jolt catches up with the present... In the fairy tale, however, Sleeping Beauty arises with a smile and is as young and beautiful and light-hearted as she was 100 years ago.[2]

It is the second of these observations which is to receive our main attention, as it appears to aim at, and provide a fairy-tale solution for, one of our basic human dilemmas: our inadequacy, inability, frustration — call it what you will — in dealing with time, our preoccupation with youth, our immaturity in confronting the process of aging, our fears of death. In our three-dimensional existence we are so inextricably caught up in the passage of time, so painfully and continuously aware of our temporal and temporary existence, that it becomes almost impossible to lead full and present-oriented lives. Hankering after a paradise which is lost, and striving for a heaven which is to come, we perceive the Golden Age as gone, or as still to be attained, but never in the present. We become ineffective in the existing moment because, to us, it is no more than an infinitesimal point at which the future turns into the past, and the Sleeping Beauty tale of time suspended, creating the possibility for an extended, extensive present, therefore has for us an irresistible attraction. Here is a world which achieves what we have failed to accomplish 'even in our wildest dreams', to use a popular cliché.

Nor, according to Lüthi, is the symbolic gesture of a long and formulaic sleep (100 years) a necessary prerequisite to permit the *Märchen* this miraculous, literally wonder-ful(l) interference in the inexorable, seemingly unstoppable realisation of one of nature's fundamental laws. The 'characteristic disregard for the passage of time,' he claims, is an aspect of 'the style of the popular fairy tale'.[3] Elsewhere he uses formulations such as 'The fairy tale conquers time by ignoring it', or 'the fairy tale seems to portray a timeless world',[4] or 'the fairy tale, to all intents and purposes, completely lacks the dimension of time'.[5] He also speaks of 'the fairy tale's essential timelessness',[6] of the 'meaninglessness of the passage of time',[7] and of a 'triumph over time',[8] or over what, in another context, he calls 'the power of time', which he sees as 'a function of psychic experience'.[9]

These are attractive phrases which gain in persuasiveness through happy variation. They undoubtedly express a fundamental truth about the nature of folktales, and yet should perhaps not go totally unchallenged, or at least unexamined and unmodified. After all, as the Finnish School has taught us, folktales are basically episodic, presupposing therefore some kind of concept of temporality, and their actions are portrayed sequentially. Repetition is one of their hallmarks, and what would repetition be without time ('and again and again and again')? It is a journey, that essential ingredient of almost every *Märchen*, not also the movement through space in time?

In the restricted context of this presentation — the usual phrase 'in the limited time available' seemed to be an unwarranted and unwelcome pun, under the circumstances — it is naturally impossible to explore this multi-faceted problem fully, or even extensively. Selectiveness, on the other hand, by its very nature, encourages the use of personal criteria, resulting in potential distortion. To ensure as much randomness as possible, I have therefore chosen as my sample the first ten stories in Stith Thompson's *One Hundred Favorite Folktales*,[10] comprising variants of AT122-314 from Norway, Italy, France, Spain and Russia; from these I have extracted all direct or indirect references to time, in order to provide substance for this little investigation. Here are some of my findings:[11]

As is to be expected, the sequential arrangement of events — Axel Olrik's 'single-strandedness' — finds its most frequent linguistic expression in the adverb *then*, which punctuates a series of main clauses: '*Then* John the Bear threw the master, who had scolded him, through the window.' '. . . he . . . *then* went to another blacksmith.' 'John the Bear *then* told the blacksmith goodbye. . .' '*Then* [the giant] knocked down John of the Mill.' 'John the Bear *then* started to look about the castle.' '*Then* Hold-up-Mountain was lowered.' And so on, and so on. Altogether I counted forty-six 'thens' in these ten stories, and it is reasonable to assume that the co-ordinating *and*, as well as the absence of any overt adverbial reference to sequential action, also imply many hidden, unspoken 'thens'.

The equivalent of *then* in subordinate syntactic structures is *when*, allowing the interweaving of two closely related events: '*When* [the snake] was at liberty, it said to the man.' '*When* they arrived in a wood, they met another young man.' '. . . *when* they found in one of the rooms a table laden with fine food, they seated themselves.' '*When* the giant

heard that, he said no more about it.' '*When* the doors were opened, he came to where the princess was.' '*When* he was walking around the tower, he noticed the good woman.' '*When* she saw the young man enter, she wanted to escape.' '*When* he had taken his bride home, he presented her with a . . . bouquet.' Obviously the inner relationships between the introductory *when*-clause and the following main clause differ greatly, but, not infrequently, the event narrated in the former makes the action of the latter possible, or the latter is the consequence of the former. In all instances the presentation is still serial.

In a way, the employment of *then* and *when* might be regarded as the most primitive, at least the simplest, of narrative devices to relate, or even stress, sequentiality, and storytellers have many other less bare means of creating the same effect. 'So *first of all* came the youngest billy-goat Gruff to cross the bridge . . . *A little while after* came the second billy-goat Gruff to cross the bridge . . . But *just then* came the big billy-goat Gruff . . . *after that* he went up to the hillside.' 'They *afterwards* happened to find a mulberry tree.' '*Afterwards* they met a fox.' Some time afterward, the next morning, after this feat, at the end of three days, the following day, soon, after many compliments and many thanks, first . . . next . . . now, after a while, after they had lain a while, once more, again, at last, later, after much travelling, finally, a few months after, after the wedding, at the appointed time, several days later, and many other variations and similar phrases intimate, mostly vaguely, but sometimes very precisely, that time has passed between succeeding actions. There is undoubtedly an 'earlier' and a 'later', and an 'even later' in the world of the folktale.

Instead of being 'timeless', its pertinent events are presented in relationship to a very human time scale. The next morning, at midnight, at the end of three days, three weeks, two days and two nights, these two years, when night came, in the evening, when the time came for the giant to come home, while it was still gray dawn, the first day — the next day, at night, at nightfall, on the stroke of midnight, all night, after a few days, on the third day, within a year and a day, during all the night, by this evening, toward the middle of the day, the following evening, today, each day, within a month, during the meal, for eight days, one night of the full moon, the same day, several days later, at the end of a meal — these and similar phrases indicate a chronological microcosm that permits the audience to orient itself with ease. Naturally, journeys and other proceedings of indeterminate and often considerable length — 'many, many days', 'for a long time' — separate the chunks of recounted action, i.e. the so-called episodes and sub-episodes, but the portions of narrated time are directly relatable to the perceived temporal structure of regular human events. In this respect, the day turns out to be the basic unit of time in folktales. In *The White Cat*, a French version of Tale Type 313C,[12] for example, the central events take place in the following sequence: a certain day, during the night which follows, the next morning, the following day (punctuated by help in the middle of the day and a deadline by evening), the next day, the following evening, during the night, and the next morning and day. The daylight hours are understood in terms of work to be accomplished and tasks to be performed; even giants and devils have a working day, for which they have to leave the house early in the morning and from which they return at nightfall. During the night one is supposed to sleep and rest in bed, although one's vulnerability and openness to the forces of the other world are especially great in the dark, midnight, of course, playing its usual ominous role in this respect. Indeed, three successive days or three successive nights, or both, are favourite structuring devices, designed to give the tale its episodic form: 'John of the Mill was *the first* to guard the lodging ... *The following day* Oak-Twister remained at the castle ... *The following day*, just as John the Bear was about to ring the bell, the giant arrived. ... she asked him if he would carry three chests for her to her parents' house, without putting them down or resting on the way ... So *the next morning* she put one of her sisters in a chest, and laid it on her husband's shoulders ... The same thing was repeated *the next day* with the second chest. On *the third day* she herself was to be taken home in the chest.'

Like the folk who listen and the folk who tell, the folk in the stories live from day to day, lead daily lives, have daily routines. Non-structural repetition — repetitiveness is, by definition, time-bound — is therefore also frequently expressed in a diurnal or nocturnal time frame: '*Each day* the

bear brought them food.' 'There was once a fisherman who went fishing *every day*.' '*Every night* these princesses went away, no one knew whither; and *every night* each of them wore out a new pair of shoes. The king could not get shoes for them fast enough and he wanted to know where they went *every night* and what they did there.' That such regular and uninterrupted repetition can have the effect of accumulating days into weeks or months, or even a year or two, is only to be expected, and still creates time spans that are easily conceivable in terms of ordinary human lives. On the other hand, concepts like morning, midday, evening, midnight — in addition to the binary division into day and night — are clearly sufficient as organising principles, and a further fussy breakdown into hours is not required.

The chosen units also allow without difficulty the narrative encapsulation of a pervasive preoccupation with definite beginnings and endings: 'The needy nobleman *began* to doubt.' 'John *began* to visit the rooms.' '... he now, *for the first time*, really loved her.' Or, '... *at the end* of three days he asked for his pay.' 'Finally, *just at the end* of a year and a day.' '*At the end* of a meal...' Folktale protagonists do not simply slide in and out of periods of narrated time; they enter and leave them at clearly marked points. Time is not, in this sense, even to a Presbyterian's secret delight, the famous metaphorical 'ever-rolling stream', uninterrupted and uninterruptable, outside ourselves, continuing whether we are or not; it is rather, as a function of the mind, a periodic, divisible, organising element of our subjective existence.

Folktale characters, therefore, do not experience time in a tick-tock, clock-on-the-wall, objective fashion, but react to its seeming slowness or rapidity: 'As his companions found time long...' '[the king] could never bear to be parted from them.' 'The king waited.' '... the more he waited the longer they stayed away.' 'Next morning the giant got up cruelly early.' '[Boots] took a long, long farewell of the princess.' 'They came at last to the lake.' 'Finally the day came when she was due to have her child.' '... she could scarcely wait for the moment to come...' 'The mule walked a long time and became tired out.' As for us, the audience, time for the folktale characters is an elastic commodity. Waited time is doubly long and claws at our patience, partings are prolonged to snatch the last few moments from unbearable separation, absences are like long, never-to-be-cured pains, pregnancies are physically demanding, but full of hope and expectation, the anticipation of a pleasant event makes the trivial present insufferably pointless, long hours of hard work are tiring and make us long for rest. As a result, folk-narrative time is clearly-lived time, not just described time, and it can be as inimical or frustrating or releasing or relentless, as the time that bounds our own little lives.

As a consequence, time is to be struggled with, to be overcome and cheated. As in real life, the surrogate which suggests to us an apparent victory over the 'auld enemy' is speed. The faster we run, swim, ride, fly, the closer we come to breaking the fetters of our existence. Speed records excite us and make newspaper headlines, Olympic sprinters and long-distance runners carry our identities around the track, supersonic planes and hurtling space capsules give us the illusion of having opened a crack in eternity. For this reason, references to velocity of movement and rapidity of action are frequent in the folktale: 'He soon rang the bell to be pulled back.' 'He soon sent guards to find John the Bear.' '. . . as soon as ever he squeezed it, the giant screamed out.' 'So fast he had never ridden before.' '. . . away they went till the wind whistled after them.' '. . . in a trice the raven came.' '[He] killed him forthwith.' 'As soon as the good woman had left, he said. . .' 'It was not long before the wedding was celebrated.' '. . . scarcely had he begun to put the chest down, when the sister inside cried out.' 'He hastily delivered the chest, and then hurried home. . .' '. . . she quickly slipped into the chest.' 'He hastened home to breakfast.' 'As he was running through the corridors. . .' '. . . he immediately ran to inform her parents.' 'The child developed very fast.' 'He had started in pursuit upon a horse much faster than the mule . . .' '[The cork] immediately formed a pond.' 'The mule quickly crossed it.' Speed as matter of life and death, leisure as a destructive force, he who hesitates is lost. This is time used to one's advantage, time employed and exploited, rather than suffered and succumbed to. After all, there may only be a limited amount available for one's personal usage, an allotted span, so to speak. 'It is time for you to serve your apprenticeship.' '. . .

the Bear did not give him time. . .' '. . . if in the time allowed the balls are not ready, you shall die.' '. . . as the time drew near. . .' 'The godfather returned at the appointed time. . .'

By now the point which I have been trying to make must be abundantly clear. Lüthi's comments concerning the treatment of time in the folktale are apposite, but only partially so. They undoubtedly apply to the outer hull of a story, signalled to us by the formulaic 'Once upon a time' beginning and the 'ever after' ending. Timelessness here means the removal of the events to be narrated from the datable, calendar bound, documentable chronology of history. It also indicates the absence of any physiological, architectural, genealogical or other outward changes usually expected as the result of the passage of time. Thirdly, it is an essential characteristic of the brief portions of discourse bridging the sections of narrated time. What timelessness does not, and cannot, mean, however, is the lack of a temporal dimension in the episodic presentation of the story. Quite the contrary, for, within the outer frame of timelessness, we have an inner frame of sequentially structured time that relies on the day as its basic unit of reference, and quite pointedly and necessarily invites comparison with the daily lives of the audience and the storyteller. Let me illustrate: 'Once upon a time there was a woodcutter and his wife. One day, when she was taking soup to her husband. . .' The first sentence provides the outer frame of unhistorical, unnarrated time, the second begins the first portion of narrated time. Or: 'Once on a time there was a king who had seven sons, and he loved them so much that he could never bear to be parted from them all; at least one must always be with him.' (End of outer frame). 'Now, when they were grown up . . .' (Beginning of narrated time). Or: 'There was once a fisherman who went fishing every day.' (End of outer frame). 'And one day he caught a fish and the fish said to him. . .' (Beginning of narrated time). Or: 'Once upon a time there was a young man named John; his parents were rich and did not work for a living.' (End of outer frame). 'One day they gave him two thousand franks . . .' (Beginning of narrated time).

Once the general conditions for an extended present have been created, and the suspension of historical time has been signalled, it is possible and expected that, within this cushioning bulwark,

317

known and understandable categories of time, reflecting the existential embeddedness of human lives in temporality, be restored in terms acceptable to the world of the folktale. Ruthless time is out, gentle time is in. Chunks of time must be of manageable duration and must have precisely marked beginnings and endings. They must be sequential, may be repetitive and incremental, and, in their goal-orientatedness, may also be important criteria in the structuring of quests and the successful accomplishment of tasks. Narrated time, on the other hand, is never continuous, impersonal, objective, or hour-glass determined. It is lived time, but choice time, in the way in which memory selects; it is therefore never off-peak time.

In my view, these characteristics make it quite distinctive from both the kind of suspension which a sleep implies, and whether this lasts 100 years or 308 years is immaterial in this respect, when time for the persons affected literally stands still. It also has to be clearly distinguished from the distortion, usually shortening, of time experienced by people who, let us say, step into a fairy mound or into a fairy ring, or the like. Almost a century ago, Edwin Sidney Hartland called this 'The Supernatural Lapse of Time in Fairyland' and devoted three chapters of his *Science of Fairy Tales*[13] to its discussion. The essential difference lies in the fact that, for the afflicted, the passage of time has been unaccountably and, what is more important, imperceptibly slowed down, normally in directly relatable proportions. What seem like ten minutes or ten days in fairyland are ten years in human terms; two days of fairy time represent two years — sometimes also seven or ten years — of 'real' time; a single hour is really a whole year. A few hours or days can even be measured against seventy or a hundred years, or the passing of seven generations. A dance on a wedding day has taken up 200 years of calendar time; listening to the singing of a bird has lasted 300 years; within one hour, three leaves fall slowly, one after another, off a large tree in a garden — and 300 years have passed. Sometimes, but much less often, in reversal, what seems like a long time has only been a moment. The legend has many neat ways of making this discrepancy outwardly visible or tangible — the heap of human dust, the outmoded clothes, the faded entry in a church register — always in terms of our normal experience of decay, aging, change, and so on, but these need not concern us here in detail.

What must be stressed, however, is that in contrast to the concepts and realisation of an extended present and of narrated time in the folktale, the dramatic comparisons made in the legend are designed to demonstrate the incompatibility of the two time frames, which exist as parallel systems. Fairyland time is clearly, on the whole, much 'slower' in its passage than human time, although its flow is never totally arrested. Perhaps even more extremely, just as the concept of eternity cannot be expressed in terms of our time — eternity is, after all, not our time 'for ever and ever' — so fairyland time, and our time, have no common denominator that makes the former accessible to our sense of temporality. The danger lies in trying to move freely from one system to the other. One gets the impression that the enviable, but potentially disastrous sluggishness of movement, the definite proportions mentioned and the obvious outward changes described in the legend are a desperate, and not really successful, attempt at accomplishing an impossible task, i.e. to find a natural analogue for the supernatural, to use our sense of time metonymically.

In my view, not the difference of treatment but the centrality of the phenomenon of time in both folk-narrative genres is in the end the most significant fact, for this centrality speaks of our continued, demanding, vain, disappointing endeavour, which I alluded to at the beginning of this paper, to come to terms with time in our lives — to confront it, to understand it, to live with it, to mature in it, to wither in it, or more unreasonably to see it as a restrictive prison, escape from which brings ultimate freedom. As long as we, as folk, are tethered to time, our stories will tell of it, will transform it, will use it as a major organisational and structural principle. True timelessness is beyond our imagination. Maybe these stories, whether legends or folktales, will teach us to live fuller and more effective lives in the present, so that the Golden Age may be now.

Notes

1. Max Lüthi, *Once upon a time: On the Nature of Fairy Tales* (Bloomington, 1976), 45.

2. *ibid.*, 44.

3. *ibid.*, 32.

4. *ibid.*, 44.

5. *idem, Volksmärchen und Volkssage* (Bern, 1961), 33 ['*Dazu kommt nun, dass im Märchen auch die Dimension der Zeit so gut wie völlig fehlt*'] ; see also 34.

6. *idem, Das europäische Volksmärchen* (Bern, 1947), 21 ['*dem Märchen wesenseigene Zeitlosigkeit*'].

7. *loc. cit.*, '*Bedeutungslosigkeit des Zeitablaufs*'.

8. Lüthi, *Once upon a time*, 44.

9. Lüthi, *Das europäische Volksmärchen*, 22 ['*die Macht der Zeit*', '*eine Funktion des seelischen Erlebens*'].

10. Stith Thompson, *One Hundred Favorite Folktales* (Bloomington, 1968), 1-36. The reader is invited to consult this edition for the verification of particular passages quoted and their contexts, since, for the purposes of this paper, it seemed superfluous to identify each quotation. References are here given in the order in which they appear in the anthology.

11. Naturally it is always hazardous to make an argument on the basis of translations, but a translator's stylistic idiosyncracies are, it seems to me, just as important as those of the 'original' storyteller or editor.

12. Emmanuel Cosquin, *Contes populaires de Lorraine* (Paris, 1886), No.32.

13. Edwin Sidney Hartland, *The Science of Fairy Tales* (London, 1891), Ch.7-9. See also the entry on 'Time in Fairyland' in Katharine M. Briggs, *A Dictionary of Fairies* (London, 1976), 398-400; and, most recently, the fine first chapter 'The Supernatural Passage of Time in Fairyland' in her study of traditional fairy beliefs in *The Vanishing People* (London, 1978), 11-26.

Storytelling by the Very Young

JOHN NILES   **University of California, Berkeley**

IN the past, folklore has been defined half-playfully as 'a way of getting to know your grandparents'. To the extent that folklorists have been encouraged to meet with older generations and to become familiar with their ways and wisdom, the definition is based on truth. Especially in the early years of the field, when folklore was regarded as a set of of survivals or 'popular antiquities,' fieldworkers turned toward the old as keepers of a precious inheritance, which was in danger of being lost unless it was soon recorded. But, if folklore is to be regarded not as a set of fossils but as a set of ongoing cultural processes, then the lore of the young calls for as much attention as the lore of the old. In other words, the study of folklore also can be a way of getting to know your children. Particularly in the field of oral narrative studies, if we wish not only to record handed-down tales but to examine the workings of human creativity, then we might profit from looking at the stories of the young. If the genius of the old is to preserve, the genius of the young is to create, and I would argue that, in the stories of the young, we come close to the wellsprings of the creative spirit.

Despite the outstanding achievement of such students of childlore as Iona and Peter Opie in England and Brian Sutton-Smith in the United States,[1] the storytelling competence of young children remains largely a *terra incognita*. In an attempt to post a few landmarks in this terrain, during the first half of 1978 I collected 100 stories from children aged 4 to 6 in Berkeley, California, at my own home and at the Harold E. Jones Child Study Center. Some stories I took down on tape, while most I recorded longhand.[2] The age group from 4 to 6 seemed an attractive group to study, chiefly because children so young still display a largely preliterate mentality. The idea of a fixed, printed text has not yet impressed itself fully on their consciousness, as it has among older children, who are drilled in the printed text in school. By choosing this age group, I was able to test my impression that human beings enter the world of storytelling viewing tradition, not as Holy Writ, but as a point of departure for their own imaginative lives.

The stories which have been told me could be grouped into three broad and interlocking categories: free fantasies, traditional tales, and transitional tales (or free fantasies which draw on handed-down motifs or handed-down plot structures).[3] Of the three groups, only the first has received attention in the published literature.[4] There is a good reason for this fact. Most persons who have collected children's stories are practising psychologists, or have written for journals of developmental psychology, and such persons have valued free fantasies as the most uninhibited expressions of a child's fears and desires. Traditional tales, on the other hand, they have explicitly rejected.[5] As my own orientation is less toward psychology than toward the study of human storytelling *per se,* I have been concerned not only with the content of children's tales, but with their structural dynamics. For this reason I have made a point of seeking out traditional tales as well as free fantasies. Whatever the type of tale collected, above all I have tried to avoid fitting my data into a preconceived theoretical mould, as a weakness of some prior work in the field has been a tendency toward the doctrinaire interpretation of tales and toward what might be called 'symbolic overkill' in the search for hidden meanings.[6] My own approach to children's storytelling has been empirical in the extreme. When I began this study, I had next to no idea what I would find. Two questions provided a point of departure. First, What do children know when they know a story? Second, To what extent do children regenerate traditional tales as they tell them, as opposed to repeating such tales by rote?

Let us turn to specifics. One of my willing informants has been a girl of age four whom I shall call Rachel. She is from a white, urban, professional family. Unlike some of my informants, who seem to have spent much of their waking lives in front of a television set, and who have a repertory of few, if any, tales, she has been accustomed to hearing stories told and read to her from an early age. She has a brother two years older. At the beginning of the present study period she could have been characterised as a mildly withdrawn child, who often played by herself, but by the end of the study period she had become a sociable member of two pre-school groups, one of which was the Berkeley Child Study Center. She would not strike one as either an atypical child or a typical child, if there exists any such thing as a typical child. She is simply one of several children I encountered, who especially enjoyed telling tales.

Of my various informants, Rachel has supplied the greatest number of traditional tales. It is these which I wish to single out for attention in the present paper.[7] Almost all her traditional tales are recognisable versions of well-known fairy tales. What she knows when she knows a tale is not necessarily what we know, however, nor does her performance remain constant from day to day. Here, for example, is a version of 'Jack and the Beanstalk', which she told at the age of four years and five months. The chief elements of the tale are numbered from 1 to 10, for clarity of reference.

Example 1. 'Jack and the Beanstalk', recorded long-hand, January 24, 1978

(1) Jack and the beanstalk were really poor. (2) So Jack's mother said, 'Jack, go up into the fields and get some money for milk.' So Jack said 'OK', and he went. (3) Soon he saw this man with a bag full of little tiny b. . . buds. So he said, 'Hey, if I give you this cow, will you give me all of those beans?' So he said 'Yeah'. (4) So his mother said, 'How foolish you are', and they went to bed with no dinner. That night when they were sleeping, (5) he woke up in the morning and said to himself, 'I'm going to climb up that bean-

stalk.' So he climbed up until he was up at the top. (6) He saw a giant castle. So he went in it and a skinny tall woman answered the door, and he said, 'I came here to get something to eat.' And the woman said, 'This isn't really my castle, this is the giant's castle.' So the giant was about to step in, so she hided him quickly in the oven.[8] (7) So the giant stepped in, and he said, 'I smell the blood of an Englishman, I'll blind his muscles to make my bread.' So the woman told him it was only his breakfast. So she said, 'Here, here's your breakfast.' (8) He was so tired he fell down asleep, so Jack looked out and he came out and he stealed his magic autoharp and his magic chicken what laid gold eggs, and he ran away, and the autoharp was crying out 'Master, master!' (9) So the giant was hearing him and he came, but Jack jumped down the beanstalk and the giant was so scared he fell down dead. And they chopped him up. (10) And Jack and his mother lived happily ever after. The end.

Taken as a whole, the story shows real narrative competence. The entire fairy tale is told, from the initial situation to the formulaic close of 'happily ever after'. There are surprising gaps, of course, as Rachel tended to skip from highlight to highlight. Between the parts numbered 3 and 4 there exists no narrative transition, while in part 4 one would have expected some reference to the throwing of the beans out of the window or the growing up of the giant beanstalk. The omission of these features leads to a curious time warp between parts 4 and 5 ('That night while they were sleeping, he woke up in the morning. . .'). There are other idiosyncracies as well. The magic harp of tradition is turned into a magic autoharp, a more familiar instrument in present-day Berkeley. The traditional formula 'I'll grind his bones to make my bread' is turned into 'I'll blind his muscles', a mistake which in a retelling Rachel corrected to 'I'll blind his bones'. The linguistic irregularities ('hided', 'stealed', 'the chicken what laid gold eggs') are very nearly standard in the speech of Rachel and her friends. In spite of these quirks, what we have is a recognisable version of 'Jack and the Beanstalk'.[9]

The next two times I asked Rachel for this story, she told me something far different. First she told a story about Jack, but (as she assured me) 'This was a different Jack.' The story went as follows:

Example 2. 'Jack', recorded longhand February 2, 1978.

(1) Once upon a time there was a boy named Jack. (2) And his mother said, 'Jack, you go to town today to get some money.' (3) And so he got some beans, (4) and his mother said, 'Oh, you foolish boy. You have to go to bed.' And she got the beans and threw them out the window. (10) The end.

On this particular day Rachel's storytelling was not inspired. Of the four stories which she told me, 'Jack' and three free fantasies, all were equally perfunctory. If one suspects that Rachel was teasing me by telling a deliberately defective tale, the suspicion may be justified. For the next time I asked for the tale, she told it as follows:

Example 3. 'Jack and the Beanstalk', recorded longhand February 5, 1978.

(1) Once upon a time there was a boy named Jack. (2) And Jack's mother said, 'Sell a cow for some money.' And Jack said 'OK.' [*5 seconds silence.*] (10) The end. [*Laughter.*] It was short, really short. And Jack lived happily ever after.

At this point I found myself reminded that the tale-taking situation is a speech-play situation, which at any moment can cross the line into nonsense, tricks, and laughter, often at the expense of the tale-taker. Given Rachel's sense of the comic, I had almost despaired of her giving me another full version of 'Jack and the Beanstalk'. On two later occasions, however, she was in the mood to try again. Each time, she made the tale her own. The first occasion was a week later.

Example 4. 'Jack and the Beanstalk', recorded longhand February 12, 1978.

(1) Once there was a boy named Jack. And his mother was very poor. (2) His mother said, 'Jack, go out to the village and sell our cow for money.' Jack said 'All right.'

(3) Jack went out. He saw a man selling beans. He was calling 'Beans for sale! Beans for sale! Fifty cents apiece! Beans for sale! Beans for sale! Fifty cents apiece!' So he [Jack] said, 'Are those magic beans?' And the man said, 'Yes, they are.' 'May I take those magic beans out of your p...' What's it called, what you hold things in? [*JN: A pocket?*] Yes yes yes, a pocket. [*JN: A pouch?*] Yes yes. 'May I take those magic beans out of your pouch?' 'Yes, you may take as many beans as you like.' He said, 'I'll take three.' The man said 'All right.' (4) His mother said, 'How foolish you are', and they went to bed without any dinner. And his mother threw the beans out the window. (5) The next morning Jack woke up and he found a big beanstalk out of his window. He climbed up that beanstalk (7) and he found a giant at the top. (9) So he climbed quickly down and (10) the end. And they lived happily ever after.

An unexpected addition here is the playful expansion of the encounter between Jack and the man with the beans (part 3) to include an extended dialogue concerning the price and quality of the beans. The expansion owes much to a similar passage in a children's book titled *Caps for Sale*, which·had been read to her several times previously.[10] As if to compensate for this addition at the start, the end of the tale almost disappears. Parts 6 and 8 vanish without a trace. The giant's friendly wife drops from the story; there is no hiding, no breakfast, no blustering threats on the part of the giant, no falling asleep, no theft, no flight, no magic harp or autoharp, no chase, no killing. Even truncated so drastically, however, the tale has a certain completeness. Jack meets the giant, and Jack escapes. Tensions are aroused, and then they are laid to rest. The essentials are there; only the adornments are missing.

Rachel volunteered the story of 'Jack and the Beanstalk' one last time during a session several months later, when she had reached the age of four years and ten months. This version is the longest and the most free of all. Parts of it are confused, especially toward the end. Like the preceding example, it is characterised by a certain deliberate inventiveness on the part of the teller.[11]

What follows is a verbatim transcription from the tape, with all the false starts and the confusion of personal pronouns, which tend to be smoothed out when a tale is taken down by the slower method of longhand.

Example 5. 'Jack and the Beanstalk', recorded on tape June 2, 1978.

(1) Once upon a time there was a little boy whose name was Jack. And his mother was very poor and so was he. (2) So she said to Jack, 'Go out and give this . . . and sell this . . . and give this cow away, and bring me back the money.' So he went walking away, and he said 'OK', so he went walking away (3) and he saw a man. He said, 'Could I have that . . . that cow for magic beans?' 'Are they magic?' 'Yes.' 'Are they *really*?' 'Yes.' So he took them and gave them [= *him*] the cow. (4) So he went back home. So she said, 'Did you get any money?' And he said, 'I got magic beans.' 'Now you foolish boy!' And he threw them — and she threw them out the window. (5) And the next morning, Jack woke up and got dressed and peeked out his window, and he saw the beanstalk. They were really magic. So he — he went and he saw . . . [*whispers*] I forget . . . [*normal voice*] he climbed up the beanstalk. (6) And he saw . . . a castle. So he went — he knocked on the door, and it was a very tall woman and a very big castle. So he said, 'I came to get something to eat.' So she said, 'What would you like?' 'I would like a milkshake and a hamburger and that's it.' So she gave him that. Then right when he started eating, the giant came home. So she said, 'Quick! Hide in the oven!' So he hided in the coven [*sic*] oven. So he hided in the oven. (7) So the giant came in. He said, 'I smell a English. B. . . b. . . I'll grind his bones to make my bread. Fee fie fo. I smell the blood of a Englishman, I'll grind his bones to make my bread, be he alive or be he dead.' So she said, the woman said, 'It's only your breakfasht . . . breakfast.' So he — so she gave him his breakfast, and he said, 'I'm still hungry!' So he [*sic*] gave him ten more pancakes. And he said, 'I'm *still* hungry!' So he [*sic*] gave him twenty more pancakes. And he said,

'I'm *still* hungry!' So he — she gave him eleven more pancakes. Then, 'Now I'm not hungry.' So the woman said 'OK!' (8) So Jack peeked out. He saw the giant. He . . . ran away. And he . . . and the ge. . . and the giant was so tired, and he fell asleep. So . . . he said, 'Bring me my magic hen!' So she brought him his magic hen. Jack got it quick. Then he got . . . then he said, he said, 'Lay, lay, lay!' So the hen laid golden eggs, as gold as they could be. So then he said, 'Give . . . bring me my magic harp!' So it said — so she said 'OK.' So — so the ge-ge-giant, the giant said, 'Sing, sing, sing!' So the ge — so the harp singed. So he said, 'Bring me my magic . . . harp.' So he [*sic*] bringed her — bringed him his magic harp. And he said . . . 'Bring' . . . so . . . she said, 'Lay me' . . . um [*8 seconds' pause; Rachel looks around room in desperation, sees my pen*] so he said, 'Lay me my . . . pen!' So it laid him a pen. And Jack got out and put one under his arm and holded one and did all that stuff and then he ran quickly out. The Jack — he her — the — the harp cried out, 'Master, master, master!' (9) So the giant heard and he came running running out. Jack quick quick got — got down first, and the giant was too scared to get down. So Jack got a hammer and cut him — smushed him to pieces. (10) Then Jack and his mother lived happily ever after.

Through section 5 the tale remains fairly tame. Sections 6 and 7 are adorned by several culinary digressions which are purely Rachel's. We hear first of Jack's choice of a menu, as the giant's castle momentarily is transformed into something resembling an American hamburger stand. Then we hear of the giant's prodigious appetite. After these digressions the traditional tale resumes, but it does so with another curious time warp. First Rachel fastens on the essential information: Jack peeked out from the oven, and he ran away. Then she backs up to recount the essential prerequisite to this action: 'the giant was so tired, and he fell asleep'. Finally she relates the preceding incident of the magic hen and the singing harp. As she does so, however, she nearly loses track of her story, thanks to a misplaced striving toward triadic form. Triadic form is evident elsewhere in the story in the threefold formulas 'Lay, lay, lay', 'Sing, sing, sing,' and 'Master, master, master,' as well as in the giant's threefold repetition of the statement 'I'm still hungry'. In example 4, the same concern with the number three is reflected in Jack's choice of exactly three beans. In the present example, the pull toward triads, which is so characteristic of fairy tales,[12] leads Rachel to try to invent a third magical object after the appearance of the hen and harp. First she has the giant's wife produce the harp for a second time, but such a solution clearly is inadequate. Then she searches desperately for some other solution and ends with the hen (or is it the harp?) laying a ball-point pen — whether a golden pen or not, we are not told. After this temporary impasse is resolved, Rachel continues at a rapid pace (note the repetitions 'running running' and 'quick quick'). To conclude the tale, she puts a definitive end to the giant by combining the alternative fates, which we have seen in examples 1 and 4. First the threatening figure is evaded ('the giant was too scared to get down'). Then, in defiance of realism (for Jack is on the ground), but in accord with the tendency of many traditional folktales to see that evil is fully exorcised, Jack dispatches the enemy with a hammer. No comparable violence occurs in Rachel's printed source for the story, in which Jack simply chops down the beanstalk until the giant falls dead to the ground.[13]

The sense of freedom with which Rachel handled the story of 'Jack and the Beanstalk' on five different occasions is characteristic of her storytelling art in general. To Rachel and to certain other young storytellers, a tale is not a fixed set of plot elements to be repeated from A to Z every time the tale is told. Instead, each performance represents a new re-visioning of the theme. New motifs may be added, old ones may be dropped. Faulty memory may play some part in this instability of the text, as in episode 8 of example 5 above, but, over and above such mnemonic slips, a skilled four-year-old storyteller seems to delight in his or her new-found powers of verbal creativity. As additional examples of Rachel's creativity in the handling of traditional fairy tales, I will cite three examples of 'Cinderella' which she told at intervals of about a week (examples 6-7-8). To adult ears, only the first performance will sound complete. Here the whole tale is told, from the

mean sisters, to the fairy godmother, to the magic coach (here transformed into a magic *couch*), to the prince's ball, to the midnight flight home, to the final recognition by means of the glass slipper. The other two versions will seem defective. They lack the flight home and all which follows. In their own way, all the same, these versions have a certain completeness as well. Each accomplishes what it sets out to do. In place of a complex story of two moves, from Cinderella's home to the ball and from the ball to Cinderella's home, we have a simple story of a single move.[14] The heroine was rejected; in the end she triumphs. 'Cinderella' has become a simple tale of lack and recompense. Although the episode of the glass slipper is lacking, there is something almost fitting about Rachel's ending the story at the moment of the heroine's greatest triumph, when she dances with the prince, before the admiring eyes of others, in her apotheosis as 'the beautifullest lady' of them all.

Examples 7 and 8 were told in response to a request for 'Snow White', hence the confusion of names at the beginning of each tale.

Example 6. 'Cinderella', recorded longhand January 22, 1978.

Once upon a time there was a girl. Her name was Cinderella. Her sisters were really mean to her. They took all of her pretty things away. They made her have to clean the fire, the ashes. And there was a ball. And so she wanted to go to the ball. She was crying outside in the woods. Soon her fairy godmother came. She turned her horses into the pretty couch what you sit on. She turned her into pretty clothes and glass slippers. So she went to the ball and she stopped crying.

There was the prince's ball. He looked at all the ladies. There was nobody he wanted to marry. So she came in. He didn't know what her name was, but they danced together. Her fairy godmother said, 'Come back at twelve o'clock', and so the ball turned DING, DONG, DING, DONG, DING-DONG DING-DONG DING-DONG DING-DONG. She ran downstairs, but she lost one glass slipper. And the prince was saying 'Wait for me!' She ran and ran down the steps, but they saw the shoe. So they brang it to her house. They brang it to everybody's house. Some were

324

too skinny, some were too fat. So they went to her house. And so her mean sisters opened the door. They tried it on and their feet were too fat. So Cinderella ran down the stairs and she fitted it on and the prince and Cinderella lived together and got married. And the end.

Example 7. 'Snow White' (= 'Cinderella'), recorded longhand January 26, 1978.

Once upon a time there was a girl named Snow White. She was a fairy godmother. [*JN: She was a fairy godmother?*] Yeah. She was a different Snow White. She went to the ball one day. Her wicked fairy godsisters said, [*imitates witchy voice*] 'Hey, you go to the ball? You have to get *us* ready, not you. You could go after you get *us* ready.' So Snow White had to do everything they said. So she went outside in the woods and started to cry. She was unhappy cause she didn't have any pretty dress. She went outside and she saw her fairy godmother, her other fairy godmother who was nice. She turned her into a pretty, pretty girl, pretty dress. She went as soon as she got her pretty glass slippers on. She got into the coach and she went there so quickly she wasn't late. So she was there at one minute. She ran up the stairs, and the prince was so happy to see Cinderella they danced all night. The end.

Example 8. 'Snow White' (= 'Cinderella'), recorded longhand February 5, 1978.

Once upon a time there was a girl named Snow White. She had a stepmother and two mean sisters. They made her have to do all the work. She couldn't have fun. And parties, she could never go to parties. One day there was a ball. Her mean sisters said, 'Help me get on my clothes! Help me get on my dress! Curl my hair! Put a ribbon in my hair!' They were all ready. Cinderella was in a raggety dress. Cinderella said, 'I guess I can't go.' She went outside in the garden and cried. Her fairy godmother said, 'Why are you sad?' 'Because I can't go to the ball.' She made all her friends turn into one thing for Cinderella to ride in to go to the ball.

'Now you are all set.' 'But my *dress*,' said Cinderella. 'Oh, you may not go in that raggety dress.' She turned her dress into a beautiful dress. And she turned two little shoes into beautiful glass slippers. 'Now you may go.' So she went. Cinderella was dancing all with the prince. She was the beautifullest lady. The end.

As with Rachel's different performances of 'Jack and the Beanstalk', there simply is no question of word-for-word repetition, except for the most formulaic of phrases, such as the first sentence of examples 7 and 8. Dialogue between the different characters belongs to the ephemeral part of the tale, and may or may not appear, depending on the teller's whim. At times the narrative progression is disarmingly naive, as in the description of the fairy godmother's work in example 6 ('She turned her [Cinderella] into pretty clothes and glass slippers'). For this particular young storyteller, evidently, you are what you wear. In example 7 this same concern with external appearances and with the contrast between beauty and plainness sounds like a leit-motif ('she didn't have any pretty dress', 'She turned her into a pretty, pretty girl, pretty dress', 'she got her pretty glass slippers on'). For Rachel, the fascination of 'Cinderella' seems to lie less in the theme of recognition by a token (the slipper) than in the simple joys of dressing up and looking beautiful at a party. The theme of marriage is expendable, but not the pretty dress.

As a last pair of examples of Rachel's storytelling ability, there follow two versions of 'Snow White', which she told at an interval of about seven weeks (examples 9 and 10). For months I had been trying to persuade her to tell 'Snow White', and all I could get was 'Cinderella'. Evidently the two female heroines are linked indissolubly in Rachel's mind. When the true 'Snow White' finally arrived, it was the longest story which I had yet recorded from a four-year-old. With its 353 words, it far exceeds the average of 104 words per story told by four-and-a-half-year-old girls as recorded by Louise Bates Ames.[15] Even so, it is shorter than its sequel (example 10), and shorter than her most complete version of 'Jack and the Beanstalk' (example 5). In example 9 the end is lacking, while example 10 resumes the story approximately where the previous telling leaves off.

Example 9. 'Snow White', recorded long-hand April 14, 1978.

Once upon a time Snow White was a pretty little girl who had a mean stepmother. 'Mirror, mirror, on the wall, who is the fairest of them all?' 'You think you are the prettiest. Snow White is eight times more prettier than you.' She got so mad she stamped her foot, she put a needle in her nose. Then she said to the woodsman, 'Take Cin. . . Snow White out in the woods and take her brain out of her and leave her there.' And she said to Snow White, [*imitates sweet voice*] 'I'll take you for a little walk in the woods.'

So 'Mirror, mirror, mirror, on the wall, who is the fairest of them all?' 'Snow White is eight times more prettier than you.' She stamped her foot, she put a needle in her nose, she put a needle right up her nose and in the middle of her eye. Then she said to the woodsman, 'Where is Snow White?' 'She is at the seven dwarves's house.'

She [Snow White] took a bite of each soup and a drink of each wine, then she went up to the bedrooms. She was so tired she took a nap. She fell right down, and then the seven dwarves came home. They said, 'Who's been eating myyyyy soup? Who's been drinking myyyyy wine? Who's sleeping in myyyyy bed?' She woke right up, and she said, 'Oh, I'm sorry. I didn't have any place to live except my own stepmother's. She's so mean, she always sticks a needle in her nose.'

And then the light turned on. And then Cinderella . . . [*laughter*] Snow White . . . went out. And then some dwarves went to Snow White's house and then . . . so . . . the . . . Snow White's stepmother said, 'Oh, you came. Now I can't do this trick with Snow White. You dummies, you banana splits.' 'We came to know if you are a good witch or a bad witch.' 'I am a bad witch, so get out of my house!' So the house — the palace — was drinking some milk. The end. Banana split.[16]

Example 10. 'Snow White', recorded on tape June 5, 1978.

Once upon a time there was a girl named Snow White. Her stepmother she asked sumpin [= *something*]. She said, 'Mirror, mirror, on the wall. who is the fairest of them all?' 'Snow White is twenty more prettier than you.' She got so mad she stamped her foot and she wanted to smash herself. So she disguised herself into a old lady, and . . . and she was . . . 'Selling combs, selling combs!' Snow White said, 'They're so pretty, I'll take one.' So she used — she put it — when she — when she got upstairs she put it right into her head . . . hair. She fell down. By this time the seven dwarves were home. One name was Piglet, another name was Polyette, another name was Gobbyette, and the — and the last name was Coolyette. Snow White . . . so the seven dwarves saw her lying on the floor. They saw the comb in her hair, so they took it, and she came right up. They said, 'Now never take combs by old ladies. They may be poisonous.' So she said, 'OK, I'll never ever do it again.'

So . . . um . . . she disguised herself. She said, 'Mirror, mirror, on the wall, who is the fairest of them all?' 'Snow White is twenty more prettier than you.' She got so mad she stamped her foot. She disguised herself into a old lady. She was selling poison — she was selling apples. She cutted off the poison, and she — she cutted off the — the not poisonous part, and she ate the not poisonous part and Snow White was eating the poisonous part. So she rode her boat all the way over. And she said, 'Apples for sale, apples for sale!' So she said, 'Oh, I like those beautiful apples.' So she gave her one. And — and she got upstairs, and she put it in her mouth. She — she felled right down. And the seven dwarves came home by themselves. So there was no comb in her, there was no s— . . . there was no pin and hole, and there was nothing wrong. They couldn't find what was wrong with her. So they made a golden bed for her to lie in. So she lied in it. They took her up. Hand by hand they holded her, they lift[ed] her up. Then a beautiful prince was coming. And he saw that she was so beautiful. And he took her, and she — and they got back down. But she was saying, 'Where am I?' 'You're with me.' Then they were riding home on the horsie.

Of the two complementary versions, the second must be considered more competent as a version of a traditional fairy tale (or the second half of a traditional fairy tale, for the episode of the woodsman is lacking). The influence of the Disney version is recognisable in Rachel's search for fantastic names for the dwarves.[17] A rowboat appears from nowhere, and there is a bit of uncertain chronology in the part which tells of the poisoned apple. Apart from these idiosyncracies and the usual examples of non-standard English, the narrative proceeds in a fairly straightforward fashion. The same is not true of example 9, with its extraordinary violence,[18] its animated dialogue, and its bizarre interweaving of elements from three different fairy tales. After an auspicious beginning, this version proceeds to an unexpected close. Somehow Rachel lost track of the traditional plot at about the time that the seven dwarves came home. Like any wanderer in the woods, a storyteller who leaves the beaten track is likely to get lost. Once Rachel lost her plot, she soon found herself in the wilds of free fantasy. The next thing we know, we seem to be in the house of the Three Bears, while it is not long until the stepmother's house is drinking milk. Hardly the *dénouement* that one had expected. In its own way, still, the story reaches completion and narrative tensions are resolved. The stepmother's evil is negated by the simple presence of the dwarves at her house. As the stepmother herself says, *'Oh, you came. Now I can't do this trick with Snow White.'* In another sense, the stepmother's words could almost be considered a comment on Rachel's own storytelling experience. Once tradition is defied and the dwarves have come to the stepmother's house, the tale has reached an impasse. It is almost as if Rachel herself were saying, 'Now that the dwarves have come to the wrong house, I can no longer do this trick [that is, tell this story] with Snow White.' In such a case a quick ending is the best ending, and any nonsense will suffice.

The stories of Rachel cannot be taken as typical of all children. They reflect the abilities and mental processes of a child who, like all human beings, is unique. Others of my informants have told tales of a different type, while some children have volunteered nothing that could be called a tale at all. Two of my other talented informants, for example, have been a girl aged 5, named Alexandra, and boy aged 6, named Walter. Alexandra excells, not at the telling of traditional fairy tales, but at the telling of stories of her own invention, which utilise traditional motifs and plots. Her stories tend to abound in witches and castles and magic, but these traditional elements are simply the building blocks of her own free fantasies. As for Walter, he never has offered to tell a traditional fairy tale, and he never has told the same tale twice. His stories are more disciplined than Rachel's, and his fantasies tend to have closer links to contemporary popular culture than to the storybook world of fairy tales. In his tales, for example, the giants and witches and helpful animals of fairy tales tend to be replaced by robbers and kidnappers and police.

Whatever their unique and idiosyncratic character, the stories of Rachel (together with the stories of Alexandra, Walter, and my other informants) have led me to appreciate that the term 'children's literature' need not encompass only literature created *for* children. The term also can be used to signify literature created *by* children out of the materials of tradition, and out of the rich resources of their own minds. It is my hope that the present study has helped to prepare the way for an awakening of interest in children's literature in this second sense, by calling attention to a few specific examples of how fairy tales are perceived and retold by the young. My conclusions are not startling, but they are important:

1. *The ability of young children to tell coherent stories has been underestimated.*

Everyone knows that children have fantasies. What is not so well known is that even young children are capable of organising their fantasies into long, coherent narratives, in which tensions are first aroused, then resolved.

2. *Storytelling by the young is marked by creativity at every level.*

Invention is natural; tradition must be learned. Children do not learn tales by rote. They learn plot structures, and even these plot structures they tend to look upon as variable. The linguistic creativity of young children is paralleled at every point by a comparable creativity in the handling of plot.

In addition to these two conclusions, two hypotheses seem plausible on the basis of my experience so far. Each hypothesis will have to be tested as more data becomes available in this still largely uncharted field.

1. *Storytelling by children can have a therapeutic value.*

At the very least, some tales will reveal phobias which the child otherwise might never express. When Walter told me fantasies about kidnapping or about loss of the mother, for example, he articulated fears which otherwise were not finding expression at the conscious, verbal level. In a more general way as well, the telling of a successful tale may contribute to a child's sense of self and sense of mastery of the world. The telling of a good tale — and in this category should be included traditional tales, as well as free fantasies — is a creative act, an act of ordering of the chaotic materials of the imagination. I would give my wholehearted assent to those psychologists who claim that a child who can tell a good story already is on the road to mental health.[19]

2. *A knowledge of traditional fairy tales may provide a valuable model for the child's own fantasies.*

In other words, as Bruno Bettelheim has claimed in *The Uses of Enchantment,*[20] fairy tales themselves may have a therapeutic value. Any motif from a folktale may provide a child with a spark which will kindle his imagination. More important, a child who has become familiar with the structure of folktales is likely to have assimilated narrative patterns which will help him to deal constructively with crises in his own psychic life. There never yet has existed a true folktale which did not turn out well in the end. By hearing folktales, children may be assimilating habits of thought which will offer them hope in the midst of terror and despair. In this way they may be reminded that the ogres and evil stepmothers of their world are not inseparable companions, but can be evaded, as in any fairy tale.

Notes

1. Iona and Peter Opie, *The Lore and Language of Schoolchildren* (London, 1959); *ibid.*, *Children's Games in Street and Playground* (London, 1965); Brian Sutton-Smith, *The Folkgames of Children* (Austin, 1972); *ibid.*, *The Folkstories of Children* (Philadelphia. Forthcoming from Univ. of Pennsylvania Press). Note also the articles by Sutton-Smith cited in note 4 below. An awakening interest in the study of childlore is reflected in the recent (1978) formation of a Children's Folklore section of the American Folklore Society; in the decision of the University of Pennsylvania Press to establish a series of publications in the area of children's folklore; and in the current planning of a special Children's Folklore issue of *Western Folklore*.

2. As the two methods yielded somewhat different results, it seemed advisable to use both. Tales taken down on tape tended to be expressive but confused, while tales taken down by the slower method of longhand tended to be more careful in their construction. The method of longhand also provided the storyteller with the opportunity for self-correction, for my method was to repeat each phrase aloud as I wrote it down. In addition, if the informant was willing, when each tale was finished I would read it back to him or her to see if I had recorded it correctly. In general I found no necessary correlation between tale length and method of tale collection. There did exist a tendency, however, for tales taken down longhand to end abruptly after an elaborate beginning. One factor contributing to this tendency may be the limited attention-span of young children. After a long time dictating, a child could call an end to the story session by the simple declaration 'the end'.

3. One of my informants (Rachel, to be introduced below) reduced these three categories to two: in her own terms, 'real' stories or handed-down fairy tales, and 'other' stories.

4. Evelyn Goodenough Pitcher and Ernst Prelinger, *Children Tell Stories: An Analysis of Fantasy* (New York, 1963); Louise Bates Ames, 'Children's Stories', *Genetic Psychology Monographs*, LXXIII (1966), 337-96; Richard A. Gardner, *Therapeutic Storytelling With Children: The Mutual Storytelling Approach* (New York, 1971); Rosalind Z. Scheffler, 'The Child From Five to Six: A Longitudinal Study of Fantasy Change', *Genetic Psychology Monographs*, XCII (1975), 19-56; Brian Sutton-Smith, 'The Expressive Profile', *Journal of American Folklore*, LXXXIV (1971), 80-92, reprinted in *The Folkgames of Children* (Note 1 above), 521-40; Sutton-Smith et al., 'The Importance of the Story-Taker: An Investigation of the Imaginative Life', *Urban Review*, VIII (1975), 82-95; Sutton-Smith et al., 'Developmental Structures in Fantasy Narratives', *Human Development*, XIX (1976), 1-13; Sutton-Smith and Gilbert J. Botvin, 'The Development of Structural Complexity in Children's Fantasy Narratives', *Developmental Psychology*, XIII (1977), 377-88; Sutton-Smith and David M. Abrams, 'The Development of the Trickster in Children's Narratives', *Journal of American Folklore*, XC (1977), 29-47; Sutton-Smith and David M. Abrams, 'Psychosexual Material in Stories Told by Children: The Fucker', *Progress in Sexology* (1977), 491-504; Sutton-Smith, 'Listening to Little Stories', *Harper's*, CCLVI (April 1978), 53-55.

5. Pitcher and Prelinger, Ames, and Scheffler make a specific point of excluding traditional tales from their studies. Ames, 347, reports an occasion when a four-and-a-half-year-old girl started to tell the story of 'Little Red Riding Hood', but was interrupted by the examiner, who explained that 'it must be an original story'.

6. As an example of what I would call 'symbolic overkill' on the part of a writer whose orientation is psychological, one might note Martha Wolfenstein, *Children's Humor: A Psychological Analysis* (Glencoe, Ill., 1954), 43. Wolfenstein quotes the following story as told by a five-year-old boy:

> Once there was a red field. A farmer went in. And you know where the seeds were? In his mouth. And he couldn't plant because there were no seeds. You know why? Because he ate all the seeds up. So he dug a hole and buried himself. And he grew to be a carrot and a tomato and a potato.

Wolfenstein interprets this as 'a funny story in which . . . the female genital appears as a huge red field in which the male is completely buried . . . The farmer having swallowed the seeds probably expresses fantasies of fellatio and oral impregnation. But the farmer with the seeds inside is also the penis, which must be buried in the red field so that the seeds may be planted. This expresses the fantasy that the father's penis is incorporated by the mother. However, in the reassuring conclusion a carrot (penis) and a tomato and potato (testicles, which had apparently also been incorporated) re-emerge.' It is not my present purpose to dispute this interpretation. Instead, I would simply point out that interpretations of this kind stand or fall on the basis of an *a priori* theoretical system, in this case a system which is derived from Freud's analyses of adult fantasies. Whether or not Freud's approach is suitable to the fantasies of five-year-old children is a question which Wolfenstein does not raise.

7. In a separate essay I plan to discuss the very interesting group of transitional tales.

8. When I read the story back to Rachel, at this point she interjected by way of clarification: 'She didn't cook him.'

9. For purposes of comparison, the reader may consult the printed version, which served as Rachel's chief source: *Jack and the Beanstalk,* illustrated by T. Izawa and H. Hijkata (New York, 1968). Rachel had heard the story told freely as well as read from the printed text, and several details of her version seem to derive from oral tellings, as they are not present in the book. These details are (1) the oven as opposed to a closet, (2) the giant's 'I smell the blood' threat, and possibly (3) the chopping up of the giant, although this last may be her own addition.

10. Esphyr Slobodkina, *Caps For Sale: A Tale of a Peddler, Some Monkeys and Their Monkey Business* (New York, 1940), 5. The passage in question reads as follows: 'He [the peddler] walked up and down the streets, holding himself very straight so as not to upset his caps. As he went along he called, "Caps! Caps for sale! Fifty cents a cap!" ' The same call is repeated twice later.

11. That this inventiveness is self-conscious and deliberate is shown by the conversation which preceded the dictation of the tale:

> JN. OK, let's try it again. Now you say you'd rather do a made-up story, or one which you've heard before?
> R. One that I heard.
> JN. One that you heard before?
> R. Yeah, I'll just make up part of it.

12. See Axel Olrik's *Gesetz der Dreizahl* as expressed in his essay 'Epische Gesetze der Volksdichtung', *Zeitschrift für deutsches Altertum,* (1909), 1-12, reprinted in translation in Alan Dundes, ed., *The Study of Folklore* (Englewood Cliffs, 1965), 129-41, and note further the works cited by Dundes, 133, footnote 4.

13. Rachel's addition of the detail of the hammer suggests that violence is not purged from the imagination of children by purging violence from the stories which they are told. Occasionally, I have found, children telling stories will invent violence where none existed in their source, while at other times they will exaggerate violence which was only suggested in their source. Evidently many normal children have violent fantasies, and these fantasies can be self-generated as well as learned. Parents, teachers, and psychologists, who hope to

shield children from violence by white-washing children's literature may be overly optimistic about the control which they can have over the minds of the young. Part of the appeal of fairy tales to the young may lie precisely in the way in which such tales articulate violence. In this way they may speak to deep-set needs by articulating feelings which otherwise might go unexpressed, at the same time as they channel these feelings by associating violence with an evil stepmother, giant, or ogre who is overcome.

14. The term 'move' I am using in the sense in which it is used by Vladimir Propp, *The Morphology of the Folktale* (Austin, 1968), 92-96.

15. Ames, 377.

16. The probability is strong that Rachel's use of the epithet 'banana split' is to be traced back to a children's television programme titled 'Banana Splits', which is broadcast in the Los Angeles area. In a subsequent discussion relating to this point, Rachel reported to me that she had not seen this programme, but she had heard friends talk about it.

17. Rachel had seen the Walt Disney film version of 'Snow White' once about a year previously. In addition, details from the Disney version may have been incorporated into versions of 'Snow White' told to her at home. Rachel also had heard the Grimm version of 'Snow White' read to her at home.

18. See Note 13 above. In the case of this particular storytelling performance, the element of violence may have been heightened, thanks to the presence of Rachel's older brother in the room. Her brother was under strict instructions not to interrupt the proceedings, but he could not help laughing when Rachel told of the stepmother putting a needle in her nose. Aware that she had an appreciative audience for this detail, Rachel repeated it several times.

19. A persuasive case for the therapeutic value of children's storytelling is made by Gardner (Note 4 above).

20. Bruno Bettelheim, *The Uses of Enchantment: The meaning and Importance of Fairy Tales* (New York, 1976).

The White Man in African Proverbial Sayings

J. O. OJOADE   University of Jos, Nigeria

THE purpose of this paper is to collect and interpret the scattered references to the white man in African proverbial sayings.[1] Some statements listed here include what some people would call proverbs. Others call them mere sayings, ethnophaulisms, local pleasantries, *blasons populaires*, ethnocentric proverbs, or ethnic slurs. Throughout this paper, therefore, the term proverbial sayings embraces all of the above.

Regarding the veracity of these sayings, they need not necessarily be true for all times, or even for today. In fact, in some cases, the sayings simply reflect the attitude, if sentimental and gossipy, of colonised Africans to their white colonial masters; they show the kind of social relationship or symbiosis that existed between the two peoples; they are African observations of some peculiarities of the whites. Some also allude to episodes in the history of the natives in which both the white man and the native were dramatis personae, thus shedding light on some important events in the history of the natives which otherwise may have been shrouded in obscurity or left in the limbo of scholarship.

Generally, some of these proverbial sayings are no more than quarries of facts associated by Africans with the whites, what the natives admire or abhor in the behaviour of the whites, observations about their dress, food, private and public life, trading activities, mode of travelling and their idiosyncrasies. But proverbs also, and this is very important, tell us as much about the people who coin them as they do about the people about whom they are made. Thus although the proverbs here are made by Africans about the white men, the proverbs tell us much more about the Africans themselves.[2]

Regarding the white people about whom the proverbs have been made, they were in evidence at least on the west coast of Africa from the fifteenth century onward (the nineteenth century was the great age of African exploration), first as slave traders, and with the passage of time, as merchants, miners, teachers, policemen, soldiers, missionaries, judges, governors, tourists, etc. Some white settlers wanted to live in Africa, but for one reason or other they could not live among the natives. Thus they distanced themselves from the natives. This separate parallel development of white colonies within African communities made their behaviour easier to observe for ridicule or admiration.

Indeed, Africans have seen the truth of the psychoanalyst's theory of repressions, by seeking through proverbial sayings, an outlet for their feelings which might otherwise have become a dangerous complex. Every facet of the white man's behaviour was studied. Nothing was sacred. Some facets were highly applauded, others lampooned. All this helped the natives to survive some of the aspects of colonialism which they strongly detested. Hostilities could be expressed in a socially acceptable way. Humour relieves tension. Poke fun at the cause of your troubles and you don't feel quite as bad afterwards. This is one way of coping with the unpleasant aspects of colonialism.

Finally, it may be noted that African peoples are very hospitable to the white men; but also they are suspicious of them. Naturally, the colonised natives detest the white colonisers *inter alia* from political and religious antagonism. But this has not blinded them from seeing the good things that the white masters have done. Africans are not satirists who emphasise only the darkest behaviour of the people they portray, they have also praised the praiseworthy achievements of the whites, achievements which are emulatable.[3]

Certainly it cannot be gainsaid that these proverbs do provide valuable data to the folklorist, the sociologist or the anthropologist, the social historian, the social politician, the psychologist, and any scholar for that matter whose interest concerns the social relationships that exist between peoples, nations or countries, colonisers and colonised.

Therefore, these proverbs, distasteful though some of them may be, need to be preserved before they are lost like some African folktales and music. This is more so, as conditions of life today are changing fast, technologically and socially.

Here are a few examples:

1. *When the pot boils for a man back from the colonies, it means the dividing of white money.* (Jabo)

This is an allusion to the practice, among the Jabo, whereby, when a native employee of the white man returns he has to give presents to his close relatives. Other relatives – for in Africa almost one tenth of all the inhabitants of a village are closely related – who desire similar presents also begin by 'boiling pot', that is to say, preparing meals to which the returnee is invited. The returnee labourer, on sensing the hint, in turn gives out some presents to the hosts.

This proverbial saying is very revealing in the sense that, as I said in the introduction, it tells us as much about the makers of it as of the white employers about whom it was made. *Inter alia* this proverb shows the mentality of the Jabo who expect something from any worker whenever he comes home on holiday. Thus they look forward to some profit from the practice of the white man's employment of their relatives. It implies clearly that the family appreciates the employment of their member by the white men.

2. *With the coming of the white men even the tortoise eats beans with spoon.* (Idoma)

The implication of this proverb is that with the coming of the white man even fools become wiser and more civilised. A good number of Africans seized the opportunity of Western education to improve their social position.

The proverb may be used to describe a person hitherto considered hopeless who suddenly surprises others by rising up the social ladder owing to the intervention of someone else.

3. *If you slap a white man in the face, he will not be angry; but let him who wishes to see his anger beat his dog.* (Igbo)

The saying simply reflects the white man's fondness for his dog, and can be applied in any situation in which somebody wishes to emphasise the degree of his affection for something.

4. *The white man looks at the black man in the face, but at the black woman in the buttocks and the breasts.* (Igbo)

This is used to describe flirtatious white men some of whom must have been sailors at the ports. This reminds one of the Swahili name for a European which is 'Mzungu'. Literally it means a person who does not show good manners in his sexual relation with women. Originally this applied only to the early European sailors who had contacts with Zululand. After a number of months at sea they became rather randy and thus could not control their sexual desires on seeing Swahili women. Unfortunately this is the name by which any white man is now called among the Swahili-speaking people.

I owe this information to Prof W. T. Morgan, Professor of Geography in the University of Jos.

5. *If you wish to know whether a white man loves his wife, go to his house when his wife is ill.* (Igbo)

Indirectly, here the black man is comparing himself to the white man. Normally the white man is monogamous, whereas the African is customarily polygamous. It is natural therefore for the white husband to dote on his only wife whereas the black husband has his love shared by a number of wives.

6. *A woman is queen.* (Igala)

This is a reference to both the queen of England and the first queen of Igala. The Igala had realised that a woman could reign as queen in the white man's country. Incidentally the first Attah of Igala also happened to be a woman named Ebelejonu, who became queen at a very young age. She was later very powerful — 'no one with power like her own'. In truth, it is on account of the fact *inter alia* that a woman had reigned Attah that subsequent Attahs, all males, still have their ears pierced like a woman's.[4]

The proverb can be cited by any woman who is being despised by males to remind them that women can hold very high positions in society.

7. *The British owned the land, the Portuguese the slaves.* (Yoruba)

The proverb is based on the observations of the Yoruba. They had observed that the Portuguese were mainly interested in slave trade, whereas the British had come to stay in their country.

The coiners of this proverb apparently were not unaware that the slave-trade was forbidden to British subjects in 1808, whereas the Portuguese and Spaniards were still continuing the trade.

8. *When a white man agrees to go to the native doctor, then he is almost dead.* (Agbede)

The white man despised the local medicine. But after his own had failed to effect the desired cure, he would resort to the local one. Malaria fever is a case in point here. If a white man who has not been taking a prophylactic is attacked by it, it is always serious, and may be fatal in spite of the white man's antidote. But the natives have very effective antidotes which the white man takes as a last resort.[5]

The proverb may be cited to ridicule a person who finally accepts what he at first despised.

9. *The white man improves the world but has no panacea for 'magun'.* (Owe)

Magun is a kind of poison which makes it impossible for a man to separate himself after copulation from his female partner. It is thus used to injure adulterers.

The basic point of the proverb is that, although the white men have done so much in improving the life of people, there are certain aspects of the native life and culture against which they cannot do anything effectively.

The text might be quoted to show that a man cannot do everything no matter how powerful he may be.

10. *If you eat or drink too much at a white man's party, you will not get a second invitation.* (Igbo)

This proverb clearly shows the difference in the attitudes of Africans vis-à-vis the white man to entertainments. The proverb suggests that the African gives more lavish entertainment than the white man.

The proverb cautions against abusing opportunities.

11. *White is never ugly; black has denied me beauty.* (Ogoni)

This is one occasion in which the African compares his colour to that of the white man. To the African the skin of a young European (on account of his colour) looks more beautiful than his African peer. But this is not the case with an old European as compared to his African peer. The wrinkles of an old European (at least those exposed to African weather) are more conspicuous than those of a black person.

12. *It is the white man who sells knives (razor blades), yet his head is overgrown with hair.* (Ashanti)

The proverb, which has the nuance of 'Physician, heal thyself' finds apt application in any situation in which a person fails to use to advantage that which he produces in abundance.

13. *On account of food-looking into, the white men emigrated to Europe.* (Ashanti)

The proverb originates from the belief of Africans that man was created in Africa where both whites and blacks had lived harmoniously together. But, as time went on, the blacks began to molest the whites. In particular the blacks always pried into the affairs, particularly the food, of the whites, as a result of which the whites emigrated to Europe.

How did the black man explain the difference in the complexion of both peoples especially as they had both lived together before the whites came to their present country? Cain, who represents the white men, was originally black. But after killing Abel, who stands for the black men, he was reproved by God. As a result Cain became pale with fear. This is how the white man got his colour.

The proverb cautions against undue curiosity.

14. *If Europe knew no poverty, the white man would not leave his people to live in the black man's country.* (Akan)

This is the Akan explanation for the coming of the white man to Africa.

Says Abraham: 'This reveals that the spirit with which some of the Akans defended themselves against European attempts to settle or alienate their land was not always due to the metaphysical entanglements in which they involved land in their thinking.

'The appreciation of the relevance of economic wants and motives to the brutalities of colonialism was quickly made.'[6]

15. *I have not seen even a penny to buy a rope to hang myself; what more to contribute to the rich white men in the name of tax.* (Igbo)

This alludes to the story of an Igbo pauper who refused to pay tax when asked by court-messengers. The generality of the Igbo did not take kindly to taxation imposed on them by white administration. Thus tax was generally collected in an 'atmosphere of resentment and protest'.[7] It was worse still when a pauper was asked to pay tax 'to rich white men'.

The proverb can be applied whenever a man is requested to give out of the very little that he has.

16. *He whom the white man shoots and misses; when he sees an anthill, it looks to him like a white man.* (Igbo)

The proverb which is used in the sense of 'Once bitten twice shy' reflects the series of gun battles between the white colonial masters and the recalcitrant natives. The natives used local guns, bows and arrows while the whites used more sophisticated guns and rifles.

17. *When a man who runs away from the white men dies he must still meet the white men when he reincarnates.* (Igbo)

During the First and Second World Wars some Nigerians were conscripted.[8] Those who could,

escaped by hiding in caves while some committed suicide. The proverb was thus coined as propaganda to discourage the run-aways, the idea being that you will still meet the same white man whom you are trying to avoid. The Igbo, like other Africans, strongly believe in reincarnation.[9]

18. *The tortoise says: If I had known that the German Wars would come I would have made a steel helmet for myself.* (Igbo)

The wellerism is used in the sense of 'Forewarned is forearmed'. The German Wars refer to the First and Second World Wars, for both of which Africans were conscripted.[10] The tortoise is always a central figure in African folklore, especially in proverbs, myths and folktales.

19. *If you wish to kill a white man without being questioned, send him to Dahomey.* (Igede)

This means that, if you wish to execute a bad plan, use appropriate or legitimate means to achieve it. The menace of African mosquitoes is itself proverbial, and one would have been surprised if this phenomenon is not reflected in African proverbs.

Nigerians had trading contacts with their neighbours such as Dahomeans, Ghanaians, etc. The makers of this proverb probably noticed that Dahomean mosquitoes were more dangerous than their own. The idea that mosquitoes are deadly enemies of the white man is not lost to the Igede!

20. *Tomorrow, tomorrow does not kill the white man.* (Ijo)

This proverb alludes to John Lander, who with his brother Richard, was captured in 1830, near Asaba on the River Niger, by some armed natives, who took them to the Obi of Aboh. Incidentally, they were ransomed by King Boy of Brass, who brought them to Nembe. King Boy was obviously urged to produce John, perhaps, as Alagoa suggested, for sacrifice,[11] but King Boy thinking that 'when I took you from the Eboe country, . . . he would be overjoyed to see me, and give me plenty of beef and rum . . . I gave a quantity of goods to free you from slavery of Obi'[12] procrastinated the release of John Lander to his own regret, as the promised ransom was never paid to him, when he finally handed John over to Captain

Thomas Lake. When asked by his chiefs to produce John, King Boy probably promised to release him, saying 'Tomorrow, I will do that' or some such thing.

The proverb is used in the sense of 'Procrastination is the thief of time'.

21. *When a white man is drunk and he invites you to trade, then trade with him.* (Mende)

That is, you are likely to get the best out of the deal. The English version is 'Take time by the forelock'. Whenever a person hesitates to seize an opportunity from which he will derive some advantage, this proverb may find application.

This is another example of a proverb which tells us as much about the maker as about the person about whom it is made. The proverb certainly shows that the Mende of Sierra Leone would cheat if the opportunity occurred in their commercial dealings with the European traders.

22. *The question that a European asked Agbonika.* (Igala)

Agbonika was an Igala man, who was an interpreter to one European. He was witty and so liked by his master. During a journey in Igala land they came to the Umaboro-Anambra River, which has its sources near Ankpa, in Benue State of Nigeria. The European master asked Agbonika where the river was flowing to. Agbonika then asked him to remove his hat (*oroji*) and throw it into the river and then he would know where the river Umaboro was flowing. The European laughed and shook his head at Agbonika.

The basic idea here is that a ridiculous question elicits a ridiculous answer. Similarly a ridiculous statement elicits another ridiculous statement.

This shows the cordial relationship between the white boss and his interpreter. Not all white masters were so much on their dignity they could not make jokes with their junior employees.

23. *Don't behave like Nwakpuda who, in the course of challenging the white man, got himself killed.* (Igbo)

Nwakpuda was a chief of Umuahia in Imo State of Nigeria. When in 1912 the British administration in Nigeria began to build the railway from Port Harcourt to tap the coal deposits at Udi and Enugu[13] it apparently did not consult the owners of the land, through which the lines would pass, for compensation. For fear of the white man's gun some people affected kept quiet.[14] But not Chief Nwakpuda who after the completion of the project (in 1916) stood on the lines waving at the moving train to stop. In the process he was crushed by the train.

The idea here is that the white man did not impose his authority on the natives without some opposition, the advantages derived from such projects — 'easier communication ... marked increase in trade and circulation of coin'[15] — notwithstanding.

The proverb itself can be used when A wants B to cease a certain action that is fraught with danger.

24. *To prevent the eyes from seeing evil is not by running away; prayer must be offered. That is how the white man won the Dahomean War.* (Yoruba)

In 1851, when William More arrived in Abeokuta from Sierra Leone, he heard the news of the impending attack on Abeokuta by the King of Dahomey. Another white man, Rev Townsend, distributed arms to the Abeokuta chiefs for the defense of the town. The attack by the Dahomean army came again in 1862. This time the danger was so great that some Europeans left Abeokuta. But the missionaries stayed at their posts and called their Christian followers to fervent prayer. A plague broke out among the Dahomean army, which turned back with a great loss of life. The event was taken by the people of Abeokuta as an answer by God to the prayers of the Christians. The mystery of Christianity increased, and more converts were made. The Europeans and some natives, who fled the town for dear life, thought it was by running away that they could save their lives. But those who stayed behind and prayed, and won the battle, proved that it was through prayer, which is more effective than running.

25. *If death doesn't take the head, it will don a European hat.* (Edo)

If a person does not die (young) he may still wear a European hat.

This is a reference to the kind of hat that used to be worn by Sir Bernard Bourdillon, Governor of Nigeria (1935-43).

In fact the hat was simply called Bourdillon. This is a periphrastic way of saying, like the English, 'While there is life, there is hope' or 'Never say "die" '.

It may be noted here that a number of educated Nigerians during the colonial days were fond of wearing European dress, including Bourdillon.

26. 'Perhaps, perhaps' prevents the white man from telling lies. (Hausa)

This proverb lampoons the cautious practice of the white man, who sometimes prefaces his replies to delicate questions with 'perhaps', in order that he may not be implicated in the matter in question. The white man prefers to say 'perhaps' when he does not wish to say either 'Yes' or 'No' to a question.

The proverb is used to describe a person who vacillates.

27. Even the white man farts. (Agbede)

This implies that if a white man breaks wind (in public?), how much more do I, who am inferior to him.

The proverb can be used as excuse for doing a wrong thing just because a superior officer does the same thing with impunity.

28. After God come the white men. (Yoruba)

With this we may compare a cognate Caribbean saying. 'After God, then the white people'.

The two proverbs arose from the black man's belief that only God can surpass the white man on account of his technological and scientific achievements.[16] On the other hand the proverb may have been based on the black man's notion that the white man is holier than himself, because of his introduction of Christianity, which preached against traditional religion, especially certain obnoxious traditional practices like human sacrifice, killing of twins, etc.

29. The white man can walk, but the African must run. (Julius Nyerere, President of Tanzania)

This statement must be regarded as a proverb, because it has received such general acceptance by all Africans in practice as to guarantee that the sentiment it contains expresses a consensus of (African) opinion on the technological and other achievements of the white man vis-à-vis those of the black man.[17] In other words the saying is the wisdom of all Africans and the wit of Julius Nyerere.

The underlying idea is that, because of the stage which the white man has reached technologically, as compared to the African, the white man can afford to walk, consolidating his gains, whereas the African, who has achieved virtually nothing, must run fast to achieve anything at all.

The proverb would be especially appropriate in any situation involving a comparison between an outstanding achievement of one person (or a group of persons) and the lesser achievement of another.

30. When a white man (Priest) says 'Amen', you must know that that is the end of his talk. (Igbo)

This means that the white priest does not wish to go further with the matter in hand. The proverb, which is used when a person wishes to put an end to a discussion, may as well serve as sufficient warning to bring this paper to an end.

Geographical Locations

Tribe		Country	Tribe		Country
Agbede	–	Nigeria	Igede	–	Nigeria
Ashanti	–	Ghana	Jabo	–	Liberia
Edo	–	Nigeria	Mende	–	Sierra Leone
Hausa	–	Nigeria	Ogoni	–	Nigeria
Idoma	–	Nigeria	Owe	–	Nigeria
Igala	–	Nigeria	Yoruba	–	Nigeria
Igbo	–	Nigeria			

Notes

1. I wish to thank the Research Grant Committee of the University of Jos for the Research Grant, which enabled me not only to collect the data for this paper, but also to travel to the Conference where it was read.

   I am grateful to my students who contributed to the list, and I am also most indebted to the following colleagues for their constructive criticism and suggestions: Professor K. D. White, Professor John Figueroa, Dr Grace Robinson and the Rev Dr T. Mason.

2. See, e.g., Nos 1, 5, 10, 21.

3. Cf. No.29.

4. J. S. Boston, *The Igala Kingdom* (Ibadan, 1968), 17.

5. Cf. W. N. M. Greary, *Nigeria Under British Rule* (London, 1965), 22.

6. W. E. Abraham, *The Mind of Africa* (London, 1962), 73.

7. E. Isichei, *A History of the Igbo People* (London, 1976), 153.

8. Cf. No.18.

9. F. A. Arinze, *Sacrifice in Ibo Religion* (Ibadan, 1970), 17-18; J. S. Mbiti, *African Religions and Philosophy* (London, 1976), 164f.

10. Cf. No.17.

11. E. J. Alagoa, 'The Use of Oral Literary Data for History. Examples from Niger Delta Proverbs', *Journal of American Folklore*, LXXXI (1968), 235-42.

12. R. Hallett, *The Niger Journal of Richard and John Lander* (London, 1965), 276.

13. J. C. Anene, *Southern Nigeria in Transition 1885-1906* (Cambridge, 1966), 297 (No.1).

14. Isichei, 134.

15. Sir Alan Burns, *History of Nigeria* (London, 1972), 217.

16. Cf. No.29.

17. Cf. No.28.

The Ritual Entry to the House in Wales

TREFOR OWEN   Welsh Folk Museum

I WANT to discuss in this short paper one of the characteristics of certain folk customs in Wales which seems to have had a special significance. I do not suggest that this feature was in any way restricted to Wales: in fact, I am fairly sure one could discover parallels in other cultures, but, looking at the historical scene in Wales, one cannot help being struck by the prevalence of this feature and the social context in which it was to be found. I am referring to the way, in traditional Welsh society, in which entry into peoples' houses was governed by certain rules and, in particular, to the way in which, when many folk customs were performed – if I may use that word – the whole question of access was transformed into a ritual and poetic battle of wits between those inside the house and those seeking entry.

Before turning to the ritual form of entry, let me first look briefly at the social context, and at the normal ways in which people visited each others' homes. The late Alwyn D. Rees in his classical study of *Life in a Welsh Countryside*, identified the dispersed nature of Welsh society and its inherent centrifugal tendencies as one of its strongest and most influential features.[1] Social life was most active, not at the centre, but at the extremities, not in towns (of which there were, until recently, very few of any size) but in the isolated farmsteads and cottages. Those Welsh institutions which emerged in the nineteenth century, such as the National Eisteddfod, the University, and national establishments such as the Museum and Library, as well as religious assemblies, were either peripatetic or dispersed. And even at the local level, the parish centre – the *llan* – was neglected in favour of the individual homestead. It was there, around the hearth, that Welsh life flourished – even when new religious influences transformed that social life in the nineteenth century.

Alwyn Rees also showed how important the hearth and its fire had been in Welsh folklore and, indeed, in Celtic folklore generally. In many Welsh farmhouses the fire was reputed to have been kept burning continuously for centuries, and to let it go out was to invite bad luck. The tasks of *anhuddo* (covering) and *dadanhuddo* (uncovering) the fire every evening and morning were taken very seriously. The 'seed of the fire' a glowing ember of peat or wood was singled out and replaced on the hearth, which had been previously swept clean, before it was covered up with ashes for the night. In the morning this was the nucleus of the new day's fire. And, of course, the fire in a new house was symbolically kindled with embers from the fire in the old house, thus emphasising continuity. The squatters' cottage (*tŷ unnos*) hastily built overnight was not complete – and his right to ownership was not established – until smoke issued through the chimney the following morning. According to the Welsh Laws, the *pentanfaen* (hearth stone or fireback stone) once placed in position might not be removed, even though the house were deserted: 'it stood as a perpetual sign that the site was once that of an occupied homestead'. Chalked patterns drawn on the hearth and carved figures near the doorways 'protected' the hearth, as Eurwyn Wiliam has shown.[2] Indeed, much more evidence could be marshalled to underline the central significance of the hearth in Wales (and other Celtic countries) from antiquity.

This ancient social tradition of the hearth, Rees showed, came into its own during the winter half of the old Celtic Year. Story-telling, one of its highest cultured expressions, took place between Winter's Eve and May Eve to an audience of assembled neighbours. Alwyn and Brinley Rees have pointed out how time was seen by the Celtic-speaking peoples as the alternation of opposites — light and darkness, warmth and cold, life and death — and how this was at the level of day and night, as well as winter and summer. And the hearth tradition belonged to the dark hours of the day and to the dark half of the year.[3]

How did one enter the house and gain access to the hearth, to partake of its activities, to participate in this tradition? Normally, assemblies of neighbours in Merioneth, for example, took place on moonlit nights, when walking across the fields was easier. The visitors called out the usual question 'Are there people here?' and let themselves in. Easy access and hospitality went together: a visitor might stay three days before being asked who he was. A place at the table was set for 'Morus Trawsfynydd' — 'Morris from over the mountain' — the unexpected guest. That interesting personage, the marriage bidder, whose task was to invite people to weddings and to remind them of their wedding debts, was entitled to walk into every house unannounced, and to tap his staff of office three times on the living-room floor to announce his presence, before beginning his address of invitation. The visiting poor who came to beg were brought into the house, even among the gentry, among whose inventories the dole-chest often figures; and the early eighteenth-century devotional books suggest that one should give alms oneself instead of entrusting this soul-enhancing duty to one's servants. All the evidence suggests that in normal everyday experience entry into the house was easy, informal and unrestricted. The hearth tradition in this dispersed cultural pattern flourished on the basis of this fact.

It is against this everyday background of un-hindered access that the question of ritual entry — and prolonged entry at that — needs to be examined. First of all, I want to refer briefly to a somewhat specialised form, that is, what was termed 'setting for the marriage chamber' which took place on the eve of a wedding. This was the reverse of a 'stag party'. It was the women-folk who came to the house of the young couple, bringing them gifts of foodstuffs to prepare the wedding feast, to be held the following day. This was the evening, too, when the furniture was brought to the house, and there are indications in certain parts of Wales that there was a recognised order in which the furniture should be brought in and that the ceremony was supervised by the two mothers — or the two mothers-in-law, if you take a pessimistic view! On special occasions such as setting up home, it seems, entry was formalised, ritualised, if you like — certainly given a structure which it clearly lacked in everyday life.

The most dramatic form which this ritual entry took was, as I suggested earlier, the mock poetic contest between those inside one house and those seeking entry. This took place at weddings, where it constituted a special form of the 'quintain' or ritual hindrance of the wedding itself, and also in several folk customs associated with the winter half of the year. I use the adjective 'mock' because the contest is merely a prolongation of entry. Hardly ever, it seems, were the contestants outside turned away.

In the context of the wedding celebrations, the ritual entry forms part of the so-called capture of the bride and the chase on horseback when the 'young man's party' came to fetch her on the day of the wedding. Obstacles were placed in the farm-yard and across lanes to prevent access; the door of the house was bolted and it was there in the doorway, through the closed door, that the contest in verse took place. The practice was to engage the services — freely given on an occasion of this kind — of local characters, who were well-known versifiers, to act as 'guiders'. In an example recorded in 1894, in Betws, near Ammanford, the verses of demand and response — five of each — are given in full, and may be paraphrased as follows: The party outside announce that they are messengers sent by the bridegroom to fetch the beautiful young woman. But there are numerous young women inside, of high and low estate — which one do you want? We want the one who has promised to become a wife. But the young girl now sees that you're only pagans — she'd rather stay as she is than take the yoke of slavery. But she's promised to come with her sweetheart to take an oath before the priest. A promise of that kind is only binding when she wishes to keep it. The party outside persists: but the maiden has promised this morning to keep her word that they will both take this bond until death. The inside party then draws upon scripture — the apostle Paul said it was better to be widowed (i.e. single)

340

than to get married. The reply comes: But Paul didn't know the virtues and gifts of women. Solomon and I praise women, so please open the door, and if we do any harm we will pay for it. The final answer comes – since you're so reasonable and your plea so clever, come in to fetch the girl, so that she can get married.[4] In this particular case the bride to be was handed over amidst considerable celebration, but in other areas she still proved elusive, hiding herself in a chest or cupboard, or even in a grandfather clock – or, possibly, she had disguised herself as a boy. An earlier account by Peter Roberts (1815) describes how the bridegroom's friends, having negotiated the quintain outside, hastened to the bride's abode:

> and if the door was shut against them they assailed it, and those within, with music and poetry, particularly the latter, in strains of raillery. If the latter could not be retorted from within, the door was opened; and by a little management, the bridegroom's friends contrived to draw the bride out of the company and bear her off as in triumph. Her friends at a convenient time, discovered her flight and pursued, and if they overtook the other party a mock encounter took place, in which the pursuers acknowledged their own inferiority and the bride was brought safely to the bridegroom's house and the whole party received with great kindness and welcome.[5]

Roberts describes the ritual entry as taking place after the wedding ceremony, but later writers make it clear that the chase on horseback ended up in the parish church. What I want to emphasise is that the ritual entry on the occasion of a wedding is only one of a series of three mock contests (or possibly four, if we include the concealment of the bride), as well as the quintain and chase. It was also found, as I have already mentioned, in an even more highly structured form in some of the traditional calendar customs, particularly variants of wassailing, including the *Mari Lwyd*, Candlemas singing and, to a lesser degree, the wren ceremony.

I will not describe these customs in any detail. However, it is worth noting that, what they have in common with each other and with certain other calendar customs belonging almost entirely to the winter half of the year, is the taking round from house to house of a ritual object – horse's head, wassail bowl, new year's gift, new year's water, a wren on a bier, a *perllan*, egg clappers, *crochan crewys* (Lenten crock), Easter lifting, may bough. In their simplest forms, these customs involve displaying the ritual object at the door, having first sung or knocked, so as to draw attention or to greet the householder. One extreme thus takes the form of socially approved begging at feast times – souling, Thomasing, *blawta a blonega* (collecting flour and fats on Shrove Tuesday), collecting Easter eggs. At the other extreme, the greeting and wishing-well is spun out in a highly elaborate way, with musical and poetical embellishments, the aim being not so much the collection of food or money, as to enjoy the company of the household on the hearth and their hospitality. The best known example is probably the *Mari Lwyd* custom, found mainly in Glamorgan and Gwent. As many as fifteen verses, if we include both question and answer, were sung at the door before the horse's head, the leader, sergeant, merrymen, Punch and Judy – the whole motley party – were granted access. Then, before the *Mari Lwyd* actually entered, a further song of seven verses was sung by the party outside. At the end of the celebration and junketing in the house after the *Mari Lwyd* and her attendants had performed their tricks and partaken of the hospitality, a final verse of thanks and of well-wishing was sung before the party finally left.[6] The most elaborate example of all, however, among Welsh calendar customs of this embellishment, comes from another part of Wales, Caernarfonshire, and relates to Candlemas wassailing. Here in the eighteenth century, the first carol – the 'carol at the door' – consisted of the usual ritual contest; this was followed by a second carol – the 'chair carol' – while the party which had now entered the house filed in twos around a chair, in which was seated a young girl representing the Virgin Mary. This might even be preceded by a preliminary carol before the small procession began. One example of a carol (or, rather, a series or carols) belonging to the second half of the eighteenth century, was sung consecutively to five different ballad tunes, each of which marked a stage in the ritual in the house. As in the *Mari Lwyd* custom in the opposite corner of Wales, here again, in Caernarfonshire, a carol of thanks was sung at the end of the feasting — 'a wassail carol on departing'. Indeed, one is left with the impression of an orchestrated sequence of secular carols, which prolonged the musical and poetical celebration of the occasion far beyond the original ritual of entry. A native folk tradition of contest in verse, which was a central part of the hearth entertainment itself, seems to be linked with the riddle tradition and the performing of feats, and applied to the gaining of access on a ritual occasion. Some of the secular carols recorded by Rhisiart Morris in Anglesey in the early eighteenth century belong to this latter tradition, notably the well-known folk song 'Counting the goats', and similar tongue-twisting verses.

One final point which I wish to raise is the faint echo of some kind of battle between the sexes, which is descernible in some of these ritual contests. It was the menfolk, invariably, who formed the party outside the door in every example I have come across. Women simply did not wander the countryside. Many of the carols sung at the door refer not only to the food and drink and warmth which the singers looked forward to, but also to the presence of young maidens inside, who would provide entertaining company. Professor R. L. Greene discusses the use of Holly and Ivy as male and female symbols in the old English carols.[8] *Holin*, or ivy, in fact, occurs as a greeting in Welsh carols sung at the door: *Olin olin weithiau. Agor ddrws yn llydan, ni ddown i fewn i fynu yn llawen fel gollwng ŵyn o'r gorlan*. Another Welsh carol refers to the contest between Holly and Ivy to be sung at Christmas time. Indeed, there seems to be an early and probably widespread symbolical contest between the sexes, which needs to be explored and explained in the relationship between ritual entry to the house in the form which I have briefly discussed here. As I stated at the outset, the practice to which I have referred probably has a wider significance than is generally realised, and the instances I have cited are probably best viewed as Welsh examples of a more widely recurring phenomenon which needs to be further examined, linked with the winter season and with weddings, and perhaps accentuated because of the strength of the dispersed and dominant hearth tradition.

Notes

1. A. D. Rees, *Life in a Welsh Countryside; a social study of Llanfihangel-yng-Ngwynfa* (Cardiff, 1950), 100.

2. E. Wiliam, 'To Keep the Devil at Bay', *Country Quest* (1975), 34-6.

3. Alwyn Rees and Brinley Rees, *Celtic Heritage* (London, 1961), Ch.3.

4. D. Trumor Thomas, *Hen Gymeriadau Plwyf y Bettws* (1894), 8.

5. Peter Roberts, *Cambrian Popular Antiquities* (London, 1815), 163-4.

6. Trefor M. Owen, *Welsh Folk Customs* (Cardiff, 1959), 49-57.

7. *idem*, 'The Celebration of Candlemas in Wales', *Folklore*, LXXXIV (1973), 238-51.

8. R. L. Greene, *The Early English Carols* (London, 1935).

Circumambulation and Medieval English Literature

MARTIN PUHVEL   McGill University

CIRCUMAMBULATION — that rather forbidding-sounding latinistic term — refers among folklorists to ritual circling — on foot or sometimes on horseback — of objects or people, not infrequently objects that have been people, for example dead bodies in their final repositories, or lying-in-state. The intent behind the practice varies greatly; at times it is a question of honouring, propitiation, appeasement, or consecration, while at other times it is prophylactic, self-protective in one way or another — often an attempt to check or neutralise some hostile influence — or, again, the intent may be actively malevolent, a matter of cursing or laying a harmful spell.

It is not possible here to enter into detailed theorisation about the basic ideas underlying this widespread and intriguing ritual; suffice it to say that authorities on folklore by and large agree that a prime moving force — and many think the main one — is a reflection of the movement of the sun, the basic cosmic moving light of the universe — in popular conception, of course. Thus it seems to be a question of an invocation, through the workings of sympathetic magic, of cosmic power favourable, or again unfavourable, to man, or certain men.

This type of magic circling is manifested in a number of English and Scottish ballads and tales, which, though recorded in the Middle Ages, are, according to ballad authorities, of ancient origin and doubtless point to time-honoured manifestations of the tradition of circumambulation reflected in them. Thus, for example, in 'The Broomfield Hill', according to Sir Walter Scott's ballad of undoubted antiquity, the heroine, in most of the numerous variants, walks a number of times, mostly three or again nine — another magic number — around her sleeping lover, or would-be lover. This is to prolong and deepen his slumber

and thus to preserve her chastity, something she has vowed or wagered she will do. Somewhat diluted, perhaps, as a magic practice but still reflective of the circling ritual is the compassing with holy water of the area about Miles Cross — possibly a crossroad — by Lady Margaret in the old Border ballad *Tam Lin*, generally associated with Thomas the Rymer, in order to recover her love from the power of the fairies. And in the story of Childe Rowland recorded by Robert Jamieson, the one possibly referred to in *King Lear* — a reference that inspired Browning's great poem — the hero circles the fairy hill in which his sister is held captive three times *widdershins*, or contrary to the movement of the sun; upon the completion of each circuit he cries, 'Open door! Open door!'

The manifestation here of circumambulation and the magic circle so closely and clearly associated with it is quite obvious and these examples may suffice. I want instead to deal in more detail with what appear to be reflections of the circumambulation tradition in two of the greatest works of medieval English literature — *Beowulf* and *Sir Gawain and the Green Knight*.

In the great Anglo-Saxon epic it is told that after Beowulf's cremated body has been interred in its splendidly prepared and equipped barrow, a chosen group of retainers ride around it, uttering a noble eulogy:

Then the brave in battle rode around the mound, children of nobles, twelve in all, would bewail their sorrow and mourn their king, recite dirges and speak of the man. They praised his great deeds and his acts of courage, judged well of his prowess. So it is fitting that man honour his liege lord with

344

words, love him in heart when he must be led forth from his body. Thus the people of the Geats, his hearth-companions, lamented the death of their lord. They said that he was of world-kings the mildest of men and the gentlest, kindest to his people, and most eager for fame.

Funeral or post-funeral eulogies are too common in ritual and tradition of all periods to require notice or comment as a folkloric practice, unless it be that speaking only well of the dead has its roots in a desire to propitiate the potentially dangerous ghost and avoid offending it. Yet circling of the grave in conjunction with eulogising is far more startling. Indeed the sole possible literary parallel, and not a very close one, is found in the 49th chapter of Jordanes, where it is stated that after the great Hunnish king Attila's body has been placed in a silken tent, 'the best horsemen of the entire tribe of the Huns rode around in circles, after the manner of circus games, in the place to which he had been brought and told of his deeds in a funeral dirge in the following manner' — whereupon follows a summary of his royal and heroic career. On the basis of this critics, notably Friedrich Klaeber,* have perceived here a parallel to the circumambulatory eulogy of Beowulf. Klaeber wonders whether it is here a question of indebtedness of *Beowulf* to Jordanes, to surviving tradition concerning Attila's funeral, or to funeral customs familiar to the poet, moulded, perhaps, by his own imagination. I prefer the last possibility. It seems likely to be a case of funeral horse races, a common fixture in ancient funeral games — combined with the usual funeral eulogy — or even of the two practices unsynchronised and un-combined. Klaeber himself admits that the account allows of interpreting the eulogy as being detached from the whirling of the doubtless rather breath-less riders; as the best riders of the nation were picked, it must have been a question of a highly athletic performance, hardly conducive to con-current singing. Nor, again, is it altogether certain that the horsemen circle the pavilion; they may simply ride around in circles in a 'circus-like' performance — thus it may here not even be a

matter of circumambulation.

In short, there seems to be no need to perceive any direct, or even indirect, influence of the funeral ceremonies of Attila in connection with the noble tribute paid to Beowulf by his mourning thanes — particularly so since the circling of the grave of the dead, not just his reposing body as in Jordanes, if indeed there is a circling there, is not uncommon in later Germanic tradition. Thus in East Frisia it used to be the custom for the mourners at the end of all other ceremonies at the grave to circle it once. The same custom was prevalent in Mark Brandenburg; after this final rite of circling everybody would go to the church, presumably for a final prayer. In Altmark the filled-in grave would be circled thrice.

Circling the corpse prior to interment has also been a not uncommon practice. Its best-known reflections come from the great classical epics. In *Iliad* XXIII the body of Patroclus is circled thrice in slow procession by the chariots, while Achilles himself leads the lamentation — not improbably involving tribute to the dead. In *Æneid* XI the burning pyre of Pallas is ridden around by the mourning warriors: 'Thrice, girt in resplendant arms, they ran their course round the burning piles; thrice circled the sad funeral-flame on their steeds, and cried from wailing lips.' And in the *Thebais* of Statius the Greek princes similarly thrice circle the funeral pile of Archimeros.

Circling the corpse prior to deposition was also practiced in modern times in Europe. Thus the Prussians would walk three times, wailing and lamenting, around the hearse on its arrival at the burial site. In Saxony, again, the relatives would circle the body lying-in-state three times, each time touching its great toe; this would help prevent the dead from returning.

Circling the corpse or its burial site may be intended to weave an imaginary magic or sacred circle — akin perhaps to the magic circle of con-jurers — around it, maybe in order to keep demons away and, at times at least, also to keep the dead from haunting or otherwise disturbing the living; thus it might serve as a two-way barrier against evil influences. Noteworthy in this connection is a custom formerly practiced among the Romanians

* Friedrich Klaeber, 'Attila's and Beowulf's Funeral', *Publications of the Modern Language Association*, XLII (1927).

in the Empire; after burial a relative of the deceased, or an old woman hired for the purpose, would for six weeks daily circle the grave thrice while fumigating it.

While the rite of circumambulation in *Beowulf* thus appears unmistakable, its reflection in *Sir Gawain and the Green Knight* is considerably less manifest. Let us look at the relevant element within its context and in the light of what follows. Sir Gawain arrives, as directed, at the so-called Green Chapel, dismounts and ties his horse:

> Then he makes his way to the mound and
>   walks around it,
> Pondering what it might be.
> It had a hole at the ends and on either side,
> And was all overgrown with grass in tufts,
> And was all hollow inside, nothing but an
>   old cavern,
> Or the crevice of an old crag, he could not
>   properly determine. . .
>
> 'Now certainly the place is deserted,' said
>   Gawain;
> 'This is a hideous chapel, over-grown with
>   herbs;
> It well befits the man in green
> To practice here his devotions in the Devil's
>   fashion.
> Now I feel in my five wits that it is the Devil
>   himself
> Who has made with me this appointment, to
>   destroy me here!
> This is a chapel of mischance — may destruction befall it!
> It is the most accursed church I have ever
>   come upon.'

Gawain's procedure on his arrival at the Green Chapel seems characterised by a deliberate, methodical approach reflective of prudent caution as well as firm courage. Not for him the flamboyant tactics employed by his adversary the Green Knight on entering Arthur's hall — on the contrary, Gawain dismounts and ties his steed before approaching the mysterious mound. This accords of course with his wonted courtesy but may also reflect proper religious respect for what is after all styled a chapel — and Gawain is yet to investigate its nature. Even if he is already dubious of its religious connotations, however, it would still be a matter of wisdom to approach it with a circumspection due to all that has an aura of the supernatural, be it a place of worship or ritual observance, a fairy mound, or a 'chapel perilous', a place of adventure and trial common in medieval romance.

Such circumspection at times involves specific rituals or ceremonies intended as safeguards against potentially malignant preternatural influences. In the light of such traditional precautions it may be asked whether Gawain's walking around the mound may not harbour a deeper significance beyond the apparent one of observing it while pondering what it might be. Could it have any connection with the ritual of circumambulation in any of its manifestations?

While, as we have seen, the practice of circumambulation is at times intended to honour or propitiate, it is not infrequently used as a protective measure, serving as a rite to ward off malignant influences, for example as already seen, to protect from haunting. I will give some more instances. In Ireland the old, originally pagan, ritual of *desiul*, i.e., sunwise circumambulation, was practiced around holy wells, churches and rude stone monuments, apparently to derive for the circlers the benefit of whatever sanctity these objects were thought to possess. In an account of a visit to the Western Islands of Scotland at the end of the seventeenth century, Martin mentions the practice of religious processions moving sunwise round cairns and stones raised for objectives unknown even to tradition.

In Ireland, again, it was customary right up to this century to walk sunwise round the graveyard with the coffin, at least once, sometimes thrice. Here it seems to be a question of an attempt to benefit those moved and/or moving, that is the dead and the bearers, perhaps through the sanctity of the consecrated place, or by propitiating the dead buried within the circle. It may be intended to gain rest for the dead and thus freedom from haunting for the living. Similarly, in Ireland and on the Isle of Man, wedding processions would circle the church before entering it.

The practice of *desiul* by a host to achieve victory was condemned by St Columba in connection with a battle near Sligo in 561; the hostile army is referred to by the saint in anathematising terms as 'the host which has taken judgment of us, a host that marches round a cairn.' Yet, ironically, St Findchua, the war-like patron saint of Brigoun, is said to have instructed a defensive party to perform *desiul* around a force of British pirates, prior to attacking and annihilating them.

While examples could easily be multiplied, it is already obvious that the practice of *desiul* was one of great prevalence and versatility in Celtic lands formerly and was thought to possess great virtue and efficacy in various ways. A relic, if vague and indefinite, of it in *Sir Gawain* hence looms as a manifest possibility, not least in view of the Celtic affinities and associations widely attributed to it. As we have seen, the rite was often practiced around objects of dubious or obscure sanctity, such as cairns and rocks, a category to which the so-called chapel in our poem could easily be seen as belonging. And it was at times engaged in to overcome or foil an adversary, something Gawain badly needs. Then, again, if the allegation that the forbidding mound is a chapel of sorts is to be taken seriously, and Gawain at least initially seems to do so, the practice of circling churches might be relevant.

The issue is, however, complicated by the fact that we are not told in which direction the hero walks around the mound; hence it is not clear that his circumambulation resembles a *desiul*. It may, on the contrary, be imagined to reflect a *tuapholl*, a circular movement 'widdershins', i.e., 'contrary-wise' — counter to the direction of the sun, a manoeuvre that in Irish tradition generally involved an intent to cause ill luck, constituting in affect part of the ceremony of laying a curse. This was accomplished by moving counter-clockwise around some object of magic efficacy while utter-ing a malefic incantation, spell, or charm. Such a practice is also reflected in the Icelandic *Grettis-saga*, where a witch cuts runes on a tree-stump and mutters a spell over them. 'After that she walked backwards against the sun round it and spoke many potent words.' Subsequently the stump drifts, apparently magically, to Grettir's island and when the outlaw tries to use it for firewood, his axe glances off it and inflicts a fatal wound.

It is interesting to note here that Gawain does utter strong imprecatory words during or just after his walk round the Green Chapel ('This is a chapel of mischance — may destruction befall it! It is the most accursed church I have ever come upon.'), and this in the generally laconic hero's longest soliloquy. Could this constitute a relic of a ceremony like the *tuapholl*, intended to counteract and foil diabolic magic in the manner of curses and spells which act as antidotes or countercharms — in this case to the evil connected with the unholy so-called chapel.

Or is it indeed impossible that the ideas of both types of circling may be reflected, performed consecutively, just for greater efficacy. Such is indeed the case in an ancient Indian funeral-rite. Clearly, whatever specific motif or motifs may be of significance in our poem, we may well have to be content with speculation; the requisite evidence does not exist and we may, of course, be dealing simply with *disjecta membra* of more or less distant source elements. Yet the hints that we can glimpse, in Gawain's *modus operandi* on reaching the environs of the Green Chapel, a relic or echo of the ritual of circumambulation in some form or other, seem to me most striking and intriguing.

Pattern Recognition, Data Reduction, Catchwords and Semantic Problems

ANNA BIRGITTA ROOTH   University of Uppsala

IN a paper entitled 'On the Difficulty of Transcribing Synchronic Perception into Chronological Verbalization' I commented on problems connected with the verbalisation of materials and situations that are not easily verbalised. Here I would like to draw attention to some problems concerning the verbalisation of ideas or notions in narratives. In this case the material is suited for narration — in fact its whole *raison d'être* is to be told as narratives.

It is not a problem that concerns good or bad, or active and passive, tradition-bearers or story-tellers only. It also involves human thinking and cognition, and for the scholar the problem of arranging data in a taxonomic way. While we are waiting for physiologists, especially brain physiologists, to give us the ultimate solutions, I would like to draw attention to some problems. The first is the pattern recognition of the human mind, and the second is the data reduction that this mind can undertake.

The terms are from computer language. As there are some similarities between a computer and the human brain, I will point out some similar ways of operating. It was after my experience of field-work in Alaska and my way of presenting a couple of story-types that I had to ask myself — why am I doing it in this way? After considering it, I reached the conclusion that my mind must have worked according to the processes or principles that are so obvious in computering.

It seems that the two processes of pattern recognition and data reduction are what scholars work with consciously or subconsciously.

It was no solution to me that I had worked with some sort of 'historical-geographical' method. We always have to consider time and space — the problem was how scholars operate in analysing the narrative. What ideas, thoughts, and notions in the story do we scholars extract and express verbally as catchwords for later references, mapping etc?

Is it the concept of the whole story — the type in itself — or is it just parts of the story, smaller or larger parts or entities in the story? Whatever it is, we then face a semantic problem. How much of the story and what parts of it are we thinking of? How do we verbally formulate the catchwords for the parts that include ideas and notions in the story? The answers to these questions are important, because the recognition of likeness or similarity depends on these formulations or catchwords, for example the basis for the pattern recognition which in turn is fundamental in the discussion of genetic relationship or polygenetic origin.

The latter problem can also be phrased in another way: pattern recognition may differ with different people according to their knowledge, and this in turn may explain why some scholars see a pattern where others do not, and vice versa.

Verbal formulation of the catchwords, to denote traits or motifs or whatever we want to call the small entities in the story, involves a semantic problem, namely that of describing the idea or part of development of events in the narrative. How big is that part? Is it a catchword for the whole story, like a title that can be given to a special narrative like 'Cinderella', 'The Dragon-slayer', 'Snow White' or, for example the two stories that I called 'Wolverine's Trap' and 'Giants' Wrestling', where two important traits were used in the title for my own orientation.

Or do the catchwords cover smaller parts *within* the story, like 'main motifs' or 'detail motifs', motif complexes, episodes, or parts? How big or how small are the entities that the catchwords are supposed to cover? This is very important for the further discussion of similarities or dissimilarities in the stories, so that we do not compare entities of a different order of magnitude.

As I will show, we can play verbally with ideas and notions in the story and describe them in many different ways. Hence it is important to formulate catchwords that are not too wide nor too narrow.

The possibility of verbally diminishing or magnifying the ideas or parts of the development of events in the stories probably helps to confuse the discussion. You may not know from the beginning whether you are studying a motif – an episode, or a type of story, or whatever that special entity should be called. It is probably more convenient to regard the different traits and small entities that stand out through our pattern recognition as motifs and adjust the terms later, if necessary. To me these terms are operational, and they are not absolute in themselves. I use the same terminology as in the Cinderella Cycle, and the terms in themselves are uninteresting since they are just instruments for my research and analysis of the tale.

If, however, we want to analyse the scholar's way of working, how his or her mind operates, we should not study the tale itself but the scholar's relation to his material. Then we work with another dimension, namely the scholar's ability to recognise patterns and his way of formulating catchwords for different striking entities in the story. Whether we call them motifs or motif complexes, episodes, parts, or scenes, is then of secondary importance. Then we are interested in why the scholar's brain emphasised some of the traits, while reducing others that could also have been used.

The interaction between pattern recognition and data reduction is of paramount interest, but this is a problem that will probably be solved only with the help of brain physiologists. We will have to use inadequate terms that are perhaps hermeneutic to this way of operating, and we may be using them both consciously and subconsciously. This means that when we do research, we get familiar with material that the brain stores and sorts.

Which entities does the brain choose as outstanding, characteristic or important to the story? How big are they, and how clear are these entities or segments in the scholar's mind?

As I worked with the Cinderella tales once, I will show how I used the term 'main motif' in that research. I finally singled out 9 main motifs, but mapped only 6, since I found them sufficient for my purpose. This data reduction was made to save time and work.

What I called the *main motif* (for which I formulated the catchwords or key-words below as expressions for the skeleton or structure of the story) are necessary for the whole narrative. However, they are not stressed in the story itself. It is the scholar who extracts the underlying idea in the story and gives it verbal expression. Two examples of main motifs will be presented here: 1. in the Cinderella story, 2. in the Wolverine's Trap.

Example 1. Main motifs in the Cinderella story.

If the Cinderella story was told with the catchwords I used for the 9 main motifs,[1] it would run:

9 main motifs

1 = orphan (stepdaughter)
2 = helpful animal
3 = helpful animal is slain and buried
4 = fine dresses
5 = sorting grain etc.
6 = visiting a feast (or a church)
7 = dropped shoe
8 = shoe test
9 = wedding

Of these, I only mapped 6 main motifs.[2] I could leave out the feast or church visit, since that was the reason for her being dressed in a fine dress and shoes, i.e. motif 4. Furthermore the shoe test (no. 8) and the wedding (no. 9) could be left out since they were dependent on motif no. 7, i.e. the dropped shoe.

6 main motifs

1 = orphan (stepdaughter)
2 = has a helpful animal
3 = helpful animal is slain
4 = fine dresses
5 = sorting grain
6 = dropped shoe

Obviously I used 'data reduction' here for practical and financial reasons. Both lists give a synopsis of the Cinderella story, but it certainly would not be worth while telling in this way, and it is not the way we think of the Cinderella story.

Now to turn to the Wolverine's trap. For my analysis I had made a synopsis of the story in parts or main motifs. I preferred the neutral term parts, as I wanted to avoid a debate on terms like motif, motif complex, episode, type. In the synopsis I structured one story in five parts.

Synopsis 1

Part I   Hero lets himself get caught in trap or grave
Part II   Hero is carried to home of ogre (or wolverine)
Part III Hero is to be butchered
Part IV   Hero slays ogre and family – except one member or
Part V   Hero escapes, ogre pursues him (= Tale Type 313), drinks the river or the lake and bursts, causing origin of fog.

Later, pondering upon why I had done it in this way and if I could have done it differently, I realised that I could have structured the story in three, and even two parts, resulting in the following two synopses:

Synopsis 2

1   Hero is caught and carried to home of wolverine (or ogre)
2   When hero is to be butchered, he slays wolverine
3a One wolverine cub escapes = Aetion: that is why there are still wolverines in Alaska or
3b Magic flight (Tale Type 313) + Origin of fog.

Synopsis 3

1   Hero fights ogre
2   Aetion results

The third type of synopsis is too simplified for pattern recognition of type or episode, or motif complex or motif. It is also too simplified as a structure; it is of no significance for a scholarly approach. Later I asked myself if I could have structured the story in more parts than three and five. It turned out that I could have structured it in e.g. 8, 12, or perhaps even 17 parts. Thus, it is possible to magnify and diminish different entities or segments in the narrative to suit our mental decision.[3]

It is standard scholarly procedure to find a comprehensive term (main motif = catchword) which covers all the detail motifs, pertaining to or clustering around the main motif. The process of finding entities and catchwords on them is related to that of making systems for catalogues for libraries or archives: to arrange details within groups that can in turn be found in a still larger and more extensive group — like a dendrogram with branches emanating from the trunk. It is not relevant to compare millimeters with miles since they are entities of different magnitudes. The same thing applies to the study of stories. There are traits or entities of different order of magnitude and hence importance, and for a valid analysis only traits or motifs of similar order or importance or magnitude may be compared.

That is why a detail or small entity may not be compared or identified with a superior entity by means of a verbal technique, which is very easily done. We must not compare incommensurable entities as Freund did. This is important for the discussion of structure, archetypes, genetic or polygenetic origin, because, just as in mathematics, it is necessary that a similar order of magnitude and the same quantitative entity be used and compared.

Consequently we cannot compress a whole story into a few striking catchwords, compare them with a detail motif picked from another type of story from another country and then compare them with a custom or a rite in a third country, and to prove the point, take a value from say, a proverb from a fourth country. Such a mixture of material from different genres is not based on pattern recognition but rather on flimsy associations. We must know the distribution of a story type and its motifs before we use it for any comparison.

Since man is a symbol-using animal, he has the ability to conceptualise and memorise verbal art, such as narratives, and retell them at his pleasure. 'Have you heard this one?' That phrase is a simple reference to the pattern recognition of the audience. The story-teller will remember the plot or the pattern of the story as he understood it or conceptualised it, and so will his audience. The scholar will be subject to the same procedure, but when he hears the same story in different villages he will most probably recognise it as a *type*. He

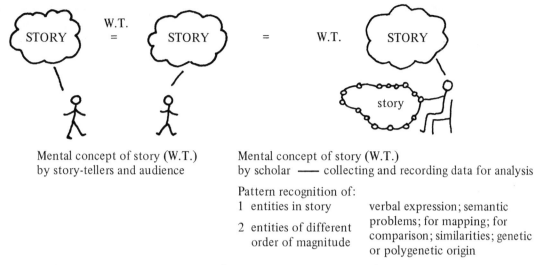

Mental concept of story (W.T.)
by story-tellers and audience

Mental concept of story (W.T.)
by scholar —— collecting and recording data for analysis

Pattern recognition of:

1 entities in story

2 entities of different
order of magnitude

verbal expression; semantic
problems; for mapping; for
comparison; similarities; genetic
or polygenetic origin

Figure 1. *Pattern recognition of the story Wolverine's Trap, here called W. T.*

has then experienced pattern recognition of a type. We recognise patterns daily, and that is one basis for a sort of symbol system. I have tried to exemplify pattern recognition in a simple drawing (see fig. 1).

Folklorists usually — as I did in the investigation of the Cinderella tales — rely upon the pattern recognition of scholars like A. Aarne, S. Thompson, J. Bolte, and K. Polivka. They have obviously done a good job, because we have been able to use their terms and the semantic form in which they expressed the types and the motifs they worked with.

We scholars mentally divide folk poetry like stories and tales into entities or characteristics, or group them into major or minor segments. We conceptualise and recognise the tale and the story as one entity containing all the details and characteristics. However, when we want to analyse the story and its contents, we divide it into segments or entities that we make the objects of our investigation. This is usually done chronologically, part by part or segment by segment, since the verbalised narrative always has to be presented chronologically. The synchronic, holistic mental notion of the story which is stored in the brain, once heard in a chronological order as well, cannot be synchronically expressed as it is bound to be chronologically verbalised when retold.[4] I have tried to illustrate this in the picture representing

our 'pattern recognition of the whole story' and also the way we have to handle it in entities of different size in our analysis.

The picture also shows how we use the entities, giving them a verbal expression (catchword) which involves a semantic problem, and how these catchwords are used both as traits ('motifs') for mapping and as objects for the morphological-analytical method in the process of comparison, which in turn leads to solutions concerning a genetic or polygenetic origin.

After doing field work in Alaska, I encountered the problem of presenting and investigating a story-type new to me but based upon my own pattern recognition. I had recorded several versions of the same story (which I called the Wolverine's Trap) in different Indian villages.

I will present the actual story in order to demonstrate the problems that are involved in the process of data recording or pattern recognition in the verbal formulation of the conceptualised structure and the catchwords used in the presentation. These problems are of consequence for scholars and their work, as well as for their often fierce debates.

To me it is of interest why we can sometimes agree upon or recognise the same 'pattern' and sometimes disagree as to pattern, likeness, relationship and genetic relationship. What one scholar cannot see as a 'pattern' is to another at least 'an echo of the same fable'.

Philip Freund writes about the Cree story of the virgin Kwaptahaw, who survived the Flood.[5] She was carried in the claws of a bird over the water and was dropped on a cliff where she gives birth to twins, a son and a daughter. As Freund puts it: 'An echo of the Greek fable of Leda and the Swan is heard here, but how can we account for the Greeks and the Crees sharing a story, or even a theme?'

I cannot accept his statement that the Greeks and the Crees share a story. The 'Skywoman' is quite different from Leda and appears in a different set of motifs and development of events. The woman who has fallen from the sky, or the sky-woman, is usually a motif that follows a long introduction about how the hole in the sky was created and how she fell through it. In the east Woodland area, it is usually two swans or geese or other birds that rescue her, carry her on their wings to the sea level and ask the sea animals to help create a world for her in this primeval water. The animals then dive in turn to the bottom of the sea and eventually succeed in bringing up some sand or soil and magically make it grow. The 'Sky-woman' is placed on this earth. She is pregnant by the sun or by some other means. In several myths she is pregnant when falling and then gives birth to for example a daughter or a pair of twins. The version that Freund refers to without giving the source, is of course related to this Earth-diver myth, which is often intermingled or mixed with the Flood-story. This latter type can be used as an introduction to explain why and how the earth was flooded.

When single motifs are taken out of their context — as Freund has done here — as well as out of their geographically traditional form, a 'similarity' with the Greek notion of Leda and the Swan is achieved, and this is exactly my point. We must not make this kind of analogy with a small unit by verbally diminishing a whole long epic story until it suits our purpose for comparison. If the Greek tradition had a long narrative story of the same structure and detail motifs, then we may discuss the possible genetic relationship.

If I say that I have found the same story, that of Wolverine's Trap, in Alaska, Northern Canada and Greenland, I am using my pattern recognition of a long narrative story to solve the question of a genetic relationship versus a polygenetic development. The story is not exactly the same, as we shall see, and instead there are some interesting differences. Part IV, for example, is geographically distributed in western North America and part V in eastern North America and Greenland (see maps 7 and 8 on pages 362-3). It was not until I did field-work in Alaska that I had to analyse, use my own ability to recognise patterns and give a special verbal form to the catchwords I decided to use.

When you have recorded a couple of stories containing more or less the same traits, as a folklorist you recognise it as a kind of type. In Alaska I recorded eight versions or data of the same type of story, which for my pattern recognition I identified as one type and called it 'The Giant's Wrestling', using the most important trait as a title for the story. The other type of story, of which I have recorded several versions, I called 'The Wolverine's Trap'. These two types were, to my knowledge, not described in Thompson's types of the North-American Indian Tales, so I had to describe them by the entities that struck me, in order to show what occurred over and over again in the stories, and in an attempt to find proper catchwords for these different motifs and traits or entities. Not until the scholarly analysis did I have to use terms like motif, motif complex, part or episode. I had to try to describe the pattern as I recognised it in the stories. In order to show the different problems connected with data recording, pattern recognition and the verbal expression of the pattern of different entities, I will give my examples here. I will use them in order to demonstrate how it is possible to use words like motifs and types in different ways according to your aim and scope. I will also point out how motifs and types might be used for the mental synopsis of the type of story or of the motifs of which the story consists. These operating terms can vary according to what the author wants to stress and is interested in, in his different investigations.

How we verbally formulate the catchwords for the motifs is also of importance for the mapping of those motifs. The reading and analysis of the maps is important for the following problem: what is the distribution of the different motifs? And this, in turn, is of importance for the problem of genetic relationship or polygenetic origin.

The verbal formulation of the catchwords for

the motifs turns out to be very important. What are we mapping? Is it a synopsis, a verbally expressed form of the head motifs or something else, such as the significant or discriminative motifs? Are the significant motifs based only on their numerical appearances, or are there other qualities that make entities discriminative? The problems of discrimination as well as numerical appearances are dealt with in another context.

I now want to draw attention to some difficulties that I encountered when I tried to structure or describe this story, which I recorded in Alaska several times. It was told by different story-tellers from different villages.

What happened was the following: I recognised the story – to me it was the same story or it was a type of story of which I had heard slightly different presentations or tellings, that is to say what I call data, versions or variants. How do I present a story-type that is not presented by Stith Thompson or Antti Aarne?

Like a computer, our brain can store and recognise patterns, and like a computer, it can reduce data considered of minor or no interest. But what is it that makes certain parts of a story interesting while others are not? To me it was evident for the first time that some of my students found it difficult to recognise what I recognised as a pattern, and what I considered unimportant could be important to them and vice versa. We were apparently differently programmed depending upon our different experience, and that made me ponder how different scholars work consciously or subconsciously.

The problem of using the right catchwords is the one pointed out above: they must be comprehensive enough for the purpose – they must not be too wide or too narrow.

If we look at motif G, i.e. the catchword 'Wolverine stumbles and breaks wind', and motif H, i.e. causing the hero to laugh, motif G was not recognised by my assistant. He corrected me and said – 'no, in this version, Wolverine did not "stumble" – he "jumped".' It is, however, of no importance which physical movement caused him to break wind.

In another situation, for example when a patient describes to the doctor how he happened to break his leg, it might be very important for the doctor to know if the patient jumped or stumbled. If he stumbled, this could be an indication of a disturbance in the patient's health or condition.

Because of these difficulties, I tried different verbal possibilities to formulate catchwords in order to show their importance for analyses and theoretical discussions concerning terms like motif and type.

After having demonstrated the possibilities of multiplying/diminishing and simplifying/magnifying the parts or segments in a story, I will present the structure of the story in motifs and parts. These terms are operational and relative and mean nothing but entities or segments of different magnitude. The catchwords used are presented here in a list, together with the letters A-X to denote the motifs or segments that I have used in my analysis. The list of motifs is based not only upon my own recorded material but also on related or similar data known in ethnological or anthropological literature.

Motifs and catchwords in the 5 parts of Wolverine's Trap

1. A   Hero lets himself get caught in a trap
   B   or in a grave
   B1 or in a cache
   C   He smears the trap with blood
   D   or puts his coat in the trap

2. E   Hero is carried to the home of the ogre or wolverine
   F   Hero is tickled (or licked – he pretends to be dead)
   F1 and keeps his breath
   G   Wolverine stumbles and breaks wind
   G1 – because hero holds on to branches –
   H   which makes the hero laugh

3. I   Hero is to be butchered
   K   Wolverine must look for a knife
   L   because hero wishes that it will disappear
   N   Children say the victim looked up
   P   Father complains the victim was too heavy

4. Q   The hero kills all wolverines except one
   Q1 often the youngest
   R   He tries to burn down the tree
   S   The youngest, or one of them, escapes
   S1 The youngest, holds out her hand against the arrows

T   The young wolverine defecates/urinates on
     the hero
U   Aetion: Still wolverine in Alaska etc.

5. V   Magic flight (Aa 313)
   V1   mountain
   V2   river
   V3   cheated to drink — bursts
   X   Origin of fog[6]

The motifs presented above, within the five parts into which I structured the story of Wolverine's Trap, are also of interest as to their spatial distribution as shown in the maps.

We have recognised the pattern of the story of Wolverine's Trap, and wherever we find two data of this type, we have to conclude that they are genetically related to each other. They imply a spatial tradition, that is to say there has been a transmission in space from one place to another.

How can this tradition within the distribution area be explained? Was one form prior to or older than the other? This is not always possible to tell. We can only establish where a subtype has developed, and as such it must be secondary to the type. It is only from the internal evidence based on a comparative morphological-analytical method that we can deduce which forms of the types, and possibly which forms of the motif or rather the motif complex, are the original ones and so prior to the others.

By means of this internal evidence we may explain the direction in which the story type has spread, for example from east to west or from west to east within the distribution area.

The spatial distribution of the type and its motif is also of great importance when we want to compare it with a study of choice, in other words the acceptance and refusal mechanisms at work when people choose or the mechanism behind studies of acceptance and innovation. Unfortunately most of these studies are based on mercantile products or social group patterns in the mobile culture of today. We see only part of this mechanism of human choice if we exclude all the immaterial, mental or verbal elements like rites, superstitions, beliefs and narratives, proverbs, formulas etc. I have commented on these problems in another study. I have concluded from the motifs on the maps that the type as such belongs to the arctic and subarctic area in Alaska, Canada and Greenland. I have not encountered it south of the Canadian border (see maps 1-8). Furthermore we can conclude that the Western tradition area, in this case Alaska and western Canada, must present an earlier form of the story than we find in eastern Canada and Greenland. These conclusions may be drawn from the existence of the many detail motifs in the western area (see maps 2, 4, 7).[7]

The analysis and method used in the research on the two arctic/subarctic types are thus based on three components:

1. Pattern recognition

2. Morphological-analytical method of the recognised type and its motifs and parts

3. The spatial distribution related to the material used.

When I started to collate other data of the Giants' Wrestling, a rather long and elaborate story for the Eskimos, I noticed one entity or segment in the material returning now and then. At that stage of my work I had recognised it as a discriminative feature or entity, but I had not yet given it a designation in mental nor verbal form.

When I started analysing this story-type, I assigned to it letter D, thus denoting that it belonged to the exaggeration motifs where bear and fox were related to the giant's size. The literary function of the entities or motifs that were to be recognised as exaggeration motifs or 'priamelen' was to point out the giant's size in a playful way. He was so big that:

A   he could put the man in his boot (*kamik*)
     or cover him with his boot-lace
B   he calls whales cod or catfish etc.
C   he calls moose hare/rabbit
D   he calls bear fox/lemming
D1   Giant's lice as big as lemmings or musk-
     rats etc.
E   Giant's finger huge (almost crushes the
     boy's head)
E1   Giant's helper will wake him up with a
     stone when bear comes
F   Giant takes whales in his hand
F1   Giant carries *kayaks* into his house
G   Moose hang from his belt like rabbits

When I analysed the exaggeration motifs or priamelen in this story, I thought of the feature

354

here marked E1 as a motif or entity among others, explicitly describing the size of the giant in relation to different animals and things as well as to the hero in the story. Later in the research process, in the analysis of the forms, meaning and functions of the exaggeration motifs in the story, it turned out that some of them seemed to belong to the Eskimo tradition of the story. What I had worked with vaguely as a motif or entity among other priamelen could, as I then found out, be structured as a narrative form of its own, often with 'motif A' as an introduction. In the first stage of this analytical process I could not assign a name to this entity, and at that stage it was of no interest to my work.

Later on, after sorting, checking and mapping, it turned out that what had been designated by the letter E1 was a product of data reduction that my mind had worked with at this stage of the analytical process. I asked myself if I could structure the notion behind E1 in a different way, and it then turned out that I could even structure it into 13 traits or entities from a-m (see scheme of the mental data reduction, stage III).

Data reduction of notion in stages I-III

I   Pattern recognition when collating material for comparison

II   Subconsciously compressing several traits (13: a-m) into one motif designated by the letter E1 in the first stages of the analysis

III Later analysis of E1:
     a. the giant tells the hero
     b. to rouse him
     c. by hitting him with a stone on the head
     d. when a bear approaches
     e. which is so big that it darkens
     f. a cleft, passage etc.
     g. the hero rouses the giant
     h. who laughs:
     i. the bear is so small that he calls it a fox
     j. the giant falls asleep again
     k. the passage is filled with darkness
     l. the giant is roused with a stone
     m. and now kills the huge bear.

What at earlier stages — I, II — I had worked with as a trait or entity among others, that at those stages could be called an exaggeration motif among others, could later properly be called a motif complex or a type of its own.

With this presentation I wanted to stress that it is futile to try and show that the terms are fixed and that you can give them a proper definition. The terms might well vary with the analytical process, as I have shown here. And because of the way the brain works in solving problems, we should not over emphasise the words, terms and their definitions. They are just temporary analytical tools that vary as the analysis progresses towards the final conclusions. In this process the terms are of minor importance, as there are, to me, other much more important questions to be solved from an ethnological/folkloristic point of view. Consequently I have tried to avoid words like motifs and types, so as not to be entangled in a fierce debate. To me so many problems are involved that the terms motif, motif complex, episode, and type are just the tip of the iceberg.

I have written this in order to elucidate the many problems that arise from taking field-notes[8] all the way to the last analytical processes and syntheses and the place of the scientific terms in the process. Many of my learned colleagues have not had the opportunity to do field-work in a 'primitif' society and have not encountered the practical obstacles and *modus operandi* that are an introductory and highly important part for the verbalising of texts. This then is stage III, at which most scholars begin. I suggest that it is very important for us all to know this 'pre-text stage' if we want to know how we work as scholars, depending on our different experiences, from the field (and the library) to the final product.

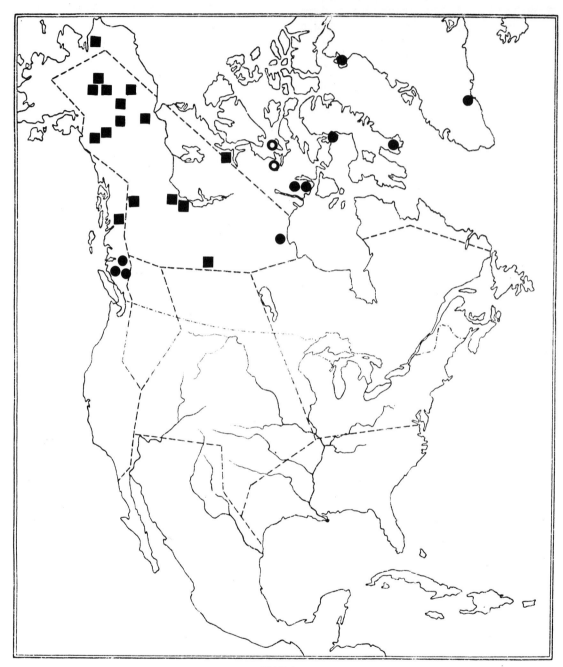

MAP 1

PART 1:1   ■ = A   = Hero (Beaver) lets himself get caught in a trap
             ● = B   = or in the grave
             ○ = B1 = or in a cache

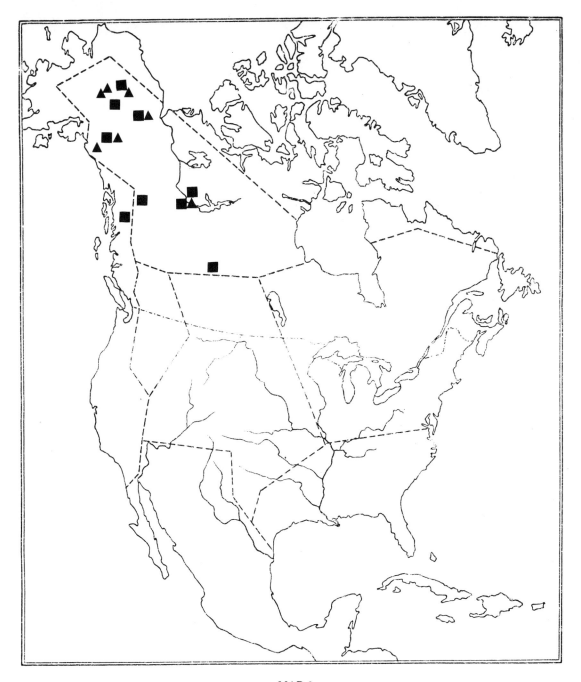

MAP 2

PART 1:2 ▲ = C = Hero smears the trap with blood
　　　　　■ = D = or puts his coat in the trap

357

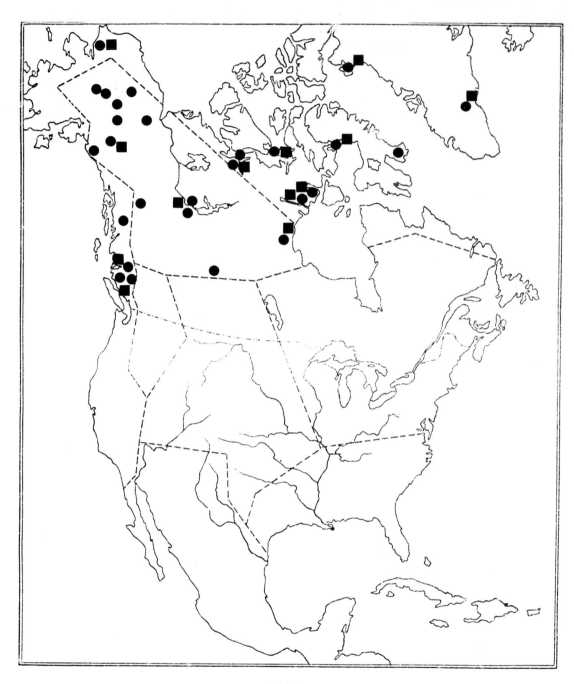

MAP 3

PART 2:1   ● = E   = Hero is carried to the home of the ogre or wolverine
　　　　　　■ = G1 = Hero holds on to branches

358

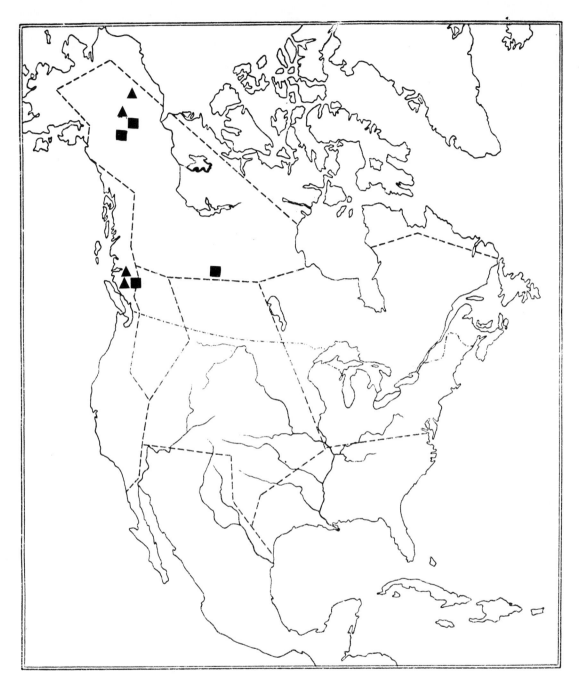

MAP 4

PART 2:2   ■ = G = Wolverine stumbles and breaks wind
▲ = H = and makes the hero laugh

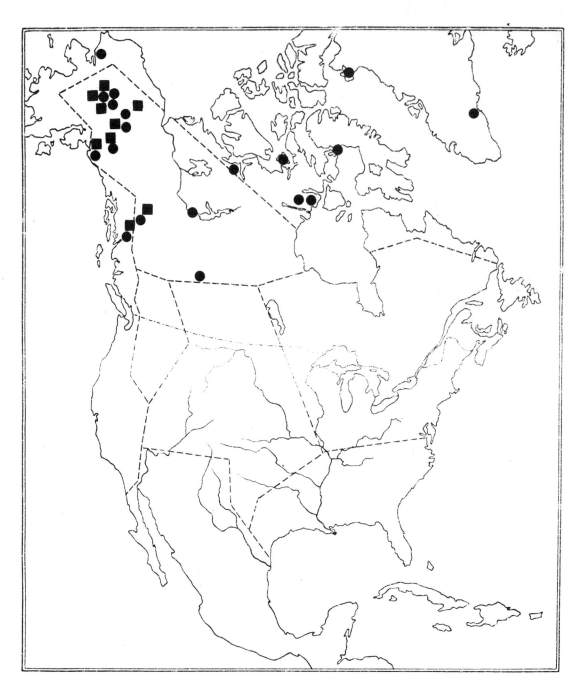

MAP 5

PART 3a   ● = I   = Hero is to be butchered
            ■ = K = Wolverine must look for knife (axe)

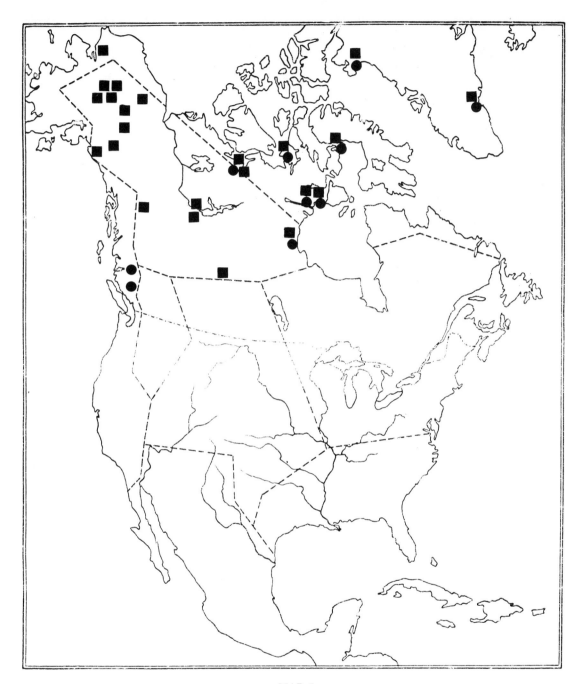

MAP 6

PART 3b   ■ = N = Children say the victim looked up
                ● = P = Father (wolverine) complains that the hero (victim) is too heavy

361

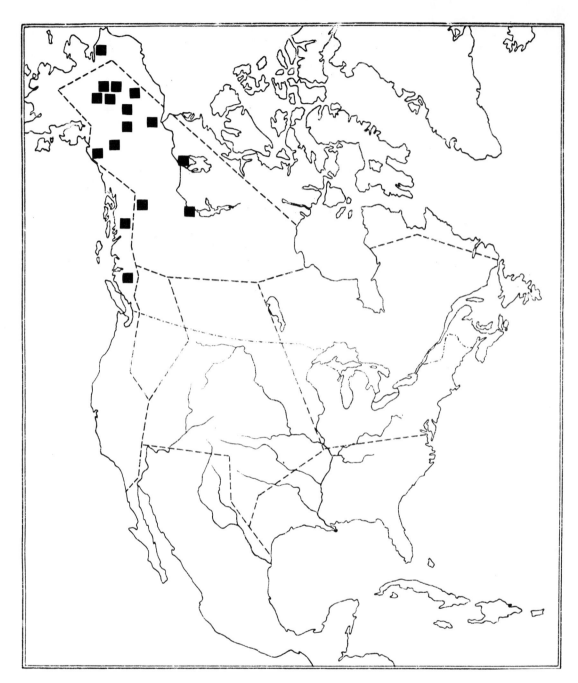

MAP 7

PART 4 ■ = Hero kills all wolverines (except one).
Aetion: Still Wolverines in Alaska etc.

362

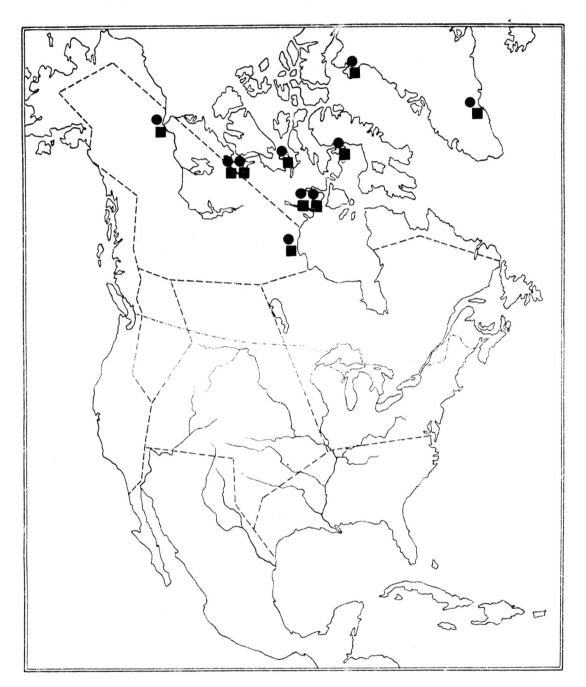

MAP 8

PART 5   ● = V3 = Cheated of drink
            ■ = X   = Origin of fog

Notes

1. A. B. Rooth, *The Cinderella Cycle* (Lund, 1951).

2. *ibid.*, 'Tradition Areas in Europe', *Lokalt och globalt*, II (1969); *ibid., ARV*, XII (1956).

3. A definition of terms like motif, motif complex, type, is premature at this stage.

4. A. B. Rooth, 'On the difficulty of transcribing synchronic perception into chronological verbalization' (1977).

5. Philip Freund, *Myths of Creation* (London, 1964), 105.

6. The 'motifs' presented here have been transferred to maps 1-8 to show their geographical distribution.

7. Seven detail motifs are covered by the symbol for 'part IV'.

8. A. B. Rooth, *The Alaska Expedition 1966. Myths, Customs and Beliefs among the Athabascan Indians and the Eskimos of Northern Alaska* (Lund, 1971), 365.

A Study in the Folk Symbolism of Kinship; The Tooth Image

CLAIRE RUSSELL

THE Reverend Robert Kirk of Balquhidder is known for his remarkable book about the fairies, *The Secret Common-Wealth*: it has recently been edited from new sources by Stewart Sanderson.[1] On March the 25th 1679, Robert Kirk had a striking dream. He wrote about it in a little manuscript notebook, which turned up at the sale of a private library in the twentieth century. 'I thought', he wrote, 'I felt a great tooth in my head break into two halves part by part and come off; on the morrow (my father being removed twenty years before) my mother took bed and on Monday thereafter about 2 a clock, gave up the ghost. Who knows if some courteous angel gives us a warning by our imaginations or senses, of extraordinary accidents.'[2]

The death of a relative is here symbolised by the falling-out of a tooth. This is a common symbol, listed, for instance, in Gertrude Jobes's *Dictionary of Mythology, Folklore and Symbols.*[3] My interest in this symbol started when reading about a recurrent veridical dream in a book called *The Mystery of Dreams,* by William Oliver Stevens.[4] Unlike many books with such titles, this one is full of interesting, well-authenticated and well-arranged facts. Stevens mentions three cases of 'the teeth dream, in which a dream about teeth was the harbinger of tidings of death in the family'.[5] The case he reports in full was that of a correspondent and friend of his, born and bred in Ireland, but living in a New York suburb. This was a Death Dream, and it was always essentially the same. The woman dreamed she went to the mirror of her dressing-table. A tooth was loose, and she took it out. She actually said it was decayed, but this, as we shall see, was a cover-up. Her teeth were excellent at the time. If there was no blood in the dream, a distant relative would die. A front tooth meant a young

person, a back tooth an older one. 'If a river of blood flowed from the tooth', a close relative would die, causing her much suffering. She 'never knew after the dream who was to die, as the dream always came well in advance of sickness'. But the dream always came true, according to the rules of the symbolism.

This woman also had a very explicit Death Dream giving, correctly, the sequence in which her near relatives would die. In this dream, they were all in a 'Long car', a kind of motor-coach, which visited a number of churchyards in succession. Each person got out at one of these stops, and walked into the churchyard. This happened in the order in which they subsequently died; the dreamer herself was in the last seat. In spite of this more explicit dream, the more symbolic tooth dreams continued, and once she had 'three in a row'. Her great grandmother too had veridical teeth dreams, so her mother told her when she was nineteen, and had a tooth dream which foretold the death of a younger sister. And this mother also requested her not to tell her dreams at the breakfast table. It seems possible that in the families of such dreamers there is often a curious mixed attitude to realistic awareness, permitting it, but not allowing some helpful direct form of discussion. This may help to account for the insight being repressed, and returning in disguise, in more symbolic form. I am not concerned in this paper with the question whether the insight itself was due to precognition in any paranormal sense, or simply to the dreamer being a superlative natural diagnostician. What interests me at present is the symbolism. In Stevens's words, 'Why should a loose tooth being removed mean impending death in a family?'

Naturally, I can only pick up the bits and pieces that I can actually refer back to reality. For instance, the woman talked of taking out a decayed tooth, and stressed that her teeth were in fact in perfect health at the time. She therefore associated the dream teeth with losing them in her old age, with deterioration. But the fact is that she had already undergone the experience of losing her baby teeth or milk teeth, and that these teeth do not decay, but come loose and fall out, and in making this wrong association, she repressed an actual experience.

Moreover, as far as I can remember, it is not normally painful to lose these teeth. Nor is the growing of the second set of teeth really painful. It may occasionally be uncomfortable, due to sore gums. But though not easy to remember, it is easily observable that the growing of the first set of teeth is painful, and a baby is much upset and cries when these teeth grow.

At this stage of the enquiry, there still remained the question: why teeth? And here I obtained a flash of illumination from a poem by the American writer Lila Karp. She has kindly permitted me to quote it.

EXTRACTIONS   February, 1965

Rooted in gum, resisting
separation from incisors
and other structures white and similar
This tooth against the poet with a hammer
wages a fight
to cling to territory deeply familiar.

Rooted in rock, adhering
by a cloudy part
to its universe of stone
This emerald fears
removal and transformation
into ornamental gem, alone.

Rooted in heart, barricaded
by the years
This smile, this laugh, this pleasure
the child so easily extracted
Now surfaces in restricted measure
Balancing joy against penalties re-enacted.

There are upper and lower rows of teeth, all rooted in a territory they have in common — members of the family, of a clan or a tribe, have certain things in common as against other people — all similar, differently positioned, arriving and departing at different times, and living there together for a considerable while. Teeth stand for kinsfolk.

I may quote here two passages from H. R. Ellis Davidson's second Presidential address to the Folklore Society in 1975.[6] First, 'folklore is an integral part of literature, not an intrusive element in it, something which may affect the language, structure and themes of outstanding works in both poetry and prose'. Second, 'as Derek Brewer has been demonstrating in his lectures, there is a marked parallel between the imagery of the folktale and romance and that of dreams'.

The imagery of dreams and literature is therefore often folk imagery, which children meet in fairy tales. By studying the dreams and the poem, I have thus far established that teeth can stand for kinsfolk, and it is not hard to find corroborative evidence. 'A tooth for a tooth' is a classic formula of reparation in clan vendetta. The emergence of men from sown dragon's teeth, as in the story of Cadmus, is listed by Stith Thompson as a folk motif.[7] A beautiful visual illustration is provided by a superb credence, made at Nuremberg in about 1500, figured by Kenneth Oakley in his monograph on the *Decorative and Symbolic Uses of Vertebrate Fossils.*[8] Credences were tree-like structures hung with fossil sharks' teeth. Sometimes they were hung over children's cots as a magical protection.[9] They were mainly in use, however, from the fifteenth to the eighteenth centuries, at mealtimes in palaces. The teeth were believed to change colour when dipped in poisoned drinks, or even neutralise the poison — a singular combination of credulity about the natural and wariness about the social environment. At the symbolic level, however, it would be a reminder that all Christians belong to one tree, and that thou shalt not kill. The beautiful Nuremberg credence is in the form of a Tree of Jesse, with Jesse at the root and the Madonna and Child at the top. In the usual Tree of Jesse, for instance the one in Dorchester Abbey, the branches are laden with intermediate ancestors. In the Nuremberg credence, the sharks' teeth hang in the place of these ancestors: once again, teeth stand for kinsfolk.

This established, I can return to the growth and loss of teeth in relation to the dream symbolism. Judging from observation of babies, there is no human being who has not found the growing of the first set of teeth painful, and there is no growing relationship among human beings that has not its painful aspects. How constructively or destructively this painful experience is handled eliminates or adds further stresses and strains. For instance, any adult who happens to suffer from sore gums will rub them; yet many a baby has been persecuted for sucking on his thumb to alleviate the unpleasant irritation.

In the meantime, it is to be noted that the woman in her dream dispassionately and objectively without pain took out her loose tooth, and yet the gum sometimes profusely bled, and then she knew she would find the loss of the relative painful. While the bleeding gave her this definite, to her unwelcome information, it is nonetheless an interesting inversion that the losing of the tooth, not the growing of it, was painful. To recapitulate, I consider the fact that she takes out a tooth, in the manner described, clearly refers to the loss of baby teeth. And yet she associates it with the loss of a tooth from the second set of teeth. This is relevant in that the first set is replaced, but the second set is not. Therefore she suffers an irreplaceable loss – but this too has to be qualified, for she only suffers an irreplaceable loss when the gum bleeds, and not when it does not.

This matter of unravelling symbolisms is a painstaking job. So far it has emerged that the experience with the first set of teeth is mixed up with that of the second set, a painless and replaceable loss with a painful and irreplaceable one. If that were all there is to it, however, there is every reason to repress the future possibility of losing the second set of teeth and all that is connected with that set, and none to repress the experience of losing milk teeth. And yet this woman plainly repressed her experience of losing these teeth. Why? And further, it is the growing, hardly ever the losing, of milk teeth that is painful. It surely seems that it is the painful aspects of the growing relationships in the family that are more repressed, than the loss of such relationships.

In tribal societies, when boys are initiated, and introduced abruptly to the necessity for forming a whole array of new relationships in society, it is a widespread practice to knock out one of their teeth, sometimes an upper incisor (common in Australia), sometimes a lower incisor (common in Sudan).[10] In Britain, in 1966, the journalist Anne Allen asked for, received and analysed letters (totalling 5,000) about honeymoon experiences,

clearly a critical occasion for the growth of a relationship. She was surprised to find that 'reader after reader recalled that – of all things – toothache turned honeymoon bliss into misery.'[11] Presumably a honeymoon is liable to touch off painful experiences in the growth of earlier relationships in the family.

But from the general I must return to the particular. There is, of course, even granting the detailed analogy, the overriding question: why are relationships transformed into a person's set of teeth? The answer seems to be that parents' attitudes and reactions to a child may be interchangeable, in some respects, with their attitudes and reactions to the child's teeth. This kind of transmission process helps to account for the persistence of folk symbolisms in which objects stand for human relationships.

I can show this by means of the case history of an intelligent woman who came to me for analysis, whose associations about actual experiences provide some clue to the interchangeability of her mother's attitude to her and to her tooth. I shall call her Renée. This particular episode took place when Renée was about seven. She was playing in a park, riding on the back of a little boy's tricycle. She fell off, and fell on her mouth. A milk tooth in the front thereupon got loose, hanging by a thread, and she bled profusely. Her mother, enormously agitated and berating the child, impressing on her the error of her ways and stressing that this was her fault, marched her to the dentist. She held the tooth in place with her finger, and one wonders how they walked. The dentist cleaned up the blood and told the mother to take Renée home, put her to bed, and wait for the tooth to come out. So Renée was taken home and put in the big parental double-bed and further admonished not to suck her thumb, which was a very bad habit anyway, but this time even worse, for she would be responsible if the tooth came out. The next morning the tooth was out.

Further horrors were in store, for in due course the new tooth, though fully grown, was ugly and discoloured, and Renée was given, as a special treat, it was stressed, a cap to hide this ugly tooth. The treat involved suffering some of the tooth being sawn off to fit the cap. That was not all, because somehow or other, by knocking it perhaps, the cap came off and yet another cap had to be fitted.

Finally, an added detail; naturally, before the cap was fitted, Renée tried to hide the tooth when talking and smiling.

A main and obvious point in this context is that Renée's mother was so anxious to hold the front tooth in position, that she admonished Renée, and told her it would be her fault if she lost it. Since the tooth was a milk tooth, it was going to be lost anyway sooner or later. Desperate attitudes that members of the family should stay around the same territory, well, ill, dead or alive, cared-for and uncared-for, are all summarily pin-pointed on to this one front tooth — a milk tooth that would come out sooner or later. But, according to Renée's mother, its leaving had something to do with Renée's wickedness, just as, later in life when Renée was grown up, her living a long way from home was taken by her mother to indicate that there was something seriously the matter with her. There is, of course, nothing the matter with a milk tooth leaving the mouth; the contrary would be the case, namely, if it persisted in staying there, and had to be forcibly removed. If this, additionally, were painful, it would add to the complication. Just so, there really is something the matter with children in the modern world who, on growing up, cannot leave their parents and set up their own home.

This mother's relationship with members of her family was clearly interchangeable with her relationship with teeth. Why should her attitude to people be converted into an attitude to teeth? Teeth are objects. Can certain of a mother's attitudes more easily relate to objects than to live independent persons? It seems so. In that case Renée was in many respects not treated by her mother as a person, but as an object which the mother disposed of as she pleased. The object should be available, be around, fit into the household, be paid attention to or no attention to, as and when the mother felt like it. In the course of her analysis, Renée was much upset to recall childhood occasions when she came home and her mother was evidently absent. She did not know where her mother was; she was left to amuse herself as best she could in the halls and corridors of the vast apartment building in which her parents had a flat; and she had to ask the hall porter for the key, if she wished to get into the flat. Here, too, she had an accident, and there was much trouble in finding somebody to look after her. Her

mother eventually arrived and made a big scene, taking her to the hospital and at the hospital, again paying little attention to Renée's distress, while 'efficiently' attending to the inefficient hospital. On such occasions, Renée wondered whether she was there at all, whether she heard and saw right, for the shock of pain and the shock of being treated that way bring about this weird feeling. This too is expressed in something she wrote about losing her front tooth, a phrase that came to her mind when she caught sight of herself in a mirror as an adult with an expression that appeared the same as that she had when seven years old — 'my front tooth — it wasn't there at all.' This is equivalent to her feeling of not being there at all herself, and getting mixed up about whether it is the here and now or some other time in her life.

I might interpolate here, in relation to wider social behaviour outside the family, that the attitude of Renée's mother to poor and under-privileged classes was interchangeable with her attitude to Renée. She did not concern herself with the problem of poverty at all, but, if it was brought up, she ventured the opinion that the Government was well capable of looking after it. Equally, she did not concern herself with Renée, if she could help it, and Renée made friends at school whose mothers looked after her. If anything went wrong, however, Renée's mother became highly agitated, and blamed Renée or somebody else for what had happened. This reaction was at its most vociferous in connection with communism and sex, particularly if she could make associations to coloured people or lesbians, which she regarded as matters of about equal abnormality. This vociferousness of Renée's mother at something wrong came out fully in the accident to the front tooth, for which she blamed Renée. When the new tooth grew, it looked bad and discoloured, and that was Renée's fault too, just as later it was Renée's 'bad blood' that showed when she made friends with underprivileged people, visited them in the slums, and interested herself in left-wing activities at the university. Most significantly, the whole attitude was repeated when Renée was adult in connection with a miscarriage she had, and in this case her mother asserted it was Renée's husband's fault, for taking her on a long car journey to stay with her parents.

Now this brings us back to dream symbolism again. Before discussing the case of the teeth dreams, Stevens refers to a well-known case of a recurrent veridical dream of a different kind, reported by the dreamer, a Mrs Burton, of Longner Hall, Shrewsbury. She dreamed of a baby in a bath shortly before, usually less than twelve hours before, hearing of a death. It is therefore interesting that tooth and baby were linked in a none too roundabout way in the analysis of Renée. She talked of the tooth, damaged by hitting her gum, emerging ugly and blackened, and how her mother said it was her fault that this happened, and she talked next of pregnancy, of being careful during pregnancy in order not to damage the embryo, and finally of the miscarriage. This final link appears natural enough in the light of the previous material. Clearly it is important to treat the baby 'pregnant' with teeth gently, and the woman in childbirth considerately. In 1967, I watched a television programme about the medical use of hypnosis.[12] The programme began with a dentist and ended with a birth. These are, in fact, the two chief contexts in which hypnosis is used for medical purposes, in both cases to relieve pain and facilitate a calm, relaxed state. The painful emergence of teeth is readily connected with painful childbirth. Above all, the birth of a baby is an obvious example of the birth of a new relationship. The association of birth and death in the bath dream is, then, yet another case of confusion between loss and growth, between bereavement and the growing pains of a new relationship, stemming from painful experiences during the growth of relationships in childhood.

This final link, teeth and childbirth, is widespread in folklore. As my husband heard a few days ago from an Indian family-planning expert, Ghansyam Dass Rai Kakar, there is a widespread belief among Indian peasants that, if a man is sterilised, his teeth will fall out. Since men generally do lose their teeth if they live long enough, this is a difficult notion to overcome. Then again, the Victorians, so prudish about reproduction, were also oddly uneasy about teeth. False teeth, in particular, were never to be noticed or referred to in public. As a dentist complained in 1845, both those who wore false teeth and their acquaintances maintained 'the most profound mystery' on this subject. In 1880 a woman called on a doctor complaining of a pain in the throat, but could not bring herself to admit, what he luckily discovered himself, that she had swallowed her top set of teeth.[13]

I shall close this account of the tooth as a folk symbol of kinship with a piece of folklore from Cambridgeshire.[14] In that county, according to Enid Porter, a husband often took to his bed during his wife's pregnancy, a phenomenon known to anthropologists as the *couvade*. In the Cambridgeshire version, the husband's complaint was, 'most frequently, tooth-ache'. A story was recorded in 1936 of a young man who 'had a terrible time while his wife was carrying. He thought at first it was his teeth so he had them all out; but of course it wasn't and he might as well have kept them in. It lasted all through the nine months and then stopped as soon as the baby came. And you know, he would never have another child after that one'.

Notes

1. S. Sanderson, ed., *The Secret Common-Wealth and A Short Treatise of Charms and Spells, by Robert Kirk* (Ipswich and Cambridge, 1976).

2. Sanderson, 5; D. B. Smith, 'Mr Robert Kirk's Note-book', *The Scottish Historical Review,* XVIII (1921), 237-48; quotation from 239-40.

3. G. Jobes, *Dictionary of Mythology, Folklore and Symbols* (New York, 1961), 1587.

4. W. O. Stevens, *The Mystery of Dreams* (London, 1950).

5. Stevens, 29-31.

6. H. R. Ellis Davidson, 'Folklore and Literature', *Folklore,* LXXXVI (1975), 73-93; quotations from 91-92 and 75.

7. S. Thompson, *Motif-Index of Folk-Literature* (Helsinki, 1932-6), A 1265.

8. K. P. Oakley, *Decorative and Symbolic Uses of Vertebrate Fossils* (Oxford, 1975), 7, 19 and frontispiece.

9. V. Penrose, *The Bloody Countess,* tr. A. Trocchi (London, 1972), 72.

10. N. Miller, *The Child in Primitive Society* (London, 1928), Ch. 9.

11. A. Allen, 'Honeymoon Verdict', *Sunday Mirror,* (17 July 1966), 24; *idem, People on Honeymoon* (London, 1968), 20, 116.

12. 'Horizon', *BBC 2* (18 July 1967).

13. J. Woodforde, *The Strange Story of False Teeth* (London, 1971), 2-3.

14. E. Porter, *Cambridgeshire Customs and Folklore* (London, 1969), 13-14.

Plutarch as a Folklorist

W. M. S. RUSSELL   University of Reading

THE late Victorian scholar Frank Byron Jevons was a folklorist of some distinction; he was one of the eight experts chosen to review the second edition of *The Golden Bough* in *Folklore* in 1901.[1] In 1892, Jevons published a new edition of Philemon Holland's seventeenth-century translation of Plutarch's *Roman Questions*. 'On the whole,' writes Jevons at the opening of his Introduction, 'Plutarch's *Romane Questions* may fairly be said to be the earliest formal treatise written on the subject of folklore. The problems which Plutarch proposes for solution are mainly such as the modern science of folk-lore undertakes to solve; and though Plutarch was not the first to propound them, he was the first to make a collection and selection of them and give them a place of their own in literature.'[2] This view of the *Roman Questions* was endorsed in 1898 in that classic of folklore, *Tom Tit Tot,* by the stormy petrel of the Folklore Society, Edward Clodd.[3] In view of all this, I thought it worth while, as the Society celebrates its centenary, to spare a few thoughts for this pioneer, who died more than one and three-quarter millennia before the Society was founded; and I shall begin with some account of Plutarch's life and other works, as the background to his achievement in the field of folklore.

Plutarch was born, somewhere around A.D. 40, into a leading family of the town of Chaeronea, in northern Boeotia, not far from Delphi. In the Roman Empire, it was generally true to say that happy was the writer who had a dull biography. Plutarch, who wrote of so many eventful lives, had an agreeably uneventful one himself. On the whole, he seems to have kept well out of trouble.[4] He was still a young man when Nero paid his celebrated visit to Greece, in A.D. 66-7.[5] Apart from extracting large sums of money and priceless works of art

from some of them, Nero was on his best behaviour with the Greeks. Plutarch, who was luckily unaffected by these exactions, remembered with pleasure Nero's famous proclamation at Corinth, in November 66, when he solemnly gave the Greeks home rule and freedom from taxes. The Emperor did this to ensure good will for his sporting activities there the next year, when he convened all four national Greek games at the wrong time. He succeeded admirably in this, for he won every single event, including one race in which he fell out of his chariot and never reached the finishing line, and several for which he was not even entered. Luckily he was recalled to Rome by news of revolts before he could erase the good impression he had made; the taxes and provincial government were of course soon restored by the next secure Emperor, Vespasian.

The next bad Emperor, Domitian, was a home-loving tyrant, quite content to torture and murder people in or near the capital. However, there is circumstantial evidence that Plutarch had a narrow squeak in this reign, specifically in A.D. 93.[6] By that time, he had visited Rome more than once, as well as Asia Minor and Egypt, and made friends with a number of influential people.[7] In 93, Domitian killed one of Plutarch's friends and banished another, and expelled all philosophers from Italy. It is possible that Plutarch was in Rome at the time and had to get out fast. Still, he certainly survived. During the reigns of the unmurderous Emperors Nerva and Trajan he lived happily in Greece, enjoying a relaxed family life, visiting friends, working in local government, and turning out his huge output of literary works.[8] At the beginning of Hadrian's reign, another of Plutarch's Roman friends was executed, but this was probably without Hadrian's wish or knowledge – he was not in Rome at the time[9] — and, by the time this Emperor went berserk, Plutarch was safely out of the way, having died at the age of about 80 in around A.D. 120.[10] He enjoyed great fame in his lifetime, and, thanks to this and to his influential friends, he obtained in turn Roman citizenship, the status of a Roman knight, nominal consular rank, and finally the office, probably also nominal, of Imperial procurator of Greece.[11] But he himself perhaps valued most of all his appointment, probably held for decades, as one of the two permanent priests of Delphi.[12] His enormous influence on later generations, especially through his *Parallel Lives,* is a large story, which I shall only touch on incidentally in this paper.[13]

Plutarch took his Delphic priesthood very seriously, and was deeply concerned with religion and morals. With due allowance for all the great differences between pagan and Christian civilisation, I think you get the feel of him if you make a comparison with a gifted and unconventional nineteenth-century English clergyman, that extraordinary body of men that included talents as various as those of Robert Malthus, Charles Dodgson, and Sabine Baring-Gould. It is, of course, irresistible to look for a parallel to the author of the *Parallel Lives,* and I am impressed by the number of features he had in common with one particular Victorian parson, Charles Kingsley.[14]

Plutarch and Kinglsey have some obvious things in common, such as their interest in old myths, or the biographical approach to history evident in the *Parallel Lives* and in Kingsley's lectures as Professor of Modern History at Oxford. They were both superb narrative writers. Oddly enough, when they retold old myths, Kingsley was by far the better story-teller, as is clear when we compare Plutarch's dry and academic *Life of Theseus* with the rousing tale in *The Heroes.* But of course this comparison is unfair to Plutarch, who reserved his wonderful narrative skill for his factual biographies.

But they have far more in common than these traits. Kingsley was appointed tutor to the Prince of Wales; Plutarch was honoured by Emperors, and his nephew tutored the Emperor Marcus Aurelius.[15] To be a Priest at Delphi was perhaps the nearest thing in the Roman Empire to being a Canon of Westminster in Victorian England. Both were devoted family men, and both were active educationalists, and also wrote much about education.

Kingsley was a keen feminist, particularly active in promoting the acceptance of women as medical practitioners. Plutarch was most unusual among Greeks in treating his wife at least as a near-equal.[16] He wrote much about the abilities of women, and advocated higher education for them. Kingsley was extremely humane in his outlook as evidenced by his sermons and social novels, his active philanthropy, and his love of animals. Plutarch wrote about the rights of slaves,[17] and even animals — he was the first great advocate of animal welfare. Yet both men had odd outbursts of militarism and insensitivity. Kingsley was a real jingo nationalist at times, and vigorously defended the repressive measures of Governor Eyre of Jamaica. Plutarch wrote a whole treatise to prove that Athenian exploits in war were more glorious than Athenian achievements in literature;[18] and he recalls, without a flicker of disapproval,[19] actually watching the revolting show with which the Spartans entertained foreign tourists, in a theatre built for the purpose, by flogging their own children at the altar of Artemis, awarding a prize to the boy who endured the greatest number of strokes without flinching, crying out, or dying. Then there is another, more attractive, contradiction common to both. They were both models of Victorian propriety, but both had unconventional moments about this. Kingsley openly declared his enthusiasm for Rabelais, whose work greatly influenced *The Water-Babies* (for instance, the long comic catalogues). In one of Plutarch's dialogues, somebody priggishly complains of the statue of the courtesan and model Phryne, put up at Delphi by her lover, the great sculptor Praxiteles.[20] Another character promptly declares she has more right to be there than all the monuments put up to celebrate murders, wars and plunderings.

Finally, both Plutarch and Kingsley tried their best to combat superstition, and were fully abreast of the rational sciences of their times. Their attitude to superstition appears again and again in their works, but most notably in Plutarch's specific treatise on the subject and Kingsley's sermon on science and superstition at the Royal Institution in 1866. They were both particularly indignant at the idea of a literal hell after death.[21] Kingsley's great involvement in natural science, especially biology, and scientific education is a large subject I cannot discuss now; he was, among other things, one of the leading champions of Darwin and evolution. Plutarch's interest in natural science was equally deep and wide, ranging from astronomy to animal behaviour.

It must be admitted that dislike of superstition and an up-to-date appreciation of science were not quite the same things in the England of Darwin and in the Roman Empire in its middle period; Plutarch stands in fact at the turning-point when rational Greek science (which still included plenty of mistaken ideas) was beginning to give place to the demon-haunted world view of the Neoplatonists. Plutarch reflects this situation, and is full of beliefs considered wildly superstitious by Kingsley's day. Nevertheless, he does know a great deal of the scientific information available in his time, and much of his science is quite sound. His dialogue on the face on the moon is a case in point.[22] Here he discusses the markings visible on the moon, and concludes, quite rightly, that they are depressions in a solid, planet-like object. His conclusion is carefully argued, and was far from self-evident in the age before the telescope. The dialogue ends with an explicit myth, or imaginative excursion in the manner of Plato, on the moon as the destination of souls after death. This dialogue has had momentous influence in the history of both science and science fiction. Bernard de Fontenelle, the versatile poet who was Secretary of the Académie des Sciences and a foreign member of the Royal Society,[23] was certainly under Plutarch's influence when he wrote his charming conversation about the possibilities for life on other planets and satellites, published in 1686.[24] Earlier in the seventeenth century, the dialogue caught the fascinated attention of Johann Kepler, who had read it before he wrote his famous science-fiction story about the moon. Kepler obviously appreciated both the science and the fantasy in Plutarch's dialogue. Shortly before his death, he made a Latin translation of the work, with a commentary.[25]

The variety of subjects I have mentioned so far give only a first impression of Plutarch's great versatility. There is a catalogue of his works, compiled probably in the fourth century, with 227 titles.[26] Many of these are, unfortunately, lost; as the poet Dryden observed,[27] one cannot look upon this catalogue without the same emotions that a merchant might feel in perusing a bill of freight, after he has lost his vessel. But even the surviving works cover a wider field than I have yet indicated. If the ancient Greeks and Romans had had the choice of one author to represent ancient civilisation, in a time capsule or a monastic scriptorium, they could have chosen worse than Plutarch. He gives, of course, no clue to the glories of Latin literature; he read Latin only with difficulty, and only quotes two lines of Latin verse in his entire output.[28] But, apart from this gap, no other author tells us more about ancient civilisation. The surviving *Parallel Lives* give a pretty consecutive account of Greek and Roman history from legendary times to the Battle of Actium in 31 B.C. His *Lives of the Caesars* would have carried the story well into the first century A.D., but only two survive. The *Parallel Lives* were my own favourite childhood reading, and I can vouch for the extensive background of ancient history I possessed when I started my formal classical education. In addition, one can learn a great deal from Plutarch about the social and economic life, beliefs and customs, arts and crafts of the ancient Greeks and Romans; and a good general impression of ancient mathematics and science. On top of this, he quotes a considerable amount of Greek literature, including verse. He even goes outside Graeco-Roman civilisation, with a life of one of the Achaemenid Persian kings. Passionately interested in comparative religion, his book on *Isis and Osiris* is the most complete account surviving in any language of this crucially important myth of ancient Egypt.[29]

His most famous work is, of course, justly, the *Parallel Lives*. These biographies are full of the touches that bring history to life. We hear of the great artist Apelles, for instance, literally speechless at the sight of a wonderful painting by Protogenes, and finally recovering his voice to gasp out that it had not quite the beauties that lifted his own paintings out of this world.[30] Or there is the moving passage of the birds beginning their dawn chorus as Cato takes his last nap before committing suicide.[31] The best tribute to their literary quality is the fact that Shakespeare used long passages from North's translation of the *Lives* in his Roman plays with so little modification.[32] But the great importance of the *Lives,* and their relevance to a discussion of Plutarch as folklorist, lies in his use of the *comparative* method. Others before him had roughly compared Greek and Roman celebrities,[33] but nobody before him, and nobody after him until William Bolitho in the twentieth century, made detailed comparisons to bring out detailed parallels. It was obvious enough to compare Caesar with Alexander, or Cicero with Demosthenes. Plutarch's genius appears when he makes unexpected, but completely successful matches, like the *bon vivants* generals Cimon and Lucullus, or the champions of lost causes, Sertorius and Eumenes. We know he often chose one hero, Greek or Roman, and carefully looked around for a matching life.[34] Some of his comparative essays survive, and in them he shows a wonderful eye for differences, as well as similarities. Thus Demosthenes was exiled for embezzlement, Cicero for suppressing a dangerous conspiracy, but Demosthenes spent his exile working for his cause, while Cicero dithered about unhappily.[35] Thus Plutarch pin-points the difference between the corrupt and single-minded Greek, and the honest Italian who was always looking for a dramatic role, like an actor, and was quite at a loss when he was, so to speak, 'resting'.

Plutarch's use of comparison has been so little appreciated, even in modern times, that translations of the Greek and Roman lives are sometimes published *separately,* losing the whole point. For what Plutarch discovered was the extraordinarily repetitive automatism of human behaviour in politics, especially under stress. Political activities are so stereotyped and repetitious that individuals in different periods and societies can have almost identical careers, by a process of extremely detailed convergence, like two animal or plant species occupying closely similar ecological niches. 'It is no wonder', he observes,[36] ' as fortune moves hither and thither over unlimited time spans, that automatic behaviour often issues in identical incidents.' He applies this generalisation, with his tongue in his cheek, to the rather trivial observation that one-eyed men are often clever and tricky generals; he lists Philip II of Macedonia, Antigonus, Hannibal and Sertorius, and we might now add Nelson and Moshe Dayan. But the sentence, in a far more fundamental sense, is really the clue to his major discovery and the significance of the *Parallel Lives.*

Plutarch's antiquarian and folklore interests appear in many of his works, including some of the *Lives,* such as Theseus, Romulus and Numa.

But his main contribution to folklore, as Jevons and Clodd observed, was his *Roman Questions,* in which he lists 113 Roman customs or beliefs, and supplies alternative explanations for each. Certainly he includes some bizarre and really old-fashioned explanations, as Jevons notes in a charming passage about Philemon Holland's translation.[37] 'To say in modern English', writes Jevons, 'that "five is the odd number most connected with marriage," is to expose the Pythagorean doctrine of numbers to modern ridicule. But when Philemon says, "now among all odde numbers it seemeth that Cinque is most nuptial," even the irreverent modern cannot fail to feel that Cinque was an eminently respectable character, whose views were strictly honourable and a bright example to other odde numbers.' As H. J. Rose points out, in his translation and commentary of 1924, many of Plutarch's explanations are vitiated by the fact that ' "Roman mythology" is almost altogether Greek, at least in so far as it concerns the gods, and therefore quite worthless for establishing the facts of cult';[38] moreover, many of the explanations are, so to speak, folk folklore — explaining a custom as commemorating a historical event, an explanation so rarely true, or at least wholly true, in fact.[39]

However, I am not now concerned with the correctness or otherwise of Plutarch's explanations, or with the true explanations of the customs concerned, which are thoroughly discussed in Rose's commentary. We must remember that new knowledge is always accruing, and before we patronise Plutarch we might note that on one question both Jevons in 1892[40] and Rose in 1924[41] are exactly as ignorant as Plutarch and Rose admits the fact. This is Plutarch's Question 95, 'Why is it normal for those living in a holy manner to abstain from legumes?'[42] We now know that many people in the Mediterranean suffer from the genetically determined disease of favism. This is a severe allergy to the broad bean *Vicia faba*: eating the bean raw or inhaling the pollen produces anaemia, which may be fatal in twenty-four hours. The enzyme deficiency causing favism, however, affords some protection against malaria, since the red blood cells of the sufferer lack a substance essential to the malarial parasite. In malarious regions, there is a balance of advantage, and favism is found in malarious regions all over the world, but notably in the Mediterranean, where malaria was widespread till very recently, and probably still more widespread in ancient times.[43] Pythagoras of Samos, the most prominent ancient philosopher to prescribe abstention from beans, probably had favism himself: it is said that he was fleeing from his political opponents when he came to a bean-field, presumably in flower, and sooner than cross it he waited for his enemies to catch up and kill him.[44] The taboo generated in this way could easily spread to other legumes. Obviously Plutarch could know nothing about all this, and neither could Jevons or Rose.

But what interests me now is the methods used by Plutarch, irrespective of whether they led to the right answers, and it is his methods which, I believe, entitle him to be considered a pioneer of folklore study. To begin with, he gives several alternative answers to every question. This in itself casts scientific doubt on the standard sorts of folk folklore explanation, such as commemorating an event, just as Peter Abelard weakened medieval blind faith in authority by listing contradictory opinions of the early Christian Fathers on many topics.

Next, Plutarch includes many explanations of quite different kinds, and it is in these that he often anticipates modern approaches. He raises the interesting possibility of spread or contagion of a culture pattern. Thus, he asks why Romans do not like to travel on the day after the Kalends, Nones and Ides of the month, gives a possible reason for the case of the Ides, and suggests the taboo was then extended to the other two dates.[45] Then he is aware of the possibility of a vestigial custom, anticipating Tylor. Thus he suggests ambassadors to Rome register at the treasury as a vestige of more hospitable days when they used to be given gifts and other benefits by the treasurers.[46]

Plutarch often advances explanations we should now call anthropological, sometimes with considerable insight. Thus, after asking why Romans do not marry close kinsfolk, he suggests two reasons perfectly valid and acceptable today — that exogamy multiplies useful social connections, and that marriages of close kin give rise to disputes.[47] After asking why women kiss their kinsmen on the lips, he first suggests it was a means of detecting women who committed the misdemeanour of drinking wine. But besides this breathalyser test, he also suggests it is a relic of a former wider exogamy

than the present one, when even cousins were in a prohibited degree, but were allowed to express their kinship by kissing.[48]

Above all, Plutarch again and again uses the comparative method. Rose notes a good example of this, Plutarch's Question 5,[49] where a commemorative explanation is 'rather contemptuously rejected (and rightly so) as "sheer mythologising", There follows an explanation which (again quite rightly, with genuine feeling for the Comparative Method) puts forward a Greek parallel.'[50] I have found at least half a dozen cases of this comparative use of Greek customs to illuminate Roman ones. For instance, Question 14 asks why sons cover their heads at the funeral of their parents, while daughters attend with bare heads and unbound hair.[51] One of his suggestions is that this is a reversal of normal procedure, since men normally go out with bare heads and women with their heads covered. For in Greece, he observes, men usually cut their hair and women let it grow, but they do just the reverse when mourning some disaster. In one case, Plutarch even uses a Phoenician parallel, from Tyre.[52] One of his lost works was called *Barbarian Questions,* and would no doubt have yielded more examples of the comparative method.

Finally, as Plutarch compared different regions in space, he was also unusually sensitive among ancient writers to change in folk beliefs over time. This appears especially in his dialogue on the decline of oracles.[53] Here he considers why there are so few oracular shrines in Greece in his day, whereas there had been many more in the great days of the Persian wars in the fifth century B.C. The main answer given is a very sensible demographic one: there are fewer oracles because there are fewer people. 'The whole of Greece', observes one character,[54] 'could now scarcely supply the 3,000 heavy infantry supplied by the single city of Megara at the Battle of Plataea' in 479 B.C. The depopulation of mainland Greece was certainly a fact. The overpopulation crises of archaic and classical times had left the country by the third century B.C. with an impoverished land and exhausted mines, while industry had been exported to the Greek settlements abroad.[55]

But Plutarch is not wholly satisfied with this explanation. He senses that there is also some fundamental change in beliefs taking place. The discussion of this involves the fascinating idea, characteristic of the age, that minor deities have a finite life span. We learn, for instance, from a calculation based on information in Hesiod, that a Naiad normally lives for 9,720 years.[56] But above all, the dialogue includes perhaps the most dramatic story ever told about change in folk beliefs. The story is fittingly ascribed to the reign of Tiberius, whose acts, of course, included the appointment and recall of Pontius Pilatus as procurator of Judea.[57] It is vouched for as true by one of the speakers in the dialogue, a historian called Philip,[58] and several others said to be present, who had all heard it from their teacher, a Greek orator who, like many in his age,[59] had taken a Roman name, Aemilianus. This teacher had in turn heard the story from his own father, Epitherses. Here, then, is the story.[60]

"Some of you have studied under Aemilianus the orator; his father was Epitherses, a fellow-citizen of mine who taught grammar. Epitherses said he was once travelling to Italy, and went on board a ship carrying cargo and a lot of passengers. It was already evening and they were near the Echinades islands, when the wind dropped and the ship drifted near Paxi. Most people on board were still awake, and many were still having an after-dinner drink. All of a sudden, a voice was heard from the island of Paxi, calling loudly for Thamus, so that they were astonished. Thamus was an Egyptian pilot, not known by name even to many people on the ship. Twice he kept silence when he was called, but the third time he acknowledged the call. Then the caller said, more loudly still, "When you are opposite Palodes, announce that great Pan is dead."

"When they heard that, said Epitherses, they were all dumbfounded, and considered whether it was better to carry out the instruction or not to meddle and let well alone. Thamus himself finally decided that if there was a breeze he would sail past without speaking, but if there was no wind and a calm sea when they got to the place, he would pass on the message he had heard. So when they came opposite Palodes, without a breath of wind or a ripple on the sea, Thamus looked towards the land from the ship's stern, and repeated what he had heard, that great Pan was dead. He had not finished speaking when there came the sound of many voices groaning in lamentation, mingled with cries of amazement.

"Since there were many people present when this happened, the story was soon spread around in Rome, and Thamus was summoned by Tiberius Caesar. The Emperor was so impressed by the story that he had inquiries made about Pan, and the many scholars at his court concluded that he was the child born of Hermes and Penelope.' And Philip had several witnesses to this story, former pupils of old Aemilianus, among the people present at our dialogue."

With this wonderful story, I may conclude this account of Plutarch as a folklorist. The achievement of every great creative artist or scientist is, after all, unique, whether it be *The Water-Babies* or *The Parallel Lives,* so, despite my comparison of Kingsley and Plutarch, I will end by quoting Dryden's version of the verses by the sixth-century poet Agathias, imagined to be written on a statue erected by the Romans:-

Chaeronean Plutarch, to thy deathless praise
Does martial Rome this grateful statue raise,
Because both Greece and she thy fame have
    shared,
(Their heroes written, and their lives
    compared).
But thou thyself couldst never write thy own;
Their lives have parallels, but thine has
    none.[61]

Notes

1. R. M. Dorson, *The British Folklorists* (London, 1968), 284.

2. F. B. Jevons, ed., *Plutarch's Romane Questions. Translated A.D. 1603 by Philemon Holland* (London, 1892), V.

3. E. Clodd, *Tom Tit Tot* (London, 1898), 63.

4. Birth, family, town: C. P. Jones, *Plutarch and Rome* (Oxford, 1971), 3-14; writers in the Roman Empire: W. M. S. Russell, 'Sound Drama before Marconi', *Papers of the Radio Literature Conference 1977,* ed., P. Lewis (Durham, 1978), 1-26, *passim.*

5. Jones, 16-19; G. Finlay, *Greece under the Romans* (Edinburgh and London, 1857), 82-83; A. Garzetti, *From Tiberius to the Antonines,* tr. J. R. Foster (London, 1976), 183-4.

6. Jones, 23-25.

7. *ibid.*, 15 and Ch. 3.

8. *ibid.*, Chs 4 and 5; D. A. Russell, *Plutarch* (London, 1972), 5-6.

9. Jones, 53-54, 32; Garzetti, 383.

10. Jones, 137.

11. *ibid.*, 22, 29, 34.

12. *ibid.*, 26.

13. e.g. G. Highet, *The Classical Tradition* (London, 1957), index, *s.v.* Plutarch.

14. For the information about Kingsley, see W. M. S. Russell, 'Biology and Literature in Britain, 1500-1900. II. The Victorians', *Biology and Human Affairs*, XLIV (1979), 114-33, and the sources given there.

15. Jones, 11.

16. H. J. Rose, *The Roman Questions of Plutarch, a New Translation, with Introductory Essays and a Running Commentary* (Oxford, 1924), 61; D. A. Russell, 6.

17. Rose, 60.

18. Plutarch, *Moralia,* 345 ff.

19. Plutarch, *Lives,* Lycurgus, 18.

20. *Moralia,* 401.

21. D. A. Russell, 78; Rose, 58.

22. *Moralia,* 920B ff.

23. W. M. S. Russell, 'Biology and Literature in Britain, 1500-1900. I. From the Renaissance to the Romantics', *Biology and Human Affairs*, XLIV (1979), 50-72.

24. A. Calame, ed., *Fontenelle, Entretiens sur la Pluralité des Mondes* (Paris, 1966).

25. H. Cherniss and W. C. Helmbold, ed. and tr., *Plutarch's Moralia,* Vol. 12 (London, 1957), 21, 104, 138.

26. D. A. Russell, 18-19.

27. J. Langhorne and W. Langhorne, tr., *Plutarch's Lives,* Vol. 1 (London, 1819), lviii-lix.

28. Rose, 12.

29. A. W. Shorter, *An Introduction to Egyptian Religion* (London, 1931), 10-11.

30. *Lives,* Demetrius, 22.

31. *Lives,* Cato Minor, 70.

32. K. Muir, *Shakespeare's Sources. I. Comedies and Tragedies* (London, 1957), Ch. 7.

33. Jones, 105-6; D. A. Russell, 106-7.

34. Jones, 104-5; D. A. Russell, 113-4.

35. *Lives,* Comparison of Cicero and Demosthenes, 4.

36. *Lives,* Sertorius, 1. All translations in this paper are my own, except two specified later, from Philemon Holland and Dryden, respectively.

37. Jevons, viii.

38. Rose, 68.

39. *ibid.*, 52 ff.

40. Jevons, lxxxvi ff.

41. Rose, 207.

42. *Moralia,* 286 D,E.

43. W. R. Aykroyd and J. Doughty, *Legumes in Human Nutrition* (Rome, 1964), 65-66; A. G. Motulsky, 'Metabolic Polymorphisms and the Role of Infectious Diseases in Human Evolution', *Human Populations, Genetic Variation and Evolution,* ed. L. N. Morris (London, 1972), 222-52, esp. 240-6.

44. R. D. Hicks, ed. and tr., *Diogenes Laertius, Lives,* Books VI-X (London, 1925), 354-7.

45. *Moralia,* 269 E,F.

46. *Moralia*, 275 B,C.

47. *Moralia,* 289 D,E; see C. Russell and W. M. S. Russell, 'The Social Biology of Totemism', *Biology and Human Affairs,* XLI (1976), 53-79, esp. 58-63.

48. *Moralia,* 265 B-E.

49. *Moralia,* 264 D-F, 265 A.

50. Rose, 23.

51. *Moralia,* 267A,B.

52. *Moralia,* 279A.

53. *Moralia,* 411 E ff.

54. *Moralia,* 414 A.

55. Finlay, 63, 97-98; W. M. S. Russell, *Man, Nature and History* (London, 1967), Chs 8 and 9; C. McEvedy and R. Jones, *Atlas of World Population History* (Harmondsworth, 1978), 110-12.

56. *Moralia,* 415 D.

57. Garzetti, 76.

58. *Moralia,* 418 A.

59. Finlay, 81.

60. *Moralia,* 419 B-E (my translation).

61. A. H. Clough (revised), *Plutarch's Lives: The Dryden Plutarch,* Vol. I. (London, 1910), xxv-xxvi.

Why Was It a de Soto?

STEWART SANDERSON   University of Leeds

STUDENTS of the modern urban legend will recognise that the title of my paper refers to a tale cited in the course of discussion at the 1960 meeting of the Texas Folklore Society, and which has at various times attracted the attention of a number of American folklorists, including Professors Louie Attebery, Jan Brunvand, Americo Paredes, and Barre Toelken. My immediate referent is Attebery's article 'It was a de Soto.'[1] which he opens with characteristic scrupulousness by saying that ' "Was it a de Soto?" or "Maybe It Was a de Soto" would more honestly reflect the content'[2] of his contribution.

The tale is the well-known one about the driver of the ready-mixed concrete truck who deposits his load of concrete on top of a parked motor-car, in most versions because he suspects that the owner of the car is engaged in an adulterous association with his (the truck-driver's) wife. Toelken has given the story the title of *The Solid Cement Cadillac,*[3] which explains in part Attebery's cautious offer of alternative titles in place of the asseverative one under which he published his article. Only in part, however. Attebery has actually seen what one can hardly avoid calling a concrete example of one of the principal elements in the tale, a 1946 de Soto encased in cement and used to advertise the product of the Centennial Concrete Co. of Denver, Colorado: there is no doubt, in view of the press reports of 5th, 6th and 7th August 1960 in the Denver *Post* and of Attebery's own presence in Denver at the time, that the car was truly a de Soto. Attebery's alternative titles were prompted mainly by the content and contention of his article, that the concrete-covered de Soto was an instance of what one might term 'applied folklore', in which a pre-existing oral tale was exploited in advertising, and the oral circulation of the oral tale was itself, in turn, reinforced through dissemination of reports of the de Soto by the news media. The discussion at the Texas Folklore Society meeting at San Antonio took place in April 1960, the Denver incident in August of that year: nature clearly — or advertising — was following art.

The focal point of the discussion of our American colleagues, however, is slightly different from my own in this paper. They were concerned primarily with the historicity of this and similar legends, whereas I wish to focus also on certain aspects of performance. But let us first consider this matter of historicity a little further.

Brunvand, discussing what he terms 'urban belief tales',[4] cites the solid cement Cadillac story amongst others, and points out that such tales 'may spring from verifiable history', mentioning in this context Richard Dorson's having traced the 'Death Car' story back to 1938 in Mecosta, Michigan; 'but', Brunvand goes on to say, 'the facts get lost, and new localisations are provided.'[5]

The search for origins, we are often told nowadays, is an outmoded nineteenth-century preoccupation which we would all do well to abandon; but attempts to prove the historicity of tale material are surely merely one aspect of 'the search for origins', and, it seems to me, a perfectly respectable intellectual quest. The critical study of source materials — which is after all what attempts to investigate the historicity of oral traditions are about — is something that none of us need be ashamed of; and around the time when the aforementioned American scholars were discussing the solid cement Cadillac tale, I myself drew attention to a parallel problem regarding the tale I have called 'The Sale of the Car for the Husband's Mistress.'[6] Perhaps I may be allowed to digress for a moment and to take this opportunity of reporting further on my attempts to trace the original source of this particular legend.

In summary form, a standard version of the tale is as follows: A man sees a second-hand car advertised in the newspaper for a nominal sum. On going to the address indicated, he finds that the widow of the owner of the car is selling it cheaply because her husband's will instructs that the proceeds of the sale are to be given to his mistress.

I first heard this tale in 1948 or early 1949, when I was a student at Edinburgh University (though not yet a student of folklore); and I have collected many variants of it since, from both sides of the Atlantic. Late in 1969 I was informed by a Bradford journalist that he knew the story was true. He claimed that when he was a young reporter in 1948, or so, working on the Wakefield evening paper, he was sent to investigate an advertisement offering a three-weeks-old car, a Standard 9, for £5 – its going market price then would have been about £500. The person who had placed the advertisement was the wife of a man who had absconded with another woman to the Cumberland Hotel in London, and who had written to ask that his car should be sold and the money sent on to him. The journalist could not, after an interval of twenty years, remember the woman's name nor her precise address; but he said he had published the story in his paper, and added that the national dailies had picked it up, which would no doubt account for my having heard of it in Edinburgh. 'You'll find it in the files', he assured me. 'If, on checking, this proves to be so', I wrote in a footnote at the time, 'this will probably be the first of these folktales to have its *point-de-départ* traced.'[7] I must own that the task of combing both the advertising and the news columns of a year's or perhaps eighteen months' issues seemed so daunting that I flinched from it for a long time; but eventually in 1974 one of my post-graduate students, a thoroughly methodical and conscientious worker, undertook the task for me; and she failed to find any trace of either the advertisement or the story. This did not altogether surprise me, though I have no doubt that the journalist in question told me his tale in good faith. All sorts of people have imperfect memories; all sorts of people can confuse the details of events after twenty days, let alone twenty years; and all sorts of people, not by any means excluding journalists, have creative imaginations, powers of narrative artistry, and a habit of patterning the recall of their experiences.

To me the real value of investigations into the historicity of legend material lies not so much in pushing back chronological frontiers, as in considering the implications of all this for such aspects of folk narrative research as transmission studies, innovation studies, and performance studies, and for the study of behavioural aspects of folk culture. I feel fairly confident that the American folklorists I have mentioned would for the most part share this view, though I do beg leave to wonder whether some yet earlier versions may not have lain behind Dorson's 1938 'Death Car' report and Alexander Woolcott's 'Foreign Hotel' story source, which he traced as far back as a report in *The Detroit Free Press* in 1899; and I also beg leave to raise with Brunvand the question of whether it's usually the facts that get lost when new localisations are provided, or whether perhaps it's not more commonly true that what gets lost is a different set of fictions.

The search for historicty, then, I regard as often a useful and valuable search, not so much as an end in itself as for the way in which it can be used to illuminate some of the more obscure corners of folklore studies and some of the darker passages in the history of ideas, as has been done with such brilliance by Professor Stuart Piggott in his recent paper 'Background to a Broadsheet. What Happened at Colton's Field in 1685?',[8] where he shows how the seventeenth-century report of the discovery in Gloucestershire of subterranean chambers furnished with various archaeological finds – urns, coins, medals with Latin inscriptions, and statuary – was a learned hoax incorporating a number of traditional folklore motifs, deployed in the manner of our modern urban legend material, and possibly the work of his namesake, the 'forward and mercurial' (as Anthony Wood described him) Mr Thomas Pigot of Wadham College, Oxford.

So much then for historicity in approaches to the study of modern urban legends. But, to return to our solid cement Cadillac and the title of my paper, *why* was it a de Soto? Or rather, since folklife studies are concerned with specimens of the typical rather than of the idiosyncratic, and the Denver de Soto is certainly an idiosyncrasy, why was it, in the majority of the American versions known to me, a Cadillac, and in the majority of the British versions a Jaguar? The answer, at one level, is fairly clear, at any rate to those who know something about motor-cars. Both Cadillacs and Jaguars are rather grand cars, rather expensive cars, cars which suggest affluence, worldly success, and The Good Life. They symbolise, in short, attributes or characteristics of the successful amorist whom the truck-driver suspects of seducing his wife. And if we examine this answer more closely, we can surely see one of Olrik's narrative laws in operation here, that Law of Contrast which is a correlative of the Law of Two to a Scene, the Contrast between the characters of the seducer and the cuckold. Or, if we care to update our folklore theory, and to move from Olrikian narrative laws to the binary oppositions of structuralism, we see the multiple oppositions of the seducer and the cuckold, the man at leisure and the man at work, the moneyed man and the weekly wage-earner, the private motorist with the expensive car and the transport driver employed trucking cement. Structural theory is, without doubt, great intellectual fun: you can go on playing with it ingeniously for ages before you finally get bored with the game.

There is, however, an important point to be made about this particular answer. It is an answer which operates only within certain limitations. The referential symbolism is clear only to those who know the socio-economic difference between a Cadillac and a Concord, a Jaguar and a Chevette. For such people the symbolism works; but for others it doesn't. So we are now getting into the fashionable worlds of performance theory and communication theory, into the interaction between story-teller and audience, and into rather subtle matters of lexical choice, semantic denotation, and language codes. There is, I suggest, a good deal of work to be done in this area of folk-narrative research by folklorists and linguists together; and the modern urban legend would seem to constitute very suitable research material.

But there is also another and more basic level at which we might profitably look for the answer to our question. And we can usefully begin by asking another, more fundamental, question. Why is the make of the car mentioned at all?

The answer to that, I suggest, is best approached by reminding ourselves of one of the classic sum-mary studies of legend material, Friedrich Ranke's article *Grundfragen der Volkssagenforschung,*[9] where he defines the *Sage* as a tale which demands belief or credibility on the part of the narrator as well as on the part of the listener, as a narrative that, while objectively untrue and fanciful, represents in direct statement the events and incidents as actual facts. Now one of the ways in which this is done, one of the devices which a narrator deploys in recounting his tale, is to furnish it with supporting credentials — I may as well quote myself accurately here, since Professor Piggott or his printers somehow managed to drop a couple of words when quoting me — to furnish it 'with such supporting credentials as details of places, names and dates',[10] and often with an introductory preamble — one can hardly, I think, dignify it with the name of 'formula' — in which the narrator mentions who told him the tale. This last mode of proceeding is, of course, quite familiar to students of mediaeval literature; but whereas mediaeval writers usually ascribe authority to some classical author — 'First folowe I Stace, and after him Corynne' — or else observe at large that 'It is well wiste', modern storytellers usually name a specific friend, relative, or work-colleague as the immediate source of the tale, which has of course happened to characters at one further remove from the story-teller and his audience.

It is the necessity to give as much credibility as possible to the tale that dictates the naming of the make of the car. That, I submit, is why it was a de Soto — or Cadillac, or Jaguar, and not just an innominate motor-car. The fact that it was a Jaguar (or Cadillac), and that the incident took place in Birmingham (or Binghampton) a week ago last Thursday, gives authenticity to the story. Knowledge of these details means that the narrator unfolds his story with confidence in its truth; and his confidence is communicated to his audience, who recognise the truth of the story when they hear these details. Some old car, in some old place or other once upon a time, doesn't sound so convincing: the Jaguar in Birmingham last Thursday week and better still the blue Jaguar coupe, XJS model, outside a semi in Handsworth — you know, the north side of Birmingham — simply must be true.

This particular device — the specification of details of places, names, and dates, or to put it in other (and perhaps not inappropriate) terms, resort to concretisation of the image rather than abstraction and generalisation, is one of the outstanding stylistic features of the performance of modern urban legends; and it seems to me that the investigation of such stylistic features, and their functions in legend performance, is a much under-researched field of study.

But let us return to Handsworth — you know, the north side of Birmingham. That gloss on the place-name is another typical feature of modern legend performance. As a rhetorical device, its purpose is to win the corroborative assent of the audience and thus again to reinforce the credibility of the story. I have not time here to go into the details of an experiment I made — rather mischievously, I suppose — at a branch meeting of members of MENSA, that self-elective association of highly intelligent people, which I was once asked to address. Briefly, the experiment was designed to test the operation of this rhetorical ploy. The experiment was not as strictly set up as I should have liked — mischief and sudden improvisation are not the best bases for scientific work — in that I recounted a selection of these tales in discrepant situational contexts. Having discussed a number of them, presented in summary form, in the course of my address, I told another to a small group during a break for coffee, appealing to one member of the group for corroboratory details about a particular place and its name which localised the scene of the events in the tale. He supplied these with further expansion; and I am convinced that these details — surface carving, as it were, on a structural beam of the tale, rather than the load-bearing beam itself — supplied by a member of the in-group, made the outsider's tale acceptable and accepted. Here too there is certainly room for further research.

Fieldwork in this genre, however, presents great difficulties. One never knows just when, or in what sort of gathering, examples of these tales will crop up. Usually they are performed casually in the most informal circumstances, when attempts to record them on tape would necessitate the kind of intrusion and disruption which would fundamentally alter the performance, if not indeed put a stop to it altogether. Nevertheless, if I were asked to identify the most important research needs in the study of modern urban legends, I should put high in my priorities — much higher than the investigation of historicity — the need for close study of texts in performance context, with particular attention to those rhetorical and stylistic devices employed by the storyteller — not forgetting paralinguistic features such as facial expressions and gestures — in projecting to his audience his own belief in the veracity of his tale. One at least of these features — the giving, in Shakespeare's phrase, of a local habitation and a name — I hope I have been able to isolate, in my attempt to explain why it was not just a car, but a de Soto.

Notes

1. Louie W. Attebery, 'It was a de Soto', *Journal of American Folklore,* LXXXIII (330) (1970), 452-7.

2. *ibid.,* 452.

3. J. Barre Toelken, 'The Return of the Cement Truck Driver', *Oregon Folklore Bulletin,* I (2) (1961), 2-3.

4. Jan Brunvand, *The Study of American Folklore: An Introduction* (New York, 1978; 2nd ed.), 110-12.

5. *ibid.,* 110.

6. Stewart Sanderson, 'The Folklore of the Motor-car', *Folklore,* LXXX (1969), 241-52; see esp. 249.

7. *ibid.,* 249, footnote 12.

8. Stuart Piggott, *Ruins in a Landscape: Essays in Antiquarianism,* Essay V (Edinburgh, 1976), 77-99.

9. Friedrich Ranke, 'Grundfragen der Volkssagenforschung', *Niederdeutsche Zeitschrift für Volkskunde,* III (1925), 12-33.

10. Sanderson, 248.

Traditional Song Current in the Midwest

A. E. SCHROEDER   University of Missouri-Columbia

IN an excellent article in the Richard M. Dorson *Festschrift*, Edson Richmond compares Telemark ballad texts collected by Sophus Bugge in the 1850s and 1860s with those made by Moltke Moe a generation later.[1] He concludes that Moe was correct in assuming that ballad singing was a dying art in his time, but' points out that the tradition did not die suddenly as Moe believed. Texts of individual ballads were found to have become shorter and shorter until the narratives were reduced to their essentials, and when especially memorable stanzas also lost significance, they, too, were forgotten. A collector in the early twentieth century found proportionately fewer ballads. In short, Professor Richmond says, the song tradition was ended, but the memory lingered on.

Collections of traditional British and Euro-American songs made in the central part of the Midwest during the past twenty years, or from 1957 to the present, show that the tradition of singing and the memory of ballads and songs have lingered on to the present day in much the way the memory of medieval ballads lingered in Telemark. In many current versions only what Tristram Coffin called the 'emotional core' of the ballad has remained,[2] and many of the forces of variation he noted, such as loss of detail, localisation and confusion of texts are apparent in current versions.[3]

The history of ballad and folksong scholarship in Missouri has been curiously circular in its development. With Phillips Barry of Massachusetts, Henry M. Belden of the University of Missouri was a leader in the collection and study of traditional balladry and native song in the United States. In 1903, at an English Club meeting, he became aware that his students knew versions of old English and Scottish ballads and began his collec-

tion on the spot.[4] In 1906 he formed the Missouri Folk-Lore Society, the second state folklore society to be established, and with the assistance of the pioneering folklorist, Mary Alicia Owen, who served as President and sponsor of the Society from 1908 until her death in 1935, he established a network of student and other contributors which resulted in one of the richest and most comprehensive of the regional collections.[5]

Associations between the Missouri scholars and English and European folklore scholars were remarkably close in the early days of collection. Mary Alicia Owen attended a meeting of the International Folklore Conference in London in 1891, where her lecture on voodoo tales she had collected was so well received that she had no trouble finding a British publisher for her first book.[6] Miss Owen had the unique distinction of being awarded honorary membership in the English Folklore Society and tribal membership by the Sac Indians, two honours that may have seemed equally exotic to her home town of St Joseph, Missouri.

Belden met Cecil Sharp during a Sabbatical year at Harvard in 1916-17 and after that frequently corresponded with him on ballad problems. Two of his early articles were published in the *Archiv für das Studium der neueren Sprachen und Literaturen*,[7] and in 1952, toward the end of his long and productive life, he wrote to Louise Pound, his old ally in the Midwestern ballad war against the Harvard communalists: 'About a year ago John Meier sent me the latest ... of his *Jahrbücher für Volksliedforschung* ... Meier I have always had a great feeling for; his *Kunstlieder im Volksmunde* helped me not a little, forty-five years ago, in your fight, and mine, against Gummere's theorizing.'[8] Belden was one of the most brilliant strategists in the fight against Gummere's 'theorizing', as demonstrated in his review of *The Popular Ballad* in 1909.[9]

Interestingly, three of the giants among midwestern collectors, Belden, Pound, and Albert H. Tolman of the University of Chicago, who started Miss Mary O. Eddy on the collection which was to be one of the most interesting and perhaps least appreciated in America,[10] did their major work in the first two decades of the twentieth century. During his year at Harvard in 1916-17 Belden copied out his collection for George Lyman Kittredge, including a section of folksongs of blacks which has never been published.[11] Not much was added to the collection of the Missouri Folk-Lore Society after that. Our great Vance Randolph started collecting songs in 1920. By 1934 he thought his collecting days were over and wrote that 'these parlous times have reduced me to writing pot-boilers about Boy Scouts. I shall never be able to work with the old ballads again unless I get a Guggenheim Fellowship or something like that.'[12] The fellowship never came, but by the early 1940s he was in the field again, collecting for the Library of Congress. Part of Randolph's remarkable work was published in the 1950s by the State Historical Society of Missouri,[13] although his extensive collection of 'Unprintable Songs' has not yet seen print.[14]

The major emphasis in the collection and study of folksong in the United States has traditionally focussed on Anglo-American materials. In 1917 Belden wrote that the folklore of Missouri contained French, German and other elements, as well as British, and that some material had been 'worked up',[15] but little was published and unfortunately the Missouri Folk-Lore Society Archives, which then reposed in a box in the Belden home, have not been located. In the 1930s, however, scholarly attention was drawn for a few years to the French Canadian settlements in Missouri, which had been established in the mid and late eighteenth century. It was found that a vigorous oral literature flourished in the quiet little villages south of St Louis into which the French had withdrawn as heavy immigration of Anglo-American settlers from the eastern states began. Particularly impressive was the survival of the traditional *conteur* as a community resource. During the summers of 1934-36 Joseph Carrière, a French Canadian scholar, was able to collect seventy-three tales in the local dialect, sixty-five from one contributor and eight from another.[16] The *conteur* was an important personage in the life of the community, enjoying enormous prestige among his neighbours even in the twentieth century. Ward Dorrance, who undertook field work in the area in the mid-1930s[17] considered the tales the 'core' of the tribal identity and believed they would survive much longer than the songs, a theory not borne out by recent research.[18]

Collecting activities in general were minor in the United States during and after the Second World War, but after a hiatus of almost two decades both academic and non-academic collectors took up the work again, particularly among Anglo-American groups. One of the most successful of the non-academic collectors working today is Max Hunter of Springfield, a native of the region, whose business takes him travelling in the Ozark area. Largely unaware of the theories concerning the death of folksong and unlike Moe, not knowing what he was looking for and unable to prompt his contributors, he was remarkably perceptive and thorough in his work, locating a large number of traditional singers and returning to them again and again during his early years of collecting. His approach has been characterised by a meticulous scholarship and the most rigorous of standards. His collection of a thousand ballads and songs from the Ozarks includes excellent versions of Child ballads, British broadside ballads, and Anglo-American song.[19] It constitutes an excellent resource for the study of ballad survival, as his version of the rare Child 214, collected in Missouri in 1957, demonstrates:

> There were five sons and two were twins,
> There were five sons of Yarrow;
> They all did fight for their own true love
> In the dewy dens of Yarrow.
>
> 'O Mother dear, I had a dream,
> A dream of grief and sorrow,
> I dreamed I was gathering heather bloom
> In the dewy dens of Yarrow.'
>
> 'O Daughter dear, I read your dream,
> Your dream of grief and sorrow;
> Your love, your love is lying slain
> In the dewy dens of Yarrow.'

She sought him up and she sought him down,
She sought him all through Yarrow;
And then she found him lying slain
In the dewy dens of Yarrow.

She washed his face and she combed his hair,
She combed it neat and narrow;
And then she washed that bloody, bloody wound
That he got in the Yarrow.

Her hair it was three-quarters long,
The color it was yellow;
She wound it round his waist so small,
And took him home from Yarrow.

'O Mother dear, go make my bed,
Go make it neat and narrow;
My love, my love he died for me,
I'll die for him tomorrow.'

'O Daughter dear, don't be so grieved,
So grieved with grief and sorrow.
I'll wed you to a better one
Than you lost in the Yarrow.'

She dressed herself in clean white clothes,
And away to the waters of Yarrow;
And there she laid her own self down,
And died on the banks of the Yarrow.

The wine that runs through the water deep
Comes from the sons of Yarrow;
They all did fight for their own true love
In the dewy dens of Yarrow.[20]

Interestingly in a version of the ballad collected a year later in Arkansas the male participants have been transformed into cowboys, and the location to Arrow. The last stanza of the Hunter version, which as Mary Celestia Parler has pointed out, is unparalleled in Child, does not occur in the second Yarrow ballad.[21]

An academic collector-performer, the late Joan O'Bryant, worked throughout the central Midwestern and mountain states, and in 1958 recovered a version of the British broadside ballad, 'Down By the Sea Shore' in Kansas. The Laws data indicate the song is common in the Missouri-Arkansas area, but rare elsewhere.[22] Miss O'Bryant's version is related in imagery to Belden's 'B' version from South Central Missouri and to a variant collected by Max Hunter in Arkansas.[23] Her contributor knew the song as 'Fair As the Fairest'.

She's fair as the fairest
She's dressed like a queen
She's the handsomest creature
That ever was seen.

Crying, 'Oh, my lover's gone
He's a lad I adore
He's gone where I never
Shall see him any more.

'The shells of the ocean
Shall be my death bed
The fish of the ocean
Swim over my head.'

Crying, 'Oh, my lover's gone
He's a lad I adore
He's gone where I never
Shall see him any more.'

She plunged her fair body
In the waters so deep
She closed her pretty blue eyes
In the waters to sleep.

Crying, 'Oh, my lover's gone
He's a lad I adore
He's gone where I never
Shall see him any more.'[24]

In the massive effort to collect British and Anglo-American song in the first seven decades of the twentieth century, Euro-American population groups have been largely neglected, except for the Pennsylvania Germans, probably the most thoroughly researched immigrant group in America. In the past decade or so, however, as the concept of the 'melting pot' comes increasingly into question, scholars have turned to European immigrant groups with results that seem to bear out Richmond's conclusions. Researchers in the French communities of Missouri have found that the memory of the old songs lingers on, although seemingly many are in the final stages of existence. Most are in fragmentary form and are only recovered with some prompting from Dorrance and French Canadian texts. As one could expect, the song which has survived most tenaciously is one that was for many years associated with a community activity, the New Year's Eve 'run' in which a group went from house to house to perform the traditional ritual of 'La Guignolée'. There are various theories concerning the origin of the custom, and the etymology of the name is disputed, but the tradition was widely practiced in French Canada and the early settlements of Upper Louisiana. At one time the custom died out among the whites in Missouri and Illinois but was carried on by the blacks.[25] In the 1930s during one of the great revivals of interest in the American past that occurs from time to time 'La Guignolée' was taken up again by various residents of the area. There were French, German and English versions of the song.[26] The following version was collected by the Missouri Friends of the Folk Arts from Rose Pratt, a resident of Old Mines, whose native language is the French dialect of the region.

Bons'r le maître et la maîtresse, y'etent le
    bonne du logis.
Pour la dernier jour d'l'année, c'était la
    guignolée vous vous duévez
Si vous voulez rien nous donnez, dites-nous le,
Si vous voulez rien nous donnez, dites-nous le,
On vous demande seulement une échinée,
Une échinée n'est pas grand chose, aux deux
    quatre vingt dix pieds de long,
Une échinée n'est pas grand chose, aux deux
    quatre vingt dix pieds de long.
Va-t-aller dire à ma maîtresse qu'alle ait tou-
    jours,
Qu'alle ait toujours le coeur joyeux, point de
    tristesse.
Toutes les figures qui ont point d'amant,
    comment vieillent eilles?
C'est les amours qui la réveillent, hon que
    l'empêchent de dormir,
C'est les amours qui la réveillent, hon que
    l'empêchent de dormir.
Quand on arrive au milieu du bois, no fumes
    à l'ombre.
J'ai attendu le cou-cou changer, c'est la
    colombe.
On te fera faire bonne chaire; On te fera
    chauffer les pieds.
On te fera faire bonne chaire; On te fera
    chauffer les pieds.[27]

One of the most popular songs in French Canada and Missouri was 'La Rose D'en Bois', and two versions were collected in Old Mines in 1977 by Rosemary Thomas.[28] Anna Pashia sang the following:

Mon père et pis ma mère, N'ont pas d'enfants
    que moué.
Mon père et pis ma mère, N'ont pas d'enfants
    que moué.
N'ont pas d'enfants que moué, la destinée, la
    rose d'en bois;
N'ont pas d'enfants que moué; N'ont pas
    d'enfants que moué.
Ils m'enouie à l'école, à l'école du roué.
Mon maître qui m'ensagne, d'vient amour-
    eux de moué.
S'est mis à m'embrasser, Dans le chemin du
    roué.
C'est la place des filles, d'embrasser les
    garçons.
C'est la place des filles de balier leurs
    maisones.
Quand la maisonne est propre, les amoureux
    ils viennent.
S'en viennent quatre à quatre, faisant grand
    carillon.
S'assisent d'ssur le coffre, Z'en cognant du
    talon.
Quand le coffre ils défoncent, les amoure
    s'en vont.
Ils s'en vont quatre à quatre, faisant grand
    carillon.[29]

A second version of 'La Rose D'en Bois' was collected in Old Mines from Joe Thebeau in June, 1977.[30]

In 1771 Goethe sent Herder twelve songs he had collected, with a comment that has been echoed in spirit by almost every collector since his time: *Ich habe noch aus dem Elsass zwölf Lieder mitgebracht, die ich auf meinem Streifereien aus denen* [sic] *Kehlen der ältesten Mütterchen aufgehascht habe.* Goethe considered it great good fortune to have recovered the songs, for in 1771 young people sang only popular stuff.[31]

Over two hundred years later, in May, 1978 Mr Lawrence Weigel of Hays, Kansas, a German from Russia, sent me a tape of his favourite songs. Mr Weigel is a business man, a collector-performer, who has been very active in the current movement among the Germans from Russia to document their unique history and traditions, preserved throughout their long search for a home. Immigrants from Germany established towns, villages and daughter colonies in Russia during the eighteenth and nineteenth centuries, and then emigrated to North and South America in the 1870s, after universal conscription was instituted and their agreement with the Czar was abrogated. Large and cohesive settlements were established in the Plains states, and traditions maintained in linguistic enclaves in Russia were transplanted to the new environment. One of the songs brought along was a variant of *Ich stand auf hohe Berge*, collected by Goethe in 1771. Mr Weigel's title for the song is *Der Graf und die Nonne*:

Ich stand auf hohen Bergen, Bergen
Schaut hinunter in das tiefe Tal.
Da seh ich ein Schifflein schwimmen,
    schwimmen
Darauf drie Ritter war'n.

Der jüngste unter den dreien, dreien,
Der in dem Schifflein war,
Der gebot mir eins zu trinken, trinken
Guten Wein aus seinem Glas.

Was gebietst du mir eins zu trinken, trinken,
Guten Wein aus deinem Glas?
Das gebiet ich dir zu trinken, trinken
Weil's du die Geliebte sollst sein.[32]

In 1973 the University of Missouri-Columbia established a Missouri German Folklore Project to collect life histories and folkloristic data in the many communities in the state settled by German immigrants. In addition to a large body of sayings and beliefs, we have found children's rhymes remembered in low German dialects; songs associated with holiday observances, such as Christmas, New Year, and Pre-Lenten festivities. A few popular dance songs are remembered. Mrs Fritz Theissen of Rhineland, Missouri sang *Zu Lautebach hab ich mein Strumpf verloren* on 12th July, 1974:

Zu Lauterbach hab ich mein Strumpf verlorn
Und ohne Strumpf geh ich nicht heim.
Dann geh ich schon wieder zu Lauterbach hin
Und hol mir ein Strumpf für mein Bein.
Tri lala, lala lei. . .[33]

One of the most interesting discoveries we have made is an excellent version of *Das Kartoffellied*, 'The Potato Song', which is very close to a broadside printing of a piece by Samuel Friedrich Sauter, popular in Southern Germany during the Napoleonic occupation. Mrs Gerhard Hilkemeyer, age 92, of Westphalia, Missouri sang *Das Kartoffellied* on 28th March, 1977:

Herbei, herbei zu meinem Sang
Hans Görgel, Michel, Stoffel
Und singt mit mir das frohe Lied
Dem Stifter der Kartoffel.
Heissa, hopsa, sa; valla tri vi tralala
Und singt mit mir das frohe Lied
Dem Stifter der Kartoffel.

Franz Drake ist der brave Mann
der vor zweihundert Jahre[n]
Von England nach Amerika
als Kapitän gefahren.

Von Strassburg bis nach Amsterdam
Von Stockholm bis nach Brüssel
Kommt Johann mit der Abendsupp'
und die Kartoffelschüssel.

Gebraten schmecken sie recht gut,
mit saurer Brüh' nicht minder.
Kartoffelklöss, die essen gern,
Die Eltern und die Kinder.

Hat jemand sich die Hand verbrannt
Und hilft doch hier kein Segen,
So tut man auf die Hand sogleich
Kartoffelschartig legen.

Wie nützlich sind sie nicht für uns,
Das Vieh damit zu mästen.
Viel Sorten gibt es, hier und dort,
Die guten sind die besten.

Und selbst die schlechten kann man noch
für etwas Guten brauchen.
Man tut sie in ein Fass hinein
Und lässt sie gut verstauchen.

Und wenn sie dann verstauchet sind,
So lässt man sie noch schweitzen
Das gibt dann den Kartoffelschnaps,
der Fusel wird geheissen
Heissa, hopsasa; valla trivi tralala
Das gibt dann den Kartoffelschnaps,
der Fusel wird geheissen.[34]

The ballads and songs surviving in Anglo-American and Euro-American communities in the central Midwest provide the folklorist with important data for textual studies and analyses and offer insight into the creative life of the modern world. Belden believed that the spirit of balladry was immortal. Certainly we have found that in the immigrant communities songs remain even after language has been eradicated and surface acculturation achieved. The memory lingers on.

Notes

1. W. Edson Richmond, 'But the Memory Lingers On', *Folklore Today*, ed. Linda Dégh et al. (Bloomington, 1971), 425-35.

2. Tristram P. Coffin, ' "Mary Hamilton" and the Anglo-American Ballad as an Art Form', *Journal of American Folklore*, LXX (1957), 209-11.

3. *ibid.*, 'A Description of Variation in the Traditional Ballad of America', *The British Traditional Ballad in North America*. Publications of the American Folklore Society: Bibliographical Series, Vol.II (Philadelphia, 1950), 3-25.

4. Henry Marvin Belden, 'Autobiographical Notes', 6th July, 1948. Typescript in collection of author.

5. H. M. Belden, ed., *The Ballads and Songs Collected by the Missouri Folk-Lore Society* (Columbia, Mo., 1940).

6. Mary Alicia Owen, *Voodoo Tales as Told Among the Negroes of the Southwest* (New York & London, 1893).

7. H. M. Belden, 'Folksong in Missouri — Bedroom Window', *Archiv für das Studium der neueren Sprachen und Literaturen*, CXIV (1907), 430-1 and 'Popular Song in Missouri — The Returned Lover', *ibid.*, CXX (1908), 62-71.

8. Letter to Louise Pound, 16th July, 1952 in Pound Papers at the Nebraska State Historical Society, Lincoln, Nebraska.

9. H. M. Belden, '*The Popular Ballad* by Francis B. Gummere', *Journal of English and Germanic Philology*, VIII (1909), 114-27.

10. Mary O. Eddy, *Ballads and Songs from Ohio* (New York, 1939). In an interview with the author on 23rd February, 1964, Miss Eddy reported that she had sent her manuscript to Kittredge and that it was returned unopened. She had the book published at her own expense. Although she was often referred to as an 'amateur' Miss Eddy's work was reprinted by Folklore Associates, Hatboro, Pennsylvania in 1964 with an appreciative foreword by D. K. Wilgus.

11. This typescript is in the Houghton Library at Harvard University.

12. Letter to Warren Douglas Meng, 16th October, 1934 in the Western Historical Manuscript Collection, University of Missouri, Columbia. Mr Meng had written to report that 'crime songs' were current among the blacks in the Missouri State Penitentiary.

13. Vance Randolph, *Ozark Folksongs*, 4 vols (Columbia, Mo., 1946-50).

14. An early copy of the MS. is in the Western Historical Manuscript Collection, University of Missouri-Columbia. Others were deposited by Randolph at the Institute for Sex Research at Indiana University and the Library of Congress. There is a microfilm copy at the University of California-Los Angeles.

15. Letter to Louise Pound, 6th February, 1917, in the Pound Papers.

16. Joseph Carrière, *Tales From the French Folk-Lore of Missouri* (Evanston and Chicago, 1937).

17. Ward Dorrance, 'The Survival of French in the Old District of Sainte Geneviève', Dissertation, University of Missouri, 1935.

18. Rosemary Thomas in a letter to the author, 8th July, 1977 reports: 'I have 12 taped interviews, so far, all of which have something of interest, 10 of which are in French. I probably have 5 songs that are reasonably complete, titles and fragments of another 4 or five, and maybe 7 or 8 old tunes; 3 or 4 stories; a fairly good stock of information on nicknaming customs ... folk medicine and horoscopic information for planting, cutting trees, etc. ... so many people have forgotten the stories and wish they could learn them again.'

19. The Hunter collection has been deposited in the Springfield Public Library, Springfield, Missouri. For a review of the collection see Rebecca B. Schroeder, 'Springfield Public Library Acquires Valuable Collection of Ozark Folksong', *Show-Me Libraries* (April, 1972), 1 ff.

20. Max Hunter, *Ozark Folksongs and Ballads*; notes by Mary Celestia Parler and Vance Randolph (Huntington, Vermont, 1963), 3-4.

21. Mary Celestia Parler, 'Two Yarrow Ballads From the Ozarks', *Southern Folklore*, XXII (4) (1958), 195-200.

22. G. Malcolm Laws, Jr., *American Balladry From British Broadsides* (Philadelphia, 1957), 148-9.

23. Belden, *Ballads and Songs*, 167-8, and Hunter, 18-19.

24. Max Hunter and Joan O'Bryant, *Songs of the Ozarks*. Produced by The Three Dials, 1962.

The transcription is from a tape made by Max Hunter who has a copy of this rare recording.

25. Ida M. Schaaf Collection in Music Papers, Missouri Historical Society, St Louis. Mrs Schaaf wrote to scholars in France and Canada to gather information on the custom. Rosemary Thomas has written an excellent but still unpublished article on 'La Guillonnée'. 'La Guillonnée: Its Survival in the Mississippi Valley and Some Observations on its Antecedents'. Typescript sent to the author.

26. *Ste. Genevieve Herald*, Bicentennial Edition (17th August, 1935).

27. *I'm Old But I'm Awfully Tough*, collected by Missouri Friends of the Folk Arts (New Haven, Mo., 1977), Notes, No.22.

28. See Marius Barbeau and Edward Sapir, *Folk Songs of French Canada* (New Haven, Conn., 1925), 111-4; Dorrance, 127.

29. Tape from Rosemary Hyde Thomas sent to author in May 1978.

30. MS. of text from Rosemary Hyde Thomas.

31. Johann Wolfgang Goethe, *Goethes Werke* (Weimar, 1887), IV, Part 2, 2.

32. Ludwig Erk und Franz Magnus Böhme, *Deutscher Liederhort*, 2 vols (Leipzig, 1893), I, 313-7.

33. Erk und Böhme, II, 768-9.

34. Mrs Hilkemeyer recited a fragment of the song on 2nd June, 1974, but was able to recall a more complete version on 28th March, 1977.

The Value of Ibn Zabara's 12th-century Sepher Sha' ashu' im ('Book of Delight') for the Comparative Study of Folklore

HAIM SCHWARZBAUM   The Institute for Jewish and Arab Folklore Research, Kiron

JOSEPH Ibn Zabara of Barcelona (born circa 1140 A.D.) is the author of the many-faceted Hebrew *Book of Delight,* revealing a vast erudition in all genres of classical Jewish and Arabic folk-literature. This work constitutes not only a fascinating anthology of recreational material full of gleams of fancy and poignant satire, but it is also an admirable corpus of pious Jewish folklore, a sort of guide to moral, ethical living. Ibn Zabara was well-versed in Biblical and Talmudic-Midrashic literature, and as a physician he was extremely conversant with medieval medical lore, the popular aspects of which are extensively dealt with in his *Book of Delight.*

A great deal of medieval-European folklore, particularly many medieval popular narratives, as well as gnomic lore, should be studied against the background of Ibn Zabara's Hebrew masterpiece, which may be called 'a literary Bohemianism', or rather a semi-autobiographical romance. The author, together with his companion Enan, are portrayed as fanciful, ready-witted hikers or vagabonds, wandering from place to place, relating their queer vicissitudes and adventures and debating all kinds of life-issues, bearing on proper conduct and adequate moral behaviour. No wonder that this book occupies a unique position in medieval folk-literature. Ibn Zabara was one of the first Hebrew writers who adopted the remarkable form of rhetorical rhymed prose, interspersed with strict verse, sometimes a kind of doggerel. It thus admirably imitates the classical Arab *Maqamat* style, a diction splendidly displayed in such Arabic masterpieces as those of al-Hamadhani (967-1007 A.D.) and al-Hariri (1054-1122), which are famous in the history of both Arab and world literature.

The *Sepher Sha'ashu'im* consists of folk-material bearing on diverse matter, such as astronomy, physics, mathematics, music, folk-medicine, and so on. It is also a real treasure-trove of folktales, fables, anecdotes and all kind of quips and gibes, thus presenting medieval-Hebrew folk-literature in full flower. In addition it is very rich in epigrams, witty sayings, pointed proverbs and folk-apophthegas and maxims derived from ancient Greek 'sages' — Socrates, Diogenes, Aristotle and others, known from Arab authorities. Recent scholarship has traced Ibn Zabara's gnomic material and his *bons mots* to their Arab models and sources.[1] It has, however, failed to point out the wider folklore ramifications and international parallels to his anecdotes. 'A philosopher', says Ibn Zabara, 'fell sick of a grave disease, and his doctor gave him up, but nevertheless the patient recovered. The convalescent was walking in the street when the doctor met him. "You come", said the doctor, "from the other world." "Yes," rejoined the patient, "I do indeed come from there, and I saw there the awful afflictions put upon physicians, for they kill their patients. Yet, be cheerful and don't feel alarmed. You will not suffer, because I told them on my oath that you are neither physician nor know anything of the healing art. . ."' This is nothing other than Motif J 1432, 'No physician at all.' Elsewhere[2] I have indicated numerous parallels to this anecdote, which is also very popular in modern Jewish folklore, as indeed it was in antiquity — note, for example, its pattern in the Aesopic fable corpus of Babrius.

Again, in one of Ibn Zabara's interludes[3] we come across the following jibe, which is also well-known in world folklore: 'A doctor and the Angel of Death both kill, but the doctor charges a fee. . .'[4] Ibn Zabara cites some Arab anecdotes illustrative of Socrates misogynic attitude: 'The wife of the "wise" Socrates was short and thin. They asked him: "How could a man like you wed such a woman as this?" He replied: "I have chosen of the evil the least possible amount..." Israel Davidson, the Hebrew editor of Ibn Zabara's masterpiece, was unable to find any parallels to this famous anecdote which is already cited by Plutarch.[5] In another anecdote Ibn Zabara tells us that Socrates was walking with his disciples by the banks of a river, where a certain woman was washing clothes. 'She cried out at him, cursed and reviled him; then she threw some of the water upon him and drenched him. He said: "Surely she has cast her lightning and hurled her thunder, and now she brings forth rain."' J. Bolte[6] provides a comprehensive bibliography bearing on this theme, but overlooked Ibn Zabara's version, just as Thompson in his *Motif-Index,* under Motif T 251.4, failed to refer to our version, though it is instanced by Diogenes Laertius and many ancient sources.

In another anecdote Ibn Zabara tells us about a nobleman, who built a new house and wrote over the door: 'Let no evil enter here.' Diogenes, the philosopher, passed and saw the inscription, and then wrote underneath: 'And how will thy wife enter?'[7] Another anecdote quoted by Ibn Zabara is about Socrates, who was walking upon the way and saw a woman hanging from a fig tree. He commented, 'Would that all the fruit of this tree were the same.'[8] This rather sardonic anecdote is already recorded by Cicero[9] and Plutarch,[10] in the *Gesta Romanorum*[11] and in many other references given by J. Bolte.[12] Motif J 1442.11 'The cynic's wish. When he learns that a woman has hanged herself from a tree he says, "Would that all trees bore such fruit!"' Both Thompson and Rotunda[13] have overlooked Ibn Zabara's version and Bolte's copious notes.

In another witty anecdote Ibn Zabara tells us about a certain wicked lad, whose mother was a harlot, casting stones. Diogenes said to him: 'Forbear, lest thou smite thy father!' Both Thompson (J 1442.7) and Rotunda have overlooked Ibn Zabara's version. Among the numerous 'parables and saws' in Ibn Zabara's 7th chapter we have the following significant anecdote: 'A man of noble birth reviled a sage for being of humble birth. He replied: "My birth is a disgrace to me, but thou art a disgrace to thy birth!"' In another version, also quoted by Ibn Zabara, the sage rejoins: ' "My family distinction begins with myself, thine ends with thee!"' I have already traced this anecdote to

various sources.[14] In this case, too, Rotunda, Motif J 1289.9.5.1, 'The two lines — philosopher's and king's. To ruler: "My line begins with me, yours ends with you,"' has overlooked Ibn Zabara's version.

The structure of the *Sepher Sha'ashu'im* is very interesting. All the stories are subordinated to the underlying framework tale of the daemonic hero, Enan, who tries to persuade Ibn Zabara to forsake his own country and accompany him to a place where his wisdom will be properly recognised. At first Ibn Zabara declines to set out, lest there befall him what befell a certain leopard with a fox. Here follows the illustrative tale of the cunning fox which persuaded the leopard to leave for another rich country, where he ultimately perishes during a flood, and thus the sly fox gets rid of him. This form of presenting stories within a framing tale reminds us of the widespread Arabic story books, such as *Kalilah-wa-Dimnah,* or the literary pattern of *Alf Laila wa-Laila* (1001 Nights), or Chaucer's *Canterbury Tales,* Bocaccio's *Decameron,* and others. The following five stories are inserted into the basic frame tale of Ibn Zabara. One of them is told by the leopard's wife in order to prove the fox's cunning, while four are told by the fox in order to illustrate the infidelity and wickedness of women. This is reminiscent of the famous *Sindbad* or *Seven Sages* stories, where tales are employed in effect as 'weapons', in the combat or controversy of the heroes of the framing story.[15] These are the stories:

1.   The leopard's wife tells the story of the sick lion beguiled by the sly fox, who promises to cure him by binding him hand and foot, and then kills him.[16]

2.   The fox then takes up the story of the silversmith of Babylonia, who follows his wife's counsel and offers the King's daughter a statue fashioned by him — that is to say an image of the princess. He thus violates the strict Islamic religious precept, forbidding the representation of the human form in art.[17]

   Accordingly the king orders the silversmith's right hand to be cut off, and the smith exclaims: 'Take warning from me, ye husbands, and obey not the voice of your wives.'

3.   He follows up this story with another tale showing how an obstinate woman, through her

misplaced ambition, brings death upon her husband and herself. This is the story of the woodcutter of Damascus[18] who is nagged by his wife, urging him to hew the wood with his left hand, but, while doing so, he strikes the thumb of his right-hand and cuts it off. Then he takes the axe and smites her on the head, and she dies. He is stoned for this crime. Therefore, continues the fox, I declare unto you that all women are deceitful; they ensnare the lives of all.

4.   The fox reinforces his argument by relating a more drastic story in which a contrast is drawn between man's love and woman's.[19] An Arab king, hearing his courtiers praise the virtue of women, expresses his view that even the best of the female sex are faithless. He proves his assertion by offering a merchant the hand of his daughter, if the merchant will first kill his own wife. The merchant cannot bring himself to do this. When, however, the king proposes to marry the wife, if she will first murder her husband, the only thing that prevents her from committing the crime is the king's foresight in giving her a tin sword for the purpose.

5.   The fox follows up this story with the widespread tale of the *Matron of Ephesus* (Tale Type 1510). Ibn Zabara, however, has a rather gruesome form of this famous story: the widow solicits the favours of the guard. Notwithstanding her lover's protests, she digs up her husband's corpse, and she does not hesitate to mutilate the 'beloved' corpse to make it resemble that of the hanged man. This is in conformity with those versions of the story studied by me in my forthcoming book on Rabbi Berechiah's *Mishle Shu'alim*, 'Fox Fables' of the thirteenth century,[20] indexed as Tale Type 1352: 'The Woman's Coarse Act. The widow mourns for her husband. When the new suitor tells her to knock out the teeth of the deceased with a stone and she obeys him, he leaves her' (see also Motif T 231.4). In Ibn Zabara's version, when the guard of the stolen corpse points out that the corpse which he had watched was bald, the perfidious widow at once tears her husband's hair out, with execrations, and then hangs him on the tree.

Here ends this cycle of inserted stories and Ibn Zabara finally joins his companion, Enan, on a roving expedition. On their way, Enan says to his friend, namely to our author: 'Carry thou me, or I will carry thee', and, in order to explain this enigmatic statement, he relates the long story of the clever peasant girl and the king's queer dream. This story is extremely popular, both in world folklore and among diverse Jewish ethnic groups — see, for example, Tale Types 875 and 875D, as well as the IFA (Israel Folktale Archives) Type 895 epitomised by Heda Jason in Fabula VII, 176. Only those features extant in Ibn Zabara's version are given here: a King dreamt that he saw a monkey among his many wives and concubines. One of his eunuchs goes to fetch a sage who can interpret the dream. On the way he meets a peasant and makes a series of queer remarks to him, including the saying: 'Carry me, or I will carry thee', which the peasant's daughter cleverly interprets as signifying that he who beguiles the way with stories and proverbs and riddles, carries his companion, relieving him from the tedium of the journey (see Tale Type 875D, item IIc). The peasant's daughter correctly explains all the queer remarks of the eunuch, and finally is taken to the king, and tells him that the monkey of his dream is a man disguised in female garb. This being found to be true, the king's wives and the disguised man are put to death, and the clever girl marries the king.[21]

Ibn Zabara and his companion journey on, and the latter weeps as they near a town. Here, he says, a friend of mine, an extremely wise judge, died. And he starts telling a new cycle of stories about the clever judge:

1.   The dishonest cantor and the ingenious judge. The latter reveals that the cantor is guilty of burglary.[22]

2.   Another story of the judge's sagacity — the tale of the merchant Jacob of Cordova who permits a nobleman to have a precious chain (or necklace) taken into the latter's house for his wife's inspection. When Jacob applies to the nobleman for the return of the chain, the latter professes ignorance of the transaction and the merchant is unable to recover his property. He complains to the clever judge, who thereupon calls a conclave of all important citizens. The deceitful nobleman comes with the rest and, after Islamic fashion, leaves his shoes at the door, whereupon, obeying the judge's orders, a servant, taking the nobleman's shoes as a token,

goes to the wife of the latter and gets the chain, which is duly returned to the merchant.[23]

3. The third story of the judge's cleverness is also narrated by Enan. A merchant dies, leaving a single son abroad. In the absence of the true heir, the late merchant's slave takes possession of everything, and when his master's son returns home he drives him away, denying his identity. The case is brought to our ingenious judge, who tells both litigants to bring him the deceased's bones in order to burn them for his neglect in failing to leave a will. The slave agreed to do so, but the true son refuses to desecrate the corpse. He is recognised by the judge as the rightful heir.[24]

This story is extremely widespread and very popular in Jewish and world folklore; see Tale Type 920C: 'Shooting at the Father's Corpse, Test of Paternity' (Motif H 486.2). Similar stories are often ascribed to King Solomon, who is the ingenious, wise judge in the story of the two women (Tale Type 926) graphically outlined in the Biblical account (I Kings, 3:16 ff).

Ibn Zabara and Enan arrive at a certain city, where an old man offers them hospitality, and entertains them with the well-known 'Story of Tobit.'[25] Ibn Zabara's version of this Apocryphon differs considerably from the Apocryphal one; Compare Tale Types 506, 507 A, 507 B and 507 C. Their entertainer also tells Enan and Ibn Zabara another story of piety connected with the burial of the dead: the miracle of the paralytic who lives on the road to a graveyard and whom God permits to rise up and pray whenever the corpse of a righteous man is carried by. If the dead man has been wicked, the paralytic is unable to arise. On a certain day, as a supposedly pious man is being borne to his grave, our paralytic finds that he cannot rise from his bed. On the following day, however, he is able to stand up and pray at the passing of the corpse of a notoriously sinful butcher. Upon investigation it is discovered that the butcher had always honoured and served his old father, while the allegedly 'pious' man had been secretly a heretic. Elsewhere[26] I have dealt in a comprehensive manner with this type of story in Jewish and world folklore, stories illustrating the notion that folk appearing to be of a saintly and righteous character are in truth wicked trans-

gressors, and vice versa: while alleged sinners on the contrary rather prove to be holy men — see, for example, Tale Type 756A, 'The Self-Righteous Hermit', as well as Keller Motif V 512.2, 'Man whose only good deed was unintentional sees the deed outweigh all his evil in the scales of judgment.' This is taken from J. E. Keller's *Motif-Index of Mediaeval Spanish Exempla* (1949). Keller has however overlooked Ibn Zabara's story.

Next day our wayfarers reach Enan's own city. Here, in the course of lengthy, elaborate discussions, Enan tells Ibn Zabara the story of the king who held a feast to celebrate the blooming of roses in the winter season. He sends for his daughter to rejoice over the joy of the roses. She stretches forth her hand to take a rose to smell it, but a serpent that was among the roses leapt at her and startled her, whereupon she died. Israel Davidson,[27] the editor of *Sepher Sha'ashu'im,* was unable to find any parallels to the story. In my *Studies in Jewish & World Folklore* (1968), I have given many analogues and parallels to this story exemplifying the idea of the inevitability of inexorable Fate, which is current in folklore.[28]

When Enan sees that Ibn Zabara consumes a great deal of food he gets very angry and says: 'Disease will leave its mark in thy bowels, and thou wilt rue thy gluttonous eating when thy malady is great, and thou wilt return to thy leanness and thy poverty . . .' Finally he adds: 'and what befell the fox will surely befall thee also.' Here Enan tells the famous story of the fox over-eating in the garden. As a result he cannot escape through the hole he has entered by. He has to fast three days so as to depart by that same hole;[29] see Tale Type 41, 'Fox in the Orchard.'

In the course of their discussion of women and their qualities, Enan tells Ibn Zabara the rather gruesome story of a certain washerwoman, a crone who was able to accomplish what the devil himself could not perform, causing strife and discord between a husband and his wife, who is eventually murdered by her spouse, and creating in the town dire commotion and warfare, so terrible that hundreds of people were killed. This is the widespread Aarne-Thompson narrative Type 1353, 'The Old Woman as Trouble Maker', narrated in Ibn Zabara's masterpiece with much pathos, picturesqueness and vividness, as well as with exuberant humour.[30]

Notes

1. cf. Yehuda Ratzabi in the *Annual of the Bar-Ilan University,* VI (1968), 320-5, as well as his comprehensive study in the *Haim Schirmann Jubilee Volume* (Jerusalem, 1970), 371-92, and in the Hebrew periodical *Bikoret u-Parshanut,* IX-X (October 1976), 176-96.

2. See H. Schwarzbaum, *Studies in Jewish and World Folklore* (Berlin, 1968), 316-7. Cf. also 'Babrius' (No. 75), B. E. Perry, ed., *Aesopica,* (1952), 447 (No. 317); *ibid.*, *Babrius and Phaedrus* (1965), 92 f. (No. 75): Halm 168, Chambry 133; S. Span, *Mishle Aesopus* (Jerusalem, 1960), No. 344.

3. Israel Abrahams, *The Book of Delight and Other Papers* (Philadelphia, 1912), 12.

4. cf. H. Schwarzbaum, 'The Physician in Jewish Folklore', *Mahanayim,* CXXIII (1970), 158-65.

5. See Stith Thompson, *Motif Index of Folk-Literature* (Bloomington, 1966), J1442.13: 'The smallest woman makes the best bride. Of an evil choose the smallest part.' Both Thompson and D. P. Rotunda, *Motif-Index of the Italian Novella in Prose* (Bloomington, 1942), J1442.16, have overlooked Ibn Zabara's significant version.

6. See the Notes to Johannes Pauli, *Schimpf und Ernst,* ed. J. Bolte (Berlin, 1924), II, 366 (No. 471).

7. cf. Israel Davidson, ed., *Sepher Sha'ashu'im* (Berlin, 1925; 2nd ed.), 31 (11. 304-6); also Moses Hadas, tr., *The Book of Delight* (New York, 1932), 67. Hadas refers to Diogenes Laertius' similar anecdote in *Jewish Quarterly Review,* XXVII, 152.

8. cf. Hadas (*JQR*), 152.

9. In his second book, *De Oratore.*

10. *Life of Antony,* 70.

11. *Gesta Romanorum,* No. 33.

12. Pauli, II, 394-5 (No. 637).

13. Rotunda, 60 (J1442.14.1).

14. cf. H. Schwarzbaum, 'International Folklore Motifs in Petrus Alphonsi's *Disciplina Clericalis'*, *Sefarad,* XXI (1961), 296. *Sefarad* is published in Madrid.

15. This important structural feature of Ibn Zabara's misogynist cycle of stories reminiscent of the form pattern of the *Seven Sages* (*Book of Sinbad* or *Sendebar*) has been overlooked by Judith Dishon in her study of the women in Ibn Zabara's *Sepher Sha'ashu'im, Annual of Bar-Ilan University,* XIII (1976), 188 ff. Dishon has published several other important studies (in Hebrew) dealing with Ibn Zabara's *Book of Delight.*

16. See H. Schwarzbaum, *The Mishle Shu'alim* ['Fox Fables'] *of Rabbi Berechiah Ha-Nakdan, a Study in Comparative Folklore and Fable Lore* (Tel Aviv, 1978), 196 f., & 199 Note 10, as well as the author's *Studies* (see Note 2, above), 355 f., No. 497. In Tale Type 8A 'the trickster [the fox] pretends to make the dupe beautiful, and then injures him'. Cf. also Aarne-Thompson 'irregular' Tale Type 125A: 'The ram wants to scratch the wolf's side with his horns to rid him of lice. He horns the wolf to death.' In T. L. Hansen, *Types of the Folktale in Cuba, Puerto Rico, the Dominican Republic and Spanish South America* (Berkeley & Los Angeles, 1957) Type 24, 'the fox agrees to make shoes for the monkey. He takes strips

of new leather, wraps them around the monkey, and tells him to lie in the sun. Monkey is at the mercy of fox.'

17. cf. F. Buhl, *Handworterbuch des Islam* (Leiden, 1941), 706-8.

18. See the humorous Islamic story in W. A. Clouston, *Flowers from a Persian Garden* (London, 1894), 64-5 ('whatever a wife advises her husband the latter should do the contrary . . .').

19. The *Qur'an* also emphasises, in accord with other ancient religious texts, that 'a male is not as a female', III:36: *wa-laisa al-dhakaru ka-l-untha.* For parallels to Ibn Zabara's tales see Schwarzbaum, *Studies,* 113 (No. 33), and extensive bibliography bearing on the present story.

20. 'Fox Fables' of the thirteenth century; cf. also Schwarzbaum, *Mishle Shu-alim,* 394-417 (Ch. 80).

21. Ibn Zabara's version is very important for the comparative study of the famous 'Seven Sages' or Sindbad (Sendebar) frame story. In this context the 'irregular' Type 875D (based on two Lithuanian specimens) is rather interesting. In Aa-Th we have the following succinct synopsis: '*The Prince's Seven Wise Teachers.* The stepmother, rejected by her stepson, unjustly makes a complaint against him to his father' (cf. Motif K 2111: 'Potiphar's Wife', in the famous Joseph story, Gen. 38:7 ff.). 'On the advice of his tutors, the prince at the gallows proves to his father, that *amongst the queen's maids there is a man dressed as a maid* – the queen's paramour. The queen and her lover are hanged.' This is given by Aarne-Thompson, and is an oral, popular retelling of the famous frame story of the 'Seven Sages' (Sindbad, etc.). In Giovanni Sercambi's version epitomised by Rotunda, Motif K 1825.1.1., a girl disguised as a doctor exposes the queen's paramour, who is masquerading as woman, cf. Thompson's Motif K 1825.1.1.1. See also Motif K 1836, 'Disguise of man in woman's dress'; K 1321.1, 'Man disguised as woman admitted to women's quarters (seduction).' Of particular interest is M. Gaster's *Exempla of the Rabbis* (New York, 1968), 131 (No. 354). Here a king dreams a peculiar dream but soon forgets it. Maimonides, though still a child, is brought before the king, and reminds the latter that he had seen in his dream a table decked with all kinds of food; a swine came out of a corner of the room, ate from all the dishes and disappeared. The dishes stand for the king's wives, while the swine is the king's slave dressed in female clothes. Cf. Tale Type 875D, item III, 'The clever girl explained that the fish laughed because there is a man dressed in woman's clothes in the harem.' See also Motif N 456, 'Enigmatical smile (laugh) reveals secret Knowledge'; Motif D 1318.2.1, 'Laughing fish reveals guilt'; and cf. Further Eberhard-Boratav, *Typen turkischer Volksmärchen* (Wiesbaden 1953), Type 100, as well the following IFA (*Israel Folktale Archives*), items hailing from the various Jewish communities' ethnic groups: IFA 854 & 4135 (Moroccan Jews); 2996 (Yemenite Jews); 292, 2674 & 6251 (Iraqi Jews); 2036 & 6618 (Afghan Jews); 6367 (Libyan Jews); 7353 (Persian Jews); 7572 (Jews from Persian Kurdistan), etc. For Ibn Zabara's version, see again the comprehensive bibliography given in Schwarzbaun, *Studies,* 394-5, which enables us to reconstruct the rather intricate 'life-story' of this widespread folktale. The data given in the present Note supplements that presented in *Studies.*

22. For Cantors in Jewish folklore see Schwarzbaum, *Studies,* 511 (Index) and Yehudit Dishon in the Hebrew periodical *Sinai,* LXXIV (1974), 242 f. See also Perry, *Aesopica,* Nos. 121, 448 & 529; cf. Motifs J 953.2, and J 953.3, as well as 'Schwarzbaum, *Mishle Shu'alim,* xliii, No. 43.

23. For numerous parallels to this detective story see Schwarzbaum, *Studies,* 80 n. 19, 216, 240, 476, No. 281. See also Babylonian Talmud, *Nectarim* 25 a, Yoma 83 1 as well as *Pesikta Rabbat,* ed. M. Ish-Shalom (Vienna, 1880), 116 and 113a; *Midrash Vayikra Rabbah* VI: 3; *Midrash Haggadol* on *Exod.,* ed. M. Margaliot (Jerusalem 1956), 411. Cf. also Tale Type 961B; Motif J 1161.7; F. C. Tubach, *Index Exemplorum, a Handbook of Mediaeval Religious Tales* (Helsinki, 1969), Nos. 3352 and 3769. See also the IFA versions summarised by Heda Jason, *Fabula,* VII, 205, as follows: 'Rascal cheats man (does not return deposit, etc.). Cheated person learns about rascal's last meal from the remnants on his beard (hands), or overhears the code used between rascal and his wife. He approaches the wife, gives her the sign from her husband and gets back his

things.' The versions hail from Turkish, Yemenite, Iraqi, Afghan Jews (and from some other Jewish ethnic groups). This cycle of stories belongs to the Master-Thief or Clever Man Type; Aarne-Thompson, 1525, Jason 1525 J. For another Mediaeval Hebrew version see the well-known eleventh century *Hibbur Yaphe mi-Hayeshua'h* of Rabbenu Nissim of Qairuan, 60 f (of the Hebrew stories).

24. cf. Tale Type 920 C: 'Shooting at the Father's Corpse (Test of Paternity). Youngest of supposed sons refuses to shoot and is judged the only genuine son of the dead emperor.' Motif H 486.2, for which see Schwarzbaum, *Studies,* 209, 216, 295 & 474; also B. Heller in *M.G.W.J.,* LXXX (1936), 479 (No. 10).

25. See S. Liljeblad, *Die Tobiasgeschichte und anders Märchen mit toten Helfern* (Lund, 1927); Tale Type 507A (full bibliography); F. Zimmermann *The Book of Tobit* (New York, 1958), 5-12 ('Folk Themes in Tobit'); Gaster, *Exempla* No. 334; Schwarzbaum, *Studies,* 593 (Index s.v. 'Tobit, Book of').

26. cf. *ibid.*, 128-32 (No. 52), 465 (addenda to No. 52); *Fabula,* VII, 167; Types 809 and 827A.

27. Davidson, 98. n.1 (of the Hebrew text); Schwarzbaum, *Studies,* 275.

28. cf. Schwarzbaum, *Studies,* 259-276; Tale Type 934 ff. (Tales of Fate).

29. See H. Schwarzbaum, *Mishle Shu'alim of Rabbi Berechiah Ha-Nakdan, a Study in Comparative Folklore and Fable Lore* (Tel Aviv, 1978), xvi, xlv n.73, 213, 217 n.18.

30. J. E. Keller, *Motif-Index of Mediaeval Spanish Exempla* (Knoxville, 1949), 34, Motif K 1085, 'Woman makes trouble between man and wife', refers to *Conde Lucanor* No. 42 (by Juan Manuel, 1282-1349) and to P. de Gayangos, ed., *Libro de los exemplos* (Madrid, 1912), No. 370. He has, however, overlooked Ibn Zabara's version. See also W. Liungman, *Die schwedischen Volksmärchen* (Berlin, 1961), 286-8, 374-5, No. 1353 (with a copious bibliography); Tubach, 405, No. 5361, and 343, No. 4511; J. Krzyzanowski, *Polska bajka ludowa* (Warsaw, 1963), 50, No. 1353, and 69, No. 1514. Albert Wesselski, *Märchen des Mittelalters* (Berlin, 1925), 194-7, refers *inter alia* to Ibn Zabara's fascinating version, which he regards as the earliest one. An exquisite Arabic version of Tale Type 1353 is extant in J. E. Hanauer, *Folk-Lore of the Holy Land, Moslem, Christian and Jewish* (London, 1935), 182 f., 'About Woman'; cf. also V. Chauvin, *Bibliographie des ouvrages arabes,* II, 158, No. 78, and 195, No. 20; VIII, 210.

Aspects of Contemporary Ulster Fairy Tradition

LINDA-MAY SMITH   Ulster Folk Museum

THE fairies have, for some time now, attracted the attention of theorists; or rather, attention has been attracted by belief in the fairies. It is important to bear in mind the distinction between the two. The cover notes to the recently published *A History of the Irish Fairies* remarks, 'Having no stories directly from the fairies themselves, we must rely on descriptions by mortal men and women.'[1] For the folklorist, the important issue is what people believe, or say, about the fairies. Tales of the fairies, and what people are prepared to believe about them are matters quite distinct from their actual, physical existence, a question which, for present purposes, clearly is irrelevant.

With reference to what the fairies represent to the people who believe in them or tell stories of them, we may accept Stewart Sanderson's view that fairy belief springs 'from the same source as religion':

> ... its major function is to afford an explanation of the inexplicable and the unknown, for those whose modes of thought operate more by patterns of association than by logic and the verifiable sequence of cause and effect.[2]

Fairy belief is a medium through which the world may be described, an alternative to the modern 'scientific' description. This alternative description may itself be purely empirical. One county Fermanagh farmer, discussing elf-shot, made the remark:

> I spend a fortune dosing cattle against fluke and worms and all this, whereas you have to remember my father never dosed cattle. He'd be mad if he saw me dosing cattle, or to think that an animal would take fluke on his land. He'd be highly indignant, you know? I suppose the farmer has got a lot more enlightened, like everyone else, maybe good or bad.[3]

However, this man himself retained his belief in fairies, a point which illustrates that the belief in fairies serves more than a purely practical purpose.

Evans Wentz, applying to fairies what he described as the 'Psychological Theory', accounted for fairies as the perception of a reality, the awareness of which was restricted to 'seers', who had developed, or who had not destroyed, the necessary psychological apparatus with which to achieve this perception.[4] According to this theory, they form a part of a spectrum of beings inhabiting the earth alongside, but not normally perceived by, human beings. This may, of course, be the case. It may also be the case that the human psyche has, of itself, the power to generate such apparitions. Such arguments, however, cannot be taken much further than themselves. It is here intended to consider what certain individuals have said about fairies, and to see what may be deduced from this. In Evans Wentz's book, *The Fairy Faith in Celtic Countries,* sample stories are provided from Celtic areas which clearly indicate that parallel stories exist in each of them. Basic to that author's argument is the idea that man in general may conceive of, or perceive, a 'spiritual realm', and, while descriptions of this may become racially distinct, it is generated by some basic human instinct.[5] In so far as this describes the 'Psychological Theory', it is an aspect of that theory which is here applied.

Of the Irish fairies in particular, Yeats asked himself the question, 'Who are the fairies?'; his reply supplies for them a succinct classification:

'Fallen angels who were not good enough to be saved, nor bad enough to be lost', say the peasantry. 'The gods of the earth', says the Book of Armagh. 'The gods of pagan Ireland', says the Irish antiquarians, 'the Tuatha De Danann who, when no longer worshipped and fed with offerings, dwindled away in the popular imagination, and are now only a few spans high'.[6]

This categorises the entire matter rather too neatly. In the first place, whether or not the antiquarians were responsible for generating the idea that the fairies were once the Tuatha De Danann, this belief has now some currency among the 'peasantry'; furthermore, ideas about the development of fairy beliefs deduced only from the beliefs themselves, and without reference to the holders of those beliefs, might be felt to be of questionable validity. Finally, even preliminary reading in the field of Irish oral narrative brings to light several tales in which the Tuatha De Danann, far from dwindling away, retain their own identity. The Tuatha De Danann are figures of the old Celtic mythology, known from mediaeval manuscript sources.

There is a tendency to slot Irish fairies into an historical background. For example, the quasi-historical Danes of Irish folklore are often associated with fairies. Forts and small clay pipes are regularly attributed to both. A tenuous link is sometimes made between Danes and De Danann, by analogy of sound, and thus, using the antiquarian argument, between Danes and Fairies. This, if it is a reasonable deduction, seems liable to account for only a part of the picture. It seems that in some cases, there is a desire to rationalise the fairies, by putting them into an historical context. One informant, describing a local archaeological excavation, mentioned some 'wee fairy boys' wearing pottery hats, whose graves had been unearthed in the course of the excavation.[7] This is an interesting extension of the association of the fairies with places known to be of ancient origin. It is of particular interest here, as on another occasion the same informant, a blind fiddle player, said he often heard fairy music in glens and lonesome places.

Folklore has, of course, its own way of dealing with history; the past is curiously pliable, and may be telescoped or extended, an issue not without relevance here. However, without side-tracking into an examination of ideas of how folklore handles the concept of history, it is intended to refer to the fact that history and mythology can be drawn together by folklore, and to follow that up by presenting some samples of modern Ulster fairy tradition.

The general connection between clay pipes, fairies and Danes was mentioned above. Being aware of this connection, when a certain informant mentioned these small clay pipes, I asked if they were ever associated with the Danes.[8] His reply was, 'No, I don't think so. They were more associated with the Milesians, those pipes.'[9] The Milesians are, like the Tuatha De Danann, figures from Celtic mythology. Another set of mythological beings is here finding a place in the spectrum of fairy beliefs.

The same informant, questioned on forts, which are commonly referred to as Danes' forts, remarked:

Inf. Well you see the fort itself was constructed not by the little people.

L.S. Mmm mmm.

Inf. They were constructed by em shall we say the Milesians, they were a race of people that were in this country. Have you heard any reference to them?

L.S. Ah I have heard reference to them yeah, but you wouldn't have heard the old people talking about the Milesians would you?

Inf. Yes.[10]

Referring to the Danes' Cast, the ancient earthwork on the borders of the Ulster counties of Down and Armagh, traditionally known by this name, and also as the 'Run' or 'Race of the Black Pig', or the 'Black Pig's Dyke', he commented:

And the Danes' Cast like I thing it was eh there were two distinct people that infiltrated into Ireland were at the building of the Danes' Cast and I remember one of them was the Milesians. I read that somewhere, in some old book. The Milesians, they were small people, very small in stature and very numerous and where they came from I don't know, they belonged em I don't know where they ... they, but the old people referred to the Milesians. The last man I heard talking about the Milesians was an old man called James Shevlin and I went to see him when he was sick, and while talking to him he turned round and he said to me he says, I says, 'Are you alone?' 'No,' he says, 'I am not,' he says, 'I have the Milesians with me.' He turned round and looked back into the room, but whether it was a figment of his imagination or not I couldn't say. And he said, 'I have the Milesians with me in the room, I'm not lonely.' So at eh... the Milesians it was common knowledge you know in those days about the Milesians.[11]

For this informant, the Milesians are not the same as the fairies, however, they have attributes in common with the fairies, thus helping him to slot the fairies into a background which is actual, and historical, according to his concept of history. On another occasion, he associates Milesians and Fallen Angels.[12] These extracts show an aspect of Irish fairy belief not in accordance with the commonly accepted classification as put forward by Yeats. It is interesting that in this instance the Milesians, not the De Danann, are the mythological characters resembling the fairies. For some informants, the De Danann occupy this position. For others, whether by the application of antiquarian ideas or by the presentation of an independent tradition, the fairies are the modern counterparts, or descendants, of the ancient Tuatha De Danann. The important point here is the lack of standardisation.

While, for this informant, the Milesians occupy a position by others assigned to De Danann or Danes, being in some way fairylike, he is aware of the eschatological background commonly supplied for the fairies:

Inf. Yes, I've heard they were a race of the 'Fallen Angels'.
L.S. Mmm mmm.
Inf. ... and that they had a lo... that they had a time to do on this earth before they were recalled back to their original places. It was said by the old people that that's what... that's what the fairies actually were, 'Fallen Angels'.
L.S. I see, yeah.
Inf. ... that were cast out of Heaven that eh the bible refers to the 'Fallen Angels'.
L.S. Mmm mmm.

Inf. ...and eh where cast out of Heaven for pride and arrogance and been taken back.
L.S. They've been taken back now have they?
Inf. I would say that they have gone for ever.[13]

The spiritual, cosmological significance of the fairies is of interest in itself. The vast majority of believers in fairies see them as having many characteristics in common with human beings, but consider them to be spiritual in nature. In Irish thought, this generally means that they must be fitted into the conventional spectrum of religious ideas, a process which can be seen at work in various fairy tales and traditions. There is, for example, the story in which the fairies seek advice about the possibility of their attaining ultimate salvation, and lament on hearing they are unlikely to achieve it. However, there is not universal agreement here. Several stories have an anti-clerical bent, expressing a contradictory attitude.[14]

It can be seen that the County Armagh storyteller ended his tale of the origin of the fairies by saying that they had been taken back (which contradicts the often-cited idea that they cannot return) to Heaven. He remarked that the fairies had gone for ever. Following up this theme of the departure of the fairies, the informant was asked:

L.S. Mmm you were saying there about the fairies having been taken back em into Heaven, I've heard stories where the fairies had battles with other fairies. Did you ever hear any talk like that?
Inf. Well eh I haven't heard eh anything about that but eh I did know about the last night, the farewell party, that... that farewell was a lamentation which was described by the old people as a lamentation of sorrow on that night that I described to you before. When on that hill at eh Glenlochin, I can see the hill yet, I know it very well, and that's where it took place, and it was a night of lamentations, just as might have taken place with the ordinary folk of losing a friend or going away, emigrating. These fairies were leaving.
L.S. And they were sorry to be leaving?
Inf. And they were sorry to be leaving.
L.S. Ha ah.

400

Inf. They must have been called back because eh they had a that eh gathering on this hill and eh they made their way and eh their first stop was as I said before in Williamson's Back Rock, it wasn't Williamson's then and on . . . in that rock or the back field there was a fairy tree and it was round this eh fairy thorn at times that they met. But this particular night they em they had em stop there at that and they left there they went on and headed for the village of Acton and eh they went down and they went into McBride's Hill, and in that hill was another fairy thorn and they had their last, that's the last place that they had a gathering at that thorn. So they left there sometime early in the morning, they crossed McBride's Hill and headed for County Down, but that's the last now was heard of the fairies.[15]

Some of the more precise details of this geographical description of the route taken by the fairies have been edited out. It is, however clearly enough, of some importance to the story-teller. He has repeated it, with the same details, on several occasions, and has taken me to photograph the various landmarks mentioned.

Admittedly, this tale is not of necessity contradictory to a tale told on another occasion by a member of the informant's family, and in the informant's company. However, in the last extract, the informant himself stated he had not heard this fairly common tradition:

Inf. There's a well outside the house and he was in contact apparently with the fairies, and they told him they were all leaving, they were going to Scotland, they were going to a battle, between the Scots and the Irish.
L.S. Yeah.
Inf. And that if the water was clear in so many days they'd be back, all would be well.
L.S. Mmm.
Inf. But if the water turned red in the well, they would hardly be back for they would have been defeated, and eh so he told me that that his grandfather went out and

there the water began to turn reddish and he got no more trace of the fairies in his part of the country from that . . .[16]

Of course, these two traditions of the departure of the fairies could be combined. In fact, the second story-teller was reminded of his tale on hearing a recording of the first version of the departure tale, and neither man challenged the other as to the veracity of this tradition. On closer examination, however, it can be seen that the tales are incompatible. In the second, the fairies do not know whether they will return or not, while in the first, it is stated '. . . they were sorry to be leaving, they must have been called back'. The important point would then seem to be not the details of the departure, but the fact that the fairies were around at one time, and have now departed.

The picture which is beginning to emerge shows that fairy belief is in fact a very vague, ill-defined area, embracing subtleties no classificatory system can hope to encompass. For one informant the tale of the departure of the fairies is a matter of such significance that he has carefully pinned down the route travelled. However, that is apparently a personal matter. Providing that both informants are in agreement that the fairies were at one time present, the rest becomes insignificant. The Armagh stories cited so far have all referred to the disappearance of the fairies. Consider however, the following extract. The 'Terry' mentioned in this incident is the teller of the last tale:

Terry and Paddy, both of them, along with myself, that we saw that . . . these little people, or leprechauns, or whatever they are, are still in existence in places, in isolated places and we were coming home from working late at . . . at . . . I recorded this for you before . . . and this little person was on the roadside and eh dressed in a kind of cape which went to the ground and a little hood over the head and what seemed to me to be . . . well, it was red in colour from this down . . . from the waist right down to the ground, but I could see . . . I couldn't see the feet or anything like that but I did walk up close against this, and looked down and saw it and when I . . . my attention . . . they spoke out of the car, attracted my attention, I looked round when I went back it was gone.[17]

401

This is told despite the categoric statement, '. . . that's the last now was heard of the fairies',

What conclusions may be drawn from this? The most obvious is perhaps that the informant, spotting an apparently gullible collector, decided to have some fun by inventing, rather than by retailing 'proper', traditions. No doubt this happens on occasion, but in this case, such a deduction would be more than unfair to the informant concerned. Rather, these contradictions lead to the conclusion that there is a great deal of flexibility underlying fairy beliefs.

Before going on to consider this flexibility, it is necessary to say something about the light that the Armagh extracts throw on the processes involved in formulating contemporary fairy belief. This informant has drawn together what he has heard from 'the old people', what he has read, and what he has gleaned from direct personal experience. This interrelation of written and oral sources is of great importance, especially when the circulation of magazines and pamphlets containing printed folk material is considered. In addition, it is necessary to consider the influence of other mass media, which affect folklore, sometimes profoundly. As the most glaring example of this, more than one informant has linked up fairy traditions and the appearance of U.F.Os.

This leads to one of two conclusions. It may be that, in looking for fairy lore in the Ulster of the 1970s, a collector is liable to come up only with half-remembered, bastardised scraps, the remnants of a once vital tradition. On the other hand, it may be that there is something misguided in this view of a 'once vital tradition'. It is, of course, true that as living conditions change, folklore develops to fit its changing context. It is also true, however, that this is not the first generation to regard itself as moving away from fairy lore.

The Ordnance Survey Memoirs of the mid-nineteenth century contain several references to fairy lore as a thing of the past; in other places, of course, the same Memoirs record examples of contemporary fairy traditions. Jeremiah Curtin, collecting in the Kerry of the late nineteenth century, records the opinion of the owner of the house in which he stayed:

My host was a man who retained a belief in fairies, though he did not acknowledge it —

at least explicity, and in words. 'When I was a boy,' said he, 'nine men in ten believed in fairies, and said so, now only one man in ten says that he believes in them. If one of the nine believes, he will not tell you, he will keep him mind to himself.'[18]

Familiar words to modern collectors, who are all too often told that the really good story-tellers are dead. This view of fairy tradition as a thing of the past is itself a part of folklore. Fairy tradition of today is dynamic, open to new influences which develop, rather than bastardise it. While, in the past, the influences may have taken different forms, there is no reason to suppose that the process itself has differed. An informant may be unaware of the source of his material, and is certainly not going to be aware of influences subsequent to his first hearing of a story — assuming his first hearing to be his source.

One aspect of this dynamism is, of course, the flexibility which fairy stories and beliefs themselves display. Even the small selection of quoted extracts show not only apparent conflict between traditions of the fairies but having told how not all the fairies are gone, for he has seen one, the same man concludes a different tale by remarking 'That's the last was heard of the fairies' — the tales, as quoted, follow a thematic rather than their chronological order. One man holds mutually contradictory beliefs, but has somehow reconciled the contradictions. He can reconcile contradictions both in his own system in itself, and as it conflicts with the system of another story-teller, as is evidenced by the contradictory departure tales. It seems that, to the tellers, these contradictions are unimportant, so long as the tales concur in the fact that the fairies actually exist. This general vagueness makes it possible for contradictory tales to be told, without any sense that they do conflict.

Clearly, the word 'fairy' must communicate something, but fairy beliefs allow for a vast range of elaboration and interpretation, depending on by whom they are handled. Thus, while there must be a commonly agreed concept 'fairy' — and there are commonly agreed ways in which fairies believe, appear and the like — precisely what the word means to any one individual, and whether its meaning is constant, even for that individual, are matters of conjecture. It is here claimed that vague, ill-defined ideas can be crystallised through stories in which fairy manifestations can be explored in a manner and form which is commonly intelligible. The very fact that the background is so vague allows almost infinite scope for the development expectations which are commonly understood. These commonly understood expectations could be seen as Evans Wentz's characteristically Celtic aspects of the fairy faith, but the individual's ability to conceive of fairies, or fairy-like creatures, is common to all humanity; or at least, to all believers and sympathisers, for of course, believers and non-believers live side by side.

This general background vagueness also allows for other folklore developments. The hero of one story, for example, may thus acquire the attributes of another. It may also account for matters such as the acquisition of plot elements of one story by another. This flexibility, making many elements of of folklore defy classification, is a marked aspect of contemporary folklore, a good reason for believing that flexibility has a respectable, 'traditional' background.

In conclusion, I wish to thank both Frank McCourt and Terry Murray, for all their generous help and hospitality, and for the permission to reproduce material recorded from them.

Notes

1. Carolyn White, *A History of the Irish Fairies* (Dublin and Cork, 1976).

2. Stewart Sanderson, *The Secret Commonwealth* (Cambridge, 1976), 46.

3. Ulster Folk and Transport Museum cassette archive, C75.1. The tapes are references below as U.F.T.M.

4. W. H. Evans Wentz, *The Fairy Faith in Celtic Countries* (London, 1911), *passim.*

5. *ibid.*, 396.

6. W. B. Yeats, *Fairy and Folk Tales of Ireland* (Gerrards Cross, 1973), 11.

7. U.F.T.M. R76.7.

8. Here another problem of a historical nature is raised. Logically, clay pipes cannot predate the introduction of tobacco. Taking oral tradition at its face value, George Benn, *History of the Town of Belfast* (Belfast, 1823), remarks of clay pipes: 'If these pipes belonged to the Danes, as their name would appear to prove, it is another proof of the universality and antiquity of that most absurd of all practices, smoking. If this be the case, it becomes a matter worthy of the inquiry of the antiquary, what root or herb was used for the purpose . . . it is certainly a curious subject of speculation, to see civilised man of the present age, using for the same purpose, the very instrument which had graced the mouth of a savage a thousand years before.'

9. U.F.T.M. C76.72.

10. U.F.T.M. C76.71.

11. U.F.T.M. C76.72.

12. *ibid.,*

13. U.F.T.M. C76.71.

14. B.B.C. Recorded Programmes Library, *The Fairy Faith,* Record No. 17941.

15. U.F.T.M. C76.76.

16. U.F.T.M. C77.13.

17. U.F.T.M. C76.76.

18. Jeremiah Curtin, *Tales of the Fairies and of the Ghost World* (London, 1895), 3.

The Collection and Study of Folktales in Twentieth-Century China

NAI-tUNG TING   University of Illinois

ALTHOUGH classical Chinese literature contained many, and made use of more, folktales, the collection and study of tales *per se* has had a brief history in China. It was not until the May Fourth Movement of 1915, when classical Chinese was taken down a peg or two, that stories told in the simple language of the peasants gradually became respectable in print. The earliest centre for folklore research was also the cradle of the above movement — Peking University, where the president, as well as some of its most distinguished faculty members, all displayed great interest in folklore. Their favourite subjects, however, were at first the folk song (regarded for centuries as the weathercock of public opinion), the myth, and the repertoire of professional storytellers. The lowly folktale did not appear in print until three years later,[1] and did not graduate from magazines for children to serious periodicals until the middle 1920s.[2] Of the two important periodicals containing folk narratives, the one published by Sun Yat-sen University at Canton adopted the anthropological approach;[3] the other, published in Hangchow, was principally humanistic.[4] Collections came out apace between 1928 and 1936. Besides the thirty-seven books edited by Lin Lan,[5] there were also those representing various provinces[6] and towns.[7] Although this period of fervid activities lasted scarcely a decade, it gathered and published several thousand narratives.

In attitude as well as method, Chinese collectors of those years resembled their counterparts in nineteenth-century Europe or India. Since no systematic field-work was carried out, most of the authors relied principally on memories. Very little, if anything at all, was said about the informant, who was usually a relative, a servant, a pupil, or a colleague. Sometimes, even the area of circulation was omitted, the author taking for granted that the readers knew where he hailed from. In style, the majority of the versions tend to be laconic and prosaic, although some, presumably by young contributors, contain florid descriptions and editorial comments. The language used by the collectors ranges from classical and semi-classical to vernacular Chinese, but rarely mixed with colloquial or dialectal phrases as one often finds in peasants' oral communications. Because all the centres of folklore activity were situated along the Pacific coast, most of the versions came from the coastal provinces — especially Chekiang and Kwangtung. The vast interior was left untouched. For the tales of the minority races within China, such as Tibetans and Mongolians, Chinese readers had to rely on European sources. Besides, the collectors being mostly students and teachers of Chinese literature and history, many of the stories they knew and liked were naturally concerned with the *literati*. Those that centre around the triumph and the wisdom of certain men of letters could have filtered down from the professional storytellers to the folk and been popular among them for some time. Those built on elegant and subtle verses, though, could not have been well known to illiterate peasantry. At any rate, a very high percentage of the narratives that saw the light during those years were jokes, which the low in China enjoyed as well as the high, even though the humble folk themselves might be presented as the dupes of unconscionable *literati*.

Remarkable in recording, this period was not so strong in folklore research. The works of German, Finnish and other Continental folklorists were apparently unknown to the Chinese, since English was the only foreign language which the majority of Chinese scholars could read. An American professor did publish an article on the historical-geographical method,[8] but only one of his colleagues – an expert in the folk song – seems to have referred to it.[9] As for the other folklorists, almost all the Western authorities that they mentioned and respected were British: Hartland, Clouston, Jacobs, Byrne, etc. Theoretically, they could be classified as followers of evolutionary anthropology, using frequently such terms as cultural relics, primitive mentality, historical evolution, and so on. From the viewpoint of the folktale, the best among them were probably Chao Ching-shen and Chung Ching-wen, both of whom made valuable studies of certain Chinese tales and legends and suggested ways to classify Chinese tale types,[10] the former using the method of Joseph Jacobs.

This prolific, promising period was unfortunately brought to an abrupt close in 1937 by the Japanese invasion of China. Chinese intellectuals who moved with the universities to the interior became so preoccupied with the survival of the nation and their own problems that most meaningful cultural activities came to a halt. A few folklorists, who migrated to West China, however, used this opportunity to record folk narratives among national minorities.[11] After World War II, China remained in the throes of civil strife until 1950. The inauguration of the People's Republic heralded for many Chinese a new period of folk narrative work, for most of the enthusiastic proponents of folk literature in the Republican Period had shown leftist leanings and Mao Tse-tung had openly praised the literary expressions of workers, peasants and soldiers.[12] The government was expected to promote the publication and research of folk narratives; and it did. Under official sponsorship, the Chinese Folk Literature and Art Research Society was set up in Peking in March, 1950. Its first effort in periodical literature resulted only in three issues.[13] But, when it picked up again in 1955, its new organ, *Folk Literature* (*Min-chien wen-hsüeh*), was to continue publication for almost twelve years.[14] Meanwhile, literary magazines in other parts of China also started to carry folk narratives, some of them in many issues between 1956 and 1959.[15] Collections in book form appeared in large numbers. Every province and almost every nationality were investigated for folk narratives and represented in print. Though usually smaller in size, these collections far exceeded those of the Republican Period in volume number. Works appearing in the previous period can be counted in dozens; works of this period in hundreds.

Unlike those of the earlier period, the folk narratives published in the 1950s and the early 1960s were apparently collected from the peasantry. Besides the teams organised by universities and literary societies and sent to the countryside to search for oral literature, many other Chinese intellectuals who had to live among the peasants also knew them well. Everybody seemed to be in agreement that complete fidelity should be observed in recording. The versions collected during those years, therefore, are often accompanied by concrete information about the actual raconteurs in either the notes or descriptions of field trips. The language used tends frequently to be idiomatic and animated, thus seemingly closer to speech. The systematic quest unearthed the narrative treasures of many remote parts of the land, especially in West and Southwest China. Animal tales and legends of various professional groups, hitherto thought to be very rare among Han-Chinese, proved to be quite common. International tale types, believed once to be sporadic and alien in China, proved now to be well-established residents. The extensive recording of the tales of the national minorities aided and corroborated this discovery, since versions found along the border areas often resemble their Indo-European counterparts quite closely and may supply the missing links in hypothetical historical reconstructions, as my work on the Cinderella Cycle[16] has suggested. Investigation of minority folklore also brought to light many long verse narratives. Some of them are concerned with the myths and the migrations of obscure races, interesting to ethnologists as well as historians. Those gathered in Southwest China mostly centre around love stories; they are valuable not only for their possible connections with ancient Han lyrics, but also for their varied, fascinating rhyme schemes, China being one of the first countries to use rhymes. The heroic epics of the Mongolians may be affiliated with similar productions from Central and West Asia or the legends of the Ural area, the importance of which are being increasingly felt. In short, because of the contributions of the collectors of those years, we can understand much better now not only the entire Chinese tradition, but also its relationship with its neighbours and its place in the whole world.

Such brilliant achievements probably would not have been possible without state support and, as in all other countries, government financing always brings government supervision. Mao Tse-tung's views on folk narratives may be best represented by the following directive: 'We must separate the musty products of the ancient feudal ruling class from the excellent traditonal elements of folk culture, elements that are more or less democratic or revolutionary in nature.'[17] Interpreted in proper historical perspective, not many Chinese folk narratives would fail to measure up to this standard. As one folklorist put it: 'In folk literature, such as folk songs and folktales, those containing unhealthy elements superimposed by the feudal ruling class are, after all, in the minority; the main stream consists indisputably of democratic and revolutionary elements.'[18] Some extremists, who were later to cluster around the Gang of Four, however, lacked historical perspective and could not tolerate anything seemingly irrelevant to their goals.[19] As they had always been powerful in literary circles, their attacks led to the disgrace of Chung Ching-wen[20] and brought on, during the latter half of 1957 and the early half of 1958, a spate of radical articles in the official organ — some of which were probably penned by moderates in order to save their research society.[21] Real radicals, though, were probably only a small minority; for volumes of traditional tales kept coming out with only short or no apologetic notes. To forestall hostile criticism, the moderates had to toe the party line in introductions to multi-volume anthologies, to avoid materials which consist of praises of kings and ministers, harmful superstitions, pornography, etc., but to favour jokes satirising corrupt officials, allusions to social injustice, complaints of the sufferings of the poor, stories of righteous rebels, and so on. Seemingly 'progressive' narratives, incidentally, had always been part and parcel of the oral tradition. Even stories of farm hands or servants outwitting their employers, though denounced by some Western folklorists as fake, had actually appeared in collections published before 1937,[22] and could boast of many analogues.[23]

The vast majority of the traditional tales published during those days, scrupulously separated from the so-called 'new' legends in *Folk Literature*, were definitely *Märchen* and *Novelle*, which had no obvious connection with any modern political philosophy.

Like their counterparts in other countries, Chinese folklorists of this period were often engaged in disputes. The longest one revolved around a problem not unknown to the West: How true should a printed version be to its original? Many Chinese collectors felt that folk narratives, which came from common people, were meant for the enjoyment of common people; consequently, a little modification or processing in published versions might be necessary. To some folklorists, processing meant only improving the readability of crude originals.[24] To some others, apparently all young people accustomed to *belles-lettres*, artless folk narratives needed embellishment. Of the best-known proponents of this view, one professed to follow the example of A. Tolstoy and sometimes exhibited a tendency to amalgamate different versions of the same tale.[25] The other resorted to the obsolete practice of pointing morals, improving characterisation, and so on.[26] The twosome were obviously 'problem children' to the editorial board of *Folk Literature*, who had insisted all along that every contributor must turn in the original transcript together with the finished manuscript. A Soviet-trained folklorist also pointed out that Tolstoy's method was fit only for authors of children's literature.[27] The replies of the twosome are not worth repeating, except that they all insisted, like their critics, that the basic plot of a narrative must remain intact, and that tape recorders, though desirable, were too few in number to be distributed among Chinese collectors.[28] This dispute seemed to peter out after 1961, when a leading folklorist maintained that 'cautious processing', as approved by the majority of his colleagues, 'would by necessity rule out wilful revisions.'[29] He gave those who wanted to take undue liberties a very damaging title: 'captives of bourgeois thought.'[30]

When working on my *Types of Chinese Folktales in the Oral Tradition and Classical Non-Religious Literature* (soon to come out in Helsinki as Folklore Fellows Communications No.223) I carefully compared Chinese tales recorded in the

People's Republic with those collected during the Republican Period or by foreign writers. I discovered that all the entries in my book can be represented with the same code numbers and letters. Semantic changes that did not require modifications in the rest of the story, such as calling a rich man a landlord, were not uncommon, but very, very few versions displayed any violent departure in basic plot. I regret therefore the deep suspicion that existed once in the United States in regard to the reliability of Chinese folktales published in China after 1950. The principal source of this suspicion[31] re-echoed Kuomintang propaganda in its terminology.[32] It did not try to be fair because, at least in its section on the folktale, it used an extreme case to represent the whole and quoted only from essays induced by an unusual crisis.[33] It was not based on very thorough research and thus misinterpreted a vital issue.[34] Following the example of similar surveys from Taiwan,[35] it exaggerated the merits of the Kuomintang regime, and magnified the faults of the People's Republic. Certainly, because of the complex political situation, folktale activities in the People's Republic were not free from imperfections, which the moderates there acknowledged and bewailed.[36] But to deny its great contributions because of these imperfections seems to me the same as throwing away the baby with the bath water. In any event, the concessions made by the moderates in order to preserve a part of their national heritage apparently deceived only their foreign critics, not their domestic foes. When the Cultural Revolution spearheaded by the extremists gained the upper hand, all folklore publications became indefinitely suspended, and their authors and editors vanished from view. No new Chinese folk narrative has seen the light since then.

As to theory, the harrassed and bewildered Chinese folklorists of those days apparently had no time to formulate systematic and comprehensive hypotheses of their own. Of Western theories, they were mostly opposed to evolutionary anthropology,[37] which they could have learned from their predecessors. In this, incidentally, they were like many folklorists in the other Third World countries, unhappy about the implied racism and social snobbery. In regard to their alleged antipathy to the Finnish School, which their American critics have regarded as quite serious, all the arguments to this effect in the above-mentioned source were drawn from articles criticising Chung Ching-wen — and Chung never showed any knowledge of the historical-geographical method.[38]

Finally, since the downfall of the Gang of Four in October 1976, the dust is settling rapidly in China. 'Let a hundred flowers bloom; let a hundred schools contend' is again the watchword to abide by. With the infantile leftists out of the way, China may enjoy a cultural renaissance for many years to come. In art and literature, traditional Chinese culture is coming into its own, and historical persepctive is being restored. For instance, the adoration of a Southern Sung-dynasty general, once the symbol of Chinese patriotism irrespective of class distinctions, has again received official blessings.[39] Landscape and still-life paintings in the classical style have become very popular and mythology and legends are again featured in art objects, the only subjects still frowned on being the subversive, the obscene, and the ugly[40] — standards not far removed from those of Western censorship. I have recently heard that the Folk Literature and Art Research Society has been re-established. If this news is true, folktale collection and research may start again under happier and freer circumstances, and the coverage of all phases of the Chinese tradition, once an urgent plea,[41] may become reality.

Notes

1. T'ang Hsiao-p'u, *Ching-yü t'ung-hua* (*Tales for Children in Mandarin*; Shanghai, 1918); *Fu-nü tsa-chih* (*The Ladies Journal*), IV (1918). Both, it is interesting to note, contain European as well as Chinese tales.

2. The following magazines began to publish folk narratives in the following years: *Hsiao-shuo shih-chieh* (*The Story World*), 1922; *Hsiao-shuo yüeh-pao* (*The Short Story Magazine*), 1925; *Yü-ssu* (*Brief Discourses*), 1925; *Pei-ching ta-hsüeh yen-chiu-so kuo-hsüeh men chou-k'an* (*Bulletin de l'Institut Sinologique de l'Université Nationale de Pekin*), 1925.

3. *Min-su* (*Folklore*; Canton, 1928-33, 1936-7, 1943).

4. *Min-chien yüeh-k'an* (*Folklore Monthly*; Hangchow, 1931-7).

5. All of these volumes appeared between 1928 and 1935.

6. For instance, Hsieh Yün-sheng, *Fu-chien ku-shih* (*Stories from Fukein*; Amoy, 1929); *Shan-tung min-chien ch'üan-shuo* (*Legends from Shantung*), ed. Bureau of Mass Education of Shantung (Tsinan, 1933); W. Eberhard, *Volksmärchen aus Södost-China* (Helsinki, 1941): tales collected by Ts'ao Sung-yeh in south and east Chekiang.

7. Sun Chia-hsün, *Wa-wa shih* (*Baby-shaped Stone*; Shanghai, 1929); Lou Tzu-k'uang and Ch'en Te-ch'ang, *Shao-hsing ku-shih* (*Tales from Shaohsing*; Canton, 1929); Liu Wan-chang, *Kuang-chou min-chien ku-shih* (*Folktales from Canton*; Canton, 1929); Wu Tsao-t'ing, *Ch'üan-chou min-chien ch'üan-shuo* (*Legends from Chüanchow*; Chüanchow, 1929-32).

8. R. D. Jameson, 'Comparative Folklore Methodological Notes', in *Tsing-hua chou-k'an* (*Tsing Hua University Weekly*), XXXI.

9. Chu Tzu-ch'ing, *Chung-kuo ko-yao* (*Folk Songs of China*; reprint, Taipei, 1965), 30-1.

10. Chao Ching-shen, 'Chung-kuo min-chien ku-shih hsing-shih fa-tuan' ('Types of Chinese Folktales: First Attempt'), *Min-su*, VIII (1928), 1-10; *ibid.*, 'Chung-kuo min-chien ku-shih hsing-shih' ('Types of Chinese Folktales'), *Min-su hsüeh chi-chien* (*A Collection of Essays on Folklore*), Series I (first published in 1931; reprint, Taipei, 1970), 353-74.

11. For instance, Chuang Hsüeh-pen, *Hsi-k'ang Yi-tsu tiao-ch'a pao-kao* (*Report on a Field Trip for Studying the Yi People in Sikang*; Kangting, 1941), and his *K'ang Tsang min-chien ku-shih* (*Folktales Recorded among the Tibetans at Kangting*; Shanghai, 1950); Kuan Te-tung, *Hsin-chiang min-ko min-t'an chi* (*Folk Songs and Folktales from Sinkiang*; Shanghai, 1950).

12. *Mao Tse-tung chi* (*Works of Mao Tse-tung*; Hong Kong, 1975), VIII, 122-3.

13. *Min-chien wen-i chi-k'an* (*Publications in Folk Literature*); Peking, 1950-1.

14. *Min-chien wen-hsüeh* (*Folk Literature*); Peking, April 1955 to February 1966.

15. For instance: *T'ien shan* (Urumchi), *Shan hua* (Kweiyang), *Pei-ching wen-i* (Peking), and *Yen-ho* (Sian).

16. Nai-tung Ting, *The Cinderella Cycle in China and Indo-China* (Helsinki, 1974).

17. Quoted by Chou Yang in *Min-chien wen-i chi-k'an*, II, 11.

18. Liu K'uei-li, 'Tsai t'an min-chien wen-hsüeh sou-chi kung-tso' ('On Collecting Folktales Again'), *Min-chien wen-hsüeh* (May 1960), 89.

19. For a contemporary description of such people, see *Min-chien wen-i chi-k'an*, II, 20.

20. Chung's difficulties, which started late in 1957, seem to have been the result of a power struggle. From the evidence available, he had not been tactful enough in his dealings.

21. There was a suggestion that the Folk Literature and Art Research Society be abolished. To my knowledge, friends of the disgraced man might also join the verbal barrage in order to save not only themselves, but also the intended victim. Chung, it may be added, was to stay on as a director of a writers' league for another five or six years.

22. *Min-su hsüeh chi-chien*, I, 281-5; Ch'iu Yü-lin, *Ch'ih-jen ↵yü chiao-jen ku-shih* (*Stories of Foolish and Cunning People*; Shanghai, 1930), II, 20-4, 31-2; Lin Lan, *Min-chien ch'ü-shih hsin-chi* (*Amusing Folktales*; Shanghai, 1932-4), I, 12-16; Lin Lan, *T'an-tsui ti fu-jen* (*A Gluttonous Woman*; Shanghai, 1933), 44-9; *Min-su*, new series, I (1936), 150-63.

23. One of those analogues has been recorded in Eberhard, *Chinese Fairy Tales and Folktales* (London, 1937), 280-2. See also *Chung-kuo hsiao-hua shu chi-shih-i chung* (*Seventy-one Chinese Joke Collections*; Taipei, 1961), 331, 407.

24. Cf., *inter alia, Min-chien wen-hsüeh* (April 1961), 8.

25. Tung Chün-lun and Chiang Yüan, *Shih-men k'ai* (*The Door on the Cliff is Open*; Shanghai, 1955), 149.

26. Chang Shih-chieh, in *Min-chien wen-hsüeh* (Nov. 1958), 65-71, and *ibid.* (Dec.1956), 90-4.

27. Liu K'uei-li, 'T'an min-chien wen-hsüeh sou-chi kung-tso' ('On Collecting Folktales'), *Min-chien wen-hsüeh* (June 1957), 35-6.

28. Tung Chün-lun and Chiang Yüan, 'Ts'ung Liao chai ch'a-tzu shuo-chi'i' ('On the Derivatives of *Liao chai*'), *Min-chien wen-hsüeh* (Dec. 1959), 89.

29. Chia Chih, 'T'an ko min-tsu min-chien wen-hsüeh sou-chi cheng-li wen-t'i' ('Problems of Collecting and Processing Folk Literature from Various Nationalities'), in *Min-chien ku-shih ti sou-chi ho cheng-li* (*On Collecting and Processing Folktales*; Changchun, 1963), 26. See also *Min-chien wen-hsüeh* (May 1961), 28.

30. Chia Chih, 47.

31. Alsace Yen's master thesis (Indiana University, 1964), and his two articles based on the same data in *Literature East and West*, II/III/IV (1964), 72-86, and *Asian Folklore Studies*, XXV (1967), 1-62. All subsequent references to Yen's work are to the second article.

32. For instance, it asserts that Mao Tse-tung had been a brigand (Yen, 24; cf. also 34). It also suggested that the coverage of minority folk-lore in China was motivated by expansionism (Yen, 62). Since the vast majority of these minorities dwell only in Chinese territories, China could not possibly encourage them to rebel against herself. By the same line of reasoning, any majority group studying the folklore of a minority (such as white folk-lorists investigating American Indian folklore) could likewise be accused of expansionism.

33. The example given is Chang Shih-chieh's 'Yü-t'ung' ('Fisher Boy'; *Min-chien wen-hsüeh* (April 1958), 81-6), followed by Chang's description of his own method, *Min-chien wen-hsüeh* (Dec. 1959), 93. The essays quoted (Yen, 45-8) are the unusually radical ones written after the disgrace of Chung Ching-wen (cf. *supra*, 5, in the present study). Yen did not point out the critique of Chang's method by the leadership (Chia Chih, 44-5, 56-7, 62) and by other folklorists, or the cir-cumstances that prompted these frantic essays.

34. With regard to the controversial motif essential to the quoted legend — a Caucasian seizing a magic object from a Chinese — Yen evidently did not realise that the same motif had appeared before in both nineteenth-century and Republican Period literature (cf. Nai-tung Ting, 'Chinese Folk Narrative in an East-West Context' [a mimeographed paper presented at the annual conference of the American Folk-lore Society in 1968], 4), or that it may have circulated very widely in China because it has been found also in Szechuan, a province far removed from Hopei. (See Tan Ling, *Chin ya-erh* [*Golden Duck*; Chungking, 1955], 1-8 and postscript.)

35. See Lou Tzu-k'uang and Chu Chieh-fan, *Wu-shih nien lai ti Chung-kuo su wen-hsüeh* (*Chinese Folk Literature in the Past Fifty Years*; Taiwan, 1963).

36. Partisan attacks such as the above were anticipated and rejected in Chia Chih, 23, 25, 36.

37. See, inter alia, *Min-chien wen-hsüeh* (May 1960), 88, and Chia Chih, 19-20.

38. Cf. *supra*, 3, in the present study.

39. *Ta-kung pao* (Hong Kong), English Weekly Supplement (11th-17th May 1978), 6.

40. *1978 Spring: The Chinese Export Commodities Fair* (Special edition, No.3), edited by the newspaper *Ta-kung pao* (Hong Kong, May 1978), 3.

41. See Chia Chih, 26-7.

The Lion, The Unicorn and The Fox

KENNETH VARTY   University of Glasgow

TALES and folklore about the Lion and the Unicorn, or about the Lion and the Fox are, I suppose, well-known: but was there, once, a tale featuring all three? This is the question I asked myself when, in the mid-1960s, I came across a misericord carving in Knowle Parish Church, Warwickshire, on which these three creatures are depicted (see plate 18) — it is probably early sixteenth century, possibly late fifteenth century. At that time I decided that this carving did not reflect any story featuring these three animals, but was simply an example of late medieval symbolism. In 1967 I wrote: (A misericord at Knowle) 'shows the lion in the centre, glaring from beneath half-lowered lids. To the onlooker's left is a unicorn distinguished by his single horn. To the right is a proud-looking fox, distinguished by his brush. The unicorn was a symbol of virtue, the fox one of vice. The lion probably represents temporal power here, as he does in the medieval French stories centred on Reynard the Fox and their derivations. The lesson, surely, is that the ruler of the land has it in his power to do great good or great evil. Perhaps it is a good sign that the unicorn stands on the lion's right. Perhaps it means that the fox has not achieved supreme power here, but is very near to doing so.'[1]

I made this last remark in the context of a general survey of fox-literature and lore in later medieval France in which the royal favour shown to the fox, however evil he may be seen to be to all the other animals and to the reader, is emphasised as part of the satire which saturates later medieval Reynard-the-Fox literature. An example is Rutebeuf's 1261 poem, *Renart le Bestourné* ('Reynard the Corrupt'), which begins with words which, in translation, read: 'Reynard is dead, Reynard is alive; Reynard is foul, Reynard is vile; yet Reynard reigns.' In the *Couronnement Renart* ('The Crowning of Reynard'; c.1263-70), the fox usurps the lion and reigns in his stead, while in *Renart le Nouvel* ('The New Reynard'; 1289), the fox is the lion's completely trusted, right-hand man. The unicorn, however, never appears in any fox-centred literature which I know.

Imagine my surprise, then, when, in the early 1970s, I rediscovered the so-called 'lost' cycle of woodcuts which illustrated Wynkyn de Worde's 1499 edition of *Reynard the Fox* and found among these illustrations a unicorn seated right by the crowned lion and opposite the fox.[2] This brief paper is to show you this evidence, and to tell you why, nevertheless, I have finally come back to the conclusion that my 1967 interpretation of the Knowle misericord is right, and that there never was any lion-unicorn-fox story as such.

One of the chief characteristics of the woodcuts which Wynkyn de Worde had made for his 1499 edition of *Reynard the Fox* is their faithfulness to the text of the narrative. The artist clearly knew the text, and illustrated it carefully. A second, quite remarkable characteristic, is that he must have observed most of the animals; they are, again and again, quite realistically depicted, though, obviously, their 'humanisation' occasionally veils the artist's evident first-hand knowledge of most of the animals depicted. The appearance of the unicorn amongst the animals in these woodcuts is therefore quite unusual, and doubly so because there is no mention of the creature in the texts which the woodcut is supposed to illustrate. Even allowing for the fact that the unicorn was not — to people in 1499 — the mythological creature it is to us, its appearance in the illustration of a 1499 edition of *Reynard the Fox* is quite remarkable. How to explain it?

Plate 18. Misericord in Knowle Parish Church, Warwickshire, showing the Lion, the Unicorn and the Fox.

Plate 19. Woodcut by Wynkyn de Worde, described overleaf, showing the Lion, the Unicorn and the Fox.

A typical and, artistically, one of the best examples of Wynkyn de Worde's woodcuts, depicts the unicorn, along with the lion and the fox. (See Plate 19, previous page.) The fox is about to be hanged for his crimes; a cat pulls the cowled fox backwards up the gallows ladder; a bear stands below, his arms on the ladder, at the foot of which a doggy-looking wolf gives assistance. Prominent in the foreground is the crowned lion who has condemned the fox to death. And by his side, even more prominently, is the unicorn. The stag behind the unicorn is an important detail, I think, as I shall try to show.

Woodcuts in other, early English and continental editions of *Reynard the Fox* usually repeat this pattern. For example, there is a fairly crude version of the same scene, to be found in a cheap, clearly popular English edition of *Reynard the Fox*, dated c.1550. Here the triangle lion-unicorn-fox is very plain to see. The stag's presence is particularly clear and prominent. There is another, quite sophisticated but somewhat confused version to be found in a Danish edition of *Reynard the Fox*, dated 1555. Here the unicorn is immediately behind the lion, and the stag behind the unicorn. There is also a much less fussy, clearer version in a German edition dated 1562. The lion-in-front-of-the-unicorn-in-front-of-the-stag situation is particularly evident. There is a further example from another German edition, this one dated 1567 and illustrating a Latin version of the text. This depicts a particularly fussy, confused grouping of the animals, and one in which the unicorn seems to be about to leave the scene with, significantly, I think, the stag. This iconographical tradition was a particularly persistent one, as yet another version of the scene appears in an English illustration dated 1735 and published in London. This 'popular' edition groups the significant animals in a very clear if somewhat crude manner.

However, in some modern editions, the earliest being late seventeenth century, the unicorn is dismissed from the scene, whilst the deer, curiously, is retained, for example in a 1681 English edition. In an eighteenth-century Dutch edition, even the stag is missing. I do wonder, however, if the curious wand held by the lion in this woodcut is not some kind of recollection of either the stag's or the unicorn's horn, or both?

Now I have drawn your attention especially to the stag, and earlier I said it was rather curious that, when the unicorn was dismissed from some relatively modern editions, the stag was retained. Why important? Why curious? Because the stag plays no part in the narrative of any of the versions of the story of which the woodcuts purport to be illustrations. The stag and the unicorn are, moreover, the only animals in any of the illustrations who do not play a part in the narrative. Why then, do the artists include them in their illustrations? Once done, it is not surprising that their reappearance goes on being depicted. Book artists, as is well known, copied each other. But why, even in the earliest cycle of illustrations, did an artist who clearly illustrated the text so closely and so realistically, include both deer and unicorn in such proximity to each other and in such obvious relationship to the lion, such obvious counterbalance to the fox?

The lion and the unicorn were first brought together, it seems, as symbols, in Flemish town emblems and heraldry — the lion representing royal power, authority and strength, the unicorn righteousness, truth, purity and goodness. A Professor van Winter has shown in an article published in 1957[3] that, to begin with, the Virgin was often depicted in an enclosed area, the enclosure being shown by a wattle fence, to represent the protected, and to some extent, to protect, the medieval township. The protected area once represented visually became connected in some viewers' minds with the enclosed garden, the garden of Eden etc., and often a tree — perhaps the tree of life — a pole, or a fountain appeared at its centre, by the side of the maiden or Virgin protectress. Gradually a lion, sometimes with a drawn sword, would be depicted, protecting either the entrance to the enclosure, or the maiden herself — symbolising the royal protector of the town. The maiden figure, however, recalled the Bestiary story of the unicorn, and soon the unicorn came to join the lion, simply to indicate that the maiden was pure, was *the* maiden, the Virgin herself. Thus there grew up in Flanders and the Netherlands especially, in the late Middle Ages, many a town emblem or coat of arms in which an enclosed garden containing the figure of a woman, a lion and a unicorn play an important role. This, incidentally, was much earlier than the coming together, by the accident of union between England and Scotland, of the English lion and the Scottish unicorn in the United Kingdom's royal heraldic imagery.

The way in which the lion of royal power and the unicorn of righteousness, that is, of right and justice, came to be combined is informative where our Knowle carving and our Reynard-the-Fox woodcuts are concerned. This is especially the case with the latter illustrations when we take into account one of the very long-lived symbolic roles played by the stag.

As Adrian Blanchet has shown in his 1949 article, entitled *Cernunnos et le Cerf de Justice*,[4] that is, the god called Cernunnos and the Stag of Justice, there is a tradition going back into Celtic, pagan times in which a stag-like deity was associated with the just and even distribution of wealth, a deity which, in medieval Christian times, became quite simply a stag, and, moreover, the stag associated with justice and equity. We have quite a lot of evidence for this, especially dating from the late fourteenth century, and France. For example, the historian Jouvenal des Ursins, writing about Isabel of Bavaria's entry into Paris in 1389, said: 'The people of Paris led the procession with the Merchants' Provost at their head; and the crowd shouted "*Noel, noel*" and, it is reported that a "bed of justice" (*un lit de justice*) was carried there, a big one, and a richly ornamented one, with a stag in the middle, as big as the one at the Palace of Justice, entirely white, admirably made with gilded antlers and a crown about its neck. . .' There was, in fact, a gallery in the Palace of Justice in Paris known as the Gallery of the Great Stag; and though the statue of the stag was destroyed in the fire of 1618, the Gallery in which it stood continued to be so called after its reconstruction. Thus, well into the seventeenth century, the stag was renowned, especially in royal and Parisian quarters, as a symbol of justice.

Let us return to the woodcuts illustrating the fifteenth- and sixteenth-century editions of *Reynard the Fox*, English and continental. The stag, who plays no part in the narrative, appears in a few illustrations in which the dispensation of justice is the main narrative topic, Let us consider just one other example from a point near the end of the story of Reynard the Fox, and many chapters removed from the episode with which we

have till now been concerned. At the end of the story, the wolf challenges the fox to a duel to decide the right or wrong of their quarrel. It reflects the primitive medieval belief that a dispute could be decided by duelling and that only the one who was right would win, provided the duel was preceded by prayer, etc. Here we see that the stag, though not in the narrative, appears in the illustrations of the wolf's duel with the fox (see Plate 20, following page).

I therefore suggest that, just as the Reynard-the-Fox artist drew on age-old, symbolic lore concerning the stag to supplement his illustrations of scenes in which justice was being dispensed, he also drew on a similar heritage where the unicorn is concerned to supplement those scenes in order to draw attention to the antithesis between good and bad, vice and virtue. In those scenes in which the unicorn is seated beside the lion, he simply shows that, momentarily anyway, the royal power is acting rightly, virtuously.

To press this point, let me draw your attention to woodcuts illustrating one other scene in which the unicorn sometimes appears. After the fox has managed to tell a terrible lie from the gallows ladder about hidden treasure which the lion can have only if he will forgive him and spare his life, the lion seats the fox by his side on a raised platform and tells his assembled animal-peers that the fox is indeed forgiven; not only that, but henceforth he will hear no evil spoken about the fox — from now on, the fox cannot be incriminated, and this by royal decree. In the earliest scenes illustrating this subversion of justice, the artists illustrate it thus, with the stag of justice — or, simply, the stag representing a place where justice of a sort is being dispensed — facing the lion, the representative of royal power, now corrupt (see Plate 21, following page). Similar compositions appear in a German (Lübeck) woodcut dated 1498, and a Danish woodcut dated 1555. However, in a German woodcut of 1562 the unicorn appears among the animals gathered before the platform party, while in another of 1567, we see the unicorn seated by the stag, opposite the lion. This is also the case in a German woodcut of 1549.

Thus, we see in a particularly vivid way how graphic material could be used in these early times in two different ways:

Reynard the Fox.

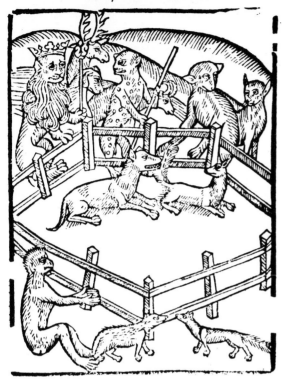

Plate 20. The duel of the Wolf and the Fox, from the Wynkyn de Worde series.

Plate 21. Wynkyn de Worde illustration of the Lion sparing the Fox's life, following a promise to reveal the whereabouts of hidden treasure in exchange.

(a) to illustrate a scene in a narrative, realistically.

(b) to illustrate a narrative situation symbolically.

Here, the artist first has age-old symbols for justice and right side by side with that for royal power, opposite to and opposed to a customary symbol for evil and vice; then he reverses the situation. Here then, we have, in these early Reynard-the-Fox woodcuts, some very clear evidence of the ability and, indeed, the tendency, of medieval and Renaissance man to think literally and symbolically, to tap deep-rooted traditions. And it should be remembered that these stories, just like carvings in parish churches, were meant for the common people, for the mass.

Late Reynard-the-Fox woodcuts also show how this ability and tendency got lost over the centuries; I am therefore now just as sure as I was in the mid-1960s that the misericord at Knowle has little, if anything, to do with Reynard the Fox proper; but I am equally sure that it reminded its viewers, mostly 'ordinary' people, of fox lore, lion lore and unicorn lore, and that it depended on their ability to put the elements together and make of them at least a brief, moralising story. It may, of course, have recalled more than the basic, most fundamental knowledge of symbols, and reminded some of its viewers of the stories they knew of Reynard the Fox, perhaps even of some woodcut illustrations made for that story.[5]

Notes

1. Kenneth Varty, *Reynard the Fox* (Leicester, 1967), 88.

2. For details of this discovery, see E. Rumbauts and A. Welkenhuysen, eds., *Aspects of the Medieval Animal Epic* (Leuven, 1975), 252-4.

3. P. J. van Winter, 'De Hollandse Tuin', *Nederlands Kunsthistorische Jaarboek* (Bussum, 1957). I am grateful to T. Hagtingius for drawing my attention to this article.

4. Adrian Blanchet, 'Cernnunos et le Cerf de Justice', *Bulletin de l'Académie Royale de Belgique*, Lettres XXXV (1949), 316-28. I am grateful to Michael Bath for drawing my attention to this article.

5. I would like further to stress my gratitude for the help of T. Hagtingius of Haarlem and Michael Bath of Strathclyde University (see Notes 3 and 4, above).

Folklore and 'Folklorism' Today

VILMOS VOIGT   Eötvös Loránd University, Budapest

IT is possible to be theoretical or purely practical in the way that one tackles the problems of the phenomenon that I shall call 'folklorism'. This paper[1] will try to outline the basic thinking involved. It will give a brief description of the most important ideas which have influenced research, and concludes by summarising the work being done at present in Hungary.

I will begin by trying to define folklore and 'folklorism'. If we contrast folklore with non-folklore, and pay particular attention to artistic phenomena associated with the first, we can assume a two-way correlation. 'Folklorism' begins in folklore and moves in the direction of non-folklore, whereas the folklorisation process begins with non-folklore and moves in the direction of folklore. This can be expressed in the form of a diagram as follows:

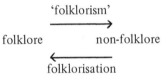

In each case the process is characterised by the adoption and spread of various styles, motifs and formulas, usually in modified form.

'Folklorism' is manifested in various ways: modern research in folklore and ethnology has shown us how folk costume, folk art, folk music, folk dance, even folk food and certain aspects of folk belief and custom, can be popularised in non-folkloric form. Scholars have discussed the phenomenon but, so far, there has been no publication of any significance devoted to the underlying theory and its development and function.

The modern form of 'folklorism', which I call 'neo-folklorism', has preoccupied German scholars of *Volkskunde* (folk life) for the last 20 years. Theoretical statements have appeared in monographs, and some thought has been given to the problems created by tourism and the significance of reviving local traditions. Nevertheless I feel that insufficient attention has been paid to 'folklorism' in literature and art; nor has there been any attempt to formulate a satisfactory theory.[2]

The authors of the various books on folklore

* Full summary by the Editor. The term 'Folklorism' may seem obscure to some British readers. It is used by German folklorists, and is widely known throughout Europe, though not, as yet, in the British Isles. At the 1967 Conference of the International Folk Music Council, Dr Felix Hoerburger spoke of the distinction to be drawn between folk-practices as wholly belonging to the innermost life of the people, or as something adopted or imposed for some understood or ulterior reason. This he categorised as the first and second existences of the custom. Hans Moser has defined folklorism as 'the presentation of folk culture at second-hand'. Often, though not necessarily, it is linked with tourism, entertainment, and business or political interests. Folklorism may be used for commercial, patriotic, romantic, propagandistic, and genuinely artistic purposes. It is a growing, world-wide phenomenon and is not unique to our time. Examples of folklorism, and they are legion, would include: television displays of 'picturesque' folklore; the conscious wearing of national dress — for instance, at political demonstrations; the use of folk melodies by composers like Chopin, Vaughan Williams, and Bartók; the use of ethnic ornamentation in architecture; folklore and myth in the work of T. S. Eliot, Thomas Mann, Bertold Brecht, and James Joyce; the 'ethnic' souvenir industry; intellectuals who decorate their homes with examples of folk art, and so on (Ed.).

theory have shown little interest in 'neo-folklorism', I ought to mention in passing the work of Albert Marinus[3] in France, the two Greeks E. D. Mazarakes[4] and Demetrios Loukatos,[5] and the Russian, Viktor E. Gusev.[6] But otherwise it is only the late Giuseppe Cocchiara, a Sicilian scholar, who has discussed the subject at any length, in his book *L'Eterno Selvaggio*, where he also takes a look at the role of folklore in modern art.[7]

In this short paper it is impossible to refer, even briefly, to the many traditional folklore studies that have paved the way for a discussion of 'neo-folklorism'; they would in fact have helped to clarify certain aspects of the problem. A number of these studies have been published in France, Germany, England and America, as well as in Spain, Italy, the Soviet Union, Hungary, Czechoslovakia, Poland and Romania, though these last are perhaps less well-known. Someone should make a survey of the work that has been done.

Scholars involved in the discussions of *Gegenwartsvolkskunde*[8] (contemporary folk culture) have wondered whether anything comparable to the folklore of the past is to be found in modern culture, but this is another problem that has not been satisfactorily resolved. In Eastern Europe, where I live and work, scholars investigating the folklore of workers have come to certain conclusions. But they are far from being unanimous — even those who accept that some form of working-class culture can be described as 'the folklore of the workers'. We shall find a similar problem with regard to 'neo-folklorism'.

Of course the techniques used to evaluate folklore do not remain the same. Within the last 20 years or so the number of publications dealing with mass culture has enormously increased. This has led to new thinking in the fields of communication and human relations, which may well in turn influence attitudes towards 'neo-folklorism'. Ethnologists have taken a look at the latest theoretical findings in the field of mass culture and failed to come up with their own model of 'folklorism'. This is why scholars involved in mass culture have taken little more than a passing interest in folklore and can hardly be expected to provide us with an overview of the problems of 'neo-folklorism'.

We know that 'folklorism' and 'neo-folklorism' increase and decrease at certain times. The optimistic attitude so charactertistic of critical theory when they are on the increase can usually be explained; it was prevalent at the turn of the century and made a reappearance several years ago. Immediately after World War II fundamental concepts of art and culture altered and became international in character; cultural traditionalism and exclusiveness were fashionable. The period was seen as a golden age of folklore and 'folklorism', with new forms of national culture emerging. But in fact, if we compare it with national culture, folklore was on the decline, and this was also true of the Soviet Union and Eastern Europe.

Interest in *Art Nouveau* and Naive Art during the last few years has given a fresh impetus to 'folklorism'; laymen are becoming increasingly interested in folklore as it was ten years ago. This of course represents a revival of interest in 'folklorism', not folklore, and we must evaluate it accordingly.

Various problems arise when we try to understand 'neo-folklorism' and I will confine myself to asking two questions: first, how do we define 'neo-folklorism' in art and, second, how can we then apply our definition to the actual creators of folklore? 'Neo-folklorism' in art refers to the fine arts, music and literature. Similar phenomena exist in dance and other art forms, but they are so complex that I shall not deal with them in this paper.

Non-folklore selects and absorbs appropriate elements from folklore: traditional 'folklorism' and 'neo-folklorism' need to be distinguished in the light of this. The first question to be asked is: when did 'folklorism' first appear? The most likely answer is that it dates from the recognition and acceptance of folklore as an independent discipline. This can be related to the age of European Romanticism, the result of a relatively widespread and prolonged process in the history of European thought. Of course traditional 'folklorism' makes its appearance under varying circumstances in different countries and at different times. But the essential purpose is the same: to contribute to the development of non-folklore art in the on-going socio-historical system of art, and to improve and protect folklore art within that system. This is closely associated with the assumption that artistic emancipation can be equated with social emancipation; in this sense 'folklorism' is the artistic equivalent of democracy and progress. The same idea is expressed with clarity and precision by Hungary's greatest poet, Sándor Petófi (1823-1849), in his first letter to János Arany (1817-1882), another distinguished poet, written in February 1847: 'Undoubtedly the poetry of the people is the true poetry. Let us work to make it dominant. If the people dominate in poetry, it is only a short step to domination in politics as well. This is the task for our time, and for every noble-hearted man who is tired of seeing several thousand idle, while millions of the poor suffer. To heaven with the people, and to hell with the aristocracy!'[9]

It is well-known that the words 'domination in poetry can be equated with domination in politics' were adopted outside Hungary. The underlying philosophy can only be appreciated after a comparative analysis of some of the theoretical implications of 'neo-folklorism'. In 1928 Béla Bartók characterised the relationship between modern music and folklore as follows: 'There are two common features shared by all forms of modern music, which are related by cause and effect. On the one hand there is a radical departure from the music of the past, especially romantic music, and at the same time there is an attempt to approximate to the musical style of earlier periods. In other words there was a reaction against works from the romantic period. This was followed by efforts to find new points of departure in complete contrast to romantic modes of expression.'[10] Thus it is possible to analyse the influence of folk music on the work of Bartók and Kodály in some detail, and to distinguish similar features in Stravinski's 'Russian period'. Bartók's remarks are all the more interesting since only once in his life does he refer to motifs which he had adopted from folk music.

The decisive factor, in his opinion, is that new music reacts against old: it is seeking something entirely different, which it finds in folklore. It also looks to primitive art, to the creative work of children and the insane, even to technical art and the purely haphazard art of *objets trouvés*.

On the basis of what has so far been said, we can compare traditional 'folklorism' and 'neo-folklorism' as follows:

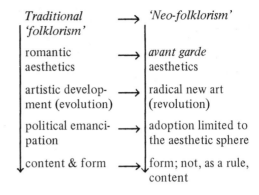

Of course there are examples of traditional 'folklorism' in twentieth-century art as well; but without a discussion of the underlying thought in 'neo-folklorism' the work of leading artists like Kandinsky, Klee, Chagall, Picasso, Moore, Brecht, Joyce, Pound, Stravinski, Bartók and others becomes unintelligible. 'Neo-folklorism' in art is the 'folklorism' of new art. This is underscored by the fact that several artists were strongly opposed to traditional 'folklorism'. However a detailed analysis of these complex processes would merit separate investigation and falls outside the province of folklore. At the same time, folklorists must recognise that modern *avant garde* art has stimulated new and effective forms of folklorism.

It is clear from recent investigations of folk art and folk music that traditional folklore research is unable to provide a uniform definition of folklore art. Recently there have been attempts to clarify the terms 'creativity' and 'tradition': they have not been particularly successful. However it is worth noting that recent surveys by Robert Wildhaber, Lenz Kriss-Rettenbeck, Dieter Kramer, Ernst Klusen, Walter Wiore and others, all refer to 'folklorism' in their attempts to define art within the general framework of folklore.[11] Scholarly interest is in fact centred on the aesthetics of folklore art, and the aesthetic consciousness of the creative process.

Now I would like to mention certain important features of structural ethnography. Exponents of Czech structuralism like Mukařovský,[12] a historian of literature and aesthetics, and the enthnologist Václávík,[13] have often considered the problems involved in an aesthetic evaluation of folk art and fine art. The distinguished ethnologist,

P. G. Bogatyrev — who is Russian by birth, but worked in Czechoslovakia between the two World Wars — has studied this question in great detail. He came to his theory of aesthetics in folklore via lengthy analysis of 'folklorism', and it took him 10 years. It was in 1923 that he first compared professional and folk literature, while analysing folklore in Pushkin's poem *Hussar*.[14] He developed the comparison further, along the lines of de Saussure's structural theory of language, in papers written in collaboration with Roman Jakobson in 1929 and 1931.[15] In 1932 he went a stage further and elaborated the theory of functional shifts in ethnology. In 1938[16] he expanded it and set up the following categories: active-collective, passive-collective, productive, and non-productive ethnological. Thus, although Bogatyrev's position was synchronic rather than diachronic, it helps us to see changes that took place in folklore in the nineteenth and twentieth centuries.

In the first period the categories of active-collective and productive are dominant; in the second period passive-collective and non-productive ethnological are dominant. In other words, when folk culture becomes better known it is not practised collectively, and is accepted but not created. At the same time, especially with regard to dress, custom and belief, there is a functional shift and the former function — ritual, magical or religious — which is characterised by traditional usage, is replaced by the aesthetic function. Bogatyrev himself only explored this functional shift in new fields, but subsequent investigations have revealed a large body of material whose original function can be termed semi-traditional as well as magical and religious, or where such features predominate; whereas the second category can be termed representational, and here the best known form aims to achieve nothing more than aesthetic effect. We can relate this process to the shift in 'folklorism' from content to form, and from social to aesthetic. Thus, to conclude, the phenomena involved in 'neo-folklorism' can be expressed as follows:

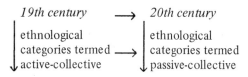

In Hungary ethnography and folklore[17] are usually concerned with traditional themes, though not long after the great social and political change that took place in 1945-1949 there were attempts to alter this and research into contemporary folk life was begun. A theoretical framework soon emerged, based on the Soviet model, but the 1950s were not the most appropriate time to publish all the results of this detailed analysis. It was only in the 1960s that interest in modern folklore research revived and we see it in evidence at conferences and in debates.

It is not difficult to give a brief account of research in this field in Hungary to date. The relationship between folklore and non-folklore prior to this period has already been examined by many scholars. It was the popularism of the nineteenth century in particular that achieved such remarkable results in literary history: problems connected with the history of aesthetics, ideology and society were also referred to. But the word 'folklorism' does not appear in these early studies and this shows that our terminology needs to be clarified. If we were to examine twentieth-century examples of 'folklorism' like the poems of Endre Ady (1877-1919) and Attila József (1905-1937), the music of Béla Bartók, the work of writers active in the 1920s and 1930s who depicted the life of Hungarian peasants, and the campaign to promote naive peasant artists, they would provide us with valuable material. There are short studies and various monographs which examine the relationship between folklore and the gifted artist, but the subject still lacks a succinct and analytic overview. Only one essay on 'folklorism' in art has been published in Hungary.[18] It discusses examples from art, literature and folklore theory, but fails to provide a picture of non-artistic 'neo-folklore'. Tekla Dömötör has written about 'folklorism' in the everyday life of the 1960s, but no-

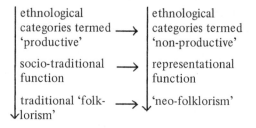

one has followed her example.[19]

I will conclude by emphasising once again that the most urgent task is to provide a critical survey of the work being done in other countries; and there should be proper discussion of 'folklorism' in Hungary too. This would involve all the national minorities in Hungary, and research within these groups needs to be conducted separately. The theoretical aspect of 'folklorism' in Hungary must also be considered. The cultural changes which took place after World War I and the way in which Austrian, Czech, Slovak, Rumanian, Serbian, Croatian and Hungarian 'folklorism' developed could form the basis for this research and would provide an opportunity to discuss similarities and differences; Hungarian 'folklorism' would also be easier to understand. Research should focus on the period beginning with 1945 and continue into the present, since here some effort has been made to provide an account of the history of society and some of the most significant features can be described. The transition from capitalism to a highly developed form of socialism would provide the social framework for the research: the data and phenomena of 'folklorism' need to be viewed as part of the process of change. The phenomena of 'folklorism' in the socialist countries — i.e. the countries of Eastern Europe — need to be studied, and Hungarian 'folklorism' must be considered within this context.

Finally I should like to draw attention to a Conference which will be held from 27th-29th July, 1978, at Kecskemét in Hungary,[20] in association with the VIth Folklore Festival of Danube Peoples, on the theme *'Folklorism', Past & Present*. Three separate sections will consider the function of Hungarian 'folklorism', the forms that it takes, results of international research, and the whole phenomenon of international 'folklorism'. The lectures will be published and we hope that this conference — the first of its kind — will provide a new impetus for future research and scholarly debate.

Notes

1. Based on my earlier papers, i.e. *A magyarországi folklorizmus 1945-1975 közti szakaszának kutatási problémái* (Budapest, 1977).

2. See the chapter providing a summary in Hermann Bausinger, *Volkskunde* (Berlin-Darmstadt, 1972), 159-209, 287-90.

3. Albert Marinus, 'Le néo-folklorisme', *Isidor Terlinck Album* (Louvain, 1931), 231-37.

4. E. D. Mazarakés, *Symbolé sté meleté tés laografias. É sémeriké topothetésé* (Athens, 1959).

5. Démetrios S. Loukatos, *Synkhrona laografika* (Athens, 1963).

6. V. E. Gusev, *Problemy fol'klora v istorii estetiki* (Moscow-Leningrad, 1963).

7. Giuseppe Cocchiara, *L'eterno selvaggio. Presenza e influsso del mondo primitivo nella cultura moderna* (Milan, 1961).

8. Cf. Herman Bausinger, *Volkskultur in der technischen Welt* (Stuttgart, 1961); Ingeborg Weber-Kellermann, *Deutsche Volkskunde zwischen Germanistik und Sozialwissenschaften* (Stuttgart, 1969).

9. Sándor Petöfi, 'levelezése', *Petöfi Sándor Összes Müvei* (Budapest, 1964), VII, 42.

10. Béla Bartók, 'Magyar népzene és uj magyar zene', *Zenei Szemle* (1928). Quoted from *Bartók Béla összegyüjtött irásai. I. Kiadta Szöllósy András* (Budapest, 1966), 750.

11. Walter Escher, Theor Gantner and Hans Trümpy, eds, *Festschrift für Robert Wildhaber* (Bonn, 1973); Lenz Kriss-Rettenbeck, 'Was ist Volkskunst?' *Zeitschrift für Volkskunde,* LXVIII (1972), 1-19; Dieter Kramer, ' "Kreativität" in der "Volkskultur" ', *Zeitschrift für Volkskunde*, LXVIII (1972), 20-41; Ernst Klusen, *Volkslied. Fund und Erfindung* (Cologne, 1969); Walter Wiora, *Das deutsche Lied. Zur Geschichte und Ästhetik einer musikalischen Gattung* (Wolfenbüttel, 1971).

12. Jan Mukařovský, *Estetická funkce, norma a hodnota jako sociálný fakty* (Prague, 1936).

13. Antonín Václavík, *Výrocní obyćeje a lidové umění* (Prague, 1959), 9-44.

14. P. G. Bogatyrjov (Bogatyrev), 'Stihotvoreniie Puškina "Gusar", ego istočniki i ego vlijanije na narodnuju slovesnest', *Očerki po poetike Puškina* (Berlin, 1923), 147-95.

15. R. Jakobson and P. Bogatyrjov (Bogatyrev), 'K probleme razmeževanija fol'kloristiki i literaturovedenija', *Lud Słowianski*, II-B (1931), 230-3; *ibid.*, 'Die Folklore als eine besondere Form des Schaffens', *Donum natalicium · Schrijnen* (Nijmegen-Utrecht, 1929), 900-13.

16. P. Bogatyrev (Bogatyrjov), 'Die aktiv-kollektiven, produktiven und unproduktiven ethnographischen Tatsachen', *II. Congrès international des sciences anthropologiques et ethnologiques* (Copenhagen, 1939), 343-5.

17. Vilmos Voigt, 'Napjaink néprajza', *Magyar Filozófiai Szemle*, XVI (1972), 282-92.

18. *ibid.*, 'Vom Neofolklorismus in der Kunst', *Acta Ethnographica Academiae Scientiarum Hungaricae*, XIX (1970), 401-23.

19. Tekla Dömötör, 'Folklorismus in Ungarn', *Zeitschrift für Volkskunde*, LXV (1969), 21-3.

20. Cf. Vilmos Voigt, ed., *A folklorizmus egykor és ma*, 2 vols (Kecskemét, 1978).

Guineas and Other Englishmen; Folklore and Race in a Tri-Racial Community*

BARRY WARD   West Virginia University

WHEN in the summer of 1975 we began our study of the West Virginia Guineas,[1] we knew that we were faced with a formidable task. The Guineas, a tri-racial group (Caucasian, Negro, American Indian), whose ancestral home is tucked away in the isolation of the Appalachian mountains, are not reputed for their hospitality to outsiders, and to our knowledge no-one had successfully gained entry to the community to conduct any professional, in-depth research.[2] Local Appalachian whites repeatedly warned us that we would be greeted by overt hostility and possibly meet with physical injury if we set foot on Chestnut Ridge, the largest Guinea settlement. The enterprise was judged futile and downright dangerous. Why, it was argued, should we want to waste our time on that group of 'ne'er-do-wells and welfare cheats', those black Guineas who did not share the values of their neighbours?

Certainly, the futility aside, it was these very things which drew us as folklorists to a study of the Guineas. Their reputation for being exotic outcasts, for holding an alien value system, for being outside the law, these attitudes and our curiosity to know the truth behind them, drew us to the Ridge. How and why, we wondered, did this particular group[3] with such a bizarre racial heritage come to be living there, in the state of West Virginia, which is otherwise essentially racially homogeneous? Indeed, the official history and recorded lore of the state both celebrate and document the predominant Scots-Irish, Welsh, and English ancestry of its people, and residents take quite literally the assertion artlessly designating

them all to be of the 'purist Anglo-Saxon stock'. That is, all excepting the Guineas. The Guineas are relentlessly denied 'Anglo-Saxonness' in custom, mores, and folklore. The question which initially impelled us into this study is the very one which lies behind scores of folk narratives we have collected from and about the Guineas, and it confronts the local region's major social issue: that is, what social relationships, using race as the major criterion, are appropriate between the Guineas and the local Appalachian white majority? Can the Guineas lay claim to being 'other Englishmen'?

If we accept the Structuralist assumption that a corresponding relationship exists between myth and culture and that each can be illuminated by the other, we should be able to seek some answers in the narratives of the two parties. I will begin first with those told about the Guineas.

The majority population in central West Virginia has developed narratives about the Guineas to make them seem mysterious and exotic, but inferior. We were initially struck by the large number clustered around the name 'Guinea' itself. One narrative holds that the group originally came from New Guinea. A second contends that they resemble, both physically and metaphorically, the black and white spotted fowl, the Guinea hen, and hence their name. A third explains that they are the issue of the miscegenation between Italian railway workers and Negro women and are 'the Guineas' children', thus playing on another more general, yet separate, discriminatory use of the word for Italians and other Mediterranean peoples.

Other narratives do not purport to be concerned

* This paper derives from a joint research effort by Professor Avery F. Gaskins of West Virginia University and myself. I also wish to express my

gratitude to Dr Rand Bohrer for his suggestions and encouragement.

about the origin of the name but rather are exoteric attempts to assign reasons for the mixing of the races. One, fraught with irony, tells how the Guineas are but the pitiful remnants of a nineteenth-century utopian experiment to eliminate racism itself, through planned interbreeding of Caucasians, Negroes, and American Indians. Another, more cynical, story recounts how the ancestors of contemporary Guineas supposedly registered as Negroes after the American Civil War in order to take advantage of a tax-break offered newly-freed slaves. The ploy backfired, it seems, because no-one but Negroes would marry, or even socialise, with them thereafter.

It is not possible for me to test the veracity of these exoteric narratives during this brief presentation. Let it suffice to say that no story is factually accurate.[4] Yet each one reveals a truth about social relations: each places the Guineas primarily in the Negro race and assigns to them a set of negative qualities.

At first one might think that the Guineas, when confronted by the overt racial typing of the local Appalachian white society, would counter it either through inversion − such assertions as 'Black is beautiful' − or negation of the values present in such racial typing − for example with facts such as that, proportionally, more Appalachian whites than Guineas are on welfare. These have been the strategies of Blacks in the United States, and they have been very successful ones. But, as revealed in their own narratives, Guineas do not accept the outside view that they are at least part Negro and adamantly reject these explanations of their origins and racial ancestry.

First, I will detail for you the family origin story of the largest of the eleven Guineas families, the Mayle family, variously spelled Male, Males, Maley, Mail, Mehl, and Malee. They are all said to have descended from a Wilmore Male who settled in what is now Barbour County, West Virginia, in the vicinity of Chestnut Ridge. Wilmore Male's story, as it is told by his descendants, is one of adventure and heroism, and it denies that there is Negro ancestry in the family. It consists of the following episodes:

> Wilmore Male, the first Male, was a British general on the government side in the Jacobite Revolution.

When one of his men mistreated a captured rebel soldier, Wilmore Male killed him in what was judged a treasonous act.

He fled, stowed away in a hog's head (barrel) with food, water, and an axe.

After six months in the hog's head, he ran out of supplies, chopped his way out with great difficulty because other barrels had been piled upon the one he was in, and delivered himself to the Captain. The Captain, who was en route to Jamestown, Virginia, had no sympathy for him and vowed to return General Male to England once he had made his stop at port.

General Male, realising that to return meant death for him, contrived to escape.

He fled first to Louden County, Virginia, then to Hampshire County where he married a half-Indian named Priscilla Harris (another Guinea surname). Eventually the family settled in present-day West Virginia where Wilmore is said to have died at the age of 108.

We have extensively traced all records available, to test the historical facts of the Male story, but very little unquestioned proof can be offered to confirm or deny it. As many as three Wilmore Males lived in the Virginia, Maryland, West Virginia territory in ·the late eighteenth/early nineteenth centuries but not at the time of the supposed flight from England. None were generals, at any rate, and though their records hopelessly overlap, in no case is it possible to establish their racial identities.

Our sources are more certain than we about the historical accuracy of the narrative, and one further contends that Wilmore Male's descendants are entitled to the insurance money he must have left behind when he cast off in the hog's head. He describes his inquiry about the money in this way:

> I written awhile back to Queen Elizabeth. [Wilmore Male] got a billion dollars insurance... [The Queen was] to take the money and send it here to bank. I didn't want to handle it. [We were going to] build him a monument, where he's buried below Philippi, two miles there in the field. I know

where he's buried, ya see. Written back, she's a very good Queen, is very good, she written back to me, 'Mr Norris, that's out of my jurisdiction'. They were to send the money to the M – A – Y – L – E race, for there hain't no M – A – L – E – S now. Any that I know, they're M – A – Y – L – E. Changed their name. M – A – L – E, Wilmore Male was M – A – L – E. I written away to England – half of England's one-thirds Male.

The sincere, even fierce, emphasis on family ancestry is a critical one. It is important to remember that both the Appalachian white and Guinea sub-cultures are anomalies so far as the total American majority culture is concerned. Both emphasise kinship bonds and 'blood ties' in their structures and hence cannot possibly reject race as an operational factor in their social structure. To invert or negate the racial values posited in the Appalachian whites' narratives would require the Guineas to forsake what they share with them as opposed to the American majority culture, that is, blood ties, strength of kinship bonds, and extreme endogamy.

Actually, another related step in this whole scheme has occurred which may help us see the roots of conflict. American majority culture assigns positive value to such qualities as discipline, mobility, career orientation, improvement through education, and peer-group standards. It sees white Appalachians, an officially designated minority group, as a people who do not adhere to these qualities and hence require special government programmes to pull them into the mainstream. Some of the qualities American majority culture assigns to Appalachian whites are extreme endogamy with consequent physical deformities in offspring, ignorance, shiftlessness, immorality, welfare dependency, reliance on cunning rather than education, and Anglo-Saxon ancestry. With only one exception these are precisely the qualities the Appalachian whites have displaced upon the Guineas. The one they withold is Anglo-Saxon heritage. It is, of course, the quality that the Guineas most seek after because it epitomises the centrality of kinship and blood ties.

The positive value of kinship and of the endogamy of society is reflected in their narratives, which reassert the importance of blood descent.

And because the critical Appalachian culture and their own culture are homologous on kinship, they insist on their Anglo-Saxonness. It is no less than a function of their fundamental commitment to this blood society. A symbiotic relationship exists between the Guineas and the Appalachian white majority. The Appalachian whites are able to displace the negative values assigned to them by American majority culture onto the Guineas; the Guineas in turn can tie into the Appalachian white Anglo-Saxon descent line. The social commitment to kinship is replicated on the level of myth.

This process reinforces for the Guineas their participation in the Appalachian white culture which surrounds them, but they are still faced with a dilemma. If they are part of the English blood descent line so valued by the Appalachian whites, why do some members of their group have darker-than-average skin tone, intense black hair, and other non-Anglo-Saxon physical features? Why are they discriminated against? There are two social realities, then, they must confront: the ways they are like the majority culture and the ways they are obviously different. They wish to circumvent the Negro racial issue without undercutting their own ties to the Appalachian culture. They do this through a double descent system. Two myths work together to explain the social realities: on the one hand is the English line we have been following; on the other is an American Indian descent line which to the Guineas accounts for their differences from the Appalachian whites.

The Indian descent line takes several forms. One ties them to Sir Walter Raleigh's Lost Colony; another fanciful story contends that they are the direct descendants of the lost tribes of Israel which bear remarkable similarity to American Indian tribes of the frontier; yet another traces their descent from a race of giants, who crossed the land bridge between Africa and South America, migrated northward, and ultimately established the Indian tribes of the United States. As appealing as these imaginative narratives may be, they are impossible to corroborate and not as widely believed as the following clear and rather straightforward account [here summarised] :

In 1750 a family of Englishmen named Norris captured an Indian boy who was part of a group coming through what is now the Morgantown, West Virginia, area from the east. The boy declared himself to be 'seventeen moons' old. Since the boy had been abandoned by him companions, the family took him in. In due course a Norris daughter, Betsie, in the words of our source, 'got something the matter with her by this Indian boy', apparently when they went down to tend the cows together. When it was discovered that the Indian was the prospective father of Betsie's child, her brothers killed him. The half-breed child was not murdered but was sent south to what is now Barbour County with another family which laid claim to land on the west bank of the Tygart's Valley River. The child, named Sam, took his mother's name, Norris.

Sam Norris had two wives. The first was a full-blooded Delaware Indian named 'Pretty Hair'; the second was a white woman named Ambler. Altogether Sam was the father of eight children. Apparently he was quite vigorous and healthy up to the end of his life, since, according to legend, he was courting a possible third wife at the age of ninety-four. His courting required him to ride from his home on the west bank of the river two miles to cross at Philippi, then three miles back up to Chestnut Ridge on the east side of the river. Surely men of lesser age could have expected Sam Norris's fate: 'His lungs burst and he fell off his horse in the middle of the road'.

Sam belongs among those hardy souls who populate the legends of the frontier during the Colonial period and the days of the early Republic. His struggles to overcome the wilderness no doubt toughened his body and assured that he would live in vigorous health up into advanced age. The tale and the circumstances of his death are obviously designed to confirm this fact, and, more importantly, to reveal how the Norris family of today is descended from the most rugged of English and Indian stock.

One might justly ask if the Guineas have not merely avoided one set of negative racial stereotypes, those associated with Negroes, for another, those thought of where American Indians are concerned. 'Half-breed' children have long been objects of contempt since the days of the frontiersmen, and Appalachian's have a huge store of legends recounting Indian savagery, stupidity, and moral depravity. The gain in status seems minimal because Indian blood descent among Appalachian whites is generally of low standing. But American majority culture also has operating the simple reversal of the drunken Indian stereotype, the Noble Savage. It is this image which the Guineas draw upon to account for their differences from their neighbours. The Noble Savage is a man of character, of honour. He is at one with the land and possesses physical stamina and courage. It is no accident that the stories of Chiefs Tecumseh, Red Cloud, and Cornstalk are well known to the Guineas.

When we first collected the stories of Wilmore Male and Sam Norris, we did not immediately see how they corresponded and complemented one another. They simply seemed two bizarre and unrelated family stories. Yet they must be taken together because they deal with the two primary social realities faced by the Guineas.

I have been implying throughout this paper that there was an audience for these Guinea narratives, which some may have assumed to be the local Appalachian white population. Perhaps, it may have been felt, if they heard the stories of Wilmore Male and Sam Norris, they would have seen the error of their ways and accepted the Guineas as part of the larger community. Or, if that was not assumed, perhaps it was supposed that the Guineas believed this would happen. In truth, they do not. They know that so long as they remain in their home area in West Virginia, they will be the objects of discrimination. The Appalachian white population simply will not accept them. Thus, the stories are not functional in the crude sense that they will instruct a hostile outside group. That is possibly a secondary, but fruitless, use. The social situation is such that it will not work.

Rather, the stories are an intra-cultural means of expressing the social realities they encounter. They become a method of communication to and among the Guineas, to account for how they are both like and unlike their neighbours. In this sense the narratives are functional for them. What is not provided for, obviously, is a means either to integrate the Guineas or give them equal status.

Before concluding, we may wish to ask ourselves if the case of the West Virginia Guineas tells us anything about folklore and race. I would submit that it does. Certainly, it clearly tells us that ethnic and racial studies may, and often do, overlap. It tells us that folklore-rich areas such as the American Appalachian region, which have been tapped for years for ballads and tales, can also yield important racial materials. It documents that the folklore of groups such as the Guineas, whose racial identity is open to question, can provide data on race relations not apparent when racial identity is certain. And it shows how structural analysis is useful in understanding complex race relations. Without this strategy we would be left uttering commonplaces about how myth and legend infuse communities with pride and identity as readily as can history, and how narratives in oral circulation take life and soon operate as effective truth. That is exactly what happens with the Guineas, of course, but now we can add that these narratives of the Mayle and Norris families, together with others too numerous and extensive to recount here, order the social reality of the Guineas' world, resolving oppositions, and explaining it to them in terms of kinship, which is at the centre of Guinea culture.[5]

Notes

1. In the following discussion the word 'Guinea' is used without quotation marks in its ethnographic sense, and in no way should its use be construed as supporting any opprobrious connotations.

2. In 1952 an Ohio State University graduate student, John F. Burnell, completed an M.A. thesis on the group entitled, 'The Guineas of West Virginia' (Columbus). Most of his material was collected from the local population rather than the Guineas themselves.

3. See Brewton Berry, *Almost White* (London, 1963), for information on other mixed-blood groups in the United States.

4. See Avery F. Gaskins, 'An Introduction to the Guineas: West Virginia's Melungeons', *Appalachian Journal,* I (3) (Autumn 1973), 234-7, for a fuller discussion of the factual accuracy of the legends.

5. Obviously I have had to move rapidly through this subject. With more time at my disposal, I might have developed with greater clarity the implications of the suggestions above, or I might have submitted the two narratives to close scrutiny, commenting on such internal elements as the cask (confinement) — escape sequence of the Wilmore Mayle story and how it replicates the Guineas' efforts to break out of their social situation. Additional texts, ethnographic details, and further analysis will be published separately.

Witchcraft and Politics in Macbeth

KARL WENTERSDORF · Xavier University, Cincinatti

AMONG the more intriguing controversies in the realm of Shakespeare studies is the long-standing debate over the nature of the Witches in *Macbeth*. Are they the goddesses of destiny, or demons in the guise of witches? Are they merely expressionistic devices to body forth the secret desires of Macbeth? Or are they merely ugly old women, capable of hexing men and animals but claiming powers greater than they actually possess? In his discussion of Shakespeare's Witches, Bradley (1904) reviewed nineteenth-century speculation and came to the sober conclusion that they are in no sense supernatural beings: 'They are old women, poor and ragged, skinny and hideous, full of vulgar spite, occupied in killing their neighbours' swine or revenging themselves on sailors' wives who have refused them chestnuts ... There is not a syllable in *Macbeth* to imply that they are anything but women. But, again in accordance with the popular ideas, they have received from evil spirits certain supernatural powers.'[1]

Bradley's judicious approach to the problem did little to settle the controversy. Allardyce Nicoll (1931) was torn between the demonic interpretation and the expressionistic theory: 'We can see in [the Witches] evil ministers tempting Macbeth to destruction, or we can look on them merely as embodiments of ambitious imaginings.'[2] And it was the considered opinion of Kittredge (1939) that the Witches were not 'hags in the service of the Devil', nor were they 'mere personifications of a man's evil desires or his ruthless craving for power'. They were in fact the Norns or goddesses of destiny found in Nordic mythology, who not merely prophesied the future but also shaped human events: 'These were not ordinary witches or seeresses. They were great powers of destiny, great ministers of fate. They had determined the past; they governed the present; they not only foresaw the future, but decreed it.'[3] Subsequent critics have almost unanimously accepted Bradley's view that Shakespeare's Witches do not determine fate, since the Witches' prophecies are not concerned with actions to be taken by Macbeth, and Macbeth himself never charges the Witches with responsibility for his evil deeds. But there has been little willingness to accept Bradley's view that the Witches are nothing but old women, nor has there been much support for the opinions of Nicoll and Kittredge.

There are two modern schools of thought on the subject. According to one, Shakespeare was deliberately vague as to the precise nature of the three strange creatures, who are referred to in the play both as 'Weird Sisters' and as 'Witches'. For Dover Wilson (1947), 'they have, as all critics have noted, something at once sublime and abysmally evil about them, which marks them sharply off from the ordinary mortal witches such as his England and especially his Scottish king were thoroughly acquainted with. ... Too witch-like to be Norns, too Norn-like to be witches, what then are they? ... The Weird Sisters in *Macbeth* are the incarnation of evil in the universe, all the more effective dramatically that their nature is never defined.'[4] In the opinion of McGee (1966), that nature cannot readily be defined because there was no single or simple Elizabethan witch-image: in Shakespeare's age, 'witches were associated, identified, confused with the Furies of classical literature, with the biblical demons, and with the fairies of folklore'.[5]

Other critics of the same persuasion are less explicit as to the reason for the dramatist's vagueness concerning their character. According to West (1956), Shakespeare treats the Witches and their

431

role 'as awesome mysteries which we may feel and in part observe, but for which we have no sort of formula'; furthermore, he 'does not look behind these mysteries' but rather 'shows us the phenomena in a piercing way that conveys a sense of their ghastly significance without bringing us much the nearer to a rational account of them or of it'.[6] For Barnet (1963), although the 'Weird Sisters' resemble traditional witches in some ways, they 'seem also to merit the title Macbeth gives them, "juggling fiends"'; but the debate as to their real nature is futile since 'the play does not provide unequivocal answers'.[7] Similarly, too, with Ribner (1971): 'Shakespeare never really explains his Weird Sisters, but it is obvious that in the scheme of the play they can be regarded only as symbols of evil.'[8]

The other popular modern view is that the Witches are demonic spirits. In an important essay on the diabolic element in *Macbeth,* Curry (1937) finds it reasonable to suppose that 'Shakespeare's Weird Sisters are intended to symbolise or represent the metaphysical world of evil spirits'. He observes that this supposition implies three possibilities as to their nature: one may consider them 'as human witches in league with the powers of darkness, or as actual demons in the form of witches, or as merely inanimate symbols' – a view evidently corresponding to the expressionistic or symbolic interpretation already mentioned. Curry opts for the second of these possibilities: 'in essence the Weird Sisters are demons or devils in the form of witches'.[9] In one of the most detailed discussions of the subject, Farnham (1950), while agreeing with Bradley that the Witches do not control Macbeth's destiny – they merely tempt but never force Macbeth to do wrong – believes that they are nevertheless 'not mortal witches such as the law might get its hands upon and put to death [but] ... supernatural agents of evil, and ... reveal both the capacities and the incapacities that the Christian tradition has attributed to devils'. Farnham feels that their demonic quality has not been given the attention it deserves: he notes that Holinshed, Shakespeare's major source for the play, is non-committal as to the nature of the prophesying Witches (they could have been 'either the weird sisters ... or else some nymphs or feiries'); that the term *nymphs* and *fairies,* used also by others writing on the topic, denoted creatures with supernatural powers who were in reality devils; and that Shakespeare's age distinguished between human witches, usually old women who had made a pact with the Devil, and demonic witches, who looked like crones but were actually furies or demons able to foretell the future. According to Farnham, Shakespeare's Witches are demons.[10]

Similar views have been expressed by several more recent critics. For Bradbrook (1951), Shakespeare's Witches 'are able to sail in a sieve, to assume animal forms, and control the weather'; 'they have powers superior to those of common witches'; and their ability to vanish 'suggests a demonic power assuming and discarding human shape'.[11] To Jorgensen (1971), Shakespeare's three strange women have the loathsome appearance of ordinary witches but 'possibly retain some association with destiny'; these mysterious beings are 'far more than filthy women ... [and] there is always a feeling, which grows as the play advances, that the Witches are demonic manifestations of the dark part of a supernatural world'. He agrees there is a possibility – a 'plausible' one – that the Witches are merely old women, simply the instruments of demons who can take the form of cats and toads, yet concludes: 'But may not the Witches themselves be demons?' He notes with evident approval that 'Curry thinks so', that 'Farnham presents extensive evidence for his conclusion that they are "demons of the fairy order such as the Elizabethans also called hags or furies"', and that Farnham supports his conclusion – 'They are fiends in the shape of old women' – with the observation that Macbeth himself finally calls them 'juggling fiends'.[12] And in a more recent evaluation of the role of the Weird Sisters, Kermode asserts (1974) that they are neither 'mere allegories' nor 'mere witches': though produced by nature, they share with angels a freedom from limitations of space and time, a power to perceive the causes of things, and to see some distance into the human mind, and they can 'assume bodies of air or mist ("the earth hath bubbles")'.[13]

The arguments offered in the controversy over the nature of the Witches in *Macbeth* illustrate the intricate nature of the available evidence, from the complex and often contradictory accounts of witchcraft in Elizabethan and Jacobean treatises to the textual ambiguities in the play.

The numerous sixteenth- and seventeenth-century works dealing with the story of Macbeth refer to the three prophesying Witches by a variety of terms. Thus Holinshed (1587) describes them as 'the weird sisters, that is (as ye would say) the goddesses of destinie, or else some nymphs or feiries, indued with knowledge of prophecie by their necromanticall science'; for Warner (1606) they are '*Fairies*' or '*Weird-Elfes*'; and Heylyn (1625) refers to them as 'Fairies, or Witches (*Weirds* the *Scots* call them)'.[14] There are semantic difficulties with all of these terms: *fairies* were preternatural creatures, sometimes young and beautiful but sometimes old and hideous, possessed of magic skills; *weirds, weird sisters,* and *weird-elfes* were preternatural creatures somehow connected with the Fates — either instruments used by the Fates or forms taken on by the Fates themselves; *nymphs* were preternatural creatures associated with seas, rivers, and wells, who were able to cause bad weather; and *witches,* beautiful or ugly, could be human or demonic, but in either case possessed powers not at the command of ordinary mortals. And even if there were no semantic difficulties in the references to the 'Weird Sisters' in Holinshed or any other sources possibly used in the writing of the play, there could be no *a priori* certainty that Shakespeare would not have intended to modify the meaning suggested by those sources.

The interpretation of the dramatic text itself must likewise take into account ambiguities both of meaning and of reference. Thus Shakespeare makes Macbeth call the Witches 'midnight hags' (IV.i.28); the term *hags* may signify 'female demons', but it can also mean 'human witches',[15] Particularly noteworthy as an example of fallacious inference from an ambiguous reference is the argument that the Witches must be regarded as demons because Macbeth describes them as 'juggling fiends' (V.viii.19). There can be little doubt that *fiends* does mean 'demons' in this context; but in the passage from which the citation is taken Macbeth is not referring to the Witches at all. During the cauldron scene (IV.i) he has been encouraged by prophecies of the Spirits to the effect that 'none of woman born / Shall harm Macbeth' and that he will never be vanquished 'until / Great Burnan wood to high Dunsinane hill / Shall come against him' (IV.i.69-100). Now, just before the final battle, he has learned that Burnan

Wood is actually moving toward Dunsinane (V.iv.29-47), and his comment on the fiends is evoked by the even more unsettling discovery that Macduff was not born of woman by a natural emergence from the womb. He cries out in anguish:

> Accursed be the tongue that tells me so,
> For it hath cow'd my better part of man!
> And be these juggling fiends no more believ'd,
> That palter with us in a double sense . . .
> (V.viii.16-20)

Those referred to here as 'fiends' who juggle with the truth are not the Witches but the demonic Spirits who appeared to Macbeth in the cavern and who were acknowledged by the Witches to be their 'masters' (IV.i.62-63). It was surely from these same masters that the Witches obtained the prophecies passed on to Macbeth and Banquo at the beginning of the play (I.iii).

From the spate of Elizabethan and Jacobean materials dealing with witchcraft, three basic concepts emerge. Witches might be simply women, often old and ugly, capable of brewing poisons or supposed love philtres and able — through the use of spells or incantations — to 'wish' bad luck or ill-health on those who had aroused their anger or spite. Secondly, witches were regarded by some authorities as entirely spiritual in nature, not creatures of flesh and blood at all, but demonic in origin and power, and capable of assuming human appearance, either attractive or repulsive. Finally, they might be flesh-and-blood creatures who had entered into an agreement with the Devil, as a result of which they had obtained certain preternatural powers. The precise nature of those powers varies with the authorities but generally includes the ability to raise storms (cf. *Macbeth* I.iii.11-25), to cause diseases (*ibid.,* I.iii.19-23), and to conjure up demonic spirits who could provide the witches with insights into the future (*ibid.,* IV.i). The latter belief derived originally from the biblical story of the Witch of Endor (1 Samuel 28: 7-20). The Witches in *Macbeth* must belong to either the second or the third of these categories: demons in human shape or human beings with diabolic skills.

There is considerable support for the view that Shakespeare's weird sisters are preternatural demons looking like hags, whose superhuman nature is indicated by the circumstance that they are able to vanish by assuming, in Kermode's words, 'bodies of air or mist'. It is certainly true that after the Witches have delivered their 'prophetic greetings' to Macbeth and Banquo, the Folio stage direction says *Witches vanish,* and the two generals speak of them as having vanished or melted into the air (I.iii.78-82). But are these comments intended to do anything more than characterise Macbeth and Banquo as credulous? It is quite likely that Shakespeare did not expect his audience, or at least, the more sophisticated members of his audience, to think of the Witches as literally dissolving into air rather than just cunningly disappearing. Whatever the manner in which the vanishing was handled in the Globe playhouse (disappearance behind a curtain, through a trap-door, behind smoke?), it was widely believed that witches in touch with the Devil were able to create illusions of various kinds, including the illusion of disappearance. According to no less an authority on witchcraft than King James I, whose *Daemonologie* (1597) was well known in Shakespeare's day, witches cannot vanish, but the demons whom they serve can 'thicken & obscure so the air, that is next about them, by contracting it strait together, that the beames of any other mans eyes cannot pearce thorow the same, to see them'.[16]

Are the Witches in *Macbeth* proved to be demons by their ability to fly, to set sail in a sieve, and to transform themselves into animal shapes? Again, the ability is more apparent than real. The Witches lay claim to such skills (I.i.12, I.iii.1-10), but the text is in part ambiguous. For example, the First Witch asserts that to get revenge on a sailor's wife, she will follow the sailor to Aleppo and 'like a rat without a tail / I'll do, I'll do, and I'll do'. If, as Jorgensen suggests, the phrase 'I'll do' is a hitherto unrecognised sexual euphemism, the implication is that she will approach the sailor, not in the guise of a rat but in the form of a woman (a succubus), as sexually aggressive as rodents were commonly believed to be.[17] As for the alleged ability to hover through the air or to sail in a sieve, these claims – like the business of vanishing – are not necessarily to be taken as representing truths. At their trials, witches certainly answered affirmatively when questioned, often under torture, about their possession of such abilities,[18] and some authorities accepted their confessions uncritically. However, the Devil and his associates were reputed to be great liars, and it was believed by many of Shakespeare's contemporaries that some at least of the witches' claims were based on illusions produced by trickery, like the already mentioned illusion of vanishing. King James, credulous as he was to begin with, did not believe that witches could fly, though he was willing to agree that they might be borne through the air by their demonic masters.[19]

If, then, Shakespeare's Witches are not themselves demonic creatures possessing their own insights into the future, they must be human beings dependent for such insights on demonic spirits, whom they are able to summon by means of necromantic spells. There would seem to be a clear case of witchcraft of this kind in English politics in the fifteenth century. Significantly enough, it was dramatised by Shakespeare in *2 Henry VI* (I.iv). There, the politically ambitious Duchess of Gloucester, married to young King Henry's uncle, desires to be queen and wishes that her husband would seize the throne. She sends for the witch Margery Jourdan and the wizard Roger Boling-brook, in order to discover what the future holds for her. With the aid of Mother Jourdan and a conjuring priest named Southwell, Bolingbrook summons a Spirit who appears and replies to questions about the fate of King Henry and two of his noblemen; the answers are equivocal in a manner remarkably similar to that in which the Spirits respond to Macbeth's questions, spoken and unspoken. In *2 Henry VI,* the necromantic session is interrupted just after the Spirit has answered the third question and has disappeared below; the conjurers and the witch are arrested and taken away to their deaths. Obviously Boling-brook and Jourdan are not themselves demons but human witches, dependent on demons for knowledge about the future. There is no compelling evidence that the Witches in *Macbeth* are in any essential way different from those in *2 Henry VI.*

The political aspect of the element of witchcraft in *2 Henry VI* and *Macbeth* is strikingly paralleled by some late sixteenth-century political happenings in Scotland, occurring shortly before that country's King James VI became James I of England. The main outlines of the affair became known in Shakespeare's London through a fairly detailed account published there in 1591 with the title *Newes from Scotland,*

After coming of age in 1587, James VI, the son of Mary Stuart, decided to marry and ensure the continuation of his dynasty by begetting an heir to the throne. His choice of wife fell on the Danish Princess Anne, and a wedding took place in Denmark between Anne and James's proxy in August 1589. Storms prevented Anne from crossing the North Sea to her new kingdom; and since it was becoming increasingly unlikely that Danish ships would bring her back to Scotland before the winter set in, James ordered his Lord High Admiral, the Earl of Bothwell, to send a Scottish convoy to escort her. When Bothwell kept delaying the expedition, James decided to fetch Anne himself. Setting sail in a single ship at the end of October, he crossed the sea safely, in spite of severe storms, and was married to Anne in person. It was not until April 1590, however, that James was able to return to Scotland with his bride, and even then his ship was nearly wrecked by a tempest.

As James was later to discover, the storms had been preceded (and allegedly caused) by incantations of the witches of North Berwick, and the man who had instigated the witchcraft activities was Francis Stuart Hepburn, 5th Earl of Bothwell, who was King James's cousin and who considered himself heir-presumptive to the throne.[20] Bothwell, like Macbeth, was a powerful nobleman and a successful soldier. His attempts to prevent James's marriage or to bring about his death by drowning were obviously meant to vitiate James's hopes for an heir and to expedite Bothwell's own accession to the throne.

After James's safe return with his queen, the North Berwick witches, again at the instigation of Bothwell, continued their attempts on the King's life: a wax image of James was made and cursed, and a deadly poison was prepared for him. But divine providence, so James believed, brought the plot to light; the witches were forced under torture to confess to their crimes, and in doing so they implicated Bothwell. In 1591 they were burned to death and Bothwell himself was arrested; but while awaiting trial for witchcraft and treason, he was helped by his supporters to escape. Ultimately, after capturing the King, being pardoned, and having his pardon revoked, Bothwell fled the country and died in exile.[21]

What the melodramatic story of Bothwell's involvement with the witches offers is not, of course, a parallel in detail to the story of Macbeth: Bothwell used the witches in an effort to get rid of his royal cousin, while Macbeth, who was Duncan's cousin, merely seeks out the witches — as does the Duchess of Gloucester — primarily to gain knowledge of the future. What we do have in the Bothwell affair is the story of a sixteenth-century Scottish nobleman of royal blood who goes to witches to solicit their aid; these witches, as King James himself believed and testified, were able to stir up storms and to encompass death by magic; they even had knowledge, again according to the King's testimony, of secrets known only to James and his wife.[22] And evil though their deeds and intentions were, they were not demons but human witches who, like their English counterparts in the reign of Henry VI, admitted to being in contact with the Devil, and were finally burned to death.

Once it is granted that for the bulk of the people in Shakespeare's age, human witches could perform or seem to perform wonders with the aid of demons, and in some cases could literally conjure up spirits so as to gain insights into the future, it cannot be argued convincingly that Shakespeare leaves the nature of his Witches in doubt. There is no uncertainty of a dramatically significant kind surrounding their role. They may well be — ultimately — symbolic figures, visible embodiments of evil, and especially of the evil desires in the heart of Macbeth; but they are primarily warped human beings, in league with Satan and functioning realistically in a world of ruthless political and social opportunists.

Notes

1. A. C. Bradley, *Shakespearean Tragedy* (London, 1904; repr. New York, 1949), 340-9.

2. Allardyce Nicoll, *Studies in Shakespeare* (London, 1931), 123. The expressionistic theory is developed in Henry N. Paul, *The Royal Play of 'Macbeth'* (New York, 1950), 61-74, where the author suggests that Shakespeare intended the judicious to interpret the Witches as figments of the imagination of Macbeth and Banquo: they are 'very real subjectively, but objectively non-existent'.

3. *Macbeth,* ed. George L. Kittredge (Boston, 1939), xviii-xix.

4. *Macbeth,* ed. John Dover Wilson (Cambridge, 1947; repr. 1951), xx-xxi.

5. Arthur R. McGee, ' "Macbeth" and the Furies', *Shakespeare Survey* XIX (1966), 56-65.

6. Robert A. West, 'Night's Black Agents in *Macbeth*', *Renaissance Papers 1956* (Columbia, South Carolina, 1956), 24.

7. *Macbeth,* ed. Sylvan Barnet (New York, 1963), repr. in *The Complete Signet Classic Shakespeare* (New York, 1972), 1229.

8. *The Complete Works of Shakespeare,* ed. Irving Ribner and George L. Kittredge (Waltham, Mass., 1971), 1290.

9. Walter C. Curry, *Shakespeare's Philosophical Patterns* (Baton Rouge, 1937; repr. Gloucester, Mass., 1968), 58-61.

10. Willard Farnham, *Shakespeare's Tragic Frontier* (Berkeley, 1950; repr. New York, 1973), 81-104.

11. M. C. Bradbrook, 'The Sources of *Macbeth*', in *Shakespeare Survey* IV (1951), 42-43; Farnham, 99.

12. Paul A. Jorgensen, *Our Naked Frailties: Sensational Art and Meaning in 'Macbeth'* (Berkeley, 1971), 116-22.

13. Frank Kermode, 'Macbeth', *The Riverside Shakespeare,* ed. G. Blakemore Evans *et al.* (Boston, 1974), 1309. Citations from Shakespeare in this paper are from the *Riverside* text.

14. Farnham, 82-92.

15. *ibid.,* 96-97.

16. King James the First, *Daemonologie* (Edinburgh, 1597), repr. and ed. G. B. Harrison (London, 1924), 39.

17. For a detailed discussion of the sexual aspects of this and other statements by the Witches, see Dennis Wiggins, 'Sexuality, Witchcraft, and Violence in *Macbeth*', *Shakespeare Studies* VIII (1975), 256-63.

18. *Newes from Scotland* (London, 1591), repr. and ed. G. B. Harrison (London, 1924), 13.

19. King James the First, 38-39. In support of this belief, King James could cite the biblical fact that Jesus was transported to a pinnacle of the Temple by Satan.

20. Bothwell's father was Lord John Stuart, half-brother to Mary Stuart. His mother was sister to Mary Stuart's lover and third husband, James Hepburn, 4th Earl of Bothwell.

21. See H. Ross Williamson, *King James I* (London, 1935), 55-57; David H. Willson, *King James VI and I* (New York, 1956), 103-6; David Mathew, *James I* (London, 1967), 75-80.

22. *Newes from Scotland,* 15.

Fact, Fancy and the Beast Books

BEATRICE WHITE   University of London

FACT, fancy, and folklore share common ground in the *Physiologus* and its descendants, the *Bestiaries* of the twelfth, thirteenth, and fourteenth centuries. Bernard of Chartres said, long ago, that moderns in any age are like dwarfs seated on the shoulders of giants. That is true, though the additional height enlarges the scope of vision. Even so it is a mistake to adopt a condescending attitude towards earlier centuries whose fanciful notions may, perhaps, become realities.

Popular beliefs, it seems, frequently rest precariously upon an insecure basis of untested investigation. General uncritical repetition of what are alleged to be true facts and may actually contain some truth, ultimately results in a widespread acceptance of inaccurate, even irrational statements which, constantly employed to explain away unusual circumstance, coincidences, or phenomena, lose nothing as they pass from place to place, from person to person, but gain accretions of more or less relevant fancy. Medieval imagination encouraged the 'deceiving elf' to new inventions and fancy 'bodied forth the form of things unknown'. The shaping instrument of this process is the pen, and in the Ages of Faith or, rather, Acquiescence, it was a very powerful instrument indeed, procuring for the written word, regarded as unassailable Authority, in immense reverence.

The universal deference to 'Authority' as much as the prevailing intellectual climate of the time largely accounted for the unquestioning acceptance of the remarkable assertions alleged in the medieval *Bestiaries* to be true. If they did not exist, Authorities were invented as required, just as Chaucer, presumably conforming to convention, invented Lollius. He certainly appeared to accept Bestiary statements without scruple when they were needed:

Chauntecler so free
Soong murier than the mermayde in the see,
For *Physiologus* seith sikerly
How that they syngen wel and myrily.

The poet's use of the word 'sikerly' (with certainty) implies, sardonically, perhaps, in the context, a due respect for 'Authority'.

It has been repeatedly maintained that the second-century(?) treatise on animals, the *Physiologus* alluded to by Chaucer, had a moral rather than a definitely scientific purpose. But the anonymous author surely had both. They are interdependent. The name bestowed on him and his book suggests that he was regarded as a reputable natural historian as well as a moralist who put his rudimentary knowledge of the animal world at the service of the Christian church. This worthy undertaking meant that human standards of behaviour were inevitably imposed on the animal kingdom which was divided into 'goodies' and 'baddies' in a thoroughly arbitrary manner – a practice which went to preposterous lengths in the Middle Ages[1] and has continued ever since, evincing itself in fable, fantasy, fiction and sometimes in serious discourse[2] down to recent times.

When we remember that Western civilisation has its roots in the East with its wealth of marvels, wonders, and fantasies, then a firm realisation of a provenance in the neighbourhood of Alexandria helps to explain the ingenious and purposeful exaggerations of the *Physiologus*, further improved on by the medieval *Beast Books* and Encyclopedias.

A craving for and delight in the strange and marvellous presupposes a deep human need which is supplied today not only by the harmless delights of Disneyland, *Watership Down*, Hobbits, Wombles,

438

and *The Lord of the Rings*, but by those impressive modern scientific developments incomprehensible to most of us, that take the place of the grotesque and fabulous creatures that thronged the *Bestiaries* and frightened and amazed our ancestors. The magic of fact (radio, cinema, television, aeroplanes, spaceships), has supplemented and surpassed the magic of fancy. *King Kong* has overtaken the Mantichor and *Jaws* has supplanted St Brendan's Whale. The Physiologus would gladly have found room for both in his menagerie.

The significance of the seminal *Physiologus* lies in the genuine attempt made by a devout Christian observer to note down, with pardonable manipulation in view of his serious dogmatic purpose, the typical behaviour of animals in his immediate vicinity — creatures which were obediently fulfilling the Divine will:

> Omnis mundi creatura
> Quasi liber et pictura
> Nobis est, et speculum.

All created things, however bizarre their habits and appearances seemed, were regarded as specifically designed to lead man heavenward. It was easy to accept the postulated wonders of the invisible world, when those of the visible one were there at hand, waiting to be studied and recommended as possible guides to a pleasant eternity by providing examples of behaviour to be imitated or avoided.

The 'Vulgar Errors' of the illuminated *Beast Books* of the Middle Ages, valued as much for their decorative and explanatory pictures as for their contributions to zoological knowledge, eventually provoked, by their challenging absurdities, a healthy curiosity which, in time, was bound to lead to a truly scientific approach to the study of natural history. Superior knowledge and equipment allowing for close, accurate, and lengthy investigation of animal life have now removed the more daring conjectures of the *Bestiaries*, replacing exuberant fancy with exuberant fact. Modern observers are well-trained specialists and because we rely on their dedicated researches we no longer believe that the hyena hangs around imitating human voices in order to lure men to their doom. We are certain that lion cubs are not born dead and after three days revived by their father's roar. We known that weasels do not conceive at the ear and bring forth through the mouth (or *vice versa*), that bear cubs are not actually licked into shape by their mothers, and that crocodiles do not shed hypocritical tears. And yet the proved facts are often as hard to believe as the former fiction, which relinquishes very slowly its power over the mind as we gradually revise our ideas about lions, tigers, panthers, hyenas, crocodiles, wolves, and all the rest of the beasts, wild and tame.[3]

What Sir Thomas Browne called 'credulity, supinity, and adherence unto Antiquity' was only partly responsible for the misreportings, misunderstandings, and misinterpretations of animal habits by medieval writers. The prevailing influence of a church indifferent to the advance of science, the ascendancy of Realist philosophy, and the obsession with allegory and symbolism made it difficult for men to tell hawks from handsaws when their accepted 'Authorities' were the Scriptures, so rich in animal analogies, and the works of scholars and historians like Pliny, Solinus, and Isidore of Seville, whose main aim was not accuracy of observation. By mingling the credible with the incredible the compilers of the popular *Bestiaries* produced from such mixed origins a remarkable and enduring progeny.

The swan's song, the crocodile's tears and the licked-into-shape bear's cubs enliven the metaphors of today's colloquial speech. The unicorn remains with us. The pelican still exhorts us with its piety. The elephant and castle is a familiar landmark to Londoners and the phoenix is a universally recognisable symbol. Old ideas inherited from the *Physiologus* and scarcely altered are still met with in country districts where the tricks of the fox, the habits of the badger (now protected), and the hedgehog's curious antics with fallen fruit make fecund subjects for lively arguments over convivial mugs of beer.[4]

To conclude — it looks as if the *Beast Books* confront us with a paradox. In the causes of their decline as reliable zoological treatises lay hidden the seeds of their revival. The 'prostration unto Antiquity' which involved their authors in bold and fertile imaginings, at length, in a more sceptical age, reduced their popularity and withdrew their authority. But the ancient legends which they incorporated and lavishly embellished, lived on to secure for the *Physiologus* and its medieval successors deserved recognition from scholars who, while giving due credit to their appeal as picture-books, find beneath the extravagant trappings of uncurbed fancy a splendid store of valuable folklore.

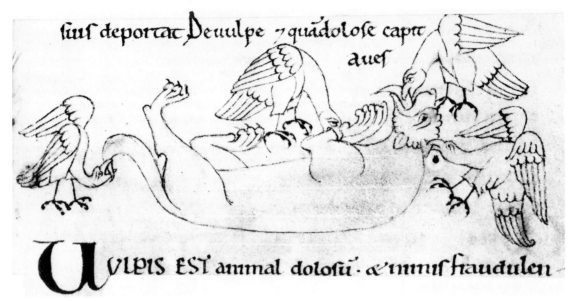

fiuf deportat Deuulpe ~quadolofe captr
auef

ꝟVLPIS EST animal dolofu· ⁊ minufraudulen

Plate 22. The fox as trickster; see Note 4. The manuscript illustration shows the fox in the moral role assigned to him by medieval compilers of bestiaries. Reproduced by courtesy of the Courtauld Institute.

Plate 23. A carving from New College, Oxford, showing hedgehogs gathering fallen fruit on their spines; see Note 4. Reproduced by courtesy of the National Buildings Record.

Notes

1. Judicial executions of and legal proceedings against animals, both wild and domestic, for violence, murder, mayhem, and trespass were extreme instances of this tendency. Cf. B. White, 'Medieval Beasts', *Essays and Studies Collected for the English Association*, ed. Sybil Rosenfeld (London, 1965), 36 n.2.

2. See Isaiah Berlin, *The Hedgehog and the Fox* (London, 1953). His 'hedgehogs' are 'monists' (Dante, Dostoievsky), and his 'foxes' 'pluralists' (Shakespeare, Molière).

3. The practice of repeating unverified statements about animals persisted long after Sir Thomas Browne's *Pseudodoxia Epidemica* (1646) and the foundation of the Royal Society (1660). The hyena, once considered detestable, is now revealed and admired as a skilful hunter. The animal was supposed to understand human speech and the curious will find an interesting reference to a strange Turkish method of capturing it in *The Four Epistles of A. G. Busbequius* (London, 1694; anonymous English translation, ed. with a dedication by Nahum Tate), 79.

   Concerning the wolf see Farley Mowat, *Never Cry Wolf* (London, 1963). His account of blameless Canadian wolves should be compared with an article in the *Times* for 21st March, 1978, describing the ferocious behaviour of Russian wolves, so dangerous and threatening as to call for a revival of the traditional wolf-hunt.

   In his *Topography of Ireland* (1187), Distinction II cap.XIX, Giraldus Cambrensis outdoes the most inventive *Bestiary* wolf-description with his vouched-for story of a wandering priest accosted by a wolf, which asked for the viaticum for his dying mate. It appears that the pair had been forced to take wolf form by Saint Natalis, an irate Abbot of Ossory. The Irish, says Giraldus, saints and all, are of a vindictive nature. Belief in lycanthropy was common in the Middle Ages and is still met with in remote regions. The Romulus-Remus legend has occasional modern echoes.

4. The fox's trick of shamming death is confirmed by W. H. Hudson, *The Naturalist in La Plata* (London, 1903), 202: 'The deception is so well carried out, that dogs are constantly taken in by it, and no one, not previously acquainted with this trickery of nature, but would at once pronounce the creature dead.' John Clare tells of a 'weary fox' to all intents and purposes lying dead in a furrow and seized by a shepherd for its skin:

   > The old fox started from his dead disguise
   > And while the dog lay panting in the sedge
   > He up and snapt and bolted through the
   >   hedge.

   (*Poems*, ed. J. W. Tibble, 1935; II, 334)

   The bestiarists describe the badger as a resourceful beast and picture him in process of digging out his sett by communal effort. Giraldus, *Topography of Ireland*, Distinction I cap. XX, confirms the story: 'Some of them, whose natural instinct it is to serve the rest, have been seen, to the great admiration of the observers, lying on their backs with the earth dug out heaped on their bellies and held together by their four claws, while others dragged them backward by a stick held in their mouth, fastening their teeth in which, they drew them out of the hole with their burdens.' (Cf. *Historical Works*, trans. T. Forester, ed. T. Wright; London, 1863.) Beavers, he says, in Distinction I cap.XXI, have a similar practice. He may have derived the information from a *Bestiary* (see MS. Bodley 764) or from earlier sources such as Pliny. The same story is told of beavers acting as thralls in the Danish fourteenth-century *Annals of Lund*.

In sober fact the ways of the hedgehog are more extraordinary than the *Bestiary* writers supposed. It can successfully fight a stoat; it can run faster than a rabbit; it can climb like a cat, and, apart from its appetite for fruit, will eat anything from snakes and frogs to household vermin. So good is the hedgehog as rat-catcher and cockroach devourer that, in earlier centuries, it was kept in London kitchens as a sort of ambulatory Rentokil. (Thomas Bell, *British Quadrupeds*; 1837.) For the strange habits of the hedgehog see *The Aberdeen Press*, 27th June, 1925, *A Country Diary*. The fruit-raiding story is as old as Pliny and appears in the *Greek Anthology*. John Clare repeats it:

Many often stoop and say they see
Him roll and fill his prickles full of crabs. . .
He makes a nest and fills it full of fruit
On the hedge bottom hunts for crabs and
    sloes
And whistles like a cricket as he goes.

(*Poems*, 1935; II, 337)

'Making his deduyt' says Caxton, while Topsell is less polite — 'making a noise like a cartwheel'.

Folklore and Regional Identity

JOHN WIDDOWSON   University of Sheffield

IN the hundred years since the founding of the Folklore Society we have witnessed not only the development of a unique discipline, but also its extension into areas of cultural tradition quite outside the scope of its original focus and fields of interest. These new developments, which have gathered impetus remarkably since the unsettling arrival of linguistics in the early 1950s, are particularly evident in North America where they have provoked a vigorous debate about the definition and delimitation of folklore and at the same time have explored its relationships with allied disciplines in the social sciences, sciences and humanities. This exploration has been especially fruitful in stimulating a re-examination of subject boundaries and identifying points of contact and possibilities for inter-disciplinary co-operation. The effects of this dialogue are to be seen, for example, in numerous recent works in anthropology and linguistics, as well as in the substantial number of major North American contributions to the redefinition of folklore as a discipline, and to the reappraisal of its whole theoretical basis. The rapid evolution of folklore theory since the 1950s draws heavily upon linguistics for its methodology. It is significant, however, that folklorists have tended to modify and even misinterpret some of the theoretical premises borrowed from linguistics, and evidently find it difficult to escape the trammels of a now dated structuralism and explore, for example, transformational-generative, stratificational or systemic models. Some recent publications nevertheless indicate that these newer analytical models may be of use to the folklorist,[1] and we should be prepared to draw on methodologies across the full range of the sciences and social sciences in developing our own theoretical framework for the study of cultural tradition.

These recent developments in folklore theory and the challenging and exciting extension of the boundaries of the subject have been slow to take root in Europe, and especially in the British Isles. Even the growing contribution of European scholars to the burgeoning fields of what may be termed 'the new folklore' (for those who find 'folkloristics' an unpalatable term), has failed to stimulate a corresponding enthusiasm among British folklorists to join in those debates which have advanced this field of study so dramatically in the past thirty years. In particular there has been a singular lack of research by English folklorists into the form, structure, function and context of their data.[2] The strength of English folklore scholarship has lain for the most part in the richness of its collected data, as attested by numerous volumes of collectanea from individual regions, not least the county folklore series initiated and published by the Society.[3] Unfortunately most of this data, interesting though it is both intrinsically and historically, is virtually devoid of contextual information, and its presentation almost invariably lacks any analysis of structure and function. We are much to blame for failing to take note of the tremendous strides forward made by folklorists elsewhere in their efforts to relate the data to its social context and to explore its relevance to culture and to life as a whole.[4] The comparative inertia of English folklore scholarship inevitably means that, a hundred years after the foundation of the Folklore Society, the vast majority of our endeavours are still to a large extent hidebound by nineteenth-century concepts of the discipline and of the role of the folklorist in both the academic world and the real world.

443

While recognising our past strengths in the publication of collectanea and of major studies on aspects of folklore and literature, we need to adopt a comprehensive and more flexible approach to our subject and dare once again to enter the arena of theoretical debate, from which we have perhaps understandably retreated since the eclipse of the solar mythologists, which destroyed at a stroke the credibility of folklore as an academic discipline in England. If the phoenix is to rise again from these ashes we must first restore that credibility. One way in which this can be done is by initiating large-scale surveys of our cultural traditions as they exist now throughout England, a country whose culture is very different from that of the nineteenth-century antiquarians, who, for the most part, viewed the picturesque life of the working classes from the comfort of their armchairs.[5] Such surveys would need to take account of traditional aspects of our culture as they operate in all social classes, all age-groups and all geographical regions. They would be primarily synchronic, investigating the traditions as they now exist and function in urban, as well as rural, areas. Their selection and sampling procedures would be as rigorous as those in other social sciences and would take account of form, function and context. Most important of all, they would be holistic — attempting to gather information on all aspects of cultural tradition, right across the social spectrum throughout the country. Such surveys would indeed approach the ideal and represent the kind of activity in which the Folklore Society should be engaged, whether as initiator or sponsor. In practice, however, in the absence of sponsorship and the financial support so desperately needed for folklore research in England today,[6] such surveys would have to rely on numerous small-scale investigations throughout the country, which would yield accurate and comparable primary data for a nation-wide study. Whichever way the surveys were carried out, it would then be possible to identify the principal features of our traditions as they are today at both national and local level, something conspicuously lacking in published sources. Indeed the investigation of the form and function of tradition at the local level is an essential prerequisite to the study of English folklore as a whole. One way in which such national features and regional variations could be demonstrated graphically is by the production of an Atlas of British Folk Culture,[7] or a series of such works, provided that these publications did not merely content themselves with mapping variations in the collectanea alone, but concentrated also on form and function.

As folklore is the common inheritance of a culture, it is natural that most, if not all, of its genres will be manifested throughout that culture and may be studied as a whole. Such supposedly national forms, however, may also be found in kindred societies such as those in other parts of the English-speaking world, and may even reflect or be indistinguishable from those which are increasingly recognised as cultural universals. Man in society evolves broadly similar traditions, as manifested for example in the universality of language and ritual, although local conditions and situations inevitably mean that the traditions are practised in various ways in different cultures. Within these so-called universals the specific forms of folklore differ in a multitude of ways from culture to culture, and from place to place within each culture. This multiplicity of variant forms represent microcultural, regional or individual diversity at its widest extent and at the same time form the basis for generalisations and the development of stereotypes at the national or macro-cultural level. Conversely, such national or general stereotypes may permeate to the regional and individual level, offering models, guidelines and frameworks capable of accommodating the maximum possible variation of local and individual forms, functions and contexts.

Setting aside the obvious ethnic and cultural differences between the English, Irish, Scots, Welsh and more recent immigrant cultures in the British Isles, each of which is worthy of separate study, it is clear that within England itself traditions vary considerably from one part of the country to another, whether for instance 'the north' is contrasted with 'the south', a given county compared with another, or a town, village, smaller community, family or individual is singled out as having a unique tradition. This apparent uniqueness may of course be fallacious, since similar, if not identical, traditional forms may occur elsewhere. Even so, these differences, slight though they may be, often constitute the essentially local feature of the form, and are part of a complex of traditions central to the sense of identity which typifies a community or other reference group.

I should now like to discuss in general terms some of the principal categories of English cultural tradition with particular reference to their form and function in the establishment and maintenance of regional identity. In order to make the transition from a descriptive approach to a functional one as smooth as possible, it seems best to base this outline on major genres[8] already exemplified in existing collectanea and the few recent studies which take account of form, function and context. It should then be possible to single out those aspects of tradition which have a significant part to play in maintaining a sense of identity in a given region, and so pave the way for systematic and detailed investigations of this important function of folklore within specific reference groups. I shall therefore ignore at this elementary stage the very real problems of using a genre-oriented approach, with all the inherent difficulties of its inevitably arbitrary and intuitive semantic categories, which are the very antithesis of structural and functional classification systems. By this means I hope it will be possible to draw parallels from and discover supporting examples in the wealth of collected material already published or in archives, despite the inevitable lack of rigour and contextual information in the original collecting process.

Folklore functions integratively within a reference group and it is therefore reasonable to study specific groups in depth to discover more about the social significance of traditions. By studying what is traditional at the family, group, village, town, city, county and regional levels we can identify not only those features which are essential to the structure of each reference group but also those which, taken together, are part of the Englishness of English people. It is significant that, in a superficial sense at least, we are able to identify certain general features which typify, or are said to typify, the Irish, the Scots and the Welsh, although we may be less sure of what is typically English. We can recognise an Irish, Scots or Welsh accent without being aware that this generalisation subsumes many different varieties of speech within each culture.

If we say that the use of Standard English or Received Pronunciation typifies the speech of those who live in England, are we perhaps thinking of an ideal, or creating a stereotype to which many English men and women might aspire, but do not in fact conform? Certainly the general characteristics of English speech, like those of Irish, Scots or Welsh, are integrative within each separate culture in that, on the surface if not more deeply, they are part of a behavioural complex which binds each group together.

On the other hand, those traditional features which are integrative within the group are divisive in their function outside it. This is seen, for example, when a group boasts about itself or makes claims for itself at the expense of another. The inter-group rivalry so typical of the *blason populaire* tradition in the British Isles is part of the assertion of local and regional identity, which is reflected in most, if not all, folklore genres.[9] Not only is this rivalry seen when the English, Irish, Scots and Welsh are vying with each other, whether seriously or jocularly, in certain situations, but it is also found at the level of the smaller regional unit, county, city, town, village or other group within a culture. The rivalries, however, may be forgotten when the sub-groups band together to support some national or corporate enterprise, such as a team representing the whole of the country in a competitive sport. In the same way the English, Irish, Scots and Welsh, in certain circumstances, may unite in their support of a joint enterprise against some outside body. In all these situations, whether internally cohesive or externally divisive, certain traditional usages, including local placenames, nicknames, *blasons populaires*, proverbial and idiomatic expressions, rhymes, chants and other linguistic forms, have an important part to play in the expression of inter-group rivalry. On the other hand there is tacit agreement to minimise the more dissonant and provocative of such usages when co-operation is called for across the group.

Of all folklore genres, language and other modes of communication such as gesture and the full range of paralinguistic, kinesic and proxemic features are central to the function of tradition in society. Being the medium of transmission in most of the other genres, language is indispensable to the maintenance of tradition, yet it has received little serious attention from English folklorists, many of whom tend to take it for granted, rather than recognising its role in moulding and modifying the forms of our traditions and of our attitudes to those forms. Our sense of regional and national identity is bound up with the fact that our language consists of many dialects, both regional and social, all of which, in turn, reflect our attitudes to our speech and to our culture as a whole. Linguistic usage functions as an index of social stratification, and provokes heated debates between reactionaries and progressives as to what is, or is not, 'correct' or acceptable. It is at such points that the mosaic of regional variations in our language is seen at its most complex and deviant from a national standard, if such there be, and the variations clearly indicate that a term or expression may not only be isolated to a particular region but may also be fundamental to the expression of that region's identity. Yet in spite of vigorous and challenging recent research in socio-linguistics in Britain, English folklorists have failed to take up Hymes's crucial suggestion, voiced as long ago as 1962, that we should investigate the use of language as a cultural system. Such an inter-disciplinary study of language within a speech community, which aims to present a partial or comprehensive ethnography of communication, is the obvious starting point for the discovery, description and analysis of spoken traditional usages, which are crucial to the identity of that community. From a practical point of view such usages reveal attitudes, prejudices and preferences, for example, which need to be taken into account by political, administrative, religious, commercial or other external organisations and groups which wish to extend their influence into the area concerned. Failure to recognise the importance of local attitudes, which are often deeply entrenched, may result in concerted resistance to such external influences, as the group closes ranks in an attempt to preserve its identity. The investigation of traditional language forms, as they exist today within a speech community, would yield valuable information about the group's sense of individuality and provide a dynamic model for evolving and assessing the strategies which will be most effective in penetrating the community from the outside. Unfortunately most work in English folklore studies tends to be based on static rather than dynamic models of social structure, and we fail to see survivals and modifications of older traditions as a means of accounting for present-day attitudes and behaviour, or as a means of predicting future trends. We need to view the whole process as a continuum, our task as folklorists being primarily to monitor the evolution of our cultural traditions, especially in times of rapid change such as those we are witnessing in England today.

The expression of regional identity in nick-names given to places and to their inhabitants is a focus for the maintenance of the *blason populaire* in all its forms. County nick-names like Norfolk/Devonshire/Derbyshire dumplings, Wiltshire moonrakers, Lancashire loiners, Lincolnshire yellow-bellies and Yorkshire tykes, along with nick-names given to people who live in cities and smaller places (Sheffield Sharpies, Austwick Carles, Oldham Roughyeads, Mossley/Wibsey Gawbies, Greenfield Whacks, Worral Mules, Oughtibridge Swilltubs, Wadsley Flatbacks) are obviously integrative for the reference group and non-integrative for outsiders. Local sayings, proverbs and rhymes, which refer to places well-known to those within the group, function in a similar way and, like the test-pieces of regional dialect served up to baffle 'foreigners' they help to maintain the group's identity and resist its penetration by outsiders. An obvious example of this regional chauvinism is the frequent accusation that an individual was not born and bred in the community, implying that therefore he is really not accepted as a member of it. The constant denigration of one neighbouring region or community by another provides a further widespread example of the typical functions of *blason populaire*, e.g. 'Foreigners begin at Watford/the Barnet bypass/St. Albans etc.'; 'All the way to Barnsley to be laughed at'; 'What's the best thing that ever came out of A? – The road to B'. As with many local proverbs and sayings, and indeed most of the traditions outlined here, the basic linguistic structure of these usages is similar all over England, but the local names and references which fill the slots in such structures give them a sharper cutting edge in everyday interaction. Indeed, people within the community concerned may feel that the usage is unique to their region, because of their strong sense of identification with the local referents.

In children's language, partisanship and regional or group chauvinism are also of great importance.

Regional dialect words, expressions and pronunciations used by mothers and other adults in their interaction with the pre-school child, are fundamental in familiarising him with accepted usages typical of the area. He is introduced to local names of people and places, which outsiders may be unaware of. Adults may refer to people and figures of authority in the neighbourhood in traditional threats to control a child's behaviour. In Sheffield, for instance, because he is still remembered in the area, the murderer Charlie Peace has been used in such threats, and references to local place-names give these verbal social controls added immediacy: 'Charlie Peace is comin' dahn t' Wicker' and 'Charlie Peace is comin' dahn past t' Salt Box'.[10] When children start school the partisanship between schools, parts of the town, villages and even streets is often expressed in local terms, the pejoratives used being frequently based on some specific knowledge or feature known only to those in the areas concerned.

Turning now to custom and belief as a second major genre set, it is obvious that such traditions have localised characteristics and functions, even though their underlying structure may well be similar throughout the country. In spite of the immense quantity of data on custom and belief assembled by English folklorists over the years, their detailed regional distribution remains uncertain. This is partly due to the fact that writers tend to reiterate details of customs and beliefs which obtained in the past, but give little or no indication of whether these are still practised today. The picture is further confused by the lapse of customs in some places and their revival in others, a constant process of evolution, which is itself highly deserving of study, if only to confirm that people apparently continue to feel the need to revive local customs. The reasons underlying such revivals are fundamental to any study of the function of folklore in England today. It is obvious, for example, that such revivals function as a focus for local or group identity. A place which celebrates certain occasions on a regular basis, and becomes known in the neighbourhood and further afield for this celebration, is drawing attention to itself and re-emphasising its existence and its institutions. A community which lacks such customs may be diminished in status and this in itself may attract derogatory comments, which

become part of local *blasons populaires*. On the other hand communities which have a long tradition of such customs are justly proud of them, and this in turn aggrandises their status. Indeed many places claim several centuries of unbroken tradition for their local customs, even though such claims are by no means always authenticatable.

General patterns of regional distribution are apparent in English calendar customs, but detailed information on the whole network is lacking and generalisation may therefore be misleading. To take a few instances at random, the custom of hurling seems now to be confined to the south and south-west, but not dissimilar customs, in which a different kind of ball is used, can be found, for example, at the Shrovetide football game at Ashbourne in Derbyshire. Should we therefore regard all customs in which a ball is used in this broadly similar way as one national form with regional variants, or should we distinguish between them? If, as at the Haxey Hood Game in Lincolnshire, for example, a roll of leather is used instead of a ball, but the game itself has obvious affinities with that at Ashbourne, where do we draw the line of demarcation? By contrast, the distribution of well-dressings is confined almost exclusively to Derbyshire, although each village has its own individual ways of dressing the wells. The observances on 5th November are broadly similar throughout the country, yet the use of such terms as *Plot Night, plot toffee, chumping/progging/chumping for prog/going bunnywooding* (collecting material for the bonfire) distinguish parts of west and south Yorkshire from other regions, even before we consider what food is traditionally eaten on Bonfire Night or Guy Fawkes Day/Night, whether a guy is burnt on the bonfire or just displayed by children asking for 'a penny for the guy', whether people go to a communal bonfire, or have a smaller one in their garden or other available ground, or whether, in predominantly Catholic communities for example, the custom is not practised at all. Wherever such customs do take place, however, they again function integratively for the group or region.

Patterns of regional variation are also distinguishable in the performance of the major rites of passage, despite the institutionalisation and officialdom which, as with many calendar customs, have clearly modified their observance even during this century. This institutionalisation obviously leads to the superimposition of general patterns over the whole country, but regional variations nevertheless persist. In Lincolnshire, for example, stuffed pork chine is still the order of the day at the homecoming after a christening, just as the things given to a very young baby as a 'blessing', as it is called in Derbyshire, used to include many other objects, apart from the no-longer-silver coin which typifies such gifts. Whatever is given is felt to be appropriate within the community, and not to behave appropriately is to invite censure as an unworthy person, or someone who has recently come into the community from elsewhere and therefore 'does not know any better'. Customs at weddings reveal remarkable differences across the social classes and in various age-groups, as well as exhibiting regional features such as the practice, still common, especially in the North East, of tying the church gates together before the couple leave church, their further progress being permitted only after money has been thrown to children outside the gates. Although the formal modification of funeral ceremonial has swept away many older traditions this century and established a fairly set routine, local variations are still to be found, not least in the typical fare eaten at the funeral tea. The erosion of superstition and older folk beliefs has also left a residue of practices which exhibit local variation. Beliefs, for example, may be attached to people and places in a neighbourhood and a community may even be proud of its ghosts, ineradicable bloodstains and topographical features, said to have been formed by the devil or by giants. Indeed such items often find their way into guidebooks and official brochures, not to mention popular compendia in which such phenomena are listed for the visitor's or tourist's delectation.

Local phenomena, like local characters, architectural features and the like, naturally act as a focus for stories, legends, anecdotes and jokes. Published work on folk narrative in England reveals not only the existence of numerous basic types and motifs, both national and international, but also an extraordinary wealth of local legends. While many of these legends conform in both structure and content to well-recognised general types, the vast majority are also distinguished by their local referents, which fix a particular recension of the tale in a specific region or community, where the relevance of these contextual features will be immediately appreciated by the regional audience. The references may be highly restricted, or, if a place and the stories attached to it become more widely known, it is sufficient to identify the place by name, and listeners anywhere in the country may be able to react appropriately. This is the case, for example, with such cycles of tales as those about the Wise Men of Gotham which, like so many other tales, have been widely disseminated in printed form, and so reached a much wider audience. For those who live in or near such a place today, however, the notoriety of local people for their supposed foolishness is a mixed blessing. It certainly puts the place on the map (seven miles southwest of Nottingham, incidentally, for those who, like myself as a child, had often heard the name but were not sure where the place was, or even if it was real rather than fictional), but not for reasons which would usually call for admiration. Even so, some communities which are the butt of *blasons populaires* and jokes may still tolerate such abuse and even appreciate it to some extent, perhaps in mock self-depreciation, so complex are the functional patterns in different communities. National and regional stereotypes are also of course prominent in tales and jokes about Englishmen, Irishmen and Scotsmen, or about 'representative' individuals from any community, emphasising and reinforcing either the integrative or non-integrative patterns determined by tradition over the years. Integratively, like the other genres already mentioned, these narratives bind the group together and give it a sense of its own status. Nonintegratively, they may lead to dissention, fighting and the kind of rivalry typical of footballcrowd behaviour at its worst.

Here we might also note in passing that the usual present-day milieu in which such tales are told is often that of the pubs, the sports clubs, the working men's clubs and the football ground — contexts of situation which are a far cry from those in which most of the tales in Enghish published collections were told, yet we have taken little note of these developments. Indeed the published collections virtually ignore the storytelling context and treat the tales as literature, rather than as the dramatic interaction between teller and audience, often in a specifically local setting, in the context of living speech.

A fourth genre set which, like the others comprises several major semantic categories, each of which could also be separately defined, is that which we might designate by the composite title of music, dance and drama. The complex interrelationships between these forms in English tradition suggest that in a general survey such as this it is reasonable to take them together. Like the genres already discussed, one of their primary functions is to entertain, but they also play their part in maintaining regional and group identity, notwithstanding the fact that their general structure may be similar in many parts of the country. The dissemination of regional forms to a wider audience through print, and later through the mass media, again means that songs and tunes originally local may have achieved national currency. On the other hand traditional instruments such as the Northumbrian pipes, regional styles of playing and singing, as well as the re-emergence of local dialect in a folksong revival earlier dominated by a mainly south-eastern linguistic stereotype, are indications of regionally distributed features, which may be identified with a specific locality. As is the case with many folk narratives, songs concerning local people, places and events are obviously important from this point of view, especially when the song is sung locally, and also when it is performed outside the area by a local person, as every Yorkshireman asked to sing *Ilkla Moor Baht 'At* to an audience outside the county is well aware. In such situations, however trivial they may be, the singing of such a song, whether it is an ancient ballad or a more modern piece, is not simply a matter of entertainment, or even of sociably taking one's turn in a singsong. It is a public affirmation or reaffirmation of an individual's association with a specific place of origin and/or allegiance. To the singer it functions as a means of retaining and re-emphasising his roots within that place, a process which is ultimately essential to most, if not all of us — the need to feel a sense of belonging, of calling a place our home, with all the mixture of pride, sentimentality, nostalgia, and even regret, which such an affirmation may hold for us. Local songs, like local legends, make specific reference to local matters and therefore have a direct bearing on the history of a community, although this important function is often ignored by folklorists, and even by oral historians.

Folk dances also play a part in the assertion and promulgation of regional identity. The careful choice of distinctive costume, for example, marks out each of the morris teams in the current revival, and, as is the case with calendar customs, strong claims, sometimes exaggerated ones, are made for the longevity of a local dance. Nor, of course, are such dances confined to rural areas. The sword dance teams at Grenoside and Handsworth[11] on the outskirts of Sheffield are excellent examples of urban teams, which claim a long history for their dances and which exhibit a marked contrast in both dress and performance. There are, of course, exceptions to this insistence on local traditional forms. One example is the Barnsley longsword dance team, which has adopted a dance collected from Kirkby Malzeard near Ripon. Such migrations could also have occurred in the past, just as a modern folk dance team may perform a number of nationally or regionally known dances, in addition to one or more dances or versions which it may regard as its own.

A similar fusion of local and general features is found in present-day performances of folk plays. In this case, however, we are in a better position to discuss the regional distribution of forms and variants, thanks to the geographical index compiled by Cawte, Helm and Peacock,[12] and to the more recent work which continues to provide further details of local recensions.[13] While many mumming plays clearly have localised features of performance and of text, it now seems probable that textual variation often represents comparatively minor deviation from earlier chapbook versions, which were widely disseminated throughout the country. As is the case with other genres, one could therefore argue that local variations are unimportant, and merely blur and confuse the form of the suggested chapbook originals. It is still a matter for conjecture, however, whether or not the chapbook versions, which are thought to be the basis for many texts handed down by oral tradition and in manuscript, were originally composed by specific writers or were written down and/or modified from an already existing oral tradition. Although the regional distribution of hero-combat, wooing and animal-disguise plays shows some regional patterning, the reasons for this remain obscure. Certainly local recensions incorporate local features and characters and, as with all spoken folklore, their performance usually reflects local dialectal usage. It is features of the performance and its context, however, which are of the greatest importance in assessing the role of folk drama as an aspect of regional identity. Unfortunately, and again typically, we lack detailed knowledge of the context of performance. Insofar as the function of these plays can be determined, however, it is certain that, in addition to their presentation as entertainment, they also in the recent past provided a means of obtaining money, and/or food and drink, in common with many house-visiting customs. This was of particular value to youngsters, and especially young apprentices who, in South Yorkshire at any rate, were the usual performers of such plays in the early years of this century. The organisation, performance, choice of venues, and so on, would be decided by common consent within the group, just as the members would also agree on how to share out the rewards received for their performance. Many of these decisions, like some features in the text and in the performance, depended on local situations and conditions, and not least on the reception of the audience, who often regarded such performers as bringers of good luck — yet another function scarcely investigated in the principal studies of this genre.

The fifth and final genre set in this brief survey is that of material culture and the work techniques, arts and crafts which produce it. Such a category would include not only traditionally hand-made objects and artefacts, but also, for example, vernacular architecture, traditional art forms and decorations, costume and all traditional usages within manufacturing processes, even in those which are primarily technological. It is possible here only to mention a few instances of the role played by such traditional forms in the affirmation of regional identity. In spite of the enormous increase in purpose-built housing of similar basic design during this century, for example, it is still possible, when travelling around the country, to see distinctive house-types, farm-buildings and cottages, which characterise a particular region, or even county. The variation is partly due to the availability of building and roofing materials in

different places, and the use of local materials is itself one of the principal features of an individual's identification with his home environment. One only has to cross the border from Cheshire into North Wales, for example, to become aware of the distinctive colour of local stone, and the steeper pitch and unusual design of roofs. The contrast may be less marked within England itself, but contrasts there certainly are. The distribution of old crafts, whether rural or urban, is also part of local identity and may depend on the availability of movements and sources of power, as well as on the necessary markets for the products. While the regional variations of, say, farm carts and wagons, and indeed almost all the artefacts and implements used in the days when horses dominated the agricultural scene, are now part of our history, there are many aspects of material culture which remain distinctively local. The notion that Cornish pasties, Lancashire hotpot or Yorkshire pudding are best made by people from those respective counties is a not uncommon claim by those of such ancestry, even though these dishes are found nation-wide. The design of boats around our coasts varies from place to place, as for instance the high-stemmed clinker-built cobles of the north-east coast demonstrate, and the men who fish from these cobles still wear the blue or brown fisherman's smock, and guernseys knitted in distinctively local traditional designs. Nor is such distinctiveness by any means confined to rural areas. It is to be found in virtually every industry and occupation, as for example in the design and manufacture of certain knives in the Sheffield cutlery trade, in a city still world-famous for its long tradition in this particular industry, just as Nottingham is still known for its lacemaking, Bradford for woollen goods and Lancashire for cotton, despite the change and decline in these trades in each of these localities.

In a brief and superficial survey such as this it is possible only to hint at some of the more overt functions of folklore in, among other things, the establishment and maintenance of regional identity. Reliable and recent data on the functions of folklore in England is conspicuously lacking, and, if we are to make headway in the development of folklore studies in this country, we must first turn our attention to the collection of data in the fullest possible social context, and investigate its functions in, and relevance to, our daily lives. We need to recognise the crucial role which traditions play in fostering a sense of identity, whether for the individual, within the family or other small group, the community, village, town, city, county or region, as well as in different social classes and age-groups, and indeed nationally. Such an investigation would help to shift the emphasis of folklore studies in England away from their obsession with data — especially data which emphasises the rustic, the archaic, the picturesque and the bizarre — towards an appraisal and analysis of its practical applications to the lives of people today. For each one of us is rooted in tradition. It informs our lives and infuses itself throughout our institutions. We can no longer be content merely to note its surface manifestations; we need to examine its deeper structure, and discover why it persists and what its essential functions are, in a changing world where a pervasive sense of anomie threatens our traditional allegiances and patterns of identity.

451

Notes

1. For examples of the scanty essays into these fields by English folklorists see P. S. Smith, 'Tradition – A Perspective', Part II, Transmission, *Lore and Language*, II (3) (July, 1975), 5-14 and Part III, Information, Perception and Performance, *Lore and Language*, II (8) (January, 1978), 1-10; J. D. A. Widdowson, 'The Language of the Child Culture: Pattern and Tradition in Language Acquisition and Socialisation', *They Don't Speak Our Language*, ed. S. Rogers (London, 1976), 33-61; *ibid., If You Don't Be Good: Verbal Social Control in Newfoundland*, St John's, Newfoundland, 1977, esp. 42-66.

2. In the issues of *Folklore* from 1968 to 1978, for example, most articles by British contributors are primarily descriptive, and only a handful focus on structure, function and context. These include: Doris E. Marrant, 'Some Functions of Narrative in Yorkshire' (Autumn, 1968), 202-16; Anthony Jackson, 'The Science of Fairy Tales' (Summer, 1973), 120-41; Jacqueline Simpson, 'The Function of Folklore in "Jane Eyre" and "Wuthering Heights" ', (Spring, 1974), 47-61; H. R. Ellis Davidson, 'Folklore and History' (Summer, 1974), 73-92; Venetia Newall, 'The Allendale Fire Festival in Relation to its Contemporary Social Setting' (Summer, 1974), 93-103; Roger Elbourne, 'The Study of Change in Traditional Music' (Autumn/Winter, 1975), 181-89.

3. The influence of this series on English folklore study has been immense, although unfortunately such massive compendia as that of Mrs Gutch and Mabel Peacock for Lincolnshire tend to serve mainly as sourcebooks for small popular booklets and articles, often without due acknowledgement.

4. For the few examples in *Folklore* during the last decade, see the articles by Marrant, Ellis Davidson and Newall, in Note 2 above.

5. For comments on the myopic obsession with the lower class and the failure to investigate middle and upper-class traditions, see Georgina Smith, 'Literary Sources and Folklore Studies in the Nineteenth Century: A Re-assessment of Armchair Scholarship', *Lore and Language*, II (9) (July, 1978), 26-42; J. D. A. Widdowson, 'Folklore – What's That' and 'Folklore – Who Cares?' *The Month in Yorkshire*, VII (9) (June/July, 1977), 7, and VIII (2) (November, 1977), 12-13.

6. See Widdowson, 'Folklore – Who Cares?'

7. See S. F. Sanderson, 'Towards an Atlas of British Folk Culture', *Folklore*, LXXXII (Summer, 1971), 89-98.

8. The genre classification used here is based on that of Herbert and Violetta Halpert, (St John's, Newfoundland, 1971), a revision of Herbert Halpert's *Folklore Classification* (Murray, Kentucky, 1948), adapted by him from L. C. Jones, and incorporating ideas from W. D. Hand, A. Taylor, V. Randolph, H. W. Thompson, S. Thompson *et al.*

9. See J. D. A. Widdowson, 'Language, Tradition and Regional Identity: *Blason Populaire* and Social Control', paper presented at the British Sociological Association Conference, Brighton, 1978.

10. These and the other examples drawn on in this paper are from my own field-work, and from the archives of the Centre for English Cultural Tradition and Language at the University of Sheffield.

11. See Geoff Lester, *Handsworth Traditional Sword Dancers* (Sheffield, 1978).

12. E. C. Cawte, Alex Helm and N. Peacock, *English Ritual Drama: A Geographical Index* (London, 1967).

13. See, for example, P. S. Smith, 'Collecting Mummers' Plays Today', *Lore and Language*, I (1) (July, 1969), 5-8; Peter Wright and Peter F. M. McDonald, 'The Cheshire Soul-Cakers' Play', *Lore and Language*, I (3) (August, 1970), 9-11; T. Chambers, 'Further Notes on Antrobus Soul-Cakers and Other Cheshire Souling Plays', *Lore and Language*, I (5) (July, 1971), 11-15; M. J. Preston, M. G. Smith and P. S. Smith, 'A Classification of Chapbooks Containing Traditional Play Texts', *Lore and Language*, I (7) (July, 1972), 3-5; David Buchan, 'The Folk Play, Guising, and Northern Scotland', *Lore and Language*, I (10) (January, 1974), 10-14; M. J. Preston, M. G. Smith and P. S. Smith, 'An Interim Checklist of Chapbooks Containing Traditional Play Texts', *History of the Book Trade in the North* (Newcastle, 1976); M. J. Preston, M. G. Smith and P. S. Smith, 'The Lost Chapbooks', *Folklore*, LXXXVIII (2) (1977), 160-74; M. J. Preston, M. G. Smith and P. S. Smith, *Chapbooks and Traditional Drama, Part I, Alexander and the King of Egypt Chapbooks* (Sheffield, 1977).

Some Problems Concerning the Folklore of Polish Fishermen

MARIA ZNAMIEROWSKA-PRÜFFEROWA   Ethnographic Museum, Toruń

ONE only needs to look at a map of the world to realise that oceans, seas, lakes and rivers provide a natural environment which determines the way of life of millions of people all over the globe, providing their chief source of income and dictating their work techniques, their tools, and even, to some extent, their personalities.

The present paper is an attempt to point out the connections which exist between the environment and conditions of life and work of a sea-fisherman, his lore, beliefs, customs and rituals, as well as magical rites that are supposed to protect him from evil and bring good luck.

I am omitting the rich oral lore on the subject because its range is too wide. My examples have been chosen almost entirely from the Cashubian villages of the Hel peninsula and a little further West, supplemented by rather rare written sources.[1]

These coastal Cashubian communities, which have existed for centuries on the Hel peninsula, have been chosen for this study because they constitute the only distinct ethnographic Polish marine group which has lived in strict isolation for a considerable time and has preserved the ancient folk fishing traditions. Thanks to their wide overseas contacts, their folklore shows the influence of the cultures not only of their immediate neighbours but also those of distant nations. In some respects it also resembles the agricultural cultures of Poland. These old traditions have been preserved in the form of many implements, utensils, a distinct dialect and rich, interesting folklore.

Until about the middle of the nineteenth century the Cashubian fishermen retained an old form of fishing co-operatives, known as far back as the fifteenth century, called *maszoperia*.[2] They were small working groups, chiefly formed on a family basis, organised for the collective catching of certain kinds of fish, such as salmon, sprat, eel and herring. They also used specific fishing gear, as for example the seine or fyke nets. These *maszoperias* had an important social function. In case of illness, they provided the fisherman with aid, either financial or in kind (fish), and they took care of widows, orphans and the aged, the last receiving a permanent 'pension' in the form of half the regular earnings.

The role of women in the fishing communities has been active. Even very old women help the fishermen in their work by tying the nets, untangling and cleaning them after their return from the sea, helping to prepare the bait, sometimes helping in the drawing of salmon seine, and so on.

Considerable changes followed as a result of the introduction of cutters at the turn of the nineteenth and the twentieth centuries. Their owners went fishing further out into the sea, employing hired labour and thus becoming an economic and social élite. Another major factor was the use of motors in coastal boats after World War I. Today *maszoperias* have persisted in only a very few villages and in a rather limited form.

I will consider first the fisherman's profession and knowledge. Traditionally, a fisherman-to-be gets his professional training from his early childhood, in his own home. He gains his professional knowledge not only by observation and by helping in the lighter kinds of work, but also through participation in the actual fishing itself. At the age of six a boy learns to tie the nets and at fourteen he would already be sailing out and fishing.

This is what Augustyn Necel, an experienced fisherman and writer, my informant, said about the profession: 'The fishing profession is better than any other, because a man must be both clever and physically fit, as well as brave and courageous.

It satisfies his ambition. Moreover, it is an optimistic occupation. No luck today, never mind, tomorrow will be better. That is why I would never change my profession; if I were to be born again, I should still be a fisherman.' 'The sea is always different. It is alive. The mountains are dead, they are the same every day, while the sea is always new.' The Cashubian fisherfolk of the Baltic coast are deeply attached to their profession, which is frequently passed on from father to son, as can be seen from statistics.[3]

To be able to cope with the hardships of work at sea and to ensure success, a fisherman has to be equipped with sound knowledge, based on keen observation and experience. This knowledge was passed down through the generations, each generation enriching it with new additions. Nowadays, such knowledge can be learned at specially organised classes. The Cashubian fishermen have rich traditional lore pertaining to meteorology, hydrography, the biology and ethology of fish. Of the many kinds of fish that they can distinguish, thirty are already extinct;[4] they know the environment in which particular kinds of fish live, they know the best places for fishing, the topography of the sea bottom, fish migrations influenced by winds, currents and thermal conditions, and much more besides. They have also observed that fish of one kind will grow different features in different environments — as, for example, in the open sea, or in the gulf.[5]

They know very well the favourite food eaten by particular kinds of fish — an important point when selecting bait. They know the fish's eyesight and hearing, their spawning sites, their behaviour during storms, and so on. They also have extensive knowledge as to the best times of the year and day, as well as the best places in which to catch particular kinds of fish. They are very good at forecasting the weather by the look of the sun, the moon, the clouds, the force and direction of the wind, the behaviour of animals — for instance frogs, gulls, or other birds — the appearance of fish, etc. From these, they are able to predict storms and to draw conclusions as to whether the catch will be good or bad.

The Cashubian fisherfolk of the Baltic coast frequently fit their houses with mobile wooden weathercocks in the shape of a fish, perched high over the roof. Even quite recently in some houses in certain villages of the region one could find a curious weathercock inside the house: a dried fish, hung from the ceiling on a piece of thread. It was said to be 'always facing the wind'. For this purpose they used a fish popularly known as the sea devil (*Myoxocephalous scorpius*), or the sturgeon (*Acipensor sturio*) or else a bone of a wild duck or the backbone of a gull.

Traditional folk medicine of the rational type once consisted mainly of herbal cures and, in the coastal villages, curing with the entrails of fish and other sea animals — for example, the liver, gall, entrails and fat of the cod, tench, porpoise and seal. These are now rarely used, but the memory of such medicines is still alive in the minds of old people along with a variety of superstitions. Among these a very widely accepted belief was that in the 'evil eye'. A good protection against it was to tie a piece of red ribbon to the net, the trawl wing, or the boat, or even onto the wrist of a new-born baby. Women were particularly notorious as bringers of bad luck. It was a very bad omen for a fisher to meet one when starting out for fear of the 'evil eye' and an unsuccessful catch.

A very interesting superstition is connected with the pike: the bones in its head are supposed to represent the instruments of the Passion of Christ and were worn as an amulet. The pike was considered sacred by some people and lightning could never strike a spot in the water where a pike was hiding.[6]

With the ever-present threat of death by drowning, the fisherman found great support in religion. 'A fisherman can sense and perceive God at sea better than on land,' said Necel. In moments of stress or at the beginning of work, he would pray to God and the patron saints. As a protection against evil, he placed holy images on his boat, or pious inscriptions, censed the boat with sacred herbs, had the priest bless both it and the nets, especially at the opening of the fishing season. Prayers were offered for the safety of those at sea by the fisherman's families and their mates, who remained on land. Frequently a mother would wake up her children in the middle of the night to pray together for their father's safe return.

Particular honour was paid to the patron saints of the fishermen, those of the *maszoperias* and of individual fishing villages: St Barbara, St Peter, St Nicholas, St Antony and others. Protection was often sought from the Holy Virgin, particularly at special feasts in her honour; examples are the feast of Our Lady of the Fishermen on 16th August, the feast of Our Lady of the Eels on 7th October, and others. These were festive occasions for the village: relatives and guests 'from inland' arrived and were ceremoniously received by the local fisherfolk.

Besides religion, which was resorted to in situations of extreme danger and of major importance, the fisherman's hazardous life gave rise to various protective magical practices which centered mainly around ensuring a successful catch. These took the form of, for instance, special rites during net-making, launching new boats, and the opening of the fishing season. To give an example, blood was regarded as a powerful charm for repelling evil and helping to ensure a good catch. For that reason, members of less fortunate *maszoperias* on the Cashubian coast would sometimes stealthily gather the blood-splashed sand where their luckier neighbours had killed salmon and bury it on their own part of the beach to bring luck.[7] I have heard in Jastarnia that they made it a practice to throw clotted blood into the sea so that nobody would steal it. Necel quotes instances of curious fights held by the fishermen as late as 1914, when they beat each other with heavy sticks (*karkuleca*) until they bled, so that the 'salmon would catch well'. The ceremony of sewing up the seine, which traditionally took place at Shrovetide, was another major occasion. There was a religious service and a great feast, and the Dance of the Devils was performed.[8]

Other protective practices of the past included some that sprang from fear of the dead. The Cashubian fisherfolk used various means to prevent the dead from returning and harming living relations. They would put a piece of net into the coffin to keep the corpse engrossed in untangling the knots; or it was provided with poppy seeds, which had to be counted, and the corpse could not leave the coffin until the task had been completed.

Protection against witches was also needed. At Christmas and New Year it was the custom to shoot in the air to frighten them away.[9] On St John's Eve witches were said to ride on brooms to their meeting-place at the crossroads. Fishermen lit bonfires on the beach and put barrels filled with tar on tall poles, while holy water was sprinkled in the four corners of the house to keep the witches away.[10] A superstition that is also widely known in other countries forbad whistling while fishing, for fear of raising a wind.

From the examples quoted, it is evident that the customs connected with fishing bear the signs of both Christian and pre-Christian origins, as well as elements peculiar to the cultures of many nations not unique to the Baltic coasts. Some of the customs illustrate magical practices widely known all over the world. Such syncretism is typical of certain aspects of spiritual folk culture, where the magical outlook of some old fishermen is mixed with a rational approach or with experience of a metaphysical, transcendental nature.

At present, the growth of modern civilisation is naturally causing a gradual extinction of old customs and rituals that are an external manifestation of magical beliefs. The essential mental and emotional reactions remain hidden and mostly invisible to the rest of the world. Contemporary Cashubian fishermen, especially the young ones, know and appreciate the old traditional knowledge related to fishing and navigation, but they look critically at the old magical practices.

With the development of education and technology, most traditional nineteenth-century fisher folklore is now becoming irretrievably lost. Unfortunately the fishing profession seems to be generally underestimated, as can be inferred from the paucity of material found in museums and archival records, and from the fishermen's own statements in reply to sociological questionnaires.[11] There are also very few open-air museums devoted to traditional fishing in any detail. Consequently there is an urgent need for research into the disappearing fishermens' lore, as well as the material which has already gone and the evolving and modern forms of their lore, particularly in the fields of medicine, meteorology, rare magical practices, and other forms of folklore which are not discussed here. The publications and material gathered by P. F. Anson, W. Gregor, G. Pitré, or P. Sébillot are too few. We need more studies analysing the spiritual life and work of fishermen, in the light of various scientific disciplines, so as to place them in a proper perspective.

Notes

1. To amplify this, I cite here the names of selected authors who, in many cases after World War II, devoted considerable attention to the problem. I do not here refer in detail to my own work, which consists mainly of unpublished material, also collected after World War II, and confirms in a different way the facts, mostly preserved in the memories of sea-coast Cashubians. They were taken down on the Hel Peninsula, including the village of Dębki on the Baltic coast. See, in addition to the following, the works cited in the further notes, below: P. F. Anson, *Fisher Folk-Lore* (London, 1965; the author has published other interesting books on related subjects); Z. Dulczewski, *Rybacy bałtyccy. Zagadnienie stabilizacji społeczno-zawodowej* (*The Baltic Fishermen. The Problem of Social and Professional Stabilization*; Warsaw, 1973); W. Gregor, *Notes on the Folk-Lore of the North-East of Scotland* (London, 1881; also other related works by the same author); K. Moszyński, *Kultura ludowa słowian. Część II – Kultura duchowa* (*The Folk Culture of the Slavs. Part II – Spiritual Culture*; Crakow, 1934); G. Petré, *Spettacoli siciliane* (Palermo, 1881; also other related works by the same author); P. Sébillot, *Le Folk-Lore des Pêcheurs* (Paris, 1968; also other related publications of the same author); B. Stelmachowska, *Rok obrzędowy na Pomorzu* (*The Ritual Year in Pomerania*; Toruń, 1933); B. Sychta, *Słownik Gwar Kaszubskich* (*Dictionary of Cashubian Dialects*; Wroclaw-Warsaw-Crakow, 1967-73); M. Znamierowska-Prüfferowa, *Przycsynek do magii i wiersen rybaków* (*A Contribution Concerning Fishermen's Magic and Beliefs*; Lublin, 1947); *ibid.*, 'Przyczynek do znajomości nadmorskiej ludności rybackiej' ('A Contribution to the Knowledge of Coastal Fishing Communities'), *Materiały Zachodniopomorskie*, XIV (1968).

2. J. Kucharska, *Tradycyjna organizacja rybołówstwa zespołowego na Wybrzeżu Kaszubskim* (*The Traditional Organisation of Cooperative Fishing on the Cashubian Coast*; Wroclaw-Warsaw-Crakow, 1968), 555-6.

3. Z. Batorowicz, 'Stosunki społeczno-ekonomiczne w kaszubskim rybołówstwie przybrzeżnym' ('Social and Economic Relationships in the Cashubian Coastal Fishery'), *Lud*, XLIX (1965), 201-3.

4. J. Kucharska and Z. Batorowicz, 'Rybołówstwo przybrzeżne w Kuźnicy' ('Coastal Fishery in Kuźnica'), *Studia i Materiały do Historii Kultury Wsi Polskiej w XIX i XXw (Biblioteka Etnografii Polskiej)*, I (1958), 148.

5. *ibid.*, 147.

6. E. S. Gulgowski, *Von einem unbekannten Volke in Deutschland* (Berlin, 1911), 102.

7. T. Guttówna, 'Obrzędy, wierzenia, zwyczaje i przesady wśród rybaków Polskiego Wybrzeża' ('Rites, Beliefs, Customs and Superstitions among the Fishermen of the Polish Coast'), *Prace i Materiały Etnograficzne*, VIII/IX (1950-51), 479.

8. *ibid.*, 464-6.

9. *ibid.*, 465.

10. *ibid.*, 469.

11. e.g. L. Janiszewski, 'Rybacy dalekomorscy. Studium socjologiczne' ('Deep-sea Fishermen. A Sociological Study'), *Ziemie Zachodnie, Studia i Materiały*, X (1967).

INDEX

advertising and folklore 114-15
African proverbial sayings 332
agitprop, and folklore 135-42
Amerindian mythology 192-6
animal disguise 172
animal kingdom, in fanciful popular belief and in the *Beast Books* 438-9
antiquarianism 8, 250, 444
archaeological sites, the folklore of 213-15
axis mundi 253-7
    and the phallus 256-7

ballad
    of Thomas the Rymer 247, 249
    and Japanese material 247-9
    survival in the Midwest 384-8
Beast Books, Bestiaries 438-9
blason populaire 154, 445-8
Book of Delights see Sepher Sha'ashu'im
breast feeding practices 44
Britain
    British folklore, founders of 7-13
    racist images in 308-11

children, lore of
    child rhymes 65-7
    story telling by the very young 320-8
Chile, foxhunting in 167-8
China
    collection and study of folktales in twentieth-century China 405-8
    Chinese Folk Literature and Art Society 406, 408
Christianity
    Christian sacraments, heathen basis of 11
    Christian cult-crosses 250-7
    pagan survivals in 250-3, 256-7
    phallic worship and 250-3, 256-7

circumambulation 344-7
    magic circling 344-7
    sacred circles 344
    desiul and *tuapholl* in Ireland 346-7
clowning *see* folly
comparative method, and Plutarch 373, 375-6
cosmogony 255
culturally based science 204-12
    team approach in 208-9
    potential for the natural sciences 209-10
    potential for folklore 210-11
    folklore's potential contribution to 211-12
cunning folk 183-6
    táltos in Hungary 184
customs
    in transition 69-70
    survival of 70-1
    some Spanish 234-5
    associated with dress in Ireland 284-5
    and regional identity 447-8

Denmark, Danish folklore 236-9
developing countries, modernisation and folk culture in 177-81
Devil
    Devil-Child theme 228-9
    devil lore 226
diffusionist theory 12
dress, belief and customs associated with in Ireland 284-8
drinking habits 42

eating behaviour 260-3
    food as a symbol of human relationships 261-3
    food as a basis for interaction 262-3
eating habits 43
Ecuador, Turkey Buzzard tales of the Quichua 240-6

England
    English fairies 144-5
    English witch trials 185
    in Danish folklore 236, 239
    academic development of folklore in 443-4
    regional variation and identity 444-51
envy, and the evil eye 40-57
ethnoscience 205
evil eye, the 37-57
    preventive measures against 37, 40, 46-8, 53-5
    distribution of folk belief in 37-8
    and envy 40-57
    structural principles of thought relating to 41-2
    symbolic associations with eyes 42, 46-57
    benevolent use of 55
    belief in among Polish fishermen 455
evolutionary theory 8-12
    applied to religion 11

fairies
    good fairies, their malevolent potential 143
    malevolent fairies 143-5
    otherworld 147-51
    and the dead in Ireland 287
    belief in, in contemporary Ulster 398-403
fairy tales
    The Science of Fairy Tales 10
    otherworld in 147-51
    time in 314-18
    told by the very young 321-7
fancy, in popular beliefs 438-9
fertility ritual 54
festivals
    festive functions of Hungarian pottery 269-71
    weddings 270-1
    and dress in Ireland 284-5
    in Wales and ritual entry to the house 340-2
fictions and play 119-22
fire ritual 234-5
folk art, artists
    silversmiths in Yemenite Jewish society 199-202
    Hungarian pottery 269-71
folk culture, in the developing counties, new possibilities for 177-81
folk dance
    Morris 128-33
    Rey dance 128-33
    and regional identity 449
folk history 291-9
folklore
    as an academic discipline 1, 2, 5-6, 12
    and national ideology 12
    evolutional theory of 8-12
    diffusionist theory of 12

    the science of 10
    concept of motif in 17-30
    transmission of 64-6
    origins in 66-7
    definitions of 67-8
    enduring features in 72-3
    study of 73-4
    and advertising 114 15
    and agitprop 135-42
    and folly 170-4
    in the developing countries, new possibilities 177, 181
    Jewish 195
    dialogue in 195
    and culturally based science 210-12
    ethical codes in the discipline of 210
    potential applications of the discipline 210-11
    of archaeological sites 213-15
    the snail motif in European 81-7, 101-3, 104-6
    opposition and contrast in 236-9
    Danish 236-9
    semiotics applied to 266-8
    Greek 278-81
    in relation to racial prejudice 311
    and history 399-400
    and folklorism 419-23
    and race 428-9
    and regional identity 443-51
    theory, recent developments of 443
    inter-disciplinary cooperation and 443
    the academic development of in England 443-4
    functions of, in regional identity 445-51
    social context, the importance of 443-51
    and language 445-7
    revivals 447
    environment and, among Polish fishermen 454-6
Folklore Society 1-6, 67, 73, 278, 281
    role and purpose of 1, 8
    history of 2, 7-13
    and academic study of folklore 2, 5-6
    and collection of material 3
    and publication 3-4
    and regional groups 4-5
folklorism 419-23
    neo-folklorism 420-1
folklorisms 114-15
folk plays, and regional identity 449-50
folk saints 123-6
folk song
    British and Euro-American songs in the Midwest 384-8
    ballad survival in the Midwest 384-8
    and regional identity 449

folktales
 analysis of 17-20, 25-30
  Ur-form 17
  minimal narrative units 17-20, 25-30
  historic-geographic method in 17-20, 25-30
  classification in 18, 19
  motif in 18-20, 25-30
 story radicals in 19
 theme of twins in 192-6
 Welsh folk-narrative tradition 218-23
 Danish, the collection of 238
 popular belief and 240, 241, 244
 narrative patterns in 240-6
 acculturation in 241
 transformation between 241
 Japanese 247-9
 Buddhist 248-9
 the Old Yiddish Ma'aseh 289-90
 didactic elements in 240, 241, 289-90
 in twentieth-century China, collection and
  study of 405-8
 see also Turkey Buzzard tales, fairy tales, legend
folly 170-4
 and taboo 173-4
 language of 174
Fool 170-4
foxhunting, in Chile 167-8
framing, in play 120-2
'fun' 120-1
funerals
 funeral games 173, 235
 circumambulation at funerals 344-7

Greece
 Greek folklore 278-81
 the Hellenic Folklore Society 279
 ancient Greek folklore and Plutarch 373-6

Hellenic Folklore Society 279
historic-geographic method 17-20, 25-30
homeopathic magic 50-1
house visiting 171-3
 ritual entry to the house in Wales 339-42
 in South Yorkshire 450
Hungary
 Hungarian witch trials 183-6
 Hungarian pottery 269-71
 ethnography and folklore in 422-3
 folklorism in 422-3

iconography
 the lion, the unicorn and the fox 412-17
 the stag 416
imitation
 fish imitation 131-3

of supernatural beings, taboo against 226
India, early Indian cosmogony 255
Iran, passion plays in 188-91
Ireland
 Irish fairies 143-5
 beliefs and customs associated with dress 284-8
 contemporary Ulster fairy tradition 398-404
Islam, early history of 188
Italy
 foreign folk attitudes to Italians and Lombards
  76-9, 95-8
 ancient Roman folklore and Plutarch 373-6

Jewish folklore
 Yemenite Jews 195
 the silversmith as folk artist 199-202
 Old Yiddish folk literature 289-90
 Yugoslav Jewish embroidery and costume 303-7

legend 10, 71-2, 273-5
 war-time 123-6
 miraculous 123-6
 fairy 147-51
 the Colbek legend 158-63
 in Welsh folk-narrative 281-20
 the Urashima legend 247-8, 249
 and oral folk history 291, 296-7
 a modern 311
 time in 314, 318
 modern urban 379-82
limited good 41, 42-57
liquid, life dependency on 41, 42-57
literature
 oral and written, continuities between 272-6
 medieval English and circumambulation 344-7
luck 170, 172

Macbeth, the Witches in 431-5
magic
 and the Yemenite Jewish silversmith 199-200
 in Welsh folk-narrative tradition 219
 magic circling 344-7
 protective, among Polish fishermen 456
 homeopathic 50-1
 in names 11
Märchen 11, 18, 30, 219
 and Dickens 283
 time in 314, 315
memorates 219, 230, 231
minimal narrative units 17-20, 25-30
miraculous legends 123-6
Missouri Folk-Lore Society 384-5
motif
 in folklore 17-30
 and the German romantics 20-1

461

motif *cont.*
    and Ruskin's aesthetics 21-2
    in literary research 22-5
    classification system 23
    and cultural characteristics 22-3
    in iconography 30, 79-81, 84, 98-100, 104
    in Jewish legends of war-time 123-6
    the 'Forgotten Fiancée' 248, 249
    supernatural beings in 249
    in oral folk history 296-7
    symbolic, in Yugoslav Jewish embroidery 305-6
    as an analytical tool 349-55
    mapping of motifs 352-4, 356-63
    exaggeration motifs (priamelen) 354-5
    see also snail motif
mumming 171-3
myth
    Amerindian mythology (twins and the trickster in) 192-6
    British myths about Africa 308-9
    and culture, and race relationships in West Virginia 425-9

narrative
    minimal narrative units 17-20, 25-30
    Welsh folk-narrative tradition 218-23
    value of collecting folk-narratives 223
    narrative patterns in Turkey Buzzard tales 240-6
    the social in narrative folklore 266-8
    oral folk history 291-9
    time in 314-18
        sequential arrangement of events 315-16
        the day unit 316
        beginnings and endings 316
        speed 317
        timelessness 317
        distortion of 318
    recording and analysis of
        pattern recognition 348-55
        data reduction 348-55
        semantic problems 348-55
        catchwords 348-55
        motif as an analytical tool 349-55
        order of magnitude in 350
        mapping of motifs 352-4, 356-63
    and race relationships in West Virginia 425-9
    and regional identity 448-9
national characteristics 22, 444
    of Italians 76-9, 95-8

oral tradition
    and written sources 237
    oral folk history 291-9
    three-fold repetition in 297

otherworld
    the visit to in folk narrative 247-9
    fairyland 247, 249
    the sea world 248, 249
    the land of the dead 248-9
    see also fairies

passion plays
    Persian 188-91
        the ta'ziya 189-91
        the rouze-khani 189, 190
phallic symbolism
    and the evil eye 40, 46-58
    phallic pillars 250-3, 256-7
Physiologus 438-9
play 119-22
Plutarch 371-6
Poland, the folklore of Polish fishermen 454-6
Project on Native American in Science 204-5
proverbial sayings, African 332
proverbs 236-7
Providences 230-1

race
    racist images in Britain 308-11
    the white man in African proverbial sayings 332-7
    relationships and narrative in West Virginia 425-9
    racial typing 426
    and folklore 428-9
regional identity 445-51
    the functions of folklore in 445-51
    language 445-7
    custom and belief 447-8
    folk narrative 448-9
    music, dance and drama 449-50
    material culture 450
religion
    and evolutionary theory 11
    pagan survivals in Christianity 250-3, 256-7
    sacred pillars 253-7
    phallic worship 250-3, 256-7
    religious supernatural sanctions 229-31
    in Spanish customs 235
    sacred circles 344
    religious ideas and belief in fairies 400-1
    among Polish fishermen 455-6
    see also Christianity, Islam
rhymes
    nursery 64-7
    child 65-7
    their functions 153-6
    their classification 154-6
Reynard the Fox
    and the snail motif 79, 81-2

Reynard the Fox *cont.*
    illustrations to in literature, and animal
        symbolism 412-17

Sagen 30, 219
    and the modern urban legend 381
semiotics 266-8
Sepher Sha'ashu'im 391-4
    value of for comparative study of folklore 391-4
sexual practices 51-3
Shakespeare, and witches 431-5
snail motif 76-106
    and folk attitudes to Italians 76-9, 95-8
    as an iconographic theme 79-81, 84, 98-100, 104
    in literature 79-81, 84-5, 95-6, 97-8
    and Topsy-Turvey Land 80, 81, 83, 87-8
    in European folklore 81-7, 101-3, 104-6
    Tardif 82, 83, 100-1
    in narrative 87-8
Spain, some typical Spanish traditions 234-5
spiritualism 11
story radicals, in folktales 19
survivals
    the concept of 8-12, 67-8
    pagan 250-7
symbolism
    phallic pillars 250-3, 256-7
    teeth and kinship 365-9
    dream 365-9
    the lion, the unicorn and the fox 412-17
    the stag 416
    the Witches in *Macbeth* 432
    see also evil eye

Tardif 82, 83, 100-1
three-fold repetition 297, 316, 324
time, in folk narrative, *see* narrative, time in
traditional code of right and wrong 227-31
traditional science *see* culturally based science
triads *see* three-fold repetition

Trickster 170-4, 193-6
Turkey Buzzard tales 240-6
    popular belief and folktale 240, 241, 244
    narrative patterns in 240-6
    acculturation in 241
    transformation in 241
twins, in folktales and myths 192-6

United States of America
    American Association for the Advancement of
        Science 204-5
    American Indians (Native Americans) and West-
        ern Science 205-8
    Midwest, British and Euro-American songs in
        384-5
    Missouri Folk-Lore Society 384-5
    West Virginia Guineas 425-9
    in relation to the Appalachian whites 425-9
universals, cultural 444
    variations from 444

wakes 173
Wales
    Welsh folk-narrative traditions *see* folktales
    Welsh Folk Museum 218
    ritual entry to the house in 339-42
    the hearth in Welsh folklore 339-40
witches
    in Hungary and England 183-6
    the Witches in *Macbeth* 431-5
    Elizabethan and Jacobean concepts of 432-5
    in English and Scottish politics 434-5
witch trials
    Hungarian 183-6
    English 185

Yugoslavia
    Yugoslav Jewish embroidery and costume 303-7
    Jewish Historical Museum in Belgrade 306, 307